The
AMERICAN
INDIAN

The
AMERICAN INDIAN

by COLIN F. TAYLOR

AN IMPRINT OF RUNNING PRESS
PHILADELPHIA · LONDON

© 2002 Salamander Books Ltd
8 Blenheim Court
Brewery Road
London N7 9NY
England

A member of **Chrysalis** Books plc

This edition published in the United States by Courage Books, an imprint of
Running Press Book Publishers
125 South Twenty-second Street
Philadelphia, Pennsylvania 19103-4399

9 8 7 6 5 4 3 2 1

Library of Congress Cataloging-in-Publication Number 2002100366

ISBN 0-7624-1389-1

CREDITS

Editor: Phil Hunt
Art Director: John Heritage
Designer: Heather Moore
Indexer: Chris Bernstein
Project Manager: Antony Shaw
Production: Susannah Straughan
Color reproduction: Anorax Imaging Ltd

This book may be ordered by mail from the publisher.
But try your bookstore first!

Visit us on the web!
www.runningpress.com

ADDITIONAL CAPTIONS

Page 1: An ivory model of a three-hole baidarka from the Arctic region. This unique style of
kayak was developed by the Aleutian Eskimo to transport non-Native travelers.
Page 2: A Tsimshian ceremonial T'Kul rattle and a woven Chilkat tunic from the
Northwest Coast region.
Page 3: An Ute cradle from the Plateau and Basin region.
Page 5: A Bella Coola pole from the Northwest Coast region.

CONTENTS

The
AMERICAN INDIAN
PEOPLES

INTRODUCTION

A HUNDRED thousand years ago the world was suffering from the last part of the Ice Age: great ice sheets covered much of North America, and sea levels fell dramatically revealing land corridors. During this time Neanderthal man developed fire for warmth and cooking. *Homo sapiens sapiens* evolved around 35,000 years ago, a big game hunter with a sophisticated tool kit and great intellectual capacity. Though less robust physically than Neanderthal man, he was more adaptable to climatic variations. Families lived in substantial dwellings and buried their dead with grave goods. Evidence for *homo sapiens sapiens* first occurred in Africa, Asia and the Near East, where they absorbed and replaced the Neanderthal populations. Several millennia later they appeared in Australia and Siberia. At the time when Europe was under glaciation, Northern Asia was cold, dry and free of glaciers.

The date of man's arrival in America is open to discussion, though archeological evidence from sites suggests a date after 14,000 years ago. *Homo sapiens sapiens* (fully modern man) was the first to inhabit the Americas during the latter part of the Ice Age. Anyone living in the region needed to have the right technology: warm clothes and shelter, strategies for food storage, a means of traveling over snow and ice and a mobile way of life.

Geologists agree that for two long periods between 75,000-45,000 and 25,000-14,000 years ago, the Bering land bridge was exposed. The first Americans migrated from Siberia over the Bering Strait. Research has shown that common linguistic and cultural traditions survive to this day on both sides of the Bering Strait, and fauna and flora are almost identical in these land masses.

Central Beringia was dry land for several thousand years. It was a cold place, with strong winds and thin snow cover, believed to be treeless, but with enough vegetation and grasslands to support the late Ice Age mammals (mammoth, bison, wild horse, and caribou). The study of fossil pollen grains has indicated that the vegetation may have been areas of steppe or tundra where reindeer roamed. Beringia may have been a refuge for animals and humans during the cold intervals of the last glaciation, and when conditions changed the animals moved on followed by the humans.

Around Beringia 11,000 years ago the inhabitants had adapted to a variety of different environments: maritime, tundra, river valley and mountain. Thus during the Ice Age there were several cultural groups living in northeast Asia, with diverse lifestyles under different environmental conditions. Of those groups, some scholars say it was only the big game hunters who crossed over on the land passage between the ice masses following the animals south into America, and later evolved according to the landscape, climate and available resources.

The sea levels rose about 14,000 years ago and by 9,000 years ago the land bridge had vanished. It is generally accepted that the American Indians migrated from Siberia.

At Paleo-Arctic sites by the Yukon and in Alaska, there is evidence of post-glacial occupation around 11-12,000 years ago. Artifacts (small cores and microblades and bladelets) have been discovered similar to those found near Lake Baikal in Siberia. At such settlements people stayed in tent-like houses and lived by hunting, fishing and gathering wild fruits.

The skulls of Indians found by the great mounds were examined and compared with modern recent Indian and Mongolian crania. It was claimed that they were the same peoples, and that the first Americans were descended from Asian origins. Biologists have discovered that there is a relationship between the teeth of humans from North China and those from North America. Apparently there was a single early migration of hunter-gatherers who evolved by cultural differentiation. Two further migrations took place later, and gave rise to the Athapaskans and the Eskimo-Aleut populations.

According to Christy Turner (1984), an expert on the physical characteristics of prehistoric

Key:
1 The Southeast
2 The Southwest
3 The Plains
4 Plateau and Basin
5 California
6 The Northwest Coast
7 The Subarctic
8 The Arctic
9 The Northeast

This map shows the ten geographic areas of Native North America (the Plateau and Basin appearing together in this book) within each of which the aboriginal cultures were broadly similar. Color-coded in the map are the nine cultural areas into which chapters in the book are divided. More detailed keys to tribes and their tribal lands are shown on maps which appear on the first pages of each chapter.

Above: *Seminole – 'The unconquered' – man of the Southeast. A Muskogean tribe, the Seminole split off from the more northern Creeks and mixed with the remnants of Florida's original Indians, before 1600 consisting of more than twenty-five separate tribes.*

Above: *Face of the Southwest. A Quechan man, more popularly known as Yuman who lived on both sides of the Colorado River in SW Arizona and eastern California. They were linguistic members of the Yuman subfamily of the Hokan family.*

Above: *A Cheyenne warrior of the Plains. The Cheyenne belonged to the Algonquian linguistic stock. They migrated from Minnesota c.1750 and finally settled on the central Plains, becoming a typical nomadic Plains tribe.*

man's teeth, the earliest penetration of Alaska by Asians took place over 14,000 years ago. They were followed a few thousand years later by two waves of immigrants from Siberia: the ancestors of modern Athapaskan Indians and northwest coast peoples; and the ancient Eskimo-Aleut.

Various bodies of research have divided the American peoples into three distinct pre-European groupings: the Paleo-Indians (Puebloans, Pimas, Pai); the Athapaskan speakers (Apache and Navajo); and the Eskimo-Aleut. Neither the Athapaskans nor the Eskimo-Aleut penetrated deep into the Americas: the Central and South American Indians were Paleo-Indians (Fagan, 1987). All three peoples came from North East Siberia, but there were three language groups: Amerindian (most North American and all South American languages were part of one Amerind family); Na-Dene; and Eskimo-Aleut. According to certain scholars these three linguistic groups correspond to the three waves of migration. The Amerindian group arrived before 11,000 years, the Na-Dene around 9,000 years ago and the Eskimo-Aleut around 4,000 years ago.

There is more linguistic diversity in extreme northwest America where there are more contrasting environments than in the recently deglaciated northeast. It is suggested that the Eskimo-Aleut, Na-Dene and Algonquian languages spread from the periphery of the ice sheets into the newly unglaciated lands. The later two migrations limited their settlements to the north and northwest coast without penetrating further into the interior of the Americas.

The period between the first proposed crossing by man approximately 14,000 years ago, and the arrival of the so-called Clovis peoples around 11,500 years ago, is a subject

fiercely discussed by archeologists. There are widely accepted and precise dates for 'Clovis' artifact sites throughout the Americas from around 11,500 years ago.

The following passages set out a few of the sites around which this controversy rages.

In the western United States, there may have been settlement of the US Pacific coastal and inland regions in the very early post glacial period, 14-13,000 years ago, for humanly made stone fragments have been found. In California, on Santa Rosa Island, there were temporary encampments where hunter-gatherers butchered mammoths and settled for a few days during their seasonal migrations. This site is firmly dated around 7,500 years ago, though claims have been made for much earlier settlement. Pre-Clovis man may have occupied China Lake sites in California, but the stratigraphy is questioned by scholars. Other sites on the high plains of Colorado and in Texas may have been visited by pre-Clovis man but scholars have put

Left: *America 11,500 years ago, showing the migration of the Paleo-Indians through North and South America. The first Americans migrated from Siberia across the Bering Strait; research shows that common linguistic and cultural traditions still survive on both sides of the Strait.*

Ice sheet cover, 9500 BC. Area later settled by early Athapaskan and Eskimo–Aleut peoples.

Passage used by Paleo-Indians during first wave of migration.

Migration path through America over the first thousand years.

forward a plethora of arguments against this.

In the eastern United States, Meadowcroft Rockshelter on Cross Creek by the Ohio River was one of the earliest occupied sites in North America, from which were found 45 species of mammal, 68 birds and 30,000 plant fragments. The environment there was stable for 11,000 years, and the rockshelter is known to have been used from 12,000 to 700 years ago, though archeologists claim it was used much earlier.

In southern Florida, the area was cooler and drier than it is today; Paleo-Indian sites at sinkholes are today submerged below sea level, but may date from before 11,500 years ago. There the peoples camped for short periods while hunting game and may have exploited huge territories using pre-Clovis artifacts.

Although not directly relevant to this book, it is interesting too to note archeological evidence of human occupation in Central and South America. In Central America archeologists such as MacNeish (1986) are convinced that human occupation in Mexico can be dated back to 20,000 years ago, though the most reliable record begins 11,000 years ago, when the hunting groups are found to the south of the Rio Grande with Clovis-type points. In South America very early settlement dates of 14,000 years ago have been given for Pikimachay Cave in Peru, but these are highly controversial. In Brazil beautifully painted rockshelters have

been found, mostly dating to between 7,600 and 8,000 years ago.

Evidence from artifacts for humans inhabiting the Americas prior to 14,000 years ago is open to debate. Scholars argue that the 'early' artifacts are intrusive, accumulations are natural, the association between mammoth bones and flakes is tenuous, or that dating materials are excavated from earlier levels and radiocarbon readings are inaccurate. It is agreed that after 12,000 years ago Paleo-Indians settled in South America, bringing with them their stone technology from the North.

Clovis peoples were hunters who followed the migratory paths of the larger mammals. They camped by rivers and streams where big game came to drink, and in the winter they stayed in rock shelters. People collected wild foods including fruits, berries, vegetables and nuts, to supplement their diet. They also ate the meat of both large and small mammals as is indicated by the discovery of these bones from their occupation sites. They were expert stone workers and artisans, renowned for producing beautiful translucent stone points with

Below: People of the in-between land: Umatilla and Palus of the Columbia Plateau. Such eastern groups as these were heavily influenced by the Plains tribes after what might be called 'The Equestrian Revolution', which occurred c.1750.

fluted bifaces, known as Clovis points.

These Paleo-Indians arrived approximately 11,500 years ago and within a few centuries spread to the North American coasts and as far south as Mexico. On the Great Plains of America Clovis culture stone artifacts have been found, in direct association with bones of large extinct Ice Age mammals.

While it is generally accepted that Clovis people came from north of the ice sheets and migrated south as the glaciers melted, the problem for archeologists is to trace their origins. The mystery exists because they appeared at sites with their fine, highly-developed stone tools, for which there appears to be no precedent. Scholars believe that the Clovis point was developed on the Plains and not in the Arctic (Alaskan points are different). Clovis points have been found in the Canadian Provinces, throughout the United States, on the Great Plains, in North America, Mexico and South America.

The Clovis people (the big game hunters) flourished on the Plains for about 500 years, then around 11,000 years ago abruptly vanished. They were replaced by a multitude of different hunting and gathering peoples. Various reasons have been put forward to explain their disappearance. It was suggested that the climate had changed resulting in reduced water availability. Consequently animals

clustered around the remaining springs, were easy prey and were over-hunted.

However, Paul Martin (1974) claimed that when the first Americans arrived they found themselves in an extremely favorable environment, with large herds of mammoth and other mammals who were not wary of hunters. As a result the human population exploded, and the rapidly expanding human population quickly depleted the slower breeding mammal groups. As big game became scarce the hunters moved on across America, and once the big game became extinct a population crash followed. Martin developed a computer projection that suggested that Paleo-Indians arrived in Panama by 10,930 years ago, and at Tierra del Fuego by 10,500 years ago. He suggested that the population of the entire continent south of the ice sheets took a mere 1,000 years.

After the disappearance of the Ice Age mammoth, the people who had preyed on them turned to bison (buffalo) hunting, and for over 10,000 years the successors of Clovis pursued bison on the Plains. By 10,500 years ago, bison were the most dominant species found at all

Below: *Faces of the living past: Ute Indians of the Great Basin region. The Utes were the most southerly of the Basin culture which was essentially unchanged and isolated for thousands of years, with few rivers seeking the sea.*

Above: *Face of a land of migrants and wanderers: a Yurok woman of northern California. This was an area of great contrast with perhaps the highest population density in North America and at least six different linguistic stocks.*

Above: *Faces of the Northwest Coast: Tillamook of northwest Oregon. Early 19th century they were a prominent Salishan-speaking tribe occupying some eight villages, with a population of about 2,200. By the 1850s that had been reduced to around 300.*

archeological sites in the region. Bison survived because they adapted to feed on grass land in post-glacial times.

Mass bison drives took place: in Colorado the Olsen-Chubbock site held 152 carcasses in a canyon into which bison had been stampeded 8,500 years ago. Such bison hunts were communal affairs that may have been conducted once annually. When the bow and arrow reached the plains in AD 500, communal bison hunting reached its greatest prehistoric intensity. In 1547 horses were introduced by the Spanish, and their use brought about dramatic change: bison herds were further reduced, the nomadic population grew and placed greater demands on the farm produce of sedentary populations. Tensions surfaced, different cultural values took hold and raids were prevalent. During the nineteenth century, Europeans with their muskets joined the bison hunt and herds were decimated. In the twentieth century great efforts have been made to save the bison, which were largely successful, and there are now herds on the Plains again, although not in the large numbers there used to be.

In the far north, the environment could only support a small population, so people moved regularly depending on the season. Na-Dene speakers came first. They were forest hunter-gatherers and spread south and west and into the interior, where they became known as Athapaskan. Later some split off, moved south and became the modern Navajo and Apache. The Eskimo-Aleut came after the Paleo-Indians, before the land bridge was severed (though some say that they arrived by boat). They are the most Asian of North Americans, and their language has Siberian roots.

The Eskimo spread over thousands of miles of mainland and probably split away from the Aleut about 4,000 years ago. Ties weakened as each group adapted to different environmental conditions. The Eskimo hunted using skin kayaks, traveled by dog sled and occupied land from the Bering Strait to Greenland between the tenth and eleventh centuries AD. Their predecessors hunted caribou and musk oxen on land, walrus and whale in the sea. They dug their houses into the ground to protect them against the arctic winter, with trap doors to shield them against the cold. The Aleut were maritime hunters and fishermen, excellent boatmen, hunting seal, sea lion and otter on the open seas.

The first wave of settlement to the newly exposed northwest coastal regions were forest hunter-gatherers from Alaska, distinct from the Eskimo-Aleut. The climate and sea levels stabilised 5,000 years ago: there was a predictable supply of maritime food and more elaborate hunting and foraging societies developed in which wealth and social status assumed a vital importance. Powerful individuals came to the fore, and it was they who regulated ceremonial

life and controlled commodities.

People lived in villages all year round in substantial log houses, and used canoes to move between settlements such as early sites on the Queen Charlotte Islands. Another coastal site was excavated at Ozette in Washington State where a mud slide buried a whaling village 500 years ago, and all household artifacts were preserved in mud. Baskets, nets, fish hooks and looms were found in cedar longhouses which had been divided into small rooms using low walls and hanging mats.

The Native American Indians occupied the entire American continent whether rain forest, desert, plains or arctic by the time Europeans arrived on the scene. In the desert and woodland areas, the first inhabitants had been dispersed bands living in seasonal camps, though more intensive foraging developed from 9,000 to 4,500 years ago, with people returning to the same location year after year. Maize cultivation developed 1,500 years ago: the cycle of planting

and harvesting reduced people's mobility and greater storage was needed. Trade networks also developed.

The Eskimo-Aleut had settled on the islands and coasts of the central Canadian Arctic by the twelfth and thirteenth centuries, and the climate had warmed. Norsemen traded in the area in AD 1000 and remained until a new wave of Westerners penetrated the land in the sixteenth century.

In the eastern woodlands, the farmers of 4,000 years ago developed a preoccupation with burial: Adena people built earthworks and ceremonial compounds. The Hopewell burial mounds were even more elaborate than those of the Adena, and a flowering of artistic tradition came about. The Mississippian Culture emerged around AD 700, with both farmers and hunter-gatherers. The population grew to around 10,000 peoples and powerful chieftains ruled the valleys. This was contemporary with Mexican civilization when heavily fortified

Left: *Faces of the great Subarctic: Ahtna of the Copper River Valley, Alaska. Typical of many Subarctic tribes, they spoke the Athapaskan language and practiced a semi-nomadic way of life; hunters of small game, their main subsistence was fishing.*

Below: *Regalia of the Northeast: early Chippewa (Ojibwa) costume worn by the son of a Mississaugi leader. Typical of the region, it is of buckskin embellished extensively with bead- and quillwork.*

communities with temple mounds and plazas were built. These were seen by the Spanish in the mid-sixteenth century.

In the Pacific coastal regions most societies lived by hunting and foraging up until European contact. In seventeenth century Mississippi the Cherokee were living in the north, with 100 settlements of around 60,000 people. In California people lived off the land and sea, and with rich resources large, permanent villages grew up ruled by local chiefs, and the population grew.

In Arizona in the southwest around 2,000 years ago the Hohokam people began planting their crops to coincide with the rainfall patterns: they dug terraces, canals and dams to control water flow. By AD 900 the Anasazi (ancestors of the Hopi, Zuni and other Pueblo Indians) were farmers living in multi-room structures in New Mexico.

Today ethnologists generally divide North America into nine culture groups, mostly based on geographical location, for the early peoples adapted their skills to suit environmental conditions. This book offers the following breakdown: Southeast; Southwest; Plains; Plateau and Basin; California; Northwest Coast; Subarctic; Arctic, and Northeast.

The arrival of the Europeans changed the face of the entire continent and the lives of its indigenous peoples irredeemably. Vikings,

Below: Faces of a resourceful race: Eskimos of the Bering Strait region. Modern-day Eskimos refer to themselves as Inuit, meaning 'humans', the word Eskimo deriving from the Algonquian meaning 'raw meat eaters'. In common with other groups of this vast region, they displayed a wide variety of subsistence patterns but a good proportion of their raw materials were obtained from the caribou and from sea mammals. These people have moved rapidly with the times; by 1982 many of the young had completed technical and professional courses in high school and local colleges.

English, French and Spanish explored the coasts of America and then settled there permanently. Colonists, missionaries, and explorers arrived, spreading disease, destruction and disruption which affected the traditional Indian way of life. Within a few mere centuries the old Indian way of life had been swept away forever.

Change came slowly. After World War II, increased awareness of the multi-cultural nature of society came about. Popular interest in the country's various ethnic groups surged, and the market for Indian arts and crafts soared, a market partly kept buoyant by the poor economic situation in the reservations and the Indians' ability to adapt their work to the preferences of their customers. Today Native American Indian artifacts and the people who produce them receive world-wide acclaim. The artifacts and the importance of their original function within Indian society are now more widely appreciated than ever.

*'My people are scattered and gone; when I shout, I hear my voice in the depths of the forest, but no answering voice comes back to me —
all is silent around me.'*

COLONEL COBB OF THE CHOCTAW

THE SOUTHEAST

THE INDIAN cultures of the Southeast in the nineteenth century and the first half of the twentieth century were the products of a long period of change, disruption, and destruction – almost genocide, although the destruction was not the direct result of conscious state policies. Thousands of years of cultural development in this region were rudely diverted and truncated by the arrival of Europeans in the early sixteenth century. Little can now be known about what the lives of the southern Indian people were like when the invaders arrived, for the first literate observers left few records, and none for most of the region, and the archeological evidence cannot answer many important questions. Native traditions cannot help, for the details of an old way of life cannot be preserved by word of mouth alone over 400 years in a society undergoing very rapid social and cultural change. However, the scale of the cultural and biological disaster that was visited on the Southeastern Indians has recently become clearer from advances in archeological interpretations, filled out by scraps of information from the thin documentary record left by the first Europeans.

Certainly this was a naturally favored region.

GULF OF MEXICO

Key to tribes:

1 Atakapa	11 Chickasaw	21 Timucua
2 Caddo	12 Tohome	22 Tocobaga
3 Natchez	13 Mobile	23 Ais
4 Tunica	14 Chatot	24 Calusa
5 Ofo	15 Alabama	25 Tekesta
6 Houma	16 Yuchi	26 Keys
7 Chitimacha	17 Cherokee	27 Yamasee
8 Biloxi	18 Muskogee	28 Cusabo
9 Choctaw	19 Hitchiti	29 Catawba and Neighbors
10 Chakchiuma	20 Apalachee	30 Tutelo and Neighbors

It is in the warmest part of the northern temperate zone, and south Florida is actually subtropical in climate. Most of the Southeast falls within the broad coastal plain bordering the Atlantic and the Gulf of Mexico. In this low-lying area the rivers meander and deposit fertile alluvial soils. In the broad valleys were many oxbow lakes and vast swamps of cypress and cane. Fields were easily cleared in the bottom lands along the rivers, and their productivity was rapidly renewed by the silt from seasonal floods. Fish were plentiful especially in the river backwaters, and migratory water fowl were easily taken. In some areas such as along the lower Mississippi River fish and water fowl provided at least half the protein in the Indian diet. Other animal food came from white-tailed deer, raccoons, and other mammals. Wild plant foods – nuts, fruits, berries – were a very important resource. Cultivated corn, beans, squash, sunflowers, and gourds were a major source of food everywhere except in south Florida, where, at least on the southwest coast, fish and shellfish were so plentiful that they allowed the Calusa to develop a complex sedentary society of a sort that normally depends on agriculture. The northeastern part

This map shows approximate territories of tribes and tribal groupings at about 1600 in Florida and along the Atlantic coast, and about 1700 in the rest of the region. After that, all tribes lost territory, many disappeared, many moved west, some new tribes arose.

Above: *Ben P. Harris, a prominent Catawba man, c.1899, in the traditional accoutrements of a participant in a 'medicine show': non-Catawba turkey-feather headdress, fringed cloth jacket and trousers, Plains-style beaded vest, bow and arrows.*

of the area includes the piedmont above the fall-line, and the low mountains of the Appalachian highlands. The environment here was different but also favorable. The valleys are narrower, but still fertile, and fish abounded in the river shoals. The economic cycle in general depended on growing crops and fishing during the warm season, then hunting deer during the cooler season.

What one sees now in the region is far different from the aboriginal situation. The forests and cane brakes are gone, many rivers are dammed and swamps drained, and the soil is much degraded and eroded from exploitative commercial farming of first indigo, then tobacco, cotton, and corn. The passenger ~igeons are extinct, and other birds, fish, and ,nost wild animals are far less plentiful than they were even at the beginning of the nineteenth century.

The radical, disastrous changes in Indian life occurred before most of the environmental degradation. In the early period precipitous depopulation was the result of the introduction of European diseases, such as smallpox, to which the Indians at first lacked immunity. In many communities half or more of the inhabitants died within a period of weeks. The social and psychological effects of this disaster can scarcely be imagined, in general and in the loss of the bearers of knowledge and tradition. Later, after immunities to the new diseases had been established, the Indian societies were

SOUTHEASTERN TRIBES

Ais. A small tribe on the east coast of south Florida, numbering perhaps 1,000 in 1650 and extinct by the 1720s. They grew no crops, being mainly dependent on fish. There is no evidence whatsoever on the Ais language.
Alabama. Their language, belonging to the Muskogean family, is very close to Koasati, the two being perhaps dialects of a single language. The Alabama population was less than 1,000 in 1704; after 1763 they were dispersed, some joining the Seminoles and Creeks and most going to Texas with the Koasatis. By 1910, there were only about 300 Alabamas in addition to those among the Creeks.
Apalachee. Speakers of a Muskogean language, missionized by the Spanish, their population was perhaps 5,000 in 1676. They were destroyed in the eighteenth century by English and Creek raids, a few survivors joining the Creeks.
Atakapa. The population was about 1,000 in the early eighteenth century, and the group was extinct by 1900. The Atakapa language was an isolate, that is, without demonstrable relationship to any other language.
Biloxi. Amounting to perhaps 1,000 people in 1650, the Biloxi spoke a language belonging to the Siouan family. By the end of the nineteenth century there were very few identifiable survivors, in Louisiana, Oklahoma, and eastern Texas.
Caddo. This term includes several tribes, mostly in three confederacies, all speaking the Caddo language which is the southern branch of the Caddoan language family of which the other languages were spoken on the Plains. The Caddo population may have been 8,000 in 1700; by 1910 there were only about 550 Caddos, in Oklahoma.
Calusa. This was a non-agricultural chiefdom in south Florida, which may have included as many as 10,000 people in the 1560s. By 1750 there were none left. So little of the Calusa language was recorded that its affiliations are unknown.
Catawba. This tribe of the South Carolina piedmont is the descendant of several small tribes that joined together in the seventeenth and eighteenth centuries. Speakers of several different languages were probably involved, but only Catawba, a language of the Siouan family, survived into the twentieth century.
Chakchiuma. A small tribe, now extinct, probably speakers of a Muskogean language (perhaps actually Choctaw).
Chatot. Another small tribe, also probably speakers of a

Muskogean language, driven by the Creeks to Mobile and then Louisiana. They probably merged with the Choctaws in Indian Territory (Oklahoma).
Cherokee. The largest Southeastern tribe from the eighteenth century until the present, speakers of an Iroquoian language. Some survive in their Appalachian homeland in western North Carolina, while most today live in Oklahoma.
Chickasaw. Numbering about 8,000 in 1650, they were removed to Oklahoma where they live today. The language is a variety of Choctaw, although the two groups have always been politically different.
Chitimacha. The population may have been 4,000 in 1700, while less than 100 survived in 1930. The language is an isolate, not known to be related to any other.
Choctaw. Speakers of a Muskogean language, they numbered about 15,000 in 1650. In 1930 there were about 18,000, mostly in Oklahoma but some in Mississippi and Louisiana, their original homeland.
Creek. This is the English name for the political Confederacy centered on the Muskogee and including the Hitchiti and others.
Cusabo. A small tribe, totalling 535 in a 1715 census and now extinct, whose language is entirely unknown.
Hitchiti. A Muskogean language, spoken by seven or so large towns incorporated into the Creek Confederacy.
Houma. A small tribe in Louisiana, numbering 600-700 in 1700 and about the same in 1930. The language, now extinct, perhaps belonged to the Muskogean family.
Keys. The inhabitants of the Florida Keys seem to have been politically independent of their larger neighbors. Nothing of the language they spoke was ever recorded. They were extinct by the end of Spanish Florida in 1763.
Koasati. A Muskogean tribe numbering perhaps 250 in 1750, of whom in 1910 there were about 100 in Texas and one town among the Creeks in Oklahoma. The language is very close to that of the Alabamas, perhaps even the same.
Lumbee. Now one of the largest Southeastern tribes, numbering about 30,000 in 1970, the Lumbee are descended from the Cheraw and other Indian neighbors of the Catawba, as well as from Black and White refugees from the European frontiers. By the eighteenth century no Indian language survived among them. In most respects they are culturally the same as their White and Black neighbors,

although socially and politically they are definitely Indian.
Mikasuki. About two-thirds of the Florida Seminoles speak Mikasuki, which is the same language as Hitchiti, as did many Seminoles in Oklahoma formerly.
Muskogee. This is the dominant element in the Creek Confederacy. The language, in the Muskogean family, is also spoken by about one-third of the Seminoles in Florida, and by most of the Oklahoma Seminoles.
Natchez. Numbering about 4,500 in 1650, the survivors were eventually amalgamated with the Creeks and Cherokees. The language is an isolate, not known to be related to any other.
Ofo. Speakers of a Siouan language, they were driven south from the Ohio River region by the expanding Iroquois.
Seminole. This tribe originated in the eighteenth century, when settlers from the Creek Confederacy moved into Florida. The Seminole Wars of the 1830s and 1850s resulted in most being deported to Oklahoma, while a minority survived in southern Florida.
Tekesta. A small, non-agricultural tribe inhabiting the Miami region, they became extinct in the eighteenth century. Their language is entirely unknown.
Timucua. A large group of northern Florida tribes, they numbered some 13,000 in 1650 (and many more a century earlier). The language, well recorded by Spanish missionaries, is not known to be related to any other. The last few Timucuas left Florida when the Spanish withdrew in 1763.
Tocobaga. A small tribe, nearly totally unknown, of the Tampa Bay region in Florida.
Tohome and **Mobile.** Two groups that evidently spoke a variety of Choctaw.
Tunica. Numbering perhaps 2,500 in 1650, less than 50 survived in 1910. Their language, although well recorded, is not related to any other.
Tutelo. Speaking a Siouan language, they numbered some 2,700 in 1600, but by 1800 the descendants had joined the Iroquois in Canada.
Yamasee. Perhaps speakers of a Muskogean language, they numbered about 1,200 in 1715, but soon fled to Spanish Florida where they had disappeared by 1763.
Yuchi. A tribe originally in the Appalachian highlands, they numbered about 1,500 in 1650, and by 1930 only about 200 among the Creeks in Oklahoma. The Yuchi language is an isolate, unrelated to any other.

further disrupted by the complex effects of European and Euro-American intrusion: trade, new kinds of warfare, enslavement, the usurpation of food supplies, of goods, and then of land, epidemics of new diseases, and finally actual replacement of the Indian populations by people of European and African origins.

A good deal is known about southern Indian cultures over the last 100 to 150 years, but probably less than in any other region of the continent can this knowledge be taken as indicative of the ways of life before European influence was felt. The first shocks came in the middle of the sixteenth century. The first good written descriptions of Southeastern Indians date from more than 200 years later at the end of the eighteenth and the beginning of the nineteenth century, after massive realignments and restructuring of the societies had taken place. Really thorough records (and representative museum collections, and extensive series of photographs) begin still another century later, at the end of the nineteenth century and the beginning of the twentieth after most of the surviving Indians in the Southeast had been deported to quite different cultural and natural surroundings in Indian Territory west of the Mississippi (present Oklahoma).

The table above includes all the tribes on the map (p.14), as well as those mentioned in the text and captions but not on the map.

The first contacts of Europeans with southeastern Indians are unknown. The first recorded visit was by Ponce de Leon, who landed in Florida, probably in the Calusa area, in 1513. But the hostile reception the Indians gave him strongly suggests that they had previous experience with some Europeans who left no

Below: Benjamin Paul, a Chitimacha chief, c.1910. This small tribe lived on the Mississippi delta of Louisiana. Mr Paul was J.R. Swanton's principal authority on traditional culture of his people. Photographed by Swanton in his home in Louisiana.

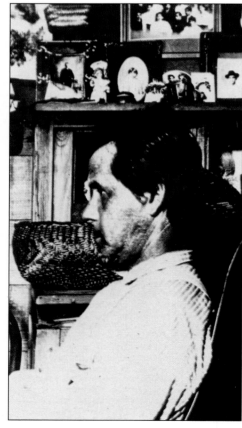

Above: A Caddo camp, probably near the Washita River, Oklahoma, c.1869. The Caddo occupied parts of what is now Arkansas and Louisiana. This scene is traditional Caddo, with conical-shaped dwellings thatched with grass or bark (as left).

other record. Other brief contacts followed, in Florida and along the Atlantic coast, which left very scanty records although they probably had serious effects on the Indians: European diseases were probably introduced, and more Indians learned how dangerous the strangers could be. Finally, in 1539-43 came Hernando de Soto's long incursion far into the Southeast. He arrived at Tampa Bay with some 700 men, 200 horses, a herd of hogs, and a huge quantity of weapons and supplies, and proceeded inland north across what is now Georgia and South Carolina, into Tennessee, then down through Alabama, back north again and across northern Mississippi, across Arkansas, then south again to the lower Mississippi River in Louisiana. This expedition was a disaster for de Soto and his men, and even more a disaster for the Indians he met, hundreds of whom he and his men killed and kidnapped, and for many others, surely many thousands, who died from the diseases introduced.

The several contemporary written descriptions of the de Soto expedition are sufficient to give us a narrow window on the aboriginal societies of the Southeast, but these records are frustratingly brief and imprecise. Archeological research provides more information, but of rather different sorts, and there are many problems in identifying specific archeological remains with the poorly localized descriptions in the de Soto accounts. In recent years archeological theory has suggested reasonable integrations of these two kinds of data, in part by looking at much later societies in the Southeast and by considering comparable societies in other parts of the world.

A reasonable reconstruction of the aboriginal Southeast when Europeans first arrived shows many chiefdoms spread all across the interior and reaching the coast in several places. These were complex societies, each with a capital town containing massive earthworks in the form of mounds supporting temples and council houses, often surrounded by large canals and usually stockaded. Each chiefdom normally included several smaller towns with only one or two mounds, subordinate to the principal town. The largest of these chiefdom capitals was at Cahokia, in present Illinois across the Mississippi River from St Louis. This is well outside the historic Southeast, for one of the consequences of early contacts with Europeans was a retraction of the area covered by chiefdoms. Cahokia seems to have reached its height by about 1250 AD, after which its population declined. At its maximum Cahokia

Right: *Johnnie, a Choctaw man visiting New Orleans, by Karl Bodmer (1833). At the time of Bodmer's visit, many Choctaw had been 'removed', but some survived in Louisiana and Mississippi.*

Below: *Temporary Choctaw camp on the Mississippi River, near Natchez, by Karl Bodmer (1833). These travelers are cooking in metal vessels with typical canepack baskets near one lean-to.*

covered more than five square miles and may have had a population of some 10,000. This was surely the largest town north of central Mexico, and in it was the largest artificial structure in North America. The central earth mound here rose in four terraces to a height of 100ft (30m.), where a large building was built on the flat top, while the base of the mound measured about 700 × 1000ft (215 × 305m.) and covered sixteen acres. More than a hundred other mounds were grouped around plazas. Most were platform mounds supporting public buildings and perhaps the houses of leading people. There were also conical burial mounds. The central 200 acres of the town were surrounded by a large wall of upright logs set in a deep trench, with watchtowers and gates spaced along it.

Another chiefdom had its capital at Moundville, about sixty miles southwest of present Birmingham, Alabama, on the northeastern edge of the territory of the Muskogees in later times (whose ancestral capital it may have been). Moundville covers 300 acres on a bluff on the Black Warrior River. Here are twenty major mounds on two sides of a rectangular plaza covering some eighty acres. These mounds are more or less pyramidal, although with flat tops, and the largest rises almost 60ft (18m.) above the level of the plaza. On the tops of these mounds were buildings, probably both temples or ceremonial structures, and houses for the rulers. A wall divided the plaza from a nearby settlement area, and the whole was surrounded by a palisade. High ranking individuals, probably especially the holders of ritual

offices, were buried in about half the mounds along the edges of the plaza. These burials were often accompanied by those of infants and of skulls or heads without bodies. Houses were built outside the plaza but within the surrounding palisade. Controlled from Moundville were about twenty smaller settlements, most of them with one small mound apiece, which were located within the valley for a few miles north and south of Moundville. In addition, the Moundville center dominated hundreds of small residential hamlets. It has been estimated that Moundville drew labor from as far as forty-five miles away, and much tribute especially from the secondary centers within ten miles or so.

Another, smaller archeological site represents a chiefdom in what was later Cherokee country; it may itself have been subordinate to a larger site well to the south. Toqua, on the Little Tennessee River about thirty miles southwest of Knoxville, contains two flat-topped mounds, one 24ft (7m.) high resulting from eight enlargements after it was first raised, and the other, about 300ft (90m.) distant, only 6ft (1.8m.) high and built in two construction stages. Both served as burial mounds as well as supporting structures. The village, consisting of some forty households, covered about fifty acres.

Construction of such large sites must have required well-organized labor. There is other evidence that these were heirarchical societies, each under a high chief ruling in a large town, which was surrounded by smaller towns and villages headed by subordinate chiefs. The chief and his relatives were considered to be descendants of the sun. The chiefs had great power and prestige, with many perquisites in the form of special insignia and possessions. They were surrounded by retainers, offered tribute, and deferred to by their subordinates. Each chiefdom was expansionist, fighting with its neighbors. There were graded ranks within the nobility, while most of the populace were commoners. Everyone belonged to one of a set of clans, each of which included both nobles and commoners. These were totemic in that each was associated with a tutelary spirit, usually an animal, and members were considered to share character and behavior with this totem. The clans were matrilineal – each person's membership in the mother's clan was acquired at birth. The clans were exogamous, that is, marriage within the clan was prohibited. But the clans were not organized groups, and every clan was spread through many villages,

Below: *Joe Silestine (Toshkachito), Choctaw, of Bayou Lacombe, La., 1909, demonstrating a cane blowgun. The wooden dart used, feathered with thistle down, had a range of 25ft.*

with each village inhabited by members of several clans.

Although each clan was quite egalitarian – most members were equals – the clan as a whole was ranked. There were two sets or sides or moieties, the clans in each in a ranked series. Furthermore, one side seems to have been considered superior to the other. The chiefly offices were hereditary, certainly matrilineally, and offices of lesser rank were also hereditary, probably most of them matrilineally but perhaps another set inherited patrilineally, from father to son. However, nobles seemingly could only marry commoners, and the children in each generation were of lesser rank than the noble parent, becoming commoners after four or five generations.

The political and social systems surely varied from chiefdom to chiefdom, they were quite complex, and the few literate Europeans who were in a position to observe them in action certainly did not understand them very well. One striking example that was quite thoroughly investigated by a Jesuit missionary in the 1560s was that of the Calusa in southwest Florida. Here the high-chief was differentiated from the rest of the society by an exception to the incest rules: he was required to marry his full sister (to the distress of the missionary). This custom is known from only a few other societies anywhere in the world, all of them with high social

Above: *Choctaw ballgame, 1925, near Philadelphia, Miss. At far right is David Jim. This is the Choctaw form, still popular among them in the state, of the widespread SE Indian team game.*

Below: *Haylaema, a Choctaw woman in Louisiana, in 1909. Her sturdy pack basket is of split river cane, woven in a twilled technique, with a supporting buckskin tumpline across her chest.*

belongings were taken out of the house and packed to be buried with him. A special red-painted pole was hung with forty-six cane rings representing the number of enemies he had killed.

The first day the mourners fasted (this was a means for gaining spiritual strength among most southeastern Indians). Those who were to accompany him into the afterworld were prepared. There were eight of them; the Great Sun himself would have joined them but was dissuaded, with difficulty, by the French. These eight people were the Tattooed Serpent's principal wife and his second wife, five officials or servants (one called by the French the First Warrior or Chancellor; a Noble woman who was a doctor and a special friend; the deceased's Head Servant, perhaps the same as his Pipe Bearer, and his wife; and the warclub maker); and a woman who would have been sacrificed at the death of an earlier Sun had she not then been a hostage of the French. Another man who had escaped a previous sacrifice but whose French protector had left was brought forth by thirty warriors, but since he was still reluctant to die he was dismissed by the Tattooed Serpent's principal wife as unworthy to accompany her and the rest to the other world. This was described to the French as a place without hunger, death, or war, where the weather was always fine. For two or three days there were

and political stratification and all very concerned with inherited rank. Royal full-sibling marriage is especially appropriate where the nobility is exogamous and no child can inherit the full rank of the noble parent.

For a late expression of the social stratification once typical of much of the Southeast, we may summarize French reports of the death and funeral of a high ranking Natchez chief.[1] The Natchez had two social classes, nobility and commoners. Within the nobility there were three ranks, Suns, Nobles, and Honored People. These were exogamous: all could only marry commoners. Class membership and noble rank were acquired from the mother at birth, except that the children of fathers of Sun and Noble rank belonged to the next lower rank rather than inheriting their mothers' commoner rank. While rank in general was hereditary, some commoner men and their wives could achieve Honored rank through special merit. The king or highest ranking chief was known as the Great Sun, and he was succeeded in office by the son of his sister. There is much evidence for the deference and special privileges afforded to this man. The other high civil, military, and probably religious offices were also filled by Suns. When any Sun died, his or her spouse was willingly sacrificed – one could say committed suicide – to accompany the spirit of the dead to the afterworld.

In 1725 a man named Tattooed Serpent died. He was the Great War Chief and a much-beloved brother of the Great Sun. As soon as he died, the news was relayed by death cries from village to village. His body was laid out on a cane bed in his house, probably on a small mound near the town plaza, dressed in his finest and with his face painted vermilion. His weapons were tied to his bed and around it were arrayed all the calumets (peace pipes) he had received during his career. All his other

Yuchi

From at least the early 18th century the Yuchi were part of the Creek Confederacy, and they were removed with the Creeks in 1836 from their ancestral lands in Georgia to Indian Territory, in present-day Oklahoma. Their long association with the Creeks resulted in much cultural similarity, although they retain a distinct identity and until the mid-20th century they preserved their distinctive language. In 1904 and 1905 the ethnologist Frank G. Speck conducted research among the Yuchi, finding them engaged in agriculture and cattle raising and living in widely dispersed households in three settlement areas, although politically they formed a single town in the organized Creek Nation. Speck's research and the monograph on Yuchi culture that he published in 1909 described many aspects of Yuchi life as it then was; Speck paid particular attention to their medicine and rituals. The items illustrated here were all collected by Speck in 1904 and 1905.

1 Man's hunting jacket, of green cotton cloth with red calico borders.
2 Man's shirt, black cotton cloth decorated with appliqué bands.
3 Man's breechclout of red flannel, edges bound with blue cotton cloth.
4 Man's leggings of strouding, ribbons along inner seams of flaps.
5 Scratcher; six pins in turkey quill frame with leaf of button snakeroot attached.
6 Cane tube used by medicine man to impart curing power by blowing into medicine.
7 Flageolet of cedar wood, used by young men during courting.
8 Dance wand with heron feathers; pair carried by leader of Feather Dance during Green Corn Dance.
9 White heron feather attached to spring, worn in hat by men during Green Corn Dance.
10 Cloth for medicine man's

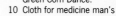

turban.
11 Medicine man's hat band.
12 Man's beaded neck band.
13 Bow of bois d'arc with twisted rawhide string.
14 Arrows; one with straight point for small game, one blunt bird bunt, one with facetted point for fish.
15 One of a pair of ballsticks for team ballgame.
16 Pounder used by medicine man to prepare ritual emetic taken by men at Green Corn Dance.
17 Pottery vessel, used for

cooking.
18 Twilled cane basket, with decorative band.
19 Twilled cane utility basket.
20 Gourd drinking ladle.
21 Awl for sewing and basket making.
22 Wooden paddle for stirring food while cooking.
23 Crooked knife for wood carving.
24 Girl's dress of calico.
25 Woman's apron.
26 Cloth bag.
27 Model of corn-grinding pestle, made by the father

at the birth of a daughter and kept to ensure proper development.
28 Man's shirt of red cotton cloth, with blue facings.
29 Man's shirt.
30 Woman's belt; design in beads and cloth appliqué said to represent storm clouds breaking up.
31 Pair of man's garters.
32 Man's fingerwoven sash of red wool.
33 Pair of men's leggings of black wool cloth with red edging.

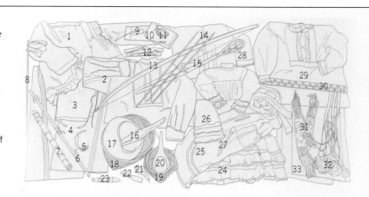

Above: *The square grounds at the Creek town of Asilanapi, Oklahoma, 1912. The busk or Green Corn Festival is in progress, with the ritual medicine being prepared near the central fire.*

dances rehearsing the sacrifices to come on the fourth day after the death. Those who were to die were finely dressed, their hair daubed red, and each carried a large conch shell. Each was escorted by eight male relatives wearing red head feathers: one carried a warclub, one the victim's sitting mat, one the cord to be used for strangling, one the skin for blindfolding, one a clay dish holding six pellets of tobacco (or perhaps it was a stronger narcotic), one a small drinking vessel of water, and finally two men who were to draw the strangling cord tight.

Those who were to die and their attendants paraded from the Tattooed Serpent's house to the front of the temple on a mound at the plaza, issuing death cries. The Chief Priest came out of the temple with a message from the Creator. The celebrants then separated into two bands led by the two wives, and the principals each sat on their mats, giving the death cry in unison, and then danced in place while their attending relatives danced behind them. This dance was repeated in front of the Tattooed Serpent's house, and the War Dance and other dances were also performed.

On the second day the dances were repeated. This time those who were to die each carried a red warclub and a bundle of red cords. Two women relatives of the man who had been dismissed by the principal wife volunteered to die

Right: *George W. Stidham and his family, 1869. Stidham was a leader of the mixed-blood Creek aristocracy in Indian Territory, a slave-owner and supporter of the Confederacy during the Civil War.*

in his place and were accordingly strangled, not only freeing him from the obligation but promoting him to Noble status.

The final day was marked by fasting and smoking tobacco (both to gain strength). The end began when the Master of Ceremonies, his torso painted red and wearing a red feather head ornament and a belt or skirt of red and

black feathers, carrying a red baton with black feathers, entered the Tattooed Serpent's house and raised the death cry, which was repeated by the crowd gathered in the plaza. The body emerged on a litter carried by six men, preceded by the Master of Ceremonies and the oldest War Chief who carried a calumet and the pole with forty-six hoops. The litter was fol-

lowed by those who were to die, and their attendants. These attendants by this service were raised from commoners to rank as Honored People and were relieved of the obligation to die when another Sun died. After circling the house, the procession slowly looped across the plaza. At each loop, they walked over the body of an infant sacrificed by his parents (by this both releasing them from the duty to be sacrificed at a future Sun's death, and raising them from commoners to status among the nobility).

When the procession reached the temple, the chests containing the possession of the Tattooed Serpent were taken inside, for burial with him. Those to be sacrificed seated themselves on their mats in a semicircle facing the temple. All gave the death cry. They swallowed the tobacco pellets with water, numbing their faculties. The leather blindfolds were placed over their heads, then the cords were looped around their necks. The ends of these were strongly pulled by the relatives assigned this task, quickly strangling them.

One account says that five more were then strangled in the plaza: the 'nurse' of the Tattooed Serpent, a doctor from a nearby town, and three old women.

The Tattooed Serpent and his two wives were buried in a trench inside the temple. The Noble woman doctor and the 'Chancellor' were buried on the mound but outside the temple. The others were carried on litters back to their home villages for burial in the temples there. Finally, the Tattooed Serpent's house was burned.

It is hardly surprising that several eighteenth-century French observers recorded these obsequies in great detail. While they said little about the Natchez beliefs that justified and maintained them, one can hardly doubt that the ideology strongly supported a heirarchical social system. A few years later the Natchez attacked the French, who retaliated and nearly destroyed them. The survivors eventually joined the Creek and Cherokee Indians, and little is heard about them until the end of the nineteenth century and the beginning of the twentieth. The elaborate social system had by then been totally replaced by one much like that of the Creeks.

The economic base which supported the dense populations and their elaborate social and political systems can be envisioned by considering the economic activities of the Choctaws at a later period. An excellent idea of Choctaw subsistence in the late eighteenth century is given by the materials collected in Mississippi in 1823-5 by Gideon Lincecum, a frontier physician who apprenticed himself to a Choctaw medical practitioner and also wrote

down and translated long historical traditions told by an aged Choctaw man named Chahta Imataha.[2]

In the eighteenth century the Choctaws had less territory than their neighbors, and were probably more dependent on agriculture. This was so productive that they were able to export corn. As in all the aboriginal Southeast there were important seasonal differences in Choctaw subsistence. In midwinter the fields were prepared for planting. On new plots, after a ceremony with dances, the underbrush and smaller growth was cut and larger trees were girdled. The dried brush was then no doubt burned, the ashes spread on the field providing the only fertilizer used. Planting was done in the spring, when the soil was turned and holes for planting the seeds were made with a digging stick, which was a short hardwood pole with a point that had been sharpened and hardened by charring in a fire. While the heaviest labor of clearing was done by men, the rest of the work was shared by men, women, and children. In much of the rest of the Southeast, however, agricultural labor after clearing was almost entirely women's work. The most important crop was corn. Also planted in the same plots were beans and squash. Crops of lesser importance elsewhere in the Southeast, and probably for the Choctaw too, were sunflowers, marsh elder, and gourds. By the late eighteenth century the Choctaws had added peas, watermelons, sweet potatoes, and fruit trees.

Below: *A Mikasuki Seminole single-family village in the Big Cypress Swamp, Florida, c.1920. Canoe trails lead to two docks. The open-ended structure is for cooking.*

After the crops were well established, it was still necessary to protect them from squirrels and crows, but most people could scatter to streams and lakes for fishing and turtling and collecting wild fruits, nuts, and berries. These included persimmons, plums, hickory nuts, chestnuts, walnuts, pecans, acorns (probably leached after grinding), cherries, grapes, and mulberries. Fishing methods included a kind of communal fish drive in shallow water, the use of a trap made by sewing a hide cover with a drawstring over a long tube of hoops, muddying the water in a pool of a river (perhaps, although Lincecum does not say so, including the use of buckeye or devil's shoestring as a plant poison to stun the fish), shooting fish with bows and arrows, and finally catching them with metal hooks gotten from the French.

When the corn first ripened in early summer, all gathered for the Green Corn Festival. Fishing, hunting waterfowl, and gathering were then resumed until it was time to return in the fall for harvesting and storing the ripe corn. The men then left for a period of hunting in the fall and early winter, while the women, children, and old people collected nuts and fruits in the woods. In the middle of the winter the hunters returned and the cycle began again with clearing the fields.

For hunting men used bows and arrows, before they acquired guns from Europeans. The most valued game was deer, which were killed in quantities. Decoys made from the skin and antlers of a buck's head were used along with special deer calls. Bear were killed in cane brakes, especially for their fat. Boys as well as men hunted smaller game too, including turtles, alligators, rabbits, raccoons, turkeys, quail, and prairie chickens. A favorite boy's weapon was a cane blowgun, some 7ft (2m.) long, with darts having thistle down at the butt ends. Meat was sun dried and also smoked and dried on racks over fires.

There were many different corn recipes. Green corn was roasted on the cob, and green corn kernels were slowly boiled with meat, with some lye added, to make a popular dish. Ripe corn kernels were pounded into flour in a wooden mortar and pestle. The Choctaw mortar was made of an upright hickory log about 2ft (60cm.) high and 1 to 1½ft (30–45cm.) in diameter, with a hollow up to 1½ft deep charred out of the upper end. The pestle was a hickory

Below: *Mikasuki Seminole men, women and children, about 1930, at a cooking fire in the center of their settlement. The radiating logs were gradually pushed in as they burned.*

pole about 5ft (1.5m.) long with a weight about 1ft long and 6in. (15cm.) in diameter left on the upper end, and a round shaft about 2in. (5cm.) in diameter narrowing to a point at the bottom. Corn kernels could be ground after parching, or else they were boiled, dried, and parched before grinding. For sifting and cleaning the ground corn there was a set of three baskets made of plaited cane: a shovel-shaped fanner, a shallow squarish sieve, and a large flat container. Hominy was made by pounding dried kernels to remove the husks, then boiling the cracked pieces (the grits) for twelve to eighteen hours in lye water. This was a favorite food called *tanfula* in Choctaw, that was customarily kept in each house ready to serve to all visitors. It was adopted by non-Indians under the name Tom Fuller. There were many kinds of bread made from corn meal, simply baking it, or letting it ferment slightly to make a sour bread, or mixing corn meal with ground sunflower seeds for the dough, or stuffing corn dough in cornhusks and baking them in hot ashes, or wrapping corn dough mixed with beans or hickory nuts in cornhusks and boiling these, or grating green corn and mixing the meal with hot water. A special dish served by the bride's parents at a wedding was made from juice from strained cooked grapes, in which small bits of corn

Above: *Fred Smith, Seminole, with a typical baby's haircut and small boy's dress with patchwork bands and front opening (small girls' dresses opened in the back). Photographed by W.D. Boehmer, 1943.*

Right: *Cow Creek Seminole women, c.1917. Their skirts were of strips of cotton cloth in contrasting colors. Patchwork was just beginning at this time. The central figure has coin silver brooches.*

dough were boiled. A lightweight, nourishing travel food for hunters and warriors (used all over eastern North America) was made from parched kernels ground in the mortar and carfully sifted. This could be eaten as a cold cereal by simply adding water to dampen a handful of the flour. The importance of cornbread in the traditional non-Indian cuisines of the American south is a legacy of the Indians.

Over most of the south documentary records are silent for about 100 years following the mid-sixteenth century, and for much of the area detailed records only begin some hundred years later than that. This was a crucial period of change, when the aboriginal chiefdoms broke up and were replaced by the towns, tribes, and confederacies that can then be followed into modern times. Archeological evidence tends to confirm that this period witnessed massive depopulation, due mainly to the spread of European diseases, with accompanying social and political reorganization, major movements and displacements of populations, and the loss of many elements of culture. The number of populated sites decreased drastically. There were shifts in the tribal balance of power, accompanying demographic changes that proceeded at different rates and to different degrees in various regions. Many sites that had been occupied for centuries were abandoned. The construction of mounds and other major earthworks ceased. The marked differences between settlements in size and, presumably, power and authority, disappeared. In

the late seventeeth century the Iroquois wars associated with the fur trade in the north had a domino effect to the south. The introduction of large numbers of firearms by the French, Dutch, and English engaged in the fur trade resulted in Iroquois expansion and the flight of many of their enemies to the south. With the founding of Charleston in 1670 new disruptions entered the area from the east, with English capture

and purchase of Indians for the slave trade in the West Indies, and the development of a massive commerce in deerskins for export to Europe. It was during this period that the Creek Confederacy arose from the broken chiefdoms, in response to these outside pressures. Another result was the total destruction of the aborigines of Spanish Florida, who lacked guns to defend themselves against the Creek and

Above: *A group of Mikasuki Seminole poling canoes, photographed near Miami, c.1920. Flat-bottomed dug-out canoes were commonly used by most SE tribes; both poling and paddling were employed.*

Below: *A Mikasuki Seminole woman grating roots of the coontie plant (Zamia, a wild cycad) from which starch was made, eaten in the Seminole soup known as sofkie.*

English invaders. During the eighteenth century Florida was resettled by Creek colonists, whose descendants became the Seminoles when their connections to the Confederacy ceased.

After a century or so, the southern Indian situation again changed radically. As non-Indian settlement expanded, especially in Georgia and Alabama, the Indians were pushed aside and their lands and fields usurped. Finally in the 1820s and 1830s nearly all were deported to Indian Territory – present-day Oklahoma. Many died during this so-called 'Removal'. A few managed to avoid the deportation: some Seminoles survived in south Florida, some Cherokees in western North Carolina, a few Creeks in far southern Alabama, and many Choctaws in Mississippi. Some tribes entirely escaped Removal: the Catawba in South Carolina, the Tunica and Chitimacha in Louisiana, and the Lumbee and other mestizo populations in the Carolinas.

In Oklahoma the deportees reorganized and established new tribal governments, especially those that became known as the Five Civilized Tribes – Cherokees, Choctaws, Chickasaws, Creeks, and Seminoles. During the Civil War many of these were divided and suffered heavily. Their governments reconstituted afterwards, and then the Five Civilized Tribes lost much land to non-Indians in the 1880s and 1890s. The tribal governments lost most of their remaining sovereignty with the arrival of statehood for Oklahoma in 1907.

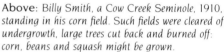

Above: *Billy Smith, a Cow Creek Seminole, 1910, standing in his corn field. Such fields were cleared of undergrowth, large trees cut back and burned off: corn, beans and squash might be grown.*

Below: *Two Mikasuki Seminole women, c.1895, using wooden mortar and pestles. The corn was ground in a log mortar hollowed by charring. The meal produced was usually used in soup.*

The Creek Confederacy was (and still is) based on so-called towns. These are social and political units more than residential ones, quite equivalent to what are called tribes elsewhere. Each town was made up of the people affiliated with a ceremonial center, a square grounds (in modern Oklahoma parlance, a stomp grounds). They often lived quite far from the center, in scattered hamlets and homesteads. The number of towns varied over time, as towns could both split, when one faction established a new, separate square grounds, and merge, by two towns agreeing to share a single square grounds. From the middle of the nineteenth century until the 1930s, there were between twenty-five and thirty Creek towns, the total depending partly on how one counted closely associated towns. Most of these were Muskogee-speaking, but some five or ten were Hitchiti-speaking (or had been until recently when they adopted Muskogee for internal as well as external use). There was also at least one town each of other languages: Alabama, Koasati, Natchez, and Yuchi. However, Muskogee was the general language of the Confederacy, through which speakers of other languages communicated with other Creeks and with outsiders.

The towns were divided into two groups, sometimes called 'sides', usually characterized as White and Red. The White or 'peace' towns were preeminent in civil affairs, while the Red or 'war' towns were conceived of as dominant in military matters. The White towns were said to control executive affairs of the Confederacy, the Red towns legislative and judicial ones. According to Creek traditions, the White towns controlled the Confederacy until the time of the American Revolution. From then through the

Seminole Ballgame, 1895

Players at a ballgame held between men and women at the Green Corn Dance, Pine Island, north of Miami. The ball is aimed at the top of the pole, and score kept by erasing a charcoal mark whenever a goal is made. Women use their hands to throw the ball, while men can use only the ballsticks. On the edge of the dance grounds is the 'bed' or ceremonial seating structure; on the other side is the frame for the ritual sweatbath. In 1895 Seminole women had used sewing machines for about five years, so that machine-sewn patchwork had not yet replaced the older appliqué. The leggings are buckskin. Heavy multiple-strand necklaces were typically worn by women at this time and for some fifty years after. The style of the boy's hairdress was also typical for Seminole men for some decades after 1895.

Civil War period the Creeks were frequently drawn into war so the Red towns ran the Confederacy. After 1865 the White towns again were dominant.

The most important Creek towns around 1900 were the following:

White	Red
Kasihta	Coweta
Hitchiti	Tukabahchee
Abihka	Laplako
Okfuskee	Atasi
Okchai	Kealeychi
Ochiapofa	Chiaha
Tulsa	Osochi
Lochapoka	Alabama
Tuskegee	Eufaula
Koasati	Hilabi
Wiwohka	Hothliwahali
Wiogufki	Talmuchasi
Tokpafka	
Nuyaka	
Okmulgee	
Asilanapi	
Yuchi	
Pakana	

The affiliation of a town as either White or Red was not permanent, however. A town changed sides if it was defeated for four successive times by a town on the other side in the important match ball games. These were the southern Indian form of the team game played between goals that is known as lacrosse in the north. In the southern form, often called 'stick ball' in English, each player used a pair of rackets rather than the single racket used in lacrosse. Like lacrosse, it was a very rough sport. The Creeks conceived it as a substitute for war, sometimes calling it 'the younger brother of war', and explaining that it kept the peace within the Confederacy.

The Creek Confederacy was modelled on the town organization, for the members of each town were also organized into two 'sides'. Here the social units of the dual organization were the clans. Every individual was born into the clan of his or her mother. There were fifty Muskogee clans, of which twenty-three were also Hitchiti clans. Most had animal or bird names, while a few were named for plants, and there were also Wind, Medicine, Salt, and Arrow clans. They were totemic in the sense that the members had a special relationship to the clan species or phenomenon, but they did not trace descent from these totems. The clans had members in various towns, which offered hospitality to visiting clan members. Among the most important functions of clans was punishment for murder, for the victim's clan members took vengeance on the murderer or another member of the murderer's clan. There was no overall clan organization. Rather, within each town the clans filled special functions and pro-vided the incumbents for town offices (not always the same ones in different towns). Each town was an independent, self-governing body headed by its micco or chief, chosen from a specific clan, usually a White clan since his duties were peaceful. Usually there was also a vice-chief or 'twin chief', and a set of assistant chiefs (sometimes from several different clans). There was also a body of sub-chiefs, usually from the micco's clan. Another set of officers directed work in the fields and on public buildings, and ran the Black Drink ceremony. These, the assistant chiefs, and a set of respected elders known as 'beloved men' formed the town council. All of these were, in most towns, from White clans. Each town also had officials from the Red clans – three grades of war officials, who gained their positions from warlike deeds, rather than inheriting them. They dealt with war and the inter-town ball games. The highest grade of warriors also served as town police.

The Creek Confederacy as a whole was governed by a council made up of town chiefs, who met at irregular intervals and not necessarily as a body. It was a loose confederation

Below: *Little Tiger's household, Mikasuki Seminole, on a small island (a 'hammock') in the Big Cypress Swamp, Florida, in 1910. In the foreground is a dock for dugout canoes. A banana plant is at right, and other crops are grown nearby. The structure in the center rear is the cookhouse.*

Seminole

When these things were collected by Alanson Skinner among the Mikasuki Seminoles in south Florida in 1910, they were living quite independent lives in the Everglades and Big Cypress Swamp, traveling by dugout canoe to stores in Miami, Fort Lauderdale, and Fort Myers to exchange alligator hides, feathers, and wages from employment as guides for sport hunters, for the cloth, coffee, salt, tobacco, sewing machines, guns and ammunition, and a few other things needed to supplement the products of their fishing, hunting, and agriculture. They were unaffected by missionaries and by government agents trying to persuade them to move to reservations. Major changes followed, with the rapid increase in the non-Indian population on Florida's lower east coast and the beginning of drainage of the Everglades. Other Seminoles lived near Lake Okeechobee speaking Muskogee, a related but distinct language, and sharing the Mikasuki way of life. Modern Florida Seminoles are descendants of both groups.

1 Woman's blouse of cotton cloth with long cape collar attached, appliqué designs, two rows of coin silver brooches.
2 Long skirt matching the blouse, with ruffles and appliqué stripes.
3 Wooden pestle for grinding corn on upright log mortar; small size, for a girl.
4 Basket for sifting ground corn, made of twilled palmetto leaf stems.
5 Winnowing/storage basket of twilled palmetto stems.
6 Fan of turkey tail feathers sewn to buckskin handle, used to fan log fire.
7, 8 Two wooden spoons used as cups to drink soupy dishes.
9 Cakes of deer brains mixed with fiber and roots, then dried and kept until needed for tanning deerskins.
10 Small girl's dress.
11 Hole-and-slot heddle, for making woven beadwork bands.
12 Man's shirt with waist band and long skirt, design of

appliquéd stripes; worn without trousers.

13 Plume of egret and other feathers tied to stick, worn inserted into man's cloth turban.

14 Woven waist belt of wool and white beads, with long red wool tassels to suspend from each hip.

15, 16 Two pairs of buckskin moccasins, each made of one piece, gathered at seam.

17 Stick wrapped with buckskin, used to buff silver ornaments by the silversmith Miami John Tiger.

18 Basket with telescoping cover, the type used only to hold medicines.

19 Bracelet of woven beadwork with wool tassels.

20 Double pendant of woven beadwork with wool tassels, worn pinned to a man's turban.

21 Shoulder belt of woven beadwork, design representing rattlesnake, worn over one shoulder and across chest, with long woollen tassels tied on hip.

22 Man's coat, with open front, large triangular cape collar, complex appliqué designs on skirt.

23 Man's straight shirt, appliqué bands on front yoke.

24 Pair of rackets or ballsticks used by man in single-pole ballgame.

25 Man's breechclout of dark cloth, edges bound with ribbon.

26 Pair of man's leggings, of red-dyed buckskin, fringed buckskin garters attached.

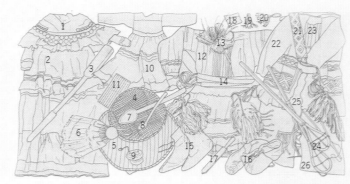

rather than a state-like organization, at least before Removal, and seemingly served mainly to keep the peace between its member towns. It did not, however, unite them in war against any outside power.

The principal ritual of the Creeks was – and for many still is – the annual Green Corn Festival or busk (so-called from its name in Muskogee, *poskitá*). This varied in different towns and changed somewhat over time, but in essentials was the same among all the Creek towns and was very similar among their relatives the Seminoles. Similar festivals were shared by the Cherokees, Choctaws, and probably other southeastern Indians. One of the best accounts we have is by John Howard Payne (actor, playwright, author of *Home Sweet Home*, and supporter of the Cherokees in their failed struggle against Removal). Payne attended the Tukabahchee busk in 1835 in Alabama, just before the Removal. His conclusion to his detailed description indicated real understanding of what he had observed, very unusual for an outsider at that period.

'I never beheld more intense devotion;

and the spirit of the forms was a right and religious one. It was beginning the year with fasting, with humility, with purification, with prayer, with gratitude. It was burying animosities, while it was strengthening courage. It was pausing to give thanks to Heaven, before daring to partake its beneficence.'[3]

Each town held its busk at a special square grounds, referred to in Muskogee as the 'big house', and evidently serving as a world symbol. The old Tukabahchee square grounds described by Payne were in a secluded location, where there were two adjacent rectangular grounds. The main square had on each side a shelter, called a 'bed', some 40ft (12m.) long, with openings of about 10ft (3m.) at each corner between the beds. Each bed was divided into three compartments, each seating a particular

Below: Jim Osceola's Cow Creek Seminole household, 1910-11. This is the traditional Florida Seminole house type, a chickee, with palm-thatched roof, no sides and so well-ventilated, and an interior platform on which people slept, ate and worked.

clan (or group of linked clans), while in front specific seats were occupied by particular town officials (without regard for their clan affiliations). Outside one corner of this square was a large semi-subterranean council house with a conical roof, on the edge of the second square which contained a ritual tall pole that served as a goal in a ball game played between men (with rackets) and women (without). On two sides of this ball square there were cornfields, on another side was an earth ridge, while the fourth side was formed by the back of one of the beds that faced the other square. In the center was a mound formed from dirt taken from the square grounds each year before a fresh layer was spread to consecrate the grounds in preparation for the busk. Outside one corner of the ball square was another mound, formed from the ashes of the central fire. The square grounds complex with its ritual structures is reminiscent of the massive ritual structures in and around the plazas of the earlier chiefdoms, and it certainly represents a much simplified descendant serving similar functions.

The Creek busk inaugurated the new year, and it was timed to coincide with the first ripe-

ning of the town's corn, for it was forbidden to eat the new crop before the busk. The ceremony was a form of renewal, of the people's relations to the spiritual world, as also to the world of plants and animals, and to other people. A feature that repeatedly struck outside observers is the amnesty afforded to those who had committed crimes (except murder) during the previous year. An important part of the ceremony was the ritual lighting of a new fire, which was distributed to all the households to relight the fires that had been extinguished as the houses were swept and cleaned. The same new fire was used to light the ceremonial fire in the center of the square grounds, where the ritual medicines were prepared.

At Tukabahchee the busk lasted eight days, with the pattern of ceremonies on the second four days being similar to the pattern on the corresponding first four days. On the first day the square grounds were cleaned, and participants and visitors gathered there. The second day was a feast day, with dances at night including a woman's dance that much impressed Payne. That night the men (only) slept in the square grounds. The third day was perhaps the

Above: *Margaret Brown, one of the last speakers of Catawba, making pottery in her front yard, 1918. Only among the Catawaba have the ancient Southeastern pottery techniques survived without interruption.*

Below: *A group of distinguished Cherokees visiting Washington in 1866 to negotiate the treaty with the U.S. that was signed on 19 July. Left to right: John Rollin Ridge, Saladin Watie, Richard Fields, Col. Elias C. Boudinot, Col. William P. Adair.*

peak of the busk. The men fasted all day, the new fire was lit with a fire drill, and men took two medicines including the emetic Black Drink. The vomiting in the square that followed was compared by Payne to a libation; it was a form of ritual purification. Young men and boys were scratched with needles on their limbs, to fortify them. The Feather Dance was performed by men carrying poles with feathers attached, signifying peace. Various dances named for animals followed, and social dances filled the whole night. On the fourth day the new corn was eaten for the first time, as part of a feast. The sacred, ancient copper plates, a palladium unique to Tukabahchee, were brought out and reverently displayed. A mock battle known as the Gun Dance was performed, accompanied by women singers. In the evening the town council met. The fifth day was devoted to a ritual deer hunt. On the sixth day there was another feast, when salt was used for the first time in the year (it was felt to be weakening and deleterious). The women danced again, wearing the typical southern box-turtle rattles attached to their calves. At the end the Old Dance was performed, by men alone, to free the

feasters from all ritual restrictions. The seventh day was again devoted to fasting. On the eighth day the chief gave a final speech and the people dispersed.

In several ways the busk reflects the Southeastern Indian emphasis on maintaining good health and on curing. Perhaps this is a result of the demographic disaster suffered by their ancestors. In traditional Southeastern cultures there was no sharp distinction between religious and medical beliefs, rituals, and practice. More is known about traditional Cherokee medicine than any other in the region. This is partly because Cherokee doctors made use of Sequoyah's remarkable invention of a syllabary for writing Cherokee. Although he was not literate in English, he was aware of the general nature of writing, or at least of the possibility of representing speech by marks on paper. After

several years of experimenting with writing Cherokee, he introduced the results in 1819. He had invented a set of eighty-five symbols, of which five represent vowels, one represents the sound s, and the rest stand for syllables each made up of a consonant plus a vowel. The system was practical, and a great many Cherokees soon could write their own language. Because the system was not introduced by missionaries (as were other writing systems for North American Indian languages), it was readily used for the fundamentally non-Christian purpose of recording the secret magical formulas used for curing. Cherokee doctors made collections of medical charms, prayers, and formulas. These provided an entree for study and description of Cherokee medicine, even though the records themselves are quite abbreviated and allusive in order to keep them secret from competing doctors.

According to Cherokee theory, illness was caused mainly by the spirits of animals, who, according to tradition, had invented diseases in order to take revenge on humans for killing and abusing them. Other diseases were caused by human and animal ghosts, spirits such as

Below: A cabin home on the Cherokee Qualla Reservation, North Carolina, 1888. The cabin belonged to Ayunini, or Swimmer, who stands at the right. He was a key informant to anthropologist James Mooney, being well-versed in Cherokee mythology, history, botany and medicine.

the dwarf-like Little People, and witchcraft. Dreams were sometimes a symptom or omen, and perhaps earlier a direct cause. Diseases were named for their causes, not according to their symptoms. A doctor diagnosed by first inquiring as to the location of the pain. Then the patient was asked whether any prohibitions or taboos had been infringed, and whether the patient had had any indicative dreams or omens, even over the preceding several months or two or three years. The doctor often had to suggest many possibilities that might fit the symptoms, and there were any number of possibilities for the same symptoms. If the interviewing still failed to reveal the cause, the doctor could resort to divination through the movement of beads he held between the thumb and forefinger of each hand. Discovering the cause of the sickness was necessary in order to choose the procedures to effect a cure.

Doctors cured by a combination of herbal remedies and the singing or recitation of magical formulas. Usually the formulas recorded in the Sequoyah syllabary indicate the cause, then often belittle the disease spirit, then threaten it with a rival spirit, who is invoked to drive it away. Frequently the formulas involve color and directional symbolism as well. Several hundred medicinal plants were recognized by skilled Cherokee doctors. Their appropriateness for curing often depended on some similarity in name or appearance to the causative agent of the disease, and sometimes on a perceived similarity between the plant and the symptoms of the disease (according to the ancient folk medical doctrine of signatures). The herbs were collected only as they were needed for a specific case, then usually boiled in water. The medicine might then be rubbed on the patient, sometimes into scratches made on the skin, or alternatively the doctor might blow it over the patient through a cane tube.

The effectiveness of Cherokee medicine is of course impossible to measure, since it depended partly on psychosomatic factors and partly on the pharmacological properties of plants (most of which have never been scientifically tested). However, Cherokee medicine was certainly at least as effective as European and European-American medicine of a century and more ago.

Left: *Tsolocha, a Cherokee man, by Karl Bodmer at Natchez (1833). Bodmer had difficulty in sketching an 'old Cherokee, who didn't want his business at first, but later complied . . . when sketches had been shown to him'. This was almost certainly Tsolocha.*

Below: *Pre-ballgame dance, Cherokee, photographed by James Mooney on the Qualla Reservation, 1888. Seven women dancers stand in a row behind their dance leader, seated with a drum. Note ball sticks hanging on a rack before the women. To the left is the men's dance leader, shaking a gourd rattle.*

JOSLYN ART MUSEUM, OMAHA, NEBRASKA

References

1 These accounts are quoted in translation on pp. 139-57 of John R. Swanton's 'Indian Tribes of the Lower Mississippi Valley and Adjacent Coast of the Gulf of Mexico,' *Smithsonian Institution, Bureau of American Ethnology Bulletin 43*, 1911.
2 T. N. Campbell, 'Choctaw Subsistence: Ethnographic Notes from the Lincecum Manuscript,' *Florida Anthropologist* 12(1): 9-24, 1959.
3 John Howard Payne (introduction by John R. Swanton), 'The Green Corn Dance,' *Chronicles of Oklahoma* 10:170-95, 1932.

Cherokee

The Cherokees have been divided since the Removal of 1838, the Eastern Band living in the mountains of western N. Carolina, and the majority, in eastern Oklahoma, being the descendants of those deported to Indian Territory. Two items shown here are from Indian Territory, the rest from the Eastern Band. Those dated 1868 and 1881 were collected by Edward Palmer. The rest were gathered by James Mooney, the great pioneer ethnographer of the Eastern Cherokee.

1 Water drum for dances, a keg of sassafras wood with groundhog skin head. 1887.
2 Wooden dance stick for dance drum. 1887.
3 Scratcher, seven splinters of turkey leg bone in turkey quill frame, to scratch limbs and chest of ballplayers to cause suppleness. 1886.
4 Eagle Dance wands. 1889.
5 Cane blowgun, about 10 feet long. 1887.
6 Blowgun darts of sharp sticks feathered with thistledown. Before 1913.
7 Bullet mold of local white talc held together with wooden pins. 1886.
8 Pair of box turtle rattles, worn by woman tied on side of legs above ankles.
9 Rattle of gourd holding pebbles, used by lead singer in dance. 1887.
10 Pair of shorts with red appliqué design, worn by ballplayer. 1888.
11 Charm worn on head by ballplayer; eagle feathers and deerhair for speed, snake rattle to frighten opponents. 1889.
12 Two stone pipe bowls carved with pocket knife then greased; with squirrel next to bowl. 1886.
13 Stone bowl pipe, bear next to bowl. 1887.
14 Sourwood pipestem. 1887.
15 Wooden mask worn in Eagle Dance at Big Cove. October 1901.
16 Mask worn in 1901; these impersonate strangers.
17 Mask of buckeye wood. 1887.
18 Ball for team ballgame, made of buckskin stuffed with deer hair. 1881.
19 Pair of ballsticks for team game, of hickory; older long type. 1881.
20 Pair of ballsticks; recent shorter type. Before 1911.
21 Ballsticks with bark wrappings for burning spiral design. Before 1911.

36

22 Toy plow, made by a twelve year old boy. 1889.
23 Awl with antler handle. 1881.
24 Hunter's deer call. 1889.
25 Twilled cane basket. 1881.
26 Muzzle for ox. Before 1913.
27 Pottery drinking cup. 1913.
28 Wooden ladle. 1900.
29 Laurel wood spoon, for hominy gruel. 1910.
30 Clay pot. 1881.
31 Clay pot. 1887.

32 Twilled cane basket. 1881.
33 Fish creel, basketry of hickory splints. 1900.
34 Divination stones, hung from string, used with charms and prayers to locate lost objects. 1888.
35 Two carved wooden combs, worn by women at back of head. 1887.
36 Carved wooden comb. 1881.
37 Pair of ballplayer's shorts. 1888.
38 Pair of ballplayer's shorts, worn in 1888 by Rope

Twister, captain of the Wolftown team.
39 Pair of ballplayer's shorts. 1888.
40 Poplar wood paddle with carved stamp, used to mark pot No. 41. 1887.
41 Round bottomed cooking pot made with paddle marked outside. 1887.
42 Netted woollen scarf from Indian Territory. 1868.
43 Woven woollen shawl from Indian Territory. 1868.
44 Band of woven beadwork. Before 1913.

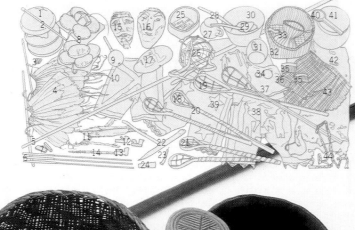

37

'There is no climate or soil . . . equal to that of Arizona . . . It is my land, my home, my father's land, to which I now ask to be allowed to return. I want to spend my last days there, and to be buried among those mountains.'

GERONIMO OF THE CHIRICAHUA APACHE

THE SOUTHWEST

THE SOUTHWEST has no specific limits or definite boundaries but can be conceptualized as the states of Arizona and New Mexico in the United States and Sonora and parts of Chihuahua in Mexico. Small parts of Colorado, Texas, Utah and Sinaloa are included in the region. Spanning two modern nation states, this is yet one culture area, characterized by a common arid environment and a multi-cultural present that is the result of a multi-cultural past. Newcomers to the Southwest of European, African and Asian ancestry meet and mingle with Native Americans to produce a distinctive and rich society. While close to a hundred groups make up the Southwest, it is the Native Americans who give the region its distinctive flavor and who provide its cultural foundations. Unlike other regions of North America, over twenty-five Native American groups have survived the onslaught of Euro-

This map shows approximate territories of tribes and language groups at the earliest periods for which there is reliable evidence: the sixteenth century for the Pueblos (the groups from Hopi to the Piro to N. Tiwa), the seventeenth century for the extreme southwestern part of the area, and the eighteenth century for the Apache, Navajo and groups on the far northwest edge.

After these dates, many tribes lost territory, some disappeared and a few gained territory.

Key to tribes:
1 Cocopa
2 Quechan
3 Halchidhoma
4 Mohave
5 Walapai
6 Havasupai
7 Yavapai
8 Maricopa
9 Papago and Upper Pima
10 Seri
11 Hopi
12 Western Apache
13 Chiricahua Apache
14 Zuni
15 R.Grande Keresans
16 Jemez
17 Navajo
18 Tewa
19 N.Tiwa
20 Tano
21 Pecos
22 S.Tiwa
23 Tompiro
24 Laguna
25 Acoma
26 Piro
27 Jicarilla Apache
28 Mescalero Apache
29 Jocome and Jano
30 Suma
31 Jumano
32 Opata
33 Eudeve
34 Jova
35 Lower Pima
36 Yaqui
37 Guarijio
38 Tarahumara
39 Tubar
40 Mayo
41 Concho
42 Toboso
43 Guasave
44 Acaxee
45 Xixime
46 Tahue
47 Tepehuan
48 Zacatec
49 Pame
50 Karankawa
51 Poorly Known Groups of the Gulf Coastal Plain and Interior
52 Ñakipa
53 Paipai
54 Kiliwa
55 Cochimi
56 Guaycura
57 Pericú

PACIFIC
OCEAN

pean expansion and been able to remain on their traditional homelands with some compliment of their distinctive customs as enclaved cultures. These groups represent almost three-quarters of the Native American cultures that inhabited the region at the time of the first Spanish explorations.

The Southwest as a region is rooted in the land and in ancient traditions. The land is varied – high rugged, snow capped mountains, fruitful river valleys, sweeping grasslands and arid deserts. The vast but often harsh landscape required many ecological adaptations. It also engendered a love of place that is so common among indigenous peoples. This love of place, the feeling of oneness with the land, conceptualized as Mother Earth, permeates Southwest Native American thought and culture as strongly today as it did 300 years ago. The land lives and all peoples respect her. Southwest Native Americans are of the land; they do not exploit it. It is this orientation that helps distinguish them for the descendants of European peoples. This does not mean that all Southwest Native Americans societies are alike, or that they are all homogeneous or never-changing. Each has a distinctive culture, one that is the result of a long historical development. All Southwest Native American cultures are independent, composed of dignified and self-reliant peoples who have wrested their living from local and regional resources. Their cultures today are a legacy of the past, the present and the future. In the Southwest, as nowhere else in North America, all that is vital in life remains as it was and as it will be.

Native Americans came to the Southwest at least 12,000 years ago. In these early times people were hunters and gatherers of wild plants. Following a nomadic way of life, they lived in small family groups and hunted first large game, like mammoths and bison, and later as the environment changed, small animals such as deer and rabbits. When this transition occurred it signalled a new adaptation and way of life and we have given them a new name, the Archaic or Desert peoples, in recognition of this change. These peoples, whose cultures emerged around 6000 BC, began to experiment with growing food around 2500-3000 BC.

Slowly the peoples of the Southwest developed distinctive cultures; those living in the mountainous regions are called the Mogollon, those on the Colorado Plateau, the Basketmakers and Anasazi, and those in the western and central parts of the region, the Patayan, Sinagua and Salado. (Unfortunately almost nothing is known about the prehistory of northwestern Mexico.) Each group became horticulturists growing corn, beans and squash supplemented by hunting and the gathering of wild foods. Each adapted in different ways to their special environments. Around 300 BC migrations brought new groups into the Southwest from Mexico. These individuals quickly developed a culture, known as Hohokam, that was based on agricultural traditions. Living in central and southern Arizona they built extensive irrigation systems, refined tools and monumental architecture. Each of the four groups centered around a geographical area – desert mountains and plateau. (Unfortunately almost nothing is known about the prehistoric groups living in

Sonora either.) Except for those people who lived in areas that could not support agriculture, all these prehistoric peoples lived in permanent and semi-permanent villages. Some were so large and complex that they resembled small towns with extensive and complex organisations.

The fourteenth and fifteenth centuries were a time of great population movement which has not yet been explained. Following a large drought, old regions were abandoned, the largest trading centers no longer used. Groups aggregated and settlements were frequently abandoned. The main Southwestern groups who developed into the peoples we recognise in the Southwest today – the Puebloans, the O'Odham (Pima) and the Yumans – settled in what is now called their traditional homelands.

Below: *Women from San Ildefonso Pueblo where some of the finest Pueblo pottery was produced and still is. They wear the classic manta adorned with jewelry (turquoise or coral), and hard soled moccasins.*

Heralded in an extensive series of clan or migrations legends, each group has a rich oral history about this period. Other groups moved into the region from the north – the Navajo and the Apaches. From the east came Plains peoples who would trade with the native peoples. Occasionally groups from the Great Basin would meet with the settled peoples in the north and along the rivers. Harassed by drought again and the new roving tribes, groups such as the Anasazi moved on to mesa tops and east to the Rio Grande, but as a region, the Southwest was characterized by much interaction and cultural borrowing.

Finally came the Europeans, first the Spanish and later the English-American. The frontiers of the Spanish and English conquests of the New World met and overlapped in the arid Southwest. When the Spaniards arrived in the mid-sixteenth century, they found the entire region inhabited by numerous groups. Some of these peoples were town-dwelling farmers called Puebloans, others were semi-

nomadic hunters and raiders; still others lived in small bands surviving by hunting and gathering. The peoples spoke a bewildering variety of languages and followed numerous ways of life. Yet all were similar in that they differed markedly from the level of political and economic organization the Spanish had encountered in central Mexico. Without the domination of agriculturally based empires like that of the Aztecs, peoples in the Southwest were politically independent and socially and economically self-sufficient farmers; all but a few hundred people on the coast of the Gulf of California and in the northern end of the Sierra Madres Mountains knew how to raise corn, beans and squash. While they differed on the extent to which agriculture was the primary mode of food production or a supplement to hunting and gathering, these peoples were quickly distinguished from the buffalo hunting peoples of the Plains to the east, from the seed-gatherers and rabbit-hunters of the north and the acorn-gatherers of California. Sporadic and small-scale trade in the form of surplus and

Above: *Children playing around open-air beehive ovens in the northernmost Pueblo of Taos. The present village was built around 1700, a testimony to the enduring qualities of Pueblo architecture.*

Left: *Two women and a child making pottery at Santa Clara Pueblo, famous for its polished black wares. Polished red pottery and red polychrome are also still made in the traditional style.*

luxury items was mutual rather than a matter of controlled tribute in food staples and people. No society maintained military or political control over another. This did not mean that groups did not form temporary alliances for warfare, but warfare was not conducted for conquest and subjugation. People fought for revenge or to gain new agricultural lands, displacing older inhabitants.

The Spanish quickly began to settle the Southwest but their advance was stopped by the Apache. Wherever they went, the Spanish established a conquest culture with programs designed to 'civilize the savages' and impose a new world view. Backed by military force and identifying civilization with specific Spanish customs, missionaries, soldiers and settlers introduced Castillian (which became the lingua franca of the region), detached houses placed around a central plaza, men's trousers, new concepts of time and work, the notions of empire, politics, and Christianity. They also established a system of forced tribute, forced labor as servants, farm workers and miners, and extensive slave trade with peoples from all over the region sent to the silver mines in Mexico. They introduced some beneficial items as well – new foods and livestock, especially sheep and horses, and silversmithing. The Spanish and later Mexican policies of concentrating the small nomadic bands in Chihuahua led to the consolidation and extinction of many groups. These changes were so drastic in Mexico that some groups, like the Opata, could no longer be distinguished from the Spanish or Mexican population by the mid-1700s. Other groups welcomed these changes. To others they meant nothing; groups that were isolated because of geographical barriers, like the Seri and the

Tarahumara, remained relatively untouched. Others reacted violently. Changes were enforced on the people so brutally that by 1680 the Pueblos were rising in revolt and successfully drove the Spanish from the Rio Grande region. While the Spanish eventually re-conquered the area, they never overcame the Apaches, the Tarahumara, the Upland Yumans or the Yaquis. It was not until the late 1880s that these groups ceased to be military threats and the final Mexican settlements occurred in northwestern Mexico. By this time, the Mexicans were interested in political and economic control, not in religious conversion. Thus groups were not forced to change and it was individuals that assimilated. Many individuals voluntarily left their native communities to find work in Mexican towns.

Anglo-Americans took over the northern half of New Spain from the Mexican government in 1848. With their settlement of the region they, like the Mexican government in the south, erected great obstacles to the retention of the old way of life for Native Americans. The most

important of these was the imposition of the reservation system which isolated groups on sections of their traditional homelands and policies of forced assimilation. Native Americans were provided with agricultural technology and sent to schools far from their families. As dependent nations, these groups were given new forms of government – constitutional tribal governments that exercise inherent and sovereign powers but are limited by treaties, statutes and agreements with the federal and state governments. They were placed in a dependency role, had a set of values superimposed with no consideration of their desires. Paternalism has meant that economic development and self-determinancy were limited, but it has not meant that any groups have died out because of government policies.

Changes in economic possibilities have also

Below: *War captain and chief hunter of the Pueblo of Nambe, New Mexico, 1880. He wears a bear claw necklace, a powder horn and pouch. His blanket of rabbit skin predates the use of woollen blankets.*

meant many changes in Native American life. The destruction of the traditional subsistence strategies and new trading patterns pulled Southwest Native Americans into the nation-state's market economy. Craft objects, formerly created for home use and minor trading of surplus goods by barter, began to be produced as supplemental or major sources of income. Craft production became important in the economic strategies of many families, even though there was a low hourly return for the labor involved. Weaving, basketry, painting, silversmithing and pottery allowed economic flexibility. People also began working for wages, on farms, on the railroad, in mines as well as in the cities.

While European groups became politically dominant, brought hardship and deprivation, had the force of laws and military might to make the old ways of life impossible, they did not eradicate all cultures. This does not mean that there were not demographic changes; many epidemic diseases raged through the Southwest and took their toll. For example, in 1883 half of the population at Hopi died from smallpox and in the 1918 influenza pandemic over half of the Jicarilla Apache and close to one quarter of the Navajo died. Since the 1920s, however, the populations have slowly and steadily increased. Other Native American groups were destroyed through internal warfare – such as the Halcidoma. But more than any other region in North America, the Native peoples have remained. They have changed, of course. There is a misconception that since Native Americans no longer follow a 'pure' aboriginal culture (i.e. one 'uncontaminated' by Europeans) they no longer exist. This is not true. Native American cultures in the Southwest are vital and vibrant. Native peoples co-exist as part of the culture of the Greater Southwest and as distinctive members with unique ways of life. They are still rooted in the past and in the land. Based on earlier lifestyles, joint ancestry, ecological adaptation, economies and linguistic affiliation we can define four basic groups of Native Americans living in the Southwest. The following pages look at the groups of the Southwest who existed in the 1600s and have survived into the present. For the core has persisted and groups – the Puebloans, the rancheria peoples, the band peoples and the hunters and gatherers – remain distinct.

In northern New Mexico and Arizona, on the Colorado Plateau and along the Rio Grande River and its tributaries, the Puebloan peoples were most in evidence – numbering over 40,000 individuals – living in ninety villages. Today there are only thirty; the others have been abandoned because of drought, disease and warfare. Called Pueblo Indians by the early Spanish explorers because of their distinctive architecture – permanent, compact, multi-chambered houses made of stone and adobe – these peoples were the descendants of the Anasazi and Mogollon peoples. Pueblo means 'village dweller' and this designation accurately reflected Pueblo life. The Pueblo Indians did not constitute a tribe; each Puebloan culture was a village that functioned as an autonomous political entity. This does not mean that these groups lived in a vacuum. They traded with one another, recognized common ances-

IN AND CHIEF HUNTER
PUEBLO OF NAMBE.

Santa Clara Corn Dance, 1950

Two dancers leave the north kiva to enter the plaza at Santa Clara, one of the Tewa pueblos. They are participating in the Corn Dance; the woman has the distinctive tablita headdress for this dance. She wears a woollen manta with a belt woven of wool and cotton, and very high wrapped moccasins. She has turquoise and silver bracelets, and a turquoise and coral necklace. Both hold spruce boughs, and the man also carries a gourd rattle. He has white and black body paint, and wears necklaces of shells and coral, a cotton dance kilt with wool embroidery, a fine woven cotton belt, and a leather belt with bells. His anklets are of skunk fur tied around his white moccasins, while a fox tail hangs behind. A very similar scene inspired a watercolor by the Santa Clara artist Pablita Velarde.

Above: *The Pueblo of Cochiti (1879), which dates from the mid-thirteenth century. Known for its pottery and fine-toned drums, Cochiti is also famous for ceremonies, kachina dances among them.*

Right: *Governor Ahfitche of San Felipe Pueblo using a pump drill to drill holes in shells and flat turquoise (1880). San Felipe lies between the Rio Grande and the foot of the Black Mesa.*

try, occasionally intermarried and shared many similar values and world views.

The Puebloan peoples speak many different languages. The largest language group is *Tanoan*, part of the Kiowa-Tanoan language family. Tanoan consists of three main languages – *Tiwa*, *Tewa* and *Towa*. The people of Taos, Picuris, Sandia and Isleta speak dialects of Tiwa. At San Juan, Santa Clara, San Ildefonso, Pojoaque, Nambe and Tesuque, Tewa is spoken. Tewa is also spoken at Hano in Hopi country because many Tewa families migrated from the Rio Grande valley about 1700 following the re-conquest of the area after the Pueblo Revolt. Jemez is the only pueblo today in which Towa can be heard. In the past the inhabitants of the famous pueblo of Pecos were also Towa speakers but the village was abandoned in the early 1800s.

Living dispersed among the Tanoan speakers are the *Keresans*. Along the Rio Grande and its tributaries are the Keresan villages of Cochiti, Santo Domingo, San Felipe, Santa Ana and Zia; farther west are the pueblos of Laguna and Acoma. Even farther west is the pueblo of Zuni where *Zunian* is spoken. Zuni is part of the Penutian linguistic stock and is unrelated to other languages in the Southwest. (Other Penutian speakers live in California.) Finally there are the Hopi in north central Arizona. Hopi consists of a series of villages located on three mesas on the Colorado Plateau. *Hopi* is a language that belongs to the Shoshonean branch of the Uto-Aztecan lan-

Zuni

Zuni pueblo has been occupied for at least 600 years. Interaction with Spaniards and Mexicans was almost continuous after Coronado arrived in 1540, but Zuni maintained its independence while adopting some European crops, sheep, and burros, and developing a secular governmental structure to deal with the outside world. This still persists, in changed form, alongside the theocratic system that controls internal affairs. The elaborate ceremonial life is organized by six kiva groups, twelve medicine societies, and two sets of priests, interacting with the fourteen matrilineal clans. In the mid-20th century the manufacture of silver and turquoise jewelry and some pottery for sale was a major source of income. However, by the 1970s weaving was extinct at Zuni and basketry nearly so. These crafts were still actively pursued when the items illustrated here were collected by A. L. Kroeber, F. W. Hodge, and H. J. Spinden between 1899 and 1916.

1 Large pottery bowl with four stepped corners with dragonfly designs inside and modelled frogs outside. 1915.
2 Food bowl. 1912.
3 Redware moccasin jars for matches and trinkets, made for sale. 1915.
4 Wooden lightning symbol carried in dance. 1915.
5 Wooden lightning symbol carried in dance. 1915.
6 Breechcloth of cotton cloth, embroidered in wool, worn by dancer.
7 Throwing club for hunting rabbits, of wood painted red and black. 1915.
8 Stone pot containing green paint. 1899.
9 Small redware jar with duck and stepped rainbow designs. 1899.
10 Pump drill for jewelry making, etc.; metal point, stone flywheel. 1915.
11 Wooden tongs for picking cactus fruit. 1915.
12 Shallow openwork twined basket. 1899.

13 Spindle with wooden whorl, spun wool thread. 1915.

14 Small basket of twilled yucca splints. 1916.

15 Pair of boy dancer's moccasins. 1915.

16 Woman's buckskin moccasins with leg wrappings made of buckskin strips. 1915.

17 Cotton dancer's kilt with pattern in wool embroidery. 1915.

18 Large pottery bowl. 1899.

19 Small wooden paddle for making bread. 1915.

20 Stone panther fetish of Hunter society. 1915.

21 Armlets of god impersonator with perforated yellow flaps and leather pendants. 1915.

22 Pair of dance moccasins with quilled heel straps. 1915.

23 Embroidered cotton cape of Shalako dancer. 1915.

24 Ornament of short turkey feathers and long white feather, worn on side of head for Hopi dance. 1915.

25 Large pottery jar with classic rainbird design. 1899.

26 Large pottery bowl. 1899.

27 Wrapped yucca ring stand for hot pot. 1915.

28 White painted naked kachina doll with flower garland. 1916.

29 Twined basket. 1899.

30 Belled flageolet for Society ceremony. 1915.

31 Wooden lightning symbol carried in dance. 1915.

32 Necklace of wooden imitation eagle claws worn in Comanche Dance. 1915.

guage family. Thus Hopi is related to Piman, Ute and Paiute in the Southwest and many language groups in central Mexico.

The Pueblos are divided into two main subgroups based on location and ecological adaptation. The Eastern Pueblos (Tanoan and Keresan speakers), who live on the Rio Grande and its tributaries, have a permanent water source enabling them to practice irrigation agriculture. The Western Pueblos (Hopi, Hopi-Tewa, Zuni, Acoma and Laguna), lacking a steady supply of water, rely on dry farming. The difference in water supply affects many aspects of culture from food procurement to religion. Economically all Puebloans are agriculturalists. Many also raise small herds of sheep and cattle, produce art – such as weaving, silversmithing, jewelry, katchina dolls, pottery and baskets. (Most Pueblo Indians, like everyone else in the Southwest, are wage earners today. This means that many must live off their land and move to the large nearby cities of Albuquerque, Santa Fe, Gallup, Flagstaff and Phoenix. All return home for important ceremonies.)

With the Pueblo Indians religion transcends and permeates all aspects of life, including interaction patterns with the land, with other peoples and with the supernaturals. All aspects of Puebloan life – arts, crafts, economics, social structure and the family – are inextricably inte-

Above: Zuni Pueblo, New Mexico, 1879. The young man stands beside an eagle cage made of adobe and stakes. The eagle was kept for its plumage which was highly valued for ceremonial purposes.

Below: The Mesa of Taaiyalone (Corn Mountain) seen from the rooftops of Zuni Pueblo. After conflict with the Franciscans in 1632, the Zunis fled to Taaiyalone, which lies southeast of Zuni.

woven and integrated under a single world view. From the simple tenet that people must live in harmony with nature, the Pueblo Indians have developed rich cultural traditions that are expressed in poetry, legends, song, dance and art. In this way central values are given outward expression. For example, many of the designs on pottery are derived from motifs connected with ceremonial life. Architecturally the center of a village, both physically and symbolically, is a special chamber called *kivas*. Here private and communal rites are performed daily and at appropriate times throughout the year. Prayers are given for blessing and to insure the germination and maturation of crops and to give thanks for good health. Through religion all else is given significance.

Secular and ecclesiastical authority are sharply delimited in the pueblos. Each village is a tightly and highly structured theocracy, organized around an elaborate ceremonial life. Based on their ancient patterns, this theocracy, whose head is called the *cacique*, is kept secret within the village. To the outside world the secular political structure is more evident. In the eastern Pueblos, the secular organization is in the hands of a *governor* who is appointed or elected each year. These governors were given canes of office by President Lincoln in the 1860s and these have become valued symbols of

office. The governor has several assistants called *principales*, a group of elder statesmen whose lifelong experience enables them to integrate wisely civil and religious matters. In all the pueblos there is a hunt chief and a war chief or war priest.

Tewa pueblos are composed of two social divisions, what anthropologists call moieties.

Membership in a moiety is through the father, though a woman may change her moiety affiliation if she marries a man of the opposite group. Each moiety has political officers. During half of the year, the governmental and ceremonial duties of the pueblos are in the hands of the Summer People, while the Winter People (the other moiety) are in charge of obligations for the other half-year. Within each moiety there are certain religious societies, but other societies cross-cut and meld the kinship divisions. Among the Keresan peoples, social organization is more unified. There is but one cacique per village and he is aided by a council composed of the heads of religious societies who all serve for life.

In all the pueblos the family is the cornerstone of life. While in the Tewa communities the extended family of either the father or mother is emphasized, at Zuni and Hopi it is the mother's that serves as the basis for the society. Puebloans, when compared to other groups in the Southwest, are non-individualistic and innovations are accepted or rejected by group decision, by consensus and persuasion. While all Puebloan peoples share many common values, ideas and traditions, each is distinct. A pueblo village is a closely united and highly systematized organization. Each village favors marriage within its own group. There are variations in the ceremonies of each group, and the pottery and stylistic designs are distinctive. (The artifacts on pp. 44–5 offer good examples of just such outstanding pottery and stylistic designs from one Puebloan group – the Zuni.)

Below: *The Hopi Natashka or Bean Planting ceremony at Walpi Pueblo, First Mesa, Arizona (1893). These kachinas are ogres who frighten children into obedience to their parents.*

Above: *A Hopi spinner making a twist in his yarn even by means of a spindle, which is placed under his foot, and by pushing the twist up along the thread (photograph undated).*

At the time of Spanish contact, the rancheria groups – the Cahitans, Tarahumarans, Pimans and Yumans – comprised the largest subgroup in the Southwest, over 150,000 individuals or approximately three-quarters of the peoples in the Southwest. They lived in widely spaced settlements along rivers or in well-watered mountain and desert areas in southern Arizona and northern Mexico. Relying on irrigation and flood waters, rancheria peoples were farmers. The extended family, rather than the village, formed the basic social unit; each family owned a house and fields dispersed along the river as much as half a mile apart. Kinship was generally bilateral or patrilineal. Nevertheless, the members of each settlement still thought of themselves as a community, moved as a unit, and symbolized their unity by placing a community house in the center of each settlement. Rancheria peoples frequently had more than one village, shifting from one settlement to another depending on the season of the year. All rancheria peoples are very interested in social gatherings, disdaining structured situations and displays of wealth, however. They are sensitive to the maintenance of form and custom in social intercourse. While this meant there has been a weak development of religious leadership – the important religious leaders were shamans rather than priests, and political leaders were senior men who were influential speakers – there is a respect for all who have knowledge and wisdom. This has led to a highly developed native literature in myth, song, folk stories and formalized oratory. Among the most famous for these skills are the Huichol.

The rancheria groups belong to two basic linguistic groups – the Uto-Aztecan and the Hokan. The Uto-Aztecans rancheria speakers can be divided into four basic language groups: Pima, Cahita, Opatan and Tarahumaran. The Pimans live in southern Arizona – Upper Piman, Tohono O'Odham, Sobaipuri – and in Mexico – the Pima Bajo and Tepehuan. The Cahitan speakers (the Mayo and Yaqui), the Opatan speakers (the Opata, Eudebe and Jova), and the Tarahumaran speakers (the Tarahumara, Warihio and Concho) live in Mexico in mountainous areas and along major rivers. The Hokan speakers live in Arizona and upper Baja California and are known as the Yumans. The Upper Yumans – the Walapai, Yavapai and Havasupai – live in the upland region of western and northern Arizona while the lowland Yumans – the Mohave, Halchidoma, Yuma, Cocomaricopa, Cocopa and Cochimi – live along the Colorado River and its tributaries. Moving constantly because of intertribal warfare, some Yuman groups all but killed each other off by the early nineteenth century. The Maricopa eventually moved in with the River Pima in the area around Phoenix because they had been displaced from the Colorado River.

In Mexico the mountain-dwelling Tarahumara are well-known. Living in shelters ranging from caves in rugged cliffs to stone masonry houses, they planted small cornfields in mountain valleys in the summer and retreated

Above: *Lieta, a Pima woman from the Gila River Reservation, Sacaton, Arizona, 1902. She exhibits a style of face painting obsolete by this time but which was reconstructed for the photograph.*

to the lowlands in the winter. Like other rancheria groups the Tarahumara also utilized wild plant foods. Only recently have the Tarahumara been affected by the outside world: the first railroad into their region did not exist even as recently as ten years ago.

On the plains and lower valleys to the west live groups like the Huichol, the Mayo, and the Yaqui at the mouth of major river systems, some of the richest farmland in all of Mexico. Favorable agricultural conditions permitted more concentrated settlements than the mountainous and desert regions and the Yaqui and Mayo developed tribal organizations for warfare and defensive purposes. So successful were the Yaqui that they were the only group in the region who were not conquered by the Spanish. Interestingly, the Yaqui were also the only group to request missionaries and voluntarily to become Christians. However, they changed much of the ritual and the meanings and developed what is essentially a new religion, Sonoran Catholicism. This is a mixture of Spanish, Mexican, and traditional beliefs and customs. The central ritual is the Eastern ceremony that lasts for forty days, culminating with the destruction of evil by good in a mock battle the day before Easter Sunday. This ritual, like many others still conducted by Southwestern groups, is done to ensure that the world will continue.

The Yaquis have another distinction in the Southwest. After years of warfare they were finally defeated by the Mexicans who occupied their territory in the late 1880s. At conquest the Mexicans deported most of the people to the Yucatan peninsula to work in forced labor camps. Some of these individuals escaped and came to the United States, building several communities in southern Arizona. The Yaquis sought and were given political refugee status and allowed to stay, even after the Yaqui were allowed to return to their homeland in the mid-1920s. One of the reasons they were given political asylum was because of their distinctive religious ceremonies.

Farther north were the O'Odham (Pima)

peoples who lived in more compact settlements than the Tarahumara. The Pima have a long history which reaches back into the archeological past of southern Arizona and northern Mexico. The Pima word for themselves is O'O*dham*, meaning The People. The Pimas can be divided into four basic groups – the River Pima who live along the rivers in central Arizona, the Tohono O'Odham (formerly called the Papago), the Pima Bajo who live in Mexico, and the Sobaipuri who lived in southeastern Arizona and were driven out by the Apache and Spanish. The survivors of this group have intermingled with the other Piman groups. All Piman groups were agriculturalists; in fact, the River Pimans were so successful that they supplied much of the food for the U.S. army during the western campaigns of the Civil War and for Anglo-American settlers moving to California during the Gold Rush of the 1860s. The River Pimans also served in the Civil War as the only Union forces in the Arizona territory; they successfully defeated Confederate troops and kept the lines to California open. After the war they served as scouts in the Apache wars. The River

Pimans remained prosperous until Anglo settlers in the town of Florence, upriver from them, appropriated their water thereby making agriculture no longer possible. The river ran dry at planting time and many people starved. Unfortunately it took the U.S. Congress until 1924 to recognize that their rights have been ignored and allot them water when the Coolidge Dam was built. It took many more years for the Pima to recover economically and socially. The Pima refer to this period as the 'Forty Years of Famine'.

Along the Colorado River lived another group of rancheria peoples, the Yumans. Like the Cahitans they had a permanent water supply and hence could have more densely settled homesteads. They also were organized as a tribe for warfare and had a strong tribal sense of identity. In civil matters, however, the local group made decisions. As groups also they relied more heavily on wild plants for their houses, clothes and food supplements than the Cahitans and their material culture was more like that of the Pimans and their neighbors to the west in California. The River

Below: *Two unidentified Cocopa men – the most southern of the Yuman tribes – on board Admiral Dewey's ship, Narragansett, 1874. Cocopa breechclouts were longer in back than in front.*

Right: *Two unidentified Yuma men, c.1870. Their main weapons were hardwood clubs; the long, weak bows and untipped arrows shown here were rather ineffective and used only for small game and birds.*

Tarahumara

The Tarahumara live in dispersed settlements in southwestern Chihuahua. They are farmers, especially of corn, beans and squash, who raise cattle, sheep, goats, pigs and burros. The first serious study of the Tarahumara was by Carl S. Lumholtz (1902), who collected the objects shown here in the 1890s (except for No. 1, the poncho, which is of more recent origin). Most of these examples have never been published, and none has previously appeared in color. Most

of the types of objects shown, however, are also widely used by the present-day Tarahumara.

The wooden cross on the necklace of Jobs-tears beads from Carichí (No.3) indicates that the Tarahumara are nominally Catholics. Pinole, mentioned in No.8, was meal made from parched corn. The spindle and whorl (No.13) were used for preparing wool thread for weaving. The cane-shafted lance (No.16) is notable because it is a rare object. The twilled palm leaves of the basket and cover (No.18) are double woven.

Peyote and bakánowa ceremonies. From Barranca de San Carlos.

12 Wooden bowl, used inverted as a resonator for musical rasps. From Guajochi.

13 Spindle and wooden whorl. From Guajochi.

14 Bow for hunting game, of elm or mulberry wood. From Carichí.

15 Quiver of mountain lion skin, and seventeen arrows, most with iron points. From Carichí.

16 Lance with cane shaft and iron point. From Carichí.

17 Gourd rattle, used by ritual chanters and matachine dancers.

18 Basket and cover, of twilled palm leaves.

19 Double-woven twilled basket, containing feathers (probably used in ceremonies).

20 Pottery dish for food, made in coiling technique, sun-dried and then fired. From Aboreachi.

21 Woollen blanket, woven on horizontal loom, used as bedding and also worn by men in cold weather. From Guajochi.

22 Woven wool belt worn by both sexes. From Carichí.

23 Woven wool belt.

24 Woven wool belt, from Narárachi.

25 Woven wool belt, from Carichí.

26 Woven wool belt, from Guajochi.

27 Pair of leather sandals, worn by both sexes, from Guajochi.

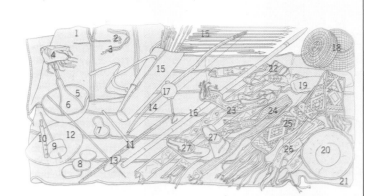

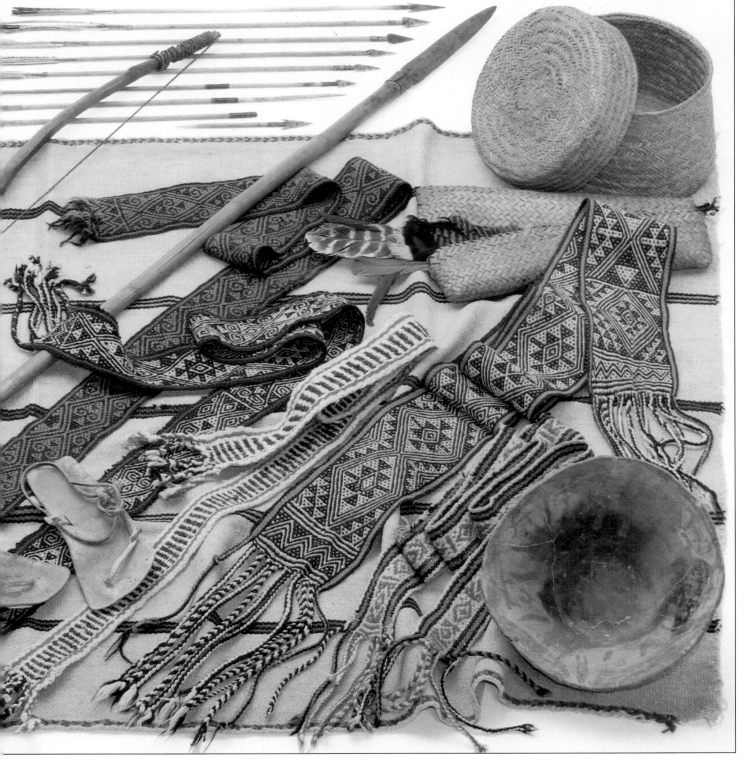

Yumans were tied closely to the annual cycle of river flooding. Since their homes were periodically washed away, they had no cultural incentive for the accumulation of wealth. Even today, the Cocopa, for example, disdain ostentatious displays of wealth. A person's goods are destroyed at his or her death. Even the goods of relatives and friends are placed in the burial fire at death and again in the anniversary festival, the most important religious ceremony. In the

historic period the River Yumans were joined by a group from central California, the Chemuehevi, who have adopted a lifestyle similar to that of the Mohave.

A final group of Yumans, the Upland Yumans, can be placed either with the rancheria peoples or the non-agricultural peoples because their homelands lacked enough water for permanent farming. The Upland Yumans – the Walapai, Yavapai and the Havasupai – lived primarily by hunting and gathering on the upland areas of western and northern Arizona. Living a lifestyle that was similar to other hunting and gathering peoples, the Walapai had a limited technological base and lived in small groups that moved often in an established

round. The Havasupai lived on the Colorado River in Cataract Canyon, next to the Grand Canyon, and have adopted many Hopi traits. The Upland Yumans had little interaction with the Spanish and Mexicans except for meeting an occasional explorer searching for minerals. Today the Yavapai and Walapai live on small reservations and herd cattle or work for wages. Through extensive intermarriage and because of their forced internment on Apache reservations many Yavapai have become intermingled culturally with the Western Apache. By 1900 the Yavapai began to drift off the San Carlos Reservation and return to their traditional homelands in areas that had not been claimed by Anglo-American miners.

Below: *Juan Chivaria, war leader and shaman, son and niece (Sye-cui-Sall), of the Maricopa, one of the Colorado River tribes. Although in close contact with the Pima, the Maricopa followed a way of life typical of Colorado River Yumans.*

Above: *Jodrava, a Havasupai man, drinking from a traditional basket water bottle. Covered inside and out with piñon gum, such bottles are strong, durable and watertight and survive years of use.*

Below: *Havasupai man dehairing a skin stretched over a wooden frame. Finished buckskin was a main item of Havasupai commerce, which they traded for horses, pottery, jewelry with the Hopi and Navajo.*

Mohave Family, 1851

The woman wears a double skirt of shredded bark fibers, the front one of willow bark. She has a multiple strand bead necklace, and carries a Pima basket on her head. Her chin is tattooed with the pattern worn by Olive Oatman while her face is painted red in the design called hotahpava and her body is also painted red. The man wears his hair in long pasted rolls, typical of the Mohave at this period and later, and wears a long cloth breechclout. His face is painted in the design called ha avkek. He carries a hardwood club used in hand-to-hand combat by those men who had dreams giving them power in war. In the background is a log house roofed with thatch and covered with sand. In front are two large Mohave pottery vessels and a shallow pottery parcher for corn and wheat.

Pima

When the Spaniards arrived in 1694 the Pimas lived in seven villages on and near the Gila R., where they used river water to raise corn, beans, squash, cotton, and tobacco, gathered wild foods (especially mesquite beans and saguaro cactus fruit), and hunted deer and rabbits. During the 18th century the Pima economy was transformed by the addition of wheat to their crops, which with efficient irrigation allowed a surplus for export. A golden age of Pima agriculture followed, during the first quarter century after American control of S. Arizona began in 1853. Then non-Indians upstream from the Pima diverted the Gila R. water, and Pima economy rapidly declined. When Frank Russell, a Harvard ethnologist, visited in 1901–2 to document Pima history and culture, especially their material world, much of what he collected and later described was obsolete or moribund. A small sample of his collection is shown here; some things collected earlier by others are also shown, with dates.

1 Blanket of homespun cotton, obsolete by 1901. Collected 1877.
2 Headband of cotton and wool; reconstruction of old type.
3 Buckskin jacket. 1877.
4 Mesquite wood war clubs.
5 Models of war club and painted rawhide shield.
6 Pair of rawhide sandals. Collected from Papago in 1895, similar to Pima.
7 Calendar stick with notches and mnemonic symbols for important events of each year from 1833 to 1902.
8 Unfinished mesquite wood ladle.
9 Farmer's spade, Mexican steel blade, Pima oak handle.
10 Stone used as anvil in shaping clay pot.
11 Stone pestle.
12 War bow, old, of mulberry wood with sinew string.
13 Arrow, collected 1885.
14 Arrows, one with stone point, collected 1877.
15 War headdress of

raptorial bird feathers, collected 1885.
16 Glass bead necklace.
17 Wooden tray for mixing bread and other purposes, collected 1885.
18 Mesquite wood ladle, form said to be Mexican, learned by Pima from Papago.
19 Gourd dipper. 1885.
20 Warrior's basket food bowl.
21 Glass bead necklace.
22 Rattle of four tin oyster-can caps set on wires in wood handles;

obtained by Pimas from Papagos or Yaquis.
23 Reed tubes for gambling; all four were filled with sand, then opposing team guessed which one also held a hidden bean.
24 Eagle feathers on short rods, used for ceremonial sprinkling of water.
25, 26 Two shaman's slate tablets.
27 Basket of coiled wheat straw, used for wheat granary.
28 Coiled basket. 1885.

29 Coiled basket.
30 Oak paddle, used with anvil to shape pottery.
31 Twilled basket, for shaman's equipment. 1885.
32 Gourd used to hold seeds. 1885.
33 Sieve of willow rods, for food preparation.
34 Notched and plain sticks – musical rasp.
35 Reed flageolet.
36 Rag doll in cradle improvised from plank.
37 Coccoons strung on cord, worn as leg rattles.

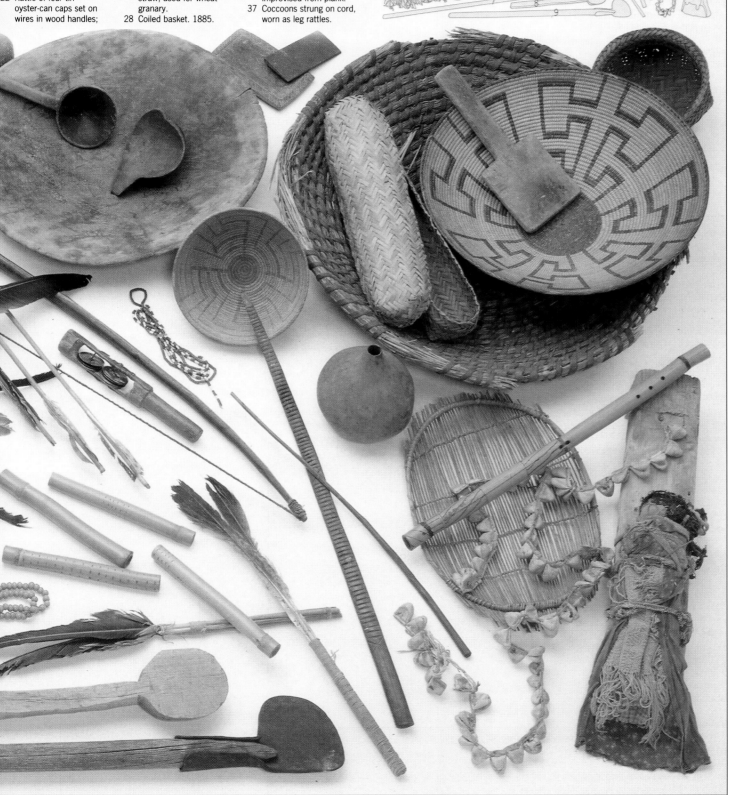

Everyone has heard of the Apaches yet few know much about them except for stereotypes, the 'warlike raiders and marauders' of so many movies. But this is a one-sided view. While the Apacheans were fierce raiders and were feared with good reason, they also had and have rich cultures that have remained unexplored. The Southern Athapascans or Apacheans were newcomers to the Southwest, arriving just before European contact. Related to other Athapascan-speakers in the north, most Apacheans lived in small units based on extended families and followed a semi-nomadic existence; their residences were temporary and seasonal. Local groups composed of several matrifocal extended families formed bands, the largest level of political organization. There were no tribes, as conceptualized by Hollywood producers and writers of pulp fiction. Today each group refers to themselves as a nation, however.

The Apaches can be divided geographically into eastern and western groups. In the east are the Jicarilla, Mescalero, Lipan (forming, in fact, a Southern Plains group), and Chiricahua Apaches; in the west are the White Mountain, Carrizo, San Carlos, Fort Apache, Pinal, Arivaipa, Apache Peaks, Mazatzal, Tonto and Cibecue bands who together are referred to as the Western Apache, and the Navajo. All share a basic world view, religious orientation and mythological cycle. Ceremonies are given to cure illness, to set the world right and to ward off possible evils. All groups are matrilineal and have elaborate and important puberty ceremonies for girls. In the Mescalero ceremony, for example, the family constructs a large, brush tipi or wickiup in which the girls dance to a series of ritual songs. This ceremony is under the direction of a shaman or medicine man, called a singer. In the second part of the ceremony, called the Sun Greeting, the girl is introduced as an adult following a period of fasting and instruction by elders.

The Athapascan-speaking peoples were the last major Native American group to come to the Southwest and the last major groups to be brought under Anglo-American political control. Originally natives of northwest Canada and Alaska, the Athapascans moved into the Southwest during the late 1300s-early 1400s AD, right before the arrival of the Spanish. By 1600 there were probably 15,000 Apaches in the Southwest. When they arrived as small bands of migrating peoples, they were undifferentiated. The groups quickly spread into the areas around the Pueblo villages and claimed areas as their traditional homes with identified sacred locales. Some groups mingled with Plains tribes – the Lipan Apache moved into west Texas and displaced the Comanches; the Mescalero and Chiricahua Apache moved into the area east of the Rio Grande Valley; the Jicarilla and Navajo moved into the northern part of New Mexico while the Western and other Chiricahua Apache moved into the old Western Anasazi and Mogollon homeland.

Apacheans lived by hunting and gathering. When they reached the Southwest they added to this economic base raiding and agriculture. All quickly acquired either Plains, Puebloan or rancheria customs as well as a reputation for fierceness. They also readily took to the horse. Much of the history of the Southwest revolves

Above: *Apache hunters, one in knitted socks probably issued by the army. Note typical Apache costume of headband and high moccasins. Arrows are much longer than those of Plains Indians.*

around Apache raids for goods and Puebloan, Piman, Spanish and Anglo-American retaliation and counter-raiding. By AD 1700 much of the Southwest was an armed camp with fluctuating alliances based on economic expediency. The Jicarilla Apaches were united with the Spaniards in their wars against the French and the Pawnee. Joining the Jicarilla were the

Below: *Eskiminzin and his wife, two Pinal Coyotero Apaches. The Coyotero lived in the vicinity of the Pinal Mountains and were known for their pleasant countenances and for the beauty of their women.*

Utes and the Tewa, especially the people of Taos, to fight the Comanche and Kiowa of the Plains. Other Apaches raided Pueblo villages to such an extent that the Pueblo communities moved to high defensible ground; many Piman communities had stockades and permanent guards. Other Apache groups raided into Mexico to such an extent that entire areas were abandoned. Because of retaliation and these economic patterns, the Apaches, in turn, lived in protected highlands, canyons and mountain valleys. They kept small communities that could be moved quickly and the situation remained thus for over 200 years until the last Apache group was defeated in the mid-1880s.

Apachean raiding was not done by a tribe but by local groups. This pattern can be loosely equated with guerilla warfare. The goal was not to kill; in fact, Apache men gained no status from killing and never took scalps. They gained status from successfully bringing back food and horses to their families. The object was to avoid encounters with the enemy. Those who led raids were men who felt the possessions in the encampment were in short supply. Apache tribes had no recognized leaders; bands and local groups did. These influential men and women had prestige because of their wealth, their abilities and personal influence. The Apacheans made a sharp distinction behaviorally between raids and warfare. A war party was formed to avenge an Apache casualty, led by a relative of the slain individual. In general, Apache attitudes toward warfare contrasted sharply with those of Plains groups; there were no warrior societies and there was no enthusiasm for standing ground in a hopeless situation or counting coup. Legendary figures like Geronimo, Naiche or Cochise became famous because of their ability to elude the U.S. cavalry. The ascendancy of tribal leaders occurred only after Anglo-American political institutions were introduced.

Some Apachean groups practiced very little agriculture and lived almost like Plains groups. The Jicarilla Apache (from the Spanish word for little basket weaver) lived in the northern part of New Mexico and the Mescalero (gatherer of agave) lived in the south central part of the state. Both groups ranged on to the Plains and hence have many cultural traits that reflect contacts with groups in Texas. For example, the Jicarilla and the Mescalero traditionally lived in tipis. (Other Apaches, who lived in forested mountain dells, built shelters of brush, called wickiups.) After a defeat by Kit Carson and the U.S. army in 1868 the Jicarilla were placed on a reservation with the Mescalero, but the two groups constantly fought and the Jicarilla were given their own reservation, in their traditional homeland, in 1887.

The San Carlos Apache, for example, began herding in 1884 when the U.S. government issued live cattle for beef rations. Men became cattlemen while women supplemented the family income by gathering wild foods and producing baskets for sale. As often happened, parts of the reservation held excellent grazing land and Anglo ranchers quickly began to encroach. By the late 1890s the Anglo-owned Chiricahua Cattle Company quietly obtained through its influence with the army permission to graze a herd of 2,000 head at Ash Flats. Other Anglo ranchers encroached illegally on San

and raiding and because of this they led a semi-nomadic life.

When the United States government annexed Navajo territory in 1849, the Navajo were feared as a warring, raiding group of bands. They were not organized into a tribe – each community and kin group was independent. For many years the government tried to stop the raids in order to allow settlement by Anglo and Mexican ranchers, but the constant raids on Navajo families by slave traders who wanted to ensure that the territory was in a constant state of flux to make capturing Navajo easier meant that warfare continued.

During the American Civil War, the U.S. government wanted to keep New Mexico and Arizona territories in the Union and ensure that the lines of communication to California remained open. To do this they felt they had to stop Apachean raids, particularly that of the Mescalero Apache and the Navajo. The campaign against the Mescalero lasted five months in 1862. The Mescalero were moved to a new military post on the Pecos River called Fort Sumner (or Bosque Redondo). The location on the edge of the Great Plains lacked firewood, good drinking water and arable land.

In 1863 Colonel Christopher Carson was commissioned by General Carleton to round up The People and move them to the new military reservation in east-central New Mexico. The military sent out peace negotiations to a few bands and local leaders telling them to move; if they refused, the general orders were to remove them forcefully. Most of the Navajo who lived in widely scattered local groups never heard the ultimatum and General Carleton made no attempt to locate them. Instead he sent Carson to destroy the Navajo economic base. Joined by Utes and Pueblos and New Mexican irregulars, Carson undertook a scorched earth policy that destroyed cornfields and orchards, hogans, water holes and livestock. Over a thousand of The People were killed, wounded or captured. The Navajo had nowhere to hide and little to eat; they surrendered in 1864.

Carlos land and shot Apache cattle. By 1900 the situation was critical, a range war was imminent and the army was called in. However, it was not for another ten years that the situation was brought until control.

With the end of their traditional economies based on raiding and hunting, all Apache groups developed a flexible economy in the twentieth century partly based on livestock – cattle and sheep.

The Navajo call themselves the Dineh – 'The People'. The word Navajo is a Tewa term 'Nava-huu' which means cultivated field in an arroyo. The Pueblos and early Spanish chroniclers of the early seventeenth century distinguished the Navajo from other Apaches living west and south of the Rio Grande because they were 'very great farmers'. This success in agriculture

Above: White Mountain Apache women in camp, one with a milling stone. A classic Western Apache twined burden basket can be seen at left; rawhide 'cut-out' saddle bags hang over the line.

was also noted by U.S. army reports 150 years later. Today we think of the Navajo as sheep herders and weavers but this did not happen until after they became agriculturalists. Like other Apacheans the Navajo raided Spanish and Puebloan settlements for sheep and horses. They quickly developed an economy and life that was based on herding, agriculture

Below: A group of Apache scouts in Arizona. Apache scouts were first recruited at Camp Apache, 1871, supplied with rifle, cartridge belt, blanket and canteen, and uniforms too – if they wanted them.

Western Apache

The Western Apaches include five independent divisions speaking slightly different varieties of the same language; one of these is the San Carlos Apaches. Each division consisted of two to five independent bands of some 50 to 700 members each (in 1880). Each of these in turn included several local groups of 35 to 200 people; these were the basic landholding and political units. The Apaches lived in a mountain and canyon country of forests, well-watered valleys, and deserts. They depended mainly on hunting deer and antelope and on gathering wild plants such as mescal tubers, cactus fruits, mesquite beans, and piñon nuts. Farming provided about a quarter of their food, from corn, beans, and squash raised on small irrigated plots in the mountains. During the Spanish-Mexican period Western Apache culture was strongly affected by the adoption of horses and horse equipment, firearms, cloth, and metal tools and implements. Trading and cattle raiding relations were established with their Indian and Spanish neighbors on all sides. For most of the second half of the 19th century the Western Apaches fought the U.S. Army. Hostilities finally ended with the capture and confinement of Geronimo in 1885. By 1909, when all the items shown here were collected among the San Carlos Apaches, many of them were working for wages, some as cowboys on Anglo ranches. Cattle raising became a major Apache industry after 1920, and lumbering became important on the reservations.

1 War club; stone head wrapped in buckskin on wooden handle.
2 Coiled basket to cook and serve food; older style.
3 Knife for trimming leaves off mescal (century plant) tubers used for food.
4 Gourd dipper.
5 Shallow old basket coated with clay for cooking corn with live coals.
6 Small twined water jar, waterproofed inside and out with piñon pitch.
7 Hide scraper, steel blade.

8 Boy's deerskin vest.
9 Awl, probably for basket making, with leather case.
10 Hat with owl feathers.
11 Very large double saddle bag with red flannel behind leather cutwork.
12 Woman's buckskin moccasins, with tops to be folded down.
13 Rope of horsehair.
14 Rope twister; strands tied to notched end of longer stick which revolves on the smaller, to twist rope.
15 Smooth grooved stone for

straightening arrows.
16 Woman's beaded moccasins.
17 Coiled basket shaped like an ordinary water basket.
18 Small twined basket water jar.
19 Small twined burden basket, a child's toy.
20 Hairbrush; tied bundle of straw.
21 Coiled shallow basket.
22 Coiled shallow bowl basket.
23 Coiled shallow basket.
24 Seed beater of twined openwork basketry.

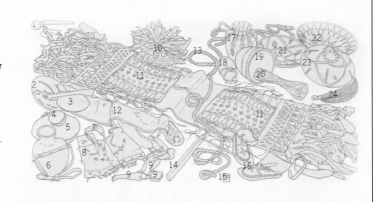

By 1864 over 8,000 Navajo had surrendered and begun the Long Walk, one of the bleakest events in Navajo history. Over ten per cent of the captives died on the way to Fort Sumner. The journey was one of hardship and terror. There were no wagons; people walked over 300 miles. People were shot if they complained of being tired or sick; women in labor were killed.

Not all the Navajo went on the Long Walk. Many were sold into slavery or hid in inaccessible locations like the Grand Canyon or moved in with other groups. Those who lived at Fort Sumner recounted their experience as a time of despair and deprivation. Army arrangements were inadequate; there was little food and no blankets. Shelter was inadequate also, epidemic disease rampant. Confined with their traditional enemies the Mescalero Apache, tempers flared and disputes were common. Droughts and poor agricultural land doomed the reservation to failure. The horror of the Long Walk and the imprisonment at Fort Sumner remained pivotal events in the history and consciousness of The People.

When the Navajo were allowed to return to their homeland five years later they quickly re-established their way of life as herders and horticulturalists. They did no more raiding; instead they developed new economic pursuits – craft production and wage labor. In crafts the Navajo are famous as weavers and silversmiths. The tribe prospered and grew so that today they are the most populous group in North America and all cannnot live on the land. Unfortunately, sheep and horses became so prevalent that the fragile land became overgrazed. By the 1930s the land could no longer support the livestock and the federal government ordered the stocks to be reduced, a tragedy for the Navajo.

Navajo ceremonies, like other Apachean ceremonies, are performed not calendrically but when necessary to restore health and secure blessings in order to insure survival. In the Navajo universe there are two classes of people – Earth People (or human beings) and Holy People (supernatural beings who are holy, powerful and mysterious). The Navajo believe that the universe functions according to certain rules that both they and the Holy People must follow. If these rules are followed there will be

Above: A Navajo mother and child wearing silver and turquoise jewelry. The first Navajo to set this stone in silver was reputed to be Atsidi Chon (Ugly Smith) in 1880. The concha belt seen here is typical of Navajo silversmithing, noted for its massive quality and simplicity of design.

safety, plenty and a world that is harmonious and beautiful. If rules are not, if disease and accidental injury affect an individual, ceremonies are held in which the Holy People are asked to restore the delicate balance of the universe. In these ceremonies, which are very complicated and intricate, sandpaintings are made and prayers recited. Sandpaintings are impermanent paintings made of dried pulverized materials that depicted the Holy People and serve as a temporary altar. Over 800 forms of sandpaintings exist, each connected to a specific chant and ceremony. Sandpaintings are made inside the hogan, the center of family life.

There are a few tribes who live in extremely marginal environments and on the fringes of the Southwest culture area who never developed agricultural ways of life. In the north, these included isolated groups who lived near the arid Great Basin – the Utes and the Paiutes, in the region – some of the Shoshonean speakers who moved from California to become farmers along the Colorado River, the Upland Yumans (already mentioned), in the south the Chemehuevi and a group of Sand Papago, a subgroup of the Tohono O'Odham already discussed, the Seri, and groups living in Baja California. There were never more than a few thousand people who existed at this level of economic development. The most well-known are the Seri.

Producing none of their own food and following a nomadic and semi-nomadic lifestyle,

Below: Pesh-lakái-ilhini, a Navajo silversmith (left), hammering silver on a steel anvil; his son stands by the bellows, probably learning the trade. The man at right is holding a pump drill. At the rear is a hogan dwelling, here of the oldest style with a forked-pole framework covered with earth.

these groups lived in small bilateral bands. Moving often, they possessed small inventories of material cultures, living off the land for all their needs. For example, the Seri, the smallest group in the Southwest, relied heavily on marine products as did groups in Baja California. They also hunted deer and rabbits, and gathered the abundant cacti fruits, greens and seaweed seeds of the desert coast and adjacent islands. Even today these groups eke out a poverty-level living by fishing and turtle hunting on the desert shores of Baja California.

In anthropology it is usual to discuss the Ute and their relatives the Paiute in the Great Basin and Plains culture areas. Both of these groups speak a Uto-Aztecan language of the Shoshonean stock and were thus in the distant past related to the Hopi.

These groups were so isolated and few in number that they were affected very little by Spanish expansion. It was only in the mid-1800s and later that European incursions changed their ways of life.

These four basic cultural groups of the Greater Southwest can be recognized in modified form today. Even after three hundred years of European contact, three-quarters of the groups have managed to preserve a sense of individual cultural identity, and a feeling for the

Below: A Navajo war captain wearing a war hat of tanned leather and carrying a lance and rawhide shield. In addition, war equipment of the Navajo traditionally included a bow and arrows and frequently a club. This photograph was taken near Keam's Canyon on the Navajo reservation, 1892-3.

land that is recorded in rich oral traditions. Indian groups have not, however, completely retained their pre-contact cultures, nor have they reacted uniformly to the attempts of Hispanic, Mexican and Anglo-American societies to assimilate them. All exist as part of either the Anglo-American or the Mexican socio-economic system and incorporate a mixture of traditional customs and European patterns. Thus, while they are distinct cultures, they are no longer separate societies. They maintain their ethnic identities in various way, such as producing distinctive forms of art and retaining feelings about, and interaction patterns with, their environment. It is this sense of continuity with the land that has helped them survive years of subjugation to conquest cultures. Zunis, for example, say that Anglo-Americans and Mexican Americans have no respect for the land and abuse it rather than work with it.

Southwest Native Americans have retained 'identity systems that have as an important element the symbol of roots in the land – supernaturally sanctioned, ancient roots, regarded as unchangeable', according to noted Southwesternist Edward Spicer. Such a perspective provides these groups with strong mythological sanctions for their residence, their right to live in the Southwest, and their views of the land. The land is not something that can be controlled and changed; it is something of which all human beings are a part.

American Indian thought is integrative and comprehensive. It does not separate intellectual, moral, emotional, aesthetic, economic and other activities, motivations and functions. Beauty is in the nature of things as well as in people, and it is the natural state of affairs. The land is beautiful by definition because the supernatural beings designed it to be a beautiful harmonious, happy and healthy place. For beauty to be maintained the Navajo, for example, feel it must be expressed in actions such as the creation of art or conservation. The land supports life, it is beautiful because of this and must be preserved. Housing and village layout reflect the visions of the land and the universe.

Native Americans face many challenges. They live both on isolated reservations and in cities for they are members of and must survive in two worlds. While European expansion has transformed much of Native American life it has done so unevenly and differentially. But never completely. Native Americans today are struggling for economic and political independence – self-determinacy in a situation where they face poverty facing other rural poor. It is a paradox that once self-sustaining and healthy populations find themselves living under poor conditions in a land of plenty. But Southwest Native Americans will adapt, as they have done in the past for the core of their lives, their relationship to the land has been preserved. No culture is static, even though we tend to portray indigenous peoples as homogeneous and frozen in time and space. But Southwest Native Americans do not regard themselves as deprived members of society. They retain a strong sense of who they are and their special place in the multi-cultural Southwest. They recognize that they have much to offer others if these others will but listen. This rich exchange will continue into the future.

Navajo

The Navajo are the largest North American Indian tribe, in population and in the area of their reservation lands. They are well known for fine rugs and blankets woven by women with wool from their own sheep, and silver jewelry made by men. Other well known features of Navajo culture include the sand paintings associated with curing ceremonies, and the distinctive earth-covered domed houses called hogans. By the late 18th century the Navajo were successful farmers, hunters, and herders, who warred against the Spaniards and Mexicans, and later the Anglo-Americans, to protect their lands, property, and families. Peace finally came with the Long Walk, when nearly all the Navajo were deported to Fort Sumner in 1864. Modern Navajo history dates from their return in 1868 to the newly established reservation within their old territory. The things shown here all exemplify Navajo material culture of a century and more ago; dates indicate when they were collected.

1 Coiled basket. 1870.
2 Woman's wool dress, of two woven rectangles sewn together at sides and shoulders. Probably made between 1850 and 1870.
3 Decorated silver bow guard, called ketoh, worn as a bracelet. 1893.
4 Silver necklace pendant, a crescent ending in hands – form called a naja. 1893.
5 Naja; the shape spread from Moslem North Africa to Spain, then to Mexico, then to the Navajo. 1893.

6–11 Six silver conchas, worn on belts and also bridles. 1893.
12 Silver buckle. 1893.
13, 14 Two silver bracelets, 1893.
15 Silver finger ring. 1884.
16 Silver finger ring with copper inset. 1893.
17, 18 Silver buttons. 1893.
19, 20 Silver brooches. 1893.
21 Hairbrush. 1870.
22 Man's moccasins. 1870.
23 Squirrel skin shirt. 1870.
24 Wool sock-leggings, 1874.

25 Knitted wool cap. 1874.
26 Batten of barberry wood, for beating down the weft while weaving. 1877.
27 Heddle to hold the warp threads on a loom. 1870.
28 Dance drum. Before 1902.
29 Warrior's hat of painted leather, feathers, and dyed hair. Old in 1895.
30 Buckskin belt and pouch. 1893.
31 Small throw used on top of saddle, woven of both Navajo-spun and German-town wool yarn, in 'post-classic' design. 1886.
32 Girth for saddle, warps directly attached to iron rings, then woven between them. 1887.
33 Well-made bow, sinew backed, reinforced with sinew bindings. 1885.
34 Bowcase attached to quiver, of mountain lion skin, fur out on quiver, in on bowcase, wood stiffener inserted in bowcase; contains two arrows. 1893.
35 Four arrows with steel points. 1893.
36 Drinking cup and pouch. Before 1869.
37 Man's shoulder blanket woven in 'chief's blanket' pattern. 1893.
38 War hat of leather, owl feather plume, abalone shells on brow. Not used after 1870; collected in 1887.
39 Cap. 1898.
40 Wool blanket, banded pattern. 1893.
41 Copper powder measure. 1887.

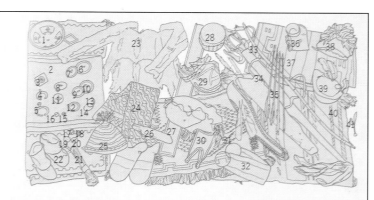

THE PLAINS

THE GREAT PLAINS form the very heartland of North America. A land of sun, wind and grass, they stretch north to south more than two thousand miles from the North Saskatchewan River in Canada almost to the Rio Grande in Mexico, while their east-west boundaries are approximately those of the Mississippi-Missouri valleys and the foothills of the Rocky Mountains, in all encompassing an area of some one million square miles.

During the eighteenth and nineteenth centuries, when contact with whites was first made, the Great Plains were largely dominated by Algonquian and Siouan linguistic groups, although others such as Athapaskan and Uto-Aztecan were also represented. The table opposite on p.65 lists the principal tribes on the Plains at this time.

The Northern Plains were largely dominated by Algonquians, the Central Plains by Siouans. These particular linguistic groups were not well represented on the Southern Plains although some Cheyenne and Arapaho formed strong military allegiances with the Kiowa and Comanche who dominated this region. The population was relatively small; in 1780, for example, the Blackfeet (name used in this chapter; also called Blackfoot), one of the largest groups on the Northern Plains, were estimated at fifteen thousand, the Lakota ten thousand and the Cheyenne three and a half thousand, while the semi-sedentary tribes such as the Omaha, Mandan and Arikara on the Missouri River have all been estimated to have been less than four thousand in 1780 (see Kroeber, 1939, and Swanton, 1952).

Climate varies on the Plains; in general the limited rainfall produces a semi-desert type terrain particularly to the west and south, where in places the arid conditions result in so-called 'badlands'. To the east, however, in the Mississippi and Missouri valleys, the rainfall is higher often producing humid conditions and green prairie lands. In these areas the grass is tall and luxuriant; further west in such regions as the present-day states of North and South Dakota, Nebraska, Montana and Kansas this gives way to a short grass; while it is generally referred to as 'buffalo grass', it is in actuality a vital food resource for many Plains animals.

Plains animals exhibit characteristics which are indicative of the nature of the country in which they live. Thus, all can survive without water for extended periods, and all, except the wolf and coyote, are grass-eaters. Most are ultra cautious and extremely difficult to approach and kill, such characteristics being particularly exemplified by the prong-horned antelope. Its acute sense of sight, great speed and ability to communicate danger by means of the white patch on its rump give it a high survival rating. In the nineteenth century and earlier, the antelope was found in vast herds across the Plains, possibly being even more abundant than the better known buffalo which, because of its size, first caught the attention of early white explorers.

The antelope was an important resource to both prehistoric and historic man on the Great Plains. When the Cheyenne, for example, first moved out on to the Plains in the late eighteenth century, they found evidence of antelope pounds – converging streams, bush or

Key to tribes:
1 Sarcee
2 Plains Cree
3 Blackfeet
4 Gros Ventre
5 Assiniboin
6 Plains Ojibwa
7 Crow
8 Teton Sioux
9 Hidatsa
10 Mandan
11 Arikara
12 Yanktonai Sioux
13 Santee Sioux
14 Cheyenne
15 Ponca
16 Omaha
17 Yankton Sioux
18 Iowa
19 Oto
20 Pawnee
21 Arapaho
22 Kansa
23 Missouria
24 Kiowa
25 Kiowa-Apache
26 Osage
27 Comanche
28 Wichita
29 Quapaw
30 Lipan Apache
31 Tonkawa
32 Kitsai

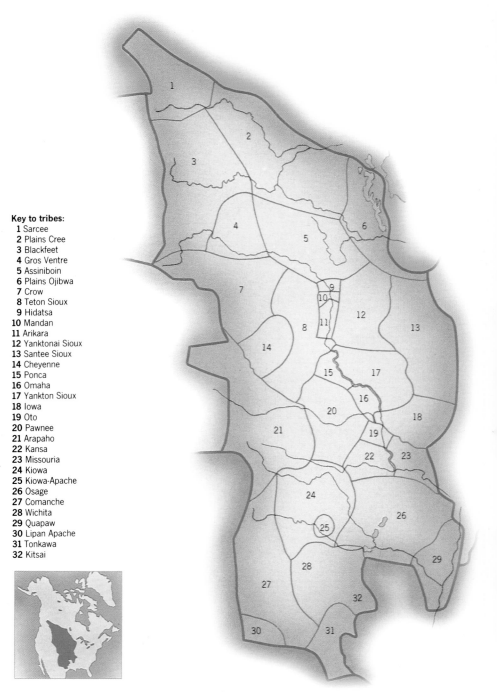

This map shows approximate territories of tribes and language groups at about 1800. After that, all tribes lost territory and some moved.

rocks terminating at a deep pit or ditch – which earlier pedestrian inhabitants had employed. The Cheyenne repaired and extended these, realizing that it was the most effective way of capturing such a wily creature. The antelope obviously greatly impressed the Plains tribes; not only were they a nutritious source of meat, but their horns were used in special head-dresses or painted on ceremonial regalia while the skins were fabricated into garments – shirts, leggings and dresses.

The animal which most dominated the Plains, however, was the bison, better known as the buffalo. Although archeological evidence and early explorers' descriptions indicate that this animal was formerly widely distributed in North America, by the mid-nineteenth century it was largely confined to the Plains region where it roamed in immense herds, the total population of which has been conservatively estimated at sixty million. The bull buffalo stood almost 6½ft (2m.) high at the shoulder and weighed 200lb. (about 900kg.); unlike the antelope, buffalo had poor eyesight and although their sense of smell and hearing was well developed they could often be approached downwind by a cautious hunter.

Early pedestrian man on the Great Plains commonly hunted the buffalo in a similar way to the antelope, stampeding the herds in to a V-shaped drive leading over a cliff edge. Evidence of such early drives is noted in the Introduction; one site in southern Alberta was used by Paleo and historic Plains Indians until about 1850, when the buffalo herds began to disappear. Called by the Blackfeet *Estipah-Siki-kini-Kots* – 'Where-he-got-his-head-smashed-in' – it was also a place of great ceremonial and ritual importance, where practical action in the trapping of buffalo was accompanied by appeals to higher powers, evoking the spirits of the mountains, winds, the raven, the latter considered by the Blackfeet to be the wisest of birds.

Thousands of buffalo were killed annually at such sites by stampeding animals, often so many at one time that it was impossible to utilize all the fresh meat and, whilst much was subsequently dried and made into pemmican

Location	Tribe	Linguistic group/comment
NORTHERN PLAINS	Blackfeet Plains Cree Plains Ojibwa Gros Ventre	*Algonquian.* Ancient inhabitants of this region. Archeological evidence suggests that there were strong Blackfeet/Cree links and there were similarities in their mythology
	Sarcee	*Athapaskan.* This small tribe, as with the Gros Ventre, allied themselves with the Blackfeet during the nineteenth century
CENTRAL PLAINS	Sioux (Lakota, Nakota, Dakota) Crow Mandan Hidatsa	*Siouan.* The Lakota were the most western of the Sioux tribes. The Dakota, Mandan and Hidatsa were semi-sedentary
	Arikara	*Caddoan.* Sometimes referred to as 'Northern Pawnees'. Semi-sedentary, living south of the Mandan on the Missouri River
SOUTHERN PLAINS	Comanche Kiowa Wichita ⎱ Pawnee ⎰ Kiowa-Apache	*Uto-Aztecan* *Kiowan* *Caddoan.* *Athapaskan*

Above: *A Blackfeet (Blood) family and tipi, c.1900. By 1870 canvas, rather than buffalo hides, was widely used. Designs such as the Maltese Cross motif were still painted in the traditional way.*

for winter use and the hides used for tipi covers, there was the inevitable waste. Thus, in December 1809, when the fur trader-explorer Alexander Henry came across a recent pound kill on the Vermilion River (in present-day Alberta), he observed 'The bulls were mostly entire, none but the good cows having been cut up' (Henry and Thompson, Coues ed., 1897:576-7).

Who the *archaic* Plains pedestrians were is conjectural. However, it is almost certain, as was discussed in the chapter on the Plateau and Basin (pp.102–129) that several tribes such as the Kutenai, Flathead and particularly the Shoshoni commonly travelled on foot to the Plains region to hunt buffalo. Some archeological evidence suggests that several bands may even have lived on the western fringes of the Plains 'for several thousand years' (Hultkrantz, 1968:70).

It was not, however, until the acquisition of the horse from the south and the gun from the east that a full flowering of historic Plains culture emerges; further, whilst the horse gave great mobility and enhanced the general quality of life – the elderly were no longer abandoned, tipis could be larger and more goods and food transported – the gun enabled the pedestrian Blackfeet and Cree to match and finally force the equestrian Shoshoni to abandon the Plains country. A decisive encounter which demonstrated the superiority of the gun, even against an enemy which had horses, was dramatically described by an aged Piegan chief, Saukamappee, to the explorer David Thompson in 1787. The battle, which occurred about 1740 (probably in present-day Saskatchewan), was between the Shoshoni and combined Assiniboin Piegan, the latter considered a frontier tribe of the Blackfeet confederacy who, armed with a few guns (but no horses), were thrusting their way into the Northern Plains. Saukamappee first briefly explained how conditions had rapidly changed in perhaps just over a decade:

'By this time the affairs of both parties had much changed; we had more guns and iron-headed arrows than before; but our enemies the Snake Indians and their allies had Misstutim (Big Dogs, that is, Horses) on which they rode, swift as the Deer, on which they dashed at the Peeagans, and with their stone Pukamoggan knocked them on the head, and they thus lost several of their best men. This news we did not well comprehend and it alarmed us, for we had no idea of horses and could not make out what they were.'
(Thompson, Tyrell, ed., 1916:330).

Saukamappee then described the formation of the combined Piegan and Assiniboin warparty, the preliminary war ceremonials and the tallying of their weaponry by the War Chiefs. In all they had some ten guns with plenty of ammunition and powder between them and those so armed were 'now considered "the strength of the battle"' (Lewis, Hallowell ed., 1942:49). After a few days march they were confronted by a large warparty of Shoshoni; Saukamappee continued:

'When we came to our allies, the great War Tent [was made] with speeches, feasting and dances as before; and when the War Chief had viewed us all it was found between us and the Stone Indians

Right: *Blackfeet painted tipis, c.1900. Such dwellings were replete with religious symbolism, many of the designs being acquired by their first Blackfeet owners in visions and dreams.*

Right: *Blackfeet painted tipis, c.1900. Such dwellings were replete with religious symbolism, many of the designs being acquired by their first Blackfeet owners in visions and dreams.*

we had ten guns and each of us about thirty balls, and powder for the war, and we were considered the strength of the battle. After a few days march our scouts brought us word that the enemy was near in a large war party, but had no Horses with them, for at that time they had very few of them. When we came to meet each other, as usual, each displayed their numbers, weapons and shields, in all which they were superior to us, except our guns which were not shown, but kept in their leathern cases, and if we had shown |them|, they would have taken them for long clubs. For a long time they held us in suspense; a tall Chief was forming a strong party to make an attack on our centre, and the others to enter into combat with those opposite to them; We prepared for the battle the best we could. Those of us who had guns stood in the front line, and each of us |had| two balls in his mouth, and a load of powder in his left hand to reload. We noticed they had a great many short stone clubs for close combat, which is a dangerous weapon, and had they made a bold attack on us, we must have been defeated as they were more numerous and better armed than we were, for we could have fired our guns no more than twice; and were at a loss what to do on the wide plain, and each Chief encouraged his men to stand firm. Our eyes were all on the tall Chief and his motions, which appeared to be contrary to the advice of several old Chiefs, all this time we were about the strong flight of an arrow from each other. At length the tall chief retired and they formed their long usual line by placing their shields on the ground to touch each other, the shield having a breadth of full three feet or more. We sat down opposite to them and most of us waited for the night to make a hasty retreat. The War Chief was close to us, anxious to see the effect of our guns. The lines were too far asunder for us to make a sure shot, and we requested him to close the line to about sixty yards, which was gradually done, and lying flat on the ground behind the shields, we watched our opportunity when they drew their bows to shoot at us, their bodies were then exposed and each of us, as opportunity offered, fired with deadly aim, and either killed, or severely wounded, every one we aimed at.

The War Chief was highly pleased, and the Snake Indians finding so many killed and wounded kept themselves behind their shields; the War Chief then desired we could spread ourselves by two's throughout the line, which we did, and our shots caused consternation and dis-

may along their whole line. The battle had begun about Noon, and the Sun was not yet half down, when we perceived some of them had crawled away from their shields, and were taking to flight. The War Chief seeing this went along the line and spoke to every Chief to keep his Men ready for a charge of the whole line of the enemy, of which he would give the signal; this was done by himself stepping in front

with his Spear, and calling on them to follow him as he rushed on their line, and in an instant the whole of us followed him, the greater part of the enemy took to flight, but some fought bravely and we lost more than ten killed and many wounded; Part of us pursued, and killed a few, but the chase had soon to be given over, for at the body of every Snake Indian killed, there were five or six of us trying to

Right: *Blackfeet delegation to Washington, 1916. Seated; Wolf Plume, Curly Bear (with hackle plume, a trade item, on headdress) and Bird Rattler, in costume beaded and fringed with buckskin and ermine.*

Left: *Blackfeet girl in buckskin dress embellished with blue and white pony beads, by Karl Bodmer (1833). Bodmer seldom painted Plains children; this one was living with the Assiniboin.*

Right: *A Cree woman, by Karl Bodmer (1833). Her deerskin dress is of the typical Plains style as are the earrings made of dentalium shells and blue beads. Her chin is tattooed, a common Cree custom.*

get his scalp, or part of his clothing, his weapons, or something as a trophy of the battle. As there were only three of us, and seven of our friends, the Stone Indians, we did not interfere, and got nothing.' (Thompson, Tyrell ed., 1916:330-32).

Under such pressures, the Shoshoni tribes gradually retreated from the Northern Plains, a process which was accelerated as the Blackfeet, Assiniboin and Cree progressively acquired more guns due to the expansion of the fur trade and also changed their warfare tactics, now successfully raiding the Shoshoni for horses.

In contrast, whilst the Shoshoni traded with the Spaniards in New Mexico, obtaining articles of clothing, iron kettles, metal bridles, stirrups and mules, the Spanish policy was not

to trade firearms to Indians. This put the Shoshoni at a decided disadvantage, as one of their distinguished chiefs, Cameahwait, complained to Lewis and Clark, 'But this should not be, . . . if we had guns, instead of hiding ourselves in the mountains and living like the bears on roots and berries, we would then go down and live in the buffalo country in spite of our enemies, whom we never fear when we meet on equal terms' (Lewis and Clark, Coues ed., 1893:559).

Whilst the time-scale and pressures varied, similar patterns were replicated across both the Central and Southern Plains. Thus, into this vast area moved Algonquian and Athapaskan-speaking tribes from the north and east – the Blackfeet Confederacy, Cree, Arapaho, Cheyenne, Sarcee and Kiowa-Apache. From the east and southeast came the Siouan tribes – the Nakota, Lakota and Dakota, Crow, Hidatsa and Mandan and from both west and southeast the Pawnee, Arikara, Comanche and Kiowa. They brought with them a diversity of cultures which, due to the impact of a new environment had, by about 1800, led to a commonality of basic lifestyle enhanced and mixed by trade and warfare, but often retaining much of their former ethos.

On the Northern Plains much, particularly that relating to horse nomadism, was obviously

Below: *Gros Ventre moving camp with a travois. Made by the women entirely of wood and rawhide, the travois had side poles of stout lodge-pole pines generally some 4-5in. in diameter at base.*

adopted from the former dominant occupants, namely the Shoshoni who, as Lewis and Clark observed in 1805, had 'within their own recollection' formerly lived on the Plains, but had been 'driven into the mountains by the Pawkees, [Piegan] or the roving Indians of the Sascatchawain' (ibid:554). Lewis and Clark's descriptions of the Shoshoni fit much of what was to become typical of the nomadic historic Plains Indian: an emphasis on warfare as a means of achieving high social status, a coup-counting hierarchy, scalping, the use of the horse in all aspects of their lives, short bows – typically about 3 ft in length (less than a meter) for effective use on horseback, given high elastic qualities by a backing of sinew – otterskin bow and arrow cases, small circular buffalo hide shields endowed with supernatura'

powers of protection derived from their ceremonials of fabrication and painting, and the use of highly dangerous stone-headed clubs. Likewise, much of the horse equipment, such as stirrups, saddles and bridles, was clearly similar in style, some of which undoubtedly being strongly inspired by the Spanish. For example, the common pack saddle was modified and given a high flat-topped pommel and cantle and, whilst popular with Shoshoni women at the time of Lewis and Clark's visit, it later emerged as a classic Crow woman's style of saddle. Further, the elaborate horse collar which became such a feature of Crow horse equipment, seemingly had its roots in the Shoshoni custom of suspending 'at the breast of his horse the finest ornaments he possesses' (ibid:563).

One important factor which led to the success in the emergence of historic Plains Indian nomadism was undoubtedly the development of the tipi. It is unclear as to the type of dwelling actually employed by the earlier Plains Shoshoni; possibly it was a small-scale conical shaped dwelling covered with pieces of elk or buffalo skins. However, the true tipi – which consisted of a large semi-circular cover pulled over a conical frame of straight poles and having a facility for regulating the draught of smoke from the central fire generally by the adjustment of the distinctive ears or wings at the top – was observed by Spanish expeditions to the Southern Plains as early as the middle of the sixteenth century. Since dogs were used for transport at that time, it is probable that these dwellings were small, possibly no more than 8ft (2.5m.) in diameter. The inspiration for such habitations may well have been based on the conical wigwam which was found throughout the boreal regions of both the New and Old World for, as one scholar has pointed out, these tipi dwellers observed by the Spanish (probably Athapaskan-speaking Plains Apaches) had only recently migrated from the vicinity of the Northern Plains (Brasser, 1982:312).

The tipi was generally pitched with its back toward the prevailing westerly wind direction, its wide base and sloping sides giving high stability to the sometimes sudden and strong winds which occur on the Plains. Whilst all tipis were similar in appearance, there were some definite tribal variations, classification being broadly based on the number of foundation poles. In the areas where the winds were particularly strong, a three-pole foundation was used, whilst in more protected areas – near the mountains or wooded river valleys – a four-pole foundation was favored. Thus, such widely spaced tribes as the Blackfeet on the Northwestern Plains and the Omaha in the Southeast employed the four-pole base whilst the Assiniboin to the east of the Blackfeet on the windswept Plains of what is now Saskatchewan and Manitoba, and the Kiowa on the Southern Plains, tended to the three-pole type. The Crow favored the use of elegant, unpainted tipis, and the Lakota those which were embellished with both realistic and geometrical paintings, but perhaps the most impressive were some of those belonging to the Blackfeet which, even as early as 1809, were described by the fur trader, Alexander Henry, as heavily embellished with pictographs of animals and birds, both real and mythological.[1]

The designs on tipis were believed to secure for their owners protection against misfortune and sickness, and definite conventions were employed in the painting of symbolic motifs which were clearly understood by the custodians of the particular tribe's religious tradition, but not necessarily by the common man. Thus, for the Blackfeet what might be called the Maltese Cross was traditionally symbolic of the Morning Star – endowed with powers to protect those entitled to employ the motif – and was painted in red at the rear top of the tipi. Ownership of a sacred painted tipi, together with all that it entailed, was an outward display of high social standing within the tribe.

High status, however, also pivoted firmly on success in warfare, the capturing of enemy horses rather than killing being a major objective in the historic period; appeals to higher powers for help in these matters attempted to evoke the spiritual forces which would help

Below: *Kill Spotted Horse, an Assiniboin warrior, c.1898. The eagle feather headdress is of quite an unusual style, the feathers being set well back from the brow so as to lie close to the head.*

attain the goal. Much of the Plains Indian cosmos centered on observed animal powers – the strength of the buffalo, the speed of the antelope, the bravery of the eagle and weasel, and so on – but there was also a recognition of an intangible power of the universe which manifested itself in varying forms from one linguistic group to the next and was embedded in ancient beliefs which, whilst modified by the Plains environment, can be traced back to the original Woodland homelands of several Plains tribes.

Widespread was the concept of three parallel worlds. Under the surface of the lake on which the earth floated, were powerful spirits which had control over animals and plants on land and in the water, whilst above the earth beyond the dome of the blue sky, lay the realm of the upper world. This world was dominated by spirits which matched those of the underworld, amongst the most powerful of which were the Thunderbirds who, by the flashing of their eyes and flapping of their wings, produced the lightning and thunder. A perpetual state of war existed between the sky and water spirits and whilst the sun was often closely associated with the Thunderbird, it was considered that it,

together with the moon, was the energy sources which controlled the day and night and the seasonal 'cycles'. On earth, the spirits of the four winds changed the seasons, their energies both sustaining and perpetrating the life 'cycle'. For hundreds of years, the symbolic and religious artwork of the Woodland tribes gave free expression to these great powers.

These ancient concepts were modified and interpreted in various forms by the historic Plains Indians, environmental factors undoubtedly having considerable influence. Thus, the Eastern Sioux replaced the underwater panther, so important to the Woodland tribes, with symbols of an underwater horned monster which had the ability to emerge from the lakes and live in trees (Carver, Parker ed., 1976:98-9), and further west amongst the Blackfeet the symbol of such powerful underwater spirits was the tadpole, its use on the costume of the owners of the prestigious Beaver Bundle being explained by a Blackfeet myth which associated the frog with the Blackfeet culture hero, Old Man, who defeated the terrible underwater enemies of mankind. The metamorphosis associated with the frog and its ability to move freely from water to land clearly has parallels with Eastern Sioux mythology.

A complex intertribal trade network was anciently developed in the Plains region and whilst there was little incentive for trade between tribes who had similar lifestyles, that between the hunters and horticulturists was beneficial to both sides. Thus, the nomadic tribes could offer dried buffalo meat and other products of the chase such as tanned deer and buffalo hides, numerous articles of apparel and buffalo hide tipis (used by the village tribes on their hunting expeditions), and in exchange the horticulturists offered corn, beans and pumpkins. With the introduction of the horse and European goods, it is probable that the newcomers to the Plains adopted the established trade patterns of those pedestrian nomads who they displaced, and simply extended the activities. Amongst the best documented of these relates to the Cheyenne and Crow, the former trading to Missouri River tribes – the Mandan, Hidatsa and Arikara – the latter mainly with the Hidatsa and Mandan. Such trade expeditions must have been colorful and spectacular affairs. For example, when the fur trader, Charles Mackenzie, travelled to the Hidatsa villages in 1805, he witnessed the arrival of over two thousand Crow Indians on a trading expedition (Mackenzie, in Masson, 1889:360). Dressed in all their finery and subsequently pitching a village of three hundred tipis adjacent to the earth lodges of the Hidatsa, the trade was elevated to the status of an elaborate ceremonial. After smoking the pipe of friendship, the Hidatsa laid before the Crow trade goods which consisted of two hundred guns with one hundred rounds of ammunition for each, a hundred bushels of corn, together with quantities of axes, clothing (probably European) and kettles. In exchange, the Crow gave two hundred and fifty horses, large quantities of buffalo robes, leggings and shirts. The trade was lucrative to both sides. Thus, the Crow sold their horses to the village tribes at double the price that they fetched at the Shoshoni Rendezvous, whilst the village tribes doubled the cost again to the Cree and Assiniboin who brought in European goods from the northeast. Recent research suggests that the rapid movement of trade goods across the Plains appears to have been facilitated by a middle rendezvous between Western and Eastern Crow bands – the so-called Mountain and River Crow (Taylor, 1984:34). This network efficiently distributed guns from the English Hudson's Bay Trading Posts (situated in present-day Manitoba and Ontario), through the Hidatsa/Mandan villages via Assiniboin and Cree, across the Plains via the River and Mountain Crow to be traded to the Nez Perce and Shoshoni for horses and Spanish horse equipment such as saddle blankets and bridles. Whilst the frontier of the gun thus moved west and south, that of the horse rapidly moved to the north and east.

Costume styles were clearly influenced by trade patterns of this sort, well beyond the regions of the Plains, and involved more than just commodities. One ancient and ever ex-

Left: *Star That Travels, an Osage, c.1897. It was the custom among the Osage to tattoo the 'mark of honor' on selected warriors to ensure that they were faithful in keeping the ancient rituals.*

panding network almost certainly introduced cultural influences from the Lower Mississippi Valley via the Mandan and Hidatsa villages on the middle Missouri River. This increasingly led to an integration of early Northern Plains ritual, cosmology and art, with that of the cosmic structure and ceremonialism of the southeast. The spread was undoubtedly via Assiniboin Indians who lived in the region of the Qu'Appelle Souris and Assiniboine Rivers of present-day Manitoba, so that Mississippian cosmology was incorporated in the world-view and rituals of the Plains buffalo hunters. As one observer recently put it, 'The role of Sun and his son, Morningstar, the cosmic struggle between thunderbirds and water monsters, virility derived from the elk spirit, and many other concepts can be traced to the southeast' (Brasser, 1987: 101). Thus, unlike the well documented *trade* of goods across the Plains, the major import from the Lower Mississippi was one of a spiritual nature. Additional evidence for this assumption is provided by petroglyphs painted and etched on cave walls and cliff faces

Below: An Osage girl wearing a robe decorated with ribbon appliqué. Although the robe is made of trade materials, the style became firmly associated with the Osage. Hands are a common decorative motif on such garments. Note the fine silverwork brooches.

found in the Plains region which, after about 1730, changed markedly from animal pictures (suggesting spiritual relationships between artist and animal spirits), to scenes of warfare. 'A new way of life emerged, made up of fragments of the old world-view changed to function in new contexts, increasingly motivated by the achieving of war honors and acquiring material wealth, to be ostentatiously displayed in warfare and tribal ceremonies. Much of this colorful paraphernalia and ceremonialism undoubtedly originated in ancient times, but owed its survival to a reinterpretation of

symbolism in terms of warfare' (ibid:106). Coupled with this emphasis, there was also cultural elaboration due to abundance of natural resources and adoption of the horse leading to a shift of regional culture from horticultural villagers to equestrian nomads.

The warlike spirit of many, if not *all*, Plains tribes was clearly motivated by something

Below: Utse-tah-wah-ti-an-kah, an Osage, c.1880. He wears an otter skin turban and holds a magnificent gun-shaped club, a weapon which tended to be a specialty of the Middle Missouri tribes.

Osage

These are the regalia and items of special occasion dress of the prominent Osage Tom Baconrind (a mistranslation of his Osage name, Washin-ha), b.1860, d.1932. Elected chief in 1912, he later served several times on the Osage tribal council. Active in both the Peyote religion and the Catholic church, he was the foremost spokesman for the cause of the Osage full-blood traditionalists during the period of greatest Osage wealth in the 1920s.

1 Studio portrait of Chief Baconrind (Washin-ha), taken in 1930, kept by himself.
2 Leather case with eagle and peacock feathers.
3 Bandolier of china tubes and blue glass beads with mink fur pendant.
4 Pair of buckskin leggings with beads and wool tassels.
5 Beaded legging strips.
6 Beaded moccasins, probably Arapaho in origin.
7 Beaded buckskin pouch for pipe.
8 Catlinite pipe bowl and stem.
9 Silk scarf with gold plated brass neckerchief slide lettered with the Osage for 'Baconrind, Osage Chief, 1920'.
10 Breastplate of bone hairpipes and blue and green glass beads.
11 Peacock feather fan, beaded handle, for Peyote ritual.
12 Beaded cloth garters, with wool fringes.
13 Fan of eagle wing feathers, with otter fur pendant.
14 Ceremonial staff of ebony in form of bow stave covered with otter fur and beadwork, with tubular case of Chinese silk.
15 Choker of shell and bone tubes, black glass beads and leather spreaders.
16 Pair of German-silver bracelets, incised eagle and star design.
17 German-silver neckerchief slide with incised design of heart and arrow.
18 Roach headdress of deer and porcupine hair, stored in usual manner on a wooden rod.
19 German-silver spreader worn with roach headdress.
20 German-silver neckerchief slide with incised design of pipe, warclub, eagle, bow, quiver.
21 Tomahawk, the shaft

covered with red felt, with wool pendant with brass bells and eagle feathers.

22 Headband of otter fur lined with blue strouding, beaded edges, and beaded buckskin placque.

23 Necklace made of white and blue beads on buckskin cord, with shell disc.

24 Silver crucifix with wood core, buckskin string.

25 Red velvet shirt with beaded yoke.

26 Leather belt covered with woven beadwork, with brass rivet edging.

27 Pair of garters, woven beadwork, yarn fringes.

28 Pair of buckskin leggings, edged with beads and nickel rivets, blue velvet lining, horsehair tassels.

29 Moccasins, beaded, metal tinklers; perhaps Kiowa in origin.

30 Headband made from fingerwoven wool sash,

with sateen lining.

31 Breechclout of dark blue strouding, red silk binding, beaded designs.

32 Peacock feather fan, for Peyote ritual.

33 White feather fan, with beaded handle.

34 Gourd rattle, handle covered with beadwork for use in Peyote ritual.

35 Whistle.

36 Feather fan.

37 Eagle feather fan, with beaded handles, pendant of brass bells.

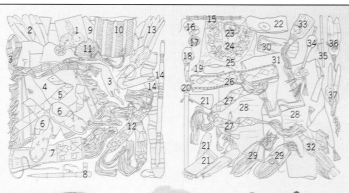

more than material wealth because a typical Plains Indian family did not require vast herds in order to supply material wants; indeed, considering their nomadic way of life, such apparent wealth could well be a hindrance rather than an asset and, in the main, it is to the Plateau tribes that we must look for individual ownership of several hundred horses. Whilst generosity could enhance a man's status, it was, above all else, the acquisition of *war honors* – an inherited craving for distinction and glory – which seems to have been the basis of Plains warfare. Analysis of the possible nature of cultural ethos input relating to warfare from the southeast shows that here war was considered to be a social institution and that warlike exploits were necessary for social advancement. The essence of much typical Plains warfare, such as counting coup on a live enemy with a harmless stick, was reported on for the Illinois Confederacy in the early 1700s.

Taking a scalp signified more than the death of an enemy[2] and ancient traditions dictated that the deed brought with it several exacting obligations. Thus, in the early eighteenth century, one missionary reported of the 'Nations of Louisiana' that those who for the first time had taken a scalp or made a capture 'do not sleep at their return with their wives, and do not eat any meat; they ought not to partake of anything but fish and thickened milk. This abstinence lasts for six months. If they fail to observe it, they imagine that the soul of him whom they have killed will cause them to die through sorcery, that they will never again obtain any advantage over their enemies, and that the slightest wounds they may receive will prove fatal' (Kenton, 1954:417).

Customs were obviously no less rigid – but with a different emphasis – amongst the pedestrian nomads who occupied the Northern Plains at about the same time. Thus, the Piegan

Right: *Pawnee earth lodge village. Lodges were erected using heavy posts, cross-beams, brush and earth. Such villages disappeared under the plow with the removal of tribes from their homelands.*

Chief, Saukamappee, told of the return of a successful warparty carrying more than fifty enemy scalps.[3] There was much discussion as to the symbolic meaning of those taken from the enemy who were found dead under their shields because no one could say that he had actually slain the enemy whose scalp he held; there was less doubt about the others, the War Chief finally decreeing that those who had taken 'the trophy from the head of an enemy they had killed, said the Souls of the enemy that each of us has slain belongs to us and we have given them to our relations in the other world to be their slaves, and we are contented'[4] (Henry and Thompson, Coues ed., 1897:332-3).

Whilst initial encounters of Plains Indians with the white man were generally friendly, particularly in Canada, the systematic slaughter of

Above: *A Pawnee earth lodge village on the Loup Fork, Nebraska. Such dwellings were typical of the semi-sedentary tribes of the Missouri River; they were generally clustered around a central 'plaza'.*

both beaver and buffalo, brought about by the demands of the fur trade together with the influx of white emigrants into and across the Plains region after about 1840, caused a progressive deterioration in relationships between Red and White. An earlier, unfortunate encounter between two Piegan warriors who were killed by Meriwether Lewis during his epic voyage as Co-leader of the Corps of Discovery after the Louisiana Purchase of 1803, caused relationships to be hostile between Blackfeet and Americans for many years. Further aggravation occurred with the American Fur Company's

policy of sending white trappers into Blackfeet country rather than, as in the case of the Hudson's Bay Company, 'depending upon the Indian supply' (Lewis, 1942:27). Not until 1846, when Alexander Culbertson – who was married to the daughter of a Blood chief – established Fort Benton near the junction of the Marias and Missouri Rivers, were relationships stabilized, at least in part, with the fierce Blood, Piegan and Siksika who comprised the Blackfeet nation: thus from that time for some thirty years trading in buffalo hides, a commodity which the Blackfeet could easily supply, was carried on, a commerce which was considered highly beneficial to both sides.[5]

The lucrative returns of the fur trade spelt the death knell of the Plains tribes as the demand for buffalo hides grew. One English observer, William Blackmore, who travelled through the valley of the Platte River in 1868, reported seeing immense herds of buffalo which extended for a distance of over one hundred miles. The Plains were 'blackened with them' and at times the train on which he was travelling was brought to a standstill to let them pass. Some five years later, in the autumn of 1873, Blackmore was to travel over virtually the same ground. This time he was confronted with an entirely different scene, the whole country being whitened with bleaching buffalo bones and in some areas 'there was a continuous line of putrescent carcasses, so that the air was rendered pestilential and offensive to the last degree ... The professional buffalo skinners had moved in.' Subsequent investigations by Blackmore revealed that even as early as 1872 the number of buffalo which were being slaughtered for their hides alone was at least a million per annum. The professional hunters formed lines of camps along the banks of the Arkansas River and *continuously shot buffalo* night and day as they came down to drink (Taylor, 1980:31-2).

The wanton slaughter alarmed and appalled the Plains Indians, as Sitting Bull was said to have observed:

'It is strange that the Americans should complain that the Indians kill buffaloes. We kill buffaloes, as we kill other animals, for food and clothing, and to make our lodges warm. They kill buffaloes – for what? Go through [the] country. See the thousands of carcasses rotting on the Plains. Your young men shoot for pleasure. All they take from dead buffalo is his tail, or his head, or his horns, perhaps, to show they have killed a buffalo. What is this? Is it robbery? You call us savages. What are *they*?'
(*New York Herald*, 16 November 1877)

Not only were the Plains tribes being deprived but, in addition, Blackmore pointed out, the settler who always looked to the buffalo for a winter supply of meat could no longer depend on their appearance and, like the Plains Indian, bitterly opposed the slaughter solely for their hides.

Adding to the decimation of the buffalo was another problem – the emigrant movement to Oregon. By 1845, it was a common sight to see the distinctive covered wagons wending their way along the Oregon Trail, which commenced in Eastern Kansas, followed the Platte River

across Nebraska and on to Fort Laramie in Wyoming. In Western Wyoming it cut through the Continental Divide following the Snake River to Idaho and then into Oregon, terminating at The Dalles on the great Columbia River which led to the Pacific Ocean. Part of the Oregon Trail – in Nebraska and Wyoming – cut across the hunting grounds of the Oglala, one of the largest and most powerful of the Lakota sub-tribes. By the summer of 1850, lured by tales of a land (now called California), where neither snow nor illness existed, and 'the black soil of Oregon was bottomless', thousands of emigrants 'cascaded up the valleys of the Platte and the Sweetwater' (Lavender, 1965:219; Utley, 1967:59).

This large influx of emigrants not only frightened away or destroyed game in the areas through which they passed but, more alarmingly, brought diseases to which the Plains tribes had little or no resistance. Within the

Below: *Quanah Parker, Principal Chief of the Comanche, shrewd politician, Peyote religion proselytizer, and his wife Tonasa, c. 1892, on the front porch of their five-bedroom house.*

space of a few years the Plains Indian and his environment was suddenly and frighteningly subjected to severe pressures, 'even the seemingly limitless bison of the Great Plains, grew suddenly less abundant and in places disappeared from their customary haunts ... Alcohol drained the vitality from those attracted to the settlements and travel routes ... Tribal ranges, ... shifted constantly as groups dispossessed or shouldered aside encroached on others' (Utley, 1967:5). The situation was rapidly getting out of hand. Protection of both emigrants and the indigenous population now became a vital Government concern and to control a potentially explosive situation urgent measures were considered: the outcome was by both Treaty and militarily.

Two major Treaties were drawn up with the Plains tribes in the early 1850s: the Fort Laramie Treaty[6] in September 1851 which led to negotiations with representatives of the Lakota, Cheyenne and Arapaho, Crow, Arikara, Assiniboin, Gros Ventre and Mandan, and the Fort Atkinson Treaty of July 1853 which attempted to stabilize relations with the Southern Plains tribes such as the Comanche, Kiowa

Kiowa

The Kiowa, traditionally among the most warlike of the Plains tribes, lived in the early 18th century around the Black Hills and the upper Yellowstone R., where they were allies of the Crow and enemies of the Cheyenne and Sioux. About 1805 they moved south to present eastern Colorado and western Oklahoma. They made peace permanently with the Comanche about 1790, the Osage in 1834, the Cheyenne and Arapaho about 1840, and were friendly with the Wichita. Their enemies included the Caddo, Tonkawa, Navajo, and Ute tribes, and the frontier settlements in Texas and northern Mexico (down to Durango), and the white overland emigrants from the east. Finally making peace with the U.S. Government at Fort Sill in 1875, they were assigned a reservation nearby that they shared with the Comanche, which they lost in 1901 as a result of the Federal allotment policy. Most Kiowa today live in western Oklahoma in the area of the old reservation. James Mooney conducted studies among the Kiowa in the 1890s, which resulted in a famous monograph that describes Kiowa history on the basis of their oral traditions, especially those correlated with the important pictographic calender histories they kept. He then investigated Kiowa heraldry, the individually owned painted designs on tipis and sacred shields, their origins and the history of their transmission from owner to owner. Part of the documentation of this research consisted of models made for Mooney, and other Kiowa artifacts he collected for the Smithsonian.

1 Hair plates – band of German-silver discs worn suspended from the hair.
2 Model shield, with design belonging to Tsenbo II.
3 Model snake shield, with design belonging to Guitonkagya (Ringboned Wolf) in period 1835-58.
4 Model dragonfly shield, with design belonging to Pa-akanti (Rough Bull), not used after about 1875.
5 Model shield, with design belonging to Setäpeto.
6 Model bird shield, with design belonging to the noted war chief Setängya (Sitting Bear), killed at Fort Sill in 1871.
7 Model shield, with design belonging to Gōtara.
8 Full-size model of shield with design belonging to Padohgai, made by his great grandson Padalti.
9 Eagle-feather warbonnet with long trailer, type worn on horseback.
10 War shirt of Dohasän (Little Bluff) the Younger, who died c.1894. Typically Crow in style (acquired from these Kiowa allies?); hair locks on right shoulder said to be from scalps of Navajo enemy.
11 Pair of man's moccasins.
12 Peyote ritual fan.
13 Metal pipe tomahawk, of Mexican origin (?).
14 Woman's dress.
15 Pair of woman's high-top moccasins, painted leather with beadwork and metal discs.
16 Pair of boy's moccasins.

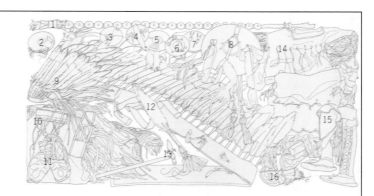

Above: *A member of the Mandan Buffalo Bull Society, painted by Karl Bodmer (1837). He wears a complete buffalo head mask, marking him as one of the leaders of the Bull dance.*

Left: *Mató-Tópe, or Four Bears, painted by Karl Bodmer (1837). His outfit a symbol of success in warfare, the carved knife in the horned eagle feather headdress represents a battle with a Cheyenne chief.*

and Kiowa-Apache. In the case of the Laramie Treaty, boundaries for the tribes were defined and Head Chiefs appointed, such as Conquering Bear, a Brulé Lakota. Generous presents, with promises of more to come, were an important part of Government policy[7] when encouraging chiefs to become signatories; it caused, together with the appointment of the 'paper chiefs' (as they became known), great discord, particularly with non-Treaty factions. The military build-up in anticipation of potential problems with this latter group, was partially achieved by purchase or garrisoning by the army of the old and established fur trade posts. Thus, Fort Laramie, purchased by the Government from the American Fur Company for $4,000, now became a strategic military post; indeed, even before the 1851 Treaty, it had been garrisoned (in August 1849) by two officers and fifty-three men. A similar pattern was swiftly replicated across the Central and Southern Plains. Whilst the established fur posts took on a military function, others, such as Forts Riley and Larned, were purpose-built by the military for protection of another famous route to the south of the Oregon Trail – the Santa Fe. Additionally, protection of the route from San Antonio to El Paso, and deep in the heart of Comanche, Kiowa, Mescalero Apache

and Tonkawa territory, was achieved by the establishment of military forts, such as Clark (1852), Hudson (1851), Stockton (1852) and Bliss (1849), near or on the Pecos and Rio Grande Rivers. An uneasy peace was established, but it would be less than a decade before, from Mexico to Canada, Comanche, Kiowa, Arapaho, Cheyenne, Sioux and other tribes, would present a formidable opposition to further expansion, which for almost a generation impeded the advance of the frontier.

Dangers and attitudes were succinctly summed up by a popular emigrant camp-fire refrain:

'The Injuns will catch you while crossing the Plains.
They'll kill you, and scalp you, and beat out your brains.
Uncle Sam ought to throw them all over the fence,
So there'll be no Red Injuns a hundred years hence.'
(Smith,1943:156)

A slow war of suppression of the Plains Indians began with a cow, so thin and emaciated that it had been abandoned by its Mormon emigrant owner. Desiring a piece of rawhide and perhaps a questionable meal in the bargain, High Forehead, a visiting Miniconjou Sioux to Conquering Bear's camp, shot the animal dead on the afternoon of 18 August 1854 'to make restitution or satisfaction for any

wrongs committed . . . by any band or individual . . . on the people of the United States . . .' (McCann, 1956:3-4).

The emigrants demanded compensation and although Conquering Bear immediately offered a horse in payment, Lieutenant Hugh B. Fleming considered the matter so trivial that no decision was reached that night. Probably the matter would have rested there, but next day Lieutenant John Grattan strongly supported the emigrants and claimed the right to command a detachment of infantry to arrest the offending Indian.[8] Reluctantly, Fleming agreed to the proposal, instructing Grattan to receive the offender, and in case of refusal to give him up, to act upon his own discretion, and 'not to hazard an engagement without certainty of success' (ibid:8).

Grattan, along with Sergeant W. Faver, twenty-six infantrymen, two musicians and a terrified interpreter (one Lucien Auguste) rode toward the Lakota encampment. Twice Grattan was forcibly warned of the potentially dangerous situation. Obridge Allen, a professional emigrant guide, rode up and pointed out to Grattan 'that the Oglalas had begun driving in their pony herds – typical Indian preparation for battle'. Shortly after, James Bordeaux, an experienced and shrewd trader at that time trading directly with the Lakota, observed to Grattan, 'Why don't you let the old cow go. It was laying there without food or water and would soon die; it was too lame to walk; its feets [sic] was worn through to the flesh. It was shot by some boys who wanted a piece of skin' (ibid:6). Grattan told Conquering Bear that he had come to take High Forehead back to the Fort. Reported Man-Afraid-Of-His-Horses, 'The Bear said to me, "You are a brave, what do you think of it?" I said to him, "You are the chief. What do you think?".' Then Conquering Bear told Grattan that High Forehead was 'a guest in his village and not subject to his authority.' Although Grattan was made further offers of ponies to

pay for the cow and was urged to delay any action until Major John W. Whitfield, the Indian Agent, arrived, he ordered his troops into the Brulé village announcing that he would 'go himself to High Forehead's lodge' (ibid:13-14). He halted some sixty yards from High Forehead's lodge which stood near that of Conquering Bear's, and then he ordered the howitzers primed and positioned his men on either side of the cannon.

The parley now became increasingly bitter and even the diplomatic Conquering Bear was beginning to lose patience with the arrogant Grattan. Reported Man-Afraid, 'The Bear said it was hard as it was a poor cow and that today the soldiers had made him ashamed that he was made chief by the whites and today you come to my village and plant your big guns . . . For all I tell you you will not hear me. I would strike you were I not a chief. But as I am chief and am made so by the whites will not do it.' (ibid:18).

Within a short time, the frustrated Grattan broke off the parley and, moving toward the

troops, gave a command that the Indians did not understand. Two or three shots were fired and one warrior was hit. Bordeaux then heard the chief's shout to the warriors not to fire, that perhaps this was just a shot to protect the honor of the troops and they would leave. Grattan, however, was now convinced of the need for a further demonstration and ordered the infantry to fire a volley. Arrows began to fly from the bowmen on the flank and Grattan's command, few if any of which had any experience of Plains Indian warfare, suddenly scattered in panic. Grattan himself crashed to the ground struck by arrows; when his body was found later, it had twenty-four arrows in it. One had gone completely through his head and he could only be identified by his pocket watch. Within a short time the entire command, except one, was wiped out. The sole survivor was Private John Cuddy who, although badly wounded, had crawled into the wild rose bushes. Cuddy died two days later without giving any account of the battle.

The clash underlined the vast differences be-

Above: *Oto warriors, c.1880. Of particular note are the superb pipe with a head of red catlinite stone (third figure) and the fine German silver brooch of the warrior on the right.*

Right: *The Crow generally employed a four-pole basic frame into which other poles were stacked, forming a conical framework for the cover. This arrangement tended to set the smoke flaps farther apart to accommodate the larger number of poles at the top. Unlike the Blackfeet, the Crow used only a limited number of painted tipis, most being a plain off-white.*

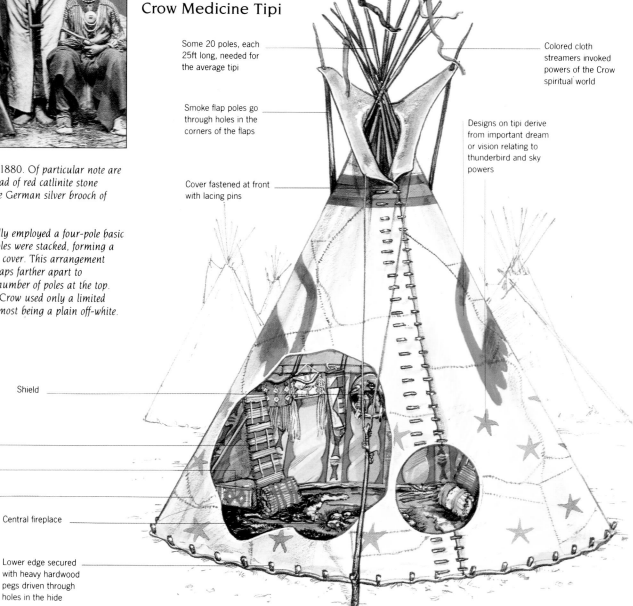

Crow Medicine Tipi

Some 20 poles, each 25ft long, needed for the average tipi

Colored cloth streamers invoked powers of the Crow spiritual world

Smoke flap poles go through holes in the corners of the flaps

Designs on tipi derive from important dream or vision relating to thunderbird and sky powers

Cover fastened at front with lacing pins

Shield

Willow back rest

Rawhide parfleche

Some 14 buffalo skins of 15ft diameter cut and sewn together to produce semicircular cover (stitching emphasized to show tailoring)

Central fireplace

Lower edge secured with heavy hardwood pegs driven through holes in the hide

tween the two cultures, and it served as a warning to other would-be 'paper-chiefs'. The uneasy peace was over. The Grattan Massacre, as it became known, heralded the beginning of spasmodic and often brutal wars which were only finally and tragically terminated almost forty years later, in December 1890, with the massacre of Big Foot's Lakota on a tiny creek in South Dakota, which the world now knows as Wounded Knee.

As early as 1834, hostility by the Comanches towards white settlers who were moving westwards from Arkansas into the Plains of Kansas and Texas initiated the formation of a Dragoon Expedition led by Colonel Henry Dodge, to lay the foundation for a Peace Treaty. They arrived at the enormous village of some six to eight hundred tipis which was pitched in the vicinity of the confluence of the Washita and Red Rivers (in present-day Texas). Dodge explained to the Comanche the friendly motives of the expedition; that he was sent by the President of the United States and hoped that a system of trade could be established 'that would be beneficial to both' (Catlin, 1926,vol.2:63). The expedition was a success and the following year agreements were ratified.

Problems, however, were looming for the Comanche, as Cheyenne, desirous of trading at Bent's Fort, moved south and joined the Arapaho. Together, these two tribes forced the Comanche, Kiowa and Plains-Apache to accept the Arkansas River as the northern boundary of their domain. Two years later, however, realizing the potential dangers of approaching well-armed eastern Indians and whites into the Southern Plains, *The Great Peace* alliance was formed; not only did it ensure that the Cheyenne and Arapaho now had plenty of horses at their disposal (from the horse-rich Comanche), and the Kiowa and Comanche access to guns and ammunition (via the northern trade), but it also led to a formidable barrier to any further encroachment by whites from the east. The Comanches had every reason to be wary of the whites and even this great alliance did not protect them. In March 1840, for example, twelve Comanche chiefs met with Texas commissioners, hoping to conclude a Peace Treaty; the Texans, however, demanded that the Comanches gave up their white prisoners. On refusing, troops were brought into the council room and in the ensuing fight all twelve chiefs, together with twenty other Comanches, were slaughtered.

After the annexation of Texas to the Union (in 1845), the Federal Government made attempts to develop a consistent and fair policy toward the Southern Plains tribes. In 1847, a tactful and patient agent – one Robert S. Neighbours – was appointed as special agent for the Indians of Texas, and for several years his friendly influence maintained an uneasy peace on the Southern Plains. However, an unratified Treaty made with the Kiowa and Comanche in April 1863 led to further discontent and Comanche, Kiowa, Cheyenne, Arapaho (and some Sioux) caused the routes to Denver and south as far as the Santa Fe Trail to become unsafe: emigration stopped 'and much of the country was depopulated' (Wallace and Hoebel, 1952:306).

Retaliation by Colonel J. M. Chivington, heading a state militia of Colorado Volunteers, led to the massacre and rout of a peaceful Cheyenne village at Sand Creek, some one hundred miles southeast of Denver, under Black Kettle, White Antelope and Left Hand. Whilst the latter two chiefs fell under the hail of bullets, Black Kettle miraculously survived but the barbarity and savagery of the militia – men, women and children were scalped and mutilated in a brutal manner – shocked the nation and the Sand Creek Massacre, as it came to be called, precipitated a policy of continuous harassment by the more militant Cheyenne Dog Soldiers[9] led by Tall Bull and White Horse, whose ranks were swelled by Northern Cheyenne under Roman Nose and Lakotas, under Pawnee Killer. By June 1867, with Denver virtually isolated, the warriors attacked Fort

Left: *Powder Face, an Arapaho chief, 1870. His crooked lance indicates membership of the Arapaho Spear Society – one of the warriors who was expected never to retreat in battle.*

Above: *The so-called Crow Dance of the Arapaho, 1893. Developed in the 1890s by the Southern Cheyenne and Arapaho, it was performed as a preliminary to the Ghost Dance, and modified from the picturesque Omaha dance of the Plains tribes.*

Wallace, just northeast of the now infamous Sand Creek site. An ensuing engagement gave an Englishman, Dr William A. Bell, an insight into the brutality of Plains warfare and made famous forever a fellow countryman, one Sergeant Frederick Wylyams. According to Bell, Wylyams, who was educated at Eton, whilst 'sowing his wild oats had made a fatal alliance in London and gone to grief' (Bell, 1869, vol.1:46, in Taylor, 1975:90-93). Wylyams had then left for America where he enlisted in the U.S. army; he was with Captain Albert Barnitz's G. Troop of the Seventh Cavalry when Bell met him. Wylyams had hoped to gain a commission and thereby get back into the good graces of his family; it was not to be. As the cavalry followed a small band of Indians beyond a ridge, they were suddenly confronted by a large body of warriors. Bell records, 'They halted a few minutes ... then, like a whirlwind, ... they rushed on the little band of fifty soldiers ... Saddles were emptied, and the soldiers forced back over the ground towards the fort ... the Indians pressed heavily cutting off five men, among them Sergeant Frederick Wylyams ... one by one the soldiers fell, selling their lives

Right: *An episode in the Ghost Dance, 1893. Due to white oppression the Arapaho turned to peyotism and the Ghost Dance religion. Repeating the dance regularly would return the earth to the Indians.*

Above: *Arapaho tipis near Camp Supply, Indian Territory, 1870. The entrances to the tipis at the right are all oriented in the same direction – almost certainly east to greet the rising sun.*

Below: *Sun Dance medicine lodge of the Arapaho, 1893. Of major importance was the lodge itself which was situated in the middle of the encampment. The Arapaho dance resembled that of the Kiowa, Dakota and Cheyenne in many features.*

dearly.' The Indians were finally repulsed by Captain Barnitz's better armed cavalry and the bodies of the fallen five discovered. The shocked Dr Bell later recorded, 'I have seen in days gone by sights horrible and gory – death in all its forms of agony and distortion – but never did I feel the sickening sensation, the giddy, fainting feeling that came over me when I saw our dead, dying and wounded after this Indian fight. A handful of men, to be sure, but with enough wounds upon them to have slain a company, if evenly distributed.' The sergeant's body had been savagely mutilated and, with scientific objectivity, Bell described in detail the different signs which each tribe had left on his body so that their presence in the battle was thus recorded; he felt that there was little difficulty in recognizing the meaning of some of the wounds. 'The muscles of the right arm, hacked to the bone, speak of the Cheyenne, or "Cut

Arms'', the nose slit denotes the "Smaller tribe'' or Arapaho; and the throat cut bears witness that the Sioux were also present. There were therefore amongst the warriors Cheyenne, Arapaho and Sioux. It was not till some time afterwards that I knew positively what these signs meant, and I have not yet discovered what tribe was indicated by the incisions down the thighs, and the lacerations of the calves of the legs, in oblique parallel gashes. The arrows also varied in make and colour according to the tribe; and it was evident, from the number of different devices, that warriors from several tribes had each purposely left one in the dead mans body.'[10] (ibid:61-4).

A Special Governmental Joint Committee, which published *Condition of the Indian Tribes* in 1867, pointed out that the major problem with these southern tribes was due to extensive white intrusion into their territory. This led to the Medicine Lodge Treaty near Fort Dodge, Kansas, in October 1867; it was a genuine attempt by the Government of the day to reconcile the vast differences which existed between the interests of both Red and White. The great Indian village of some eight hundred and fifty tipis and five thousand Indians – Cheyenne, Arapaho, Comanche, Kiowa and Kiowa-Apache were represented – was finally assembled in the vicinity of Medicine Lodge Creek, so-called because the Kiowa had recently celebrated

their annual Sun-dance nearby and the medicine lodge was still standing at the time of the conference.[11] The some one hundred whites, commissioners, interpreters, clerks and newsmen were escorted by a battalion of the Seventh Cavalry under Major Joel H. Elliott. The assembly has been described as one of the 'largest and most colorful gathering[s] of Indians and officials ever witnessed on the plains' and 'free food and plenty of coffee were provided to ensure that the Indians did not wander away' (Nye, 1968:107).

Although the Treaty was signed by such famous chiefs as Little Raven (Arapaho), Black Kettle and Little Robe (Cheyenne), Satank and Satanta (Kiowa), Wolf Sleeve (Kiowa-Apache) and Ten Bears (Comanche) and the attacks on whites ceased for several months, intertribal warfare continued. Cheyenne and Arapaho raided the Osage and Kaw, whilst the Kiowa and Comanche raided the Navajo, Caddo and Wichita. Later, they began forays to the farms and settlements of the Chickasaw[12], as one of their number wryly observed: 'The wolf will respect a treaty as much as Mr Wild Indian (ibid:113).

The problem stemmed from several misunderstandings and difficulties, a pattern which was to be repeated in later negotiations with tribes on the Central and Northern Plains. The Treaty had stipulated that in return for safe traffic across the Plains, agencies and schools would be built, and farming tools, seeds, doctors, instructors and artisans provided. At the new agencies, rations and annuities were to be regularly distributed and arrangements made so that unscrupulous agents and traders did not cheat the Indians. The Government, however, was slow in meeting the stipulations of the Treaty and it later emerged that many of the Indian signatories did not fully understand their obligations, or if they did, found it difficult to control the younger warriors, particularly those of the Comanche and Kiowa, who still raided into Texas which, since its annexation in 1845, made its people citizens of the United States. Traditionally, raiding south into these areas had been the Kiowa and Comanche warriors' path to wealth and glory and the continued hostile action of the southern tribes led to demands for more effective military protection.

The death of Roman Nose at the Beecher's Island battle in September 1867, and the slaughter of Black Kettle together with over one

Below: *Arapaho from Fort Washakie, Wyoming, and the Paiute prophet Wovoka. The ethnologist Mooney reported that the Arapaho had great 'faith in the unseen things of the spirit world' and in the early 1890s at least two delegations visited Wovoka at his home in Mason Valley, Nevada.*

Arapaho

These are among many objects collected by A. L. Kroeber in Oklahoma and Wyoming in 1899 and 1900, as part of a famous study of Arapaho symbolism. These things were typical of those made and used by the Arapaho in 1900. Hardly any like them are now made. The meanings of the designs given below are those explained to Kroeber by the original owners or makers of the objects. Color photographs of most of these beautiful things have not been published before.

1 Child's moccasins.
2 Feather bustle worn by a man in the crow dance.
3 Child's moccasins. Green triangles represent horse ears.
4 Moccasins. The design represents clouds and stars in a blue sky, with a tipi at the toe, and a red crayfish in the center.
5 Moccasins. The cross represents the Morning Star, and the bar at the instep is the horizon.
6 Boy's hair ornament worn during the Ghost Dance, made of cowhair and two brass clock wheels, the larger representing the sun, the other food.
7 Moccasins. The rows of blue triangles represent rocks, the rows of red and blue squares are hills, with three people sitting on each row shown by red squares; a blue path lined by red rocks crosses the center; the two red bars at the top sides are standing people.
8 Woman's leggings attached to moccasins.
9 Pouch for matches and other small things worn by a woman at her belt.
10 Pouch for combs, paint-bags, and other toilet articles. The three crosses represent the Morning Star.
11 Bag for the medicine called 'two babies'.
12 Pouch worn at the belt.
13 Moccasins. The green squares are life symbols, touched by red tipis.
14 Moccasins.
15 Moccasins. The zigzag line represents lightning.
16 Child's moccasins.
17 Moccasins. The green rectangle is a buffalo, standing on a white path.
18 Moccasins. The large triangles represent buffalo horns (red for bare soil, green for grass); zigzag lines are pipes; the tongues are forked, representing rattlesnake tongues, with spotted blue for the snakes' skins and

tin cones representing their rattles.

19 Moccasins. The spotted stripe are buffalo tracks.

20 Moccasins. The blue-striped areas represent fish; the small paired triangles are butterflies.

21 Child's moccasins. All the stripes represent paths.

22 Moccasins. The white background represents snow; blue triangles are tipis, with square doors; the two large triangles on top are lakes.

23 Moccasins.

24 Rattle of dewclaws.

25 Fan used during Peyote ceremony.

26-31 Six circles of quillworked leather. Each is an ornament attached to the top of a tipi at the back.

32 Ornament of quillwork on leather.

33 Moccasins. The checked red design represents the rought interior of buffalo intestines.

34 Man's beaded vest.

35 Pendant worn attached to the scalplock of a man in the Crow Dance.

36 Eagle bone whistle.

37 Girl's leggings. The triangles represent arrowpoints; those with smaller triangles attached also symbolize tipis.

38 Small girl's leggings with attached moccasins.

39 Woman's moccasins. The large stripe represents the path the wearer travels.

40 Moccasins.

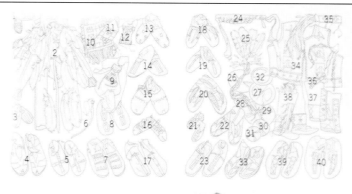

Pawnee War Dance, 1821

In 1821 a delegation of sixteen Pawnees and other western Indians performed a war dance for President Monroe at the White House, which was sketched by the Baroness Hyde de Neuville, wife of the Minister of France to the U.S. An admired member of the delegation was Petalesharo, shown here, who in 1817 had rescued a woman about to be sacrificed to the Morning Star by the Pawnees. His portrait was painted by C.B. King, providing one of the earliest illustrations of the classic eagle feather warbonnet and giving other details of his dress. He wears a James Madison peace medal, silver trade armlets, and multiple silver cones in ear ornaments, and carries a gunstock club decorated with brass tacks. His fingerwoven wool and bead sash and buckskin leggings resemble Pawnee examples in the Smithsonian collections.

hundred men, women and children, by Custer at Washita in November 1867, the progressive decline of the buffalo, superior weapons, the Cavalry's ability to strike the village communities in winter, wore the tribes down. By the early 1870s, the principal Kiowa and Comanche war leaders – Satank, Satanta and Kicking Bird were dead; new leaders – such as Feathered Lance of the Kiowa and the able Quanah Parker of the Comanches – sensing the inevitable, turned to negotiation and many visited the Great Father in Washington.[13] By 1875, warfare on the Southern Plains was all but over; less so, further north, where smoldering apathy over broken Treaties was being rapidly replaced by open hostility.

The Fort Laramie Treaty, which was finally concluded in November 1868 with Red Cloud's signature together with those of some two hundred leaders of the Lakota – Brulé, Oglala,

Right: *Cheyenne camp, date not recorded but probably c.1890. The women tan hides staked out on the ground, products of a beef issue rather than the hunt. The tipis appear to be of canvas.*

Below: *Man on a Cloud, Southern Cheyenne, 1892, probably the same Alights on the Cloud who visited Washington in the 1850s. His magnificent warbonnet and scalp shirt denote a high ranking warrior.*

Cheyenne

The Cheyenne are speakers of an Algonquian language whose ancestors moved about 1700 from the wild rice region of the eastern woodlands to establish agricultural and hunting villages on the northern prairies. About a century later they moved farther west on to the high plains where they took on the Plains way of life, living in migratory villages of tipis, hunting buffalo on horseback and engaging in raids and warfare, especially against the Crow, Pawnee,

Shoshoni and Ute. By the 1851 Treaty of Fort Laramie the Northern Cheyenne were separated from the Southern Cheyenne who joined the Arapaho. Warfare with the U.S. Army and the Colorado militia broke out as Cheyenne country was invaded by white immigrants, buffalo hunters, and gold miners. The Cheyenne joined their Sioux allies to defeat Gen. Custer in 1876. In 1879 peace was finally established. Most of the items shown here are from the Southern Cheyenne of Indian Territory. The dates indicate when they were collected.

1 Parfleche for clothing. 1868.
2 Medicine man's necklace, with imitation bear claws of carved horn. 1891.
3 One-piece leggings and moccasins, beaded. 1891.
4 Pair of beaded moccasins. 1891.
5 Buckskin pillow with beaded designs. 1891.
6 Buckskin bag for clothing with beaded designs imitating quillwork patterns. 1868.
7 Pair of beaded woman's

moccasins. 1891.
8 Saddle-blanket ornament, beaded buckskin strip. 1891.
9 Snake effigy with cord netting, worn as personal war medicine. 1891.
10 Headdress of eagle feathers and buffalo horns, with long trailer. 1881.
11 Wooden medicine bowl. 1891.
12 Pair of woman's leggings. 1891.
13 German-silver arm band.

14 1916.
14 Paint pouch of turtle skin. 1891.
15 Stone hammer for breaking bones for marrow and mashing wild plums. 1891.
16 Bone hide flesher with metal blade. Northern Cheyenne. 1901.
17 Woman's small parfleche. 1891.
18 Bow obtained from Red Eagle. 1891.
19 Five arrows, iron heads. Northern Cheyenne, 1868.

20 Flageolet. 1891.
21 Powder horn on buckskin pouch with flannel-covered strap. 1891.
22 Pair of woman's moccasins, beaded green-painted leather. 1891.
23 Necklace of bear claws, brass bells. Before 1931.
24 Necklace of dentalium shells and brass studs. 1891.
25 Girl's necklace of bone beads and 14 dimes dated from 1857 to 1888. 1891.
26 Girl's leather belt. 1891.

27 Warrior's quirt, wood with brass tacks. 1877.
28 Drum for curing; with painted design of red-wing blackbird; representing original name of medicine-man owner later called Woman's Heart. Before 1915.
29 Medicine man's cap. Old in 1891.
30 Buckskin shirt bought from Little Chief; painted, decorated with quillwork and tufts of human hair. 1879.

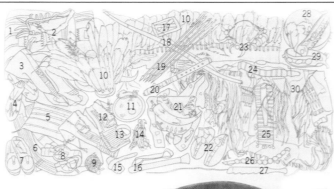

Miniconjou, Hunkpapa, Blackfeet, Sans Arc and Two Kettle – as well as Santee and Yanktonai, conceded all of Red Cloud's demands which 'for the army, it was an unpalatable but not indigestible prescription' (Utley, 1973:134). This was withdrawal of the army from the Bozeman Trail, abandonment of such forts as Fort Phil Kearny and C. F. Smith, and the granting of hunting rights on the Republican River and in Nebraska and Wyoming. It also reserved the Powder River country as 'unceded Indian territory' on which no white might trespass without Indian consent (ibid:135). As with the Medicine Lodge Treaty the previous year, it provided for the building of schools and the issuing of rations and annuities. On several counts the Laramie Treaty was a success; it ended the eponymously named Red Cloud War which had shed so much blood on both sides particularly with the annihilation of Fetterman and more than eighty men on the 21 December 1866 and the later Wagon Box of 2 August 1867 where, although white casualties were not so high, some of the men never fully recovered, mentally or physically, from their ordeal.[14]

The Government-sponsored expeditions to the Black Hills in 1874 and 1875 to investigate mineral wealth led to a largely unfounded rumor of extensive gold deposits. The Treaty of 1868 had defined the Great Sioux Reservation to encompass a vast area west of the Missouri River of what is today the state of South Dakota; this included the *Pa Sapa* or 'Black Hills', an area considered sacred to the Lakota. By late 1875, a Gold Rush had commenced; encroachment into Lakota territory was a violation of the 1868 Treaty and the army attempted to keep the miners and others out. Inevitably, the task was impossible. 'I say to you there is not power enough in this Government to stop the progress of this |our| conquering race . . . you cannot repress . . . the people of this country . . . there is not power enough to stop the migration of our people' (Senator Hurlbut, Congressional Record, July 1876. See Taylor, 1975:110).

Below: *Crow warriors dressed for dance, c.1890. Note the large brass bells tied just below the knee which together with the drum and singers added to the dance rhythm. Umbrellas for use as sun shades were also popular at this period.*

By February 1876, a new war with the Lakota was on, precipitated by Sitting Bull's refusal to leave the Powder River country and register at one of the agencies, the ultimatum being initiated by none other than Ulysses Grant himself, President of the United States: 'If they neglect or refuse so to remove, they will be reported to the War Department as hostile Indians, and that a military force will be sent to compel them to obey the orders of the Indian Office. (Chandler to Belknap, Congressional Record, July 1876).[15]

A winter campaign by Brigadier-General George Crook, who led ten companies of cavalry and two of infantry into Powder River country against Sitting Bull and Cheyenne allies in March 1876 was quickly abandoned due to severe weather conditions. On return, a spring campaign, larger and better organized, was planned by Brigadier-General Alfred H. Terry. On 29 May 1876, Lieutenant-General P. H. Sheridan reported on the projected three-pronged campaign under Terry and Crook. 'Brigadier-General Terry moved out of his command from Fort Abraham Lincoln in the direction of the mouth of Powder River . . . The total

strength of his column is about nine hundred men . . . General Crook will move from Fort Fetterman with a column about the same size. Colonel John Gibbon is now moving down north of the Yellowstone and east of the mouth of the Big Horn with a force of about four hundred . . . each column should be able to take care of itself, and to chastise the Indians, should it have the opportunity . . . I presume the following will occur: General Terry will drive the Indians towards the Big Horn valley and

General Crook will drive them back towards Terry; Colonel Gibbon moving down on the north side of the Yellowstone, to intercept . . . the result of the movement of these three columns may force many of the hostile Indians back to the agencies . . .' (Lieutenant-General P. H. Sheridan to General W. T. Sherman in Washington, 29 May 1876. See Taylor, 1975:113).

Unknown to these three forces, one of the largest concentrations of Plains Indians ever known in the historic period was rapidly build-

Above: *Crow dancers, date not recorded but probably c.1900. To the left is a man dressed as a clown; during the reservation period, such men wore gunnysacks made into leggings and ponchos. They gave much amusement to their audiences.*

Below: *Crow village, probably near Crow Agency on the Little Big Horn River, Montana, c.1910. Crow tipis are notable for the long lodge-pole pines which were cut in the Big Horn mountains. Note favorite ponies tied by some of the tipis.*

Above: *Interior of the Crow Tobacco Society Initiation lodge, showing participants with hand drums in front of them. Tobacco (Nicotiana multivalvis) was an important Crow medicine.*

Below: *A Crow delegation to Washington, 1880. Indians from left to right: Old Crow, Medicine Crow, Two Belly (standing, in beaded shirt), Long Elk, Plenty Coups and Pretty Eagle.*

ing up along the valley of the Little Big Horn, drawn by the charismatic Sitting Bull of the Hunkpapa and Crazy Horse, undoubtedly one of the most distinguished war chiefs the Oglala ever produced. A village of some fifteen hundred tipis containing between twelve to fifteen thousand Indians – mainly Sioux and Cheyenne – was strung for three miles along the banks of the Little Big Horn River. Sitting Bull's message had travelled far; a few weeks previously, he had invited the powerful and influential Blackfeet chief, Crowfoot, in Canada 'to join the Sioux in their fight against the Americans . . . after the Americans and Crows had been defeated, the Sioux would come to Canada with the Blackfeet and exterminate the whites' (Dempsey, 1972:88).[16]

The predicted retreat of the Indians from Crook's forces was foiled by Crazy Horse's attack on the morning of 17 June. Crook was camped on the headwaters of the Rosebud with more than one thousand officers and men and some two hundred and sixty Shoshoni and Crow scouts. The Indians struck without warning – Crook was playing a game of cards and his men were having breakfast. The ensuing battle lasted six hours; unhindered by consideration of their women and children who were camped some seventeen miles further north, Crazy Horse's forces employed unusual offensive tac-

tics leaving Crook's column severely depleted of ammunition and with nearly one hundred dead and wounded. Most importantly, Crook was eliminated from the three-pronged campaign.

Four days later, on the afternoon of the 21 June, Terry, Gibbon, Custer and Brisbin held a 'council of war on board the *Far West*' (Taunton, 1977:21). Later that day, Mark Kellogg sent what was to be his last despatch to the *New York Herald*; in it he outlined the next step of the campaign. Custer would 'start with his whole command up the Rosebud valley . . . and follow the Indians as long and as far as horse flesh and human endurance could carry his command . . . [he] proposes to live and travel like Indians; in this manner the command will be able to go wherever the Indians can. Gibbon's command has started for the mouth of the Big Horn' (ibid:24). Custer's Seventh Cavalry consisted of some 31 officers, 586 soldiers and in addition 33 Indian scouts and 20 employees and citizens. As Custer bade farewell, Gibbon apparently called out, 'Now Custer, don't be greedy! Wait for us!' Custer made the ambiguous reply 'No, I won't' (ibid:29).

At 12.05 on Sunday 25 June, Custer divided his forces into four columns and prepared to attack. Major Marcus Reno with 131 men was to parallel Custer's movements; Captain Benteen with 113 men to the southwest and Custer with five companies (in all some 215 men), followed a line of hills leading to the lower end of the Indian village. At the Washita battle in November 1868, Custer had divided his forces in a similar way, attacking the village simultaneously from different points and hence maximizing confusion. At 3.15 Reno struck the *southern* portion of the great Sioux-Cheyenne encampment – Sitting Bull's Hunkpapa.

. . . 'under a towering cloud of dust, they caught the glint of gun barrels, saw the flutter of a guidon, the blue shirts of the troopers . . . Lead whistled overhead, smacking the tipi poles. The soldiers were coming on the gallop straight for the Hunkpapa camp. In that camp all was confusion. Old men were yelling advice, . . . women and children rushing off afoot and on horseback, . . . fleeing from the soldiers . . . grabbed their babies, called their older children, . . . The Hunkpapa stood their ground bravely . . . Every moment reinforcements came up and the firing grew constantly heavier . . .'

(Vestal, 1948:241-2)

Several weeks earlier, during Sun-dance ceremonials on Rosebud Creek, Sitting Bull had experienced a dramatic vision; it foretold of a great triumph for the Sioux with many dead soldiers falling into camp. Inspired by the promise and imagery, the Hunkpapa stood their ground. 'Instead of running, the Indians ahead multiplied until there was a solid front before the village.' Reno's force was now pushed into a defensive position, the command was being rapidly surrounded by Sioux and Cheyenne warriors and 'the retreat now became a free-for-all' (Taylor, 1975:134). 'The fight was not at all in accordance with my ideas. The so-called charge from the valley was almost a rout. I became sick and dis-heartened with what was going on . . .' (Thomas H. French, 7th Cavalry, in Johnson, 1989:17).

Cut off by a maze of bluffs which caused the timing to be misjudged, 'Custer's luck' had run out; his regiment was fragmented and each potentially exposed to separate defeats before they could again be united. Had Reno's initial charge been sustained, victory may have ensued, but for Reno the odds seemed too great: shortly after ordering his men to dismount, he

Below: *The Hunká-Alowanpi Ceremony, Oglala, 1907. Among the Lakota this was associated with the mythological figure of the White buffalo Maiden. Here the ceremonial pipe is consecrated before a painted buffalo skull lying on a bed of holy sage.*

Crow

These pieces were collected by the anthropologist Robert H. Lowie on the Crow Reservation in Montana between 1910 and 1913. At that time, the Crow had become farmers, whose everyday material culture was largely of non-Indian origin, although moccasins were commonly worn and the old forms, if not the materials, of clothing often remained. Buffalo hunting and warfare had ceased several decades earlier, but what Lowie called the 'war psychology' remained

strong, and much of the ancient ritual was still performed, often involving special dress and implements. The Tobacco Society was important to the Crow; the Wolverine chapter (No.6) was a ritual organization of men and women devoted to planting and harvesting a special sacred tobacco. The deerclaw moccasins (No.23) were worn in a Tobacco Society dance. Social and military societies also had their place; the Lumpwoods (see No.8) were one of the two most important of these types of men's societies in about 1910.

1 Parfleche of rawhide, with typically Crow painted design. A container for storage, in earlier times especially for pemmican.
2 Beaded moccasins.
3 Beaded moccasins.
4 Rattle, a rawhide circle on a wooden handle, a distinctive type used by a young man belonging to the Crazy Dog Society.
5 A model of the red flannel sash, over 12ft long (3.5m.), of which a pair were worn slipped over

the head as emblems of rank by leaders of the Muddy Hands men's social and military society (long extinct by 1910).
6 Wolverine skin emblem of the Wolverine chapter of the Tobacco Society.
7 Horse bridle ornament, cut from an old rawhide parfleche and then covered with beadwork.
8 Otter fur dance ornament, part of the distinctive regalia of the Lumpwoods.
9 Beaded moccasins.

10 Moccasins decorated with red-dyed porcupine quills and light blue beads.

11 Woman's leggings.

12 Shirt with tassels of horsehair, a type worn by young men acting as clowns during rituals.

13 Beaming tool made from the rib of a large animal, used by a woman to soften hides.

14 Wooden bowl used for mixing sacred tobacco.

15 Spoon of mountain sheep horn, used with No.14.

16 Iron flesher, used by a woman in tanning hides.

17 Older flesher, of bone with toothed metal blade.

18 Adze with bone haft and metal blade, used by a woman for scraping skins for tanning.

19 Maul of stone with wooden handle, used to break bones to remove the marrow.

20 Quilled and beaded moccasins.

21 Cover for a rawhide shield, made of buckskin, with painted design revealed in a vision – here evidently a thunderbird (an eagle with zigzag lines).

22 Man's fully-beaded vest.

23 Moccasins with deer dewclaws.

24 Cloth shirt worn in Tobacco Society dance.

25 Beaded mirror case with quilled fringe.

26 Fur wrapper for buffalo medicine.

27 Green flannel sash, emblem of a leader of a men's society:

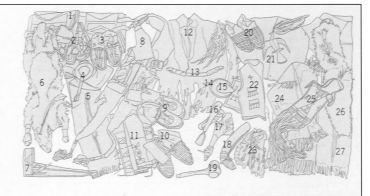

then gave the command 'Retreat to your horses men!' Confusion reigned: 'I thought that we were to charge headlong through them all, – that was the only chance. To turn one's back on Indians, without being better mounted than they, is throwing away life. When he [Reno] started to that hill he had told me, not one minute before, that he was going to fight – this was in reply to a question of mine' (ibid). Whilst Reno was in retreat, some three and a half miles away Custer attacked the other end of the village. Like Reno, he too was confronted by a mass of Sioux and Cheyenne warriors, this time Hunkpapas under Gall, Oglalas and others under Crazy Horse, and Cheyennes under Lame White Man: they repulsed his charge. Within minutes, Company L under James Calhoun, their horses stampeded by Crow King and his warriors, was annihilated. The other four Companies, C. E, F and I, many soldiers now dismounted, stood their ground on the higher bluffs. Before 5 o'clock, however, Custer and his entire force was completely surrounded and in less than an hour they were all dead. 'Custer's Field' was discovered on the morning of Tuesday 27 June and as Captain Edward S. Godfrey later recorded, it was 'a scene of sickening ghastly horror': Sitting Bull's prophesy had been fulfilled.[17]

The great Indian encampment rapidly dispersed; villages of that size could not be sustained, the grazing was soon exhausted and game driven away. Many returned to the agencies but most of the non-Treaties under

Above: *A Sioux camp, by Karl Bodmer (1833). The buffalo hide tipis are accurately depicted; for example, the details showing the characteristic heavy seams and the lacing at the front with wooden pins.*

Below: *Sitting Bull, the Hunkpapa leader, with William F. Cody (Buffalo Bill), c.1885. He thought highly of Cody, calling him Pahaska (Long Hair) and describing the scout as sincere and genuine.*

Sitting Bull, Crazy Horse, American Horse, Dull Knife and Little Wolf remained in Powder River country; their free life on American soil, however, was rapidly coming to a close.

'One repulse does not give enemies final victory . . . the blood of our soldiers demand that these Indians shall be pursued . . . [they must] submit themselves to the authority of the nation . . .'
(Maginnis, Congressional Record, July 1876)

By late summer 1876 a two-pronged campaign against the Cheyenne and Lakota started to take effect; it extended well into the winter of 1877. At Slim Buttes, 8 September 1876, Mills and Crook attacked American Horse's village; the chief was killed and the village destroyed. At Red Cloud and other Sioux Agencies, Crook subdued the Indians by a display of strength. Crook deposed Red Cloud, whose sympathies with the non-Treaties were all too apparent. Willow Creek, 25 November 1876 (south of the Big Horn Mountains), Ranald S. Mackenzie destroyed Dull Knife's village, thirty Cheyennes were killed and seven hundred ponies captured.[18] Cedar Creek, Yellowstone River, 20 October 1876, Colonel Nelson A. Miles parleys with Sitting Bull who demands peace on the old basis (freedom to roam and hunt). Miles later recorded, Sitting Bull 'spoke like a conqueror and he looked like one' (Miles, 1896:223). Wolf Mountain, Big Horn range, 8

January 1877, Miles attacks the Lakota under Crazy Horse, ... village destroyed and Crazy Horse withdraws. March 1877, Sitting Bull and some nine hundred followers retreat to Canada. Lame Deer, west of Tongue River, 7 May 1877, Miles attacks and captures Miniconjou village, chiefs Iron Star and Lame Deer killed. Red Cloud Agency, May 1877, Crazy Horse surrenders.[19] Fort Robinson, Nebraska, 7 September 1877, Crazy Horse resists arrest and is bayoneted by a guard: 'My father, I am bad hurt. Tell the people it is no use to depend on me any more now' (Vestal, 1948:272). Fort

Right: *This Lakota headdress dates from c.1875. The illustration was inspired by one which belonged to Sinte Maza, or Iron Tail, an Oglala Sioux who was born in the White Clay district of northwest Nebraska in about 1860. It contains some seventy feathers from the tail of an immature golden eagle, each tipped with yellow horsehair and white gypsum. The carefully prepared feathers are laced to a red tradecloth base which is surmounted by a skull-cap supporting a circle of feathers.*

Lakota Headdress

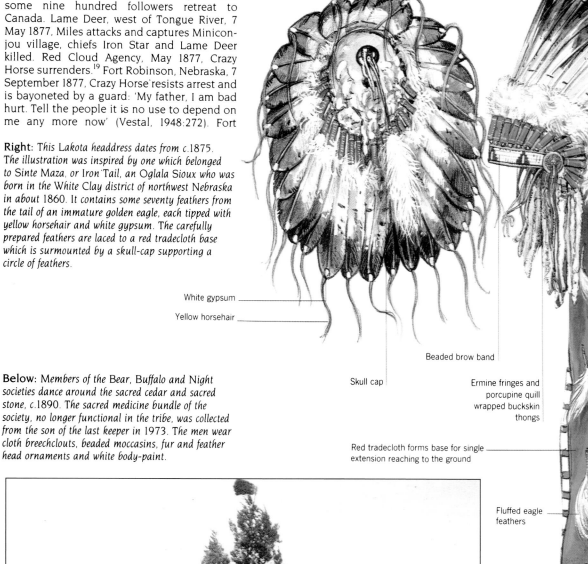

White gypsum

Yellow horsehair

Skull cap

Beaded brow band

Ermine fringes and porcupine quill wrapped buckskin thongs

Red tradecloth forms base for single extension reaching to the ground

Fluffed eagle feathers

Selvedge edging

Below: *Members of the Bear, Buffalo and Night societies dance around the sacred cedar and sacred stone, c.1890. The sacred medicine bundle of the society, no longer functional in the tribe, was collected from the son of the last keeper in 1973. The men wear cloth breechclouts, beaded moccasins, fur and feather head ornaments and white body-paint.*

Hidatsa

Between 1906 and 1918 Gilbert L. Wilson worked with several aged Hidatsa men and women on the Fort Berthold Reservation to compile a marvelous, extensive record of daily life as they remembered it when they lived at Like-a-Fishhook Village from about 1840 to 1885. Much had changed by the turn of the century, and even the rich bottomlands where the Hidatsa lived and farmed have been flooded behind dams since Wilson collected these things among them.

1 Woman's dance dress, of cloth with painted pictographic battle scenes.
2 Quill-decorated carrying case for a man's firemaking materials (flint, steel, and tinder) or a woman's whetstone. Worn tied to the belt or wrist.
3 Quill-decorated carrying case for a flint whetstone, obtained from Owl Woman.
4 Hairbrush made of a porcupine tail with the quills removed. Used by either a man or a woman.
5 Beaded moccasins.
6 Moccasins decorated with quills (probably birds').
7 Beaded and quilled moccasins.
8 Beaded moccasins.
9 Arm band decorated with porcupine quillwork.
10 Man's shirt of tanned elk hide with porcupine quill decoration, with V-shaped neck flap slightly old-fashioned when this was made about 1910. Such shirts were formerly worn only on special occasions or in inclement weather.
11 Dancing cap, probably for a woman.
12 Brush or whip of horsehair used when bathing in a sweat lodge.
13 Rake of ash wood with deer antlers, a model of the kind used about 1860 by a woman preparing her garden. Made by Maxidiwiac (Buffalo Bird Woman).
14 Hoe with elm-wood handle and blade made from the shoulderblade of a buffalo or other large animal. This type was used by a woman to hoe her garden of corn, beans, squash, and sunflowers. This is a model by Maxidiwiac.
15 Arrow point made of sinew from a buffalo's neck. According to Hidatsa tradition, this kind preceded stone points. It was considered to be especially strong, and

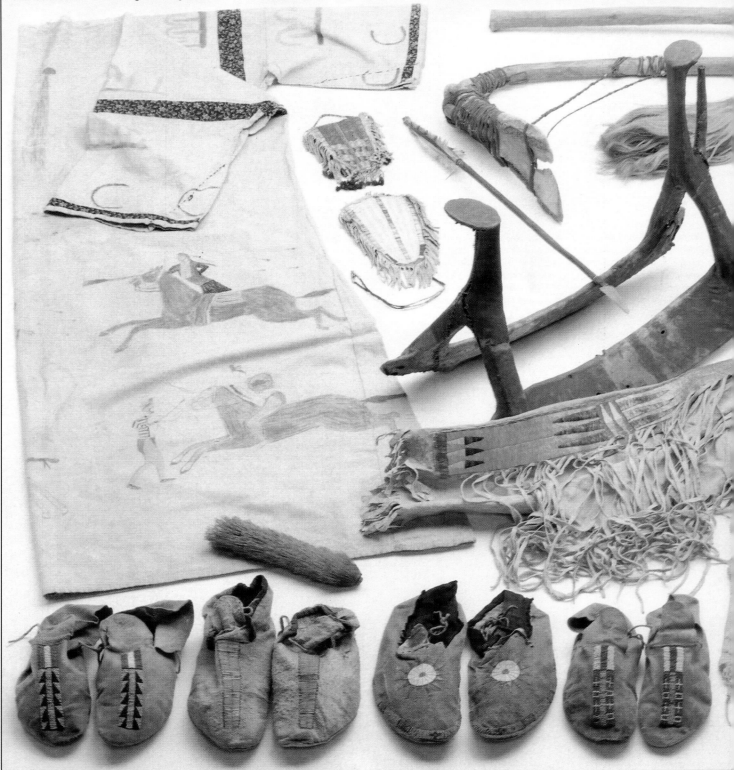

good for buffalo hunting. This is a model, for such arrows were evidently last used in the 1830s.

16 Saddle tree, for a woman's saddle.

17 Pipe of a type of black stone found on the Fort Berthold Reservation, inlaid with metal.

18 Box of painted rawhide, used to store clothing and other things.

19 Woman's burden basket, used especially to carry harvested corn, squash,

and beans. Made of dyed and undyed willow and elder bark, woven in diamond and chevron patterns on a bent willow wood frame.

20-23 Three pottery vessels resting on ring stands made of willow twigs and bark. Such pots were used as water vessels and for cooking. They were made of clay tempered with crushed rock, shaped by a paddle and anvil technique, and then fired.

By 1908 when these were made for the collector by a Hidatsa woman named Hides and Eats, no one could make the large vessels with very thin walls that were used before metal pots became common.

23 Bone hoe, as No. 14. The short handle was copied for the later iron hoes to suit the usual Hidatsa woman's method of use.

24 Ladle made of mountain sheep horn.

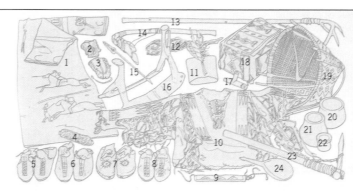

Robinson, Nebraska, January 1879, Dull Knife's Cheyenne starved into submission, break from army barracks, sixty-four killed and fifty wounded.[20]

There is little doubt that at this time it was Sitting Bull who epitomized the free and independent Plains Indian but the road ahead was to be particularly difficult as game became scarce on the Canadian Plains and gradually hundreds of Lakota crossed back to the United States to join friends and relatives at the agencies. By 1881, Sitting Bull had less than two hundred followers and finally, on 20 July 1881, at the head of his small band, he rode into Fort Buford, Dakota Territory, and surrendered: 'the

Right: *Medicine lodge associated with the Arikara Buffalo Society Medicine Bundle, 1908. Members of the medicine fraternity are seen here just about to enter the lodge; they will then be followed by the Buffalo Society shamans. The ceremonial combined buffalo calling and thanksgiving rites with curing functions.*

final surrender of his cherished independence was a hard blow to his pride, and he took it hard. He was much broken' (Vestal, 1957:232).

For two years Sitting Bull was held as a prisoner-of-war, finally returning to his people on the Standing Rock Reservation in 1883; the signs were ominous . . . Sitting Bull's return coincided with the last great Indian buffalo hunt. The immense herds had gone forever.

The continued influx of settlers and the building of the railroads exerted more pressures. The Great Sioux Reservation was increasingly viewed as standing firmly in the way of any further expansion westward and the settlers 'demanded that the Indian move aside' (Utley, 1963:42). In 1889, after much wrangling and questionable promises by the Government, vast areas of the Reservation were signed away, a move bitterly opposed by Sitting Bull.[21] The winter of 1889-90 also heralded epidemics and with frightening suddenness the full realities of Reservation life became starkly apparent: Lakota political organization was shattered, their religious ceremonials were suppressed, the hunting economy abolished and now even their children taken away to distant schools to learn the ways of the white man. Thus, all the old values became meaningless so that the conditions necessary for self-fulfilment and the attainment of happiness no longer existed. The Lakota had reached an *anomic* state, a situation which was common to virtually all other tribes throughout the Plains, and elsewhere, as they were forced to adapt to a new way of life.

Wovoka's message of the *New World* to come was simple and clear. The Son of God would punish the white man for his injustices towards the Indians, he would wipe them from the face of the earth, the dead would be restored to life, the buffalo and other game would return, 'dance four successive nights . . . you must not hurt anybody . . . when the earth shakes [at the

Left: *Black Fox, an Arikara warrior. The grizzly bear claws on his magnificent necklace are attached to a collar of otter skin. The turban headdress is likewise of otter and is surmounted by three golden eagle feathers, these undoubtedly symbolic of outstanding deeds performed in battle.*

coming of the new world] do not be afraid. It will not hurt you' (Mooney, 1896:781).

'They swore that this Messiah came to
            them in visions sleep
And promised to restore their game
            and Buffalos a heap.'

The people danced – they called it Ghost or Spirit Dance – and the earth indeed shook for shortly rifles and Hotchkiss guns also thundered.

'They claimed the shirt Messiah gave, no
            bullet could go through,
But when the Soldiers fired at them
            they saw this was not true . . .

A fight took place, 'twas hand to hand, un-
            warned by trumpet call,
While the Sioux were dropping man by
            man – the 7th killed them all . . .'
(Extracted from W. H. Prather's (I Company, 9th Cavalry) *The Indian Ghost Dance and War*. See ibid:883)

On 15 December 1890, Sitting Bull crashes dead to the ground, bullets in his head and chest; 29 December, Big Foot together with some one hundred and forty-six men, women and children of the Miniconjou Lakota, dies on the Wounded Knee Field.[22] 'Do not be afraid,' Wovoka had said; 'It will not hurt you.' But the nation's hoop was broken and scattered, there was no longer any center, the sacred tree was

dead – the conquest of the Plains Indian had become a reality. Wovoka's *new* message rang loud and clear, 'My children, today I call upon you to travel a new trail, the only trail now open – the White Man's Road' (Smith, 1975:200).

'A powerful and warlike people, proud, haughty and defiant – well over six feet in height, strong muscular frames and very good horsemen, well dressed, principally in skins and robes; rich in horses and lodges; have a great abundance of meat since buffalo, elk, antelope and deer abound in their country. They say they are *Indians* and do not wish to change their mode of living.'
Samuel N. Latta, Indian Agent, Upper Missouri, circa 1860.

References

1 Blackfeet tipis of this type might use as many as twenty buffalo hides for the cover supported on a foundation of some twenty poles, 25 ft (over 8m.) in length (those of the Crow could be even longer). See Laubin (1957) for the basic study of the Plains tipi.

2 Scalping, however, was *not* necessarily fatal. Several cases have been reported where scalped victims have survived the ordeal. Catlin, for example, sketched an individual 'who had been scalped and recovered from the wound' (Catlin, 1841, vol.1:240). Perhaps the most bizarre episode, however, was that of the brakeman, Edward Thompson, on a Union Pacific Railroad freight train which was travelling across Kansas in 1868. The train was derailed by a combined force of Cheyenne, Arapaho and Lakota warriors. Plunged into the darkness, he was felled by a bullet; later, he reported that although the bullet knocked him down, it 'did not render him unconscious and that his greatest trial in that terrible night was the necessity of shamming dead and not daring to cry out when the Indian was *slowly sawing* at his head covering with a *very* dull knife'. The rescue party later found the scalp and it was put into a bucket of water. On arrival in Omaha, an effort was made by surgeons to sew it back in place, but without success (see Taylor, 1975:93 and Dodge, 1876:400, in ibid, 1980:23).

3 This was related to the explorer, David Thompson, in 1787. It refers to an episode in Saukamappee's youth and took place about 1730.

4 Note also here as with the Louisiana people, the emphasis on the belief that the spirit or soul of the scalped person 'was somehow in and of human hair' – a concept which also prevailed amongst the Sioux (Hassrick, 1964:84).

5 Fort Benton was originally named Fort Clay, founded after the abandonment of Fort McKenzie in 1844 and Lewis in spring 1847. Renamed at Christmas 1850 in honor of Senator Thomas Hart Benton of Missouri who was a strong supporter of the fur trade, the first steamboat arrived a decade later (2 July 1860). River traffic was maintained until the late 1880s when the new railroads took over most of the freight. Although the Missouri was navigable to St Louis, it had to be continually dredged and cleared of snags.

6 The actual campground for this important Treaty was some thirty-four miles down the North Platte river at Horse Creek in present-day southeast Wyoming.

7 In return for safe emigrant travel up the Platte, west to the mountains, the United States Government agreed to 'make an annual payment to the Sioux in goods valued at $50,000 per year for fifty years, to be delivered in the Fort Laramie area . . . should any of the Indian nations, party to this treaty, violate any of the provisions thereof, the United States may withhold the whole or a portion of the annuities mentioned in the preceding Article from the nation so offending, until, in the opinion of the President of the United States, proper satisfaction shall have been made' (McCann, 1956:3-4).

8 The following account of this tragic encounter is

based on the superb research of Dr Lloyd E. McCann (1956) of Butler University, Indianapolis, Indiana, being based on data in House and Senate Executive Documents, a narrative of Man-Afraid-Of-His-Horses, now in the National Archives, and an interview with Red Cloud by Judge E. S. Ricker at Pine Ridge, South Dakota, 24 November 1906. It demonstrates so much of the attitudes and prejudices which existed at this time and gives unusual insights into the diplomacy and fair play of mature Plains Indian leaders. Conquering Bear, who emerges as a man of exceptional ability and tact, was mortally wounded in this encounter.

9 The Cheyenne have a legend which told 'how, after a disastrous encounter with some other tribe, they all decided they would become terrible fighters and so become great men'. The formation of the *Hotam itan iu*, 'Dog Men' was a living reminder of that legend. The 'Dog Soldiers', as they became known to the whites, considered that they were the watchdogs of the Cheyenne people. (See Vestal, 1948:63.)

10 Bell and Wylyams had arranged earlier on that fateful day to work together and print some photographs which Bell had taken en route. The shocked Bell later observed 'so I had to print off my negatives alone, and to take a photograph of him, poor fellow, as he lay; a copy of which I sent to Washington that the authorities should see how their soldiers were treated on the Plains' (Bell, 1869:vol.1,64).

11 The town of Medicine Lodge, Barber county, Kansas, now stands on the site.

12 This important tribe of the Muskhogean linguistic stock were originally located on the Mississippi near present-day Memphis, Tennessee. Under White pressure, together with the Choctaw, they began to emigrate west of the Mississippi as early as 1822.

13 Indian delegations were usually treated well and often given the opportunity of publicly presenting their side of the picture. Newspaper reports generally gave sympathetic coverage of such events, pointing out the difficulties confronting both races. Typical was the Cheyenne, Arapaho and Wichita delegation, led by the head chief of the Arapaho, *Ohnastie*, or 'Little Raven', who arrived early in the summer of 1871. As the New York Times expressed it (1 June 1871) 'Their main purpose was to meet the "Great Chief of the American Nation" and to have their reservation boundary lines clearly defined.' They were 'astonished by our cities; such a gathering of men all in one place . . . they do not understand our railways, telegraphs, etc. They know such things are done, but they cannot understand by what power, etc . . . they have no words in their language to comprehend all they see.' (For further details of this visit and also that of Red Cloud's in 1872 see Taylor, 1975:106-7.)

14 It was, however, a victory paid for dearly by the Lakota whose tactics were to ride down the enemy before they had time to reload. Unknown to Red Cloud, new Springfield breech-loaders had been recently issued to the troopers and more than sixty were killed and one hundred and twenty wounded under the withering fire power during a battle which lasted more than four hours. Such heavy casualties

were devastating to small population Plains tribes. Leaders were supposed not to lose any men 'if he could possibly help it' (Pakes, 1989:21). For an excellent up-to-date analysis relating to the nature of Plains Indian warfare, see ibid.

15 After the 1868 Laramie Treaty, the Lakota divided into three main factions: agency Indians wholly dependent on the Government; those who stayed at the agencies in winter and left in spring to live in Powder River country and finally those who permanently shunned the agencies, preferring their own free life in the Yellowstone and Powder River regions. This third group 'was regarded by the army as the principal barrier to white encroachment' (Taunton, 1977:7).

16 Crowfoot refused to join, almost certainly due to the fair-minded and honest treatment which the Canadian Plains tribes received at the hands of the North-West Mounted Police, which was founded in 1873 on the recommendation of Colonel W. F. Butler (Butler, 1891:378-9). Sitting Bull and Crowfoot later became firm friends and Sitting Bull was to name his son in honor of the Blackfeet chief.

17 For a detailed analysis of the aftermath of this historic encounter, see Taunton (1986).

18 This particular battle was graphically documented by Captain John G. Bourke, U.S.A. Third Cavalry. He describes in great detail the complete destruction of the Cheyenne village (which consisted of some two hundred tipis) and hence 'wiping off the face of the earth many products of aboriginal taste and industry which would have been gems in the cabinets of museums . . . Never were orders more thoroughly executed . . . (Bourke, 1890:29). It was a pattern replicated many times by the United States army in their subjugation of the Plains Indian.

19 Apparently, Crazy Horse and Sitting Bull had discussed surrender on a number of occasions but Sitting Bull said 'I do not wish to die yet' (Vestal, 1957:182).

20 Recent researches by members of the University of South Dakota and the Dull Knife Memorial College, have put a new perspective on the escape route followed by the Cheyennes supporting the oral history of the tribe (see McDonald, McDonald, Tallbull and Risingsun, 1989:265-9).

21 This reduction of the Great Sioux Reservation is considered in great detail by Utley (1963:40-60).

22 A general sentiment amongst those tribes who adopted the Ghost Dance religion was that their domination by the white race would soon end 'and that a beautiful new world was coming in which everyone would live forever' (Smith, 1975:74).

Author's note
In February 1972, a small Catholic church at Wounded Knee became the scene of Wounded Knee II, the headquarters and sanctuary for members of the American Indian Movement who tried to draw attention to the 'Trail of Broken Treaties', a cry of impatience and despair with human waste so commonplace on the Reservations for almost a century. Now, over 100 years after the death of Big Foot and his 146 Lakota, Wounded Knee II can be seen as a turning point in the restoration of Lakota values; the fundamentals of ancient beliefs are taking root once again.

'I buried him in that beautiful valley of windings waters. I love that land more than all the rest of the world.'
JOSEPH OF THE NEZ PERCE

PLATEAU AND BASIN

THE PLATEAU area stretches from central British Columbia, south and across the United States border, eastern Oregon and Washington, then across the majority of the northern half of Idaho and straddling the Continental Divide into northwestern Montana. It is laced by rivers – the names of several suggesting both their character and products, the Clearwater, Boulder, Salmon, Beaverhead and Cascade – and the Blue and Bitterroot Mountains which skirt the Columbia Plateau – the most dominant geographical feature of the area and through which runs the great Columbia River which, together with the Fraser in the north, is the lifeblood of the land and its people. The area, covering approximately two hundred thousand square miles, is one of great contrast and beauty being marked by forested mountains, deep valleys and canyons, clear rushing streams, open meadowlands and, to the south, bordering the northern rim of the Great Basin, windswept plains and desert regions dotted with sagebrush and rock.

The rivers are rich in fish resources, particularly salmon which migrate from the Pacific via tributaries of both the Fraser and Columbia; other fish also abound such as sturgeon, lamprey eel, whitefish and trout. The clear, cold waters, with their high oxygen content, support much life in comparison to the warmer and often murky rivers of the Great Plains. Whilst the area was largely devoid of buffalo, elk, deer and mountain sheep were common as well as otter and beaver.

The Plateau was dominated by two major linguistic groups: in the north, occupying the inland areas of present-day British Columbia,

were the Salishan-speaking Shuswap, Lillooet, Thompson and Okanagan, while across the border into present-day Washington and Idaho lived the Kalispel, Coeur d'Alêne, Spokane, Colville, Sanpoil and Flathead. In the middle Columbia ranged the Sahaptin-speaking Klikitat, Yakima, Umatilla, Walla Walla, Palus, Nez Perce and Cayuse. Other linguistic stocks were also represented, such as the Kutenai in the northeast who spoke a language of their own, but now shown to be distantly related to Algonquian, and in the west – although their cultural traits tend to identify them more with the tribes of the Pacific coast – the Chinookans on the lower Columbia. Associated with this latter language was the foundation of the so-called

This map shows approximate territories of tribes and language groups at about 1850, and somewhat earlier in the western and eastern edges of the Basin. After that, all tribes lost territory and some moved.

Key to tribes:
PLATEAU

 1 Lillooet
 2 Shuswap
 3 Thompson
 4 Nicola
 5 Okanagan
 6 Lakes
 7 Kutenai
 8 Kalispel
 9 Sanpoil
10 Columbia Salish
11 Yakima
12 Spokane
13 Palus
14 Coeur d'Alêne
15 Flathead
16 Nez Perce
17 Walla Walla
18 Cayuse
19 Umatilla

20 Klikitat
21 Wishram
22 Tenino
23 Molala
24 Klamath
25 Modoc

BASIN

26 Eastern Shoshoni
27 Northern Shoshoni and
   Bannock
28 Northern Paiute
29 Washoe
30 Western Shoshoni
31 Ute
32 Southern Paiute
33 Owens Valley Paiute
34 Kawaiisu

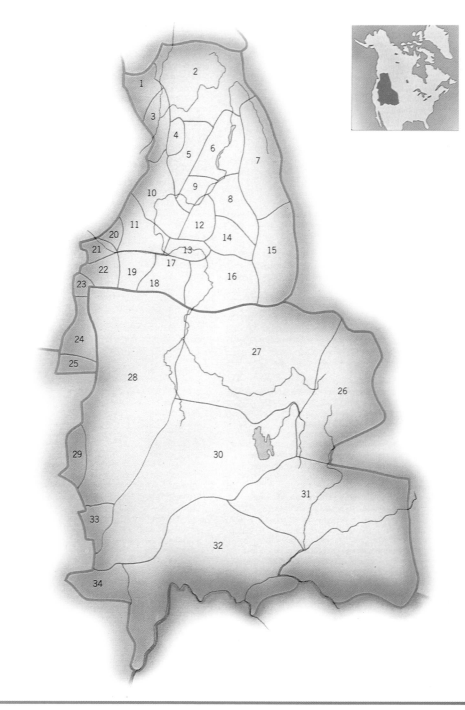

Chinook jargon, the Indian trade language of the Columbia River region, its use extending to the Pacific coast and reaching from California up to Alaska.

While gathering and hunting were important to the Plateau people, their principal subsistence depended on the salmon which were speared, netted, gorge-hooked or trapped, the latter method being by the use of weirs constructed of willows and boulders across the smaller streams. The spearing was a way of obtaining quantities of large salmon and these were caught from specially built platforms which projected over the water, or from jutting ledges of rock. The platforms were generally built above the weirs which impeded the movement of the fish. One magnificent painting by the Canadian artist, Paul Kane, vividly illustrates the various techniques used by the Spokane in the vicinity of the Kettle Falls on the Columbia River in what is now northeast Washington State. Clearly, in 1846, when the sketches used for the painting were made, the Indians highly valued this bountiful area; sadly, they lost it a century and a quarter later with the building of the Grand Coulee Dam across the Columbia whose backwater (as has happened with several other dammed rivers in the United States) has flooded forever this ancient Indian site.

The spears depicted by Kane, which were identical to a type used by the Nez Perce further south, consisted of a three-pronged gig attached to a shaft some 8ft (2.5m.) in length. Through each prong, which was made of a flexible wood such as hackberry, were pointed bone pins, these projected inward and away from the end of the prongs. The spear was not thrown, instead it was jabbed down into the water, the spread of the three prongs adding to its efficiency; it was a favorite style for night fishing, the light of pitch torches being used to attract the salmon. Another type of spear which had a detachable head was also used by the Nez Perce: here, the point was of heavy bone (cut from the thickest part of an elk leg bone) with a socket of elderberry wood, the whole being bound firmly together and attached to the shaft some 11in. (30cm.) from the head. When the salmon was speared, the head loosened from the shaft; fish, head and shaft were now easily pulled in by an attached braided cord. Whilst much of the fish caught was eaten fresh, a great deal was dried on scaffolds and smoked for winter use.

The Nez Perce, as with many other tribes on the Plateau, attended the great Dalles Rendezvous which was held every fall on the Columbia River where it cuts through the Cascade Mountain range.[1] For several environmental and historical reasons, The Dalles became one of the most important centres for a lively trade throughout the summer, reaching its peak in the fall. In the vicinity of The Dalles lived the Wishram and Wasco, both of whom spoke Chinookan dialects, and were identified as noted middlemen between the Plateau and Pacific coast tribes; they hosted many groups who came to their villages during the fall trading fair.

In order to obtain the goods they required, each tribe tended to specialize in producing or acquiring materials which they knew would trade well at The Dalles. Thus, the Nez Perce,

Above: *Nez Perce warrior on horseback. He wears a Plains style eagle feathered warbonnet. The large tipi in the background is of canvas; it is unlined and hence suggests a temporary encampment.*

several bands of which hunted on the Montana and Wyoming Plains to the east, brought along buffalo robes; others, such as the Klamath, specalized in camas bulbs, a widely used sweet and nutritious vegetal food; dentalium and other shells were brought in from the Pacific coast by the Wishram and Wasco. Although the Rendezvous appears to have been established long before white contact, according to the explorers Lewis and Clark, who visited The Dalles in January 1806, 'the circumstance which forms the soul of this trade is the visit of the whites' (Lewis and Clark, Coues ed., 1893, vol.II:787). From such contacts, Plateau people obtained access to somewhat outdated 'British or American muskets, powder, ball, and shot, copper and brass kettles, brass tea-kettles and coffee-pots, blankets . . . scarlet and blue cloth . . . brass wire |and| knives' (ibid:788). Clearly, the Plateau people became increasingly dependent on European goods which ultimately became essentials rather than luxury items.

The habitations of the Plateau Indians varied in style and emphasis, at least four distinct types having been identified. Traditionally, the northern Plateau tribes such as the Shuswap, Thompson and Okanagan, used semi-subterranean earth lodges; occupied by one or two families, they were constructed by excavating the dry sandy ground to a depth of some 2 meters and were about 13ft (4m.) in diameter, although sizes varied considerably. Poles were then laid across which were covered with grass and earth to a depth of 4in. (10cm.) or so and the entrance was generally, but not always, from the top, via a simple ladder. Further to the south amongst the Nez Perce, similar habi-

tations tended to be used by women before and after childbirth, and during the menstrual period, whilst a smaller sudatory lodge was used by boys above fourteen years of age.

A favorite habitation, however, used by many tribes on the Plateau both in winter and summer, was the conical lodge, formed by stacking seven to nine poles around a tripod and then covering the frame with mats woven from cattail (*Typha latifolia*) or tule (*Scirpus lacustris*). Such habitations gave the appearance of the Plains tipi, although on average they were somewhat smaller. For winter living these lodges were covered with two to four layers of mats and generally sunk about 2ft (60cm.) into the ground with the earth stacked around. On occasions, such habitations could be very large; Lewis and Clark reported seeing an ancient circular house ring some 30ft (10m.) in diameter, the rimmed circumference being about 3ft (1m.) in height and the centre sunk more than 3ft into the ground.

There were also communal long houses: Lewis and Clark in describing their visit to Neeshnepahkeook or Cut-nose, a Nez Perce chief, refer to the entire village of some thirty-eight families occupying two large houses. 'At a little distance from us are two Chopunnish houses, one of which contains eight families, and the other, which is by much the largest we have ever seen, is inhabited by at least 30. It is rather a kind of shed built, like all the other huts, of straw and mats in the form of the roof of a house, 156 feet long and about 15 wide, closed at the ends, and having a number of doors on each side. The vast interior is without partitions, but the fire of each family is kindled in a row along the middle of the building, about ten feet apart' (ibid:vol.III:988-9). The upright supports of these lodges separated the ridge poles by several inches so that an aperture extended the whole length of the lodge, thus serving as a smoke vent.[2] Poles were then leaned on to the horizontal ridge poles and long mats attached to these in a shingle-fashion; earth was packed against the lower part of the mat which was generally protected from decay with a covering of dry grass. The mats were carefully selected. Those of cattail were simpler in construction than those made of tule. The former were not very effective in repelling rain, thus although generally of the same size (approximately 4 × 10ft (1.2 × 3m.), the more exposed surfaces were covered with tule mats. As a safeguard against the wind, more poles were often leaned up against the mats and during cold weather – especially with the smaller habitations – the interior was lined with skins.

The Okanagan and other tribes further north also utilized a similar long house, but it was, according to one observer, a temporary shelter made to accommodate people at gatherings and at the fishing places. They were favored when communities camped together because they required a lesser number of mats than the conical tents to accommodate the same number of people. It is probable that Lewis and Clark, therefore, were describing a temporary Nez Perce camp. This is consistent with Mylie Lawyer's observations, who related that the long house (which she referred to as the Lah-pit-ahl Ain-neet) was popular when large groups of people got together, 'a gathering place for social, religious and war ceremonials' (M.L. to C.T., Lapwai: 1969).

As mobility increased with the introduction of the horse, those tribes on the eastern side of the Plateau region such as the Pend d'Oreilles, Flathead, Colville and some of the Nez Perce bands, made forays to the Plains buffalo country. There they traded for buffalo hide tipis which tended to displace the mat covered conical tent, being far more convenient for hunting and trading expeditions.

Prior to the introduction of the horse during the early eighteenth century, the Plateau was settled with small and independent bands generally on, or near, the many rivers and streams which characterized this region. As has been outlined, in adapting to their environment, they had shaped out a pattern of living – undoubtedly established over a period of several thousand years – which pivoted on the extensive use of fish and other food resources, wide travel, mutual interdependence and trade, and a limited war complex.

Travel to the great trading fairs held at such places as The Dalles, Kettle Falls and Celilo Falls, was mainly by means of canoe, portaging passed dangerous rapids such as those on the Upper Clearwater. The style of canoe varied. In the north, tribes such as the Shuswap, Thompson, and Okanagan used the sharp-snouted 'sturgeon nose' type which was made of cedar bark; the same style (as in Kane's illustration, right) was also used by the more southerly

Above: *Tum-se-ne-ho, or The Man without Blood, a Spokane chief, by Paul Kane (1847). He carries a combined bow case and quiver as well as a second bow, a custom common among the Spokane.*

Coeur d'Alêne and Kutenai. Rafts of tule lodge mats, rolled into bundles lashed together and pointed at each end like canoes, were also used on occasions. Tribes to the eastern part of the Plateau area, such as the Kalispel and Pend d'Oreilles, were particularly well known as expert canoe people and whilst these crafts resembled in shape those of the northern Salishan tribes, they differed in having the ends cut off square. Teit has suggested that this style was due to Iroquois influence, some of whom, in the employment of fur traders, 'made bark canoes of the eastern or Iroquois shape on

Flathead Lake' (Teit, Boas ed., 1930:350).

The Nez Perce (south of the Pend d'Oreilles in the valleys of the Clearwater), seem to have favored the simple dug-out type of canoe which was made from a single log and hollowed out by fires; it was propelled by either paddles or poles and could vary between about 16 to 42ft (5–13m.) in length. The former importance of water travel to the Nez Perce may be indicated by the Crow name for these people, A-pu-pe, which means 'to paddle'. However, even as early as 1806, canoes were scarce in the Nez Perce camps which Lewis and Clark visited, and some large villages were 'entirely without them' (Spinden, 1908:223). The horse, it seems, was now the major mode of travel and as with the Plains Indian it brought great cultural changes to all the Plateau people. Lewis and Clark were greatly impressed by the number of horses owned by many of the tribes whom they came into contact with during their travels through the Plateau region and, compared to the Plains Indians at this time, their wealth in horses was immense. The explorers reported that fifty to one hundred horses per individual amongst the Nez Perce was quite common, and forty years later it was reported that as many as fifteen hundred horses might be owned by Cayuse and Nez Perce family units, whilst reports for the Crow – considered to be the wealthiest of the northwestern Plains tribes – gives seven per lodge in 1805 and fifteen in 1830 (Ewers, 1955:25).

The traditions of the Flathead and Nez Perce credit the Shoshoni as furnishing them with their first mounts; the Shoshoni in turn said that they obtained them from their kinsmen, the Comanche, who, as early as 1705, raided the horse-rich Spanish settlements in what is now present-day New Mexico. The subsequent horse trade was thus via a complex route from such places as Santa Fe, probably west of the Continental Divide to the Snake River and Shoshoni Rendezvous, whence to the country of the Nez Perce, Flathead, Pend d'Oreilles, Kutenai and Kalispel. Tribal traditions of this

Below: A *study of the Kutenai Indians on the Columbia River by Paul Kane accurately showing the sharp, sturgeon-nose type canoe and temporary habitations traditionally used by Plateau groups.*

last tribe – typical of many – records the first appearance of the animal: 'Some people saw the horse's tracks where it had passed over some sand. They called other people, and discussed what kind of animal had made the tracks, which were strange to them all. Some thought it might have been a horse, as they had heard about them. Other people lower down, near the river bank, saw the man approach on the horse at a lope. They observed that he was smoking, and that he seemed to be quite at his ease. They watched him enter the river and swim across on the horse. They gathered around and examined the animal with much curiosity' (Teit, Boas ed., 1930:352).

An amusing story related by the Okanagan refers to the initial efforts to ride this strange creature, the main fear it seems was falling off! 'The first horse |we| obtained was very gentle. The first person who mounted it rode with two long sticks, one in each hand, to steady himself. Another man led the horse slowly, and the rider shifted the sticks (as one does with walking sticks) as they went along' (ibid:250).

Much of the Plateau region was fine horse country, the natural barriers protecting the animal from wandering too far and also from would-be thieves, whilst the well watered valleys, such as the Wallowa and Grande Ronde,[3] provided nutritious forage and shelter in winter. The horse also fitted well into the established seasonal movements of the Plateau people. By careful and selective breeding, such tribes as the Nez Perce and their close relatives, the Cayuse, built up enormous horse herds. Eliminating the poorer stallions by castration, the Nez Perce became justly famous for the superior speed and endurance of their horses, amongst the most distinctive of which was the traditional war-horse, which came to be known as the Appaloosa.

It was Meriwether Lewis, in 1806, who first made a definite reference to what was almost certainly the forebear of the Appaloosa, describing a few of the Nez Perce horses as being marked with large spots of white, irregularly scattered and intermixed with the dark brown or other dark shade. Later, in 1820, Alexander Ross of the Hudson's Bay Company observed that the Nez Perce preferred entirely white horses which were painted for war 'drawing a variety of hieroglyphic devices, the head and neck were dappled with streaks of red and yellow; the mane dyed black, the tail red, clubbed up in a knot and tied short . . . and the rider as well as the horse was so besmeared with red, blue and yellow ochre, that no one could tell what the natural color of either was.' (Ross, 1855:307). At this time, however, next to white, those which were speckled or white and black were in most demand, being used by distinguished warriors in preference to any other and being valued at two or three times the worth of other horses. They were more than just handsomely marked, being generally larger and heavier than the average Plateau breed, sure footed and possessing great endurance; they matched well the varying Plateau country, capable of travelling with equal ease through

Below: *The Kettle Falls on the Columbia River, by Paul Kane (1847). The highest falls on the river, they were favorite salmon fishing places for the Spokane, Colville and Walla Walla of the region.*

heavy timbered or mountainous terrain. Whilst the Appaloosa became indelibly associated with the Nez Perce, it is possible that the name derives from Palus, a tribe closely associated with the Nez Perce and Cayuse, the latter breeding a distinctive type of pony.

With the acquisition of the horse into Plateau culture – probably around the first quarter of the eighteenth century – the basic mode of travel was considerably modified, resulting in increased interaction between more distant tribes such as those on the Plains to the east, in particular the Blackfeet and Crow. It also led to an expansion on the already long established seasonal activities, in particular the scope for trade, which was greatly enhanced by an ability to transport quickly and easily large amounts of trade commodities; not surprisingly, the horse itself also became a highly valued trade item.

Unlike the Plains, neither the dog nor the travois were popular on the Plateau as a means of transporting equipment and whilst the Plateau tribes became adept horsemen, most of the horse equipment which they used, such as pack and riding saddles, bridles, cinches, whips and ropes, were adopted along with the horse from the Shoshoni. Nevertheless, when the Plateau people made their own horse equipment, it displayed some distinctive features. Men's saddles, in common with those used by the Plains Indians, were generally of the pad-type with the four corners of the saddle embellished with quill or beadwork; women's saddles, on the other hand, had a high pommel and cantel, generally with a hook or spike at the front with hanging triangular shaped flaps beautifully ornamented with trade cloth and beads. The

stirrups were made of bentwood covered with rawhide, those used by the Flathead, Pend d'Oreilles and Nez Perce women being particularly distinctive in having beaded pendants attached to the bottom. Wide cruppers and horse collars were also used, the latter again exhibiting heavily embellished flaps similar to those used on stirrups. This attractive horse equipment was also used by the Crow and has been particularly associated with that tribe (Wildschut, Ewers ed.,1959). However, the style may have been copied by them from the Plateau people, the roots of which can in turn be traced to the Spanish settlements of New Mexico and Texas. The Nez Perce women's horse equipment and mode of riding was sufficiently distinctive for the Presbyterian missionary, Henry H. Spalding, to observe that their saddles were an 'improvement upon our side saddle if we consult the ease of the woman' and the Nez Perce woman always used a blanket or robe which was 'thrown over the saddle covering the lower part of the person . . . in my opinion the more modest way of riding as also the more natural & comfortable' (Fletcher, 1930:3).

With the acquisition of the horse, tribes such as the Coeur d'Alène, Spokane and Nez Perce began to visit the Plains for buffalo hunting and trading. The goods which passed from east to west were chiefly catlinite and pipes of the same material, clothing, buffalo skins and robes. Whilst both Plains and Plateau people tended to make the same items, there was an emphasis on *quality* goods, it being recognized that one group was more skilled than the other in the production of certain items. For example, whilst the Plateau made headdresses, they considered that the finest were made by the Sioux,[4] and the Crow robes – of the softest tan and embellished with beaded or quilled bands – were greatly sought after: 'Often a horse and, in addition, a well-made leather shirt, was paid for one of the best kind of robes' (Teit, Boas ed., 1930:114). Porcupine quillwork, beaded and quilled pipe-bags, moccasins, and parfleches were all items made in quantity and *quality* which the Plateau tribes desired from the Plains people. This trade had a profound impact on their clothing styles, particularly that which was worn for ceremonial and dress occasions.

Whilst the trade in horses from the Plateau to the Plains was a major activity – and even the rare Appaloosa was occasionally traded (Ewers, 1955:217) – the Plains Indians also desired such items as salmon oil, pemmican, cakes of camas and berries, hemp and hemp twine, shells, certain types of beads, pipes of green soapstone, eagle-tail feathers, mountain-sheep horn and horn spoons, and woven bags. One of the most coveted items, however, was the highly perfected Plateau bow which the Plains tribes considered was greatly superior to those of their own make. Amongst the finest were those made from mountain-sheep horn, being a particular speciality of the Nez Perce.

The traditional dress of the Plateau was of soft tanned skins from the antelope, elk or deer, generally without the hair. The men wore soft-soled moccasins, leggings and breechcloth, shirt and a robe, whilst the women wore moccasins, calf-length leggings, a long dress and a robe. The women's dress of the Coeur d'Alène was very similar to that worn by the Nez Perce. Two deerskins formed the body of the dress, a third was used for fringing and shaping. 'The upper parts of the skins were folded down on the outside of the dress, forming a kind of false yoke at back and front. They were sewed to the body of the dress throughout, or stitched here and there with thongs. Pendants and tassels were often attached to the edges of the fold. The hair of the tailpiece was clipped in lines, and the end of the tail generally, but not always, cut off. Usually the sleeve parts were left open underneath, but sometimes they were stitched or tied here and there with thongs. Generally three rows of inserted fringe or thongs extended around the skirt below the waist. Single rows were also placed on the back and front of the dress below the yoke, but only rarely . . . Often all or the lower part of the yoke piece was beaded or quilled in lines following the contour of the edge of the yoke, or the dress itself was beaded immediately below the yoke . . . Most

Below: Kutenai Indians probably c.1900. The woman utilizes a baby carrier typical of the Plateau region, the rounded top embellished with beadwork in combined geometrical and floral patterns.

dresses reached to the ankles, . . . Some had several lines of quillwork across the breast and back of the body and many had long fringes following the edge of the yoke' (Teit, Boas ed., 1930:70). The leggings were also of tanned hide; they reached to the knee and were generally fringed on the outer edges. Most could be opened at the sides and wrapped around the leg and then fastened with tie strings, one string going around the leg above the calf to hold the leggings in place. They were often heavily beaded on the lower part with a narrower band extending up the outside of the legging.

Although Teit has identified five moccasin types which were worn by the Coeur d'Alène and adjacent tribes (ibid:72), the most popular and traditional type with wide distribution on the Plateau was constructed so that both the sole and upper were of one single piece of deerskin with the main seam extending around the outside of the sole starting on the inner side near the big toe and terminating a few inches beyond the heel seam. Near the base of the heel seam were additional strips of buckskin to enable the moccasins to be easily removed and an extra single piece of hide was sewn around the top producing flaps which could tuck under

or be attached to the leggings. The summer soft-soled moccasin fitted snugly to the foot, but those made for winter use were looser, not infrequently being made of tanned hide – deer, antelope or buffalo – with the hair left on the inside.

After sustained and extended contact with the Plains tribes towards the end of the nineteenth century, a two-piece rawhide soled moccasin became increasingly popular, particularly amongst the more eastern Plateau people such as the Kutenai, Flathead and Nez Perce, and ultimately it all but replaced the ancient soft-soled type. Lewis and Clark likened the costume of the Nez Perce to that of the Shoshoni, extending on the idea of not only a general similarity in clothing styles throughout the Plateau region, but also to the Great Basin. However, deeper analysis indicates that there were considerable differences. For example, in his studies of Nez Perce women's dresses, Wissler concluded that here were 'a number of distinct cuts for the contour of the yoke and the bottom of the skirt. Yet, there is very little variation within the tribe, . . . [each tribe] followed a definite form for the bottoms of their dresses, making it clear that they had a fixed mode, or style for the cut' (Wissler, 1915: 65-6).

Above: *Flathead boys in dance costume, c.1900, one (left) in a beaded waistcoat with a shield on his back, the others with horse and porcupine guard hair roaches of a style imported from the Plains.*

Below: *Flathead woman and girl, c.1900. The woman carries a cradle attached to the pommel of her saddle; both use (trade) metal-bitted bridles. The lavish horse regalia is typical of the region.*

Thompson

The Thompson Indians, speakers of a Salishan language, live in British Columbia in rugged country east of the Coast Range. When whites first arrived in 1858 and 1859 they were living in many villages along the Thompson, Fraser, and Nicola rivers. By 1900 they occupied some 70 villages ranging in size from only two or three families to over 100 inhabitants. Winter houses were large, semi-subterranean, earth covered structures; summer dwellings were mat-covered frameworks of poles. Hunting and trapping was important, for deer, small mammals, and birds especially, while fishing for salmon provided a substantial share of the diet. By 1900 much food was obtained from stores and the Thompson Indians also grew potatoes, peas, beans, maize, turnips, raised chickens and hogs, and kept cows. The materials shown here were collected in 1897-1904 by James A. Teit, a white man married to a Thompson woman, who was trained and supported in his anthropological research by Franz Boas.

1 Saddle bag, red and black cloth appliqué on fringed leather bag.
2 Beaver spear point of deer leg bone.
3 Coiled cedar-root carrying basket with imbricated pattern representing combs such as No. 17.
4 Cedar bark face towel used by girl during her puberty isolation.
5 Birch bark container with design in red ochre; used as berry basket, etc. for many years.
6 Tobacco pouch on shoulder strap, of red strouding embroidered in silk. 'Octopus pouch' type (because of eight tabs).
7 Pair of buckskin young man's moccasins with silk embroidered design of flowers and horse heads.
8 Adze for canoe making, etc. with handle of service berry wood; evidently a reconstruction of an obsolete type, re-using a stone used as skin pounder.

9 Deer figure made of rushes, shot at with special bow for four nights after a person's death.

10 Wooden spoon.

11 Rattle of deer hoofs.

12 Model head to illustrate warrior's face paint and hair dress.

13 Model head to illustrate woman's face paint and hair dress.

14 Riding saddle shaped like a pack saddle; antler cross pieces, braided bark cinch and stirrup straps;

used with deerskin cover.

15 Tobacco pouch of fawn or doe skin, beaded and fringed, worn tucked under belt or sash or carried on arm.

16 Woman's buckskin cap with bead and button decoration; style obsolete after about 1885.

17 Comb of wood.

18 Bone whistle used by boy or girl during puberty ceremony.

19 Sock of twined grass, worn inside moccasin.

20 Buckskin bag, design embroidered in silk thread.

21 Pair of horn tweezers for removing beard hairs, with incised design representing a butterfly.

22 Beaded tobacco pouch of Nawissatken, chief of the Nicola River band.

23 Tobacco pouch (octopus bag) on sash, ornamented with beads and Hudson's Bay Co. buttons in design of wild flowers and leaves. Bought from Neakyapamuxoa.

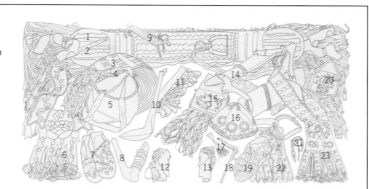

Two particularly fine women's dresses – almost certainly Nez Perce and probably amongst the earliest now extant from this tribe – were collected by the Presbyterian missionary, Henry H. Spalding, who sent them to his brother in Oberlin, Ohio in 1846. Each dress, Spalding said, was valued at three horses[5] and the dentalium shells which embellished one of them he described as 'very costly' . . . and the shells removed 'From a single dress were once taken to the mountains by a man who lives near, & sold in small parcels for $1600.00 sixteen hundred dollars. A young lady (Red one) in one of these dresses, upon a firey horse well equiped [sic] with saddle & crouper [sic], makes a fine appearance.' Spalding's description continues, referring to objects which were so typical of Nez Perce accoutrements of the period when natural materials were utilized to their best effect – both for service and decorative embellishment. The elk teeth on the other dress and the cradle which he also sent, were, he explained, from the 'Buck elk, two from an animal, after & before certain ages'.[6] He refers to the woven fiber bags for which the Nez Perce are justly famous: 'The bags are made of

the hemp of the country & used for packing roots, etc.' (Fletcher, 1930:3). Such bags were coveted trade items; in the older types, the warp and weft threads were of hemp (*Apocynum cannabium*) and the false embroidery material was of bear grass (*Xerophyllum tenax*) dyed in soft natural colours and combined in such a way as to produce attractive geometrical patterns across the surface of the bag.[7] A distinctive flat topped hat (commented on by Lewis and Clark in 1806 (Lewis and Clark, Coues ed., 1893, vol.III:1017), without a rim and utilizing similar techniques of weaving to that for the bags, was also made and worn by Nez Perce women; it has been described as the highest form of Nez Perce textile art and 'the gayest portion of their dress' (Spinden, 1908:220).

Whilst Plateau culture was profoundly affected by the horse and the extensive contacts which they subsequently made with the Plains tribes to the east, the tribal domains remained largely intact and Plateau intertribal warfare was minimal.[8] Less so with forays to the Plains, where for almost one hundred years the majority of the Plateau tribes were arrayed in war against the Blackfeet and Crow (although

Below: *A Cayuse chief known by the whites as David Young, c.1900. Note the elaborate horse mask and matching martingale. Young wears a spectacular horned headdress and ermine fringed shirt.*

Left: *Oscar Mark, or The Little Vessel, c.1870, a Wasco Indian of Warm Springs, Oregon. He wears a perforated and fringed buckskin shirt with a broad pony beaded band across his shoulder.*

at times there was an uneasy truce). The Kute-nai, Flathead and some of the Northern Shoshoni, in particular, viewed the Blackfeet and Crow as intruders into the western Plains region which for centuries they had used as intertribal buffalo country. Tribal traditions collected by Wissler and Teit[9] from Blackfeet and Plateau in the early twentieth century, confirmed the report of the explorer, David Thompson, who, when travelling in the region of present-day Calgary, Alberta, observed: 'All these Plains, which are now the hunting ground of the above Indians (Blackfoot), were formerly in full possession of the Kootenaes, northward; the next the Saleesh and their allies, and the most southern the Snake Indians' (Henry and Thompson, Coues ed., 1897:330).

Armed with guns which they obtained from the Cree to the east, the Blackfeet forced the Kutenai, Flathead and Shoshoni to abandon their former hunting grounds and some of the bands who had previously lived east of the Rockies were all but exterminated; others retreated to the Plateau. The Shoshoni were so badly decimated that for more than half a century none were 'seen on the northwestern

Above: A Cayuse woman called Kupt, with her young son in a typical laced Cayuse cradle. The hoop in the cradle could be raised to protect the child's head. Kupt wears a basketry hat and a beaded band.

Below: Edna Kash-Kash, a Cayuse woman, outside a rush-mat covered tipi, c.1900. Note the fine costume – a woven basketry hat, buckskin dress and trade blanket embellished with beadwork.

plains north of the Yellowstone' (Teit, Boas ed., 1930:126). This devastating experience had a positive and lasting effect; it greatly strengthened the interdependence ethos which was so much a part of the Plateau culture and added another – the war complex.

The Flathead invited the Coeur d'Alêne and other Salishan tribes to join them as partners when travelling to their former Plains hunting grounds, the result being a great war alignment of tribes (Plateau versus Plains). The latter were weaker in this respect because of the constant warring which occurred amongst the Plains people themselves (for example, the Crow and Blackfeet were almost constantly at war with one another). Thus, expeditions across the mountains were relatively commonplace, and parties of Coeur d'Alêne, Spokane, Kalispel, Pend d'Oreilles and Nez Perce hunted in territory now claimed by the Blackfeet and Crow. Initially, a rendezvous was made in Flathead country, then three or more large parties would travel to the Plains keeping in touch with one another during their travels. The worst enemy were the Blackfeet, but even with them the Plateau tribes would form a truce so that trading could take place for a few days. 'No one on either side was to quarrel, fight, or steal horses; but all were to be friends for the allotted number of days, and all were to play games and trade as they felt inclined . . . The conduct of the people during these periods of truce was in great contrast to their attitude at other times, when each side was always ready to attack or repel an attack. Sometimes . . . less than a day passed before one side made an attack on the other. The Blackfoot are said to have been the worst offenders' (ibid:114).

Some lasting friendships were, however, made particularly by the Nez Perce bands who commonly travelled to the Plains following the Lolo Trail[10] across the Rocky Mountains into present-day Montana and Wyoming, there to barter with a western branch of the Absaroka – the Mountain Crows. As early as 1806, Lewis and Clark referred to these contacts although they reported that of the seven groups of Nez Perce (whom they referred to as 'Chopunnish') only two travelled to the Missouri. In the 1860s, it seems to have been small bands such as those led by Looking Glass, who had the reputation of being a great wanderer, that forged and maintained these links.

The effect on these Nez Perce bands was that it led to the adoption of a number of Plains traits, particularly those of a material culture nature and it served in the second half of the nineteenth century to distinguish more clearly between two groups of Nez Perce, those strongly influenced by the missionaries and increasingly giving up the traditional religious, tribal customs and lifestyle and those who wished to maintain their independence and ethos. Henry Spalding, for example, instructed the Nez Perce 'to give up native dress before they could receive the rewards of salvation and the power of Christian spirits' and many native materials 'were abandoned or destroyed, mostly by burning'[11] (Shawley, 1974:259). Divisions increasingly became apparent; as the Nez Perce Agent, John Monteith, reported in August 1872: 'The tribe is about equally divided between Treaty and those who term themselves Non-Treaty Indians. The Non-Treaty portion

with very few exceptions reside on the outside of the Reserve along the Snake River and its Tributaries. They never ask for assistance . . . (Brown, 1967:36).

Although convenient from the white man's standpoint to regard the Nez Perce as one single body, this was entirely inconsistent with the traditional social organization of these people – the tribe consisted of bands, both Treaty and Non-Treaty, each with its own leader. Regardless of the appointment by Government officials of Lawyer as 'Head Chief of the Nez Perces Nation', the bands largely acted independently (ibid:31).

By the mid-nineteenth century, the Plateau country became increasingly subjected to white settlement and, in an attempt to avoid conflict, the Stevens Treaty of 1855, amongst others, defined Nez Perce territory. Agreement was reached with little dispute, the Treaty being signed by Lawyer, a highly respected leader and direct descendant of Chief Twisted Hair who had so well received Lewis and Clark half a century previously.[12] Forty-seven others also signed; the anticipated difficulties it appeared had thus been resolved, but sadly, not for long. Five years later, in 1860, a trader named Elias D. Pierce discovered traces of gold deposits on the Reservation and by the end of that year, Pierce had set up camp with some thirty-three recruits. The intention was to mine the following spring (ibid:30).

Anticipating a further influx of miners,

Below: *A Umatilla woman called by the whites Nellie Salmon, c.1900. Her dress is heavily fringed with beads. The corn husk bag is probably of Nez Perce make and the leggings Sioux.*

Above: *A group of Umatilla, c.1900. The costumes are a mixture of traditional Plateau accoutrements – feathered headbands, basketry hat and bag – and Plains clothing such as the buffalo headdress.*

another Treaty attempted to reduce the Reservation further. This time, an agreement could not be reached and the Lower Nez Perce – which included Looking Glass's band – walked out of the negotiations, refusing to sign. It was again left to Lawyer and others to negotiate and this time the lands of the Lower Nez Perce – largely the Non-Treaty faction – were ceded by Lawyer and the Band Chiefs closely associated with him. This included the Wallowa Valley, a traditional homeland of *Tu-eka-kas* or Old Joseph, as he was known to the whites: there were deep regrets and concern on both sides. As Agent Monteith observed in 1872: 'It is a great pity that the valley was ever opened for settlement. It is so high and cold that they can raise nothing but the hardiest of vegetables . . . It is a fine grass country and raising stock is all that can be done to any advantage. It is the only fishery the Nez Percés have and they go there from all directions . . . If there is any way in which the Wallowa Valley could be kept for the Indians I would recommend that it be done' (ibid:38).

This report was written some months after Old Joseph died, who on his deathbed charged his son never to relinquish the Wallowa and Grande Valleys. 'Always remember that your father never sold his country' (Brady, 1916:55). As Hein-mot Too-ya-la-kekt,[13] better known to the world as Joseph, later commented: 'I buried him in that beautiful valley of winding waters. I love that land more than all the rest of the world' (ibid.).

In 1872, Monteith had also reported that whilst at that time there were no white houses yet built in the Wallowa Valley, some were to be built 'this fall' . . . [Then] the question will have to be settled soon to those Indians living outside the Reserve . . .' (Brown, 1967:38).

In 1877, General Howard's[14] adjutant, Major H. Clay Wood, considered the legality of the 1863 Treaty and concluded: 'In my opinion the non-treaty Nez Perces cannot in law be regarded as bound by the treaty of 1863, and in so far as it attempts to deprive them of a right to occupancy of any land its provisions are null and void. The extinguishment of their title of occupancy contemplated by this treaty is imperfect and incomplete' (ibid:37). Nevertheless, as more whites, believing they were within their rights, moved into the valley, the situation became tense. One historian who considered the status of these incoming settlers was led to the conclusion that a number were 'human parasites of varying degrees of undesirability'; he quotes Major Wood's authoritative study of the Nez Perce problem, who had observed: 'I could fill page after page in portraying the number and nature of outrages the Indians and their families were subject to' (ibid:44-5).

In a final council meeting between Joseph and Howard, a show of military force finally caused capitulations: the Non-Treaty Nez Perce agreed to leave the Wallowa and Grande Ronde Valleys. Howard reported 'We have put all non treaty Indians on reservation by using force and persuasion without bloodshed.'

Above: *A Yakima woman and child, c.1900. The baby is in a typical hoop-protected and laced cradle; the woman wears a fine heavily woven blanket, almost certainly a trade item from farther west.*

Below: *Joseph Untush's family on the porch of their home, 1923. Although the time-honored techniques of fruit preservation have changed, traditional styles remain in the woven baskets.*

An unrealistic time limit of thirty days for the move to be completed added to the consternation and deep resentment of the Nez Perce, and young Wahlitits, whose father had been murdered by a white man some three years earlier, decided to seek revenge. As one historian put it, 'a taunt about Eagle Robe's death that was the match that lit the fuse' (ibid:65). On Wednesday, 13 June 1877, Wahlitits and two young companions killed Richard Devine: the next day they killed Henry J. Elfers, Robert Bland and Harry Becktoge. The trio were joined by seventeen others from White Bird's camp and, plied with stolen liquor, the rampage continued. Detailed analysis clearly demonstrates that the prominent leaders – Joseph, his brother Ollokot, Looking Glass and Too-hool-hool-zote – had no part in these incidents and that their attempts 'to deliver the culprits were foiled by unscrupulous volunteers. As Agent Monteith reported to General Howard, 'the fact is there is a certain class here who are afraid there will not be an Indian war' (ibid:66). In less than a week the die was cast and a war with the Non-Treaty Nez Perce was on.

The first major conflict, at White Bird Canyon on 17 June 1877, caused consternation in the ranks of Howard's force under Captain David Perry, when approximately seventy warriors 'quickly and completely routed a column consisting of four officers and ninety-nine men plus ten or eleven armed citizens. Not only did the Indians whip them soundly, but they wiped out one-third of the cavalrymen and chased the remainder for about thirteen miles' and in 'one salutary demonstration, the Nez Perce showed that not only would they fight but that they could fight with the skill, courage and determination that would have been creditable to the best troops in the Army' (ibid:139-40). Sobered

by this defeat, Howard now mustered a more than five hundred strong artillery-supported force. The chase of some two hundred and fifty Nez Perce warriors together with their families numbering about five hundred women and children was on . . . it took nearly four months and seventeen hundred miles across rugged terrain to stop them just forty miles short of their final intended destination, Sitting Bull's camps in Canada. Howard undoubtedly regretted penning the following: 'Other troops are being brought forward as fast as possible . . . [I need] authority for twenty five Indian scouts . . . Think we shall make short work of this', Howard to Division Headquarters 15 June 1877 (ibid:131).

Although supported with these further reinforcements, the Nez Perce again turned the tables on Howard; they encircled the troops and pushed on to the valley of the Clearwater and then dug in for protection. This time, however, on 11 July, assisted by the howitzers, four companies of cavalry, six of infantry and five of artillery acting as infantry, in total some four hundred and forty men exclusive of his staff, Howard, after twenty-four hours of siege, routed the Nez Perce; an enormous amount of property was abandoned and as one elderly Nez Perce woman related, 'many, many, had been wounded'. So harrowing was this attack, and probably anticipating what the future would hold, Joseph was prepared to surrender at this point, but differences of opinion existed in the Nez Perce camp in regard to a Treaty of Peace, with White Bird, Looking Glass and Too-hool-hool-zote voting to make for the buffalo country. The precedent of hanging had already been established for leaders who were involved in uprisings and this was a major fear amongst the Nez Perce, thus whilst at the Clearwater they lost so much which was vital to their subsistence, they refused to capitulate and picking up the one hundred and fifty mile long Lolo Trail, they headed through the Bitterroot Mountains toward Montana. Travelling through the Bitterroot Valley, exhausted but

Above: *Looking Glass, a Nez Perce chief, shown in a Crow camp, 1871. Looking Glass and his group of Nez Perce were firm friends of the Mountain Crow. He was killed at the Bear Paw Mountains in 1877.*

still defiant, they camped on the banks of the Big Hole River. There at dawn on 9 August, they were attacked by the two hundred-odd force under Colonel John Gibbon who, under orders from Howard – now lagging sadly behind somewhere on the Lolo Trail – had ridden out from Fort Missoula to head off the fleeing Nez Perce.

The Battle of the Big Hole on 9 August resulted in a terrible massacre of some eighty Nez Perce, fifty of whom were women and chil-

dren: 'Many women and children were killed before getting out of their beds. In one lodge there were five children. One soldier went into it and killed every one of them' (ibid:254). Andrew Garcia later related what his wife – who as a seventeen year old girl was in the Nez Perce camp – told him of her terrible ordeal: 'The bullets came through [my father's] Gray Eagle's lodge like hail and rain, and hit one of Hoot Owl's women in the head, killing her dead, and another bullet hit one of Hoot Owl's sons in the breast, so that he fell down and lay there. With this rain of bullets coming through the tepee and the noise of the soldiers' guns, with the warriors and white men's yells, . . . the scream and shrieks of the squaws and children . . . Then [we] all tried to get out of the tepee at once, . . . but the soldiers were there . . . Hoot Owl and his other woman and two of the small children were shot dead, and [my] father shot in the belly, . . . [my] sister . . . now fell dead with a bullet through her head . . .' *In-who-lise* was struck in the right shoulder and fell down near the creek bank: she recovered with a soldier standing over her and tried to get up by grabbing his leg – the surprised soldier pushed her back with the butt of his gun, hitting her in the mouth injuring her lips and teeth (Garcia, Stein ed., 1977:215).

Although the initial phase of the attack was successful, the tide of battle unexpectedly turned. One scholar of the Nez Perce has dramatically described that moment: 'Soon, at one end of the camp could be heard the voice of White Bird, and at the other, that of Looking Glass. In tones that stood out above the sounds of the fight like the notes of a bugle call, these two chiefs rallied their warriors and turned what had started as a rout into a desperate fight' (Brown, 1967:255). After the Nez Perce managed to regain their camp, Gibbon later recorded: 'Few of us will soon forget the wail of mingled grief, rage, and horror which came from the camp four or five hundred yards from us when the Indians returned to it and recognized their slaughtered warriors, women, and

Links with the Plains: Indian ponies (not Appaloosas)

Cheyenne/Lakota. Horns of prong horned antelope refer to swiftness and survival powers of one of the purest Plains animals

Cheyenne. Dragonfly symbolic of whirlwind and associated with the thunder and rain spirit. Protective

Cheyenne. Pony painted with motifs symbolic of wounds received, point of impact and bleeding emphasized

Blackfeet. Pony w[ith] figure of man on chest, symbolizing a man was ridden down in battle by owner of the hors[e]

children' (ibid:258).[15] More than forty women and children and some twenty-six warriors were dead and others would die of their wounds – including In-who-lise's father, Gray Eagle – to be buried on the Trail. But the Nez Perce would not give up, they pushed on for another thousand miles – Camas Meadow on 20 August where Ollokot and twenty-seven Nez Perce warriors stalled Howard's men by stampeding his horses and mules . . . 13 September, Canyon Creek, where Nez Perce marksmen stopped four hundred Seventh Cavalry troopers under Colonel Samuel Sturgis whilst the women and children escaped with the horses[16] . . . A respite at Cow Island, 23 September, where a raid on an Army cache, deposited because the Missouri was too low to get it to

Fort Benton, provided much needed supplies[17] . . . and finally, 30 September, on to the Bearpaw Mountains, camping on Snake Creek, only forty miles from the Canadian border. With Howard – now dubbed by the Nez Perce as General Day After Tomorrow – and Sturgis judged to be some two or three days march away, the remnants of the Nez Perce clearly

Below: *This horse was traditionally associated with the Nez Perce, but it is possible that the name actually derives from Palus, a closely associated tribe also known for their horsebreeding skills. The characteristics of this animal were the distinctive speckled markings, together with great endurance and surefootedness; on average they were larger and heavier than the typical Indian pony.*

considered themselves safe: they were wrong.

On 18 September after receiving a report – which took five days to arrive – from General Howard and Colonel Sturgis that the Nez Perce had 'left them hopelessly in the rear' (ibid:378), Colonel Nelson Miles, together with some three hundred and fifty men, rode from Fort Keogh on the Yellowstone travelling northwest towards the Bearpaw Mountains arriving within a few miles of Snake Creek on 29 September. Early on Sunday 30 September, their movements shielded from the Nez Perce by a blinding snowstorm, they attacked the village; the result was a devastating repulse with some twenty per cent of Miles' force put out of action. As Captain Snyder later recorded: 'Our loss today Capt Hale & Lt Biddle & 23 enld [en-

The Appaloosa

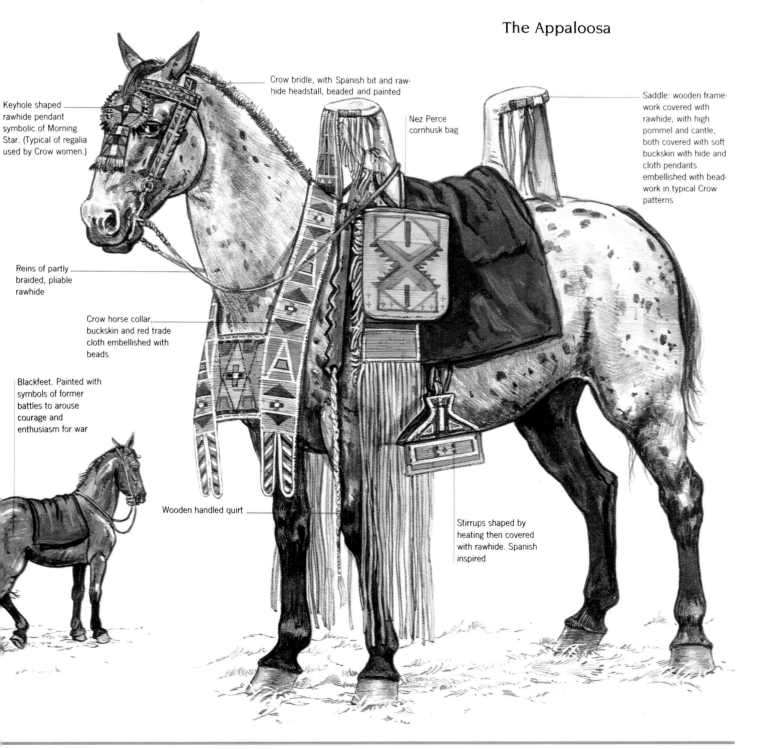

Crow bridle, with Spanish bit and rawhide headstall, beaded and painted

Keyhole shaped rawhide pendant symbolic of Morning Star. (Typical of regalia used by Crow women.)

Nez Perce cornhusk bag

Saddle: wooden framework covered with rawhide, with high pommel and cantle, both covered with soft buckskin with hide and cloth pendants embellished with beadwork in typical Crow patterns

Reins of partly braided, pliable rawhide

Crow horse collar, buckskin and red trade cloth embellished with beads

Blackfeet. Painted with symbols of former battles to arouse courage and enthusiasm for war

Wooden handled quirt

Stirrups shaped by heating then covered with rawhide. Spanish inspired

Nez Perce

Cornhusk bags are a well-known specialty of the Nez Perce. These are flat, flexible wallets made by twining without any loom or frame. The foundation warps and wefts are cords of Indian hemp bast or, less good, elderberry, willow, or other bark, twisted by rubbing across the thigh. The decoration is applied by false embroidery: as part of the weaving process a strand is wrapped around the weft each time it passes in front of the warp. The outside surface is completely covered, while the inside shows only loose ends of the false-embroidery cords. These decorative cords were originally of beargrass or ryegrass, but with the introduction of corn in the late nineteenth century the grasses were replaced by cords twisted from the pliable, slick inner parts of cornhusks. Colored designs were made by dyeing some of the false-embroidery cords with colors from minerals, barks, grasses, berries, green algae, or other natural materials. The designs are made up of geometric elements repeated in rows and columns in an all-over pattern, normally entirely different on the two sides of a bag (see No. 20 below). The designs have no meanings or significance, and the very varied patterns are only for esthetic effect. The bags were used to store and carry roots, berries and household items. They have been an important Nez Perce trade and export product at least since Lewis and Clark mentioned them in 1805. The designs on cornhusk bags are quite different from those painted on par-

fleches, which were formerly made of buffalo hide and used especially to store meat. These distensible containers were widely used by Plains tribes and in the eastern Plateau and Basin. Before Nez Perce weddings the groom's family might give parfleches filled with blankets, shawls, and calico to the bride's family, who reciprocated with the same number of cornhusk bags filled with dried roots. These artifacts are a small sample of those collected by Livingston Farrand on the Nez Perce Reservation in Idaho, 1902.

1–5 Cornhusk bags.
6 One of a pair of woman's leggings, of Cheyenne origin.
7–9 Cornhusk bags.
10–12 Parfleches – folded rawhide cases with painted geometric designs.
13–14 Cornhusk bags.
15 Parfleche.
16 Parfleche.
17 Comb.
18–24 Cornhusk bags.
25 Flat leather bag with beaded design like the parfleche designs.

listed] men killed and 4 Officers & 40 men wounded. Indians still hold their position' (ibid:389).

But one major objective had been achieved in that attack – the majority of the Nez Perce horse-herd was captured.

The next day, 1 October, under a flag of truce, Joseph attempted negotiations with General Miles; by now many of his relatives, friends and council members were dead or lost, including both Looking Glass and Joseph's brother, *Ollokot*, who had been killed the previous day. This left only the defiant White Bird and Joseph as the key leaders. Joseph stayed in Miles' camp overnight, the Nez Perce held Lt Jerome as a hostage; the next day, each man returned to his own camp, a stalemate had been reached.

According to one contemporary observer – Lieutenant Charles Erskine Scott Wood, Howard's acting aide-de-camp – the Nez Perce had literally honeycombed a portion of the site of their camp, and other transverse gulches, with subterranean dwelling places and communicating tunnels.[18] In addition, they were using their dead horses as fortifications as well as a source of food: 'Here they held their own, refusing all offers of surrender, and saying in effect: If you want us, come and take us' (Wood, 1884:141).

With the loss of most of the horse-herd, however, the possibility of yet another flight towards the Canadian border and freedom was out of the question.[19] Winter was now setting in and the freezing weather with rain and snow caused suffering on both sides. Howard and a small escort arrived on the evening of Thursday 4 October and the next day the terms of surrender were agreed, a message being conveyed by two Treaty Nez Perce who had daughters in Joseph's camp. There was little room for maneuver, Howard pointing out that his whole command was only two or three days behind him. This force, together with that of Miles', would have thus combined to a total of at least six hundred fighting men – to be arrayed against no more than one hundred able Nez Perce warriors, who had the added responsibility of protecting the women and children.[20] Promises were made of good treatment and Joseph asked if his people would be allowed to return to Idaho. 'He was told that he would, unless *higher authority* ordered otherwise'[21] (ibid). Joseph's final answer summed up the desperate experiences and now the plight of the remnant Nez Perce, its poignancy, eloquence and dignity being a remarkable tribute for all time to the people that he represented, for it was the end of an era:

'Tell General Howard I know his heart. What he told me before – I have it in my heart. I am tired of fighting. Our chiefs are killed. Looking-glass is dead. *Too-hul-hul-suit* is dead. The old men are all dead. It is the young men, now, who say 'yes' or 'no' [that is, vote in council]. He who led on the young men [Joseph's brother, *Ollicut*] is dead. It is cold, and we have no blankets. The little children are freezing to death. My people – some of them – have run away to the hills and have no blankets, no food. I want to have time to look for my children, and to see how many of them I can find; may be I shall find them among the dead. Hear me, my chiefs; my heart is sick and sad. From where the sun *now* stands, I will fight no more forever!'

(ibid)

The Nez Perce 'are among the most amiable men we have seen. Their character is placid and gentle, rarely moved to passion' . . . 'the Shoshonees are not only cheerful but even gay; . . .in their intercourse with strangers they are frank and communicative, in their dealings perfectly fair, . . . [nothing] has tempted them into a single act of dishonesty'.[22]

Left: A Nez Perce boy called by the whites Joseph Ratunda, c.1900. His otter skin breastplate, hair roach and beaded moccasins show a strong Plains influence. Floral beadwork is typical Nez Perce.

Below: Hein-mot Too-ya-la-kekt, better known to history as Chief Joseph of the Nez Perce, 1901. The mottled feather in his hair is from the tail of a maturing golden eagle.

Nez Perce Warrior, 1877

A Nez Perce warrior at the opening of the Nez Perce War that ended when the U.S. Army defeated the epic retreat toward the Canadian border led by Chief Joseph. The head-dress is of fur, ermine tails, and trimmed buffalo horns. The war shirt, sent to the Smithsonian in 1876, is of leather trimmed with yellow and red cloth, bands of porcupine quill-work and beads, horsehair tassels, and fur around the bottom. Used in the Nez Perce War were the buffalo horn cup once owned by Husis Owyeen, the bone war whistle owned by Peopeo Tholekt, and the Winchester carbine, Model 1866. The beaded moccasins came to the Smithsonian in 1876. A fine bow of mountain sheep horn (a Nez Perce specialty) is carried in a bow case attached to a quiver — an arrangement adopted from the Crow.

central and western Basin area. Here the environment varied from salt marshland to alpine herbland and the individual camp sites from large and well ventilated caves to small and open camps. Of particular interest is that more than eighty per cent of these sites were located between an elevation of about 5250 to 7550ft (1600-2300m.), only eleven per cent were located below 5250ft; for obvious reasons, the indigenous population generally avoided open desert with its lack of protective cover, intense heat and high aridity. Above 7550ft (2300m.) game was often unpredictable and limited, and winters severe. Clearly, the Basin people managed successfully to strike a balance between these environmental extremes.

Unlike the Plateau to the north where natural resources were generally predictable and abundant, leading to a subsistence economy which pivoted on intertribal trade, that of the Basin was largely characterized by a people whose lifestyle has led them to be described as 'superb resource generalists' (Harper, 1986:51). Roots and seeds were a major food resource;

Although there is no abrupt natural barrier change as one moves south from the Plateau to the Great Basin region, the declining influence of the two great rivers, the Columbia and Fraser, upon which so much of Plateau culture depended, becomes increasingly apparent. Lying as it does between the Rocky Mountains to the east and the Sierra Nevadas to the west, with only limited and widely varying precipitation – particularly to the west and south – the Great Basin with no rivers draining to the sea, includes the southern parts of Oregon and Idaho, all of Nevada and Utah, and the western halves of Wyoming and Colorado. It is a region characterized by mountains which tower above the flatlands, but the terrain varies markedly. In the central and southeast areas of this region, where the Colorado River has carved immense canyons whose towering walls exhibit richly coloured sedimentations, saltbush and sagebrush deserts dominate, whilst to the north and east in areas which are drained by the Snake and Green rivers, there are wide sweeping grasslands of varying composition and, at higher elevations, scattered open forests of conifers and alpine type herbland.

In this vast, diverse area covering some quarter of a million square miles, lived a predominantly Shoshonean-speaking people[23] whose territory once also extended to the Northern Plains and south almost into Mexico. In the northeast – at times overlapping with the Plateau Nez Perce and Flathead – were the Shoshoni and Bannock, to their west the Paviotso or Northern Paiute, whilst to the south of these tribes were the Western Shoshoni, Paiute and Ute. Unlike the Plateau people there was a great difference between the lifestyles of these various tribes, particularly after the acquisition of the horse by the more eastern Shoshoni and Ute, the latter using packhorses, although apparently not yet riding them, as early as 1650.

Recent archeological analysis of ancient camp sites in the more northern parts of the Great Basin – in the vicinity and to the west of the Great Salt Lake in Utah – gives some important insights into early Indian lifestyles, which are probably typical for much of the

Above: *The Shoshoni chief Washakie's lodge and encampment, Wind River Mountains, Wyoming, 1870. Note the wooden pins lacing up the cover at the front and pictographic symbols on his lodge.*

Below: *Interior of a Shoshoni lodge, 1878. The standing woman wears a striped Witney 'point' blanket. The baby is in a typical Shoshoni cradle; fine beaded saddle bags hang behind the figures.*

however, the prong-horned antelope was to be found scattered throughout the region and these, together with the more abundant jack-rabbit, were an important food resource, the annual family gatherings in the autumn enabling these animals to be captured by use of communal drives. In the east, the Northern Shoshoni and Bannock had the luxury of buffalo which, prior to c.1840, were to be found west of the continental divide. After this date, bereft of this resource locally, it was necessary for these tribes to travel annually to the Plains region – a hazardous venture in territory of gun-armed tribes – or accept the harsher alternatives of the more Central and Western Great Basin environment, where brush wickiups replaced the comfortable hide tipi for shelter, and a largely foraging economy that of hunting.

These central and western Shoshonean groups – largely occupying what is now Utah and Nevada – were, particularly in the mid-nineteenth century when first described by whites, referred to as 'Digger Indians', a derogatory term, drawing attention to their extensive

Below: *The exterior of a Paiute rush covered dwelling, probably for winter use, c.1900. Note the cradle with the broad covering shade. The parallel lines on the band suggest a male child.*

Above: *Paiute couple, date not recorded but probably before 1880. The man wears a buckskin shirt with decorative shoulder flaps, the woman a trade cloth dress with a heavily beaded belt.*

use of a pointed stick which was used to pry roots and wild vegetables from the ground. These people, variously designated as Gosiutes, Northern Paiute, Panamint, Kawaiisu, Chemehuevi (Southern Paiute) and Weber Utes[24] were loosely grouped according to the major type of food utilized, such as sunflower seed, root, pine nut, squirrel, sheep and even earth or dust eaters. A remarkably adaptable and practical people, they represented a culture sustained in the arid regions of the Great Basin for thousands of years, largely shut away from the outside world and little influenced by the Plateau or Plains people to the north and east. In order to survive, they utilized an immense range of plant and animal resources, some of the major root crops being camas, bitterroot, caraway, onion and Indian potato. Salad plants were miner's lettuce, sweet cicely, violets and certain brackens. Fruit, seed and nut crops which occurred in the foothill and riparian zones, were chokecherries, currants, oregon grapes, blue elderberries, amaranths, chenopods, sunflowers, acorns and pine nuts, the latter generally referred to as *piñon*, being amongst the most important for a large part of the region and a focus of great activity by groups in late summer and early autumn, particularly in the Central Great Basin.

Northern Paiute

Speakers of the Northern Paiute language once occupied some 70,000 square miles in Nevada and southeastern Oregon, as small semi-nomadic bands, not a unified tribe. The principal game animals were deer and mountain sheep. Small game also included hares, rabbits, marmots, and porcupines. Bird hunting was important, and special decoys were used to attract ducks to the hunter. In some areas fish were a major resource. Everywhere wild plants were basic – some 150 species were used. Piñon nuts were collected and processed with baskets, while special beaters were used to knock some kinds of seeds into a tray or conical basket. Seeds were usually cooked as a mush boiled with hot stones dropped into a basketry container. The reservation period for the Northern Paiutes began in the 1870s, but many people refused to move to the two or three areas set aside for them, and smaller reservations and colonies were established later. The Fallon and Pyramid Lake reservations are among those within the former N. Paiute territory. The government encouraged farming on the reservations, but with little success: the soils were unsuitable and water was lacking, especially when non-Indians began to divert streams. When the items shown here were collected by Robert H. Lowie in 1914/1915 many of the collecting and processing techniques and implements for seeds were still in use, although a decade later they were rare. In 1914 the only type of aboriginal clothing still in use was a basket hat for women.

1 Cradleboard of twined basketry with buckskin cover. Pyramid Lake Res.

2 Infant's cradle of twined willow rods. Fallon Res.

3, 4 Decoys for hunting ducks; duckskins over tule foundations. Pyramid Lake Res.

5 Twined basketry water jug, waterproofed with piñon pitch. Pyramid Lake Res.

6 Woman's dress, blue cotton printed cloth (model). S. Paiute, Moapa River Res., collected 1915.

7 Willow splints for making baskets. Pyramid Lake Res.

8 Twined basketry seed beater. Fallon Res.

9 Bent rod mush stirrer. Pyramid Lake Res.

10 Stone tobacco pipe smoked with straight wooden stem. Fallon Res.

11 Cane fire drill with sage wood hearth (model). Fallon Res.

12 Woman's dress of printed cotton cloth (model). S. Paiute, Shivwits Res., Utah, collected 1915.

13 Twined openwork basket for berries and nuts: Pyramid Lake Res.

14 Twined conical harvesting basket. Pyramid Lake Res.

15 Pair of men's sandals of twined tule (models). Fallon Res.

16 Man's cloth shirt (model). S. Paiute, Moapa River Res., collected 1915.

17 Two plain and two wrapped bone implements for team guessing game. Pyramid Lake Res.

18 Set of stick dice. Fallon Res.

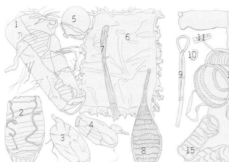

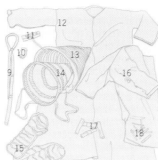

The complex subsistence technology, developed in order to render the *piñon* crop both edible and suitable for storage, commenced with the collecting of the green cones with the aid of harvesting poles, which were then transported in large conical shaped woven baskets[25] for pit roasting which caused them to open; now piled up, the cones were beaten, or individual cones tapped, to release the seeds which were then lightly parched in a tray making the shells brittle – a combined flat metate and huller, together with winnowing, finally separated the seed and husk. The seeds were then given a final parching in trays: they could now be used in this raw state or ground into a meal from which a gruel was prepared. Alternatively, the meal was moulded into cakes which were then dried in the sun and in this form they were stored in lined ground pits for winter use, a vital step for survival given the unpredictable nature of the Great Basin, since studies have shown that 'good nut years are irregular: no definite cycle exists' (ibid:59). The Great Basin people, however, held the belief that a bumper crop occurred every seven years and in this respect they were correct, since it has been recently recognized that even in a single valley, local environmental factors were such that synchrony of production from one grove to another never occurred. The *piñon* subsistence complex also involved ceremonialism – prayers before the season, dances at the harvesting and special prayers of thanksgiving over the first seeds. Ceremonials of this sort are still (even in the late twentieth century) practiced, remaining 'as one of the key features of Native identity' (Fowler, 1986:65).

In addition to the communal antelope and rabbit hunts, there are descriptions of grasshopper drives. The first priest to visit the Western Shoshoni in the mid-nineteenth century, Pierre Jean De Smet, refers to an area which swarmed with grasshoppers and was often visited by the local Indians (probably the Gosiutes who lived some one hundred miles to the west of the Great Salt Lake). He relates a fascinating firsthand description: 'They begin by digging a hole, ten or twelve feet in diameter by four or five feet deep; then, armed with long branches . . . they surround a field of four or five acres, more or less, according to the number of persons who are engaged in it. They stand

Below: Wovoka, known by the whites as Jack Wilson, c.1895. Called the Paiute Messiah, he initiated the doctrine of the Ghost Dance: 'You must not fight . . . Do no harm to anyone . . . Do right always.'

Above: *Paiute women in close woven basketry hats gathering seed, Kaibab Plateau, c.1873. They bear large burden baskets and the close twill twined trays of the type used for winnowing pine nuts.*

Below: *Three Paiute women in traditional summer dress, wearing finely woven basketry skull caps and heavily buckskin fringed skirts. The woman at right appears to have a fur cape of rabbit skin.*

about twenty feet apart, and their whole work is to beat the ground so as to frighten up the grasshoppers and make them bound forward. They chase them toward the center by degrees – that is, into the hole prepared for their reception. Their number is so considerable that frequently three or four acres furnish grasshoppers sufficient to fill the reservoir or hole' (De Smet, Chittenden and Richardson eds, 1905, vol. III:1033).

The Gosiutes preserved some of these grasshoppers for future use by crushing them into a paste which they then dried; for more immediate needs they were either made into a soup or the largest selected for roasting at the campfire. In later years, white settlers would view the presence of such myriads of grasshoppers as bordering a plague, but to the indigenous population they were clearly seen as another natural subsistence resource, quite in keeping with the unstated but widely practiced ethos which characterized the Great Basin area – if it moves it can probably be eaten! There was, however, in all this an element of conservation and environmental manipulation; widespread, for example, was the avoidance of killing female animals during the gestation and rearing seasons and the Northern Paiute and Northern Shoshoni speared only male trout or salmon on the spawning beds or runs. Complex fish weirs were used to control migrating fish; the Washoe of the Pyramid Lake region cut the upper branches of browse plants to encourage deer herds to remain in the vicinity during the winter months and, at times, antelope were kept penned and killed as needed whilst some plant life was improved and conserved by selective harvesting and pruning.

The scarcity and unpredictable nature of food resources in the Great Basin region led to the development of a World View which put emphasis on respect for plants and animals so vital for survival in an often hostile environment. In the gathering of plants, for example, prayers were offered to the plant spirits and the Northern Paiute commonly buried a small stone or bead in the hole left vacant by a lifted root, whilst slain animals were often placed with their heads facing east or body parts, such as the eyes, glands and gall bladders, laid out or buried. Special terminology which may be used in an accompanying address reflected the respect shown for the animal and at the same time it was an appeal to the spirit powers that the food resource would be sustained. The power to cure disease frequently derived from the animal spirits, whilst more than three hundred plant species, burnt, crushed and powdered, were used medicinally. Great Basin mythology was also replete in references to plants and animals, the latter's adventures and misadventures explaining such things as the creating of the earth and its people, the formation of the seasons, food taboos and the establishment of social behaviour. Of particular interest, as recently pointed out by one anthropologist who has studied Great Basin culture in depth, is the naming of constellations after animals and associating these in turn with 'tales of their adventures and misadventures in the sky' (Fowler, 1986:96).

The Great Basin religion put strong emphasis on immortality. After death, the Western Shoshoni said the human spirit went to the land of the Coyote, who together with Wolf his brother, had created the world; not until Wolf had revived and washed the spirit was its place correctly established. So strong was the belief in immortality that on occasions sutteeism was practiced; one 1861 eyewitness account refers to the killing of a Shoshoni woman in Carson Valley, Nevada, so that her spirit could accompany that of her husband to the land of the Coyote. Death and regeneration was a recurring theme in Great Basin religion. The anthropologist, Robert H. Lowie, for example, recorded the dream experiences of a Northern Shoshoni '... my body dropped, cold and dead. I looked at it for some time; it made no movement at all ... The Sun told me I would be restored to life ... I don't know how I returned. Suddenly I was back alive ... On another occasion, I went up to the clouds. The people I met there were nothing but skeletons ...' (Lowie, 1909:233). Another student of the Shoshoni reports that the predominate way supernatural messages were received was through 'unsought dreams' (Hultkrantz, 1986:44) and in this respect the experiences of the Paiute holy man, Tavibo, and later his son Wovoka, fit the Great Basin shamanistic pattern, but modified by Christian teachings.

The great communal drives for the antelope and jack-rabbit were also invariably associated with religious ceremony. Certain men were credited with the power to lure the game, their dance being accompanied by ritual and song; restrictions were associated with such rituals, for example, amongst the Paiute, women were excluded as were menstruating women amongst the Western Shoshoni, the belief being that the calling powers would thus be weakened.

The jack-rabbit was a source of both food and clothing to these interior Basin people and fine

Below: A group of Washoes, members of a small tribe living around Lake Tahoe and speaking a language unrelated to others. These people wear Euro-American clothing but traditional hairstyles.

Above: *Ute men, women and children, most in dance costume, c.1900. Dentalium shell ornaments, bone hair breastplates, beaded leggings and moccasins and roach-style headdresses are all in evidence.*

Below: *A Southern Paiute (Chemehuevi) woman weaving a basket. This tribe excelled at basketry, producing conical burden baskets and close coiled and twilled trays for sifting and winnowing.*

garments for winter use were fabricated from strips of the skins; but they were expensive, up to forty skins being required for a single robe. It was thus a garment owned only by the most prestigious and the majority sufficed with a few skins wrapping the feet and legs as protection against the harsh terrain. In summer, the men wore only a breechcloth and the women a double layered skirt woven from a fiber derived from sagebrush.

Except for the annual get-togethers, the majority of the year was spent by small family groups ranging tribal territory, and in addition to root and vegetable gathering, they snared and netted small animals, birds and fish. During spring and summer, housing consisted of temporary shelters or windbreaks made of reed mats and branches. A common form of pottery was a flat bottomed cylindrical shaped vessel with holes in the rim for suspension[26] and this, together with matting, stone metates, digging stick, twined and coiled basketry and open hooded baby carriers, made up the typical family household utensils. In winter, shelters were more substantial, some being subterranean with an opening through the mound-like roof which served as both door and smokehole; clusters of such habitations, when viewed at a distance, have been described as resembling a prairie dog town.

Such was the lifestyle which epitomized Great Basin culture: unchanged for thousands of years, a constant search for food and reduction of essentials to the minimum – an environment where survival of the fittest had a very real meaning.

Not all of this region, however, was so harsh and unremitting. To the east and north, as has already been described, the terrain changed and whilst in common with the Northern Paiute (Paviotso), Paiute, Washoe and Western Shoshoni there was still considerable depen-

Southern Paiute Elder, 1872

When Maj. J.W. Powell and his photographer John K. Hillers visited the Southern Paiute in 1872 and 1873 they saw a Kaibab Southern Paiute man sharpening a hafted chipped-stone knife while seated like this in front of a winter house with a pole foundation covered with grass, brush, and rushes. The girl behind him wears a beautifully tailored Plains-style buckskin dress made of two fawn skins and two separate pieces sewn into a yoke, which has a blue and white beaded design with two rows of perforated elk teeth below. The man wears hard-soled moccasins and fringed leggings with a painted design. The buckskin cap, tied underneath his chin, has hawk feathers attached. Powell brought garments very like these back to Washington for the Smithsonian collections.

dence on a foraging existence; the lifestyle of the Northern and Eastern Shoshoni, together with that of the Ute who between them ranged southern Idaho, western Wyoming, eastern Nevada and much of Colorado, differed to a marked degree, with a shift from bare essentials and now enhanced by intertribal trade which included Plains as well as Plateau tribes, access to buffalo country, a more complex social organization and ceremonial warfare and, from the early seventeenth century, contact with the Spanish Southwest which brought the greatest luxury of all – the horse.

The establishment of Spanish rule by Juan de Oñate in New Mexico in the period 1597-1610 led to the importation of several hundred horses to the region, within comparatively easy reach of Ute bands, particularly those in the vicinity of the San Juan river in present-day southern Utah and Colorado. These people soon acquired a knowledge of the horse and by the mid-seventeenth century used them, together with the dog, as pack animals. Ute tribal territory took in the majority of the Colorado Plateau which differed sharply from the interior Great Basin further west, having high average rainfall, giving well-watered valleys and grasslands; it was ideal pasture land for the horse and a resource rapidly exploited by the ped-

Below: A Ute warrior described as 'The messenger in full dress', c.1873. The broad bow is typical of the tribe, also the heavily fringed buckskin shirt and leggings. Note his beaded hair braids.

Above: A Ute camp on the eastern slope of the Wasatch Mountains, Utah, c.1873. The tipi was made of elk skin. At right are two conical pole frames and a sloping pole, supporting possessions and dried meat.

estrian Ute. The Pueblo revolt in 1680 and the establishment of missions by Father Eusebio Kino in Central Arizona amongst the Pima and Papago led to a further source of horses – acquired by both theft and trade – and by 1730 the horse had reached the Northern Shoshoni, who, rapidly adapting to an equestrian lifestyle, expanded their territory deep into the buffalo country of the Northern Plains and at least as far as the Belly River[27] in southern Saskatchewan. One group split off from the Eastern Shoshoni probably to be nearer the southern source of horses. Here, armed also with guns which they obtained from the French, they claimed the country from the Platte to New Mexico driving the Apaches south and, turning on their former allies the Utes, by 1755 had crossed the Arkansas. With both gun and horse they, together with the Kiowas, dominated the Southern Plains for more than a century; history knows them as the Comanches,[28] a Spanish rendering of a Ute word, *Cumanche*, 'enemies'. The Comanche never, however, completely severed their former Great Basin links and continued to visit back and forth, and some bands such as the Yamparika Comanche still had a taste for root vegetables, partially clinging to a Shoshoni foraging subsistence, but predominately now buffalo meat eaters, living in tipis – dashing and free.

By contrast, Shoshoni equestrian life on the Northern Plains was less successful. Archeological evidence suggests that as pedestrian hunters they at least made extensive excursions into Plains country 'before the birth of Christ' (Hultkrantz, 1968:59), and it was thus territory familiar to them; but the moving frontier of the horse from the west virtually coincided with that of the gun from the east and this, together with the devastating smallpox epidemic of 1781, gave the Shoshoni but transient equestrian residency. In less than a generation, under pressure from the well-armed Piegan who spearheaded Blackfeet[29] dominance of the Canadian Plains, the Shoshoni progressively retreated to the safety of the Rocky Mountains. For all their outward appearance, however, these Eastern Shoshoni retained much of their Great Basin culture – mythology, religion, forager economy, social organization and a widely intelligible language – and although it has been rigorously debated[30] there is much in one contemporary observation which attempted to distinguish between the Eastern and Western Shoshoneans: thus, when the former 'acquired a horse . . . he (became) a Shoshoni; if he found himself deprived of it, he was once again a Shoshoko (Walker or Digger)' (Trenholm and Carley, 1964:4).

Ironically, in just less than a century after the Shoshonean retreat from the Plains, it was to be reverberations from their peaceful Shoshoko kinsmen which led to the final collapse of the warlike spirit – epitomized by the Lakota – of the historic Plains Indian.

On New Year's Day 1889, during an eclipse of the sun, Wovoka, a Paiute holy man, ill with a high fever, had a vision; later, he related that

Right: *A Ute warrior, Utah, c.1873. The otter skin band across the shoulder supports a combined bow case and quiver which has a long pointed drop heavily embellished with beadwork.*

'When the sun died' he was taken up to heaven and saw God and all the people who had died a long time ago. Wovoka claimed that he was told by God that he must go back to earth and preach goodness, industry and peace to the Indians. If they followed his instructions they would be reunited with their relatives and friends who had died. A new world would be created where there would be no more death, sickness or old age (see Mooney,1896).

Much of Wovoka's experience reflected the Great Basin shamanistic pattern outlined earlier. It was, however, somewhat modified by Christian doctrine.

An important phase of the new faith was a dance for the Indians. It came to be known as the Spirit or Ghost dance, spreading to the Great Plains where each tribe put their own interpretation on Wovoka's teachings (see also Plains chapter, pp.100–01). In the case of the war-like and independent Lakota, it precipitated the tragedy of Wounded Knee and the death of Sitting Bull, both in 1890 – and inscribed forever in the annals of American Indian history the name of a gentle, Great Basin Paiute, whose vision reflected an immense and widespread yearning for a past life which was now rapidly disintegrating under the impact of the European-American.

References

1 This was some seventy-five miles southeast of a now particularly famous landmark – Mount St Helen's, Washington.
2 Mylie Lawyer, an elderly Nez Perce, direct descendant of Chief Lawyer and residing at Lapwai, said that during the Nez Perce wars of 1877 the makeshift shelters were of a single lean-to type (M.L. to C.T., 1969).
3 In present-day northeast Oregon.
4 (i) Teit reports that the Crows obtained these from the Sioux to trade to the Plateau people.
(ii) Mylie Lawyer had many items of Sioux make which were family heirlooms.
5 Spalding estimated that the dresses would sell for '$50 or $60 a piece' in the 'southern states'.
6 These milk teeth were highly prized by the Crow who used them to decorate their women's dresses; because of their rarity, imitation ones were made of bone.
7 More recently made bags are generally false embroidered with corn husk (hence the modern term 'corn husk bags'), colored with either soft toned native or the brighter (trade) aniline dyes and perhaps the addition of colored yarn. The end-product is, however, still highly attractive and the process is a time-consuming exercise. At Lapwai in 1969, Ida Blackeagle's daughter, Josephine, showed me a partially completed corn husk wallet. It measured about 7in. (18cm.) wide and she said that it took her mother 'about one hour' to do a one inch full width section. Such bags are not infrequently exchanged with the Crows for the rawhide parfleche.
8 Wissler, 1910:17, and Teit, Boas ed.,1930:304-5.
9 These tribal domains appear to have been established over a period of several thousand years. Unlike the Plains Indians, the Plateau people have no legends of ever living anywhere else.
10 An ancient Indian route across the Continental Divide from Idaho into Montana.
11 Mylie Lawyer reiterated this fact. The missionary/ school teacher, Kate McBeth, was said to have had an enormous bonfire (c.1875-6) to destroy 'leather materials'.
12 Lewis and Clark were very well received by the Nez Perce band led by Twisted Hair which formed the basis of particularly friendly relations between the Nez Perce and Americans in the years to come. Of interest is the fact that the explorers left American

flags at various places and sent one to Twisted Hair as a token of friendship (Lewis and Clark, Coues ed., 1893, vol.II:610). Research specifically on Nez Perce material culture in 1969 suggested that there was some preference by this tribe for the use of both stripes and stars in their 'decorative' work on such items as bags, shirts, women's dresses and horse equipment. The Nez Perce were greatly influenced by the flag design and incorporated it in their artwork as a mark of esteem to the explorers. At Yakima, the trader and collector Roger Ernesti showed me an unusual Nez Perce shirt which emphasized the star symbol. It had fringes of blue trade cloth, the white selvedge edge of each fringe being cut into a V shape. When the shirt was shaken, it gave the appearance of dancing stars.
13 Thunder Travelling to Loftier (Mountain) Heights.
14 Brig. General Oliver O. Howard, who was assigned to the northwestern command in 1876, was sometimes referred to as the Christian General (it was maintained by his men that he hated fighting on Sundays). Howard, who had distinguished himself in both the Civil War and on a mission to Cochise in 1872, was a man of strong humanitarian principles and largely in sympathy with the Non-Treaty Nez Perce.
15 Two years later, Garcia and In-who-lise returned to the Big Hole Battlefield – a site now scattered with human remains. They finally located the disturbed grave of Gray Eagle and reburied his bones. More than fifty years later, in 1930, Garcia returned to the site and found the lance head which he and In-who-lise had agreed to leave intact as a tribute to its former owner (Garcia, Stein ed., 1799:270).
16 Nez Perce sharpshooting was both effective and selective; cornered at the Clearwater, the elderly Otstotpoo advised not to bother with the common soldier, suggesting instead 'Shoot the commander!' (McWhorter, 1940:70). It was a technique employed time and again with great effect throughout the four month retreat.
17 This area is still remote and difficult for access. A visit by the writer to the Cow Island site in the summer of 1986 gave an opportunity to examine the deep rifle pits which are still to be found, dug during the Nez Perce–Seventh Infantry contingent skirmishes (under First Sergeant William Moelchert) on the night of 23 September 1877.
18 Some twenty years ago, it was still quite easy to

locate remnants of these fortifications and also the rectangular hospital area where the troops were buried. One surprising fact was the obvious close proximity of troops and Indians, perhaps no more than six hundred meters separated them.
19 Howard's mandate from General Sherman was a *carte blanche* to follow the Nez Perce wherever they went but *not* into Canada.
20 One of these children was Josiah Red Wolf (*Heemeen Ilp Ilp*), a boy of five at the time of the retreat. In 1969, I visited this ninety-seven-year-old veteran at the Sommerville Rest Home near Lapwai, Idaho (courtesy of Marcus Ware of Lewiston). Red Wolf was then the sole survivor of the 1877 war: it was a sobering and privileged experience to be in the company of a man associated with an historic event which took place almost a century earlier.
21 The emphasis is mine since this was a significant statement. Although it is clear that the officers of the day – Howard and Miles – made this promise in good faith, the complexities of politics prevented its implementation. After several years' exile in Indian Territory, Kansas, Joseph, together with some one hundred and fifty Nez Perce, were settled on a Reservation in Washington – some three hundred miles north of his beloved Wallowa Valley. He was granted but one visit to his father's grave in the summer of 1900 and died in Nespelem four years later – it is said, of a broken heart.
22 Lewis and Clark, Coues ed., 1893: 1017 and 556.
23 It should be noted that both the Shoshoni and Bannock languages belong to the Numic branch of the larger Uto-Aztecan linguistic stock.
24 Some of the designations were localized, for example, Brigham Young's term for the Weber Utes was Cumumbahs.
25 The Great Basin people excelled at basket-making; some were rendered waterproof and could be utilized for cooking meat or vegetables.
26 A very widespread style which was used throughout the Great Basin and reached both the Plateau and Plains regions.
27 A Blackfeet term for the South Saskatchewan River just to the west of present-day Regina.
28 The Central Numic dialect spoken by the Northern Shoshoni is comprehensible to the Comanche.
29 The Blackfeet Confederacy consisted of the Siksika, Blood and Piegan.
30 See, for example, Hultkrantz (1968).

CALIFORNIA

FROM THE sub-sea level sands of Death Valley, the continent's lowest point, to the peaks of the Sierras, where Mount Whitney rises as the highest point of the lower forty-eight states, California is a land of contrasts. Its nearly 1,200 miles of coastline makes such a dramatic swing that Eureka, to the north, is the nation's most westward city outside of Alaska and Hawaii. Yet, San Diego, at the southern end of the state, is farther east than Reno, Nevada. This is the face of the present day California. Although modern names have been applied to the towns, rivers and regions of what was formerly aboriginal territory, the following paragraphs clearly emphasize the richness and variety of the land and why it was held in such esteem by the Indians of California.

Over millions of years, subterranean plates, volcanoes, glaciers, wind, and water have shaped the countryside that helped form such features as the great Valley, perhaps California's main topographic element. The Siskiyou Mountains are now a northern barrier that serves as a border between the Golden State and Oregon in an area where timber abounds, particularly in the northwest. Lava flows provide a surreal landscape in the northeast. Farther south, the Tehachapis, the Sierra, the San Bernadinos, and other ranges divide 'the so-called Valley of Southern California, a broad strip of broken country near the coast, from arid wastes of the Mojave and Colorado Deserts in the hinterland'.[1]

The Northern Rivers, the American, Feather, Indian, Pit, Sacramento, and Yuba, owe much to Mount Shasta's annual melting snows for replenishment of their southerly flow. The San Joaquin, which shares the name of the valley it waters, runs northward from its source in the mountains of present-day Fresno County, being joined by the Calaveras, Consumnes, Fresno, Kings, Mokelumne, Stanislaus, and Toulomne Rivers, as well as by a considerable number of other smaller streams.

The Klamath, Scott, and Trinity drain the seaward slopes of the Coast Range with the Eel, Mad, and Russian Rivers carrying water north of San Francisco Bay, the marvelous 'harbor of harbors' so cherished by Spain. To this port's south run the Salinas, Santa Clara, Santa Maria, and Santa Inez Rivers. Proceeding still southward, the Los Angeles, San Diego, San Gabriel, San Luis Rey, Santa Ana, Santa Margarita, and Ventura Rivers slow to a trickle much of the year or become dry beds until spring floods bring them back to life.

These various natural elements combine to form a half dozen life zones: Arctic, Canadian, Hudsonian, Transition, Upper Sonoran, and Lower Sonoran. The first areas exist, 'in the higher elevations of the Siskiyous, the Trinity Mountains, the Sierra, the San Bernardino and the San Jacinto ranges'. Next, the Santa Cruz Mountains, along with the upper portions of the Santa Lucias combine with 'all of the coast country north of San Francisco, the heavily watered northeastern counties and a long belt, between 2,500 and 5,000 feet high in the Sierra' to form the Transition zone. In turn, the foothills of the Sierras lie within the Upper Sonoran which also contain 'the lava plateaus of Modoc and Lassen Counties, the western slopes of the Sacramento Valley, the inner chains of the Coast Range and Valleys from Medocino County to San Francisco Bay, and all of the coastal region south of San Francisco' with the exception of those segments noted as part of the Transition zone. Finally, the Lower Sonoran consists of most of the Great Valley between Bakersfield and Red Bluff, 'all of the great arid desert regions southeast of the Sierra to the Nevada and Arizona lines, and several long narrow strips extending from the Salinas Valley south'.[2]

Each of the six environments support divergent flora and fauna. The high peaks of the Arctic-Alpine are treeless, but alpine buttercup, alpine shootingstar, blue and fragrant polemonium, Sierra primrose, and steershead can be found at these lofty elevations. The Sierra rosy finch makes its regular home here. Hummingbirds and the gray and white Clark nutcrackers

This map shows approximate territories of tribes and language groups in about 1800. After that, all tribes lost territory and some disappeared.

Key to tribes:

1 Tolowa	**28** Maidu
2 Karok	**29** Yana
3 Yurok	**30** Konkow
4 Shasta	**31** Nisenan
5 Hupa	**32** Patwin
6 Chilula	**33** Lake Miwok
7 Whilkut	**34** Wappo
8 Wiyot	**35** Coast Miwok
9 Chimariko	**36** Miwok
10 Wintu	**37** Northern Valley Yokuts
11 Mattole	**38** Costanoan
12 Nongatl	**39** Esselen
13 Sinkyone	**40** Monache
14 Lassik	**41** Foothill Yokuts
15 Wailaki	**42** Southern Valley Yokuts
16 Cahto	**43** Tubatulabal
17 Yuki	**44** Salinan
18 Northern Pomo	**45** Chumash
19 Northeastern Pomo	**46** Kitanemuk
20 Eastern Pomo	**47** Tataviam
21 Southeastern Pomo	**48** Serrano
22 Central Pomo	**49** Gabrielino
23 Southern Pomo	**50** Luiseño
24 Kashaya	**51** Cahuilla
25 Nomlaki	**52** Cupeño
26 Achumawi	**53** Dieguño
27 Atsugewi	

from chickadees to mountain quail. Moreover, coyote, muledeer, hawks, and some sparrows inhabit the Canadian zone, as well as are distributed throughout some other zones.

The Upper Sonoran zone encompasses a great chaparral belt that was once the home of the California grizzly and the nearly extinct California condor. Blue and scrub oaks, California buckeyes, digger pines, ceanothus, and species of manzanita and yucca grow along with several other shrubs. Anna hummingbird, bell sparrow, bush tit, California and stellar jay, California thrasher, dusky poorwill, house finch, mourning dove, valley quail, and yellow-billed magpie typify the feathered denizens of the zone. Land animals include antelope, brown-footed woodrat, brush rabbit, as well as the ring-tailed cat.

The Lower Sonoran zone offers its specialties, too. The Colorado Desert has bigelovia, a litany of cacti, California fan palm, echinocatus, mesquite, palo verde, and screwbean. In the Mojave Desert grow other specimens with the Joshua tree (Yucca arborenscens) standing out among the plant life. Fremont cottonwoods and valley oaks flourish in still different parts of the Lower Sonoran.

The zone has a fair share of nocturnal animals as well. All sorts of rodents, kit fox, chipmunk, opossum, jack rabbit, and, in times past, tule elk, share the land with desert tortoise, lizards, and snakes. In the air, blue grosbeak, cactus wren, hooded orioles, mockingbirds, phainopeplas, and Texas nighthawks are plentiful, while the long-legged roadrunner remains earthbound, depending as it does on speed of foot rather than the ability to fly as the key to survival.

With both an array of potential food sources and also numerous climatic advantages, California proved an attractive magnet for early hunter-gatherer peoples. While no one knows for certain when *homo sapiens* first trod on California soil, some evidence points to the arrival of humans over 20,000 years before the present.[3] Despite the lack of definitive evidence as to origins, with the passage of the ages, it is certain that distinct groups emerged with highly developed territorial and cultural traits. Of these, 'about one half of California was held by Penutian-speaking people', a collection of 'small families which linguists believe were related because their languages employ some of the same grammatical tricks'.[4] In general terms, the diverse 'tribes' followed a lifestyle which took on a more uniform pattern than usually evidenced elsewhere among North American Indians. One of the chief similarities revolved around the consumption of acorn-based foodstuffs. Over the centuries, the first people to live in California unlocked the secret of turning the bitter, tannic acid laden product of the oak into 'a rich, nutritional food' which, as a soup, porridge, or kind of bread, provided the mainstay of their diet.[5]

Two basic means allowed for this process to be accomplished. Either individuals pulverized and leached the nuts in sand or a basket or they could immerse or bury acorns in water or mud, and thereby not have to crush the nuts. Since the earth provided this source free for the taking, along with other plants and animals for sustenance, agriculture really did not evolve in early California.

pass through as do the Sierra cony and white-tailed jack rabbit. Bighorn sheep also once ranged in this land.

At slightly lower reaches, the Hudsonian zone shares lodgepole pine as a mainstay of ground cover with the Canadian zone. White bark, foxtail, and silver pines grow higher up, mingling with mountain hemlock. Fowl and mammals, most importantly the alpine chipmunk, California pine grosbeak, mountain bluebird, Sierra cony, Sierra least weasel, Sierra marmot, white-crowned sparrow, and wolverine are found in the Hudsonian zone.

Besides lodgepole pine, the Canadian zone boasts yellow pine, Jeffrey pine, mountain pine, and red fir. Cancerroot, ceanothus, several species of corallorrhiza, dwarf manzanita, herbaceous vegetation, Sierra puffball, and snowplant carpet the floor. Blue-fronted jay, evening grosbeak, Sierra grouse, Sierra hermit thrush, Sierra junco, Townsend solitaire, water ouzel, and western chipping sparrow soar above. Various types of chipmunk share the zone with

Above: A Karok, one of the most northerly tribes of California, in war costume of rod armor and helmet, with an animal-skin quiver under his arm. Photographed probably by John Daggett c.1898.

mountain weasel, golden-mantle ground squirrel, Sierra chickaree, snowshoe rabbit, and yellow-haired porcupine.

In the Transition zone, however, lie most of California's great forests, the most impressive of which, the redwoods, often intermingle with broad-leafed maple, California laurel, Douglas fir, madrona, and tanbark oak. Other vegetation runs the gamut with several types of trees and many eatable plants being found to support the animal life and what was quite a complex food chain.

Black bear, bobcat, California ring-tailed cat, Columbian black-tailed deer, cougar, elk, fox, marten, mink weasel, mountain beaver, Pacific coon, and packrat once roamed in numbers. Many reptiles and amphibians find the range a suitable habitat, as do an assortment of birds

Moreover the people varied their diets by hunting, gathering, and fishing. They enjoyed resources which 'were bountiful in their variety rather than in their overwhelming abundance along special lines'. Thus, the fare contained venison, rabbit, gopher, lizard, snakes (including rattlers), ducks, and small birds, depending on local availability. These might be obtained by snares, throw stones, and such implements as could be fashioned from stone and other natural materials. Crayfish, molluscs, turtles, and an assortment of creatures from water and marsh might be procured in several ways with harpoons, nets, digging tools, and poison numbing among the means developed to take advantage of this type of bounty. Caterpillars, grasshoppers, maggots, and snails added to the possibilities for protein.

Despite the broad ranging approach to food, not everything was considered fit for meals, either because of religious beliefs or for practical reasons. For example, most northern groups would not eat dog, except the Yokuts, whose southern branch also 'relished the skunk, which when smoked to death in its hole was without offensive odor'. Conversely, these same connoisseurs of pole cats 'eschewed all reptiles, pronouncing them unclean'. Additionally, certain northern tribes rejected frogs, gopher snakes, and water snakes. Usually, the majority of groups refrained from grizzly bear

Below: *Indian men from several northern California groups in treaty at Round Valley, c.1858. The fourth white man from the left is probably Simmon P. Storms, first Indian agent of the Nome Cult Farm.*

Above: *An 1806 depiction by Georg von Langsdorf of the Spanish garrisoned Presidio of San Francisco. In the foreground is a native tule balsa, propelled by a pair of 'Ohlone' men.*

tication and diversity present among those people who made them. Examples from one of the best known practitioners of the art, the Pomo, who lived in a rather compact unit in the Russian River valley, underscore some of the points about the importance of basketry to California's past.[9] The Pomo produced baskets which gained 'the name, among Americans, of being the finest in California; according to many, in the world'.[10] Relying upon ten or twelve types of material, with five being commonly employed, the baskets often took on an intricate nature.[11] Willow normally served as the warp for both twined and coiled examples. For the woof, *Carex* (sedge root), *Cercis* (redbud bark), *Scripus* (bulrush root), and digger pine root were used, with the first named medium being the most important basic ingredient. In turn, red patterns relied upon the redbud (used most commonly with twined leaves). Dyed bulrush gave black patterns, usually for coil work. Finally, digger pine fibers, in the main, were the woof for course twined baskets. Thus, by 'convention and habit ... practically all the basketry of the Pomo' consisted of these five materials.[12]

The Pomo, unlike most other California bas-

Above; *Little Ike, a Karok man, fishing for salmon with a plunge net from a fishing platform among the rocks at pame·kyá·ra·m on the Klamath River. Photographed before 1897.*

Right: *A Talowa woman shown wearing a fine basketry hat and clamshell bead necklaces and shell-decorated skirt. This photograph was taken by Edward Curtis (1868-1952) in the early 1920s.*

and coyote, mainly because these animals figured into many spiritual tenants. Sometimes brown bear was avoided, nor did 'birds of prey and carrion from the eagle down to the crow ...' constitute common dishes.[6]

Thriving on the resources they found, California's Indian population rose, with estimates ranging from 133,500 to 350,000 inhabitants during the golden age prior to the arrival of the Spanish and others. Given even the higher figure, the average density represented only three people per square mile for those areas not considered an uninhabitable desert. These numbers would fall dramatically in the wake of later events so that 'the low point was reached between 1880 and 1900 with a recorded number of no more than 20,000 or perhaps 25,000 souls'.[7]

In their heyday though, these culturally and linguistically rich groups came into contact with each other in several ways. A major means of association resulted through the trade which occurred on an inter- and intra-tribal basis. Routes and complex exchange systems grew up where a wide assortment of commodities, tools, food, clothing, pottery, slaves, sea shells, and basketry changed hands between and among players from as far away as western Canada and the mainland of Mexico.[8]

Baskets came to be particularly prized and remain an important part of continuity between the past and the present. Serviceable, aesthetically pleasing pieces, the baskets of California's first residents served utilitarian purposes and also demonstrated the extraordinary artistic talents of their makers. These objects likewise bespoke of the level of sophis-

Hupa

The Hupa lived along the Trinity River in NW California, where they subsisted mainly on salmon and acorns. The men were wood workers, the women expert basket weavers. They shared with the neighboring Yurok and Karok the annual White Deerskin and Jumping dances, world-renewal and wealth display ceremonies each lasting ten days, and the Brush Dance to cure sick children. Hupa doctors were nearly all women. Dates of collecting are given below.

1 Drum-rattle for gambling songs. 1875.
2 Woman's hair ornaments. 1885.
3 Man's necklace, c.1928.
4 Young man's dance hat. Yurok (but collected from the Hupa). 1885.
5 Eagle feathers worn in White Deerskin and Brush dances. 1928.
6 Eagle feathers, as No. 5.
7 Headband of mink skin. 1944.
8 Headdress of buckskin and wolfskin. 1944.
9 Ornament for mouth of stuffed white deerskin for dance. 1929.
10 Eagle feather head ornament, used for White Deerskin and Brush dances.

11 Rattle belt for dance. Yurok (but collected from the Hupa). 1885.
12 Tobacco basket. 1899.
13 Pipe. 1885.
14 War bow. 1885.
15 Arrows. 1885.
16 Quiver. 1885.
17 Man's wand for Jumping Dance. Yurok (but collected from the Hupa). 1885.
1928.

18 Stone cooking vessel. 1885.
19 Stone sledge used for driving fish dam stakes. 1929.
20 Netting shuttle. 1889.
21 Nettle shuttle. 1875.
22 Stone pounder. 1928.
23 Woman's shell spoon. 1899.
24 Man's wooden spoon. 1908.
25-28 Men's elkhorn

134

spoons. 1875-99.
29 Shell beads for dance. 1928.
30 Elkhorn purse for dentalium money. 1890.
31 Dentalium money. 1875.
32 Elkhorn purse. 1883.
33 Spoon or trinket basket. 1899
34 Basket for boiling acorn mush. 1885.
35 Storage basket. 1890.

36 Acorn bread tray. 1899.
37 Salmon or meat tray. 1899.
38 Basket for acorn mush. 1899
39 Basket tray. 1899.
40 Basketry acorn flour scoop. 1899.
41 Man's apron for White Deerskin Dance, of civet skins. 1890.
42 Woman's dance skirt. 1885.
43 Woman's necklace. 1885.

44 Woman's dance apron. 1885.
45 Doctor's wand for Jumping Dance and curing. 1928.
46 Woman's hair ornaments. 1885.
47 Widow's basketry cap. 1928.
48 Woman's basketry cap. 1885.
49 Woman's necklace. 1885.
50 Woman's hair ornaments. 1885.
51 Doctor's headdress, used in curing. Very old in 1944.

ket weavers who ordinarily worked in one or two techniques, employed upwards of a half dozen approaches. Not only did the Pomo use twining, the norm for the most northern reaches and for the Achomawi, Atsugewi, Modoc, Northern Wintu, and Shasta, but also they were adept at coiling, which generally dominated the remainder of the state. It seems the Pomo alternated between the two forms with equal ease and regularity.

When turning out coil pieces, the Pomo utilized both single rod and triple rod foundations. In the twined versions they perfected five weaves: plain, diagonal, lattice, three-strand twining, and three-strand braiding, beside incorporating a wealth of decoration and design elements.

While examples of Pomo basketry demonstrate some of the spectrum of this art so often associated with California's indigenous people, other indications of the cultural medley once represented by the state's Native American population might best be appreciated through a brief survey of several of the major groups who once carried out an array of lifestyles there. (For locations of the various groups mentioned in this survery see the accompanying map to this chapter on p.130.)

Starting to the far northwest, the Tolowa people speak an Athapascan dialect from whence their name came (a designation derived from the neighboring Yurok). Living in a dozen and a half or so towns, this group sometimes feuded among themselves but a

Above: *A Karok basketmaker, 1896. Of note, to her right, is a space-twined pack basket used for packing acorns, fish etc, and on her lap and beside her two partially twined baskets.*

Below: *A Hupa village on the Trinity River in 1898 or before. In the foreground are two houses of the traditional type, built of cedar planks, with three-pitch roofs covered with overlapping boards.*

Above: *Hupa participants in the Jumping Dance at the Yurok town of Pekwon, Klamath River, 1893. The men wear traditional buckskin headbands covered with woodpecker scalps, bordered with white deer belly fur.*

Below: *Hupa White Deerskin dance, 1891, a part of one of the two great World Renewal ceremonies performed by the Hupa, Yurok, and Karok-speaking peoples in northwestern California.*

number of villages might unite if an expedition was mounted against the nearby Yurok or Karok. Such exchanges may have been infrequent, however, since the Tolowa seemed to be middlemen in the trade of dentalium shells from Vancouver Island, a highly regarded commodity which served as currency in the region. Evidently the Yurok looked upon the Tolowa as being quite wealthy.

Beside being purveyors of dentalium, the Tolowa became skilled boatsman, constructing canoes from redwood trees. The made ropes and cords from a species of the iris, practiced twined basket-making techniques, and fabricated rattles from deer hooves for accompaniment to religious ceremonies, such as the girl's adolescence ceremony and dance. Other rituals included war dances, doctor-making dances, the Deerskin dance, and the so-called 'salmon dance' which was somewhat akin to a new year celebration which entailed 'the catching and eating of the first salmon of the season; after which fishing was open to all'[13] Much later, in the last decades of the nineteenth century, they also added the Ghost Dance to their beliefs.

The Yurok and Karok flanked the Tolowa on the south and southeast respectively. The former group resided on the lower Klamath River and shared many traits in common with those around them as well as the inhabitants of the Pacific Northwest to Alaska. Living in more than fifty autonomous hamlets, the Yurok pursued fishing on the river and ocean along with hunting and gathering. They too made redwood canoes which could be bought for a pair of twelve-dentalium shell strings or ten large or sixty small woodpecker scalps. As can be deduced from this price structure, the Yurok had a sophisticated monetary system and, according to one source, they held wealth in high esteem. There was:

'Blood money, bride purchase, compensation to the year's mourners before a dance can be held ... Every injury, each privilege or wrong or trespass, is calculated and compensated. Without exactly adjusted payment, cessation of a feud is impossible except through utter extirpation of one party, marriage is not marriage but a public disgrace for generations, the ceremony necessary to the preservation of the order of the world is not held. The consequence is that the Yurok concerns his life above all else with property. When he has leisure, he thinks of money; if in need, he calls upon it'.[14]

Other standard costs provide an idea about relative value in the society. An eagle skin brought only one small shell while the 'dowry' for a bride could be as high as ten strands of shells of various lengths. This indicated the status of marriage since a fishing spot fetched only one to three strings, a house five, and a tract of land bearing acorns from one to five strings of shells. The last mentioned item, an acorn plot, indicates a concept of private land ownership. Indeed, in this individualistic culture, 'up to a mile or more from the river, all land of any value was privately owned; back of this, there were no claims, nor was their much hunting'.[15]

A number of other traits separated the Yurok from many other cultures. They observed inheritance practices, passing on much of their holdings to kinsmen. If an individual required ferrying across the water, the service customarily was granted free of charge. A shaman received considerable fees for services and those who entered the field might expect to make a considerable living. Class-consciousness existed to the degree that the Yurok made a definite distinction between rich and poor in their dealings.

Early Yurok clothing resembled that found throughout most of California. Young men regularly wore a folded deerskin wrapped around the waist while older men might go naked in warmer seasons. A buckskin fringed front piece and 'a broader apron or skirt ... brought around to meet the front piece' served as the standard garb for women. Women also wore basket caps as the rule. When weather dictated additional covering, a cape or blanket of two sewn-together deer hides provided protection. Wealthier women sported extensive ornamentation. For footgear, a plain one-piece, front-seamed moccasin sufficed, being used most commonly by women when traveling, obtaining firewood, or for dress occasions.[16]

This same physical description might be applied to the Karok, whose name comes from the adverb *karuk*, meaning 'upstream', their location in relationship to the Yurok. While outwardly very similar, the two groups differed in one major respect, their languages. The

Above: *Keintpoos, better known as Captain Jack, who served as a major leader among the Modoc in the siege of the Lava Beds, 1873. Taken by the U.S. Army, Jack was sentenced to death.*

Below: *Following the adage 'it takes diamond dust to polish a diamond', the U.S. Army employed Indian scouts (above) from the Warm Springs reservation to track down and pursue the Modoc.*

Yurok spoke an Algonquian tongue and the Karok belonged to the Hokan linguistic family.

Moreover, they could be distinguished from the culture found downstream in a number of other ways. For example, in the dance for adolescent girls, the men played a more prominent role than the males among the Yurok. Then, too, the Karok's 'world making' ceremonies were more defined. Finally, they prided themselves on the ability of their shaman, whom they claimed had no equal save among the Shasta and a few other groups located further over to the east.

This respect for the Shasta may have stemmed from a regular contact between the two peoples. Indeed, the nearby Shasta traded deerskins, obsidian, and sugar-pine nuts to the Karok for baskets, canoes, dentalia, seaweed, and tan-oak acorns.

Not all intercourse with outsiders stemmed from peaceful exchanges. The Karok raided periodically, the women sometimes accompanying the men, possibly to cook and carry provisions. The warriors occasionally donned a hide helmet or headband, along with armor of rods or elk skin as they set out to do battle.

It seems that the Shasta did not turn their aggressions toward the northeast where the Modoc made their home, ranging across the present-day Oregon and California state lines. Had the Karok attempted this, they would have met stiff resistance since 'the Modoc ... probably possessed more tribal solidarity than the great majority of California Indians ...'[17] Although the Modoc have been included in the map on page 102 as a Plateau tribe, it is suggested here that the boundary between the

Above: *Joseppa Beatty, noted Central Pomo-speaking basket maker, with her husband and son on the Yokayo Rancheria, 1892. She works on a one-rod coiled basket, the rod seen projecting to her left.*

Below: *McCloud River Wintu men and boys, c.1872, at Colchoolooloo's Rancheria. The two men standing wear traditional netted down caps and demonstrate arrow release.*

Plateau and California was not, in the mid-nineteenth century, as fixed as this. As with many hunter-gatherers, their boundaries were not restricted. For this reason, and because of the importance of the events surrounding the resistance of Captain Jack and the Modoc Indians, the Modoc and their final flourish are considered in greater depth in this chapter.

For all this, the Modoc suffered greatly at the hands of white encroachment. The steady increase in miners and settlers to their home eventually led to relocation on an Oregon reservation. In the mid-1860s, they began their short-lived, turbulent stay with the Klamath who spoke a Lutuami-based language, as did the Modoc. Friction increased between the two occupants of the reserve. The situation deteriorated even more with the killing of a Klamath shaman by one of the Modoc who would play a major part in subsequent events. Soon thereafter, some of the Modoc quit the confines of Oregon to head back to their former Lost River region in California under such leaders as John Schonchin and another key player variously known as Keintpoos, Kintpuash, or, more commonly, Captain Jack. It was Jack who had shot the Klamath healer thereby bringing about charges of murder. Under the circumstances, he saw the wisdom of returning to the traditional Modoc territory. This move, however, caused yet more conflict since 'just north of Tule Lake, white settlers had already moved in with their herds and had erected cabins'.[18]

Some four years passed with an uneasy attitude prevailing on both sides. Kintpuash, whose father had been killed by whites under Ben Wright, in 1852, could not be persuaded to rejoin the Klamath. Failing to dislodge Jack and his compatriots, local citizens turned to the U.S. army for assistance.

The local senior military officer in the area, Major John Green, attempted to speak to Captain Jack in September 1872 but to no avail. Within weeks, Green's superior, Brigadier General E. R. S. Canby decided to press the issue. He sent orders for the arrest of Captain

Wintu

The Wintu were hill people whose economy was based on the use of salmon, deer, and acorns. Objects shown are from an excellent collection made in 1872–5 by Livingston Stone while in charge of the U.S. salmon-hatching establishment on the McCloud River. At this time the Indians here were relatively undisturbed, although other Wintu had suffered greatly, from a malaria epidemic in the 1830s, from gold miners' pollution of their streams, from the intro-duction of cattle ranching, and from massacres and forced relocation to reservations. After the railroad arrived in 1875, the McCloud R. Wintu and others underwent rapid culture change with the increase in white settlement and with the introduction of several new Indian reli-gions. Stone got along well with the Wintu, and this collection is perhaps a more important re-sult of his work than was his failed attempt to use California salmon spawn for restocking sal-mon streams on the Atlantic coast. No other collection so well documents aboriginal Wintu arts and technology.

1 Twined storage basket.
2 Twined cooking basket, with lizard and rib design.
3 Twined cooking basket.
4 Twined storage basket.
5 Twined basket, probably a woman's hat.
6 Woman's hat, twined basketry, weft of natural and alder-dyed grass and fern stems.
7 Twined basket, probably a woman's hat.
8 Front part of woman's skirt, buckskin and twine strings, wrapped with vegetable fiber, pendants of pinenut seeds, tin and buttons.
9 Belt of human hair, worn by girl at puberty ceremony (a major ritual of the Wintu).
10 Fur head ornament for dances.
11 Fur strip used to tie hair on top of head.
12 Front part of skirt, type worn by women before the 1870s, of pinenut seed shells

threaded on buckskin strings.

13 Openwork twined baskets containing manzanita berries for flour, wrapped in grass.

14 Dance skirt of wild swan feathers with small squares of flicker quills.

15 Woven beadwork pouch for carrying shot or wild tobacco.

16 Feather head ornament, for dances.

17 Head ornament for dances

with small squares of flicker quills.

18 Head ornament for dances, feathers of great western horned owl and white-headed woodpecker.

19 Dance head ornament, a red wool knitted cap with feathers (including woodpecker scalp) and two rattlesnake rattles.

20 Twined basket.

21 Sinew-backed yew bow, buckskin wrap at grip, twisted sinew bowstring.

22 Arrows with glass and

obsidian points.

23 Carved wooden pipe for smoking wild tobacco.

24 Sling used for killing small game; buckskin pouch, twisted sinew cords.

25 Twined basket.

26 Drinking cup.

27 Twined basket.

28 Twined serving basket.

29 Shaman's basket.

30 Twined serving basket.

31 Twined serving basket.

32 Birdbone whistle used for dances.

Jack and two other important headmen, Black Jim and Scarface Charley. Miscalculating the effect of this directive, a detail set out in response to Canby's command. On the morning of 29 November 1872 Captain James Jackson, Lieutenant Frazier A. Boutelle, and Assistant Surgeon Henry McElderry rode with some three dozen or so enlisted men from Company B of the First U.S. Cavalry into the Modoc camp. Jack, asleep in camp along with most of the other villagers, awoke to find armed men in their presence. The would-be captors' arrival led to bloodshed. An exchange of fire left casualties on both sides. The Modoc fled. A war had begun.

In the confusion, Jack escaped as did many others of the band. Splitting into at least two different parties, the Modoc ultimately regrouped in the region south of Tule Lake, which had been called by some 'hell with the fire burnt out'. Here, 'in this wild expanse of black lava, that nature had piled into a gigantic fortress', the Modoc made their stand. They knew every fissure, cavern, and passageway. Patches of grass subsisted their cattle. Sagebrush and greasewood yielded fuel. Water came from Tule Lake.'[19] The weeks which passed before the U.S. government's forces arrived on the scene allowed the Modoc to prepare for the siege which ensued. Scarface Charley particularly would distinguish himself once the whites

Below: *Cecilia Joaquin, a Central Pomo speaker from the Sanel community at Hopland demonstrating the use of the seed beater to collect seeds in a close-twined burden basket, in the early 1920s.*

Above: *Traditional site of Pomo fish camp, Clear Lake, c.1900. The permanent house frames were covered each year with fresh tules, sometimes replaced after white contact by large sheets of canvas, as here.*

arrived to do battle.

Regulars and volunteers surrounded their foe. After their first attack on 17 January 1873, the troops found the Modoc to be tenacious freedom fighters. The opening engagement ended in a clear victory for the Lava Beds' defenders, despite the fact that they were outnumbered by an estimated seven to one. In defeat, the whites broke off to tend to their wounded and see to their dead.

Time passed. The Modoc held their own against cavalry, infantry, artillery, and militiamen from Oregon and California. New tactics seemed in order. Kaitchkona (also known as Toby Riddle), Captain Jack's cousin, and a few other courageous individuals visited the entrenched Modoc in an effort to reach some sort of settlement. In addition, a peace commission dispatched from Washington, D.C., arrived with hopes of bringing an end to hostilities. For six weeks they tried to entice Jack and his people to the bargaining table but their efforts produced no results. By this time, Canby had come from his headquarters in Salem, Oregon, to assume field command. He sought to end the whole affair, moving his units closer to the Modoc stronghold. Captain Jack finally met with the general. This exchange allowed the Modoc to state their case. They wanted the troops to withdraw; they requested their own reservation on the Lost River; and they sought protection 'from charges of murdering a number of settlers'.[20]

Nothing came of this conference. Then, on 11 April 1873, Canby again went to speak with Captain Jack. On Good Friday, Canby and other fellow commissioners resumed negotiations. In the midst of the talks Captain Jack pulled out a concealed weapon and fired point blank into Canby's face. The wounded officer attempted to flee. Another Modoc fell on Canby and finished him with a knife. Two of Canby's party, the Re-

verend Eleazer Thomas and Oregon Super-intendent of Indian Affairs, A. B. Meacham, went down in the killing frenzy. When the slaughter stopped, Canby and Thomas were dead and Meacham sustained wounds, not the least of which was the loss of his scalp.

Up to that point, the Modoc had gained con-siderable sympathy for their cause, with the military being painted as incompetent aggres-sors. Now, public opinion turned. Canby's suc-cessor redoubled efforts to dislodge the enemy. After considerable bloodshed and suf-fering, on 1 June 1873 the ill-fated Modoc survi-vors capitulated. A trial followed with Captain Jack and three others being given the death sentence. The remaining 153 Modoc received a different fate, relocation to Quapaw Indian Agency in present-day Oklahoma.

While this clash of cultures was well known, the Modoc were not the only Native Americans to suffer at the hands of Europeans and Euro-Americans. From 1769, when the Spanish arrived to establish their first settlements in Alta California, a long, unfortunate decline in the Indian population and territory began. The first long-term contact started in the south with those groups living in the north being the last to face the consequences of meeting the new-comers.[21] They would not be exempt forever though, for as Captain E. D. Townsend, assis-tant adjutant general for the Pacific Division, confided in an 1852 entry to his diary:

'If the tale of these poor wretches inhabit-ing the more Northern parts [of Califor-nia], could be impartially related, it would be a picture of cruelty, injustice and hor-ror scarcely to be surpassed by that of the Peruvians in the time of Pizzaro. In their eager search for gold the whites have boldly penetrated and explored wilder-ness and mountains far beyond the reach of settlements. They have established themselves in many cases, in large com-munities so that Tribes of Indians were left between them and the settlements. Aggression would naturally be of fre-

Above: *Pomo fisherman in a tule boat on Clear Lake, space-twined collecting basket in the prow. Speakers of six distinct languages lived around this lake in over a dozen separate communities.*

Below: *Northeastern Pomo dancers at a Big Head dance (also called Bole-Maru or 1872 Ghost Dance), at Stony Creek, Colusa County (Big Head in the center, Charlie Watham on the left), in 1907.*

Pomoan

The Pomoan tribes are famous for fine basketry. Here is a selection from those collected by J.W. Hudson in the 1880s–90s to show the shapes, materials, techniques and designs associated with specific uses. Baskets were then beginning to be made for sale, as manufactured products replaced them in everyday Pomoan use. Below, tribe is given when known, with language: CP=Central Pomo; EP=Eastern P; NP=Northern P.; SP=Southern P.

1 Meal storage bowl, plain twined basketry. Tsetum, NP.
2 Burden basket. Yokiah, CP.
3 Flail for beating seeds off plant into burden basket; of willow shoots.
4 Jar of coiled basketry. Póma, NP.
5 Feast cup. Limma, CP.
6 Fishworm pan, spaced lattice twined willow shoots; bottom mended.
7 Feast tureen. Cokowa, CP.
8 Dowry basket, boat-

shaped coiled, sedge and redbud on 1-rod foundation, decorated with quail feathers and beads. Póma, NP.
9 Feast dish, coiled, sedge and bulrush on 3-rod willow foundation, decorated with red woodpecker and quail feathers and clamshell beads. Yokaia, CP.
10 Jewel basket, decorated with clamshell beads, trade beads, and quail and woodpecker feathers.

11 Dish, coiled, sedge, bulrush and quail feathers. Yokiah, CP.
12 Jewel basket, 3-rod coiled, sedge, bulrush, quail and woodpecker head feathers, beads. Ano, NP.
13 Set of net-weaving tools, of mountain mahogany and manzanita wood.
14 Squirrel skin pouch for pipe and tobacco.
15 Arrows.
16 Sinew-backed cedar bow.
17 Sinew-backed ash bow.
18 Meal storage bowl,

diagonally twined sedge and redbud over willow shoots, decorated with quail feathers. Póma, NP.
19 Jewel basket, 3-rod coiled, sedge, covered with woodpecker, meadowlark, and bluejay feathers and shell beads. Cikom, EP.
20 Marriage token. Yokiah, NP.
21 Condiment dish, perhaps by Mary Benson. Límma, CP.
22 Ornamented cup, 1-rod coiled, sedge, bulrush,

quail and woodpecker feathers, beads. Amo, NP.

23 Jewel basket, 3-rod coiled, sedge, bulrush, quail feathers, beads. Póma, NP.

24 Necklace of clamshell and magnesite beads.

25 Man's dance plume, worn on crown of head, of tail-feathers of Lewis woodpecker.

26 Man's dance forehead band, of flicker tail feathers.

27 Woman's dance forehead band, of weasel skin with projecting pendants of beads and flicker feathers.

28 Woman's dance plume, worn on crown of head, of turkey tail feathers.

29 Jar, 1-rod coiled, sedge redbud. Póma, NP.

30 Small (child's?) boat basket, 1-rod coiled, sedge, redbud. Yokiah CP.

31 Meal cup, 1-rod coiled, sedge, bulrush. Yokiah, CP.

32 Dowry basket, exchanged with food at marriage.

Yokiah, CP.

33 Ornamented dish, 1-rod coiled, sedge, bulrush, beads. Codokai, NP.

34 Snail jar, plain twined, sedge, bulrush, redbud. Buldam, NP.

35 Basket hopper for mortar, plain twined, willow root, redbud. Póma, NP.

36 Basket jar, similar to type presented to bereaved at funeral; 3-rod coiled, sedge, bulrush, trade beads, shell beads. Yokiah, CP.

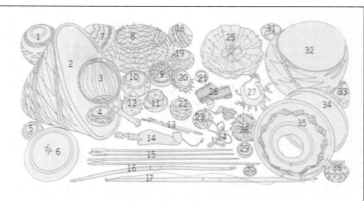

Coast Miwok Chief's Wife, 1833

Beside Bodega Bay a high-status woman offers guests acorn mush in a feast basket decorated with olivella shell beads and red head-feathers from scores of woodpeckers. Her downy feather robe, worn only by prominent women, is woven of ropes made by wrapping feathers around a doubled cord. Each robe required specific feathers from hundreds of birds (Canada and snow geese, mallards). The woman's ear ornaments have abalone shell pendants on strings of clamshell beads wrapped at the top with a pair of meadowlark scalps. She wears necklaces of clamshell and olivella beads, and a double apron of shredded tules. Two men paddle ashore in a tule balsa boat. Robe, basket, and ear ornaments are all examples collected by Gov. Gen. von Wrangell of the Russian American Fur Company in 1833.

quent occurrence on one side or the other, and the whites found it convenient to seize upon Indian lands, or to move them away for any cause, it was an easy matter to raise a quarrel in which the natives were made to appear in the wrong, and then an expedition would be fitted out against them which would butcher sometimes, thirty, fifty or a hundred men, women and children.'[22]

In these few terse sentences, Townsend summarized the fate of not only many California Indians but also that of numerous native peoples all over North America.

Before this tide swept away the old ways, however, the diversity of California's native cultures flourished. The northern peoples went about their daily lives. There were the Achumawi, Atsugawi, Chimariko, Pomo (the main bands of which were the Northwestern, Central, Southern, Southeastern, and Eastern bands), and Yana, who all shared Hokan as the base for their dialects, as did the Shasta, whereas the Hupa, Cahto, Lassik, Mattole, Nongatl, Sinkyone, Wailaki, and Whilkut had Athapascan as a base, just as was the case with the Tolowa. Another pair of people communicated in Yukian, the Yuki and Wappo, with a third practitioner of the language being a possible offshoot of the Wappo who were surrounded in a small enclave by the more numerous Eastern and Southeastern Pomo.

The remainder of the northern groups spoke in a root of Penutian. The Konkow, Lake Miwok, Maidu, Miwok, Nisenan, Nomlaki, Northern Valley and Southern Valley Yokuts, Patwin, and Wintu fell into this category, as did the Coast Miwok and Costanoan.[23] These last two peoples might be looked at in more detail to obtain a better sense of several representative traits found among many of the other inhabitants of this part of the state, along with some of the unique characteristics which set them off from others who once lived in California.

To begin with, the Coast Miwok and Costanoan territories surrounded San Francisco Bay, the former being found on the north and the latter to the south and east, and occasionally in Marin and the islands of the Bay. Besides similarities in language, they shared many attributes which provide a means for comparison and contrast.

Starting with the Costanoan, for whom considerable enthnographic information exists, some eight major subdivisions have been noted. Each of the groups had 'separate languages, as different from one another as Spanish and English'.[24] Evidently, they had no common name for themselves but 'the label Costanoan had its roots in Spanish history [the term being taken from *Costanos* or coast people] and has long since established itself as a recognized language family'.[25] More recently, 'Ohlone' has been applied to the Costanoan. Descendants of this stock tend to prefer the newer reference.

In those earlier times, when the people had

no commonly accepted single name, outer appearances nonetheless reflected their ties. Men and boys commonly went about naked while a grass or tule apron, which covered the front and back below the waist, constituted the clothing for women. When the weather dictated, capes or cloaks fashioned from deer, rabbit, water-fowl feathers, or sea-mammal skins provided protection.[26] Even mud occasionally served 'as insulation from the cold – a custom not recorded among their neighbors, the Coast Miwoks'.[27]

The Costanoans regularly walked barefooted and without head coverings, except on ceremonial occasions. Painting and tattoos provided decoration and clan affiliation, the former practice being applied in patterns which made it appear as if the people wore striped tights. Pierced ears could be adorned with beads, feathers, flowers, or grass while pierced nasal septums might hold a small bone, although the custom was not universal and seemed only to apply to men. Both sexes often added necklaces of beads, feathers, and shells (abalone and olivella) to their wardrobe.

For shelter, poles bent into a conical shape

Right: A Nisenan *boy wearing flicker feather headband, large abalone shell gorget at his neck and a belt covered with abalone pendants and beads worn as a bandolier, all objects of wealth. Photographed possibly by A.W. Chase, prior to 1876.*

Maidu

These objects are a sample from a large early collection of traditional Maidu artifacts, which was assembled in 1899-1903 by Roland B. Dixon. Most of the types of objects shown here went out of use among the Maidu during the present century. This collection comes from three distinct groups or tribes, now called Maidu, Konkow and Nisenan, which were all known as Maidu in Dixon's time. In the following list the tribal origin is mentioned where it can be identified

1 Headband of flicker feathers, worn by male dancers attached across the forehead. Konkow.
2 Cloak of hawk feathers attached to a net foundation. Konkow.
3 Rattle made of moth cocoons with small pebbles inserted.
4 Pair of split-stick rattles used to accompany ceremonial dances during the winter.
5 End-blown flute of elder wood, with four fingering holes.
6 Feather plume stick of bird scalps and the tips of quail feathers attached to a stick. Konkow.
7 A pair of tremblers, worn stuck horizontally in a ceremonial headdress, one on each side of the head. Konkow.
8 A feather bunch, made of half feathers inserted into a coiled rope of feathers. Konkow.
9 Stone found in a deer, worn around the neck by a deer hunter as a charm.
10 Wooden pipe used for smoking native tobacco. Nisenan.
11 Stone pipe, drilled by tedious tapping with an antler pick.
12 Flaked obsidian knife, considered to be a valuable and powerful object, worn by a shaman around his neck and used in curing.
13 Bow used in hunting and warfare. Made of yew, with a layer of deer sinew glued to the back to add strength. Konkow.
14 Deer arrows, two with obsidian points. Konkow.
15 Squirrel arrows, with long foreshafts. Arrows were painted in patterns unique to each owner. Konkow.
16 Quiver made of a wildcat skin turned inside out. Konkow.
17 Pair of snowshoes, used in the mountains where the snow is deep.
18 Feather bunch, made like No. 8, worn by a dancer

inside a crown of feathered rope. Konkow.

19 Coiled basket, used for cooking acorn mush or soup. Nisenan.

20 Coiled basket tray used for holding food, as a receptacle for sifting acorn meal, and as a cover for large conical baskets. Nisenan.

21 Hairbrush made of pine needles.

22 Coiled basket with arrow-feather design, used for cooking. Nisenan.

23 Four bones used in the popular hand game. Two players each have a marked and an unmarked bone, and the opposing side guesses which hands hold which kind of bone.

24 Coiled basket dipper. Nisenan.

25 Indian-made reduced-size model of a fish trap.

26 Cap of netted cord, used mainly as a foundation to which were pinned feather elements of an elaborate ceremonial headdress.

Konkow.

27 Tumpline of twine, passed across the forehead or chest to support a burden basket. Konkow.

28 Cocoon rattle for dances, similar to No. 3. Nisenan.

29 A full-size model of the sort of figure used at the annual mourning ceremony held in the autumn for five consecutive years after the death of a prominent man. Konkow (or perhaps Nisenan).

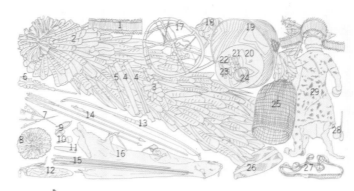

and covered in brush or tule sufficed. Occasionally, split redwood or redwood bark constituted the basic construction material. The building of balsas was another use for tule. Double-blade paddles propelled these light craft swiftly through the water.

These people produced other items as well. Baskets, frequently embellished with beads, feathers, and mother-of-pearl were typical. Wild onion or soaproot brushes, mollusc shell spoons, wooden stirring paddles, and various stone implements made many daily chores possible. Both self-bows and sinew-backed versions launched arrows with bone and stone tips.

As with other material necessities, the Costanoan depended on nearby natural resources for food. The ubiquitous acorn, available from several types of live oak, served as the basis for flour to make mush and a form of bread. Other seeds could be roasted and ground into meal too, with chia, digger pine, and holly-leaf cherry offering other forms of subsistence, and which, according to the early missionary, Francisco Palou, could be made into 'a sort of dumpling, ball-shaped and the size of an orange, which was very rich and savory, like toasted almonds'.[29] Strawberries, manzanita berries, and Christmas or the Toyon berry offered other treats in season. Roots, such as 'amhole' (soaproot or Chlorogalum), along with wild carrots, onions, and the herb chuchupate could be obtained too.

Besides vegetable matter, dog, grizzly bear, mole, mountain lion, mouse, rabbit, raccoon, skunk, and squirrel could be taken on land, with snares serving to catch the smaller creatures. The Costanoan likewise hunted deer and did so with deer's heads masks as disguises. They took seals too, although the means of hunting these mammals is uncertain. Quail, hawks, doves, ducks, and geese could be had with nets and traps, depending on the type of the bird. Nets also brought in sturgeon and salmon. Shellfish, most notably abalone, clams, and mussels, offered fine fare when gathered from December through April when they were safe to consume. Shark, swordfish, and other saltwater species may have been killed with spears or taken by hook and line. Occasionally, when a whale washed ashore, the Costanoans held a feast for this specially prized meat.

The Costanoan considered certain food taboo for new mothers who abstained from meat, fish, salt, and cold water for a number of days after giving birth. As young adolescents, females observed these same dietary restrictions. They held some sort of puberty rite as well, while males celebrated their entry into manhood by induction into what was known as a 'datura' society.

Once of age, a young man might take a wife. He and his relatives provided a gift to the bride's family. Then, the couple started their life together with no further formalities. When an infant arrived, the mother nursed for about twenty weeks, during which time the wife and husband refrained from sexual relations. Padre Palou commented on the fact that he saw many of the couples living 'in the most perfect union and peacefulness, loving their children dearly, as the children their parents'.[30] In the event two people chose to end a relationship, they simply separated. Evidently, the children remained

Above: *A Nisenan girl wearing an abalone shell necklace and headband and belt decorated with abalone shell pendants, objects of great wealth. Photographed possibly by A.W. Chase before 1876.*

with the wife. For a woman who lost a husband, mourning involved such practices as smearing the face with asphalt or black ashes and the cutting of hair. When laying the dead to rest, the women used a stone pestle to beat their breast and heads. The deceased's belongings would be destroyed or buried, while the body might be cremated but sometimes was buried, especially where a person was poor.

In the main, the Costanoan made contact

Below: *A Chumash woman wearing a back skirt of painted deerskin ornamented with shells and fringe fronted apron and prized columella bead necklace, picking prickly pears.*

with Europeans in the late eighteenth century and soon thereafter provided the population required for the establishment of several Spanish missions founded to the south of the Golden Gate.[31] Conversely, the Coast Miwok (sometimes spelled Mewuk and Meewoc) traced their association with foreign visitors to a much earlier time. Beginning in 1579, some of these inhabitants of land north of San Francisco set eyes upon Sir Francis Drake's crew who had come ashore to repair their ship. They made presents of arrow quivers, feathers, skins, and tobacco to the English and crowned Drake, treating him as a god. Descriptions by the British depicted them as tall, striking, and strong people who regularly traveled at the run. They parted their long hair in the middle or tied it behind in a bunch, the men wearing beards but scant clothing, other than a deerskin loin cloth on occasion.

The double apron favored by the Costanoan persisted among Coast Miwok women. Blankets or capes of rabbit fur and other small mammals resembled those of their southern and eastern neighbors. They likewise carried on the practices of tattooing, body painting, and adornment with feathers fashioned into belts and wristlets. Clamshell disk beads sometimes added to the display but usually this material served as currency.

For food, the Coast Miwok shared a similar diet as described for the Costanoan. They added greens such as miners lettuce, monkey flower, and watercress, and also may have consumed California buttercup and lupine either as greens or in seed form. Other seeds provided the basis for pinole or a mush. Wild cucumber or manroot and edible roots, most notably the bulbs of the wild hyacinth, found their way into the diet.

Coast Miwok diet taboos paralleled those of the Costanoan, but a new mother could have fresh fish and kelp. Sexual abstinence did not seem to last as long as the Costanoan, however, although fathers halted their fishing and hunting activities for a brief period and did not smoke during the same time of abstinence.

These people tended to be monogamous and expected fidelity. When a spouse died, her or his goods were to be buried with them, unless many children remained behind. In that case, shell money would be kept back for the use of the family. This was important since all transactions required payment.

While a monetary system existed, the concept of land ownership was foreign to the Coast Miwok. Nevertheless, they regarded food-producing sources and fishing rights as private property to be respected. So strong was this concept that the Coast Miwok marked their belongings with some sort of personal ownership symbol. They were far from totally materialistic people, however, and supported intricate religious beliefs centered around dance, doctoring, fasting, offerings, and prayer. Often they accompanied many of these ceremonies with music provided by bone whistles, bullroarers, drums, flutes, and rattles. When not engaged in religious practices or providing food, shelter, or clothing, these first residents of present-day Marin County played games of skill and chance primarily aimed at adults, while children played with dolls and other toys.[32]

Leisure time for some other groups who

Yokuts Shaman's Dance, 1880

A shaman of the Tachi tribe of Southern Valley Yokuts performs a secular Watiyod (spring dance), to entertain onlookers and collect money. Spectators put small amounts of money in the basket beside the singer, who shares it equally with the dancer. The singer marks time with two split-stick clappers of elderberry wood. The shaman wears a skirt of strings of milkweed fiber with owl down twisted in and flicker feathers on the ends, and a separate belt woven with beads. In his ears are falcon feathers; his necklace is of shells and an abalone pendant. His body is painted black and white, and he holds two feather bunches. The fine shaman's headdress rests on a base of owl feathers. The central feathers are magpie, wrapped with red wool and mink fur, with a band of crow wing feathers below.

dwelled along the coast cannot be ascertained with the same certainty. This particularly proved the case with the Esselen people who lived just south of the Costanoan. In fact, little information remains on these people who 'were one of the least populous groups in California, exceedingly restricted in territory, the first to become entirely extinct, and in consequence are now as good as unknown . . .'[33] Soon after contact with the Spanish, the people became part of the mission complex at San Carlos, eventually disappearing as a distinct, independent stock. What little data still remains about them stems from some knowledge about their language which was a generalized Hokan derivative.

So, too, did the Esselen's nearby Hokan-speaking relatives, the Salinan, suffer reductions in numbers after the arrival of the Spanish. In the period before contact with outside forces, the Salinan subsisted on birds, fish, reptiles, and most mammals in their area 'with the single exception of the skunk, and possibly dog and coyote . . .'[34] A half dozen types of acorn, grasses, clover, berries, sunflower, pine nuts, chia, buckeye, and wild oats could be had in their territory.

They took much from the Yokuts way of life in their beliefs, customs, and industries since they frequently traded and carried on other forms of interaction with these people. While friendly with the Yokuts the Salinan usually considered the Costanoans as enemies. Final-

Above: A Diegueño platform granary used for storing mesquite beans, near Santa Isabel, San Diego County. Photographed by Henry W. Henshaw in 1892 or 1893.

Below: Four Diegueño men wearing traditional feather headdresses and black and white body paint; the two women in front wear calico skirts and plaid shawls, and one also has face paint (1880s).

ly, despite a common boundary to their south with the Chumash, the Salinan remained rather aloof from this fellow Hokan language group.

The Chumash far outnumbered the Salinan and ranged over a larger area. They, nonetheless, succumbed to the mission process which at first they willingly accepted. In fact, the Chumash may well have been the first natives of California to be 'discovered' by explorers flying the ensign of Spain. In 1542-3 Juan Rodríquez Cabrillo met the Chumash, who inhabited not only the coast but also some offshore islands making them 'more nearly maritime in their habits than any other California groups'.[35] Their canoes, *tomol* or *tomolo*, consisted of planks bound together with cords and then caulked in asphalt found readily around the beaches. Light and swift, the crafts could be powered by as few as two or three paddlers but at times larger versions could be propelled by eight men and carry an additional half dozen passengers.

Besides these plank canoes, the Chumash made another important product, spear-throwers. They could be used on land or at sea, in the latter instance making it possible to harpoon seals and otters. Although these products set the Chumash apart to a certain extent from other California Indians, they did draw upon other native groups for inspiration: from the Yokuts and the Shoshoneans of the southern part of the state for their basket making.

The Shoshoneans formed a corridor on the eastern side of the state which ran almost the entire lower two-thirds of California. Another spur jutted out to the west below today's Santa Barbara and above San Diego. The various sub-elements consisted of such peoples as the Kitanemuk, Tubatulabal, Serrano, Gabrielino, Luiseño, Cahuilla, and Cupeño. Another common name assigned to eastern bands located toward Arizona and Nevada (and considered in the Plateau and Basin chapter) was Pah-Ute or Paiute. On the eve of the American Civil War, some of these people crossed swords with the U.S. army under Major James Henry Carleton. For some time, friction continued but eventually subsided as these Mojave Desert based residents dwindled in numbers.[36]

The 'cousins' of the Paiute, living in what is now the greater Los Angeles area and extending down toward San Diego (the Gabrielino and Luiseño) did not clash openly with military forces of Spain, Mexico, or the United States, 'although they had oft-times distinguished themselves in warfare with other tribes'.[37] One of the weapons the Gabrielino devised when they did engage in combat was the war club, 'which ranged from a heavy stick to a shorter form with a definitely marked cylindrical end . . .'[38] Additionally, they developed a curved stick, the *makana*, which they wielded with great effect against rabbits and birds as a sort of boomerang.

The Gabrielino were also innovative in that they had moveable stone mortars for the grinding of various plant foods rather than being restricted to bedrock mortar holes they could not be take along to enable relocation to another site when a village moved. The Luiseño also used moveable mortars alongside bedrock ones. The so-called portable variety actually constituted a large boulder of up to 200lb (90kg) which was hollowed out to form a recessed surface.

A small variation of the Luiseño mortar likewise found its way into the Diegueño society, one of the southernmost inhabitants of California, who, along with the Kamia, Yuma, Hal-chidhoma, and Mojave peoples living in an arc which ran to the east and then up the Colorado River, spoke Hokan dialects. Pottery makers as well as basket makers, the Diegueño employed other familiar aspects of California native culture, most significantly tule balsas which they paddled with double bladed oars. They made pipes of stone and pottery too, the former types presumably being set aside for religious purposes.[39] Gourd and turtle shell rattles provided accompaniment to ceremonies but the Diegueño had no drums, nor did any other southern California group for that matter. (see pp. 154–5 for examples of Diegueño artifacts.)

The Diegueño numbered among the first of California's Indians to be incorporated into the Spanish missions. While the impact of the experience took its toll, the intent was far more benign and humane that the conditions which resulted when the United States gained control of the region after concluding the Treaty of Guadalupe Hidalgo (1848), in the wake of the War with Mexico. The discovery of gold soon followed this transfer of title. With that event, pressure grew to remove the Native Americans to reservations, which:

'from their inception in 1853 until relatively recent times, is hardly a matter of pride. During the 1850s and 1860s, many of the officials placed in charge of Indian affairs were unfit for their posts. Too often, whenever a reservation contained valuable land, selfish whites were permitted to swoop in, and the Indians were driven on to rocky or sandy terrain'.[40]

In time, reactions against this deplorable situation led to reform movements. One champion of the California Indians' cause, Helen Hunt Jackson, wrote two books which attempted to bring the plight of these people to a sympathetic audience. Her publications, A *Century of Dishonor* and *Ramona*, released in 1881 and 1884 respectively, caused ripples to be felt in Washington, as did writings of Mary Hunter Austin and Marah Ellis Ryan, both of whom followed Helen Hunt Jackson's literary tradition most effectively.[41]

Redress came slowly. The Dawes Act of 1887 attempted to reverse the disintegration which escalated in the nineteenth century. Reduced to less than six dozen reservations, with as few as seventy people living on some in the 1960s, the battle to regain lost land went to the courts and Congress. One Federal commission awarded $29 million in exchange for the estimated 64 million acres which once sustained the state's Amerind population. Unfortunately, 'These legal victories came rather late . . . and have scarcely proved useful in salvaging tribal integrity.'[42] In fact, a mass exodus to cities, particularly Los Angeles and its environs, has depleted reservations even more than before such financial settlements took place.[43] In the urban environment, California Indians tend to be outnumbered by all others, including Indians from groups which originated outside of the state. Thus, the first people to tread this territory struggle to maintain an identity in the face of overwhelming odds. They confront the possible fate of Ishi, 'the last of the wild Indians' of California, whose passing ended an era.[44] Such a loss would effect not only the people of the many cultures who once thrived in California but also diminish us all.[45]

References

1 Federal Writers' Project, 1943: 9.
2 All information and quotations about the various environmental zones are taken from ibid.: 23.
3 Joseph and Kerry Kona Chartkoff, 1984, shed additional light on this topic.
4 Wissler, 1966: 202. The other main language families once extant in California were the Algonquian, Hokan (including the Isoman), Lutuamian, Shoshonean (also called Uto-Aztecan), and Yukian; Heizer and Whipple, 1971: 111. According to another source, some twenty-two linguistic families had existed at one time or another in the state, speaking 'no less than 135 regional dialects'; Rolle and Gaines, 1979: 21.
5 Wissler, 1966: 203.
6 The section on food came from Heizer and Whipple, 1971: 297-300.
7 Cook, 1976: 1, 199.
8 Davis, 1974, discusses this subject in some detail.
9 The group itself deserves more attention than just for its basket work. Some of their world views, for example, are of great interest, as indicated in Clark and Williams, 1954.
10 A. L. Kroeber, 1970: 244. To place work by Californian native basket makers in context, refer to Mason, 1976.
11 Merrill, 1980, explores this topic more fully.
12 Heizer and Whipple, 1971: 319.
13 Ibid.: 53.
14 A. L. Kroeber, 1970: 2.
15 Ibid.: 34.
16 Ibid.: 76.
17 Ibid.: 319.
18 Thompson, 1971-5. This publication provides a fine overview of this conflict and is recommended reading.
19 Utley, 1984: 171.
20 Members of the Potomac Corral of the Westerners,

1966: 196.
21 For more on this topic consult Cook, 1976a. Also refer to Heizer ed., 1974.
22 Edwards ed., 1970: 56.
23 It should be noted that gold discoveries in the acorn bearing domain inhabited by the Miwok and Yokuts led to friction between the native people and the encroaching white miners. While space prohibits further discussion of this topic, the reader should consult Crampton ed., 1975, for an excellent account of this turbulent time.
24 Lang, 1979: 3. Generally speaking, this synopsis of the Costanoan and Coast Miwok was taken from this source as found on pp.1-56.
25 Ibid.: 7.
26 An early Franciscan missionary noted many of the Costanoan men were bald and bearded and made 'a habit of pulling out the hair of their eyebrows by the roots . . .'. The same source also mentioned observing capes of beaver skins and pelican feathers for the men and 'plaited tules' skirts for the women, 'for very few skins of animals are seen among them'; Bolton ed., 1926: 121.
27 Lang, 1979: 11.
28 Heizer and Treganza, 1972, provides more details about sources of materials for stone implement making.
29 Fray Francisco Palou, 'The Founding of the Presidio and Mission of Our Father St Francis', George E. Dane, trans XIV, *California Historical Society Quarterly* (June, 1953): 109.
30 Ibid.: 110. Palou was not the only missionary to provide important commentary about early California Indians. Many of the other padres did so, one important example of this type of information being found in Geiger and Meighan, 1976.
31 The northern Costanoans could be found at Missions San Francisco Assis, San Jose, Santa Clara,

and Santa Cruz and the southern Costanoans made up the main numbers at San Juan Bautista, Soledad, and San Carlos. Here, as elsewhere throughout New Spain, the mission, a key colonial institution sanctioned by the Spanish sovereigns to deal with the native people, 'had three fundamental purposes. They desired to convert him, to civilize him, and to exploit him', Bolton, in Bannon ed., 1974: 190. For more on certain aspects of native activities at these combined religious and civil complexes, see Webb, 1952.
32 To provide an overview and some context in this area, the reader should consult Cullin, 1975.
33 A. L. Kroeber, 1970: 544.
34 Ibid.: 547.
35 Ibid.: 550
36 Casebier's two monographs, *Carleton's Pah-Ute Campaign* and *The Battle at Camp Cady* (both published by the author in Norco, California, during 1972) provide details on this short-lived military operation.
37 Reid, 1926: 49.
38 A. L. Kroeber, 1970: 632.
39 The people in this region tended to manipulate both stone and bone by inlaying the basic materials with various patterns and designs. Burnett, 1944, delves into this subject at some length.
40 Rolle and Gaines, 1976: 24.
41 Tuska and Pickasski, 1983: 12-14, 190-91, 303-4, provides basic details about the work of these three authors.
42 Rolle and Gaines, 1976: 27.
43 Wax, 1971: 36, 216-17, 222, shares some useful statistics for more recent times.
44 Theodora Kroeber, 1976, traces this fascinating, bittersweet story.
45 For further reading, Heizer, ed., 1978, remains a must.

Diegueño

These objects were collected by Constance Goddard Du Bois in 1903, 1904, and 1905 from various Indian communities (named below when known) in southern California near the Mexican border, whose members spoke a single Yuman language. The people of some of these communities were and are known as Kamia, Ipai, Tipai, or Kumeyaay. They are descendants of the groups of 'Mission Indians' who were gathered with considerable resistance into the first

Franciscan mission in Alta California, established in 1769 at San Diego – hence the name Diegueño. The missions were secularized in 1834, initiating the long Diegueño struggle to preserve their lands and livelihoods. In pre-mission times the Diegueño depended for subsistence on acorns and mesquite beans, flour made from various seeds, on berries, fruits, and other vegetable foods, and on deer, rodents, and birds hunted by the men (rodents supplying the most meat). A little corn and beans were grown on newly-flooded lands.

Important in ritual and shamanistic practices was a vision-producing drink of toloache root. Some shamans cured with herbal remedies as well. Girls' puberty rites were important in many Diegueño communities. A particularly important ceremony commemorated deceased members of a clan, with feasting, the distribution of gifts to non-relatives, dancing with images of the deceased, and at dawn burning of the images, regalia, and new goods. Shamanistic tricks and contests were a part of this ceremony.

1 Cooking pot; old type.
2 Two-mouthed jar.
3 Pottery jar. Manzanita.
4 Two-mouthed jar.
5 Pottery dish. Campo.
6 Tool to smooth pottery.
7 Pottery pipe, used with rabbit bone stem; model of old type made at La Jolla.
8 Throwing stick to hunt rabbits.
9 Woman's stick game.
10 Half of girl's skirt, of elder bark fastened with milkweed cord; worn with another such in front or

behind; model of an obsolete style. Mesa Grande.
11 Woman's basketry cap. Campo.
12 Blanket or robe of twined rabbit-skin cords. San Felipe.
13 Twined openwork basket.
14 Brush of yucca fibers for sweeping off metate (grindstone). San Felipe.
15 Pottery paint dish.
16 Pottery dish.
17 Woman's carrying bag of milkweed cords. San Felipe.

18 Pair of yucca fiber sandals. Manzanita.
19 Horsehair halter. Campo.
20 Man's carrying basket. La Jolla.
21 Net cape with pendant eagle feathers used in (obsolete) eagle dance.
22 Stick game. Mesa Grande.
23 Wand used by shaman to throw a 'pain' into an enemy, and also for curing; in the wooden handle is an archeological stone Elko Eared projectile point made c.1500 BC.

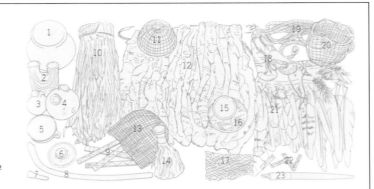

THE NORTHWEST COAST

THE NORTHWEST Coast offers a mild climate with a wide array of food resources. Several distinctive cultures developed on the Northwest Coast from the Columbia River through coastal British Columbia to the top of the Alaskan panhandle. The cultures are very similar in some ways and remarkably diverse in others. People from all regions developed a rich ceremonial and spiritual life. They invested tremendous creative energy in artistic expression, including songs, dances, legends and spectacular, philosophically powerful art work.

There are several different languages indigenous to the Northwest Coast, each with its own subdivisions or dialects. Since there were no large political units outside of the individual village, the cultures are conveniently grouped today according to language. The southern portion of the Coast, including the mainland and lower Vancouver Island, is the homeland of the Coast Salish. The Nuu-chah-nulth people live on the west coast of Vancouver Island and were formerly called the Nootka, a name originally

Below: *Interior of a Tlingit chief's house in the village of Klukwan, c.1895. The painted and carved screen known as the 'rain wall' (rear) epitomizes the high symbolic content of Tlingit art.*

given them by Captain Cook. They are closely related to the Makah on the tip of the Olympic Peninsula in Washington state, and the national boundary that separates them is a relatively recent development in the history of the Northwest Coast. The Southern Kwakiutl villages are in northeastern portions of Vancouver Island and the adjacent mainland. Branches of the Northern Kwakiutl, who speak different dialects and have some different cultural characteristics from the Southern Kwakiutl peoples, live in the central portion of the British Columbia coastline. The language of the neighboring Bella Coola people is related to

that of the Salish; they originally moved to central British Columbia from the south and adopted some cultural traits of central groups. Along the coastline and the lower Nass and Skeena Rivers to the north are the villages of the Tsimshian. The Queen Charlotte Islands are the homeland of the Haida Indians, whose large seaworthy cedar canoes kept them from being isolated. A few centuries ago a group of the Haida moved northward and settled what is now the southern portion of Prince of Wales Island in Alaska. They are now known as the Kaigani Haida but have maintained communication with their relatives on the Charlottes; here, too, the national boundary is both recent and arbitrary. Tlingit Indians live along the panhandle of southeast Alaska; some also moved into inland British Columbia. Because this chapter focuses on the eighteenth and nineteenth centuries, past tense will be used; but it should be emphasized that Northwest Coast Indians still live on the coast today and are culturally and politically active.

Northwest Coast peoples enjoyed a relatively favorable natural environment compared to most other places in North America. While the entire region can get harsh winds and rain, only the portion in the north regularly gets freezing winters and heavy snowfalls. The yearly salmon runs offer a fairly reliable food resource; and there are a variety of other fish, shellfish, sea mammals and plants, roots and berries to supplement the diet and compensate for poor salmon seasons. However, the native peoples were able to take advantage of these resources only because they developed very specialized knowledge and highly efficient tools for both harvesting and processing.[1] People stored food they harvested in the summer for consumption in the winter. Thus, like agriculturalists, they did not have to travel after food in the winter and could establish permanent villages.

Because of this environment, the region supported a relatively dense population compared

This map shows approximate territories of tribes and language groups in the early nineteenth century. After that, all tribes lost territory.

Key to tribes:

1 Eyak	**16** Makah
2 Tlingit	**17** Southern Coast Salish
3 Haida	**18** Quileute
4 Nishga	**19** Chemakum
5 Gitksan	**20** Southwestern Coast Salish
6 Tsimshian	**21** Kwalhioqua
7 Haisla	**22** Chinookans
8 Haihais	**23** Clatskanie
9 Bella Bella	**24** Tillamook
10 Bella Coola	**25** Alseans
11 Oowekeeno	**26** Siuslawans
12 Kwakiutl	**27** Kalapuyans
13 Northern Coast Salish	**28** Coosans
14 Nootkans (Nuu-chah-nulth)	**29** Athapaskans
15 Central Coast Salish	**30** Takelma

to other places on the continent north of Mexico. While population estimates are always speculative, it has been suggested that there were over 46,700 Indians in coastal British Columbia in 1835.[2] Undoubtedly the population there was greater before white diseases were introduced. In 1880 the native population of southeast Alaska was estimated at about 12,000, and again, the population was undoubtedly smaller than it had been before the arrival of Europeans.[3]

Traditionally people lived in numerous villages along the coastline and inland rivers. Often large extended families lived together in communal longhouses spread in a row along the beach. The villages were permanent settlements inhabited for generations or longer. People made excursions from them for hunting and fishing, trading, social activities and military raids. The village was the major political unit, and people identified first and foremost with the leadership in their village.

The villages were always located along waterways, either the coastline or rivers closely connected to the coast. From the sea came food, but also materials that were used in manufacturing clothes and tools – skins from sea mammals, as well as bones, bladders, and sinew. The great temperate rainforests were also vital to the cultures. Trees, especially cedar, provided the materials for large communal houses, sturdy canoes, and a variety of utilitarian and ceremonial items.[4] Women used the inner bark of the cedar and the roots of cedar and spruce to weave highly functional baskets, capes, mats, and cordage. Some of these baskets were woven so tightly that they could hold water.[5]

In addition to the food it yielded, the ocean was tremendously important for transportation. The coastline of the region is rocky and irregular, and land transportation was much less practical than travel by canoe. Again, it was the Indians' technological skill that made it possible for them to take advantage of this opportunity. They built large canoes, spreading them to a functional width with steam. In this method, water is placed in the bottom of the dugout log and hot rocks are dropped into it to create the steam. The sides of the canoe must be well balanced in width to create a stable and seaworthy vessel, and the entire process takes considerable work and skill. The canoes were vital for hunting and fishing, and also for trade and social exchange between villages up and down the coast. People from southeast Alaska may have traveled down the coast as far south as California for trade. In some Haida oral traditions there are stories of voyages to Hawaii, although these have yet to be corroborated by any archeological record.

The Northwest Coast region was probably inhabited very shortly after the ice sheets from the last Ice Age uncovered the coast line – some 9000 to 13,000 years ago. The land and water fluctuated for some time before reaching the configuration we know today. At first the human populations were nomadic, but as the flora and fauna came to resemble that of the present, they developed the food-storing technologies that make permanent villages feasible. Archeological finds suggest that the cultural characteristics known in recent times were already highly developed at least fifteen hundred years ago and probably somewhat earlier.[6] Indians on the Northwest Coast traded with other coastal groups and with inland peoples prior to the arrival of Europeans, so they were by no means isolated. Substantial contact between Indians and Europeans began to occur in the last quarter of the eighteenth century. Thus, that time is often known as the beginning of the historic era, but Northwest Coast Indians had a vibrant history and kept oral historical records long before the arrival of the Europeans.

On all parts of the Northwest Coast, family ties were extremely important. People identified closely with extended families and with

lineages, and in many places rank and political leadership were hereditary. Each lineage owned certain privileges. These ranged from the right to perform specific dances to the right to use resources in a certain geographic area. In most places on the coast there were various levels of social status, including people of high rank, people of lower rank, and slaves who were captured in battle or purchased through trade.[7]

Among the Tlingit, Haida and Tsimshian on the northern coast, the society was matrilineal, and children inherited through their mother. Thus, a leader might be succeeded by his sister's son rather than by his own son, and boys were often trained by their maternal uncles. In

the northern groups with matrilineal descent, social divisions based on kinship were especially important. For instance, the Tlingit divided themselves into two basic hereditary groups, known as moieties. One was known as the Raven, while the other was called the Wolf (or occasionally the Eagle). Everyone in society belonged to the Raven or Wolf moiety, and people could only marry someone from the opposite moiety. Thus, since the society was matrilineal, children always had the same moiety affiliation as their mother and a different one from their father. Each moiety was subdivided into smaller groups, which anthropologists often call clans or sibs. The Raven moiety had some twenty-seven clans.[8] Within each village, there would be a leader for every clan that lived there. Many clans had branches in more than one village, but leadership always remained local. Social organization among the Haida and Tsimshian was similar, with some clans also among the Northern Kwakiutl.[9]

Among the groups on the lower coast – the Southern Kwakiutl, Nuu-chah-nulth, Bella Coola and Coast Salish groups – inheritance came from both parents. Family ties and local kinship group relationships were still considered extremely important. As in the north, kinship families had recognized leaders who gave guidance about such matters as resource use and marriages.[10]

In all parts of the coast, ties between different kinship groups were politically and economically essential. These ties were solidified through trade, and often – as in Europe – marriages helped promote political and economic relationships between different kinship groups or different villages.[11]

Ceremonial gatherings also served to develop and reinforce these ties. There were many different types of ceremonial gatherings up and down the coast. Today they are often all re-

Above: *Interior of a Tlingit dwelling, Sitka, Alaska. Clothing and metal utensils evidence white contact but the open interior of the plank house is typical of many dwellings.*

Below: *A Tlingit village in Alaska, c.1883. The siting of houses in this permanent village is typical, located on low benches slightly above the high water mark of sea or flood-level of rivers.*

ferred to by one term – potlatch – which is a word from the Chinook trade jargon meaning 'to give'.[12] Actually, though, there was tremendous diversity in the nature and purpose of the ceremonies. They were very complex institutions combining social, cultural, spiritual, political and economic elements. Because of the diversity on the coast and the complexity of the celebrations themselves, it is difficult to discuss them without reducing them to a much too simplistic level.

In brief, potlatches were sponsored by a host who had saved food and material goods for the express purpose of the occasion. Guests were invited from other kin groups and other villages, and the celebrations could continue for days or considerably longer. During the potlatch, the host displayed and emphasized certain rights or prerogatives. For instance, these privileges might include the right to take the name, political title or other hereditary prerogatives of a relative who had recently died. In some potlatches parents or other relatives would confer certain prerogatives on their children. The prerogatives were expressed at the potlatch through dances, songs, oration and display of art.[13]

The guests from other lineages and other villages watched these claims to rights, acting as witnesses. The host fed them amply from the food he had stored, and gave them gifts from the material possessions he had accumulated for the purpose. When the witnesses accepted the food and gifts, it was understood that they affirmed the host's right to claim the privileges displayed during the potlatch. In effect, the witnesses were paid for publicly acknowledging these rights and for keeping the memory of the potlatch alive. People passed on stories of potlatches they had attended, creating a communal memory of the event and of the affirmation of the host's right to the privileges he displayed there. This system of witnessing, of communal memory and of oral tradition functioned very efficiently as a way of keeping records, and made a written language unnecessary.

Thus the potlatches were extremely important for validating rank and leadership. They were also vital for passing the rich cultural heritage from generation to generation, for during ceremonies children saw the songs, dances and art work that referred to the history and legends of their families and their people. The potlatches served an economic role, for they kept goods circulating in several ways. A leader saving for a potlatch would often loan goods, receiving goods of their value back with interest as the time of the celebration grew near. That leader then distributed goods to his guests in payment for their witnessing role. In return, high ranking guests would aspire to reciprocate with their own potlatch, matching or exceeding the gifts of the former host. In preparing for that event, they would loan some of their goods. Thus, the potlatch system supported a cycle of exchange of material wealth. The host of a potlatch might be almost bereft of material possessions at the end of the gathering, but his wealth measured in honor would be greater.

Ceremonies took place in the winter months, when families were living on food they had stored during the summer and autumn. Freed from the necessity of traveling for food, they were able to take the time for large social gatherings. Thus the rhythm of life moved with the seasons, with different economic, social and cultural activities in different times of the year.

Whatever the season, Northwest Coast peoples surrounded themselves with artistic expression. There was no firm demarcation between 'art' and 'daily life', as tends to exist in Western cultures today. Northwest Coast arts were functional arts, adapted to perform a task or convey a message. The purpose of the art went far beyond aesthetics, and it was intended for much more than contemplation. Northwest Coast peoples decorated tools and utensils they used in daily life, and they created spectacular and dramatic masterpieces to display crests or for use in dances. Men carved wood, bone and antler and sometimes also worked in stone. Women wove with plant and animal fibers, decorating their vessels, mats and blankets with careful designs. While most adults developed skills in making articles for daily uses, it took specialized training to create monumental and ceremonial art. Thus, carvers of totem poles, masks and similar art works apprenticed with master carvers to learn the skills. They earned high reputations for their

Below: Sitka Jake, a Tlingit, wearing Chilkat dance headdress and blanket, the latter woven by women from cedar bark and mountain goats' wool from designs drawn by men on a special pattern board.

Tlingit

The Tlingit are a nationality, not a unified political body, living on the strip of mainland and hundreds of islands just offshore, along the panhandle of southeastern Alaska. There are three main groups of Tlingit tribes or local communities, each consisting of nearby villages occupied by several matrilineal clans. Clans had territorial rights, and each one owned several crests which leading members displayed on totem poles in front of lineage-owned houses, and on many objects. Social ranks and the right to display crests were validated in potlatches, where property was distributed by the hosts to guests. Dance and feast regalia included the famous Chilkat blankets, and button blankets with designs outlined in imported mother-of-pearl buttons, often also with fine appliqué designs representing clan crests. For the objects in both spreads, the tribe of origin is given where known, along with the date when the object was collected (or when it entered the museum).

1 Rope of twisted cedar bark worn as a belt in dancing. Hutsnuwu, 1881.
2 Wooden hat with carved beaver and potlatch rings c.1883.
3 Dance cape, of leather with painted design of bear, wool tassels, deer hoofs on fringe. 1903.
4 Carved wooden box, for holding food. Chilkat, 1882.
5 Shaman's wooden rattle, representing oyster catcher. Hoonah, 1884.
6 Classic ancient style bi-pointed fighting knife, hammered from trade iron, eyes inlaid with abalone. Sitka, before 1870.
7 Northern style dagger, with bone handle carved to represent bear. Hutsnuwu, 1881.
8 Pair of small canoe paddles. 1876.
9 Dance frontlet, carved and painted wood representing a bear. Haida, Skidegate, 1883.
10 Frontlet, portrait of a

favorite daughter of a Haida chief. Haida, Skidegate, before 1903.

11 Food bowl, kerfed and bent wood, painted. Sitka. 1884.

12 Wooden spoon with carved handle.

13 Leather pouch containing set of gambling sticks. Chilkat, 1882.

14 Twined basket with cover. 1893.

15 Twined basket with cover. Sitka. 1882.

16 Chilkat blanket, twined,

of mountain goat wool. 1893.

17 Dance headband of twined cedar bark, dyed red, with abalone ornament. Stikine. 1905.

18 Carved horn comb. Sitka, 1884.

19 Carved wood food box. Sitka, 1884.

20 Wooden food dish in shape of seal. Hutsnuwu, 1881.

21 Ladle of mountain sheep horn. Sitka, 1874.

22 Carved wooden spoon.

Hutsnuwu, 1881.

23 Rope of twisted cedar bark, worn as belt in dancing. Hutsnuwu, 1881.

24 Twined basketry hat. Chilkat, 1903.

25 Wooden food dish, ends carved and painted. 1874.

26 Carved wooden dish for a child. Stikine, 1876.

27 Silver bracelet engraved with raven. Sitka, 1875.

28 Silver bracelet engraved with whale. Sitka, 1875.

29 Carved wooden berry spoon. Stikine, 1875.

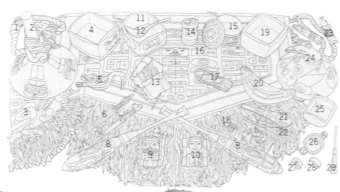

proficiency, and leaders commissioned art from these masters. In the Tlingit region, usually art was commissioned from an artist who belonged to the opposite moiety from the patron.[14]

Northwest Coast Indian art is well known today internationally. Most people associate the term either with the highly structured linear art of the northern regions of the coast, or with the dramatic and colorful dance masks of the

Southern Kwakiutl. In fact, there is tremendous diversity in artistic expression up and down the coast, and it would be much more accurate to refer to Northwest Coast Indian arts in the plural. Regional artistic styles developed, and in some cases specific styles can be traced to individual villages. There are certain characteristics common throughout the coast, and others that differ regionally.

There were three principal forms of art made

Above: *Tlingit men and boys in dance costume, 1895. Their clothing is mainly fabricated from trade cloth adorned with beads, bone or mother-of-pearl buttons in traditional patterns.*

on the coast: two-dimensional design in the way of painting or light engraving; three-dimensional sculpture, usually woodcarving; and the production of baskets, mats, woven hats, and textiles. Two-dimensional design appears on a wide variety of articles. Pigment for paints was made from minerals such as red ochre and copper mixed in a medium of fish roe; later artists adopted commercial pigments bought through trade. House fronts and canoes sometimes had motifs painted on them. Large storage chests were often painted, or both painted and engraved. Woven hats sometimes also had painted motifs, showing collaboration between female and male artists. Wood food bowls and grease dishes often had two-dimensional design engraved on their surface, and utensils such as berry spoons were also frequently painted or engraved. Ceremonial items such as masks were also painted. Two-dimensional design was practiced long before Europeans arrived on the Northwest Coast. Archeological finds suggest that the technical, highly formalized styles found on the northern part of the coast were developing there at least a thousand years ago.

Three dimensional sculpture also included a wide range of articles, from wood carving tools to feast dishes and ceremonial masks – and, on some parts of the coast, the totem poles for which the region is famous. The tradition of

Left: *Eight Tlingit men, three of them in treasured Chilkat blankets, the group at left in headdresses (with carved wooden frontlets) embellished with sea-lion whiskers and whole ermine skins.*

sculpture extends back centuries and possibly millennia. Very expressive stone sculptures have been found in many regions of the coast dating back at least three thousand years.[15] Almost certainly these same artists were practicing in wood as well, but wood deteriorates more quickly than stone and is less likely to be preserved in archeological sites.

Female artists made woven and coiled baskets, woven mats, hats, capes and textiles. After trade with Europeans started, they also practiced beadwork and appliqué, and outlined designs on commercial wool dance blankets by sewing rows of decorative pearl buttons. Until recently, these art forms unfortunately received less attention in the literature about Northwest Coast Indian arts, but they, too, required substantial skill and creativity. Like wood, basketry does not last well in archeological sites except under unique circumstances, but there are still enough indications to suggest that Northwest Coast people have made baskets for thousands of years.

Each of these three primary art forms differed regionally on the coast. The two-dimensional design made by northern artists – the Haida, Tsimshian and Tlingit – was quite different from that made by artists to the south – the Southern Kwakiutl, Nuu-chah-nulth, Bella Coola and Salish. Northern Kwakiutl villages, in a central position between these regions, produced some works resembling northern styles

and others suggesting a southern influence. The two-dimensional art practiced by the Haida, Tsimshian and Tlingit artists follows the same very technical set of conventions. It is very difficult to tell two-dimensional art from these peoples apart unless there is documentation, or unless the work also has sculptural qualities. The very complex art style is known today as 'Northern formline'.[16] Stated much too simply, artists depicted animals by using a series of standard conventions and combining them in fairly uniform ways. Basic outlines are defined by 'formlines' which are curvilinear; right angles are rare. The formlines vary greatly in width, giving the designs a dynamic sense of fluidity and motion. The lines converge and diverge to form certain shapes that recur again and again. Thus, a somewhat oval shape, called today an 'ovoid', usually depicts eyes and joints in limbs or appendages. U-forms often indicate ears, snouts, and wing feathers, and the fins and flukes of sea mammals and fish. There were very standard ways that artists combined the formlines to create these elements, and there were also standard ways in which artists placed the design within the shape of the field they had to decorate. Individual expression writ

Below: *Tlingit in ceremonial costume at a potlatch in Klukwan, Alaska. The man to the left wears an elaborately painted hide tunic over a trade shirt. Some of the men have metal nose rings.*

large was not the goal; but individual artists had personal styles that were all the more creative because of their subtlety.

Two-dimensional design in the more southern groups, by contrast, followed fewer standard conventions. Thus there is considerably more variety in style. It is usually not difficult to distinguish Southern Kwakiutl, Nuu-chah-nulth and Salish two-dimensional design from each other. Each of these groups had their own aesthetic and artistic goals. Unfortunately there is not much information about Southern Kwakiutl art in the eighteenth century. In the nineteenth century these artists experimented with elements from northern painting, varying them significantly to create a style that is distinctly Southern Kwakiutl. The early works from the Nuu-chah-nulth, found in archeological sites and collected by late eighteenth-century European explorers, suggest a tradition emphasizing rows or bands of geometric elements and liberal use of circles and dots. Some of the curves suggest more northern elements. In the mid-nineteenth century, some Nuu-chah-nulth artists also began incorporating more northern elements into their art work. The lines and shapes in Coast Salish two-dimensional design have much in common with the northern graphic art, although again there are fewer standard conventions, more wide-ranging variation between designs, and a highly developed aesthetic unique to Salish artists. It is

Tlingit

Tlingit economy in the past was a maritime one, as it still is largely today. Five species of salmon are important, especially in the summer. Halibut are taken in the spring as, formerly, were seals and otters. Waterfowl were taken in spring and summer, and the dense forests behind the beaches furnished berries, roots and deer, bear, marten, mink, beaver, mountain sheep and mountain goat. Northern style art displayed on most Tlingit artifacts follows rules governing the representation of animal and human forms that include wrapping essentially 2-dimensional designs around 3-dimensional objects, rearranging body parts in ways that sometimes made deciphering difficult, and connecting elements of designs with carefully planned form-lines. The scale of an object has little effect. Lines and forms are treated the same way whether carved or painted. Wood is the main material, with bone and ivory also used; shell inlays are common. Copper was used and valued aboriginally.

1 Cylindrical twined basket with cover. Sitka, 1882.
2 Woodworking adze, steel blade, bone handle; the straight adze type typical of southern area. Makah (not Tlingit), 1876.
3 Wooden box, painted, with fitted lid with opercula inlay. Sitka, 1884.
4 Stone maul. Sitka, 1884.
5 Wooden box, carved, with fitted lid with opercula inlay. Hutsnuwu, 1881.
6 Knife for woodcarving, 1901.
7 Woman's knife. Sitka, 1892.
8 Fish knife. Sitka, 1884.
9 Stone fish pounder, Sitka, 1874.
10, 11 Stone rubbers, perhaps for hide dressing, 1876.
12 Dress of white-tanned caribou skin. 1901.
13 Large labret, worn by woman. 1900.
14 Wooden fish masher. Baranof Is. (Sitka or Hutsnuwu).
15 Twined basket.
16 Twined basket. 1890.

17 Harpoon head and line. 1890s.

18 Buckskin shirt. Sitka, 1875.

19 Drum, hide stretched over a pine hoop. Sitka, 1875.

20 Shaman's necklace of incised ivory pendants. Sitka, 1884.

21 Bone snuff tube. Chilkat, 1882.

22 Stone carving of bear. Killisnoo, Hutsnuwu, 1903.

23 Graver's tool. 1901.

24 Awl in carved handle. Hoonah, 1881.

25 Wooden headdress for dancing. Hoonah, 1881.

26 Shaman's cape, painted, with rattles. Sitka, 1875.

27 Shaman's mask. Sitka, 1904.

28 Wooden tobacco pipe. Sitka, 1884.

29 Carved ivory charm. Sitka, 1882.

30 Copper mask, shell inlays, fur hair. Yakutat, 1926.

31 Dance helmet, carved from single block of wood, painted, with tufts of hair. Sitka, 1875.

32 Wooden collar and face mask, worn as armor; held in place by cord between teeth; notches for eyes. Sitka, 1874.

33 Body armor, of rods held together by twined cords. Hutsnuwu, 1882.

34 Knife; non-Indian steel blade, Tlingit-made handle. 1881.

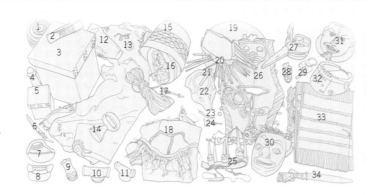

Left: Haida shaman and patient re-enacting a cure The dress of the shamans varied according to the spirit possessing them, generally consisting of an apron or cloak covered with esoteric designs.

Right: *Johnnie Kit Elswa, a Haida from Skidegate, Queen Charlotte Is., 1886. The tattoos allude to events in family history: on his chest a brown bear is represented, at each wrist a dogfish.*

possible that far back in antiquity there was once a much more uniform art style on the coast, and people in different regions chose to modify it in different directions.[17]

Sculptural styles differ substantially up and down the coast. In the north, where two-dimensional art is almost identical, sculptural styles vary considerably from language group to language group. The variations are even greater in the south, where each group has a particularly distinctive carving style and a unique genre of masks.[18]

Women up and down the coast were proficient at weaving baskets, mats, hats and capes

from plant fibers. The inner bark of the cedar, cedar root, spruce root and grasses were most often used. Twining was the technique most prevalent, although women from interior Salish villages also made coiled baskets. Dyed grasses and other dyed plant fibers were added during the manufacturing process to form decorative designs, which were usually geometric. Types of designs and forms of baskets varied somewhat from region to region. In the eighteenth century, the Nuu-chah-nulth wove a very distinctive conical-shaped hat with whaling scenes. Along with their close relatives the Makah, they were the only Northwest Coast peoples to hunt whales, and these whaling hats are unique to that region.[19]

Women in some groups – particularly Coast Salish and Tlingit – also wove blankets from animal wool. Salish women used hair from small domesticated dogs as well as wool of mountain goat, often mixed with plant fibers.[20] Tlingit women made the famous Chilkat dancing blankets of mountain goat wool and cedar bark. These blankets show elaborate figures in Northern formline design, taken skillfully from a pattern painted on a wooden board by a male

Below: *Potlatch dancers, Klinkwan, Alaska, c.1900. Potlatches, complex ceremonies involving feasts and dances, were very important to Northwest Coast tribes such as the Tlingit, shown here.*

artist.[21] When commercial beads became available through trade, women also began using them for ceremonial items.

Ceremonial and monumental art played a variety of roles in traditional cultures. Like artistic style, these roles varied from region to region. In northern areas, much of the ceremonial art displayed crests identifying the lineage of the owner. Thus, a man wearing a mask of a bear would belong to the Bear sib or clan. In some ways, the crests served much as coats of arms in Europe. In other ways, they differed from coats of arms, for they also might refer to experiences that the wearer's ancestor – the

Haida Heraldic or Totem Pole

Above: *A Bella Coola village, c.1885, on the British Columbia coast. The village shows several painted house fronts along the beach and basket fish traps behind the foreground figures.*

Watchman figures wearing so-called potlatch rings which referred to wealth and prestige

Mammal (probably a bear) holding two smaller animals

Carving was enhanced by limited painting, natural pigments being used: black was obtained from coal and charcoal, red from alder bark or iron ore

Mammal (probably a bear) holding a small human figure

Raven with small human figure on the front

person who founded the family – had had with an actual bear spirit.

In fact, much of the art refers to a primordial time when boundaries between human beings, spirits and animals were much more fluid than they are at present. During this time, animals could marry human beings, and sometimes spirits transformed themselves from animal form to human form. People who had experiences with animals and spirits in these ways could acquire the right to display an animal as a crest and to pass that crest on to descendants. Thus, a work of art that displays a crest may do more than signify genealogy. It may also speak of the history of the family and of the specific rights that family enjoys as a result of ancestral experiences. In effect, the art work makes visible all the invisible rights the family has – the rights to perform certain dances, sing certain songs, tell certain stories, and claim a specific ancestral history. These rights were carefully guarded, and it was inappropriate for any member of society to perform a dance or sing a song to which he or she was not entitled.

Crests were displayed in a variety of contexts. Masks were carved in the form of crests and worn in dances. Ceremonial frontlets with crest designs were worn on the forehead. Chilkat blankets were woven with crest designs, and basketry hats had crest designs painted on them. Sometimes house fronts were painted with crest designs. Probably the most well-known form of crest display is the totem pole, which has become a symbol for the Northwest Coast today. Contrary to popular belief, they were not carved all over the coast, and were most prevalent among the lower Tlingit, the Haida, the Tsimshian and the Kwakiutl peoples. There has been some debate as to whether totem poles existed prior to the arrival of European traders with their iron tools.

Almost all scholars agree today that totem poles were a well-established art form before Europeans arrived. However, it is also almost certainly true that the iron tools – as well as the ceremonial activities that were supported by the fur trade – increased the number of totem poles being carved.

There were many types of totem poles, varying in size depending on their function. When a high-ranking person died, often his successor, or other members of his family, raised a pole in his honor. The pole would display crest figures pertinent to his ancestry. Other poles, known as frontal poles, stood against the front of house displaying crests of a family living in it. Interior house posts, which were shorter than most memorial poles and frontal poles, supported the beams of the house. In some regions of the coast, especially among the Haida, human remains were placed in grave boxes at the top of mortuary poles. Mortuary poles tended to be relatively short, with one or two primary crest figures displayed. In places on the coast where people were buried, carved figures were often placed to mark the grave. Freestanding carvings of human beings, known as welcome figures, were sometimes placed on village beaches, especially in the lower half of the Northwest Coast, to welcome visitors.[22]

Totem pole raisings were accompanied by a potlatch. The guests who came acted as witnesses affirming that the family raising the pole had the right to do so. The potlatch accompanying a memorial pole would honor the person who had recently died, and would create a

Right: *Traditionally the heavy cedar timbers of a Northwest Coast indoor house frame as well as center gable post were carved and painted. From such features the heraldic or totem pole evolved. Widely distributed along the northern part of the coast, the freestanding pole in front of the house seems to have been quite a recent innovation, its heyday being between c.1850 and 1900. Majestic, dignified and imposing in their design, each figure on the pole referred to the crest of the owner and his family or incidents in their history.*

Haida

Haida territory is the Queen Charlotte Islands in British Columbia and a small part of Alaska immediately to the north. The traditional social organization is matrilineal, with lineage ownership of the large plank houses. There was no overall Haida political organization; regional groups of villages are recognized. Totemic crests were associated with the lineages and with individuals within them. Most were animals and birds, but some referred to natural phenomena such as clouds, rainbow, evening sky. This was a highly ranked class society, with ceremonies intimately related to individual status. These rituals included feasts, potlatches, and dance performances, during which prestige and status were achieved and maintained by the display and distribution of objects of wealth. Guests were served special foods in fine dishes and bowls. Dance regalia was varied and elaborate, including masks and headdresses, and specialized musical instruments such as drums, rattles, and whistles. Elaborate, carefully controlled artistic decoration was emphasized, and nearly every artifact was decorated, usually with zoomorphic designs. Specialists in carving and painting were highly respected. The art style is widely appreciated not only on the Northwest Coast, and is currently practiced by many fine artists. Objects illustrated in these two spreads (except as otherwise noted) were collected between 1875 and 1884 by Judge James G. Swan of Washington Territory at the localities mentioned.

1 Dance cape; wool blanket with mother-of-pearl buttons and appliquéd red flannel design of a killer whale with attached dorsal fins. Skidegate.

2 Dance mask, representing a sparrow hawk.

3 Dance mask, representing an old woman with labret in lower lip. Cumshewa.

4 Dance headdress, worn by a woman.

5 Spherical rattle, of painted wood, two pieces tied together. Skidegate.

6 Dance mask of painted wood, copper inlays, represents a bear, with collar of cedar bark and wood pendants.

7 Carved and painted figurine. Sitka.

8 Headdress for crow dance. Skidegate.

9 Carved wooden tobacco pipe. Sitka.

10 Head ornament for dance, representing killer whale, painted wood head with movable flukes, connected by cloth to painted wood tail. Skidegate.

11 Food dish, of wood kerfed and then steamed and bent. Skidegate.

12 Double whistle of wood, for dances. Skidegate.

13 Dance rattle, carved and painted wood, represents raven with man and frog on back, sparrow-hawk on breast. Masset.

14 Large wooden whistle representing mountain demon's call. Skidegate.

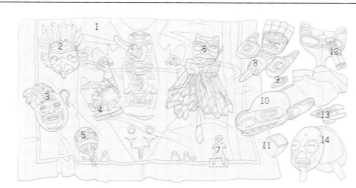

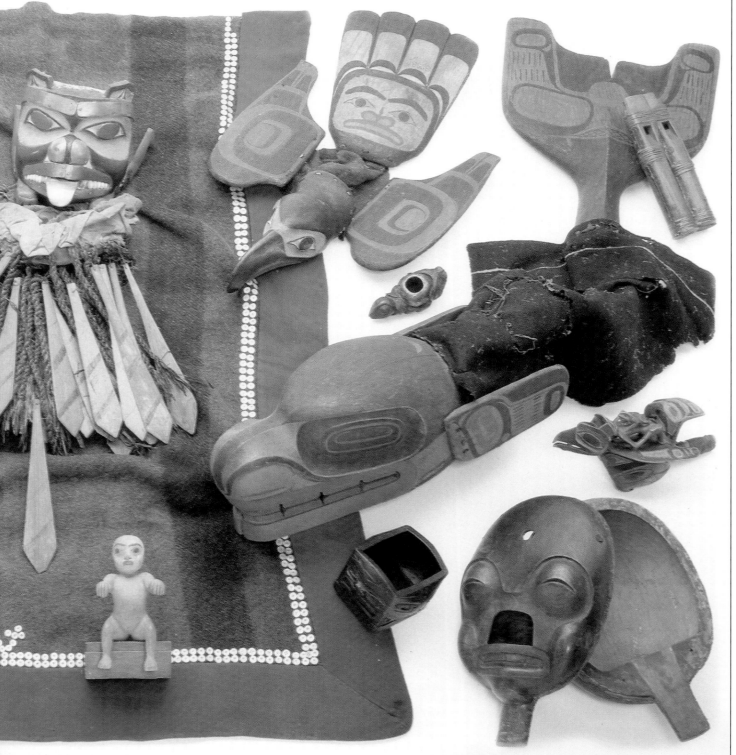

Haida

The Haida in aboriginal times depended chiefly on fish (particularly halibut, sockeye and salmon) and shellfish, and then on sea mammals (seals, porpoises, sea lions, sea otters), plant products (especially berries, also roots, seaweed, and hemlock and spruce inner bark), and land animals (deer, caribou, beaver, bear) and birds. Everyone collected shellfish and birds' eggs and hunted birds. Women gathered roots and berries, seaweed, and materials for basketry. They prepared, cooked, and preserved all foods, tanned animal skins, made all the clothing and basketry. Men fished and hunted both sea and land animals, built houses, made the large canoes, and did all the wood carving and painting. Basketry hats were woven by women and the painted designs on them were applied by men. Haida art is similar in style to that of Tlingit, Tsimshian, and Bella Bella, but carving in argillite is a Haida specialty; some basketry patterns are distinct from those of their neighbors.

1 Fine carved slate (argillite) box made for sale, top design a killer whale, added heads in front (bear), and ends (wolf).
2 Carved argillite panel. Collected by Wilkes Expedition, 1841.
3 Carved argillite, made for sale, representing a platter with a fish.
4 Dance cape, dark blue blanket with red appliqué design representing killer whales. Skidegate.
5 Carved panels of wood with bone inlays, with European (perhaps Russian) motifs, made for sale. Collected by Wilkes Expedition, 1841.
6 Feast dish of wood, carved and painted ends, opercula inlay on rim. Collected by J.J. McLean, 1882. Hutsnuwu, Tlingit.
7 Bowl of mountain sheep horn. Collected by J.J. McLean, 1884, Sitka.
8 Chief's bow and arrow, used in dances, obtained

from Capt. Skedans, chief of Kloo.
9 Twined basketry hat with painted design. Masset.
10 Bowl of mountain sheep horn, shaped by steaming then carved and inlaid with abalone shell.
11 Bowl of mountain sheep horn. Ft Simpson.
12 Dance hat, of blue-painted wood with copper inlays and eight twined basketry potlatch rings.
13 Dance skirt trimmed with Chinese coins, edged

with quillwork and fringed with puffin beaks. Skidegate.
14 Twined basketry hat, of fine spruce root fibers, a virtuoso imitation of a Panama hat. Skidegate.
15 Dance headdress, painted wood, representing duck on top of killer whale. Skidegate.
16 Food dish of mountain goat horn.
17 Food dish of mountain goat horn, carved to represent a duck.

Skidegate.
18 Iron sealing harpoon head attached to line, with wooded sheath. Collected by J.L. Gould, 1884.
19 Wooden food dish, representing a seal. Collected by Ĺt L. Curtis 1881.
20 Close-twined spruce root basket. Collected by Lt G.T. Emmons, c.1892.
21 Yew wood sealing club, carved to represent a sea lion. Masset.

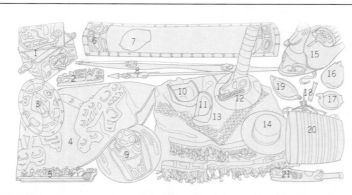

Haida Canoes

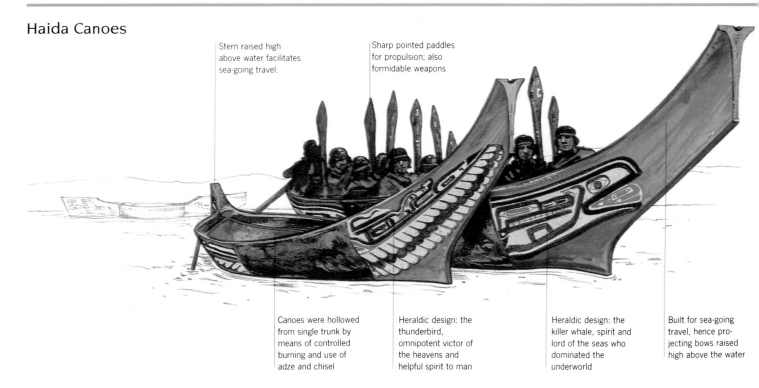

Stern raised high above water facilitates sea-going travel.

Sharp pointed paddles for propulsion; also formidable weapons

Canoes were hollowed from single trunk by means of controlled burning and use of adze and chisel

Heraldic design: the thunderbird, omnipotent victor of the heavens and helpful spirit to man

Heraldic design: the killer whale, spirit and lord of the seas who dominated the underworld

Built for sea-going travel, hence projecting bows raised high above the water

Above: *As sea-faring, island people, the Haida were highly dependent upon canoes for their daily activities. Made from the trunks of the red cedar, Haida canoes were considered among the finest available.*

communal memory that that person had been so honored. Totem poles were commissioned from master carvers who had apprenticed to learn their skills and who had earned reputations as fine artists. Between the cost of the pole itself and the potlatch ceremonies surrounding the pole raising, each pole represented a considerable expense.

The art that displays crests also displays con-

siderable wealth. Wealth on the Northwest Coast was measured by rights as well as by material possessions. Thus, art work displaying a crest suggested a much broader complex of entitlements belonging to the family that owned the crest. Not all art on the Northwest Coast displayed crests in this way, but other forms also spoke of rights and entitlements. Ceremonial masks also were worn in very pres-

Below: *The southern Kwakiutl village of Koskimo, Quatsino Sound, Vancouver Is., c.1880. Note the houses made of hand-hewn cedar planks, various shapes of canoes, and fishing gear on the beach.*

tigious dances that were inherited. People gained the right to participate in the dances and to claim the less visible wealth of their inheritance by going through initiations. The dances formed a part of this initiation. Examples of art associated with these dances are the dramatic masks used in ceremonies among the southern Kwakiutl and the Nuu-chah-nulth.[23]

The Southern Kwakiutl are particularly well known for their Tseyka dances or winter ceremonies, known popularly as the Hamatsa dances. These dances, too, refer to ancestral experiences with spirits. The Hamatsa, or initiate,

re-experiences the adventures of an ancestor who encountered the supernatural cannibal spirit Bakhbakwalanooksiwey. This spirit was attended by a number of fierce birds capable of eating human beings. The ancestor escaped and brought back to his family the right to perform dances he had learned from the encounter.[24]

During the winter ceremonies, the boundaries between human beings and spirits were temporarily transgressed, as were the boundaries between present and past and the boundaries between initiate and ancestor. The initiate relived the experiences of the first ancestor in his encounter with Bakhbakwalanooksiwey. After a period of isolation, he returned to the village during the winter ceremonies in a wild state, and was tamed and restored to his former human state in a set of specific dances. Gradually the boundaries between human being and spirit, between present and past, and between initiate and ancestor were re-established.

During some of these dances, dancers wear large masks representing the cannibal birds that attended Bakhbakwalanooksiwey. These dramatic masks were carved of wood with great strands of red cedar bark draping from them. The masks have movable beaks that the dancer opened and closed by working a network of strings. The cedar bark strands hung thick, obscuring the dancer's body and hiding his hands as he moved the strings. The clap of the beak added both sound and motion to the dance.

The Tseyka ceremonies spoke of special privilege limited to people who inherited the right to those entitlements and who had gone through a specific initiation to gain the right to

Below: *Kwakiutl village, Fort Rupert, Vancouver Is., c.1888. Note the traditional windowless cedar plank dwellings, one with a painted front (left), and several carved totem poles.*

display them. The art work helped re-enact – or to re-experience – the ancestral experiences that conferred the privileges to the descendants. A ceremony with similar function took place among the Nuu-chah-nulth and the Makah peoples. They called it the Klookwana or the Klookwalli, respectively. In this ceremony, initiates were removed by supernatural wolves, and villagers participated in dances to help bring them back. These efforts eventually succeeded and the initiates returned to dance specific dances they had inherited. The dances were performed in set orders. In some of these dances, dancers wore carved masks represent-

Above: *Kwakiutl winter ceremony speech of the leader Hō-letite, c.1894. His blanket is probably of red trade cloth with pattern insert of black,and bone and mother-of-pearl buttons adorning edges.*

ing wolves. In others, headdresses made of flat painted boards were worn on the forehead. These represented profiles of the wolf, mythological lightening snake or thunderbird. Again, in the Klookwana or Klookwalli, boundaries between human being and spirit, present and past, initiate and ancestor are temporarily transgressed.[25]

Some Salish peoples – those living on the

Kwakiutl

Kwakiutl is the language of about thirty named tribes (one of which is also called Kwakiutl) on northeast Vancouver Is. and the adjacent mainland. Today there are fifteen Kwakiutl reserves, each governed by an independent band council. All except two of the objects shown here were collected between 1897 and 1904 by George Hunt (of Tlingit and English parentage) who was raised in the Kwakiutl town of Fort Rupert, married a Kwakiutl, and was a full parti-

cipant in Kwakiutl society. For forty years he was a co-worker and colleague of Franz Boas, with whom he recorded and published massive amounts of information on Kwakiutl traditional culture, including the language, oral literature, fine art and material culture, and elaborate rituals which were the centerpiece of Kwakiutl life and are still important. Kwakiutl religious ceremonies involve dramatic performances, with masked dancers, singing, and oratory, often re-enacting myths owned and inherited within families.

1 Raven mask worn by hámatsa dancer in Winter Ceremonial. Nakwoktak tribe.
2 Shining Dawn mask. Koskimo tribe.
3 Mask representing grizzly bear kneecap. Koskimo tribe.
4 Sun mask. Kwakiutl tribe.
5 Cedar bark neck ring worn in Winter Ceremonial by partly tamed hámatsa initiate.
6 Red cedar bark head ring worn by partly tamed hámatsa initiate. Kwakiutl

tribe.
7 Woman's cape of twined yellow cedar bark. Nakwoktak tribe.
8 Pair of nose ornaments. Kwakiutl tribe (collected by Boas).
9 Young woman's cedar bark pouch. Tsawatainuk tribe.
10 Twined basketry bag. Kwakiutl tribe.
11 Spoon of mountain goat horn. Kwakiutl tribe.
12 Wooden spoon. Kwakiutl tribe.
13 Axe, weapon of nutlmatl

or 'fool dancer', participant in hámatsa ceremony. Tsawatainuk tribe.

14 Rattle with hámatsa face. Koskimo tribe.

15 Club for killing halibut. Kwakiutl tribe.

16 Wedge for splitting wood. Kwakiutl tribe.

17 Woman's bucket. Kwakiutl tribe.

18 Drinking bucket for chief's wife. Koskimo tribe.

19 Feast dish for eating boiled berries or crab-apples. Koskimo tribe.

20 Chief's daughter's dish. Kwakiutl tribe.

21 Dagger of performer impersonating Dzoónokwa, a powerful supernatural giantess.

22 Girl's work box. Kwakiutl tribe.

23 Skull-shaped rattle. Koskimo tribe.

24 Wooden comb. Kwakiutl tribe.

25 Raven mask of hámatsa dancer. Tsawatainuk tribe.

26 Frog puppet used by performer in Winter

Ceremonial. Koskimo tribe.

27 Dish for serving soaked dried salmon. Koskimo tribe.

28 Model of 16ft feast dish associated with Dzoónokwa giantess at the Winter Ceremonial.

29 Mask for the Tlásulá, so-called Summer or Weasel Dance.

30 Wasp dancer mask. Tsawatainuk tribe.

31 Woodworking adze. Collected about 1881 by I. W. Powell.

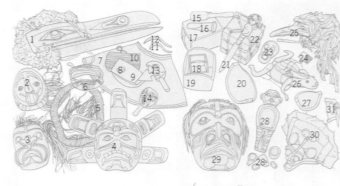

Kwakiutl Basket Making, 1850

A woman and her grand-daughter sit working on the platform raised above the beach in front of a Kwakiutl village. A dugout canoe has been lifted up (at right) and fish dry on racks below. The house fronts of adzed planks with painted designs, and the totem poles (including one with a movable beak at the door) resemble those in the village of Alert Bay. Both people show skulls intentionally shaped, the results of pressure in infancy from bundles such as those on the baby whose cradle is rocked by the woman's toe. She wears abalone shell ear pendants and a blouse of calico trade cloth. Both have skirts of shred-ded cedar bark and robes twined from cedar inner bark and edged with sea otter fur. The bark strips for weaving the baskets are kept flexible in water in the wooden box.

Olympic Peninsula near the Makah – also participated in dances of this nature. Among the Salish living along the Puget Sound, other ceremonies took place that did not feature initiates. Nevertheless, they too spoke of the fluidity of boundaries. These ceremonies, known as Spirit Canoe ceremonies, were performed to cure people who were ill. Shamans, or people in the community invested with special powers to communicate with spirit helpers, enacted a canoe voyage into the world below the earth where the souls of the dead stayed. The ceremony was intended to cause the spirit helpers of the shamans to make the actual journey and bring back the soul of the ill person. During the ceremony, distinctive wooden boards and carved figures were used to help evoke power and to bridge the boundaries between human beings and spirits. Because of their potency, these art works were kept in hiding away from the village when they were not in use.[26]

Coast Salish art often referred to personal spirit helpers, even when on utilitarian objects. Particularly in British Columbia, a very distinctive mask style was also used. This mask, known as the Sxwayxwey mask, was used by individuals at very personal times in their lives: births, marriages, deaths, and at times when they took new names. Unlike other masks on the coast, these masks have blunt cylindrical eyes that extend from the surface of the mask. They also often use the technique of 'visual

punning', incorporating bird designs into the features of a larger mythical figure.[27]

This technique of visual punning is prevalent up and down the coast, so it deserves more mention here. In 'visual punning', portions of one animal double as portions of another animal. Thus, the wings of an eagle may also

Below: *Swinomish warriors launching a canoe. Made from the dug out trunk of a cedar tree it would be up to 50ft (15m.) long, curved projections at bow and stern giving great stability in rough seas.*

portray the pectoral fin of a whale, enabling an artist to suggest shared identity.[28] Again, this artistic technique implies that boundaries can be very fluid. Two presences can occupy the same place at the same time, just as the dancer can exist in present and past at the same time.

The discussion above has often talked about initiates who gained the right to perform certain dances and claim certain privileges through inheritance. Some ritualistic art was also used by another small sector of society, the shamans or spiritual healers. These people

had special powers to transcend the contemporary boundaries between human beings and spirits and to communicate with spirits directly. They used those powers to help heal ill people and to foresee events. Each shaman had a personal spirit helper or a series of helpers, and his or her personal collection of art work that was used to call on the power of these helpers. The shamans and their art work were often buried away from villages because of the danger of their power.

The art and ceremonial expression on the Northwest Coast was integrally connected to all parts of life. Utilitarian objects and ceremonial objects alike were decorated. The art was functional art, often used in the place of a written language to convey genealogy and to preserve historical memory. Similarly, the ceremonies kept experiences of ancestors alive and also made hereditary privileges evident. Certain art work both represented and facilitated the power of shamans to cross the boundaries between human beings and spirits and to call on supernatural powers. The ceremonial life was extremely rich and varied on the Northwest Coast. Despite strong cultural oppression on the part of non-native peoples who opposed native ceremonialism in the nineteenth century, many ceremonies have survived and are practiced today.

The earliest record of contact between Northwest Coast Indians and Europeans occurred in 1741, when the Russian explorer Chirikov harbored his ship briefly in the area in southeast Alaska near present-day Sitka. The next recorded contact was in 1774, when the Spanish explorer Juan Perez reached the Queen Charlotte Islands and traded with Haida Indians there. Perez was followed by another Spanish expedition the following year, and by the English captain James Cook in 1778.[29]

The Indians on the Northwest Coast were well accustomed to trading with other indigenous groups, and were interested in the materials the Europeans brought. In the initial years of exchange with Europeans, iron – especially iron with a blade – was particularly in demand. In return, Indians traded food and furs, especially the thick fur of the sea otter.

Captain Cook's crew discovered that they could sell sea otter pelts for very high profits in China. This information became generally known in 1784 when the journals of that expedition were published, and investors began supporting trading voyages to the Northwest Coast. Very quickly, the Northwest Coast became a commercial center with Europe and the eastern United States, and the Indians on the Northwest Coast engaged in active trade in sea otter pelts. By 1820, these small sea mammals had practically disappeared.

The maritime fur trade affected native lives in a variety of ways. It was not without its incidents of violence: the sailing ships were always armed with cannon, and misunderstandings arising from cultural and language differences could lead to tragedy on both sides. Fur traders accidentally introduced diseases such as smallpox, and since native peoples

COURTESY STARK FOUNDATION, ORANGE, TEXAS

Above: *Culchillum, a Central Coast Salish, by Paul Kane (1847). His medicine cap appears fringed with ermine strips and quill wrappings, with two eagle feathers delicately attached to the top.*

lacked natural immunities the diseases hit hard. Traders introduced firearms as well: it is still unclear whether these weapons increased deaths in intertribal warfare.

In a more positive light, the maritime fur trade introduced a great influx of material wealth into Northwest Coast societies in a short period of time. This new wealth helped support ceremonialism and cultural expression. There were probably more potlatches and more production of ceremonial art in the decades immediately following the advent of the maritime fur trade than there had been previously. The fur traders were for the most part transient. They did not appropriate native resources, and they had no wish to change Indian cultural or economic activities as long as Indians kept bringing furs. The trade may have disrupted social structures somewhat by making wealth accessible to a wider range of people. However, it did not attack native culture, and in some ways it supported it.[30]

This situation began to change as European and Euro-American settlers moved to the Northwest Coast. These settlers expected to be permanent residents, and they wanted land resources that belonged to Indians. These developments happened at different times in different parts of the Coast. Except for the Sitka region, where Russians had the settlement of New Archangel, Indians in southeast Alaska did not feel great pressure from non-natives until after Alaska was transferred to the United States in 1867. In southern British Columbia, pressure was felt somewhat earlier. In 1849 the British Government started encouraging the colonization of Vancouver Island in order to keep the United States from claiming it. In the 1850s, some treaties were made with Indians in British Columbia. After that time, reserves were established without treaties. The white settlers and their government appropriated lands that belonged to Indians and restricted their access to these lands. Gunboats patrolled the coast-

Below: *The impact of the white man on Southern Coast Salish (Puyallup). Their lives were changed dramatically by the infiltration of non-Indians into their territory on the Northwest coast.*

line, ready to shell native villages if there were signs of insurrection. The first Governor, James Douglas, had recognized native title to land, but his successors denied Indians ever had title. Entering the 1990s Indian land settlement issues in British Columbia remain unresolved.[31]

In southeast Alaska the situation was much the same. No treaties were negotiated and no reserves were set aside except for one which was formed after a group of Tsimshian Indians from British Columbia followed the missionary William Duncan across the border in 1887. From 1867, when Alaska was transferred to the United States, to 1877, the U.S. army was stationed in southeast Alaska; in 1879 they were replaced by naval gunboats. In the 1870s, industrialists began moving into the region to establish canneries and mining concerns. Indians became wage laborers in these indus-

tries, working for relatively low pay and leaving villages to live in cannery or mining housing. Land issues in southeast Alaska were dealt with through a settlement in 1959 – following decades of pressure – and the state-wide Alaska Native Claims Settlement Act in 1971.

Along with the settlers, Christian missionaries came to the Northwest Coast. Russian Orthodox missionaries had been active among the Tlingit in New Archangel in southeast Alaska since the mid-nineteenth century, and in the last quarter of the century southeast Alaska also saw the arrival of Roman Catholic, Presbyterian and Friends missionaries. In British Columbia, starting in the mid-nineteenth century, missionaries from Roman Catholic, Anglican and Methodist denominations were represented. In addition to church services, missionaries ran schools for children and adults. Some, such as William Duncan,

established 'model villages' separated from existing villages, where Indians lived in European-style houses and agreed to abandon traditional forms of cultural expression such as the potlatch.[32]

Indians on the Northwest Coast had mixed reactions to missionaries. Many were interested in access to the missionary teachings – especially because missionaries could help them learn English and other skills that would equip them to survive in the new Euro-American society that was developing around them. As white settlers appropriated native lands and white industries took over native fishing streams and food resources, it became harder for Indians to continue entirely in their traditional economy, and it was increasingly important for them to be able to work as wage laborers.[33] Missionaries could help them acquire these skills and could prepare them for functioning in a society where white people were ready to exploit them. While missionaries are often condemned for their paternalistic, condescending and frequently dictatorial attitudes, they cared whether Indians survived and they believed at the time that their actions were helping the Indians.

However, missionaries and government officials did much more than teach English. They also held that traditional native culture was at the best that of 'heathens' and was at worst depraved. They waged an active campaign to stop Indians from practicing their own cultural expression and from passing on their heritage

Left: John Hunter, a Nuu-chah-nulth, in dance costume, c.1925. His heavy robe is hide, probably painted with (mainly) red and black pigments. Such fine carved and painted headdresses are rarely found in ethnographical collections.

Below: Effects of trade on the Nuu-chah-nulth. The main figure holds a trade gun, as does the man to his left who also wears a blanket which is probably not of indigenous manufacture.

Makah

The Makah lived in large plank houses in five semi-autonomous permanent villages on the tip of the Olympic Peninsula; today they mainly live at Neah Bay, one of these five. The village headmen and their immediate families occupied the top social rank and validated their positions by giving potlatches. Whaling was a particularly prestigious occupation, ritualized and hereditary. The large sea-going canoes were also used to hunt fur seals and for trading expeditions, and were exported to tribes to the south and east. Fishing for salmon and halibut provided an important part of the diet, but land mammals were little used. A major contribution to subsistence was made by women, who gathered shellfish, berries, and roots. Men engaged in complex woodworking technology. Carved food dishes were involved in conspicuous consumption by leading families. Women were versatile artists in basketry. All the objects shown here were collected by Judge James G. Swan between 1861 and 1884.

1 Braided grass tumpline, used for carrying loads on the back; the broad section ran across the forehead.
2 Model of whaling canoe, in the typical Makah shape, complete with harpoon and its inflated skin floats, and carved figures.
3 Halibut hook. (Halibut and salmon were fished especially in the summertime.)
4 Bow.
5 Arrows with brass points.
6 Two kelp fish lines with floats.
7 Knife used for splitting fish.
8 Dancer's rattle, made of scallop shells.
9 Braided grass tumpline, used for carrying loads on the back. As in 1, the broad section ran across the forehead.
10 Bow.
11 Wooden quiver and three arrows.
12 Twilled bag for spear heads and other gear.

13 Headdress for medicine dance, made from cedar bark, cut feathers, and red flannel.
14 Fancy work basket with foot and lid.
15 Large table mat, made for sale.
16 Large table mat, made for sale.
17 Woven rush bag.
18 Grass basket.
19 Carved stone with crest figures.
20 Bottle covered with coiled spruce root

basketry.
21 Carved wooden feast dish.
22 Wooden bowl in tortoise shape.
23 Small basketry table mat, made for sale.
24 Small basketry table mat, made for sale, as No. 23.
25 Short robe, twined, wefts of twisted downy bird skins.
26 Grass basket.
27 Straw basket made with three different tech-

niques.
28 Conical hat.
29 Plaited straw hat, copying non-Indian style.
30 Shaman's rattle, with carved weasel on top.
31 Shaman's rattle, with carved man's head and bird on top.
32 Fancy work basket with lid.
33 Bottle covered with fine coiled basketry.
34 Mat of checker woven cedar bark.

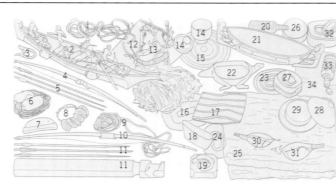

Left: *Interior of a Chinookan ceremonial lodge, by Paul Kane (1846). The spacious lodge is of hewn cedar planks; note the smoke-hole and cracks between the planks for good air circulation.*

native spirituality, native political systems and systems of hereditary rights – all of which seemed threatening to missionaries and government officials. The potlatch came to be viewed as the native custom that was preventing Indians from becoming 'civilised' as defined by missionaries and government officials, and they felt they had to destroy the potlatch if Indians were to become both Christians and citizens.[34]

Thus, in both British Columbia and southeast Alaska, missionaries and government officials launched an active campaign against native ceremonialism. In 1884, these efforts resulted in Canadian federal legislation outlawing potlatches. This law stayed on the books until 1951. Many Indians – and some white authorities – protested the legislation immediately, but to no avail. While it was not enforced regularly, the threat of prosecution – coupled with the other manifestations of cultural oppression the Indians faced – caused people to stop performing ceremonies in public. In some places on the coast, the ceremonies continued in clandestine fashion, always under the threat of prosecution. In other places, people gradually abandoned the ceremonies for the same reason.

In southeast Alaska, no legislation was passed outlawing potlatches. However, government officials and missionaries put strong pressure on Indians to stop potlatches, and many agreed to do so voluntarily.[35] Some felt that with white attitudes as they were they could not afford the prejudice that came from native cultural expression. When they were trying to find ways for their children to live with a reasonable amount of physical and psychological safety, they could not risk the prejudice they faced from whites when they expressed their culture openly. In 1904, many Tlingit leaders in southeast Alaska agreed at the governor's request to stop holding potlatches.[36]

In addition to appropriation of lands and extreme cultural oppression, white settlement brought another devastating blow to native societies and cultures. This was the introduction of diseases and of alcohol. These problems, which first developed during the maritime fur trade, increased exponentially with white settlement. As more whites came in to the region regularly, more diseases were introduced. Equally significant, native peoples from a number of villages throughout British Columbia began to gather at one city, and an epidemic that broke out in that city could be carried throughout the region.

This in fact occurred in 1862, when a ship from San Francisco accidentally brought smallpox to Victoria. When Indians camped outside the city contracted the disease, white residents drove them away. They returned to their home villages, inadvertently bringing the germ with them. The tragic epidemic wiped out at least one third of the total Indian population in British Columbia, and in some areas along the coast line villages were practically eradicated. In addition to smallpox, other diseases such as

to their children. They often forcibly removed children from their parents and communities, raising them in residential schools where they were punished for speaking their own language or celebrating their culture.

The potlatch was a particular target of missionaries and government officials both in British Columbia and in Southeast Alaska. They viewed it as a threat for a variety of reasons. Since they measured wealth only in material possessions, it seemed wasteful to give away summer earnings during winter ceremonies. Indian agents in British Columbia, who wanted Indians to become agriculturalists, would have greatly preferred to see the money spent buying farm equipment and seeds. Missionaries

charged that children were taken out of schools during potlatches, while employers complained the ceremonies made workers unreliable.

However, probably the most fundamental reason for opposition to the potlatch was the recognition that those ceremonies kept native culture alive. It was the expression of native ceremonialism that passed on native history and culture to young people. It was also the expression of native ceremonialism that affirmed

Below: *Interior of Chinookan lodge, by Paul Kane (1847), with central fire place. Meat is smoked on the heavy beam across the lodge, as are animal skins which are made waterproof by the smoking.*

Left: A Makah fisherman holding a whaling harpoon. These were generally made of yew and were about 18ft (6m.) in length. The cutting point was a mussel shell held by elkhorn.

During this period, except among the Kwakiutl and Salish peoples, very little ceremonial art was still being made. Some artists made works to sell to tourists and other non-native peoples. Some of these works remained technically excellent, especially the baskets being woven by women for white collectors. Because women had fewer opportunities to earn wages in the white economy, they could afford the time it took to make baskets, and this activity was also compatible with child care. However, with so few traditional contexts for ceremonial art and with more opportunities to work in white industries, fewer and fewer male artists could afford the time it took to become skilled carvers and painters. Also, with the population decline, there were fewer masters left with whom to apprentice. Predictably, this situation worsened as the twentieth century went on. By the 1960s, when art historian Bill Holm studied the Northern Formline style, he could not find a practicing artist from the Bella Coola region who had learned in traditional methods.[40]

Despite the extreme cultural oppression and social disruption, though, native peoples retained their sense of ethnic identity and their cultural values. Even when ceremonialism was suppressed, these values remained. Today, when civil rights and human rights are more widely acclaimed, Northwest Coast native peoples are reviving their traditional ceremonialism and are again practicing their cultural expression openly. Artists are active again making traditional forms of art, both to sell to collectors as fine art and to use in their own ceremonies. Indians are also very well organised politically and are still seeking redress of injustices of the past. They are also playing a strong role in environmentalism, for the preservation of their culture is integrally tied to the preservation of the forests in their traditional homelands of the Northwest Coast.

measles, influenza, tuberculosis, venereal disease and alcoholism had grave and disruptive effects on native societies.[37] In a short period of time, every native person almost certainly had friends and relatives who had died. Due to the social disruption, populations consolidated into a few villages in some places on the coast. The devastation made it easier for forces of cultural oppression to take their toll.

By the first decades of the twentieth century, the open expression of native ceremonialism had been effectively suppressed by white authorities. In British Columbia Indians could and were prosecuted for continuing their ceremonialism. This was particularly true of people from the Southern Kwakiutl region, who continued their ceremonialism more actively than most.[38] The cultural oppression, along with the other forms of devastation that Indian societies

faced, led to fewer and fewer ceremonies. Thus, there were fewer contexts in which traditional art was used, and fewer ceremonial art works were made.

Starting in the 1870s, museums in North America and Europe became very interested in collecting Northwest Coast Indian art.[39] Curators believed erroneously that the cultures would not survive and wanted to make a scientific record while it was still possible to do so. They sent collectors to the Northwest Coast to make 'representative' collections of the cultures. Collectors purchased art from native peoples who no longer were using it in ceremonies and who needed the money. Frequently, too, collectors took art from graves without permission. In a few decades, vast quantities of ceremonial art and of totem poles were removed from the Northwest Coast.

References

1 For more discussion of this point, see Holm, 1983: 15–16. For more detailed information on native methods of harvesting resources in their environment, see Stewart, 1973, 1977, 1984.
2 Duff, 1964: 38–9.
3 Jackson: 62–9.
4 For more discussion see Stewart, 1984.
5 Lobb: 21.
6 For more discussion of archeology of the Northwest Coast, see Carlson ed., 1976; MacDonald and Inglis, 1976; Fladmark, 1986.
7 For a succinct discussion of social organization on the Northwest Coast, see Macnair *et al.*, 1984: 15–24; Bancroft-Hunt and Forman, 1979: 25–49. The discussion that follows is based on these sources.
8 Bancroft-Hunt, 1979: 37.
9 For more discussion of Tlingit social organization, see Jonaitis, 1986: 34–9; Holmberg, 1985: 10–11; de Laguna, 1972: 212–13.
10 Macnair *et al.*, 1984: 21.
11 Macnair *et al.*, 1984: 22.
12 Macnair *et al.*, 1984: 22.
13 For a succinct discussion of ceremonialism on the Northwest Coast, see Halpin, 1981: 6–15.
14 Brown, in Corey ed., 1987: 157–75.
15 Duff, 1975.
16 This style was analysed in depth by Bill Holm in

Holm, 1965. It was here that he defined the terminology 'Northern Formline'. A popularization of his technical discussion is provided in Stewart, 1979.
17 A clear and succinct discussion of these styles appears in Macnair *et al.*, 1984: 25–42.
18 A succinct description of the various cultural styles is found in Macnair *et al.*, 1984: 43–62.
19 These hats were discussed in Vaughan and Holm, 1982: 32–3.
20 For more detailed discussion of Salish weaving, see Gustafson, 1980.
21 For more discussion of Chilkat blankets, see Samuel, 1982.
22 Halpin, 1981: 16–23.
23 Halpin, 1981: 7–12; Holm, 1987: 84, 100.
24 Holm, 1987: 100; Macnair *et al.*, 1984: 50–51, 96; Holm, 1983: 86–7. The discussion of the Tseyka is based on these works.
25 Holm, 1987: 84.
26 Holm, 1987: 48–9.
27 Macnair *et al.*, 1984: 52–3, 62.
28 A classic example is the Haida wood bowl illustrated and described in Macnair *et al.*, 1984: 46–7, 50. The bowl is in the collections of the Royal British Columbia Museum, Victoria, B.C.
29 For more discussion of the interactions between Northwest Coast Indians and European explorers

and maritime fur traders, see Gunther, 1972; Pethick, 1973; Cook, 1973.
30 For more discussion of the maritime fur trade, see Duff, 1964: 53-60; Fisher, 1977; Vaughan and Holm, 1983; Wyatt, 1984.
31 For a comprehensive discussion of government policies towards native lands in British Columbia, see Tennant, 1990. Policies are also discussed in Duff, 1964: 60–74; Fisher, 1977.
32 For more more discussion of missionaries, see Duff, 1964: 87–101; LaViolette, 1973; Fisher, 1977: 119–45; and Fisher in Veillette and White, 1977: 1–11.
33 For more discussion of native involvement in wage-labor industries, see Knight, 1978; and Wyatt in *Pacific Northwest Quarterly* 78 (1–2): 43–9.
34 For discussion of opposition to the potlatch, see LaViolette, 1973; Sewid-Smith, 1979; Hou, undated; Halliday, 1935. A book on the potlatch prohibition, written by Cole and Chaikin, is soon to be published by the University of Washington Press.
35 Hinckley, 1982: 249–53.
36 Hinckley, 1982: pp.251–3.
37 Duff, 1964: 40–44.
38 For a discussion of arrests made following a potlatch in 1921, see Sewid-Smith, 1979.
39 For more discussion of collecting, see Cole, 1985.
40 Holm, 1965: vii.

'To the south and east, in traditional Chippewa and Montagnais/Naskapi territory, full bloods and Métis all reported the same tale: "The beaver are going fast; in large areas they are already gone."'

THE SUBARCTIC

THIS VAST AREA spans the whole continent of North America from the Labrador peninsula in the east (including Newfoundland) and dipping to the south of Hudson Bay then west to Alaska. It encompasses a total area of some two million square miles inhabited by perhaps no more than 60,000 Athapaskan or Algonquian-speaking people.

Although the climatic features in the Subarctic tend to be uniform over large areas, the terrain is varied. Most dominant, however, is open woodland tundra of scattered coniferous trees, which is bordered in the north by an Arctic-alpine tundra and to the south by boreal forest, or Parkland, consisting of broadleaf trees scattered on wide expanses of grassland.

Approximately west of the Churchill River on the Manitoba shore of Hudson Bay were the Athapaskan-speaking people, and to the east the Algonquians. For successful fishing and hunting, small groups of extended families who were united by a common dialect lived together and followed the movements of the game animals; only for a comparatively short period during the summer months did these various groups briefly rendezvous, hence expressing a form of tribal solidarity. The Athapaskan speakers included the Tanaina, Tanana, Kutchin, Han, Inland Tlingit, Tahltan, Hare and Mountain Indians in the northwest and the Yellowknife, Dogrib, Slavey, Beaver and Chipewyan in the east and to the south of the Great Bear and Great Slave lakes. The Algonquians, such as the Strongwoods Cree, Western Woods Cree and Rocky Cree, were east and south of the Slave and Athabasca rivers. A broad sweep eastwards beyond Lake Winnipeg in present-day Manitoba included the Swampy Cree, Northern Ojibwa, Saulteaux and West Main Cree whose territory bordered the shores of the Hudson and James Bays. East of these bays and north of the St Lawrence River were the East Cree, Attikamek, Naskapi and Montagnais, the territory of the two latter tribes extending to the Labrador Sea. Because of the extensive area encompassed by the Subarctic region, it has been further divided into smaller regions – the Yukon, Mackenzie, Central (bordering the south of the Hudson Bay) and Eastern on the Labrador peninsula, and whilst the overall lifestyle of the people was similar, none, for example, practiced agriculture; they were all hunters and fishermen and tribal cohesion was minimal. However, the type of dwelling used, the mode of transportation, subsistence patterns, care of the elderly and warfare patterns were often markedly different. The emphasis on local band affiliation was a characteristic feature of much of the Subarctic social organization. Such bands readily adapted to the annual migrations and seasonal foraging ranges. They had a high degree of continuity, but a fluidity of composition, and one scholar of the Chipewyan has recently pointed out the great value of such organization in maintaining identity in a variety of traditional and modern environments. For example, whilst the nomadic herds of caribou were generally predictable in their movements, any erratic or unusual changes could be accommodated by the spatial distribution of the bands facilitating a communication network which could 'report on the direction of movement, dispersal and concentration of the caribou'[1] (Smith, 1978:68).

The total population of the scattered bands, which constituted a loose-knit tribe, was generally small; that for the Montagnais-Naskapi, for example, was some four thousand in the mid-nineteenth century occupying a territorial range of at least four hundred thousand

This map shows approximate territories of tribes and language groups in about 1850, and somewhat earlier in a large region west of Hudson Bay. After that, many tribes lost territory and others moved.

Key to tribes:
1 Holikachuk
2 Ingalik
3 Kolchan
4 Tanaina
5 Koyukon
6 Kutchin
7 Tanana
8 Ahtna
9 Han
10 Tutchone
11 Hare
12 Mountain Indians
13 Tagish
14 Inland Tlingit
15 Kaska
16 Tahltan
17 Tsetsaut
18 Sekani
19 Slavey
20 Beaver
21 Carrier
22 Chilcotin
23 Dogrib
24 Yellowknife
25 Chipewyan
26 Western Woods Cree
27 West Main Cree
28 Northern Ojibwa
29 Lake Winnipeg Saulteaux
30 Naskapi
31 East Cree
32 Attikamek
33 Montagnais
34 Beothuk

184

square miles. The statistics for the Chipewyan are similar: thus, a population density of one person per one hundred square miles was not uncommon in both Athapaskan and Algonquian territory.

A marked social characteristic of the Subarctic people was the great emphasis placed on personal autonomy and this gave rise to largely non-aggressive behavior in interpersonal relationships, thus avoiding domination and respecting others' freedom of action. Parents extended such behavior toward their children which led to the development of independent personalities with a high degree of self-reliance and personal initiative, traits so essential for maintaining harmonious life in the small extended family bands. However, a built-in symbolic warning that the independence must not be carried too far was another Subarctic trait; its message was conveyed in tribal mythology which warned of the dangers of extreme isolation from communal life and referred to lone forest prowlers, such as the Cree and Saulteaux Windigo (cannibal) and the Kutchin's 'bush men'.

The immense self-reliance and personal initiative displayed by the Subarctic people was underlined by a remarkable episode related early in the history of the Canadian fur trade and reported on by Samuel Hearne in 1770, who led an expedition from the Hudson's Bay post of Fort Churchill in search of the Coppermine River east of the Great Slave Lake. On their return journey, they came across a Dogrib woman who had escaped from Cree captors; alone for some seven months, she had not only built herself a small shelter, made snares to trap hares (the so-called snowshoe rabbit), fabricated snowshoes and begun work on a fish-net in anticipation of the spring melt, but had decorated her fur clothing. Hearne, obviously greatly impressed by this resourceful, brave woman, reported: 'It is scarcely possible to conceive that a person in her forlorn situation could be so composed . . . all her clothing, besides being calculated for real service, shewed great taste, and exhibited no little variety of ornament . . . as to make the whole of her garb have a very pleasing . . . appearance' (Hearne, 1958:169).

Above: Ingalik man holding a pick and scoop used in fishing, Anvik, Alaska, c.1923. These implements were used in winter fishing for cutting a hole in and clearing the ice.

Hearne's journal also gives an interesting perspective relating to the woman's lot in Subarctic culture at the time of early contact. Befriended by the influential Chipewyan chief, Mattonabee, Hearne was lectured on his misfortunes which were due, the Chief said, to the lack of women in Hearne's party. Women, he emphasized, were 'made for labor'; one of them, he maintained, could carry or haul as much as two men. They could also pitch the tents and keep up the fires at night. Further, he pointed out, although they did everything, they could be maintained at a trifling expense and, with wry humor added, that as they also acted as cooks, the 'very licking of their fingers' in scarce times would be quite sufficient for their subsistence (ibid).

The most common form of habitation was

Hudson Bay

30

33

27

34

28

31

32

ATLANTIC OCEAN

the conical tent – the 'wigwam' of the Algonquian-speaking groups – resembling the Plains tipi and covered with moose or caribou hides on the tundra, and bark in the forest regions. On occasions, the Cree used domed-shaped lodges covered with sheets of birch bark whilst the Kutchin, who had limited access to birch bark, utilized similarly constructed domed dwellings, but covered with skins. In both conical and dome-shaped lodges, the fireplace was located at the centre; an exception to this was the East Cree *shabúktowan*, 'the house that you walk right through', which resembled two wigwams joined together with a fire at each end and a smoke hole above each (Skinner, Wissler ed., 1911:14). In constructing the conical lodge, two poles were laid on the ground in the form of a cross; these were bound together at their intersection and set upright, a third pole was then placed into the crotch and this too was lashed in. By drawing the tripod closer together at the base, the top was elevated and the sides made steeper. Other poles were then laid into the foundation to support the covering of skin or bark. In the latter case, the bark was in rolls about 3ft (1m.) wide and varying in length depending on its position on the conical frame. Once the bark was in place, more poles were laid upon it, thus anchoring the cover. Skin wigwams were similarly constructed, thus mark-

Above: Ingalik caches at Shageluk, Lower Yukon River, Alaska. Caches, in which food was placed, stood adjacent to houses in the village; they were then mounted on high posts safe from predators.

Below: An Ingalik man removing fish from a trap, holding a wooden scoop. Behind him is an ice chisel and long wooden ice scoop. Large traps of this type were mainly used for ling.

edly differing from the Plains tipi which was generally of a single sewn cover and devoid of any external anchoring poles.

Wigwams were clearly not primitive dwellings, as a cursory inspection may suggest: the sewing of the bark rolls, the varying lengths, the shingle-like overlapping and the painted ornamentation referring, in the case of the East Cree, to property marks, point to a well-constructed and habitable dwelling suited to the environment and the nomadic lifestyle of the people. Likewise, wigwam organization and etiquette was well developed, poles being tied across the interior some 6 to 8ft (1.8-2.4m.) from the ground from which moccasins and utensils could be hung and it was not uncommon also to hang fish on this cross-piece directly above the fire for slow curing, whilst the place of honor for guests was recognized as directly opposite the door.

Caribou and moose, the most important large food animals, were the Barren Ground caribou of the northern transitional forest and the adjacent tundra, whilst to the south and throughout the boreal forests were the wood-

Below: Lower Ahtna Indians from the Copper River valley of SE Alaska, c.1902. The clothing is decorated with bone buttons and beadwork on the carrying straps. Note moss for the diaper (right).

land caribou, moose and a few woods buffalo.

The Chipewyan technique of hunting caribou was to drive them into the mouth of a chute consisting of bush or poles set some 50 to 65ft (15-20m.) apart, which led to a circular pound, up to a third of a mile in diameter; this pound enclosed a complex maze of bush hedging between which snares were set. Entangled caribou were despatched with spears whilst the remaining loose ones were shot with arrows.

In contrast, the enormous moose did not move in herds and a different technique had to be adopted, a method which was based on the close observation of the behavioral characteristics of the animal. In order to catch the scent of any following predator, a moose generally doubles back after feeding, resting at a spot downwind of its earlier trail. Responding to this behavioral characteristic, the Indian hunter avoids following the trail of the moose, but instead makes semi-circular loops downwind; when the moose's trail loops back, the hunter can accurately locate it. During the rutting season, moose could be attracted by use of a birch bark calling horn and in late winter immobilized by drawing them into deep snow, where they could be speared.

The main meat diet of the caribou and moose was supplemented by that from smaller animals such as beaver, hare, rabbit, muskrat

and squirrel, which could be trapped with deadfalls or snares. The Subarctic areas required large quantities of food to support families, it being estimated that at least four pounds of flesh could be consumed daily by each adult. It was essential that a high proportion of this flesh was fat in order to ensure the necessary calorie and fatty acid intake, thus the *type* of flesh eaten was important. Rabbits, for example, were little valued by some groups as sustaining food, since most of the year they had limited body fat, a common native adage being that one could 'starve to death on rabbits'! (Rogers and Smith, 1981:135). One Hudson's Bay Company trader has pointed out that to these Subarctic people, the beaver – and this would be particularly applicable to the Cree in whose territory the animal abounded – was to a large extent what the seal was to the Eskimo. The beaver, in contrast to the snowshoe rabbit, carries a large amount of fat upon its body; it was, the Indians claimed, 'just as necessary to their well-being in the cold of winter as was bacon and butter to the white men' (Godsell, 1935:114).

The availability of food resources varied with the season and in order to preserve a balanced diet a good deal of meat and fish was preserved. On occasions during the winter, sometimes flesh was frozen, but the most common

Ingalik

The Ingalik, speakers of an Athapaskan language, lived in the late 19th century mainly at Anvik on the lower Yukon River and Shageluk on a nearby tributary. They hunted caribou, moose, bear, beaver, and other mammals, and waterfowl, and depended heavily on fish which they caught throughout the year, including during the winter when they set traps beneath the ice. The fish wheel trap introduced near the end of the century greatly increased the summer take of salmon. Each winter village was centered on a large, semi-subterranean building where ceremonies were held, and men socialized and made and repaired weapons and implements. The Ingalik traditionally observed seven major ceremonies involving feasting, gift giving, and a wide variety of dramatic dances, many of them masked, such as the Mask Dance which was to increase the numbers of game animals. The objects shown here were collected pre-1905 by the Rev. John W. Chapman, missionary at Anvik since 1887 (except for No. 13).

1 Pair of maskettes used by messengers who invite guests to attend Silver Salmon Mask Dance.
2 Grouse mask for Mask Dance.
3 Fire drill; birch rod spun by cord with toggles on ends; it is pressed into the hearth by means of the mouthpiece with bone inset. Anvik.
4 Bear mask for Mask Dance. Shageluk.
5 Mask painted with ochre, for informal dance at Mask Dance. Anvik.
6 Rings with feathers held in each hand by a dancer wearing the mask described above (No. 5). Anvik.
7 Wand with carved wolf figure, used by a dance master at Partner's Potlatch. Anvik.
8 Stone ulu or woman's knife. Anvik.
9 Half-man mask for Mask Dance. Shageluk.
10, 11 Two masks caricaturing Holikachuk men, for Mask Dance. Shageluk.

12 Otter mask for Mask Dance.

13 Custom of masked dances was shared with neighboring peoples, as illustrated by this N. Alaska Coast Inuit mask used at Point Hope, c.1903.

14 Birch bark container for liquids, berries, etc. Anvik.

15 Wooden ladle used as spoon or cup. Anvik.

16 Pouch made of fish (perhaps lamprey) skin.

17 Man's leather pouch with quill decoration. From the Holikachuk neighbors of the Ingalik.

18 Fingerwoven wool belt. Anvik.

19 Storage bag of leather with bird skin inserts.

20 Woman's twined grass bag, for carrying or storage.

21 Saucer of feather-tempered pot used with whitefish or seal oil and moss wick as lamp for lighting; obsolete by 1904. Anvik.

22 Mask of Siren being, for Mask Dance.

23 Maskette used by messenger inviting guests to Otter Mask Dance.

24 Crow mask for Mask Dance. Shageluk.

25 Mask, Father of Mosquito, for Mask Dance. Shageluk.

26 Raven mask for Mask Dance. Shageluk.

27 Mask of Siren being, for Mask Dance. Shageluk.

28 Mask.

29 Mask, Mother of Mosquito, for Mask Dance. Shageluk.

30 Mask caricaturing a Holikachuk man, for Mask Dance.

methods were to smoke or sun dry. One observer described the manner of smoking moose meat for quick preservation during traveling, as being accomplished 'by drying up the juice of the flesh by the heat from the fire' (Skinner, 1911:29). The flesh was sliced up and placed on a scaffold formed of four upright sticks of green wood driven into the ground in the shape of a rectangle and at a height of about 3ft (1m.); longitudinal bars were then lashed on the long sides and these supported the green wood grill over which the thin strips were hung. A sizeable fire cured the meat within two to three hours – sufficient to preserve it for a few days – but the method required that the meat be constantly turned toward the fire and, if traveling for some time, it was necessary to repeat the process by stopping earlier in the day. An alternative technique, which gave more permanent preservation, was to smoke it on a frame built of three poles which were fastened together with cross bars near the top; the meat was hung on these bars and smoked for several days. Enormous quantities of fish were often preserved in a similar way, particularly by those groups such as the Kutchin, some of the Hare bands, Tanana and Tanaina; indeed, in the case of the latter, salmon was the very basis of their subsistence.

Hide tanning was a crucial part of Subarctic technology and, in the case of the Chipewyans, the caribou was a central component to their whole material culture complex and whilst the animal was hunted, skinned and butchered by men, the exhausting tanning process was carried out by women. Unlike the tanning of buffalo and moose hides, which were stretched or pegged out, Chipewyan women stretched the 'green' hide over a log and defleshed the inner side with a bone tool with a serrated edge. The hide was then soaked in water for several days, which loosened the hair so that it could be more easily removed with a bone beamer. The brain from a caribou skull was removed and mixed with water to produce a soup-like substance which was worked into the hide by alternately soaking and rubbing. It was necessary to carry out this step in the process with great care, ensuring that all the hide was thoroughly soaked, because it was at this stage that the chemical reaction led to the preservation of the hide and prevented subsequent deterioration. The hide was then stretched out to dry, often aided by freezing, and then soaked in water to wash out the unreacted tanning solution. It was then made pliable during the final period of drying by pulling it over a pole and working it by hand. An attractive brown color could be imparted to the hide by smoking it on a tripod over a hardwood fire which was smothered with moss; the process had the added advantage of partially waterproofing the hide – due to resin impregnation – and repelling mosquitoes and flies.

Although there were some differences in the above process (some groups, such as the Dogrib for example, used urine to remove fat surplus in the hide (Hatt, 1969:18)), the basic technique was the same throughout the Subarctic region – defleshing, perhaps dehairing, tanning with fatty substances, and rigorous mechanical handling, during the final drying sequences.

Whilst there were considerable variations within the Subarctic region in naming of sea-

Above: *Lower Ahtna Indians, the daughters of Chief Stickwan, c.1902, probably near the Lower Tonsina or Taral. They demonstrate the use of tumplines in the carrying of camp equipment.*

Below: *View of a Beaver encampment in the Peace River area, c.1920, showing an arrangment of lean-to dwellings typical of the Athapaskan groups. The tipis are a Plains influence.*

Above: *A group of Beaver hunters, c.1920. Although a late scene, it underlines the recorded fact that nomadism still persisted among these people even after the fur trade changed patterns of movement.*

sons and months, the annual cycle is fairly typical, putting emphasis on important seasonal events – the budding, blooming, leafing and fruiting of vegetation, moulting, migrating and pairing of animals and birds and the freezing of the rivers. The entry for January in the table refers to the winter as the 'old fellow' which caused the pine needles to drop, forming a covering on the snow just as pine boughs were laid on the floor of a wigwam to be used as bedding, an action referred to as 'spreading the brush' (Skinner, Wissler ed., 1911:48).

The Cree divided the year into eight seasons with twelve months or moons, producing a clearly defined annual cycle which is illustrated in the table below.

Group activities related to seasonal changes were determined by the relative abundance of fish or big game in a particular area. For example, in the case of the Tanana on the downstream sections of the major rivers which had heavy concentrations of salmon, there was an emphasis on fishing for their subsistence and they were the least mobile with a comparatively high population density. In contrast, those Tanana on the headwaters of the same rivers – perhaps less than two hundred miles away – put emphasis on hunting caribou, supplemented in July and August by the trapping of

| SEASON | | MOONS | |
Cree	English	Cree	English
Sigun	Spring before open water	Migisupizun	Eagle month (March)
		Miskipizun	Gray goose month (April)
Miluskamin	Spring, after the water is open and before summer	Aligipizun	Frog month (May)
Nipin	Early summer	Sagipukawipizun	The month leaves come out (June)
Megwanipiu	Middle summer	Opaskwuwipizun	The moon when ducks begin to moult (July)
		Opunhopizun	The moon young ducks begin to fly (August)
Tukwagun	Early autumn	Weweopizun	Wavy or snow goose month (September)
Migiskau	Late autumn	Opinahamowipizun	The moon the birds fly south (October)
Pichipipun	Early winter, just before the frost	Kaskatinopizun	The moon the rivers begin to freeze (November)
Megwapipun	Late winter	Papiwatiginashispizun	The moon in which the young fellow spreads the brush (December)
		Gishepapiwatekimumpizun	The moon when the old fellow spreads the brush (January)
		Cepizun	Old month (February)

(AFTER SKINNER, WISSLER ED., 1911:48)

Kutchin

The Kutchin in the early nineteenth century lived in nine or ten regional bands on both sides of the present Alaska-Canada border, separated from the Arctic Ocean by a narrow strip of Inuit territory. Important as food were salmon, char and herring that were caught in weirs and with fishhooks, gill nets and spears. Small mammals, mountain sheep, moose and bear were hunted. The most prestigious hunting was for caribou, driven into surrounds or corrals, shot with bows and arrows, and speared while they swam. They provided food, bones to make tools and weapons, and skins for the fine, white-tanned leather used for clothing before about 1870. Both men and women wore a pullover shirt and trousers, the latter often with attached moose skin moccasins. Many of the objects shown here were collected before Kutchin technology was much affected by their participation in the fur trade, and by other outside influences. Dates of collecting are given, and (where known) the band of origin.

1 A man's caribou skin shirt, decorated with porcupine quills. Yukon Flats (or Birch Creek) band, 1866.
2 Man's caribou skin shirt, decorated with porcupine quills, pony beads, seeds, and red ochre. Yukon Flats (or Birch Creek) band, 1866.
3 Summer trousers with attached moccasins, made of caribou skin and beadwork. Yukon Flats (or Birch Creek) band, c.1860.
4 Pair of snowshoes, of the Loucheux type. Such snowshoes became standard across the western Subarctic. Probably Arctic Red River band, before 1905.
5 Man's caribou skin shirt, decorated with dentalia and

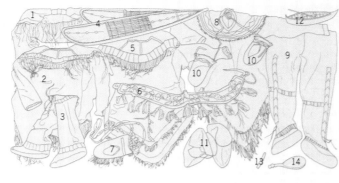

pony beads. Yukon Flats (or Birch Creek) band, c.1860.

6 Woman's shoulder band used to support a baby carried in a blanket; made of caribou skin faced with black velvet, beaded; before 1905.

7 Summer mittens on cord. Peel River band, c.1860.

8 Man's caribou skin shirt, beaded. This

fine shirt was acquired by E. W. Nelson from an Innoko River Kutchin man trading at St Michael, whom he photographed wearing it one summer between 1877 and 1881.

9 Trousers that were worn with the above shirt.

10 Pair of mittens on a cord (to run through sleeves of shirt to prevent loss), collected with above shirt and

trousers.

11 Pair of moccasins, Yukon Flats band, c.1866.

12 Model of one-man birch bark hunting canoe with spear; before 1905.

13 Knife. Yukon Flats (or Birch Creek) band, c.1860.

14 Ladle of mountain sheep horn; Han (not Kutchin) from Yukon River headwaters, c.1866.

whitefish. Such groups were amongst the most mobile following the caribou herds and had lower population densities. The general pattern was the same throughout the Subarctic region. Life was comparatively sedentary during the summer months when local bands rendezvoused along the shores of the rivers and lakes, an environment which afforded some protection from the great swarms of mosquitoes and blackflies. This was a time when social and family ties were reinforced and plans made for the coming winter. By early autumn, the gatherings dispersed, each band departing by canoe; at this time, the big game were in prime condition – the hides were at their best and the animals had an abundance of fat. Hunting was now a major activity and each band moved to its winter locality taking in meat and fish provision for the long winter months. The trapping of fur bearing animals took place in November and December when the furs were of the best quality. The pelts and hides were processed during the severest months of January and February when outside activities were virtually impossible due to intense cold and extended hours of darkness.

It was during these enforced periods of inactivity that the story makers recounted legends and perpetuated the tribal oral literature, whilst Montagnais-Naskapi hunters or shamans might assess their prospects, interpret dreams or organize discussion through the rituals of scapulimancy where moose, caribou or hare shoulder blade bones were held over a fire: the heat cracks, blackened spots and breaks were then interpreted in direct proportion to the ingeniousness of the practitioner. The custom was ancient, and has been sustained. It was reported on by the Jesuit missionary Paul Le Jeune who wintered with a

Above: A Cree Indian from the Fort Edmonton area, by Paul Kane (1846). He wears a fine shirt which is embellished with heavy bands of pony beadwork across the shoulders and down the arms.

Left: Otisskun, or 'The Horn', a Cree warrior, by Paul Kane (1846). He wears a war cap; the headdress consists of a cap covered with white ermine fur, surmounted by horns.

group of Montagnais in 1633-4 (Rogers and Leacock, 1981:184-6) and it was filmed by Hugh Brody in Pien Penashue's camp of Eastern Montagnais on the Goose Bay, Newfoundland, during the autumn of 1989 (Brody, 1990).

In addition to the tales of lone spirit woodland prowlers – the cannibals and bush men – it was also said that the spirits crossed the skies. In describing his travels with two Swampy Cree companions, one experienced observer reported that on witnessing the Aurora Borealis one remarked 'The *Choepi* [Ghosts] are having a good time to-night! ... Look how the spirits of our departed friends are dancing ... we call that *Pahkuk-kar-nemichik* – "The Dance of the Spirits!"' (Godsell, 1938:101).

In dealing with the supernatural, the East Cree, in common with most groups in the Subarctic, gave recognition to the enormous dependence on the products of the chase: this manifested itself in the form of sacrifices to propitiate the animals which they had to kill in order to survive. A widespread ethos recognized that a close bond existed between animals and human beings. Every animal was considered to have a spirit whose favor had to be sought, otherwise it could exert its influence to stop its species being killed by the hunters. Thus, the bones of beaver were carefully cleaned and cast into running water, whilst the heads of geese and ducks, the teeth of caribou and moose, the claws and skull of the bear, were cleaned and saved, serving not only as talismens and tallies, but also and, primarily, as an offering to the spirit of the respective animal. Bears, in particular, were highly honored, their skulls being carefully cleaned, dried and painted with stripes or dots[2] in red vermilion. They were then placed in trees out of respect to the animal.

At close quarters, the bear was a formidable opponent; nevertheless, because the bow was not considered powerful enough, they were

Above: *Cree hunting camp. The hide (or bark) covered conical wigwams have extra protective poles on the outside, a commonly used technique where the cover was of several pieces of material.*

hunted with club and knife. Crees reported that both the black and polar bears were particularly vulnerable when standing like a man, as they found difficulty in turning on the right side, thus an agile hunter was able to run in close and stab them in the heart. The creature was often likened to man and it was thought that they understood all that was said to them; as the hunter approached, he apologized and explained that the lack of food was the only motive for killing him and begged that the bear spirits would not be angry. At times, the bear was the winner, but the Cree explained that under these circumstances the animal could show compassion, such as in the case of a hunter who on attacking a bear was 'horribly scarred and mangled' but was finally set free when he pleaded with it for mercy (Skinner, Wissler ed., 1911:73).

In addition, the Subarctic people appealed to the powers of nature to help them with their great struggle for existence.[3] The winds were considered to be four brothers, the oldest and the most powerful being the north wind which brought the cold and had the power to punish evil doers. The other directions also had their distinctive characteristics and attributions (see table below).

For fast and effective travel, snowshoes were vital during the winter months; the style of snowshow varied, generally being described by reference to the frame shape. As a generalization, broad oval, sometimes almost circular frames, were typical of the Montagnais-Naskapi, whilst the narrow elongated shape was used further west. Virtually all such snowshoes were of a wooden frame which was netted with rawhide thong generally referred to as 'babiche', which universally took the place of vegetable cordage, almost absent in these regions. Finely cut rawhide strips were made into snares and netted game bags, whilst the heavier strips were used for burden straps, tow-lines and sometimes even extensive fencing when driving caribou into the pound. The snowshoes were not uncommonly embellished with tufts of colored trade wool which enabled them to be located in deep snow, whilst the babiche netting was colored, generally red and black, and patterns produced by additional lacing at the toe and heel sections.

In this vast area, clothing tended to become increasingly elaborate from south to north. Widespread was the use of leggings or trousers with attached fur- or grass-lined moccasins and a semi-tailored dress or hide shirt. Some of the finest, both everyday and ceremonial, clothing from such tribes as the Kutchin and Dogrib, now resides in the Royal Scottish Museum, Edinburgh, having been collected by the Hudson's Bay Chief Trader, Bernard Rogan Ross, in 1859 and 1860. Collected just prior to the white man's all-pervading influence, they provide invaluable basic data for any Subarctic material culture studies (Kerr, 1953:32-5). In the case of the Dogrib clothing, the woman's costume consists of a smoked caribou skin dress sewn with sinew and decorated with red and white porcupine quills and red flannel, with a red and white quilled belt; tube-like leggings are also made of smoked caribou skin sewn with sinew, as are the separate straight center front seam-'T' back seam moccasins (Type 2(Ab), Webber, 1989:28). The man's costume is similarly constructed, which may have a slight hint of white influence, exhibiting as it does a curious military collar.

Similar everyday clothing for the East Cree was described by the explorer Alexander Mackenzie three-quarters of a century earlier, whilst Skinner describes a fine hooded coat worn by hunters which was made of caribou skin and retaining the hair 'somewhat resembling Eskimo parkas'. Of particular interest is that they were painted *inside* by outlining on the skin, the eyes and mouth of the animal, symbolically stating that the power of the living animal – its speed, endurance or cunning – was possessed by the garment and could be transmitted to the wearer (Skinner, Wissler ed., 1911:15-17).

Ceremonial regalia was an elaboration of everyday clothing, generally embellished with porcupine quillwork, dentalium shells or painted. The quillwork was later combined with trade beads which ultimately virtually displaced the indigenous quillwork. Several garments are particularly distinctive within these areas. The Naskapi, for example, were well known for use of clothing which was painted in

WIND		ATTRIBUTION
English	Cree	
West	Nikapi-hun-nizeo	'A favorable person, good and generous to mankind. This is the best hunting wind'
East	Wapanung-nizeo	'A stingy fellow, he starves the people, and will give them nothing to eat'
South	Shawanung-nizeo	'Gives food in summer, and has charge of it. He gives the berries'
		(AFTER SKINNER, 1911)

Carrier

The Carrier of British Columbia were much influenced by their proximity to the rank-conscious, potlatching Bella Coola and Gitskan, by the 19th-century fur trade, gold mining and Catholic missionizing, and by 20th-century lumbering. Anthropologist Julian Steward documented their material culture during his field research among the Stuart Lake Carrier in 1940. The names of his sources, carefully noted at the time, are also included here.

1 Recent fish net made with fine commercial cord, made by Sophie (Mrs Sam) Basil.
2 Pair of snowshoes with single strap harness, upturned toes. Models by Keon Sagalon.
3 Snow walking stick, with sinew netted hoop, burned spiral design. Model by Louie Billy Price.
4 Recent hide flesher of moose leg bone with notched blade. Made by Mrs Puis.
5 Old scoop to remove ice from fishing holes; sinew cords. From Louie Billy Price.
6 Old shuttle for making fish net. From Mrs Stevens.
7 Man's moose skin shirt, sewn with thread (rather than sinew). Model by Mrs Alec McKinnon.
8 Man's moose skin leggings, sewn with thread. Model by Mrs Stevens.
9 Old moose skin mittens, sewn with thread. From Mrs George Todd.
10 Moose skin high-top soft-sole moccasins, sewn with thread. Model by Mrs Isadore Louis.
11 Moose skin quiver. Model by Mrs Edward Thomas.
12 Old harpoon head for beaver, of steel, three barbs. From Mrs Jimmy Stevens.
13 Canoe paddle for lake travel, burned design on handle. Model, about ¾ size, by J. B. Patrick.
14 Recent birch bark container with wood strip rim, made by Mrs Isadore Louis.

15 Old pack net of moose rawhide, used by women. From Mrs D. Todd.

16 Beaver harpoon point made from moose leg bone, two barbs. Model.

17 Buzzer toy of moose joint on sinew cords, wooden handles. Model by Pierre Sagalon.

18 Shinny stick of poplar wood. Reduced size model by Louie Billy

Price.

19 Recent shinny ball, moose skin sewn with red and blue thread. Made by Mrs Sam Sekani.

20 Recent dog's back pack, double sack of moose skin. Made by Mrs George Todd.

21 Shuttle cock, a ball of spruce bark. Model by Pierre Sagalon.

22 Snow shovel of poplar wood. Model by Daniel Michel.

23 Recent moose skin carrying bag, with lace closure. Made by Mrs Isadore Louis.

24 Recent birch bark basket with wooden rim, cloth handle.

25 Hoop of twigs wrapped with willow bark, at which darts are thrown in popular team game. Model by Mrs Edward Thomas.

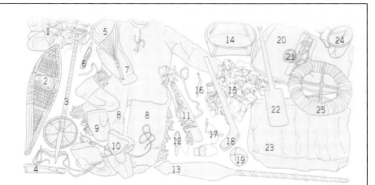

intricate patterns with tools of bone or wood, the main colors being red and yellow, but pigments were also mixed to obtain varying hues. Extended parallel lines were produced by the use of a multiple prong tool whilst fine lines were drawn with a curved paint stick; many of the designs were geometrical, but the so-called double curve motif was also commonly used. The work reached its fullest development on men's robes and summer coats, one specimen in the museum collections dating as early as 1740 (National Museum of Canada, Ottawa. Cat. No. III-B-588). This particular piece is made of soft caribou hide with fringed edges which were once wrapped with red porcupine quills. It is embellished with scores of double curve motifs in addition to straight lines, triangular figures and dots in a three-fold division, which one scholar has suggested symbolize the three cosmic zones which only a shaman, wearing the robe, could actually penetrate. Recent research has led to the speculation that such robes represented a religious microcosm and that, in donning the robe, the wearer entered into contact with the spirit world, abolishing time and entering into a primordial state. It is contended that his symbolic rebirth achieved with the robe 'was synonymous with the return of the sun, the renewal of the world, the rebirth of his people and, almost certainly the return of the caribou' (Webber, 1983:69).

Some of the earliest depictions of the magnificent prestige garments worn by the Athapaskan-speaking Kutchin to the northwest were made by Alexander Murray in his *Journal of the Yukon, 1847-48*. The distinctive pointed tailored shirts or tunics were often tailored in a complex pattern of many separate pieces of skin,

although the main body was generally made up of large pieces, front and back. The same style had also been traditionally worn by the Chipewyans who inhabited the country to the southeast. Indeed, the name Chipewyan, it has been suggested, was derived from the Cree name for this tribe, *Chepau-Wayanuk*, meaning 'pointed skins'[4] (Godsell, 1938:246; Duncan, 1989:46).

Prior to the introduction of beads, such garments were embellished with bands of porcupine quillwork, perhaps 2 to 2½in. (5-6cm.) in width, which extended across the chest and over the shoulders; similar bands were sometimes attached to the cuffs. There were variations in the quill techniques employed; in some instances the quills were held to the surface by two rows of stitches, the thread of sinew being caught into the surface of the skin between each fold of the quills. Alternatively, a markedly different appearance was obtained by a variation in the technique of folding the quills so that the quills crossed diagonally, producing a double sawtooth-like pattern. Five to six lanes of such work produced the full width bands, with patterns consisting of triangles, simple crosses, and bands predominately in red, white and blue. In addition, the lower edges were generally embellished with a buckskin fringe completely wrapped with quills near the point of attachment, for some 2½in. (6cm.), and then changing to alternate wrapped and unwrapped sections for another 2½in or so, finally terminating to a free fringe. The whole –

Below: *Northern Ojibwa camp, date uncertain but probably around 1900. The woman (right) heats water in a metal trade kettle. Note headscarves worn as protection against swarms of mosquitoes.*

sewn band and wrapped fringe – greatly enhanced the overall appearance of this prestigious and valuable garment.

An alternative quill technique was a type of surface weaving where quills were applied direct to the hide. First described by Orchard for the Tlingit (Orchard, 1916:36-7), but now rather firmly associated with the Alaskan Tanaina, the quills are laid lengthwise side by side on the hide surface. Spot stitches are concealed beneath the ends of the quills and at regular intervals a stitch is made across the surface of the quills; initially caught into the skin and under the quill on the outside edge of the decorative band, it then runs over the next quill and into the hide, running under the third quill, and so on across the entire width of the band and acting as a type of weft. At the commencement of the second row of stitches, the surface of the *first* quill is crossed, then under the second, over the third, under the fourth, over the fifth, repeating the sequence to the opposite edge. Additional quills were spliced in by bending the end of the previous quill together with the new one under the nearest spot stitch (ibid:fig.22).

A variant of this technique was to use a weft sinew such that, except for the outside quills, each rectangular exposed portion of quill was surrounded by a sinew thread. Whilst patterns were predominately made up of stripes, the techniques did lend themselves to the production of curvilinear motifs and, particularly in the older specimens, the colors were a distinctive yellow/orange, black/brown and natural white.

Such bands were also utilized to embellish mukluks (combined moccasins and leggings),

Cree Snowshoes

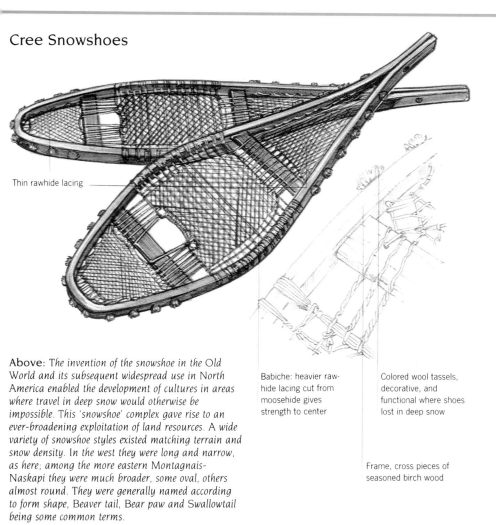

Thin rawhide lacing

Above: *The invention of the snowshoe in the Old World and its subsequent widespread use in North America enabled the development of cultures in areas where travel in deep snow would otherwise be impossible. This 'snowshoe' complex gave rise to an ever-broadening exploitation of land resources. A wide variety of snowshoe styles existed matching terrain and snow density. In the west they were long and narrow, as here; among the more eastern Montagnais-Naskapi they were much broader, some oval, others almost round. They were generally named according to form shape, Beaver tail, Bear paw and Swallowtail being some common terms.*

Babiche: heavier rawhide lacing cut from moosehide gives strength to center

Colored wool tassels, decorative, and functional where shoes lost in deep snow

Frame, cross pieces of seasoned birch wood

knife sheaths and mittens.[5] In the two latter cases, the quills were applied directly to the object, but for larger items – such as leggings and tunics – it was not unusual to work the quills on to a separate band and then sew them to the garment.

Separate woven quilled bands were, and still are, very much a speciality of the Slave and to a lesser extent, the Dogrib, who lived in the vicinity of the Great Slave Lake, North West Territories. Unlike the Tanaina work just described, this was done on a wooden bow loom. The warp threads were attached at each end of a green sapling, the tension bending the sapling into a bow shape so giving ample space below the threads for the work to be carried out unimpeded. A weft thread is now attached to the outer warp and then made to pass over and under the warp to the other side and back again; flattened quills are at the same time woven between the warp and weft threads. As the work proceeds, and each time a row is completed, the quills are pushed together so that the cross threads are hidden. Geometrical designs are produced by adding colored quills at various intervals. When the work is finished, the protruding underside ends of the quills are cut off for easy attachment of the band to an object. The finished piece has the appearance of fine cylindrical elements creating an impression that the quills themselves have been cut into short lengths and then woven in – as one could do with beads of a similar size and shape. The patterns produced in such work are wholly geometrical, commonly consisting of a series of repeated diamonds outlined in red, green, blue and orange quills. A notable feature of such work is the delicacy and repetition of the design patterns, in marked contrast to loom quillwork of some of the more southerly Algonquians such as the Cree and Métis (people of mixed Indian and French-Canadian blood) of the Red River area, where the patterns are bolder, design motifs are not quite so repetitive and larger quills are used.

A further feature of Slave woven quillwork is the occasional employment of moosehair in conjunction with the quills. Here, a number of hairs – perhaps four or five and equal to the width of a quill – are introduced in place of a quill so building up the stepped diamond patterns (Turner, 1955:38-9). Although commonly used as belts, bands of such quillwork were also attached to moosehide jackets, game bags and gun cases. This type of quilling required great skill and patience, and was much coveted, as Hudson's Bay Company factor Bernard Ross reported in 1862: 'The quantity done in a day by a skillful operative is about 2½ inches of belt size – and one of these articles is completed in about a fortnight, when it would be bartered for about 8 £-worth of goods' (Hail and Duncan, 1989:144).

The impact of trade goods on the Subarctic tribes was considerable. When Alexander Hunter Murray, a senior clerk of the Hudson's Bay Company, established Fort Yukon on the Porcupine River in 1847,[6] he made reference to the great importance of beads for trading to the

Left: *Montagnais-Naskapi winter camp, c.1910, showing the most common form of dwelling used in the region: 20 to 30 poles were used to form a conical framework covered with rolls of birch bark.*

Naskapi Hunter, 1880

A Naskapi hunter arrives home dragging a beaver he has killed. The ceremonial game carrying string, passed through the animal's nostrils, is designed to show respect for the game; red cords were used for beaver. The hunter wears a winter coat of tanned caribou skin with the fur side in, caribou skin leggings, and smoked deerskin mittens. His muzzle-loader is wrapped against the weather; he has a powder horn and a beaded shot pouch. His wife, smoking a stone pipe, has her hair wrapped around wooden blocks and wears a cloth cap and beaded cloth leggings. Her overdress is of caribou skin. The painted skin garments were brought to the Smithsonian the next year. The conical wigwams are covered with skins and canvas. A toboggan rests against one, with the front painted with a magical pattern.

Kutchin Indians, remarking 'Without *beads* and plenty of them you can do little or no good here . . . To trade here successfully, there ought to be for one year's outfit four boxes of common white beads, one box of red (same size) and one box of fancy' (Murray, Burpee ed., 1910:94). Beads were clearly a sign of wealth and prestige. 'I may here remark that all the chiefs hereabouts are young men, . . . none are considered a chief until they have 200 skins worth of beads . . . There is one man of the upper band who has between 90 and 100 skins in martens and beaver which he is keeping *all* for beads on our return' (ibid: 90 and 93). Murray further reported a competition with the Russian traders and expressed concern at the time it took to get suitable goods to the distant trading posts – perhaps up to *seven* years after the request. He also refers to the high value placed by the local Indians on the dentalium shells[7] and requests more for trading: 'They are most valuable, every Indian wears them, as nose and ear ornaments, for hair bands, etc.' (ibid:94)

Beads and dentalium shells were greatly favored by the Kutchin and Murray was impressed by the large quantities which they procured to embellish their clothing. His on-the-spot pen and ink sketches illustrate their early and extensive use as well as giving a wealth of ethnological detail which, although lacking some of the finer points relating to bead motifs, are found to be largely reliable when compared to actual specimens. The beaded bands which were attached to the garments resembled the earlier woven quillwork, the string of beads following the long axis of the band. Just as in the lanes of quillwork, patterns too were not uncommonly made up of striped rectangular figures, similar to quillwork; colors differed, however, blue, red, as well as black and white, dominated and preferences changed, sometimes remarkably quickly.[8] Actual examination of specimens reveals the use of large round-ended cylindrical shaped beads about 4 to 5mm.

in length and diameter to be common on mid-century and earlier pieces, whilst the slightly smaller and more rounded variety (generally referred to as 'pony beads' – see references to these in captions throughout the book), were more popular less than a quarter of a century later, possibly reflecting a change in trade patterns.

The coveted dentalium shell, whilst popular in the form of necklaces and carrying straps, was also combined with black or blue pony beads and sewn to the tunic or dress, generally following the contours of the shoulder cape. Whilst large areas could be covered comparatively quickly by the use of these shells, they were an exceedingly expensive embellishment. Murray, reporting from Fort Yukon in 1847, states 'these are traded in this country 6 and 8 for a beaver or 3 martens, a box of these shells here would be worth over *two thousand pounds*' (ibid:71-2).

By the 1850s, a smaller type of bead was gaining popularity in the Subarctic region. Generally referred to as a 'seed' bead, which ranged approximately 1 to 2mm. in diameter and came in a wide variety of colors, it was frequently used in combination with red and black cloth to embellish a wide variety of objects, considerably extending on the earlier artwork, which had largely been restricted due to the scarcity of natural materials.

About the same time, silk and cotton threads were being introduced, particularly in the Lake Winnipeg region, with outlets at such Hudson's Bay Trading Posts as Norway House, located on the northern shore of that great lake. Embroidering with such threads was particularly popular with the Cree, Saulteaux and Métis people of that region and, on a smaller scale, to the

Below: *Montagnais-Naskapi encampment, c.1883. Note the 'at ready' canoes adjacent to the lodge. Light and maneuverable, the 'crooked' canoe was well suited to the fast flowing rivers of the region.*

north and west, amongst the Chipewyan, Slave and Dogrib, who wrapped horsehair[9] fillers with colored threads, or used silk and colored ribbons or tape largely as decoration around the edge of moccasin vamps.

As was discussed earlier, whilst some of the pony beadwork patterns can sometimes be related to those found in the earlier quillwork, this is not the case with embroidery or seed beadwork, the dominant motifs being floral and most highly developed in the Great Slave Lake-Mackenzie River region amongst those tribes – particularly Chipewyan, Slave and Dogrib – who had firm contacts with the Hudson's Bay Company Trading Posts such as Fort Chipewyan on Lake Athabasca, and Forts Resolution, Rae and Providence, on the Great Slave Lake. The new media allowed greater freedom in the development of design motifs which had previously been largely confined to the geometrical in porcupine quillwork. Further, there were considerable outside influences, not least the missionaries, who after establishing a religious community on the Red River amongst the Plains Cree and Chippewa (Ojibwa) in 1818, expanded north to Lake Athabasca and the Great Slave Lake in 1849. It is almost certain that floral vestments, altar cloths and church paintings became the inspiration for these new design motifs. Certainly in the case of the church paintings, one Mother Superior reported: 'The native women, who enjoy silk thread, bead and quill embroidery . . . came to copy these designs from the Cathedral'[10] (Duncan, 1989:59).

Initial efforts at producing floral patterns could result in attractive but stiff designs but, in largely dispensing with a beaded background, which tended to crowd the decorative field, the motifs expand into dynamic semi-realistic, generally stemmed, patterns, which became the characteristic of much Athapaskan beadwork produced in the latter years of the nineteenth and early twentieth centuries. This

Cree

These objects were collected by the anthropologist Alanson Skinner in 1908 and 1909 in Ontario and Quebec from speakers of three different dialects of the Cree language. The Cree at Eastmain and Rupert House speak East Cree, those at Moose Factory speak Moose Cree, and those at Fort Albany speak East Swampy Cree and the rest are West Main Cree. When Skinner was conducting his research among them, they were hunters and fur trappers, living off forest products (primarily game and fish) and food obtained from the Hudson's Bay Company posts in exchange for furs. They lived in conical or domed wigwams covered with canvas, wore Euro-American clothes (hunters often used native moccasins), and hunted with guns. Travel was by birch bark canoes in summer, dog sled and snowshoes in winter. Crafts included woodworking, tanning, beadwork, and making rabbitskin blankets in a netting technique. Long missionized, the Cree were Catholics or Anglicans, though some native rituals persisted.

1 Beaming tool, for dehairing skin. Ft Albany.
2 Netting needle.
3 Wooden spoon for eating boiled caribou blood mixed with moss. Rupert Hse.
4 Toy snow shovel (full size 4–5ft long). Rupert Hse.
5 Boy's sling. Rupert Hse.
6 Crooked knife for carving; from Tom Bain, Moose Factory.
7 Old style crooked knife of beaver incisors. Eastmain.
8 Shot pouch of beaded cloth. Ft Albany.
9 Leather work bag embroidered with silk thread. Eastmain.
10 Beaded pouch for ammunition caps. Ft Albany.
11 Sealskin shot pouch. Eastmain.
12 Wooden ladle. Ft Albany.
13 Wooden ladle. Ft Albany.
14 Ladle, shape used to dip out boiled fish. Rupert Hse.
15 Spoon for boiled caribou blood mixed with moss. Rupert Hse.
16 Woman's bag made of

202

caribou fetus skin. Eastmain.

17 Pipe bowl made of red stone found on shore; 'beaver size' (trade value, one beaver pelt). Rupert Hse.

18 Birch bark container with cloth top. Moose Factory.

19 Birch bark porridge bowl. Ft Albany.

20 Model of wooden eating tray of type left in food cache at forest camp. Rupert Hse.

21 Model of net used to catch beaver. Rupert Hse.

22 Painted bear skull, hung up in forest for success in taking bears. Eastmain.

23, 24 Two lower lips of black bears; hunting charm or trophy. Rupert Hse.

25 Young bear's scapula, kept as charm and hunting trophy. Eastmain.

26 Caribou teeth charm.

27 Bone charm in bag tied to 23.

28 Stuffed goose head kept as charm or hunting trophy. Rupert Hse.

29 Beaded shot pouch. Ft Albany.

30 Beaded pouch for ammunition. Ft Albany.

31 Model of bow drill for making fire. Moose Factory.

32 Model of old style fish hook. Rupert Hse.

33 Rattling beater used with conjuror's drum. From 'Old Swallow', conjuror at Rupert Hse.

34 Woman's bag of summer caribou leg skin. Rupert Hse.

35 Child's rattle. Rupert Hse.

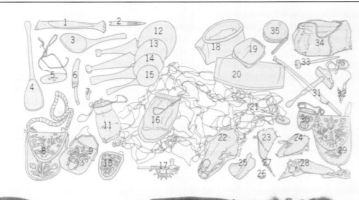

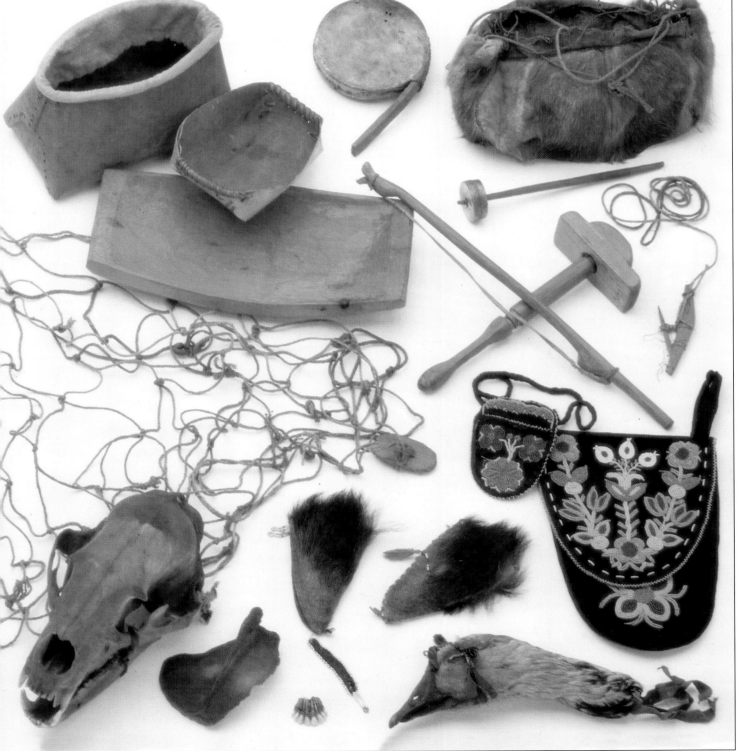

ready adoption of European technology epitomized the flexibility of Athapaskan society, developed over the centuries in order to survive in a frequently hostile and often unpredictable environment and where the natural materials required for ornamentation were difficult to obtain and use. It also became a source of revenue for the often impoverished families whose womenfolk turned their hands to the production of wall pockets, dog blankets, pouches, moccasins, mittens, gauntlets, jackets and even shelf valances, all magnificently embellished with beads and to a lesser extent, thread embroidery.[11] Much of the raw materials were supplied by 'The Bay' which,

since its foundation and Royal Charter from Charles II in 1670, encouraged the Indian people of the Subarctic to hunt and trap such creatures as the beaver, mink, ermine, fox, wolf, bear and otter, often with brutal metal traps supplied by 'The Company': all this to satisfy

Below: A view of a Montagnais-Naskapi encampment on Grand Lake, Labrador, c.1891. Note the bark and hide/cloth covered conical lodges, the bearskin frame and the strips of wood which have been prepared for canoe building. Their lodges would have an opening for smoke just above the fireplace. The canoes near the dwellings underline the vital importance of mobility to the Indians.

the demands of the European markets for exotic animal pelts. Clearly, by seemingly reconciling the ancient beliefs where animals were treated with respect and killed only for survival, Indian people expanded their hunting activities, thus obtaining some relief from the harsh Subarctic environment – expressed in utterances by the people themselves such as the Chipewyan eternal cry, 'Dow-diddla! dow-diddla!', 'It is hard! it is hard!' and the Montagnais' sentiment, 'We are poor, . . . and we live among the trees, but we have our children' (Godsell, 1938:250 and Hubbard, 1908:193).

But for this a price was to be paid because, as with the decimation of the immense buffalo

herds on the Great Plains to the south in the last quarter of the nineteenth century, so too with the fur-bearing animals of these northlands. The immense number of animals which were slaughtered solely for their furs is illustrated by the Annual Reports of the fur companies. The returns of the North West Company,[12] c.1800, in a single season were:

Beaver	106,000
Bear	21,000
Fox	15,000
Kit Fox	40,000
Otter	46,000
Marten	32,000

Whilst trade values obviously varied, particularly when there was competition, the profits could be enormous. For example, when Alexander Murray set up a trading post in Kutchin territory in 1847 (as mentioned earlier), he reported that the Russian traders gave ten blue beads 'a little larger than a garden pea' for one beaver skin (Murray, Burpee ed., 1910:71). The slaughter continued, virtually unabated, for a century. Over a nine year period (1920-29), the average number of pelts returned per year by the Canadian provinces was:

Beaver	137,400
Red Fox	56,030
White Fox	39,688
Marten	43,480

The following year, however, saw a dramatic drop to less than fifty thousand in returns on the beaver, an animal generally considered emblematic of the fur trade, and which to several Subarctic tribes, as already mentioned, was as important to their territorial lifeway as the seal was to the Inuit. The enormous profits which could be made, as with the buffalo hunters some sixty years previously, caused the influx of white trappers who not infrequently employed hunting methods which gave scant regard for a basic woodland law, which decreed that female animals were left undisturbed during the breeding season. In this, they were encouraged by traders because, although the pelts at this time were poor in quality, they were still accepted by all 'except the Hudson's Bay Company' (Cory, 1935:66).

The Dogrib and Slaves north of the Peace River, incensed at the white trappers encroachment, retaliated by starting forest fires to drive out the white invaders. To the south and east, in traditional Chippewa and Montagnais-Naskapi territory, full bloods and Métis all reported the same tale: 'The beaver were going fast; in large areas they were already gone' (Grey Owl, 1935:48).

On the Subarctic-Woodland boundary north of Lake Nipissing, one Indian hunter in the winter of 1925-6 had 'twelve white men trapping on his family hunting territory . . . As the white newcomers trapped an area until it became barren, to protect themselves from exploitation, the Indians began to do the same' (Smith, 1990:80).[13]

European diseases, and in some cases poor diet, also weakened resistance. As with the Plains tribes, smallpox had decimated many of the northern tribes in 1791-2 and again in 1837-8, whilst the influenza epidemics, against which the indigenous populations had little resistance, caused havoc. Skinner (1911), for example, found that owing to the great mortality during the influenza epidemic which swept through Northern Quebec and Ontario in the winter of 1908-9, it was almost impossible to find anyone who was able to relate the myths and legends of the East Cree. Again, in 1917, it wiped out forty per cent of the Lake Nipigon Chippewa/Cree and, in the winter of 1927, most of the Prophet River band of Sekani.

By the 1930s, the great Subarctic was witnessing a fast vanishing frontier, with several parallels to events in the United States less than a half century before. It would, however, be too simplistic to suggest that in this case it was largely dominated by avarice because this exploitation needs to be appreciated in the context of the times. The Great Depression of the 1920s caused the influx of large numbers of white trappers and traders. Lured by dreams of wealth, they tried their hand at trapping, often with little regard for any form of conservation or humane killing. It was a desperate attempt to 'escape the joblessness and despair of the Great Depression' (Irving et al., 1985:23). Traditional techniques of trapping by the indigenous people rotated trapping areas; the experienced hunter specifically designed his trap set so that only particular animals were guided

to the trap and thus few unwanted and unnecessary catches were made.

By the beginning of the 1940s the economic effects of the Depression and World War were felt in the north; markets collapsed, and fur prices plummeted. Whilst a few white traders and trappers stayed, most left, almost as suddenly as they had appeared and the fur trade reverted to the Dene, Métis and other indigenous groups of the Subarctic. The change came only just in time and today (1990s) it is claimed that no commercially trapped fur bearing species is endangered or threatened with extinction and the animal depletions which occurred during the early part of the twentieth century have now been restored and the fur bearing animals are 'as abundant as they ever were' (ibid:48).

A new threat, however, confronts the Subarctic people as they now face the great anti-killing campaigns which stigmatize their very lifestyle. Living in a land which does not lend itself to agriculture and in a land where oil, gas and mining developments are enormously expensive, they have been hardest hit by such campaigns and they are becoming a serious threat to a long-standing and sound way of life which has adapted to and produced a balanced environment.[14] It has been suggested that the Subarctic people must assert their right to manage their ancestral lands and animals based not on imposed standards but on inherited principles.

Today this message has been sent forth to the people of Canada in English, French and, as an extract below illustrates, in an almost universal written language of the great Subarctic – Cree :

ᐅᓇ ᐸᑦᐋᐦᑲᐸᒥᑎ ᐊ ᐊᓇᐊᑦ ᐸ ᐃᒥ
ᐅᓇ ᐸᐦᑕᐦᐸᒥᔭᑯᐋᑦ ᑲᐱᒪᐅᐱᑎᐦ ᐊᑕᐦᔭᒥᔭᑦ
ᐱᐦᑎᐋᑕᐦᑲᓄ ᐋᐦᐱᐋᒐᑕᐊᑕᐸᑦᐋᓄᐤ ᐋᐦᔭᑯᐤ
1000-ᐊᑦ ᐅᐦᐧᑎᐋᑦ ᑭᐊᐅᑕᐃᐅᐱᐋᑲᔭᑦᐊᑌᓇᑦ
ᐋᐦᐢ ᐊᐧᒪᐋᒥ ᐋᐸᑕᐦᐢᑕᐋᒋᐋᐸᑦ ᒐᐧᑕᐊᒥᑲ
ᐱᐦᑎᐋᑕᐦᑲᐱᒥ ᐋᑕᐱᐊᑕᐢᐱᑲᐊᑦᓇᐸᐊᐅᐅᐦᓇᑦ
ᐅᓇᐦᐸᐦᐸᐦᐱᒋᐋᑦ ᒸᐊᐤᐋᑕ ᐅᐸᐸᐸᑐᐢᑕᐋᑕᐊᑕᑦ
ᐋᐅᑎᐋᐸᐋᑕᐃᔭᓄᐊᐧ ᐸᐅᓇᐦᐢᒥᑕᐊᑦ.
ᑕᑲᐦᑲᐅᑎᑦᐸᑕᓇᐋᐧᐦᐤᑦ ᐊᐠᓇᐅᐅᐱᐱᐠᐊᓄᐤ
ᒥᐋᓇᐦᐧᓇᐦᑎ ᐅᐱᐅᐧᑕᐧᑦᐱᐧᐊᑦ ᐅᓇᐦᐊᐱᐸᓄᐤ
ᐅᑕᐅᐊᐧᐋᐸᑎᐅᐢᑕᐃᐧᐱᐋᐱᔭᐢᒥᐊᐧ ᐢᒥᐢᐸᐦᐢᐊᐋᐧ.
ᐋᑐᐦᐠᒐᐋᐠᔭᐅᐊᐧᑕᐊᒋᓄᐦᐸᓂᒨᑐ ᒪᑲᐃᐦᓇᑦ.

(ibid:3)

References

1 Band communication clearly led to efficient exploitation strategies: whilst living in a severe environment, Smith points out the Chipewyan 'do not have myths and legends which emphasize starvation' (Smith, 1978:68).

2 Frank G. Speck has discussed the distribution and symbolism of dot ornamentation on both Inuit and Indian objects (Speck, 1925:151-72).

3 See epigraph to this chapter.

4 A close observer of the Chipewyans commented on the large number of caribou hides required to make a complete outfit for one hunter – ten to twelve – and 'an even larger number to supply him with lodge, lines, snares and nets' (Godsell, 1938:246-7).

5 Speyer, 1968:Abb.2 and 4

6 This was actually within Russian territory. As Burpee observes, Murray seemed to have deliberately invaded the ground of his rivals, but it was 'all in the game of the fur trade, and that game was a rough-and-tumble affair at the best'

(Murray, Burpee ed., 1910:5).

7 Petroff refers to the very high value placed on these shells in 1802: 'The price of one pair of these shells was a whole parka of squirrel skins' (ibid:71).

8 Duncan reports that a Hudson's Bay Company trade list refers to 'amber and crystal beads, both unsalable five years earlier, are listed as now acceptable' (Duncan, 1989:44).

9 Horsehair was another valuable trade item (Turner, 1955:64).

10 I am appreciative of discussions with Katherine Pettipas of the Manitoba Museum of Man and Nature, who first drew my attention to such influences in the summer of 1977.

11 The influence of some particularly active Métis women on such artwork was commented on by Agnes Cameron, a journalist who visited Fort Chipewyan in 1909. Of Mrs Loutit, a Métis lady of mixed Chipewyan, Cree and Scottish blood, Bell reported 'She weaves fantastic belts of beads and

sets the fashion for the whole North' (Cameron, 1912:321).

12 The most powerful of all the Hudson's Bay Company's rivals.

13 The great efforts of the English born, Archibald Belaney – better known as Grey Owl – in the 1930s to reintroduce the beaver and his emphasis on conservation were to earn him the title, 'Father of Canadian Conservation'.

14 The Canadian Director of Greenpeace recently observed: 'Greenpeace, of course, is opposed at a philosophical level to the inflicting of pain on any wildlife at all for any purpose. But . . . where you still have a semblance of the natural ecosystem and where you still have an abundance of the wildlife species . . . I don't see any reason not to attempt, at least, to retain some kind of balance between the original peoples there and the wildlife resources and the plant resources that they have depended on for so many centuries' (Bourque, 1986:11).

'In one incident, the Russian ... lined up a dozen men and fired his musket ... to see how many Aleuts one bullet killed. The answer was nine. The Aleut recognized their inability to succeed against the guns of the Russians. Introduced diseases further reduced numbers ... by 1799 only an eighth of the pre-contact population remained.'

THE ARCTIC

THE ARCTIC conjures up romantic images of an untamed land of ice and snow, a land of mystery and grandeur. The Arctic is also seen as a harsh, unforgiving environment where any wrong choice is the difference between life and death. The Northwest Passage is one of many places where imagination and reality come together. Explorers have long tested themselves against the Arctic and continue to do so in the twentieth century. Nowadays, the Arctic is frequently envisioned as a refugium, one of the last pristine environments on the planet.

The Arctic is not a vast, uninhabited land. It is the homeland of three separate linguistic groups: the Aleut, the Yup'ik, and the Inuit-Inupiaq. In fact, not all of these groups live in the Arctic as defined by geographers. The Arctic is usually regarded as the region north of the treeline, the mean 10°C (50°F) July isotherm, and/or the line of continuous permafrost (Stager and McSkimming, 1984:27). Depending on the definition, some speakers of all these groups do not live in the Arctic. However, these people are regarded as the descendants of a common ancestral group, the Eskimo-Aleuts, and therefore they are all regarded as inhabitants of the Arctic by anthropologists.

Archeologists hypothesize that the Eskimo-Aleuts migrated across Bering Straits some 8-10,000 years ago (Turner,1988; Dumond, 1984). As they spread across the north the three linguistic groups evolved. First, Aleut separated from the Eskimo-Aleut stock and then Yup'ik and Inuit-Inupiaq split. Eventually these people colonized the area from Prince William Sound in southern Alaska to eastern Greenland. The peoples of the Arctic have many diverse cultures. They have never remained static and today they continue to change and adapt to new social, political and economic situations. (The title-page map shows a key to tribal territories of the Arctic; some groups or societies of the Arctic specifically mentioned in the text may be included in overall groups and will not be shown on the map.)

> My breath, I have it here
> My bones, I have them here
> My flesh, I have it here
> With it I seek you,
> With it I find you,
> But speak to me
> Say something nice to me.
> (Nineteenth-century Aleut
> love song, in Bergsland and
> Dirks, 1990:687)

In 1741 Aleut culture was changed irrevocably by the visit of two Russian ships. Captains Bering and Chirikov, on a voyage of discovery, became the first Europeans to visit the Aleutian Islands. Although Bering later died on the Commander Islands, following a shipwreck, many of his crew returned to Russia with a cargo of sea otter pelts. These pelts, highly prized by the Chinese Emperor and his court, were virtually unobtainable as sea otters had been hunted almost to extinction in the waters of the western Pacific. The discovery of a new land rich in sea otters led Russian fur traders, known as the *promyshlenniki*, to build boats and set sail for Alaska.

To the Aleuts, the visit of strangers in ships was an oddity but not a unique event. Steller, the naturalist on Bering's ship, noted the presence of iron among the Aleuts:

Two had, in the fashion of Russian peasants, a long iron knife of very poor workmanship, which may be their own and no European fabrication ... From a distance, I observed very exactly the quality of this knife, when one of the Americans unsheathed it and cut a bladder in two with it, and I saw ... that it did not resemble any European workmanship.

(Steller, 1988:103)

This iron may have come through trade from the northeast, or more likely from Japanese fishing boats blown off course and wrecked on the foggy islands (Black,1983). These contacts

Key to groups:
1 Siberian Eskimo (Siberian Yup'ik)
2 St Lawrence Island Eskimo
3 Nuaivak Eskimo
4 Aleut
5 Pacific Eskimo (Pacific Yup'ik)
6 Mainland Southwest Alaska Eskimo (Central Alaskan Yup'ik)
7 Bering Strait Inuit
8 Kotzebue Sound Inuit
9 Interior North Alaska Inuit
10 North Alaska Coast Inuit
11 Mackenzie Delta Inuit
12 Copper Inuit
13 Netsilik
14 Caribou Inuit
15 Sallirmiut (Sadlermiut)
16 Iglulik
17 Baffinland Inuit
18 Polar Eskimo
19 East Greenland Eskimo
20 West Greenland Eskimo
21 Labrador Coast Inuit
22 Inuit of Quebec

with strangers were rare and their impacts on Aleut society minimal.

In the early 1700s Aleut society was still expanding. The population for this period has been estimated at 12-15,000 (Lantis, 1984:163) spread throughout the entire 1200 mile Aleutian archipelago: a chain of active volcanic islands strung like a pearl necklace across the northern Pacific. The majority of Aleuts lived on the islands closest to the Alaskan mainland, but, even the Near Islands (those nearest Russia) were inhabited. Archeologists believe that the Aleutians were first occupied about 8,000 years ago with people reaching the Near Islands about 1,000 years ago (McCartney,1984). This vast region can be divided into two based on dialect: Eastern and Western Aleut (Krauss, 1988:146). Within these regions

This map shows the approximate territories of tribes and language groups in about 1850 over most of the region, but somewhat earlier in northwest Alaska and coastal Labrador, and somewhat later for south Alaska and Greenland. After that, many groups lost territory and some disappeared.

Above: *Aleut in two-hatch kayak (baidarka), St Paul Is., Pribilof Islands, c.1900. They tended to be of shallow draft and long in proportion to the beam, making them seem both light and fragile.*

there were many village-level societies each of which had their own territorial boundaries and their own leaders.

Relations between villages were generally cordial. Trade goods such as pine bark and birch bark were exchanged from the mainland to the treeless islands. Villagers visited each other for feasts and masked dances, usually held in December (Black,1980:89). However, relations were not always harmonious; murders, witchcraft and insults led to stealthy and deadly raids. Captives became slaves, and the raiders would quickly dismember those killed. Dismemberment dissipated the power contained within the deceased, preventing it from harming the attackers (Laughlin, 1980:103).

Aleut homes were dug into the ground to a depth of 5 to 6½ft (1.5-2m.). They were then roofed with whale bones and driftwood and covered with sod, '. . . when they have stood for some time they become overgrown with grass, so that a village has the appearance of a European church-yard full of graves' (Langsdorff, in Lantis, 1970:183). Some of these houses were single family dwellings, others were multi-family longhouses 40 to 65ft (12-20m.) long and 20 to 33ft (6-10m.) wide (Laughlin, 1980:50).

Houses were oriented along an east-west axis and the location of families within a house mirrored the importance of the east in Aleut cosmology where the east was viewed as the home of the creator (Black and Liapunova, 1988:57). The longhouses had a central passageway on either side of which were individual family compartments. All the families within a longhouse were related. The headman and his family occupied the easternmost compartment while the slaves lived at the western end. Entrance into these houses was through one or two holes in the roof; a notched log provided access to the floor.

These holes were the only means of entering and exiting houses. This left the occupants easy

Baffin Bay

Davis Strait

Foxe Basin

Hudson Bay

prey for surprise attacks. The Aleuts employed three means to counteract this problem. Firstly, villages were usually located on isthmuses or narrow necks of land with dual sea access to provide a means of escape. Secondly, lookouts were posted to watch for unexpected and unwanted arrivals. Thirdly, secret compartments were excavated into house walls. During an attack, people could escape detection by taking shelter in these compartments.

Raids were rarely over territory. They were most often retaliatory feuds. The Aleuts had no need to fight over territory as the sea and land provided them with a bounty of resources. Starvation was almost unknown although March was often a lean time. There were very few land mammals on the Aleutians, but this lack of terrestrial fauna was compensated for by the variety of flora, marine fauna and bird life. The starchy roots of several plants were made into a thick gruel; the greens of fiddleheads, mountain sorrel, cress, cowslip and others were eaten and some herbs and roots were gathered for medicinal purposes. Berries including crow berries, salmon berries and cloud berries were both consumed fresh and stored for winter use. The beach grass (*Elymus mollis*) was used to produce the exceptionally fine baskets and mats made by Aleut women. Grasses were split into thin strands by fingernails and then twined. Baskets with over 1,000 stitches per square inch were made (Hudson, 1987:64). This quality of workmanship and attention to detail was characteristic of items created by Aleut women. Finally, monkshood was known to be poisonous and aconite was probably used for whaling. The gathering of these plants, with the exception of monkshood and some medicinal plants, was women's work. The women would store these seasonal plants for use throughout the year in pokes made from seals or seal lion stomachs (Collins, 1945).

Every spring flocks of waterfowl migrate to the Aleutians. Ducks, geese, swans, murres, puffins and many others lay eggs, raise their young and then fly south in the fall. The Aleuts gathered the eggs and hunted the different species adapting hunting methods to the habits of the birds. For example, puffins nest in burrows therefore the hunters placed snares over the entrance holes thereby strangling the puffins as they left their burrows in the morning. Another example was the hunting of albatross. 'The people sail out to catch them when the weather is quiet and foggy, because in such weather the birds cannot fly so well. The hunters move against them, since they know that the birds always fly up against the wind' (Merck, 1980:62).

The intertidal zone provided shellfish, octopus and seaweeds, foods that were gathered easily by women, children and the elderly. The availability of these resources gave widows a freedom to choose their own future rather than remarrying immediately as was the case among other northern peoples (Robert-Lamblin, 1982:199). They also saw people through the lean times when stores ran low and it was too rough to go out hunting.

Salmon were harvested throughout the summer and early autumn when they migrated up the short Aleutian rivers to spawn. Although many were caught and dried for winter use, the staples of the Aleut diet were the marine mam-

Above: *Oululuk, the chief village of the Aleut on Unalaska, with two-hole baidarka, by Louis Choris (1816-17). Even at this period white influence was evident, hence the Russian Orthodox church (left).*

mals, especially sea lions (Yesner, 1988). These mammals were hunted by men from their *baidarkas* (the Russian name for the Aleut kayak). Sea lions, seals and sea otters were hunted with darts thrown overhand using throwing boards. All men hunted these species. For a successful hunt a man prepared himself both physically and spiritually. Included in his hunting equipment were amulets to attract the animals and appease their spirits. 'Their preparation and place of preservation are kept secret, otherwise the amulets will lose their power. It is necessary to protect them from wetness; if an amulet becomes wet its owner will rot' (Jochelson, 1968:78).

Only a few men who had undergone special training would hunt whales. The hunt began on shore with the collection of the whaler's amulets, and the preparation of a special potion used to coat the dart and poison the whale. Some of the amulets used included hematite, feathers of a rosy finch and fluids from mummified bodies of dead hunters. The latter were considered extremely powerful amulets but the owner of such an amulet would lead a short life (Jochelson, 1968:78). When a whale was sighted a single hunter would set out to sea in his baidarka, then he would throw his dart into the whale and immediately return home, where he would enter an isolation hut and lie under a blanket for three days motionless. 'He behaved, ... like a sick man and thus by sympathetic magic attempted to persuade the whale to be sick' (Laughlin, 1980:41). On the third day he would rise when the whale was seen to be dying. The people dispatched the whale and brought it to shore. It is not known how successful this method of hunting was. If the whale did not drift into your territory it might end up as the bounty of another village (Laughlin, 1980:41).

All these hunts were undertaken in the baidarka, a watercraft renowned for its speed and ability to withstand the rough waters of the Gulf of Alaska (Zimmerly, 1986:18). The Aleut baidarka was unique among kayaks as it had a bifurcated prow and a straight stern. These design elements are thought to have allowed the baidarka to ride over waves and counteract ' . . . the lift created when the bow meets waves'

(Heath, 1987:24) respectively. In the event of a sudden storm, Aleut would strap their baidarkas together thus creating a more stable craft.

Boys began learning kayaking skills from an early age. They had their tendons and ligaments stretched to allow them to sit in the baidarka for hours (Laughlin, 1980:28). They also played games mimicking hunting from a baidarka (Laughlin, 1980:2) and practiced with a baidarka in calm waters. Later, they would venture out in a two-hatched baidarka with an experienced hunter, often a maternal uncle. By late teens a boy would become a man by building his own baidarka. He was then considered to be ready for marriage.

Constructing a baidarka was extremely complex. First, driftwood was collected for the frame. Then the baidarka was crafted to the exact measurement of its owner. Many of the construction techniques were jealously guarded secrets passed from the father or uncle to the boy.

> In some places, where the different pieces of the skeleton are fastened together, two flat bones are bound cross-ways over the joint inside, and this the chief assured me was of the greatest use in stormy weather. As the fastenings are apt to be loosened by the shock of the waves, these bones contribute essentially towards preventing such an inconvenience; but this art is not known to all, and is kept very much secret by those who possess it.
>
> (Langsdorff, in Dyson, 1986:42)

Finally, women would cover the baidarka with the skins of sea lions. The women had to be careful that none of their hairs were caught in the seams or a sea lion, enraged by this female contamination, would bite a hole in it.

The Russian interest in the Aleuts is as much due to the versatility of the baidarka as to the presence of the sea otters in the region. When the promyshlenniki first visited the Aleutians they hunted by themselves. The Aleuts were regarded simply as useful trading partners. Then the Russians realized the potential of the baidarka for sea otter hunting. They began exploiting Aleut hunters, forcing villages to hunt by capturing hostages who were returned at the end of the hunting season (Pierce, 1988:121).

In the early 1760s the eastern Aleuts tried to rebel but they were crushed. In one incident,

Above: *Study of inhabitants of the Aleutian Islands, by Louis Choris (1816-17). Contact with traders, explorers and missionaries is already evident in these early portraits.*

Oh, what is it going to be?
What is he going to say?

Not expecting to be like this,
I entered again the end of it.

My islands, my dear islands there east!
Above them the clouds will be light in
the morning.

Over there it will be like that, too, in the
morning.
If I live on like this, endless, unceasing.

This boredom, this grief!.
(Bergsland and Dirks, 1990:697)

the Russian Soloviev lined up a dozen men from Kashega and fired his musket at point-blank range to see how many Aleuts one bullet would kill. The answer was nine (Laughlin, 1980:129). The Aleut recognized their inability to succeed against the guns of the Russians. Introduced diseases further reduced their numbers and by 1799 only an eighth of the pre-contact population remained (Laughlin, 1980:130).

The Russian American Company (RAC) was

Below: *Karluk fishing/cannery village on Kodiak Is., Alaska, c.1900. Aleut fisherman brought fish to the cannery which at this time was manned by seasonal Chinese workers from San Francisco.*

established in 1799 and granted monopoly trading rights by the Russian crown. For most Aleuts this charter meant they became vassals of the company. The RAC was allowed to employ half the able-bodied men of a village and need only pay them a fifth of the wages of a Russian (Hansen, 1982:67) although often even these provisions were ignored by the company. This led to complaints by the Aleuts to the crown and a revision of the RAC charter in 1821. The change allowed the company to employ half the able-bodied men of a village for a period no longer than three years (Laughlin, 1980:130). By the 1800s Aleuts had been settled on the Commander and Pribilof Islands (the breeding grounds of the northern fur seal) by the RAC and Aleut hunters were located in Sitka and at the company's post, Fort Ross, on the California coast. One song in particular captures the loneliness of an Aleut hunter a long way from home.

Under the 1821 revision to its charter the RAC had to provide schooling, health services, churches and missionaries. The schools provided instruction not only in reading and writing but also in trades including shipbuilding, carpentry and metal working. Many of the students attending these schools were the off-spring of Russian-Aleut unions, known as creoles. These unions led to a new class of people. At the top were the Russians, followed by the creoles and at the bottom the Aleuts. Health care was rudimentary; however, it did include a massive vaccination program following the devastating smallpox epidemic of 1838 (Black, 1980:103).

Most Aleuts were converted to the Russian Orthodox church by lay preachers who also built small churches. In 1824 the first missionary, Father Veniaminov, arrived in the Aleutians. This priest, beloved by his Alaskan parishioners, later became the Metropolitan of the church and is now Saint Innokenti. Another of the early priests was the creole Father Netsvetov, who had been educated in Russia (Black, in Netsvetov, 1980:xv). Why did the Aleuts

Aleut

These objects illustrate Aleut emphasis on sea hunting from kayaks, the use of intestines for waterproof clothing and bags, and specialization in very fine basketry twined of split dune grass. Russian influence, which began with the arrival of fur hunters in the 1740s, is evident in some of the forms and decoration. When known, the island of origin is given below. The dates are when the piece was collected or when it was received in the museum.

1 Twined dune-grass basket with false embroidery design, for carrying fish. Atka, 1882.
2 Twined openwork basket with colored thread decoration, 1903.
3 Fine twined basket with tight cover, decorated with blue, red, and yellow silk threads; probably made for sale. Attu, 1927.
4 Cigar case of very fine twined basketry with false embroidery design, a popular Aleut specialty, made for sale. Attu, 1874.
5 Model kayak, in typical two-hatch form, with paddlers wearing bentwood hats. Collected by Wilkes Expedition, 1841.
6 Conical hat of thin bentwood with polychrome painted abstract design, sea lion whiskers at back. 1868.
7 Cap of black leather, with white fur and red threads, in the shape of a Russian hat. Unalaska Island, 1868.
8 Thin wood hat with painted design of bird. Kayaligmiut (Yup'ik not Aleut), 1879.
9 Cigar case of fine twined dune grass, with false embroidery of wool thread, made for sale. 1921.
10 Basket with wool thread design near rim. Attu, 1894.
11 Twined openwork basket for carrying fish. Atka, 1879.
12 Twined basket with fitted cover, false embroidery design. Atka, 1879.
13 Woman's work basket, with fitted cover, of twined dune grass with colored wool thread design. Attu, 1920.

14 Table mat, twined dune grass, made for sale. Atka, 1879.

15 High top boots, dark and light colored leather, trimmed with fur and red and green wool. Attu, 1890s.

16 Bird spear, wood with multiple bone points. 1890s.

17 Throwing board, used to propel harpoon or spear while seated in a kayak; ivory hook and groove for butt

end of spear which is on top, hole and notches for fingers of throwing hand. Painted red on top side, black on bottom Unalaska Island, 1892.

18 Work bag of sea lion intestine. Atka, 1879.

19 Bag of sea lion intestine, with decorative bands. Collected by Wilkes Expedition, 1841.

20 Large bag made of sea lion intestine.

Collected by Wilkes Expedition, 1841.

21 Waterproof overdress, of intestine. 1896.

22 Sealskin trousers. Atka, 1879.

23 Small twined pouch with colored thread decoration. 1921.

24 Table mat, twined dune grass, made for sale. Atka, 1879.

25 Pair of boots (mukluks) with fine appliqué design. Attu, 1890s.

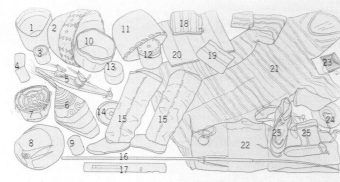

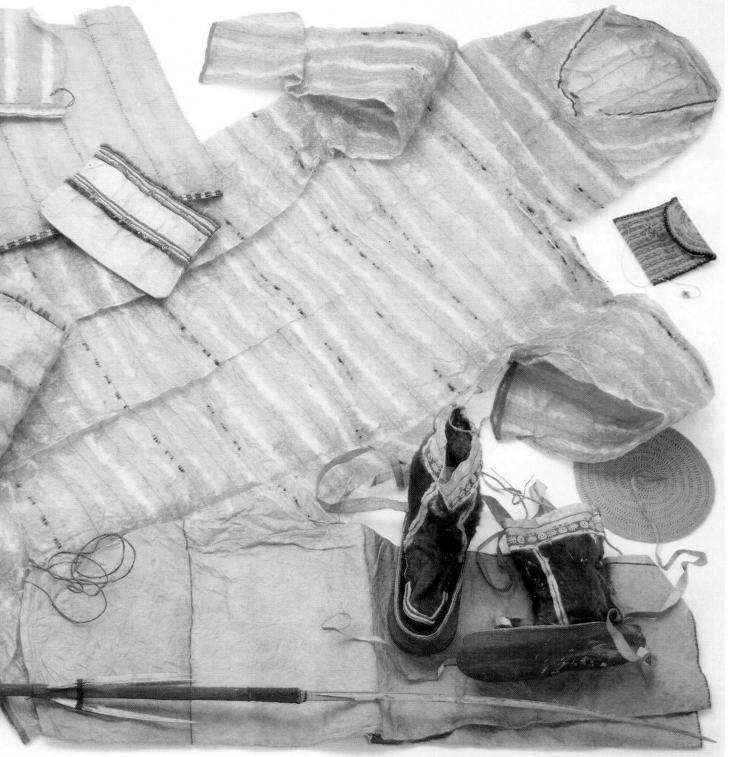

Above: *An Aleut man, by Louis Choris (1816–17). He wears a hooded gut shirt and a hat with a painted eye shade of thin wood bent into shape, stitched at the back to produce a deep, inverted scoop.*

embrace Christianity so readily? Part of the answer may lie in the church's ability to provide hope and succour. another part may lie in the god-parenting of Aleuts by Russians creating kin and economic ties of benefit to both groups (Black, 1984:94; Kan, 1988:506).

By 1867 Aleut society had adapted to the Russian presence. The population showed signs of recovery, many Aleut children received some schooling, and everyone belonged to the Russian Orthodox faith. However, the Opium Wars had caused the sea otter market to collapse and RAC efforts to diversify the Alaskan economy had proved unsuccessful (Black, 1988:80). Also, Russian America was a very long way from Moscow. Therefore, the Russian empire accepted an American offer to purchase Alaska for $7.2 million in gold.

Once again, without warning, life changed for the Aleut. The RAC was gone, the schools were closed, as were the health clinics, and many educated creoles chose to move to Russia. All that remained of the Russian presence was the church whose ministers were permitted to stay. The Aleuts were still vassals but they had lost power. The Russians had needed the Aleuts and the relationship had become symbiotic. The days of the sea otter hunt were gone and the Aleuts no longer had access to the trade goods on which they depended. The Aleutian Islands became a far flung and forgotten corner of the USA. Not until 1885, eighteen years after the departure of the RAC, was a mission with a school established (Morgan, 1980:114).

Gradually, Americans began to discover their new colony. A San Francisco concern purchased the assets of the RAC and renamed it the Alaska Commercial Company (ACC; Van-Stone, 1967:57). The ACC, interested in profits, concentrated on the lucrative Pribilof Island seal industry. The Americans expanded both the seal and sea otter hunts removing all quotas implemented by the RAC to protect these populations. By the 1880s the seal population exhibited signs of overhunting and the sea otter population was on the verge of extinction. In 1911 an international treaty curtailed the hunting of sea otter and placed strict quotas on the seal hunt.

Foxes were indigenous to a few of the Aleutian Islands and some had been introduced by the Russians. Independent American trappers and traders began leasing entire islands from the Government in 1880. With no predators and abundant waterfowl the foxes prospered and so

Below: *Aleut settlement, Karluk, Alaska, c.1900. To the left is a Russian Orthodox church and graveyard (the Russians brought their own religion to Alaska at least a century earlier); some semi-subterranean Aleut dwellings are seen (foreground).*

Above: *An Aleut woman, by Louis Choris (1816–17). There is considerable evidence of white contact in her dress, of trade cloth, and the cross, no doubt due to Russian Orthodox missionaries.*

did some of the independents. However, the collapse of the fur market in 1941 spelt the end of this industry. This boom and bust economy characterized other industries on the Aleutians prior to the Second World War. A gold mine brought a flurry of activity from 1886 to 1908. A cod salting station was built in 1876 and was soon followed by salmon canneries, and the establishment of a Norwegian shore based whaling station. This station operated from 1907 until 1939 taking an average 100 whales per season (Morgan, 1980:119).

The beginnings of the Second World War saw a collapse in the never stable economy of the Aleutian Islands.

St Lawrence Is. Eskimo, 1930

A man and his wife prepare the framework of a small umiak before fitting on the cover of split walrus hide. He has a typical Siberian and St Lawrence Island haircut, and wears ear pendants and charms on a necklace. On his belt are beads, a tobacco pouch and a sheath knife. His parka is made of caribou skin tanned and dyed red, with a dog skin collar. His trousers are of seal skin with the fur side out, and his boots have fine skin and fur appliquéd bands. The woman has tattooed patterns on her face and arms, and wears a charm on her arm-let. Her parka, worn with one shoulder freed for her work, is of dark caribou fawn skin with white caribou skin insets and fringes of white Siberian dog skin. Her boots are of red-dyed sealskin with the fur side in. Near the house is a food storage rack.

Above: *St Lawrence Island Eskimos, Bering Sea, Alaska. The boat is an umiak, constructed of driftwood and covered with walrus hides. When used for whale hunting sails were raised on such boats.*

> Only the mind
> will make a person
> continue on,
> only his will to follow
> those who are successful,
> Will bring him finally to his goal.
> Great wealth will not bring him all that
>   way
> only his will to follow those who are
>   successful.

> Whoever has very little
> must aspire to do
> as others around him who are more
>   successful do.

> He must try to imitate, follow, and
>   listen
> to those he wants to be like, and only
> in this way can he succeed in life.
> (Leo Moses, in Woodbury, 1984a:69)

Speakers of Yup'ik languages have lived for centuries on both sides of the Bering Strait. Across this narrow waterway they traded, visited and occasionally fought. Items traded from Siberia to Alaska included iron, tobacco and the skins of domestic reindeer. The mottled variated domestic reindeer skins were especially valued by the Yup'ik of southwestern Alaska as they were more colorful than the coats of the wild Alaskan caribou. Tobacco, another prized commodity, almost circumnavigated the globe from its homeland in eastern North America to Alaska. Despite these ties, the differences between Yup'ik-speaking

Below: *Pacific Eskimo settlement, c.1900, showing a semi-subterranean dwelling of turf with straw covering. Up to 20 persons lived in these houses which consisted of a main room with central hearth.*

groups are vast. There are five separate Yup'ik languages: Sireniski, Central Siberian Yup'ik, Naukanski (Siberian Eskimo), Central Alaskan Yup'ik (Mainland Southwest Alaskan Eskimo) and Pacific Yup'ik (Pacific Eskimo) (Woodbury, 1984a). In fact, the Siberian Yup'ik (Siberian Eskimo) are more similar to their Maritime Chukchi neighbors than to their American relatives (Hughes, 1984:249). This diversity extends from language to economy, social organization, belief systems and contact history. Here, only one language group will be discussed, the Central Alaskan Yup'ik, who inhabit the mainland of southwestern Alaska.

The pre-contact social organization of the Yup'ik centered on the family as did the Aleut although it was not as hierarchial, nor were slaves kept. Village societies maintained territories large enough to support their needs. The Yukon-Kuskokwim Delta teems with wildlife although much of it – the birds, anadromous fish and caribou – is migratory. This abundance enabled the Yup'ik to live in permanent villages located along river banks. During the spring, summer and fall they would travel into the country to intercept migrating wildlife. Each village consisted of many single family homes and one or two *qasgiq*, or communal men's house. Single family dwellings belonged to the women and were their domain. This is where they would sew, cook, and raise their children. At around the age of six a boy would move from his mother's home to the qasgiq. This large dwelling had an important place in the lives of the men for it was where they ate, worked, played, held ceremonies, took sweat baths and slept. The transition to the qasgiq signalled the beginning of a boy's training for manhood.

'It was good for us to hear the admonitions of those in the qasgiq who did the speaking there, though we did not always think so. Poor me! Sometimes I thought they could see right through into me, into my life, when they spoke. It was chilling, I tingled all over. How could they know me so well . . . Their instructions on how to live come up again, and again . . . It is true, the qasgiq is a place of instruction, the only place where the necessary instruction can be given in full.'
(Joseph Eriday of Chevak, 1978, as told to Anthony C. Woodbury, in Fitzhugh and Kaplan, 1982:210)

Below: *Mainland SW Alaska Eskimos at a settlement on the Kuskokwim River, Alaska, c.1880. Their winter clothing, probably ground squirrel, beaver or muskrat skins, fits loosely and lacks the tailoring of some of the more northern groups.*

These instructions were extremely important. It was not enough for the youth to gain technical skills; they had to learn their place on the universe. In Yup'ik cosmology the universe consisted of many different layers held in a delicate balance. The ill-considered actions of people could offend the spirits thus upsetting this balance. The result could be illness, poor hunting or stormy weather. Therefore, a necessary part of growing up was learning correct behavior. For example, the relatives of a dead person could not use any sharp tools in case they accidentally cut the deceased's spirit. If a spirit was cut, 'it would become very angry and bring sickness or death to the people' (Nelson, 1899:312). While boys learnt in the communal men's houser, girls learnt from their mothers and female relatives.

The Yup'ik also believed in two different worlds: the visible and the invisible. These two worlds occupied the same physical space although the spirits of the latter were seldom visible to the occupants of the former. The boundary between these worlds was permeable and at times of transition such as birth, death or puberty it was most transparent. At these times accordance with proper ritual was crucial or *tunghat*, generally malevolent spirits, could be released and would harm the people.

All objects, animate and inanimate, had

spirits or *yuas* of human form. In the past all
animals had the ability to transmute at will.

After a while she saw a fierce old wolf
coming over the rise on the bank of the
lake. His red tongue hung out. When he
came down he went over to the girl and
prodded her on her side with his nose.
Then he stood up beside her and was
transformed into a big husky man in his
prime. He wore nothing but a cape of
wolfskin.

(From *Adventures of a Young Girl*, told by
Ella Lewis, in Tennant and Bitar, 1981:173)

By the time of contact animals had lost this
power.

Occasionally, a hunter would still glimpse a
human face in the eye of an animal he was pursuing and know that he had seen its *yua*. He
would then carve a mask of his vision and at the
next festival he would sing of his encounter
while dancing with the mask. Shamans had
similar experiences with tunghat which only
they could see. The following dance was witnessed by Lt Zagoskin in the early 1840s:

But now the skylight opens, and quickly,
in a flash, a dancer slides down a strap
and with a quick leap is on the stage; two
pairs of women take their places beside
him. He is wearing a mask representing a
fantastic raven's head, and there he
goes jumping about on the stage, calling

*Above: St Lawrence Island Eskimo children, 1888.
Girls wore long hair, boys had tops of their heads
shaved, both of which aped the adult style. The parkas
are of reindeer skin with the hair side turned in.*

like a raven; the drums sound their rhythmic beat, the singers strike up a song. The
dancer at one time represents a raven
perching and hopping like bird; at
another time he represents the familiar
actions of a man who is unsuccessful in
everything. The content of the dance is
explained in the words of the song and
may briefly be described as follows. A
shaman is living in his trail camp. He is
hungry, and he notices that wherever he
goes a raven goes with him and gets in his
way. If the game he is pursuing is a deer,
the raven from some place or other caws,
startles the deer, and makes it impossible
to creep up within a bowshot of it. If the
man sets a noose for hare or partridge,
the raven tangles it or runs off with it. If he
sets a fish-trap for imagnat, there too the
raven finds a way to do him harm. 'Who
are you?' cries the shaman at last. The
spirit in the form of the raven smiles and
answers: 'Your evil fate.'

(Michael, 1967:227)

Shamans were holistic healers, treating their
patients' physical, psychological and spiritual
symptoms. Gifted individuals, they could
devine the cause of ill health or poor hunting.

When the infractions of people upset the universe the shaman would fly to the spirit world
and mediate with the spirits in an effort to restore the balance.

Shamans and elders were responsible for the
yearly ceremonial cycle. There were four major
annual festivals: the Asking Festival (*Petugtaq*),
the Feast of the Dead (*Merr'aq*), the Bladder Festival (*Nakaciuq*) and the Inviting-in Festival
(*Kelek/Itruka'ar*). The Asking Festival was an in-
tra-village event where kin relationships, particularly cross-cousin ties, were reinforced
through the exchange of requested gifts. The
Feast of the Dead ensured that the deceased
would have food, drink and clothing in the after
world. At the Bladder Festival the bladders of
all seals caught during the year were inflated,
painted and hung in the qasgiq. The souls of
the seals lived in the bladders and for several
days they were offered food, song and dances.
Finally, the bladders and the souls were returned to the water. If the seals had been
treated with respect they would allow themselves to be recaptured. The final festival of the
year was the Inviting-in Feast. For this ceremony, held when food was scarcest, the people
invited the spirits to share in what they had left.
By inviting the spirits and reminding them of
their past assistance, the people hoped to ensure successful hunting for the coming year.

Other festivals were held at different intervals. One of these was the Great Feast of the
Dead. At this festival, often held ten years after
the death, gifts were given away to honor the

deceased. During the festival the spirit of the deceased was believed to enter its namesake. Many gifts and clothing were given to the namesake and were therefore also given to the deceased.

Once this festival had been held, it was no longer necessary to remember the individuals at the annual Feast of the Dead.

> My children, where are you?
> Ai-ya-ya-yai.
> Come back to us, our children,
> We are lonely and sad.
> Ai-ya-ya-yai.
> For our children are gone,
> While those of our friends remain
> Ai-ya-ya-yai.
> Come back, nephew, come back, we
> miss you;
> Ai-ya-ya-yai.
> Come back to us our lost ones,
> We have presents for you,
> Ai-ya-ya-yai.
>   (Nelson, 1899:374-5)

The importance of the spirit world was not confined to rules of behavior and ceremonies, it permeated all aspects of Yup'ik life. Hunting equipment was exquisitely fashioned to please the yua of the prey, thus persuading it to give itself to the hunter. By carving bears, wolves and otters on to his weapons, the hunter appropriated the qualities of these predators. These disparate concepts, spiritual appeasement and appropriation of spiritual power were also incorporated into the clothing sewn by women (Chaussonnet, 1988).

Very complex concepts were contained in symbols on clothing and tools. A hole in the palm of a thumbless hand symbolized the game that the tunghat allowed to escape from the skyworld for the consumption of people. One simple symbol, the circle and dot motif, represented the Yup'ik world view. Like the universe, it had several layers of meaning; it stood for the all-seeing eye, the world and the layers of the universe, and the passageway from one world into the next (Morrow, 1984; Mather, 1985; Fienup-Riordan, 1988).

The first direct contact the Central Alaskan Yup'ik had with Europeans was with the Russians. This contact began following the establishment of the RAC's trading monopoly in 1799. The Russians explored southern Alaska and realized that beaver were available on the mainland. As the sea otter populations declined Russina interest in the beaver increased. The RAC constructed several trading posts on the mainland in the early 1800s. By 1845 Russian Orthodox missionaries had established themselves at most of these posts (Shalkop, 1987). The Yup'ik, however, maintained their independence from the RAC and some even resisted conversion to Christianity (Kan, 1988:513).

Following the sale of Alaska to the United States the RAC was replaced by the Alaska Commercial Company with very little impact on the population except an increase in quantity and variety of trade goods (VanStone, 1984:154). However, Yup'ik desire for trading goods led to a gradual change in their economy. Individuals who spent more time

Below: *Mainland SW Alaska Eskimos before store houses at Togiak, Alaska, c.1877. These were of split logs with curved roofs of cut sod and straw, here with stabilizing poles which act as battens.*

trapping beavers had proportionally less time available for subsistence hunting. Eventually, this led to a dependence on the trading posts (VanStone, 1984). In many communities, however, the subsistence economy with its seasonal hunting and gathering cycle was hardly disturbed at all.

The Russian Orthodox church continued to play an important role in Yup'ik life. Missionaries of other faiths attempted to convert the Yup'ik but were mostly unsuccessful. The work of a powerful Inuit minister led to the founding of a successful Moravian mission in Bethel in 1885 (VanStone, 1967:38).

The 'rich man's route' to the Klondike gold rush was up the Yukon River by paddle steamer from Saint Michael, Alaska. However, no gold was found in the Yup'ik territory and so the thousands of miners pouring into the Yukon Territory from 1896 to 1899 had almost no impact on the local population (VanStone, 1984).

In 1883 the first salmon cannery opened and was quickly followed by others (VanStone, 1967:67). At first these canneries employed Euro-American and Philippino workers, but by the 1920s many of the workers were native Alaskans. Seasonal job opportunities in the canneries created out-migration from some of the more northern and interior communities into Bristol Bay. These canneries and the trapping industry were the main employers of Yup'ik prior to the Second World War (VanStone, 1984).

Other than Christianity and clapboard above ground homes Yup'ik culture prior to the war was similar to the pre-contact culture. The last masked dance ceremonies were performed in the 1930s. Recently, this tradition as well as others have been undergoing a revival.

Speakers of the Inuit-Inupiaq live in four countries – Russia, the United States of America, Canada, and Greenland (formerly part of Denmark). Despite the thousands of miles, Inuit-Inupiaq is regarded by linguists as a single language with many separate dialects (Woodbury, 1984b; Krauss, 1988). The cohesiveness of the language stems from a recent migration from northern Alaska to Greenland in about AD 1000. Northern Canada and Greenland wre inhabited as early as 2500 BC, however this population was overpowered and assimilated by the later migrants who adopted their culture and language.

The patient fur-clad man poised over a seal breathing hole. The smiling baby peeking out from its mother's parka. A howling wind sweeping over dogs and an igloo. A man paddling a kayak. These images form the stereotype of the Inuit – a smiling, friendly people eking out a marginal existence in a harsh environment. This stereotype ignores the diversity and complexity of Inuit societies. The Nuvugmiut (a subgroup of the North Alaska Coast Inuit) of northern Alaska were whale hunters and lived in semi-subterranean log houses in large permanent villages. They rarely used kayaks and only made snowhouses if caught on the land in a snowstorm. Their society was highly structured with special status accorded to the *umialik*, owner of a whale hunting boat. In contrast, the Padlirmiut (a subgroup of the Caribou Inuit) lived a nomadic lifestyle on the west coast of Hudson Bay. In spring they hunted seals basking on the ice, however, the rest of the year was spent in the interior hunting caribou and musk oxen. Padlirmiut society was strongly egalitarian; knowledgeable individuals were asked for advice but each person was free to reach his or her own decisions.

British explorers' descriptions of the Central Inuit, the people of the Canadian Arctic, are the origin of the Eskimo stereotype (Brody, 1987). There are many divisions within the Central Inuit; one of these is the Iglulik Inuit. The Iglulik Inuit consist of four societies: the Tununirusirmiut (of northern Baffin Island), the Tununirmiut (of northern Baffin Island), the Iglulingmiut (of northern Foxe Basin) and the Aivilingmiut (of the northwest coast of Hudson Bay) (Mary-Rousselière, 1984:432). In this section the culture and contact history of one of the Iglulik societies – the Aivilingmiut – will be considered in more detail.

While reading about the Aivilingmiut it is necessary to realize that generalizations are being made. There are myriad ecological niches across the north, each one providing Inuit with the challenge of discovering its complexities and designing hunting strategies to exploit its resources. Inuit oral history contains accounts of individuals or groups who migrated into new regions and starved because they were unfamiliar with local conditions. In one incident, a murderer and his extended family (Tununirusirmiut) fled their home in order to escape revenge. They found an uninhabited island with abundant marine life and decided to settle. All winter they waited for the ice to freeze solid. It never did and eventually they all starved to death except one woman. In this region the local population (Iglulingmiut) had learnt to hunt on the shifting ice flows and thin elastic ice (only a few centimeters thick). The migrants, ignorant of this technique, eventually starved to death, surrounded by a sea of plenty (Mary-Rousselière, 1954).

Inuit-Inupiaq, in common with Aleut and Yup'ik, is an agglutinative language. For instance, the name Aivilingmiut is composed of *aivik* (walrus), *-lik* (place), and *-miut* (people of); it means, people of the place of walrus. The Aivilingmiut were renowned for their walrus hunting and their concommitantly strong dog teams. These teams enabled people to travel long distances to hunt, to visit relatives and later, to visit trading posts. Long voyages occurred in spring when the days were lengthening and warming, migratory birds were returning to their breeding grounds and basking seals provided relatively easy prey.

As the summer approached the hunters would move to the floe edge for walrus hunting. Walrus were harpooned either from the floe edge or from kayaks. The prow of the kayak was narrow so that the hunter could aim it between the tusks of an enraged walrus, thus preventing the walrus from ripping the skin of the kayak and drowning its occupant (G. Quluat pers.comm.). Once caught, the walrus was butchered and most of it cached for future use. Some parts were eaten immediately, either raw or cooked over a bone and oil fire. The Inuit diet is almost entirely meat. Meat contains all the nutrients required for life as long as both the fat and meat are consumed and a significant por-

Below: *Bering Strait Inuit man using a bow drill to make an ivory cribbage board, c.1902. This group produced a great deal of artwork, especially wooden and ivory sculptures to sell to sailors.*

Above: *Bering Strait Inuit in a one-holed kayak throwing a harpoon with an atlatl, c.1888. The atlatl added an extra joint to the throwing arm and gave greater projection to the harpoon.*

Below: *West Greenland Eskimo kayaks and umiaks. The subsistence of these people almost entirely depended on marine animals such as the ringed harp, spotted and hooded seal, walrus and whale.*

tion of the meat is eaten raw (Stefansson, 1946).

In autumn, people would split into smaller groups, often no larger than one or two families and travel to their summer hunting grounds. These families had areas they visited habitually (Damas, 1963) and, while there was no individual ownership of land, if others wished to hunt in these areas it was only polite to ask permission (R. Inuksuk pers.comm.). Autumn hunting varied. Generally, older men stayed on the coast hunting walrus, seals and whales until the sea ice formed. Younger men often hunted caribou in the interior (Mathiassen, 1928:24).

Caribou were hunted in many different ways. In some cases hunters would sneak up on the caribou raising their hands above their heads as if antlers. In other cases stone hunting blinds were built beside caribou trails. Yet another method required the participation of the entire family. A series of inukshuit (means: look like people) of stone were built along a caribou trail. Caribou mistook these cairns for people and were channeled into either a river or narrow valley. This method of corralling allowed people to take many caribou in a short time. The caribou provided not only sustenance but also bone and antler for tools, and fur for clothing. Caribou taken in September and October were preferred for clothing. Those taken later in the year, when the caribou had longer hair, were used for bedding.

When the sea froze (usually in the middle of September, Mathiassen, 1928:24) the older men and their families would also go caribou hunting. At this time of the year, Arctic char were caught using leisters at stone weirs. Some were dried and could easily be carried when the family moved camp. Others were cached and collected later by dog team.

In January/February the Aivilingmiut congregated in large villages of snowhouses. Snow is a versatile building material; not only is it plastic but it is also a good insulator. When traveling the Aivilingmiut built simple one-room snowhouses. In winter villages the houses could last several months. These complex houses had entrance passages and side chambers for clothes and meat storage. Sometimes houses were connected so that people could visit without going outside (cf. Rasmussen, 1929:46).

In winter, when the weather was bad, the people would live on their cached supplies. However, they took advantage of calm days to

Central Inuit

The Central Inuit, north and west of Hudson Bay, share the Inuktitut language and are culturally quite similar. The Copper Inuit and Netsilik hunted seals on the ice in the winter and caribou in the summer. The Sallirmiut (extinct by 1904), Iglulik, and Baffinland Inuit depended on large sea mammals. The Caribou Inuit lived off caribou supplemented by fish. The most important collections of artifacts (some are shown here) are those made by George Comer, under the direction of Franz Boas, while he was captain of a New England whaling vessel spending winters among these Inuit between 1895 and 1908. Inuit groups had been in intermittant contact with European and American ship crews for several centuries, but their material culture was so well adapted to the extreme environment that it remained largely unchanged except for the use of metal, beads, a little cloth, and the adoption of tobacco and some European foods. Ig. = Iglulik; CI = Caribou Inuit; LCI = Labrador Coast.

1 Snow shovel. Ig.
2 Model of kayak, with two paddles. CI.
3 Line for dragging a seal, with bone toggle. Ig.
4 Ivory case for keeping needles. Ig.
5 Ivory case for needles and pins. Ig.
6 Ivory needle case. Ig.
7 Pipe. Hudson Bay. (Ig?)
8 Line for dragging a seal, with ivory toggle. Ig.
9 Ivory needlecase on cord. Ig.
10 Harpoon head attached to skin line. Tununa (Ig?).
11 Boy's hooded parka. Savage Is., LCI.
12 Bone knife for cutting snow for melting and to build igloo. CI.
13 Saw. Netsilik.
14 Scraper of chipped flint mounted in bone handle. Sallirmiut.
15 Knife, with blade of copper salvaged from lost Franklin Expedition ship. Netsilik.
16 Wooden throwing board (atlatl). CI.

17 Bone scraper. CI.
18 Large knife, steel blade mounted in native handle. Sallirmiut.
19 Pair of snow goggles in Iglulik style. CI.
20 Woman's parka, with short flap in front, long one behind. CI.
21 Child's suit. Savage Is., LCI.
22 Wooden tray with bone mounts. CI.
23 Box of bent whalebone. Netsilik.
24 Scoop for removing snow from sealing hole in ice. Netsilik.
25 Spoon, with bone handle, musk ox horn bowl. Netsilik.
26 Copper kettle, salvaged from lost Franklin Expedition ship. Netsilik.
27 Bucket of whalebone. Sallirmiut.
28 Dish of whalebone on wooden bottom. Hudson Bay. (CI?).
29 Woman's knife (ulu). CI.
30 Dipper of musk ox horn.
31 Wooden dish. Hudson Bay (CI?).
32 Bailer. Netsilik.
33 Musk ox horn spoon. Kidlingnukniut, west of Back River (Netsilik?).
34 Large skin bag, fur side out. Southampton Is. (Ig?).
35 Hard leather box with metal trim. CI.
36, 37 Ivory combs. CI.
38, 39 Ivory combs. Ig.
40 Set of dominoes, bone. Savage Is., LCI.

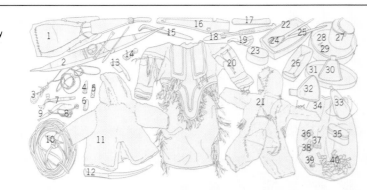

hunt seals at their breathing holes. Seals keep many breathing holes open and the Aivilingmiut practiced several methods to increase their chances of success. Usually a group of hunters would go out together and each stand at a breathing hole. Sometimes, the women and children would scare the seal away from its other breathing holes, forcing it to the hole where the hunter waited. At other times a boy would drive a dog team in a wide circle around the hole occupied by the hunter thereby frightening the seal towards it (Mathiassen, 1928:44).

Winter was also a time for socializing, telling stories and renewing friendships and alliances. A single family's home was too small for a community gathering: consequently a large snow-house, an architectural marvel, sometimes over 23ft (7m.) in diameter was constructed. In this building drum dances and shamanic seances were held. At the dances people would sing their personal songs. The following is the song of a great hunter and modest man.

> It is a time of hunger,
> But I don't feel like hunting.
> I don't care for the advice of old people,
> I only care for dreaming, wishing, nothing else.
> I only care for gossip;
> I am fond of young caribou, the age they
>   start getting their antlers;
> Nobody is like me,
> I am too lazy, simply too lazy,
> I just can't bring myself to go and get
>   some meat.
>   (Arnatkoak, in Columbo, 1981:90)

Aivilingmiut beliefs were quite similar to those of the Yup'ik. When the weather was poor or game disappeared, the shaman would hold a seance to divine the cause. During seances such as these, shamans transformed into bears and visited Uiniyumayuittuq (literally 'one who does not want a husband'), from whose hands sprang all sea mammals and who therefore controlled them. The shaman would comb her

Above: *Copper Inuit caribou hunters. Caribou were mainly hunted with bow and arrow, bows generally composite with sections joined together with sinew; wood, antler and musk-ox horn were used.*

Below: *Copper Inuit building a snow house, c.1915. Such domed houses were used from October to May. A distinguishing feature of the Copper Inuit house was the flat topped entrance, partly visible here.*

hair and ask forgiveness for the transgressions of the people.

> That woman down there beneath the
>   sea,
> She wants to hide the seals from us.
> These hunters in the dance-house,
> They cannot right matters.
> They cannot mend matters.
> Into the spirit world
> Will go I,
> Where no humans dwell.
> Set matters right will I.
> Set matters right will I.
>   (Houston, 1972:71)

Shamans were highly regarded individuals but

they were not viewed as leaders. Likewise elders were respected and their opinions sought. Also, skilled individuals were consulted. A man who combined several of these functions was known as an *isumataq* (literally 'one who thinks'). He had the ability to command individuals and create new camps. This position was held through general acknowledgement not through coercion or heredity.

Aivilingmiut society was fairly flexible; people could come and go as they pleased. This flexibility was extremely important in an unpredictable environment. When an unexpected environmental crisis occurred and starvation appeared imminent camps dispersed. At these times a network additional to and reinforcing the kinship network was required. The Aiviling-

miut maintained an elaborate alliance system that operated at many levels. Some of these alliances or fictive kin relationships were namesakes, joking partners, singing partners, trading partners, adoption, and spouse exchange partners (often incorrectly called wife exchange). 'The Eskimo ideal was to have a network, as extensive as possible, of kinship and fictive kinship relationships' (Mary-Rousselière, 1984:436). During normal times these partnerships were fun and made travel to new areas easy. In times of stress they carried the obligation of aid, usually provided as shelter and food. This obligation was often unrecognized by Euro-Americans when they participated in unequal spouse exchange alliances. In a spouse exchange the couples agreed to exchange partners for a short time. The result of this exchange was a mutual obligation for support in the future. It was also trans-generational; the offspring of the couples, whether related by blood or not, would regard each other as siblings (Guemple, 1961). This is a very different type of arrangement from that described by most Euro-Americans.

The earliest contact the Aivilingmiut had with Europeans was indirect. They were unaffected by the first British voyages in search of

Above: *Family group with dogs and loaded sled, Bering Strait Inuit, c.1880. Sleds were generally drawn by three dogs but this scene shows a particularly large sled with more dogs harnessed.*

Below: *Iglulik woman inside an igloo softening a skin by chewing. In the tanning process, fat and flesh were first removed, the skin dried. Softening could be by means of a stone scraper or by chewing.*

the Northwest Passage (1570s-1630s). In 1670 the British Crown granted the Hudson's Bay Company monopoly trading rights in Rupert's Land. The Company established forts in the 'bottom of the bay'. There were no beaver to the north and the Company was rarely interested in venturing into this area (they tried a whale fishery in Padlirmiut territory on the west coast of the Bay (1765-72; Ross, 1975) and sent the occasional exploratory expedition when their monopoly was challenged). By the early 1800s Inuit from the west coast of Hudson Bay were traveling to the Company post at Churchill to trade seals. As far as we know these were not Aivilingmiut, but, by 1821, when the first British explorers Parry and Lyon visited them, they already had iron knives and copper kettles (Parry, 1842; Lyon, 1824). Such possessions were most likely attained through trade with their southern neighbors.

Parry and Lyon were searching for the Northwest Passage by following the continental coast of North America. After two years' attempts to traverse Fury and Hecla Strait they returned to Britain and correctly reported that no viable route existed following the mainland. As a result, the Aivilingmiut remained undisturbed until 1860 when American whalers expanded their whaling into Hudson Bay. This led to a migration of Aivilingmiut southwards as they congregated around the whalers and took jobs working as crew members.

Inuit crews were not paid wages by the whalers, instead they received goods and food. If a hunter killed a whale he might be given a wooden whaling boat (Eber, 1989:102-3). Other rewards for service included shirts, guns, ammunition and knives. Women also worked for the whalers, scrubbing decks, cleaning clothes, and sewing winter clothing. Their remuneration included dresses, knives, scissors, needles and beads.

The whalers wintered over in Hudson Bay. As the sea ice formed they would allow the ship to be frozen in. A 'house' was built on the deck and became the venue for dances and theatricals. The Aivilingmiut built their villages beside the ship and went on board for meals and entertainment. During the winter the Aivilingmiut supplied the ship with fresh meat.

The presence of the whalers changed Aivilingmiut life in many ways. Guns and whale boats displaced the bow and arrow, and kayak (Mathiassen, 1928:92). Supplying the whalers

with fresh meat depleted local wildlife. The whalers introduced new foods including alcohol. Also, other Inuit groups, some former enemies of the Aivilingmiut, migrated into the region to work for the whalers. The tensions between these groups sometimes erupted into fist fights (Mathiassen, 1928:101).

As in all contact situations disease took its toll. Syphilis and tuberculosis were perhaps the most insidious, but even common diseases could have disastrous effects. In 1902 the Scottish whaler *Active* carried a sailor ill with dysentery into the region. This disease was so virulent that the Aivilingmiut of Lyon Inlet felt they had been bewitched by their neighbors (Rose, 1975:117). This same epidemic resulted in the virtual extinction of the aboriginal occupants of Southampton Island, the Sadlermiut (Sallirmiut). The deserted island was later repopulated by the Aivilingmiut (Comer, 1906).

Many of the impacts of whaling were negative, however; the Aivilingmiut and other Inuit who participated remember this period with fondness. It was a time of excitement, new

Above: *Bering Strait Inuit trading with passengers aboard the steamer Roanoke, c.1900. They use traditional one-hole kayaks with frames across the top for transport of their wares.*

things and of great hunters. When the last whaling ship sailed away in 1915 never to reappear, the people were sad.

We wondered, but we never really knew why the whalers didn't come back. We were kind of regretful because we remembered how good their food had tasted and we remembered everybody getting together like a big family. When the whalers left, that big family feeling was gone.
(Leah Arnaujaq, in Eber, 1989:105).

Below: *North Alaska Coast Inuit summer encampment showing both triangular and dome shaped dwellings. As caribou formed the staple diet of this group, the dwellings are probably covered with the skins of the animals.*

left by the whalers. With the Company came the Catholic and Anglican missionaries. The Company, Royal Canadian Mounted Police and missionaries sought to change Inuit culture. The Company depended on the hunters to bring in furs and fostered a dependence on the goods already introduced by the whalers. They realigned, but did not radically alter Inuit subsistence economy. The missionaries sought to replace Inuit cosmology with Christianity. While they succeeded in converting the people and deposing the shamans, they were less successful in altering the people's fundamental beliefs about their world.

Finally, the RCMP were in the north as agents of the Canadian Government. It was their role to ensure that justice was done. Their imposition of an unknown legal system was confusing to a people who had their own system of customary law. Although the Company, RCMP and missions were paternalistic and autocratic institutions, they had relatively few representatives in the north. As a result of this lack of representation, their impact was limited. It was only after the Second World War that most Canadian Inuit groups became more exposed to southern Canadian education, and at last began to benefit from regular health services and social services.

The Royal Canadian Mounted Police (RCMP) established their first eastern Arctic post in 1903 among the Aivilingmiut. Its purpose was to ensure Canadian sovereignty over the area and to collect duty from the American whalers. When the whalers left the RCMP remained to bring law and order to the north.

The Hudson's Bay Company, now interested in seals and white fox, moved in to fill the void

Above: *Four Mackenzie Delta Inuit with dogs and sled. Such sleds usually had bone or antler runners. They were commonly used for tundra land mammal hunting and for sealing at the floe edge.*

Below: *Men from Icy Cape, Arctic Ocean, Alaska, c.1880. Note the use of labrets – ornaments of bone and ivory – worn in holes pierced through the lips. Men's lips were pierced at puberty.*

THE NORTHEAST

THE GEOGRAPHIC AREA here under discussion, conveniently referred to as the 'Northeast', stretches approximately from the northwestern shore of Lake Superior south to the confluence of the Ohio and Cumberland Rivers and then east to the Atlantic coast. Its northern border runs just south of the Lake of the Woods and the area extends as far south as the Virginia-North Carolina coastal plain. Newfoundland, once inhabited by the now extinct Beothuks, is included in the Subarctic chapter.

While it is useful to consider the concept of cultural areas in North America suggesting an internal homogeneity, it is important to stress that – and this particularly applies to the Northeast – there was great variation in lifestyle and, while dominated by Algonquian- and Iroquoian-speaking people, some Siouan in the west – *possibly* east as well – were also represented. Recognizing the difficulties of applying an all-embracing cultural description,

recent studies have subdivided the area into three further geographic regions, Coastal, Saint Lawrence Lowlands and Great Lakes-Riverine and, while even this tripartite division has its shortcomings, it more accurately delineates common lifestyles. For example, the Saint Lawrence Lowlands was the traditional home of the powerful and famous Iroquois Confederacy – the 'People of the Longhouse' – who shared similar cultural patterns which were based on fishing and horticulture, residence in mostly fortified villages, ritual sacrifice of prisoners, similar ceremonials and a matrilineal kinship system.

The major features within these three divisions of the Northeast are given in the table opposite on p.227, which also shows the major tribes of the Northeast and their associated linguistic grouping and main cultural patterns (with events which affected the tribes).

In terms of population, tribes or groups were

small, certainly no more than sixteen thousand for the Iroquois in the late seventeenth century, twenty thousand for the Huron prior to the smallpox epidemic during the winter of 1639-40 which reduced the population by one half, and some twenty-five thousand for the Chippewa in 1760. These, however, are but estimates since, in early days, only limited numbers of the various tribes actually came into contact with whites at any particular period, such as in the case of the Chippewa whose settlement pattern in the early historic period was that of many widely scattered and small bands. The fortunes of the Indian tribes, the changes in their life styles and population, can be illustrated by reference to one tribe – the Micmac – who were

This map shows approximate territories of tribes and language groups in the seventeenth century. After that, all tribes lost territory, some disappeared, some moved and a few new tribes arose.

Key to tribes:
 1 Chippewa (Ojibwa)
 2 Menominee
 3 Winnebago
 4 Illinois
 5 Potawatomi
 6 Sauk
 7 Fox
 8 Mascouten
 9 Miami
10 Shawnee
11 Kickapoo
12 Algonquin
13 Nipissing
14 Huron
15 Ottawa
16 Petun
17 Neutral
18 Wenro
19 Erie
20 Seneca
21 Cayuga
22 Onondaga
23 Oneida
24 Mohawk
25 Mahican
26 Delaware
27 Susquehannock
28 Nanticoke and Neighboring
   Tribes
29 Va. Algonquians
30 Va. and NC Iroquoians
31 North Carolina
   Algonquians
32 St Lawrence Iroquoians
33 Western Abenaki
34 Eastern Abenaki
35 Maliseet-Passamaquoddy
36 Micmac
37 Southern New England
   and Eastern Long Island
   Algonquians

amongst the first to encounter Europeans.

It has been estimated that the population of these Algonquian-speaking people was about four thousand prior to white contact. Their territory was the area to the south and west of the Gulf of Saint Lawrence, the Gaspé Peninsula and the Maritime Provinces. This is a heavily forested region with many lakes and rivers and natural harbors along the extended coastline. By use of the canoe, scattered bands maintained strong ethnic identity between the seven districts traditionally observed by the Micmac.[1] Because the winters were so severe, only tobacco was cultivated and the subsistence was predominately one firmly based on an annual cycle of hunting and fishing. One of the most comprehensive reports on the Micmac which undoubtedly closely describes a lifestyle which had been established and little changed for centuries comes from the writings of the missionary, Pierre Biard (c. 1616). Describing those groups associated with Southern Nova Scotia, he refers to a two-phase type annual cycle now classified as 'diffuse' and 'compact' settlements.

In the first, which coincided with the winter season, the population was widely scattered throughout the seven districts; main activities at this time were beaver, otter, moose, caribou and bear hunting, which occupied the months of January to March. At the onset of spring, 'After the smelt comes the herring at the end of April; and at the same time bustards |Canada geese| . . . sturgeon, and salmon, and the great

Below: *A traditional Micmac wigwam of poles and branches bound with cedar bark fiber and covered with overlapping strips of birch bark and grass matting, photographed in 1873.*

(i) Coastal Zone. Atlantic Provinces of Canada and the seaboard of the United States to North Carolina. Separated from the interior by the Appalachian Mountains

Linguistic group	Major tribes	Cultural patterns/events
EASTERN ALGONQUIAN	Micmac Maliseet-Passamaquoddy Eastern Abenaki Lenni-Lenape (Delaware) Nanticoke Powhatan	The varying Eastern Algonquian languages appear to have constituted a continuum of variation along the coast. Population and dependence on agriculture increased southwards. Political organization varied from hunting bands in the north to rudimentary states in the south. These East Coast tribes were the first in the Northeast to come into close contact with Europeans. Because they lacked time to reorganize themselves under the impact of the Europeans, they were the most decimated or dispersed of all the tribes in the Northeast

(ii) Saint Lawrence Lowlands. Southern Ontario, Upper New York State and the majority of the Saint Lawrence and Susquehanna Valleys

Linguistic group	Major tribes	Cultural patterns/events
NORTHERN IROQUOIAN	Saint Lawrence Iroquoians Mohawk Oneida Onondaga Cayuga Seneca Tuscarora (after c.1720) Huron Erie Susquehannock	Practical intensive horticulture and fishing; often lived in fortified villages. Initially, they were sufficiently remote from the earliest centers of European contact that they were little affected and until 1760, after the fall of New France, the Iroquois maintained their autonomy. After this date, their homeland was increasingly depleted by white settlement

(iii) Great Lakes–Riverine. Adjacent to the Great Lakes of Superior, Michigan and Huron and west almost to the Mississippi

Linguistic group	Major tribes	Cultural patterns/events
CENTRAL ALGONQUIAN	Chippewa (Ojibwa) Ottawa Potawatomi Menominee Sauk & Fox Kickapoo Miami Illinois Shawnee	All these tribes depended on horticulture although the emphasis varied. Their kinship system was patrilineal. With European encroachment this area – through intertribal cooperation – became central to efforts opposing European domination, such as that of Pontiac in 1763 and Tecumseh in 1811

search through the Islets for [waterfowl] eggs... From the month of May up to the middle of September, they are free from all anxiety about their food; for the cod are upon the coast, and all kinds of fish and shellfish...' (Bock, Trigger ed., 1978:110).

At these abundant times, large groups – the 'compact settlements' – gathered at favorite camping sites along the coast or rivers. It was a time when friendships were renewed or made and, particularly, elements of tribal solidarity recognized. As Biard reported, it was principally at this time that 'they pay visits and hold their State Councils; I mean that several Sagamores [Chiefs] come together and consult ... about peace and war, treaties of friendship and treaties for the common good' (Biard, Thwaites

Above: *Group of Passamaquoddy with canoes. Virtually identical to the Maliseet, the combined group was adept at woodworking, the finest product being the light and maneuverable birch bark canoe.*

Left: *Jennie Bobb and her daughter Nellie Longhat, Western Delaware, 1910-15, in traditional Delaware women's finery, characterized by heavy necklaces, silver brooches, pony bead 'encrusted' moccasins.*

ed., J.R.3.1896-1901:89-91).

The French were greatly impressed by the Micmac and many found their way of life far more agreeable than that which they had experienced in their native land. French youths readily adapted to the Indian lifestyle and language, encouraged by the early French traders, who thus gained efficient interpreters and agents for the lucrative fur trade. The French found the Micmac a vigorous, handsome and healthy race, who were disdainful of those amongst the French who were squint or one-eyed, flat-nosed and hairy. The Micmac had few diseases; they knew nothing of fevers, gout or rheumatism and the French were impressed by their knowledge of plants, 'for wounds and other mischances' (Bishop, 1949:112). Thus, the Micmac formed strong friendships with the French[2] and they became increasingly dependent on trade goods, particularly such things as axes, metal knives and kettles. This improvement in their material possessions, however, was increasingly offset by rapid decreases in their population, due to smallpox and other diseases against which the indigenous populations had little resistance and their numbers, it has been estimated, decreased to some two thousand by the early eighteenth century.

The period 1610 to about 1760 saw an increasing dependence on the fur trade – mainly carried on with the French – and, whilst Acadia[3] was ceded to the English by the Treaty of Utrecht in 1713, the new owners found it impossible to gain control of the fur trade which had been monopolized by the French for so long; any attempted changes were fiercely opposed by the Micmac and not until 1779 did the difficulties that the English have with the Micmac actually cease.

The English trait of colonization was rapidly put into effect, the Micmac being confined to reservations and the old free hunting and fishing economy gone forever. The subsequent exploitation – further loss of lands, loss of water resources and the offer of only seasonal jobs at subsistence wages – is a shameful chapter in the settling of Acadia, but it did demonstrate the great resilience of the people. Adapting to the rapid changes, the men took to fabricating wooden craft items and baskets, whilst the women, utilizing some of their traditional knowledge and skills, together with those indirectly acquired from the Ursuline Nuns of Quebec, produced greatly prized souvenirs, which were embellished with quillwork, moosehair and beads. Thus, unlike the Beothuk of Newfoundland who were all but brutally exterminated by 1830, the Micmac population – much to the surprise of those whites who concerned themselves with Micmac welfare – actually progressively increased and by 1900 it again approached four thousand.

At least three basic central principles were shared by both the Algonquian and Iroquoian people who lived in this vast region. The first emphasized and defined the rights of the individual such that all actions of individuals were based on their own decisions and all group actions pivoted on the consensus of the participants. The second was that everybody shared, and in times of want the well-being of all was to be taken into account; charity and generosity were considered paramount principles by which all should abide. The third was that man was part of nature – not outside it – he was but part of the web of the natural world and the earth and woodlands could be neither owned nor exploited. One notable scholar, Cleland, managed to express this last principle particularly well:

'Thus a man is born and for a time becomes a cannibal, eating and taking energy from his fellow creatures; when his soul and shadow leave his body, Earth Mother takes it back to nourish the plants which in turn feed both animals and men. His debt is repayed, his spirit freed, and the cycle of life complete.'
(Cleland, 1973:XIII)

These central principles were incorporated in the famed Confederacy of the League of the Iroquois, the founding of which is still celebrated today. According to Iroquois tradition, the League was founded by the prophet Deganawida[4] who had a vision of a great spruce tree which reached through the sky to communicate with the Master of Life. The tree was considered the sisterhood of all tribes whilst its roots represented the five Iroquoian tribes – Seneca, Cayuga, Onondaga, Oneida and Mohawk – who make up the Confederacy.[5] The names which each had for themselves give interesting insights relating to their location, activities and wealth (see table below).

The League was founded in about 1570 in response to the state of continual war which existed between the tribes of the region and had a double purpose: the establishment and enforcement of peace and the acquisition of strength to oppose any would-be intruders. An eagle perched at the top of the great spruce tree in Deganawida's vision was a symbolic reference to a state of vigilance against any enemy

Right: *Micmac man and woman, Nova Scotia, c.1865. Although not identified, the woman is probably Christianne Morris who was known for her great skill in producing exquisite bead- and quillwork.*

Tribe	Name for themselves
Seneca	'The great hill people'
Cayuga	'People at the mucky land'
Onondaga	'The people on the hills' (who took their name from their position on top of a mountain or hill)
Oneida	'The people of the standing stone'
Mohawk	'The possessors of the flint'
Tuscarora (after 1722)	'The hemp gatherers' or 'The shirt wearing people'

(AFTER LYFORD, 1945:9)

who might break the peace. The League was governed by a carefully worked out constitution, the laws and regulations of which were transmitted orally from one generation to another by selected leaders. At the time of its establishment, the centrally placed Onondagas were chosen as both the 'firekeepers' and 'wampum keepers' of the League. As 'firekeepers' of the League, it was the Onondagas' responsibility to call yearly councils at which the constitution and laws were rehearsed and differences resolved. At its foundation, the League took into account the established clan system which had been used by the five tribes from ancient times; each clan owned several personal names which served to define roles within the tribes, whilst the fifty chiefs who

Micmac

The Micmacs live in many settlements within the seven traditional districts of Nova Scotia and New Brunswick that they occupied in the 16th century and before. This is a region of heavy forests, a long indented coastline, and many rivers and lakes. The climate does not allow dependence on agriculture, and in aboriginal times tobacco was the only plant cultivated. The Micmacs subsisted on shellfish, herring, salmon and other fish, moose and caribou and birds' eggs, waterfowl, partridge, seal, beaver, rabbit, otter, and porcupine acquired for food and for hides, feathers, and quills. They traveled in fine large birch bark canoes, and on snowshoes. Birch bark was an important material for vessels and containers and for covering the conical wigwams in which they lived. In the French period from 1600 to 1760, fur trapping for trading transformed Micmac life. During the 19th century porpoises were hunted for their oil that was sold to traders. Toward the end of the 19th century the Micmacs were Catholic in religion and found employment especially in lumbering and in guiding sports hunters and fishermen. Trapping came to an end. About 1900 many Micmacs engaged in harvesting potatoes and blueberries. Elaborately beaded garments were worn by both men and women on special occasions. The items shown here were collected in 1913 and 1914 by G.A. Paul, a Maliseet-Penobscot Indian of Oldtown, Maine (except for a woman's cap collected about 1916 by his friend, the anthropologist F.G. Speck).

1 Wooden gauge for birch bark.
2 Twined spruce root basket with handle.
3 Birch bark box with wooden ends.
4 Bone dice for gambling game.
5 Burl bowl used to throw the bone dice.
6 Wooden counters for dice game; the shaped sticks are equal to four and five plain counters.
7 Pair of beaded garters; old when collected.

8 Beaded garter.
9 Baby's beaded cap.
10 Woman's peaked cap of red cloth, beaded with double-curve designs. Collected by F.G. Speck about 1916.
11 Man's cape of beaded red cloth (special occasions).
12 Blue cloth coat trimmed with red cloth and beads, worn by man for special tribal occasions.
13 Necklace, woven beadwork.
14 Toy moccasins.
15 Toy birch bark dish.
16 Wooden cooking spatula.

17, 18 Wooden gauges with spaced metal blades, for cutting splints for basketry.
19 Cowhorn rattle with incised designs.
20 Cowhorn rattle.
21 Head for lashing to end of a salmon spear; iron point and two wooden barbs to hold on the speared fish.
22 Man's hat of mooseskin with long hair from the animal's throat; worn with beaded flap at back.
23 Beaded armlets, old style.
24 Carved handle for knife.

Mohawk Warrior, 1750

A Mohawk warrior runs past a tree with a pictographic war record. He carries an English Brown Bess flintlock and a metal tomahawk with scalplocks on the end. His powder horn is French, worn over a pouch woven of wool and beads like his belt and garters. His knife scabbard and black buckskin moccasins are decorated with porcupine quills. He wears a buckskin breechclout and bead-edged leggings. Around his neck is a George I Indian medal. He is tattooed like the Mohawk in Benjamin West's 'Death of Wolfe', while his clothing, ornaments, and weapons are very like those collected by George Townshend and shown in marble on two Mohawk supporters on the Westminster Abbey memorial to his son Lt Col. Roger Townshend, killed at Ticonderoga in 1759 while fighting with Mohawk allies against the French.

made up the 'Roll Call of Chiefs' were each elected from the appropriate clan members. Thus, the ancient social organization was maintained, giving stability and unification to the League, which would not have otherwise been obtained had the old social structure been discarded[6] (Tooker, Trigger ed., 1978:426-8).

The Iroquois clan system was matrilineal, emphasized by the custom of a child receiving a name belonging to the mother's clan. Of great interest is the power which the woman had in the selection of the clan chiefs: 'When one of these "federal" chiefs died, the clan mother (senior woman of the clan, that is, the "aged sensible" women recognized as such) in consultation with other women belonging to that clan in the same tribe chose the man who would assume that name and hence become successor to the deceased chief. Often she chose a man of her lineage (and of the lineage of the deceased chief), but if there was not a suitable man of this lineage, a man of another lineage in the clan might be chosen. If the clan did not have a suitable candidate, the name might be "loaned" to another clan, that is, the name give to a man belonging to another clan with the understanding that at his death the name would return to the clan that had loaned it' (ibid:425-6). Thus, although the League of the Iroquois had the appearance of a government consisting exclusively of males, each member of that governing body was in reality answerable to the women of his maternal family, which in fact consisted only of one female, the 'aged sensible' woman. There is little doubt that this power wielded by the women had its foundation in the Iroquoian subsistence patterns which were highly dependent on horticulture.

Maize, beans and squashes were the three major sources of nourishment to the Iroquois and these were regarded as sacred gifts from the Creator; called 'the three sisters', these foods played an important part in the ceremonials, particularly those associated with the spirit of gratitude. At the gathering and storing of these crops, the communities celebrated the completion of the cycle: 'The "three sisters" are happy because they are home again from their summer in the fields'[7] (Fenton, Trigger ed., 1978:301). A survey of Iroquois horticultural achievements, together with their knowledge of wild plants, leaves little doubt that as with their northern neighbors, the Huron, meat was of fairly limited importance to their subsistence. Up to seventeen distinct varieties of maize were produced, some sixty varieties of beans and some seven squashes. Additionally, they collected thirty-four wild fruits, eleven species of nuts, twelve types of edible roots, thirty-eight varieties of bark, stem and leaf products and six fungi. They also produced some twelve beverages and eleven infusions from parts of plants as occasional drinks, and whilst salt was little used, maple sap was very popular, being used to flavor corn meal, sweeten mush and as a beverage. Little wonder that culture statisticians have given the Indians of the Eastern Wood-

Right: A Mohawk girl, identified by her stage name, White Deer, wearing the neo-traditional special occasion costuming suitable for her performance as an 'equestrian wonder' at the 1901 Pan-American Exposition in Buffalo, New York.

Above: Six chiefs of the Iroquois photographed on the Six Nations reserve, Ontario, Canada, September 1871. Most of the tribes sided with the British during the American Revolution and subsequently many moved to land along the Grand River in Ontario. These men hold the tribal wampum records, belts woven of white and purple beads with motifs symbolic of agreements and treaties between whites and other tribes. The gift of a wampum string held immense value for the Indians.

lands 'a high rating in the ratio of food discoveries' when the Old and New World peoples are compared (Speck, 1945:38).

Iroquois villages were composed of bark-covered houses averaging perhaps 65ft (20m) in length, 20ft (6m.) wide and 20ft high. The Iroquois referred to these as *ganonh'sees*, the 'longhouse', which depending on its size, could accommodate between five and twenty families. There were only two doors, one at each end and lengthwise down the center ran a passageway 6½ to 10ft (2-3m.) in width, either side of which and raised 1½ft (50cm.) from the ground ran a platform which served as both seats and beds. Above this, perhaps 8ft (2.5m.) from the ground, was a second platform which could be used for storage and, if necessary, additional beds. The longhouse was divided into family apartments some 10ft (3m.) wide and either side of the passage, two families were served by a small fire set at intervals along the length of the house. In the roof were openings to allow for the escape of smoke and to give light to the interior; as necessary, openings could be shut off by use of a slab of roof bark. The longhouse was warm and weatherproof, but unlike the Plains tipi there was no direct control over the rising smoke. However, the large doors at each end undoubtedly produced a useful forced convection effect, expelling smoke through the roof apertures.

The longhouse was made from a basic framework of upright posts set into the ground and enclosing a rectangular floor area. Attached to the tops of the posts were flexible poles which were bent over to produce the roof frame. Slabs of bark about 5ft wide by 6½ft in length (1.5×2m.), preferably elm although basswood, ash, hemlock or cedar were also used, were then attached to the frame in an overlapping fashion with strips of the inner bark of hickory or basswood trees. As with the clearing of the fields the work was carried out by the men but longhouses were considered the property of the women.

Although similar houses were used by other tribes in the region – for example by the Huron to the north (who favored cedar rather than elm bark) – the longhouse was the most conspicuous feature of Iroquois villages and each was a microcosm of the whole community becoming a symbol of identity, thus the common description for themselves – with some variations – strongly conveyed the idea of them being 'The People of the Longhouse'.

By the end of the eighteenth century, there was a gradual abandonment of the longhouse in favor of single family dwellings. However, the longhouse has now become the council house of the communities; whilst today the longhouse often resembles a modern building, symbolically it states tribal unity and is the center which perpetuates the teachings of the Seneca prophet 'Handsome Lake' who, in 1799, recognizing the social disorganization which was occurring, urged return to the ancient annual ceremonials of the Iroquois. The so-called 'Longhouse Religion' has thus become a 'continued assertion of the integrity of an Iroquois ethnic identity' (Wallace, Trigger ed., 1978:442).

Early descriptions of Iroquois villages refer to elaborate fortifications consisting of a stockade and sometimes a moat. In illustrating his attack on the Onondaga in 1615, the French explorer Samual Champlain shows massive pal-

Above: *The defeat of the Iroquois in 1609 at Lake Champlain by a force of Huron, Montagnais, and Ottawa with Champlain and his guns. Palm trees, hammocks, and nakedness are the artist's inventions.*

Below: *Chiefs of the Iroquois Confederacy in the Council House at the Six Nations Reserve, c.1910, the Onondaga chief holding wampum strings. Flags above represent the deer and turtle clans.*

isades which the Iroquois had constructed by driving two rows of tree trunks into the ground, inclining each pair so that they crossed some 16½ft (5m.) from the ground, the space between being filled with logs. The trunks were bound together at their point of crossing and horizontal beams were laid into the Vs, forming a narrow walkway protected on the outer side with bark slabs. Notched poles on the inner part of the palisade were used as rough ladders giving the defenders access to the protected walkway (Bishop, 1949:232). They were formidable forts and, even with the use of a cavalier,[8] the Onondaga held off the gun-armed French and their Huron allies for nearly a week until the attackers abandoned the action, much, it must be said, to Champlain's discredit in the eyes of both friend and enemy.[9]

Other than the supporting French, the raid on the Onondaga village was typical of intertribal warfare between Iroquoian speaking tribes. Indeed, such was the nature of the Iroquoian warfare pattern, it is unlikely that the Huron would have considered the Onondaga siege a failure because hostile encounters were not generally a struggle for hunting territory or land, but a test of a warrior's bravery, to take a scalp or two and perhaps prisoners for torture.

Prior to an expedition against the enemy and agreement having been reached in council, the Hurons traditionally had a war feast which was prepared by the women. The origin of the feast – and it also went some way to explain the warlike nature of the Iroquoians – was attributed in their mythology to a giant whom a number of Hurons had encountered on the shore of a large lake. When failing to reply politely to his greeting, one of the Hurons wounded the giant in its forehead. In punishment, the giant sowed the seeds of discord amongst the Huron, but before he disappeared into the earth he recommended the war and *Ononharoia* feasts and the use of the war cry, *wiiiiii*. The feast was accompanied by singing and dancing by the young warriors who uttered abuse against the enemy with promises of victory and as they moved from one end of the longhouse to the other, 'under the pretext of doing it in jest, [they] would knock down others whom they did not like' (Trigger, 1969:46)

It was not unusual for several hundred Huron warriors to lay siege to an Iroquois village, generally the Seneca who lived closest to Huron territory. Such expeditions usually took place in the summer, when there was plenty of leaf cover and often had an air of an outing, as Champlain commented on the prelude to one Huron-Iroquois battle: 'This war had much of the character of an organized sport' (Bishop, 1949:147), the men travelling slowly towards enemy country, fishing and hunting along the way. On crossing Lake Ontario by canoe to the south shore, they would then hide, split up into smaller groups and then travel on foot to the Iroquois villages. Women and children were not infrequently captured before the village itself was put to siege. The principal weapon used in pre- or early contact times was the stone-headed or wooden ball-headed club. The latter was a formidable weapon at close range; commonly made of ironwood and up to 2ft in length (60cm.), it had a large knob or ball at the head, some 4½ to 10in. (12-15cm.) in diameter which was often carved with animal figures, perhaps emblematic of the owner's personal totem and protective power.[10] The ball-headed club was later superseded by the trade metal pipe tomahawk, and, likewise, the bow and arrow replaced by the gun, the latter having a particular impact on warfare tactics, for example the abandonment of wooden body armor (Trigger, 1969:47, illus.), and change in battle formation.[11]

In all cases, casualties were usually few in number, the young aspiring warriors laying emphasis on performing acts of daring. Generally, after a few injuries and deaths the attackers withdrew to their temporary forts which they commonly built near the enemy village. Pitched battles tended to be avoided and if reinforcements from other settlements were imminent the attackers left for home. The wounded were carried home in a makeshift basket sling, on the backs of their companions and, whilst it was a practical means of transport through the heavily wooded forest, it was appallingly uncomfortable for the injured. Champlain, who was himself wounded in the leg and knee by two Iroquois arrows, describes how the Huron men fabricated the frame of hickory or elm, attaching a seat with straps of hide or of the plaited inner bark of elm. The frame and burden were supported by a tumpline across the carrier's forehead and the wounded warrior sat on the seat, his legs under his chin and tightly bound in position. Champlain described his ordeal – undoubtedly an extremely unpleasant one experienced by many an immobilized Iroquoian warrior:

'It was impossible to move any more than a little child in its swaddling clothes... and this causes the wounded great and extreme pain. I can say this indeed from my own case, having been carried for

Below: Caroline Parker, Seneca, sister of Gen. Ely Parker, c.1850, in a studio portrait wearing traditional costume she made herself, with elaborate beadwork on a wraparound broadcloth skirt.

Seneca

The Senecas are one of the six tribes that formed the Iroquois League or Confederacy. Many have lived in Canada since 1784 when the League split into two duplicate political organizations, Canadian and American. The majority of the Senecas remained in New York where they lived on three reservations in the western part of the state. The Allegany and Cattaraugus Reservations are organized as the Seneca Nation, which seceded from the League in 1848. Senecas on the Tonawanda Reservation are not part of this Seneca Nation; rather, they maintain their political affiliation with the New York League. In other ways all Senecas are culturally very similar. A majority of the modern Senecas are Christians but a large minority are followers of the Longhouse religion that was founded by the Seneca prophet Handsome Lake between 1799 and 1815. On each of the Seneca reservations there is a longhouse, a ritual structure associated with this religion. The Tonawanda longhouse serves as headquarters. When the items shown here were collected (1905–10) on all three New York reservations, many Senecas were still farmers, growing corn, beans, and squash, the traditional Three Sisters referred to as 'our life supporters'. Several native types of implements were associated with the harvesting and processing of corn, while other traditional artifacts included the musical instruments used in Longhouse rituals. 'Traditional dress', worn only on special occasions, maintained the Iroquois styles of the early 19th century.

1 Large wooden bread bowl, used on lap to hold mealing stones and for other culinary purposes.
2 Wood splint basket for drying berries or green corn.
3 Hickory splint sieve for ground corn.
4 Fingerwoven man's belt of red wool and white beads.
5 Caribou skin kilt with embroidered floral design; part of man's formal dress.
6 Wooden cradleboard.
7 Burden strap (tumpline) of twined bark fiber.
8 Pack basket for harvested corn, with burden strap
9 Deer jaw for scraping green corn off cob.
10 Crooked knife for wood carving.
11 Washing basket for hulling boiled hominy.
12 Corn planting and berrying basket.
13 Woman's printed cotton cloth (long blouse) with beaded edges and silver brooches in four traditional Iroquois shapes.
14 Pair of woman's red flannel leggings with beaded designs.
15 Pouch or purse of cloth with floral design in raised beadwork.
16 Box turtle rattle used for Women's Dance.
17 Rattle of snapping turtle, with neck skin and head forming handle, carried by maskers in curative ritual.
18 Gourd rattle to accompany singers.
19 Cowhorn rattle used by singers for dances.

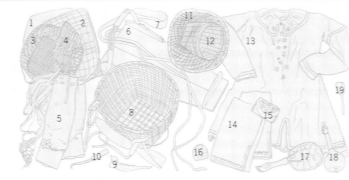

several days because I was unable to stand, chiefly on account of the arrow-wound I had received in my knee, for never did I find myself in such a hell as during this time; for the pain I suffered from the wound in my knee was nothing in comparison with what I endured tied and bound on the back of one of our savages...'

(Bishop, 1949:238)

Such journeys subjected the helpless incumbent to endless tossing, buffeting and whipping by the tree branches and half, sometimes complete, immersion in water as the bearer made his way through forest and streams, but it was greatly preferable to falling into the hands of Iroquois enemies.

Early explorers found much to admire in Iroquoian society; they describe, for example, the superb physique of the men and the beauty of the young women. There was surprisingly little internal conflict within the crowded villages and all were fond of laughter and jokes, applied good sense and justice in their affairs, showed great hospitality and, at times, great kindness. They had an acuteness of sense, great courage, endurance and were stoic to pain.

The Iroquoian treatment of prisoners was, however, another matter and many whites were stunned and appalled by what they saw. In Iroquoian war ethos, nothing was considered more desirable than to be credited with the capture of prisoners and more particularly the capture of an enemy warrior. On occasions, if several men claimed the capture of a particular prisoner, the prisoner himself would be requested to designate his official captor. In so doing, wily captured Iroquoians, who were well versed in the psychology of intertribal warfare, not infrequently named another who was less involved in his capture. In so doing, he struck a note of discord amongst his captors and sometimes, rather than allow the honor to go to the wrong man, he was helped to escape. Whilst women and children might be slain on the spot or taken back for adoption, male prisoners – unless there were too many of them – were taken back to the villages. On some occasions, men were formally adopted, receiving the name of a lost relative which 'served to dry the tears of the bereaved' (Trigger, 1969:49), but most often they were subjected to ritual torture which for some unexplained reason was part of Iroquois and Huron psychology and far less practiced by the Algonquian tribes.

The historian Francis Parkman has described in great detail the fate of one Iroquois prisoner who was captured by Hurons during the savage Iroquois-Huron war of 1648-50.[12] *Saouandanancous* was brought in by his Huron captors and adopted by an elderly chief who, having lost a son, had hoped that *Saouandanancous* might take his place; the prisoner's hands, however, had been seriously injured[13] and because of this, whilst treating him with courtesy and an outward show of genuine affection, he was condemned to die. He was put to death by fire so carefully applied that it took him over twelve hours to die. Astoundingly, his tormentors showed no signs of lack of self control and as each applied his particular torture they spoke to the prisoner in a kindly way. Equally extraordinary is that *Saouandanancous* demonstrated the courage and endurance expected of an Iro-

Above: *Now-on-dhu-go, an Ottawa chief from Lake Michigan, Paul Kane (1845). The vermilion stripes on his face are symbolic; his hair appears to be tied at the front with a piece of red trade cloth.*

quois warrior: during intervals between the torture he not only reported on Hurons who had been adopted into his tribe, but sang as well. When he finally expired, he was cut up and small pieces of his flesh distributed for eating.

In 1609, Champlain described a similar episode; after the battle at Ticonderoga, one of the dozen or so prisoners was selected for torture. The Huron harangued him with the cruelties which he and members of his tribe had practiced on them and that he should prepare himself to experience as much. They told him to sing 'if he had the heart' and Champlain reports that he did 'but it was a very sad song to hear' (Bishop, 1949:150).

Although it has been reported that on occasions the body of the dead man was burned as a sacrifice to the most powerful of the Huron supernaturals, Oki, 'the sky',[14] the ritually tortured prisoners were probably symbols of the tribe represented; as one anthropologist has recently explained it, the prisoners became a 'hate object on whom the frustrations of life and past wrongs could be expended' (Heidenreich, Trigger ed., 1978:386).

West and north of Huronia was the domain of an equally powerful, but politically considerably less coordinated, tribe – the Algonquian-speaking Chippewa – who occupied much of what is now the state of Wisconsin, southwest

Ontario and northeastern Minnesota. Unlike the Iroquois, who were too far south and so had largely to resort to elm bark for building their longhouses and fabrication of utensils and canoes, the Chippewa had easy access to a superior natural material – birch bark – and, in further contrast, depended far less on horticulture, the maize of their southern neighbors being largely replaced by superb wild 'rice' which grew in abundance in the countless streams and lakes so characteristic of the Mississippi headwaters region.

Wild 'rice' (*Zizania aquatica*) was not in actuality a true rice but an aquatic grass. Early explorers were greatly impressed by its nutritious value and it was an important component in the diet of the Western Great Lakes people, particularly the Chippewa and Menominee, whose tribal name was derived from the Chippewa for wild 'rice', *manomini*, it being the chief vegetal food for that tribe although for religious reasons they never attempted to cultivate it, seemingly as part of their unwillingness to 'wound their mother, the earth' (Hodge ed., 1907-10:843).

The rice was collected in late August or early September[15] with the people working in groups; certain areas were recognized as being the property of certain families and it was a right which was seldom disputed. Often the growth was so dense that the areas gave the appearance of enormous green meadows and the canoes needed to be poled through the torpid streams or shallow lakes, generally by a male member of the group, whilst the women gathered. Two sticks about 2ft (60cm.) long were used in the harvesting process; the women sat in the stern of the canoe and bent down the stalks (some could be over 20ft (6m.) high) with one stick and struck the kernel with the other; the process was continued until the canoe was full. On return to the temporary lakeshore camp, the 'rice' was laid out on sheets of birch bark for drying; it was then poured into a lined hole in the ground and pounded with long pestles, or curved sticks, to loosen the husks, perhaps several women participating in this part of the work. Finally, the 'rice' was winnowed by pouring from one special large bark tray to another. The quality, size and taste differed and it was recognized that certain areas produced particularly good crops, 'kernels there are small and better tasting than the ones around here' and the kernels on the La Pointe Reservation were 'finer than the ones at Red Lake' (Hilger, 1951:147). Nevertheless, whatever its type, as with the tapping for maple syrup in the spring it was an opportunity for group activities and joyous gatherings.

The collecting of maple sugar was an activity of great importance as it was used in feasts and ceremonials and everyone was expected to eat all that was set before them. The sugar was used on fruits, vegetables, cereals and even fish. Although the collecting of maple sugar – which generally commenced in March – was a time of work, it was also one of pleasure and special wigwams were retained from year to

year in certain areas. It was an opportunity for social and ceremonial gatherings and a chance to catch up on the previous year's tribal gossip.

The maple trees were tapped by making a gash in the trunk a meter or so above the ground. A cedar spike was then pounded into the tree at an angle and this allowed the sap to drip down into a birch bark bucket placed on the ground. The sap was then boiled and when it hung in strings from the stirring paddle it was

considered ready; it was then strained through a basswood-fiber matting and transferred to a granulating trough. It was worked as it cooled and the granulated sugar which resulted was pulverized into finer granules. Some of the sugar was packed into moulds to make little cakes, but most was put into *makuks* – special birch bark storage containers – and carried home for use throughout the rest of the year. In addition to its use as a highly nutritious food source, it was also mixed with water to make a refreshing drink. A small amount of the sugar was always offered to Manito[16] and this type of ceremonial – the offering of the first fruit or game – was observed with the first preparation of each seasonal food.

The vast woodland areas had an abundance of wild foods, such as cranberries, gooseberries, blueberries, black and red raspberries, cherries and grapes, hickory, hazel, beech and butternuts and also wild onions and potatoes, the former being particular favorites. Later in the summer when plants were fully developed, special attention was given to gathering herbs for medicine. The person gathering the herbs would offer tobacco to the four directions as well as to the sky and earth. Prayers were made in a low voice with promises that no more would be taken than was necessary, whilst hope was expressed that the mysterious powers would make their use successful. After gathering, the various plants were dried, each variety being separately stored. Whilst most of

Below: *Blackhawk and Winneshiek, Winnebago, before 1900. Both were prominent leaders, c.1870, among those Winnebago bands who resisted removal from traditional homelands in Wisconsin to Nebraska.*

Above: *A Kickapoo man, by Karl Bodmer (1833). At the time Maximilian met members of this tribe they had just been removed from their original homeland in Wisconsin to a reservation in Kansas.*

Below: *Winnebago woman tanning a deerskin, c.1880. The skin has been stretched on a vertical wooden frame and is being defleshed with a chisel-like tool. Note the two dwellings in the background.*

Above: *The construction of a Chippewa birch bark canoe. Birch bark was the 'skin' of the elegant and graceful line canoe. The framework of the unfinished canoe shows the process of fabrication.*

Below: *Ne Shiw Shkak (Jack Davis) and Wis Ki gete (Rising Smoke), Potawatami. Fine ribbon appliqué decoration (at which this tribe excelled) is in evidence on the leggings worn by Rising Smoke.*

that which was three or more layers in thickness was suitable for peaked or domed winter wigwams, whilst two layers for the conical summer lodge would suffice.

The domed wigwam consisted of a framework made of flexible poles or saplings of ironwood or elm which were pushed into the ground and then bent over, producing a series of arches. Horizontal encircling poles were then lashed to the vertical poles with basswood fiber producing a net-like framework. The sheets of bark, perhaps over 6ft long and 3ft wide (about 2×1m.) wide, were then laid on a lining of woven cattail (*Typha latifolia*) mats, overlapping as one would shingle a roof; a smoke hole was left at the top, the fire was small and provided by several dry logs which radiated from the central hearth and as the logs burnt they were pushed inward. By careful selection of the wood, the flame could be made virtually smokeless. The permanent lodges generally had a platform about 1½ft extending part way around the interior, which served both as seats

the herbs were used as remedies for sore eyes, abdominal problems, skin and lung troubles, some were also used as hunting charms; powdered or in the form of fine roots, they were mixed with tobacco or red willow and smoked in a pipe. During the course of tracking the deer they occasionally sat down and smoked one of the herbs 'and it is said that before long the deer came toward them sniffing the air' (Densmore, 1929:129). For so many of these subsistence activities – the canoe to collect the wild 'rice' and the winnowing trays used to separate it, the *makuk* for collecting berries, the leak-proof containers for collecting the maple syrup and water, and the fabrication of their habitations – the Chippewa very much depended on one natural and remarkable material, *wigass*, or 'birch bark'; it was the very basis of their material culture.

Although the time varied in different localities, the Chippewa knew when to remove the bark without destroying the tree, but generally it was between the end of spring and early summer. The process of removing the bark was demonstrated by a Lac Courte (Wisconsin) Chippewa lady to Sister Inez Hilger: clutching her pocket knife in her right hand and 'with blade extending beyond her little finger [she] carefully cut the outer bark (only the outer bark is removed) from a place as high as she could reach, down to the root. In removing the bark she moved clockwise around the tree, loosening it carefully with both hands so as not to break it' (Hilger, 1951:133). It was later explained that when very large pieces of bark were needed, such as were used in making canoes, trees were felled and then all the bark stripped off. The bark was then rolled or folded and tied up with a basswood fiber and transported on the back of the gatherer; rolls or folded batches of birch bark were common in or close to the wigwams, ready for use. The actual thickness of the bark determined the use to which it could be put; that removed from the large trees could have up to nine separate layers and was suitable for making canoes. Some, however, was as thin and pliable as tissue paper, but so tough and durable that it was used for wrapping. Between these extremes were several other grades, mainly used for containers and trays;

and beds; many had a medicine pole, perhaps 20ft (6m.) high attached to the top of which was a small sacrifice to the mysterious and unfathomable potentials and powers of life and the universe – the Manito.

One observer, Frances Densmore, who spent over twenty years studying the life of the Chippewa, came to view these people with enormous respect. She was moved by the beauty of the northern woodlands, familiar with its changing seasons, the material abundance and inspiration, giving, she concluded, the poetry and the spiritual essence of Chippewa culture. Densmore captured in words the warmth and beauty of the winter wigwam, where the 'winter

Above: *Chippewa woman weaving a rush mat, typical summer occupation for older women. This appears to be a cedar bark mat of a natural golden brown, the patterns worked in dyed cedar strips.*

evenings were social and pleasant. The fire burned brightly, but no work was done which placed a strain on the eyes. A favorite pastime was the making of birch-bark transparencies. The women made basswood cord or fish nets, and sometimes they made birch-bark makuks or dishes. The young men reclined in the wigwam and always had a drum conveniently near them... the winter was the time for story-telling, and many old women were experts in this

art. One old woman used to act out her stories, running around the fire and acting while she talked' (Densmore, 1929:29).

Because the Great Lakes region was dotted with lakes and laced with streams and rivers, a great deal depended on transportation by canoe, the best being made of the versatile birch bark.[17] In common with most tribes inhabiting this area, the Chippewa were considered to be expert canoemen and builders, employing one of at least three styles although it is probable that the so-called 'high-ended' type was the old tribal form resembling that of the Algonquin further east. This particular type of canoe was still used by the Chippewa on Lake Nipigon in Ontario and also by the Menominee in Wisconsin in the nineteenth century. The artist and explorer George Catlin was particularly impressed with the Chippewa canoe, and the consummate skill with which it was fashioned, observing:

'The bark canoe of the Chippeways is, perhaps, the most beautiful and light model of all the water crafts that ever were invented. They are ... so ingeniously shaped and sewed together, with roots of the tamarack, ... that they ... ride upon the water, as light as a cork.'

The skill required in handling these was not lost on Catlin:

Below: *An Ojibwa village near Sault Ste Marie, by Paul Kane (1846). The largest lodge, covered with sheets of silver birch at the top and matting near the bottom, suggests a makeshift encampment. Note child's cradle (center) with protective head bar.*

'They gracefully lean and dodge about, under the skillful balance of an Indian, . . . but like everything wild, are timid and treacherous under the guidance of white man; and, if he be not an experienced equilibrist, he is sure to get two or three times soused, in his first endeavors at familiar acquaintance with them.'

(Catlin, 1841, Vol. 2:138)

Whilst the size of the canoe varied depending on its use, the typical model was just under 16ft (5m.) in length, 3ft (1m.) wide at the middle, and 1½ft (50cm.) deep. Such a canoe could carry about six adults. All measurements were based on the distances between various parts of the human body, although one basic unit employed by many good canoe makers was the 'hand spread' or span from the end of middle finger to the tip of the thumb. It took great skill to fabricate these crafts; the women generally prepared the ground, bark and pitch, whilst the men shaped the wood for the floor, ribs, stern and bow. The whole process was customarily supervised by a highly respected, skilled canoe maker, such expertise not uncommonly passing from father to son so that the traditional skills could indeed be maintained.

In one description of the fabrication of a birch bark canoe, it was reported that it took about a week to gather all the materials together and make the craft. All the material came from trees; the framework and lining was of lightweight cedar, the cords used to keep the frame and other parts together was of spruce root and the pitch for the seams was made from spruce gum, which was generally boiled to thicken it (that which was to be used on the

Above: *Grand medicine dance at Lac Courte Oreille Reservation, Wisconsin, 1899, one of the most important ceremonies of the Midewiwin (Medicine Lodge Society) of the Chippewa. This shows a candidate and mother within the framework lodge.*

Below: *Five Chippewa and Menominee drummers and two Chippewa dancers at a drum ceremony, c.1910, Menominee Reservation. Some Menominee ceremonies petitioned the spirits through the sacred drum which stands before the seated singers.*

Chippewa

The Chippewa in the U.S. (Wisc., Minn., Mich., N.Dak.) and southern Ontario, and the Ojibwa in western Ontario and Saskatchewan all spoke the Ojibwa language (many still do). In 1900 they were mainly forest dwellers, dependent on fishing, hunting, and wild foods (especially wild rice). The main religious ceremony was the medicine Dance of the Mide society. Except as noted, all the items here were collected by Frances Densmore between 1907 and 1930.

1 Birch bark bucket. White Earth Reservation, Minn.
2 Birch bark temporary dish. White Earth Res.
3 Man and woman dolls of slippery elm bark. Red Lake Res., Minn.
4 Man and woman dolls of cattail roots. Minn.
5 Wooden cradleboard with wrappings and ornaments; baby is museum-made plaster model.
6 Piece of cattail mat of type used for wigwam covers. Bois Fort Res.
7 Small cedar bark bag. Bois Fort Res.
8 Piece of cattail mat of type used for wigwam walls. White Earth Res.
9 Birch bark dish for wild rice. White Earth Res.
10 Game: deer bones, thimble, leather with holes, tied to iron pin for spearing them. White Earth Res.
11 Wooden spoon. White Earth Res.
12 Wooden spoon to stir maple sugar. White Earth Res.
13 Leaf patterns of birch bark for beadwork designs.
14 Counting stick for gambling guessing game with bullets hidden in moccasins. Minn., 1891. (W. J. Hoffman coll.)
15 Piece of cedar bark mat of type used for floor mats. Bois Fort Res.
16 Wooden bowl for bear's head at Mide feast. White Earth Res.
17 Unfinished bag of slippery elm bark for holding wild rice. Minn.
18 Chief's cloth headband.
19 Child's toy: gray squirrel skin stuffed with wild rice. White Earth Res.
20 Piece of cattail mat of type used for floor mats. Bois Fort Res.
21 Cedar bark bag filled with wild rice, for storage.
22 Small model of snowshoes.
23 Needle for netting snowshoes.
24 Bone fish hooks.
25 Bow of oak, made in 1928 by Kawakatusk of Rainy Leech Lake Res., Minn., 1891–2. (Hoffman coll.)

Lake Reserve. Ont., for the anthropologist J.M. Cooper.

26 Five arrows with bone points. Manitou Rapids Reserve, Ont. (Cooper coll.)

27 Skunk fur garter; part of costume of Keekweechi-weepinank 'trying to throw' (Red Blanket) bought from him when he was an 1899 delegate to Washington.

28 Fur headband, and belt (?) of black velvet, white fur, and feathers. Part of Red

Blanket's costume (see 27).

29 Red woollen breechclout. (As 28, Red Blanket's.)

30 Pair of beaded moccasins. (As 28, Red Blanket's.)

31 Ballheaded club from man named Odjibwe. White Earth Res.

32 Mide rattle. Red Lake Res.

33 Mide rattle. White Earth Res.

34 Two-headed drum, and drumstick wrapped with red braid, to accompany songs for moccasin game (see 14).

35 Buckskin coat, bands of weasel tails and woven beadwork across back. (As 28, Red Blanket's.)

36 Buckskin belt with woven beadwork. (As 28, Red Blanket's.)

37 Painted and beaded buckskin knife sheath. As 28.

38 Buckskin leggings with woven beadwork. As 28.

39 Stone pipe. As 28.

40 Woman's pipe.

41 Beaded cloth pouch. White Earth Res., 1891. (Hoffman coll.)

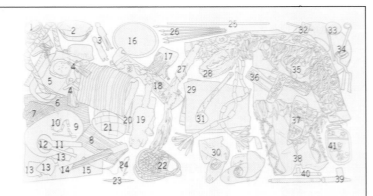

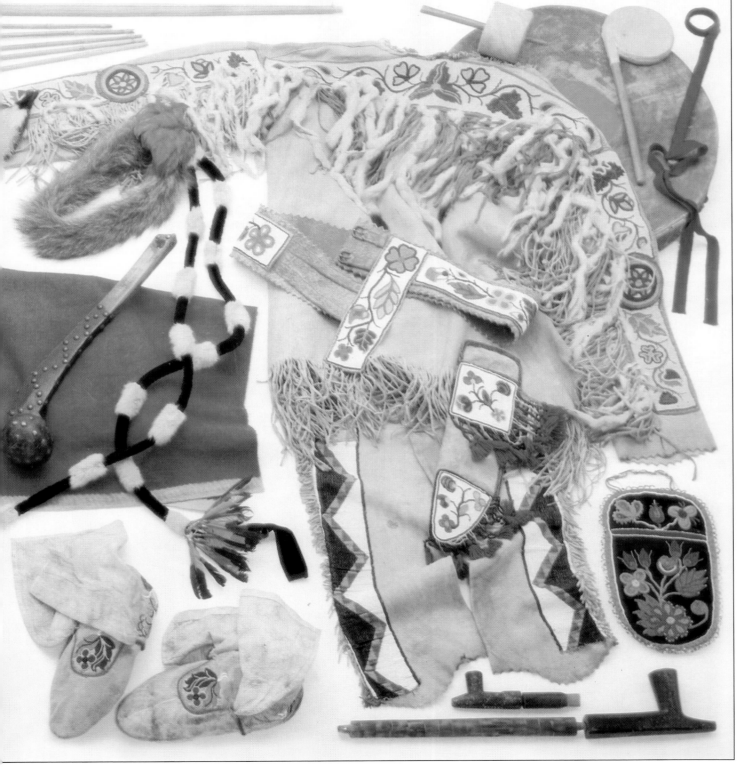

main seams being mixed with powdered charcoal which not only made the resin less brittle when it dried, but gave an ornamental appearance to the caulking). Often, the ground on which the canoe was to be fabricated was covered with a layer of sand so as to shape the canoe bottom, then long sheets of thick bark with the inner side of the bark to the outside were weighted down with a flat frame, which defined the approximate length and width of the canoe; large stones ensured that the frame and bark were held firmly in place. Seven or eight pairs of short poles were now driven into the ground, slightly inclined to the vertical, conforming to the shape of the lower frame and perhaps 3ft (1m.) or so apart at the middle; as the posts were positioned they eased the bark up at an angle and the canoe now began to take shape. The gunwales were now placed in lengthwise and the bark sewn in place with the spruce root; the gunwale gave shape and strength to the upper edges of the canoe and was prepared beforehand so as to have the correct shape and curve as were the sections of cedar for the bow and stern which were eased between the bark at each end. This was then trimmed, conforming to an approved outline. All the final sewing was carried out by the women, traditionally using a bone awl, the finer being done with split and soaked spruce root. Several women could probably complete the

Below: *Household scene, Sauk & Fox, c.1900. The men are in front of winter lodges covered with rush mats, on either side of a summer work area under a brush-covered roof.*

required sewing on an average canoe in one day; some of the stitching was deliberately of uneven length, particularly at the ends, to reduce the likelihood of the bark splitting.

It was important that all overlapping edges of the bark were toward the stern of the canoe so as to ensure streamline flow around its contours, and that all the gores and laps were firmly stuck together with spruce gum. Ribs were now cut to length and shape and eased into place with a lining of thin strips of cedar placed between the ribs and the bark as the work proceeded; this protected the floor and sides of the canoe. Ribs, lining and bark were all kept moist, but the varying width cross pieces which permanently shaped the top of the canoe were sewn in dry.

The canoe was now left to dry for several days and, if necessary, pulled into correct shape by tying it between end stakes. It was then inverted and the seams sealed with the black spruce pitch.

Paddles were of birch or cedar, some 4ft (1.2m.) in length, approximately half being the blade which was 4½ or 6in. (12 or 15cm.) wide. Both men and women rowed, generally with the man seated in the prow and the woman in the stern; however, for fast travel up to four men might paddle at one time.

A good serviceable canoe would last a family perhaps a year; some men were known for

Left: *A Sauk & Fox chief. His distinguishing turban/ deertail headdress is surmounted by an eagle feather. A further sign of his high rank is the split bear and otter hide over his shoulder.*

making and supplying canoes and a typical price in the late nineteenth century would be a three point Hudson's Bay blanket.

There is little wonder that, given the great value of birch bark in the life of the woodland tribes, there are references to it as sacred material. The Abenaki, for example, named the birch *Gluskabe* which was one of their hero gods who, it is recorded, asked the tree 'to take care of the Indians' (Butler and Hadlock, 1957:49). A widespread mythological tale explains the migrations of birds back to the northern forests after the intense winters. The birds are caged in birch bark containers which are torn open by animal-men volunteers from the north, freeing the birds who fly north bringing the summer warmth and regrowth; symbolically, life emerges from the birch container, hence the patterns, produced by a scraping technique (sgraffito), of birds, plants and shrubs embellished on their outer surface.[18]

The spiritual life of the Western Lakes tribes, so eloquently captured in the writings of Frances Densmore on the Chippewa and referred to earlier, centered around the ceremonials of the *Midewiwin*,[19] or Grand Medicine Society, which has been particularly well documented for the Chippewa. The existence of the *Midewiwin* was not recorded by the Jesuit Relations (covering the period 1640 to 1700). However, it has been suggested that special efforts were made by the ritualists to conceal a religious rite which was in direct conflict with the missionary message.[20] The probable antiquity is suggested by its extensive distribution in the Western Great Lakes region, being practiced by the Potawatomi, Menominee, Winnebago, Sauk, Fox, and Kickapoo from 'early historic times' (Ritzenthaler, Trigger ed., 1978:755).

Whilst there were regional variations in the *Midewiwin* ceremony, the principles of ethical

Above: *Kiyo' Kaga, or Keokuk, a distinguished Sauk chief and able leader who was poisoned by one of his own band. In this early image (1847), he wears a necklace of bear claws on an otterskin collar.*

Below: *Sauk, Fox, Kansa delegation, Washington, 1867. Included here is Moses Keokuk, the son of Keokuk (above). Those present had just signed away their remaining land in Kansas for $1 an acre.*

Sauk and Fox

The Sauk and Fox tribes, speaking the same language and culturally very similar, have been close allies since 1733, although maintaining their distinct identities. Traditionally both hunted and trapped during the fall and winter while living in mat-covered lodges in hunting camps, and farmed corn, beans, and squash during the summer while living in large bark-covered lodges in river-bottom villages. Patrilineal clans owned their personal names and had various ritual functions. Within each of the two tribes there were two political organizations for war and peace, that had largely the same memberships but different leaders for the different functions. The Sauk and Fox were enemies of the Dakota and Chippewa and allies of the Iowa, Winnebago, and Potawatomi. During the colonial period they fought the French until 1737. Defeated by the U.S. Army in the Black Hawk War of 1832, the Sauk and Fox were moved from Iowa to Kansas in 1837 and 1842. Many of the Fox returned to Iowa during the 1850s, where they bought land that was later recognized as a reservation, the Mesquakie Settlement near Tama. The other Fox in Kansas joined the Sauk and moved with most of them to Indian Territory (now Oklahoma) in 1869, leaving a small band of Sauk in Kansas. The objects shown here were collected in 1901–3 by the ethnologist William Jones (himself a Fox from Indian Territory) among the Mesquakie (Fox) at Tama or, if so specified below, the Fox or Sauk in Indian Territory.

1 Woman's skirt with silk ribbon appliqué on red flannel; ceremonial.
2 Wooden hole-and-slot heddle for weaving beadwork.
3 Woman's dress, ribbon appliqué decoration. Sauk, Okla.
4 Woman's leggings with ribbon appliqué, beadwork, and buttons.
5 Wooden food paddle.
6 Black gourd warrior's rattle.
7 Bag with beaded design of underwater panther and 'TAMA'.

8 Bag of woven twine and blanket ravellings.
9 Feather fan.
10 Ball of native twine.
11 Braided hank of reed fiber for weaving bags.
12 Woven bag.
13 Pack saddle.
14 Man's fur turban.
15 Twined reed mat.
16 Woven bag, thunderbird design.
17 Twined bag.
18 Hide scraper for tanning.
19 Set of bone gambling dice.
20 Wooden bowl for tossing

dice.
21 Young man's shirt with ribbon appliqué.
22 Boy's buckskin leggings. Fox. Okla.
23 Man's buckskin leggings. Fox. Okla.
24 Young man's beaded 'love bag'.
25 Bone spreader for roach headdress.
26 Boy's popgun toy.
27 Pair of woven beadwork garters. Fox. Okla.
28 Lacrosse stick. Okla.
29 Bundle of gambling sticks.

conduct, the desire for attainment of a long life, the interpretation of dreams and the phenomena of the natural world, permeated the activities of the Society. The basic ethics of the *Midewiwin* were that rectitude of conduct produced length of life and that evil conduct would eventually react on the offender. Stealing and lying and the use of alcohol were strictly forbidden, whilst respect towards women was emphasized. Male members of the *Midewiwin* were taught to be quiet in manner and moderate in speech and not hasty in action. As Densmore observed, 'this directed |my| attention to the gentle voices, the patience, and the courtesy of the old people who had been trained in the Midewiwin' (Densmore, 1929:87). The initiation ceremony was designed to inject a spirit power into the candidate, achieved by pointing a special medicine bag whereupon the candidate fell to the ground unconscious. The bags were made of animal or bird skins being distinctive of one of the four orders of degrees which could be attained in *Midewiwin* membership. The initiation of one candidate who was seated in the middle of the Grand Medicine Lodge, was described by one observer:

'The medicine men, four or five of them, came dancing in, carrying pouches. The pouches were made of the skins of beaver, otter, white martin or weasel – all elongated like snake skins. The dancers danced along the path of the wigwam and when they came near my uncle they threw their pouches at him. The "medicine" in them was so strong that he fell over and fainted. Each man then picked up his pouch and laid it on him, and he came to.'

(Hilger, 1951:69)

The *Midewiwin* medicine bags held a special small white shell called the *migis*;[21] this was considered the sacred symbol of the Society and traditionally associated with immortality. It was also the *migis* which transmitted the spirit power:

Here it is
Here it is
The weasel skin |medicine bag|
Through it I shoot the white shells.

It never fails
The shell
Goes toward them
And they fall

(Initiation songs of *Midewiwin* (Densmore, 1910:Songs Nos 52 and 63))

The ceremony was one of curing a sick individual or responding to a dream that directed application for membership should be made. The *Midewiwin* was generally an annual affair held in the late spring or early fall and lasted for up to five days, depending on the number of candidates. A possible reason for its popularity with the Chippewa is that they have been identified by one anthropologist as having an unusual preoccupation with health, a manifestation of this concern being the assortment of different roots and herbs which were used for medicinal purposes, gaining a knowledge of which was one major objective of the members of the *Midewiwin*.

A notable component associated with the Society was the use of bark rolls inscribed with pictographs, which referred to the instructions to be given to its members; they also recorded the songs and teachings of the *Midewiwin*. The rolls were some 2½ft in length by 1ft wide (75×30cm.), the pictographs being engraved with a bone stylus. To the uninitiated, they were

Below: *A Sauk summer lodge, covered with bark, photographed in Indian Territory in about 1884. An unusually large structure, it is probably the central council lodge of the village. Seated third from the left is the chief Pashipaho, otherwise known by the name 'Little Stabber'.*

virtually meaningless, but to those with the esoteric knowledge the figures were invaluable memory aids. The records were passed down through successive generations, the aged keepers initiating younger men as to the meaning of each pictograph. Such pictographic records in the Woodland region were by no means unique to the Chippewa alone, but because of their association with religious concepts of these people they have been extensively reported on (Hoffman, 1891: Mallery, 1893: Densmore, 1929).

Studies have shown that there were similarities between birch bark pictographs of all the Algonquian stock from the northeastern seaboard to west of the Great Lakes and the Abenaki in Maine even modified the ancient pictographic techniques when, in the late nineteenth century, they became 'engaged in civilized industries in which they have found it necessary to keep accounts' (Mallery, 1893:259). Extending on the nineteenth-century studies of Mallery, W.C. Sturtevant has recently demonstrated that Iroquois hieroglyphics[22] could convey extensive and sophisticated ideas to those familiar with the glyphs. Such pictographic work was perhaps the nearest approach to writing by the indigenous population of North America,[23] but the influx of Europeans caused its abandonment before further development took place.

'Had the whites delayed their coming for another century, . . . these Indians might have succeeded in establishing an enduring State based on the six foundation stones of the League – health, happiness, righteousness, justice, power, and strength of character'[24].

Above; Wakusásse, a Fox warrior, painted by Karl Bodmer (1833). In this early portrait, the warrior wears a deer and porcupine hair roach embellished with feathers as a mark of success in battle. His face is painted with vermilion and brown ochre with what is possibly a lightning symbol.

Right: Wah-com-mo (Fast Walker), a Fox warrior, in 1868. This tribe, who were closely associated with the Sauk, called themselves Meskwahki haki or Mesquaki, 'The Red Earths'. Wah-com-mo wears a grizzly claw necklace and carries an eagle feather fan and pipe tomahawk – traditional accoutrements used by high-ranking Sauk & Fox warriors.

JOSLYN ART MUSEUM, OMAHA, NEBRASKA

References

1 Cape Breton district, called Onamag by the Micmac, was – and still is – considered the residence of the head chief.
2 Although contacts with England may have occurred as early as 1497 when Sebastian Cabot was said to have taken three Micmac Indians to England, the rapport which the French developed contrasted markedly with the attitude of superiority which characterized most of the English colonists.
3 The early name for the areas of Nova Scotia and New Brunswick.
4 Deganawida was possibly of Huron descent. Closely associated with Deganawida was the Iroquois chief, Hiawatha, and the renowned woman chief of the Neutral Nation, Djigonsasen.
5 The Tuscarora joined in about 1720.
6 It has been suggested that the ideals underlying the founding of the League inspired the forming of the American Constitution because it is known that a number of the main writers of the Constitution were thoroughly familiar with the structure of the League.
7 Iroquois women's celebration song.
8 In this context, a moveable tower, overtopping the palisade.
9 This battle has been described as one of the most decisive in American history, it being suggested that had the Hurons and French won the land of the Iroquois, 'Iroquoia', would have been dominated by the French, displacing the Dutch, and the course of colonial history changed (Bishop, 1949:240).
10 One particularly fine Iroquoian ball-headed club is in the collections of Skokloster Castle, Sweden (Ryden, 1963:114-15). A similar club also with a lizard-like creature carved at the top of the handle is in the Museum of Mankind, London (King, 1982:85).
11 Champlain vividly describes the battle between the

Huron and Iroquois in which he participated in 1609 and demonstrates the useless protection which 'shields made of cotton thread woven together and wood' afforded against guns (Bishop, 1949:148).
12 War between Iroquois and Hurons dated from prior to colonial times; this particular conflict, however, finally destroyed the Huron Confederacy.
13 As soon as the Huron had an enemy in their power they tore out his finger-nails and bit or cut off the fingers which he used to draw the string of a bow. Whilst often causing serious infection, it rarely resulted in the prisoner dying before he reached the Huron settlements; indeed, he was well fed to ensure that he could 'better endure the tortures that awaited him' (Trigger, 1969:48).
14 Shamans and powerful warriors were also referred to as Oki. For a graphic 1616 description of a Huron Oki, see Bishop (1949:252).
15 This was just before the rice matured; if attempts were made to gather it later, a great deal was lost.
16 Manito, variants of which were manitto, manetto, manitoa and, more popularly as it has now been taken into the English language, manitou. It may be described as the 'mysterious and unknown potencies and powers of life and of the universe' (Hodge ed., 1907-10:800).
17 In comparison, although the Iroquois were great travelers, they were essentially landsmen, having only limited access to birch bark. Whilst they used canoes, these were fabricated of elm bark which has been described as 'a clumsy craft unsuited to long voyages, dangerous for crossing lakes, and suicide in white water' (Fenton, Trigger ed., 1978:303). The more northerly Huron (Wyandot), however, lived within easier range of birch bark country and mastered both technique of manufacture and use from their Algonquian

neighbors. (See particularly Adney and Chapelle, 1964:214-15 for more details on Iroquois styles of canoe, and their characteristics.)
18 With acknowledgement to Alika Webber (1978:57-61). The author wishes to emphasize here that there is no suggestion meant that such designs were necessarily universally read and understood; however, the roots of the symbolism could well be elucidated by tribal shamans in the mythological terms described.
19 In recording Chippewa language, vowels are indicated as: a, as pronounced in father; e, as in they; ĕ, as in met; i, as in marine; ĭ, as in mint; o, as in note; u, as in rule; û, as in but (acknowledgement to Densmore, 1929:10).
20 The diplomacy of the Algonquians was clearly not matched by the more volatile Iroquoians. It will be recalled that the missionaries' well-intentioned but zealous thrust amongst the Huron and Iroquois led to the martyrdom of several priests.
21 Hoffman states that the migis may consist of any white shell; a cowrie shell was used in one tradition (Hoffman, 1891:167) and Ritzenthaler, who observed the ceremony in the 1940s, also refers to a cowrie shell, 'mikiss' (Ritzenthaler, Trigger ed., 1978:754).
22 American Indian Workshop, Vienna, April 1989.
23 It should be emphasized here that the reference is to peoples north of Mexico. For a discussion on writing in Mesoamerica, see Brotherston (1979:15-19). The Cree writing (referred to in the Subarctic chapter) was developed by the missionary James Evans in about 1840, whilst the mixed blood Cherokee, Sequoyah, developed an alphabet in 1821.
   Both developments, however, appear to have had their inspiration from European, rather than indigenous American, roots.
24 Observations on the League of the Iroquois, Palmer, 1949:102-3.

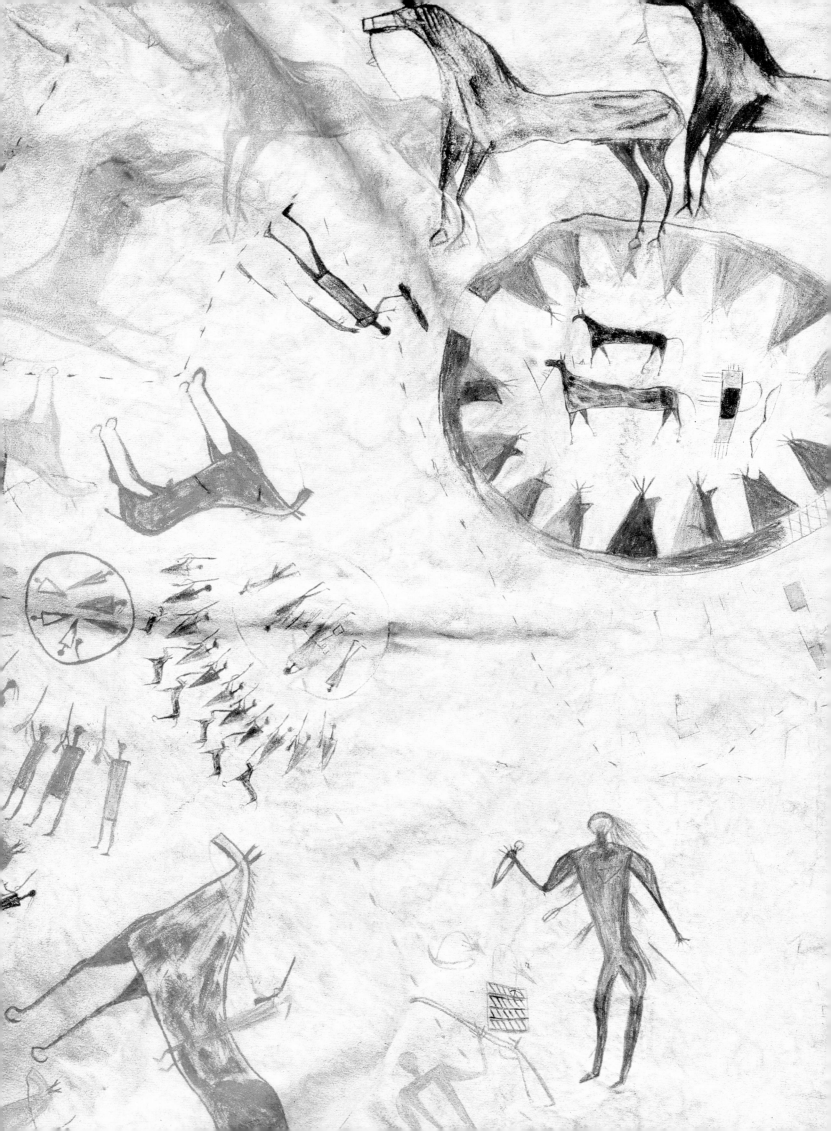

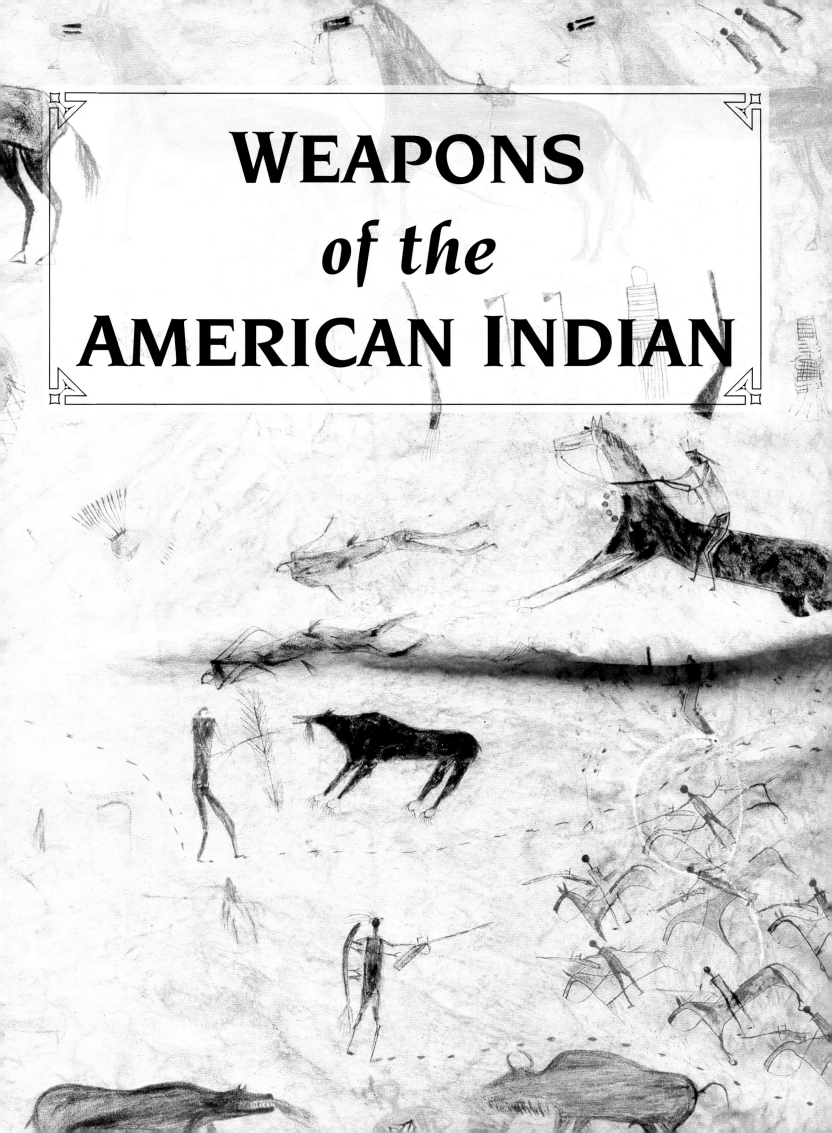

WEAPONS
of the
AMERICAN INDIAN

INTRODUCTION

THIS SECTION surveys the variety of weaponry used by the North American Indians north of present-day Mexico from prehistoric times to the late nineteenth century, by which time various weapons introduced by Euro-Americans had largely replaced those of indigenous make.

These later weapons, such as the pipe tomahawk, knives, axes, arrow and spear heads, were generally based on native designs but replaced stone, bone, horn and hardened woods with iron and steel. When adopted, however, they were generally turned into something very Indian by use of various embellishments, such as engraving, carving or the addition of paint, quillwork, and beads (p.255).

Classification has been according to five broad categories relating to function – striking, cutting, piercing, defensive, and symbolic; these form the five main chapters in the section. The use of pre-contact copper and the later significant impact of trade iron and the horse on weapon styles is dealt with in the chapters on Striking, Cutting and Piercing Weapons.

The subject is vast; a focus on one cultural area alone, even one tribe, could produce a substantial study and so this section must be viewed as a broad overview of a fascinating, but very extensive, topic. Some techniques of fabrication have been described. This includes the widespread war club, which had a stone head held in place by rawhide that also covered the handle and which was generally sheathed in soft buckskin.

Depending on the region and period, the club was then quilled or beaded (p.255 lower left). The main emphasis, however, has been on the finished weapon. The footnotes refer to further sources.

Detailed attention has been given to the pipe tomahawk, the early history of which is still quite obscure; some early pictorial evidence has suggested that the original idea of a combined weapon and pipe may have come from the American Indians themselves (p.268) rather than, as has generally been contended, invented by Euro-Americans. The various styles of pipe tomahawk have been referred to as 'English', 'Spanish', and 'French'. However, as one student of the tomahawk has observed, a large number of these were probably fabricated by local blacksmiths rather than wholesale production in Europe.

The early types of war clubs used in eastern North America, are covered in Striking Weapons and looked at in some depth since weapons such as these were often the precursors to those which were refined and enhanced by Euro-Americans. These include the anciently used clubs of a 'pickaxe' type, now to be found in the National Museums of both Denmark and Sweden and dating from the mid-seventeenth century. Possibly of Nanticoke or Delaware make, these probably had a wider distribution than is generally recognized, as did sword-shaped and ballheaded clubs. Early forms of weapons made for the Indian trade were often inspired by these various styles but replaced with

varieties made from iron, steel, and sometimes brass – a recurring theme which was generally readily accepted by the indigenous peoples.

Less so was one style of defensive weapon on the Plains. Here, attempts by traders to introduce metal shields, and replace those of rawhide, were opposed by Blackfeet holy men who contended that the designs on the shields gave far more spiritual protective power than the simple mechanical protection afforded by a disc of heavy metal. Obviously, religious and military symbolism, as well as tribal economics, entered the equation.

The section on piercing weapons looks at the use of the atlatl, or spear-thrower, which pre-dated the use of the bow in North America by thousands of years. When the atlatl was first encountered by the Spanish under De Soto, its frightening effectiveness against mail-armored soldiers – due to a

Right: *Weapons from the region of the Plains and Eastern Woodlands. The earliest weapon here is the ball-headed club (third from left), which possibly dates from 1700 and of Iroquois manufacture.*
The bows are typical of the Plains region for the mid-nineteenth century. About 40in (1m.) in length, the bow on the far left is partially covered with snake skin; the one on the far right is sinew-backed. The stone-headed club (lower left) is an Apache 'slungshot' type which contrasts with the conical stone-headed club (right) from the Central Plains region. In the middle is a trade pipe tomahawk (probably from the Crow) and adjacent to it is a so-called Missouri war axe.

Left: *A Louisiana Indian war-party, one of whom is carefully covering their tracks. Stealth and surprise were characteristics of Native American warfare. Although the bows, quivers, clubs, and hairstyles look stylized in this print, the use of guns and details of clan tattoos are accurate for the period.*

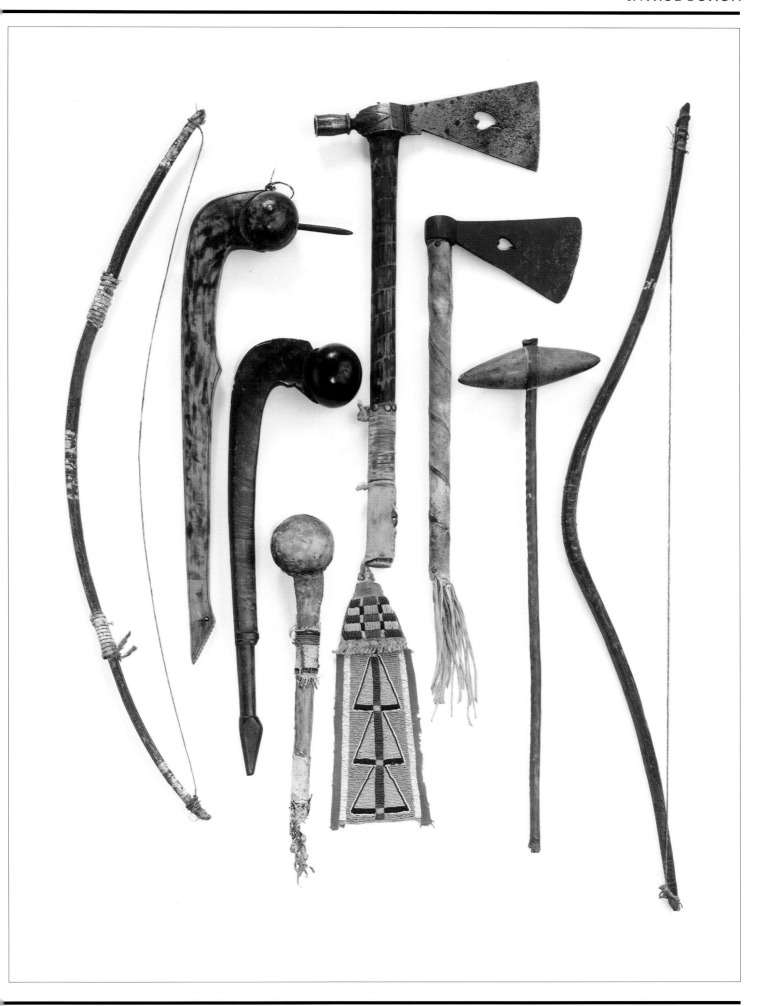

Above: *Pawnee warriors and their interpreter, circa 1868. The men are stripped to the waist and wear little restrictive clothing or accoutrements – typical of Pawnee warriors about to enter battle.*

Left: *Kutchin hunters and warriors, after a sketch by Alexander Hunter Murray at Fort Yukon, 1847-48. Of Athapaskan stock, this powerful Subarctic tribe occupied the northern regions of Alaska and Yukon territory. The use of finely tanned caribou skin for clothing was typical of the period for this region. As shown here, it consisted of a distinctive shirt and pants decorated with dentalium shells and trade beads. The man on the left carries a trade gun in a protective skin case, powder horn, and bullet pouch. The other man is armed with the more traditional bow and arrows.*

three to five times energy increase imparted to the projectile – filled the Spaniards with consternation. Little wonder, as is discussed in the main text, the spear-thrower continued in use, particularly amongst the Inuit. Not only was it a highly effective killing weapon but when used, it only required one hand.

In the chapter on defensive weapons the use of body armor is considered, together with warrior and horse shields, warfare tactics, and village fortifications. All were

Right: *'His-oo-san-ches' or 'Little Spaniard', a Comanche warrior in an engraving after George Catlin who visited the tribe in 1834. The warrior is armed with a bow, lance and shield of typical styles for the Southern Plains at this time.*

later modified with the introduction of steel weapons and the gun. Protective symbols then dominated rather than actual mechanical protection – the subject of the Symbolic Weapons chapter.

The ingenuity of North American Indian weaponry is documented and recognized; how, over thousands of years, it was developed and ingeniously matched the environment where it was used. It was highly functional, often decorative, and proudly carried in war and parade.

There is, perhaps, a slight bias present to Plains Indian weapons and warfare. This is because collections and data are particularly rich for this area and it is also more recent in the Indian-White confrontation. The use of such weapons, however, was clearly embedded in ancient styles and history when ancestors of the Plains tribes lived in the Arctic, the northern boreal forests, the woodlands to the east and, perhaps, even south into Mexico.

STRIKING WEAPONS

A VARIETY OF striking weapons were used throughout ancient North America, most of which were designated for warfare. As will be discussed, however, a number were relegated to ceremonial use or employed solely for special functions.

Whilst most of these weapons could be classified as hatchets or clubs – the term 'war club' particularly was widely used – others such as the tomahawk tended to fall into a class of their own. This was certainly true by the mid-eighteenth century. With the passage of time, the term 'tomahawk' referred to a weapon largely fabricated by whites and having a metal blade.[1]

Ancient stone clubs in North America
Early clubs of indigenous manufacture often display exceptional skills in stone- and flint-working. For example, those from the Southeast and found in the ancient mounds of Tennessee and Alabama are invariably monolithic, with both the handle and blade carved from a single piece of stone (below). Generally about a foot (30cm.) or more in length, many were made of a green stone with superb native lapidarian work. Whilst undoubtedly formidable weapons, it has been speculated that some of the finest may have also served as maces or were used in a ceremonial context. The perforated knob extending from the end of the handle (below) suggests the use of a wrist thong, reinforcing the contention of possible employment in ritual or dance. Although not exclusive to the

Above: *Three stone club heads: the one on the left is probably made of chert, the two on the right of flint. These have been grooved for attachment to a wooden handle. The resultant clubs could be formidable weapons and of a type widely used for thousands of years in North America.*

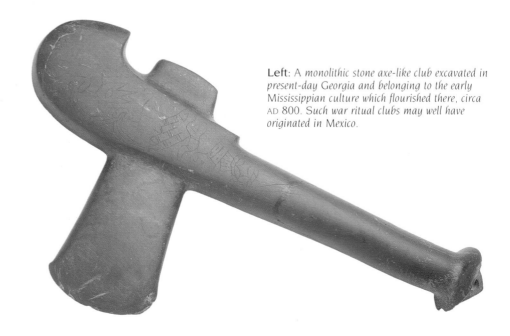

Left: *A monolithic stone axe-like club excavated in present-day Georgia and belonging to the early Mississippian culture which flourished there, circa AD 800. Such war ritual clubs may well have originated in Mexico.*

Above: *A ceremonial war mace made from jasper, a flint-like material. This particular specimen was found in Mound Spiro in the Ohio Valley.*

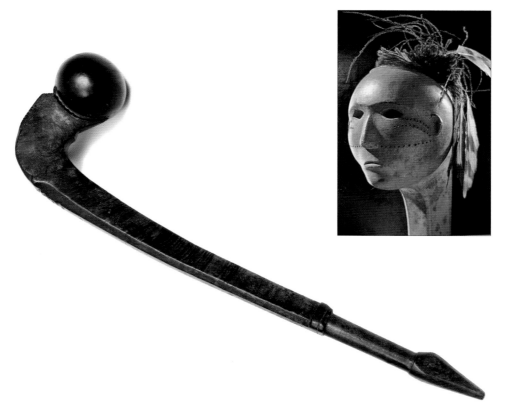

beads and porcupine quills.

An alternative, related style of stone-headed club was a heavy round-headed stone entirely covered with rawhide or heavy buckskin, which was in turn sewn around the wooden handle. It left 2in (5cm.) or so of rawhide between the end of the handle and the stone head free. When used in combat, the relatively free-moving head was able to deal a lethal blow. Such weapons were not uncommon on the Plains, in the Southwest, and on the Plateau. It has been suggested that they originated west of the Rocky Mountains, whilst its eastern limits 'were the Great Lakes where it was observed among the Menomini'.[2]

Wooden clubs

Many early clubs of indigenous manufacture were of a simple knob-stick variety (p.260, left, and p.261). Typical were those used by the Pima and Yuman tribes in the Southwest and made of a hard wood; mesquite was the most popular. The natural shape was carved to produce a very formidable weapon in the hands of a resolute man, whose technique of combat was to invariably employ a powerful upward movement in an attempt to break or crush the jaw of an opponent.

Far more elaborate wooden clubs were developed by the Northwest Coast tribes, including the Nootka and Kwakiutl. Exhibiting carvings which not infrequently made reference to tribal mythology, these types of clubs were more used in the ceremonial context rather than in action on the battlefield. Interestingly, some were referred to as 'slave killers', although there is

Above and inset: *A magnificent early style wooden club which was generally referred to by the early colonists in Virginia as a tomahawk. It is made of a single piece of wood and displays a sharp drop to the ballhead which is a typical feature of such clubs. At times the heads were elaborately carved, as in this presentation piece.*

Southeast (large monolithic clubs have been described for Northwest Coast tribes such as the Tlingit), they seem to have reached their highest development in this area. This may be due to the influence of early contact with tribes on the islands of the West Indies where such monolithic clubs were far more prevalent.

Associated weaponry was made of chipped flint or jasper, some of the finest being found in the Spiro Mounds of present-day Ohio. Dating from prehistoric times, these weapons were shaped with great skill (p.258) – razor-sharp, they could decapitate an enemy at a single blow. Masterpieces of the chipping art, some of the finest examples were obviously carried by distinguished individuals – song leaders, shamans, chiefs – but the style shows that the skills were available to make weapons for everyday use.

The stone-headed club

Of wider distribution were those clubs with stone heads generally set at the end of a wooden handle. Typical stone heads – two of which are shown on the right at the top of p.258 – were found on the banks of the Vermillion River in present-day eastern South Dakota. They are of a type commonly used by the prehistoric pedestrian Plains warriors and later by equestrian nomads who peopled the Plains from about 1750 onwards. The stone head was attached to the handle by shaving thin the upper end of the wooden shaft and then bending it around the groove which had been made in the stone; the pared wood was

then lashed into place with rawhide thongs. Alternatively, a broad band of rawhide secured the head to the shaft, which might be inserted into a hole drilled in the stone. The rawhide was generally softened by first soaking it in water and then tightly bound; when it dried, the subsequent shrinkage held the head securely in place. This technique is evident on the club shown on p.260 (right) and the handle, as was common with this style, has been covered with rawhide; additionally, it has been decorated with both

Below: *A rendering of the formation and equipment of Outina, a Timucua (Florida) war chief (Feest, 1988: 35). Note the heavy oval-headed (wooden?) clubs carried by most of the warriors; an unusual style for eastern North America.*

Left: *The Mohawk leader, Etow oh Koam, whose portrait was painted in London in 1710. He is carrying a finely carved ballheaded club which from earliest times was much favored by the Iroquois and other Woodland tribes.*

little evidence to suggest that they actually performed that function.

For everyday use – in both hunting and warfare – clubs were often spatula-shaped and made of either hard wood or carved whalebone, which was generally sharpened along the edge and sometimes embellished with carvings on the blade and handle.³ These clubs were similar in shape – although smaller – to the paddles used by the Northwest Coast tribes. The paddles shown on p.262 were collected from the Tlingit in the 1870s. Traveling in elaborately carved and painted canoes (p.262), war-parties often beat time on the gunwale during confrontation and the pointed paddles (generally made of yew or maple wood and polished smooth with sharkskin) might then be utilized as makeshift – although formidable – offensive weapons.⁴

An unusual type of carved club collected from the Kiowa is shown on p.261. Heavily embossed with metal tacks and painted red and green, the distinctive notched shape seems to have had early and wide distribution in North America and was not exclusive to war clubs. Thus, a fine quirt collected from the Southern Cheyenne in the 1870s⁵ is of this shape. Kroeber, in his description of Arapaho military societies, makes reference to a wooden sword which was 'straight along one edge, and notched in curves along the other'.⁶ The upper end was cut off diagonally, as with

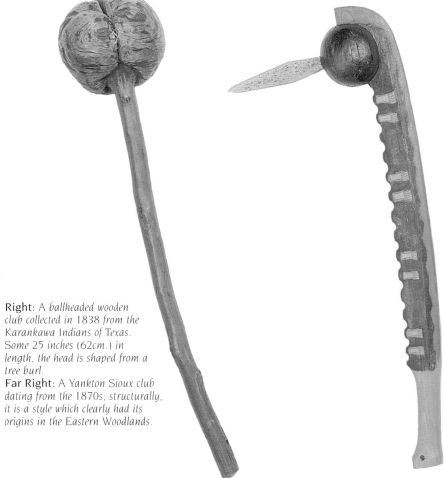

Right: *A ballheaded wooden club collected in 1838 from the Karankawa Indians of Texas. Some 25 inches (62cm.) in length, the head is shaped from a tree burl.*
Far Right: *A Yankton Sioux club dating from the 1870s; structurally, it is a style which clearly had its origins in the Eastern Woodlands.*

Above: *A short-handled stoned-headed club dating from circa 1860 and probably Sioux. The naturally shaped stone-head, probably of agate, is attached to a rawhide-covered wooden handle. The band around the head is decorated with porcupine quills and the handle partially wrapped with blue and white seed beads.*

the club on p.261. It was said to have been used in the Ghost Dance revival ceremonials and thus is probably of an ancient style, although its origin is conjectural.[7]

Some of the finest wooden clubs, generally made from a single piece of wood and obviously of considerable antiquity, are those from the Eastern Woodlands.

Styles of war clubs in eastern North America
Brasser's (1961) detailed analysis of the clubs used in eastern North America identifies four main types which, prior to the forced movement of several tribes west under the pressure of white settlers, were used mainly east of the Mississippi River. Usually made from wood, he refers to them as the pick axe, sword, gun-shaped, and ballhead types.

Pick axe styles were described as early as 1540 by the Spanish explorer De Soto, who visited groups on the Savannah. They were provided with copper or stone blades or celts. Such celts had a sharp edge on one side and a diamond-shaped point at the back; a variant was that used in the Virginia region which had a horn or stone celt that was pointed at both ends, the celt itself being driven through the wooden handle. Its use as a weapon, carried in the left hand with shield on the right arm, was illustrated by the French explorer, Samuel de Champlain, who traveled to the Iroquois on the Hudson and Mohawk Rivers in 1609.[8] (See Defensive Weapons, p.297 for an early engraving of this illustration.)

A variant of this style of club was the use of a rawhide cord or strap which attached the celt to the handle. As Brasser has observed, it suggests a possible relationship to the hammer-type club so popular further west and described earlier.

Two examples of the pick axe-type club are represented in the collections of the National Museums of Denmark and Stockholm. Described as 'unique pieces'[9] and dating from before 1650,[10] it is probable that they were acquired in the region of the lower Delaware

Right: *Early styles of wooden clubs: (1) Osage which gives the impression of the head of a bird. (2a and 2b) Sauk, circa 1760 gun-shaped type. Detail of engravings, possibly war tally marks. (3) Early Iroquoian-type ballheaded club, probably early eighteenth century.*

Below: *A wooden club collected in the early 1900s from the Kiowa by the ethnologist, James Mooney. Such clubs resemble some types of quirts or whips, particularly popular on the Southern Plains.*

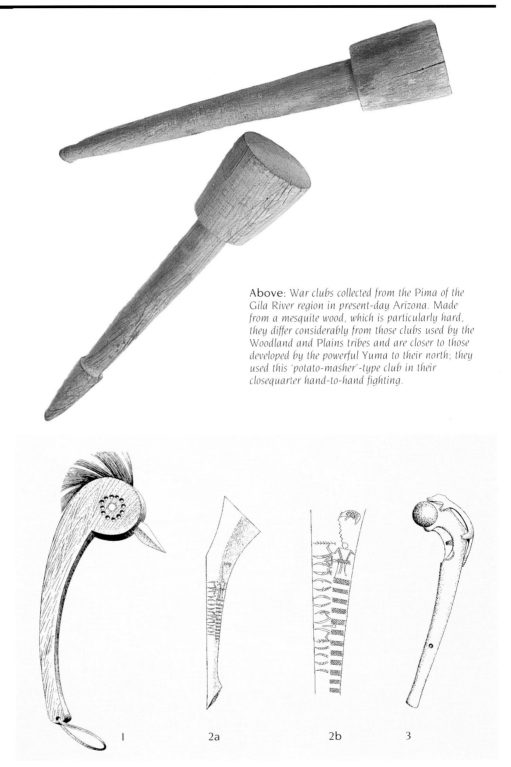

Above: *War clubs collected from the Pima of the Gila River region in present-day Arizona. Made from a mesquite wood, which is particularly hard, they differ considerably from those clubs used by the Woodland and Plains tribes and are closer to those developed by the powerful Yuma to their north; they used this 'potato-masher'-type club in their closequarter hand-to-hand fighting.*

1   2a   2b   3

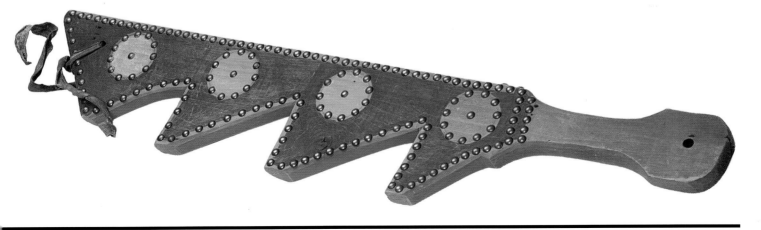

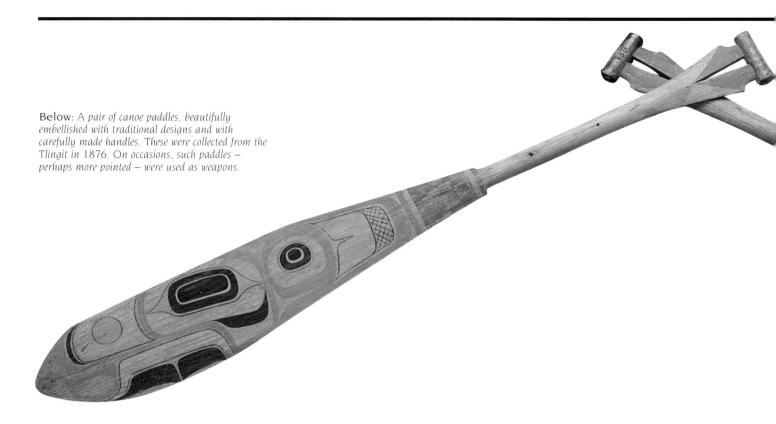

Below: *A pair of canoe paddles, beautifully embellished with traditional designs and with carefully made handles. These were collected from the Tlingit in 1876. On occasions, such paddles – perhaps more pointed – were used as weapons.*

River where a small Swedish colony had been founded in about 1650.[11]

The efficiency of these clubs as striking weapons has been questioned, particularly because of the weak attachment of the blade to the haft.[12] Nevertheless, these rare specimens probably represent a style which had relatively wide distribution – they were used not only by the Iroquois, but also by such tribes as the Nanticoke, Delaware, and Susquehannocks to their south and east, and perhaps even to tribes beyond.[13]

A club compared by early observers to a scimitar but more recently referred to as a 'sword-type'[14] seems to have had its origins in

the south. Indeed, a weapon used by the Aztecs strongly resembled the sword-club and it was a style widely used early on in the Southeast by tribes of the Florida Keys, the Muskogeans and Powhatans. Varying considerably in style[15] – some had shark teeth or flints set along the edge, others were notched or plain – the sword-club was later popular amongst the Iroquois and extended as far north as the tribes of southern New England. A relatively simple form of this club was collected from the Tuscarora by Prince Maximilian du Wied. Some 2ft (62cm.) in length, it had been preserved and used by the Tuscarora in their dances, 'as a memory to

their past'.[16] Although at the time of Maximilian's visit the Tuscarora had long been associated with the Iroquois, their earlier homeland was considerably further south, perhaps extending as far as the coast of the present-day North Carolina.

The utilization of a sword-shaped club as a symbol of the past certainly suggests that this was an important style of weapon in the Southeast – a contention supported by Brasser's 1961 research.[17] The shape, with distinctive notched edges, was used in the fabrication of the quirts used by some western tribes (alluded to earlier on p.260). It is therefore possible that this style of quirt

Below: *A rendering of Haida canoes as they may have appeared in warfare, circa 1870. Such canoes were made from a single hollowed-out tree trunk by skilful use of adze and chisel as well as controlled burning. Designs such as the Thunderbird made reference to the victor of the heavens, whilst that of the killerwhale leant toward the spirit and Lord who dominated the underworld powers, which gave confidence to Haida war-parties.*

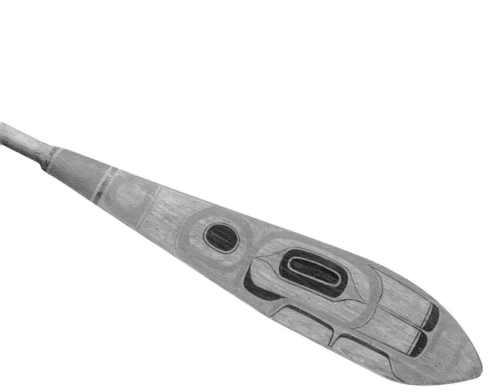

such as stylized depictions of a horned serpent, underwater panthers, Thunderbirds, and human figures. In addition, there are bands and crosses which may be indicative of tally marks – perhaps coups counted, prisoners captured, war-parties led, or even scalps taken. Such motifs on these and other early North American Indian clubs have been the subject of considerable discussion in recent years.[23]

Gunstock clubs – so called because they were carved in the form of a European gunstock – were popular and widely used in the Woodland area, Peterson recording that they were in use as early as 'the beginning of the seventeenth century'.[24] Generally some 30in (75cm.) or more in length, they usually differed from the earlier style of sword-type club by having a blade of flint, horn, or iron set into the upper end; the stock itself was often decorated with engravings or brass-headed trade tacks. This style of club continued in popularity in the Midwest amongst such tribes as the Sauk and Fox as well as the Eastern Sioux. A particularly fine example, collected by Duke Paul of Württemberg in the 1820s and probably from the Osage, is shown in on p.264; the spear-point-type steel blade used here was a very popular trade item.

By the 1850s, such clubs were to be found

derived from an ancient and popular sword-like weapon, memories of which were brought west by displaced tribes, particularly those from the Southeast such as the Delaware, Creek, Seminole, and Cherokee.[18]

Most impressive of all Eastern Woodland striking weapons are the magnificent ballheaded clubs (p.259) much favored by the Iroquois and Huron and described as early as 1635. One notable authority on the Iroquois described such clubs as 'a heavy weapon two feet (62cm.) in length made of ironwood with a globular head five or six inches (12.7 or 15cm) in diameter (p.259). The head sometimes resembled a human face or a ball enclosed by claws'.[19]

A fine example of this style of club is now in the collection of the National Museum of Scotland (p.259), although it dates from circa 1850, and thus was probably a presentation piece rather than a functional weapon. It reflects the very high degree of skill used by the Iroquois (and other tribes) in the carving of naturalistic effigies and at the same time it 'also displays an assemblage of symbolic materials and paint that has often disappeared from similar pieces collected during the early contact period'.[20] Whilst tree roots or tree knots were said to be used in the fabrication of such clubs[21], one favored source was apparently a sapling which grew from the sides of a river bank and which curved upward toward the light; clubs made of such wood were obviously of great strength and elasticity.[22]

Although not a feature exclusive to the ballheaded club, a number of the early examples exhibit a series of engraved motifs,

Right: Waatopenot, 'The Eagle's Bill', a Chippewa chief, painted by James Otto Lewis at the Fond du Lac council in 1826. This man is carrying a classic gunstock-shaped war club which is embellished with brass-headed studs. The basic club style is ancient.

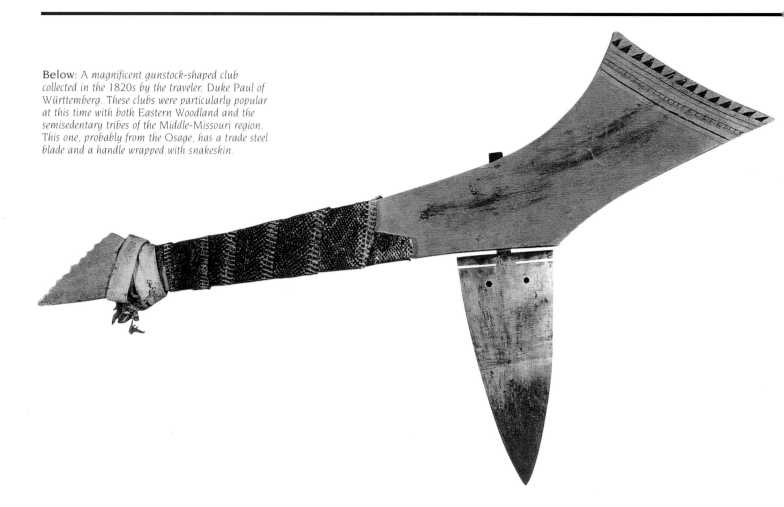

Below: A magnificent gunstock-shaped club collected in the 1820s by the traveler, Duke Paul of Württemberg. These clubs were particularly popular at this time with both Eastern Woodland and the semisedentary tribes of the Middle-Missouri region. This one, probably from the Osage, has a trade steel blade and a handle wrapped with snakeskin.

Right: The Fox chief, Nesouaquoit, 'Bear in the forks of a tree', painted in Washington in 1837. This man carries a classic Missouri war hatchet; the decorated blade is of an unusually large size.

amongst the Lakota on the western Plains, although the stock itself was generally slimmer and longer than those formerly used by the more eastern tribes.[25] A variant on this style of club was one which had two or more steel knife blades set in the edge (p.270). A particularly dangerous weapon at close quarters in the hands of a resolute man, such styles were popular in the period 1860-80; one was collected from the Hunkpapa Sioux leader, Sitting Bull, by General Nelson A. Miles and is now in the National Museum of the American Indian, Washington, D.C.[26]

The so-called 'Missouri war hatchet' was found in use by Lewis and Clark when they stayed with the Mandan on the middle Missouri River (in present-day North Dakota) in the winter of 1805-06. Meriwether Lewis was particularly interested in this style of weapon since, in his opinion, it was a 'battle-ax, of a very inconvenient figure'. Such axes, he said, were fabricated of iron, the blade being 'extremely thin and from seven to nine inches long... the eye... is circular and about an inch in diameter... the handle is straight, and 12 or 15 inches long; the whole weighs about a pound'.[27] The combination of the blade to handle length rendered such a weapon, in Lewis' opinion, 'of very little strength, particularly as it is always used on horseback'.[28]

Nevertheless, it would appear that the Mandan, as well as at least nine other tribes in the region, favored this weapon, which seems to have been introduced by French traders some time in the 1700s. The expedition's blacksmith was kept busy making such axes, mainly in exchange for corn, which helped the expedition to survive the brutal winter when temperatures often plunged to almost 50 degrees below zero. Being without a steel edge, of thin iron and often having decorative piercings in the form of a 'bleeding heart', the Missouri war hatchet, it might appear to white observers, was more for ceremonial use than for use in actual warfare. However, as Peterson observes, this may be 'an excellent illustration of the fact that European standards may not always be used in judging the use an Indian may have had for an object'.[29]

The Missouri war axe continued to be used by the Missouri River tribes as late as the mid-nineteenth century.[30] Thus, the artist/explorer Rudolph Kurz sketched an Omaha carrying such a weapon in the vicinity of Bellevue, Nebraska, in 1851.[31] Perhaps at this time, however, they were considered more for ceremonial use and indeed it has been observed they were handed down as heirlooms 'in even more recent times'; the height of its popularity, however, seems to have been 'between 1810 and 1830'.[32]

Also reported in use amongst the Mandan was the so-called 'spontoon tomahawk'. Even as early as 1805, though, it was considered an old-fashioned weapon and even more inconvenient than the Missouri war hatchet. The large blade was invariably fashioned from one piece of wrought iron which was bent round at the top to form the eye, welded on to the blade. Two sections were then cut from the body of the blade and bent outward; further decorative features were holes drilled near the top. The length of such blades could be up to 15in (38cm.), although the shape has been likened in appearance to large door hinges.

The inspiration for this form of war axe probably derives from the espontoon, a polearm which was commonly carried by commissioned officers in the 1700s. The espontoon, in turn, derived from the partizan, an officer's spear which was commonly used in the sixteenth and seventeenth centuries. Little wonder that even as early as 1805, Lewis and Clark described them as the 'older fassion'![33] The spontoon tomahawk has been described with some justification as the French type (of tomahawk), resembling the fleur-de-lis;[34] further, the earliest specimens come from areas traditionally associated with the French in North America – the St. Lawrence Valley, Great Lakes, Lake Champlain, and extending down to the mouth of the Mississippi. Such tomahawks, however, were not exclusively made by the French. Certainly after 1763, when the British took over the region formerly occupied by the French, they were probably produced by not only the British but by Americans and Canadians, mainly for the lucrative fur trade.[35]

By the mid-nineteenth century, the spontoon tomahawk (with several variations) was widely distributed, extending across the Prairies and Plains to the Plateau region. It found particular favor with the Crow and their friends, the Nez Perce, from about 1870 onwards. Steel was only seldom used in their fabrication; however, as Peterson has observed, the iron blade would 'inflict a serious wound in combat' and also that 'later specimens seem to have been primarily ceremonial in use'.[36]

A question of terminology

References to 'tomahawk', as against 'club' or 'hatchet', in the discussion of the spontoon

Below: *Battle between a Cheyenne and the Mandan chief, Mato-tope, 'Four Bears', as depicted by Four Bears in 1834. This was a particularly dramatic battle. Note the use of the Missouri war axe by the victorious Mandan chief, who himself was badly injured.*

'tomahawk' 'tends to restrict the term to metal axes'.[18] The term 'pipe tomahawk' almost exclusively refers to a combination of a pipe and weapon, made of metal, although at times there are some interesting combinations of other materials One example is the weapon carried by the Seneca chief, 'Cornplanter', in the fascinating portrait produced in 1796 (p.268)[19] – the blade is metal but the bowl appears to be clay.

The pipe tomahawk

Perhaps of all the various tools and weapons on offer from the European (and later American and Canadian) market to the North American Indian during the lucrative years of the fur trade (circa 1650-1870) nothing was more appealing than – as the English put it – the 'smoak tomahawk'. Although the term covers an immense number of styles, the basic construction combined both pipe and war hatchet in one single unit – symbols of both peace and war. It was a highly prized and exceptionally useful implement. As was observed of the Cherokee who had adopted the pipe tomahawk as early as the 1750s, 'this

blade raises several points with regard to the nomenclature used to describe North American Indian striking weapons. The word tomahawk was originally applied to a group of striking weapons which were commonly and anciently used by both the Algonquian and Iroquoian tribes of eastern North America. Early colonists mention the word from this region – with slight variations – as 'tomahack' or 'tommahick', whilst the Mahican referred to such weapons as 'tumnahecan'. The wooden ballheaded club at this time was also generally referred to as a 'tomahawk' and it clearly impressed white observers with its effectiveness; as an offensive striking weapon, one recorded that it was heavy enough 'to knock men's brains out'.[17]

Tomahawk ritual and symbolism was undoubtedly well established at a very early period. Thus, it is recorded that when council was called to deliberate war, a tomahawk, entirely painted red, was placed on the ground by the chief. If the council agreed that a war-party should be initiated, the young war-chief leader raised the tomahawk, dancing and singing war songs. This was a pattern not exclusive to eastern tribes; with some variations, but basically similar, it was replicated in a number of other regions, particularly on the Plains.

With the passage of time and with a wide variety of striking weapons to describe, in modern anthropological parlance the word

Right: The Shoshone, Heebe-Tee-Tse, photographed circa 1900. Shown here is a modified form of Missouri war axe – a triangular section is cut out of the blade, which is probably of pewter.

Above: *A fine steel pipe tomahawk (1860-80) where the classical features of the Plains Indian style have been embellished with a detailed pictographic-type warrior on horseback and enemy prostrate on the ground (above right, detail). The handle has been file-branded and additionally decorated with brass tacks.*

is one of their most useful pieces of field-furniture, serving all the offices of hatchet, pipe, and sword'.[40]

The history of the pipe tomahawk extends back to at least the first half of the eighteenth century, possibly as early as 1709-10, since a portrait of one of the Iroquois 'Kings' who visited London at this time depicts a metal hatchet with a flaring blade. At the top it appears that a pipe-bowl is attached, although it could simply be the opposing spike or hook of the halberd-type tomahawk.

Such weapons were named after an English polearm weapon developed in the late fourteenth century and modified by at least the early 1700s into the 'battle axe' tomahawk for the North American Indian trade.[41] Whatever the precise date of invention, by the

middle of the eighteenth century, pipe tomahawks were commonly used, although they were at least four times more expensive than the relatively simple war hatchet. Those inletted with steel or combined with brass seem to have been valued at almost twice that amount.[42]

Who first invented the pipe tomahawk is conjectural. In an insightful discussion, the scholar Richard Pohrt, who has made a special study of the tomahawk, concluded that the possibility that it was the brain-child of a North American Indian could not be discounted. Pohrt refers to the fact that in 1779-80, David Zeisberger, a Moravian missionary, reported that Indians in present-

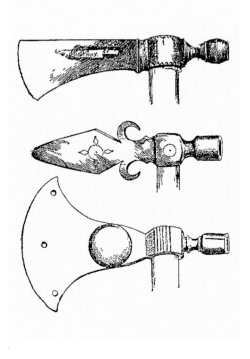

Right: *There were many different styles of pipe tomahawk. (Top) Early style of axe-like tomahawk, circa 1800. (Middle) A spontoon tomahawk. Some of the earliest specimens (circa 1750) suggest French influence. (Bottom) Flaring blade tomahawk resembling those widely used in Europe. This type may be Spanish-influenced.*

Bottom: The Seneca chief, 'Cornplanter', painted by Frederic Bartoli in 1796. This is one of the few renderings of an early style of pipe tomahawk where a clay pipe appears to have been inserted at the front of the handle (in combination with a spiked hatchet).

Below: An iron pipe tomahawk, fitted with a beechwood handle, embellished with silver. This is a particularly elaborate piece, being engraved and also inlaid with an image of a bowie knife. Probably of English make, it was collected in West Virginia, circa 1873, but undoubtedly dates to the early nineteenth century.

Above: The head of a pipe tomahawk, probably Santee Sioux. This has been carved from catlinite, a soft red stone quarried in present-day Minnesota.

Above: A fine steel pipe tomahawk with pierced blade and bowl made from a gun barrel. Probably Hunkpapa Sioux, circa 1870.

day Ohio were well acquainted with blacksmithing and fashioned metal hatchets and axes 'right well'. Additionally, it is noted the most commonly used material for pipe-stems was ash sapling, which was the same material used for the handles of pipe tomahawks. Pohrt concludes, 'It seems but a short step for an Indian, patiently fitting a handle in a hatchet head, to realize that he had the makings of a pipe stem. The addition of a pipe bowl to the poll, or back, of his hatchet blade would produce a dual purpose object – one that could be used for chopping or smoking'.[11]

The use of ash for the handle not only gave a stronger wooden stem which could take high polish, but also enabled a hole to be comparatively easily bored through for use in smoking. Ash has a soft pith center which is easily removed by burning or splitting the wood lengthwise, cutting out the pith, and then sticking the two pieces back together. The handle was often decorated with heavy brass-headed trade tacks and the lower end covered with buckskin to facilitate a firm grip. An extension of the end cover was, particularly on dress occasion tomahawks, elaborately quilled or beaded – the particular technique of embellishment (type of bead, patterns, and color) was indicative of tribal origin.

Although early Hudson Bay trade lists tabulate various types of hatchets and axes

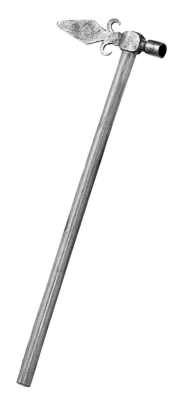

Above: *A spontoon-type pipe tomahawk of a style which dates to the mid-nineteenth century, and is possibly Sauk or Fox. Note the unusual flat strap.*

Right: *The Yankton Sioux, 'Flying Pipe' in full regalia, photographed circa 1870. He wears a quilled shirt, fringed with hair-locks, and dentalium shell necklace and ear ornaments. In his right hand is a spontoon-type pipe tomahawk, which was popular with the Sioux at this time.*

Above: *Pictograph of a Cheyenne warrior wearing a warshirt embellished with ermine fringes. He is striking a U.S. soldier with a Warrior Society membership lance. This may be more than just a symbolic coup count, as the lance appears to be pointed. Collected by the traveler, William Blackmore, from Two Lance's camp on the Platte River in 1874.*

on offer to Indians in the fur trade, there is little evidence to suggest that the pipe tomahawk itself was manufactured on a large scale in Europe.[44] The majority seem to have been made by rural blacksmiths and exhibit an enormous variety of design. The inspiration for some of these designs undoubtedly derived from early English, French, and possibly Spanish weaponry. However, as Pohrt has observed, 'Most tomahawks show a great variety in design, size, and decorative detail, and lack the standardization usually associated with quantity production'.[45] In addition, Pohrt found, after extensive examination of tomahawks over a period of more than thirty years, that it was very rare for a pipe tomahawk to be stamped with a trade mark or the maker's name, which was common practice with English (and other) manufacturers of metal weapons and tools. It seems that the pipe tomahawk, invented by either an Indian or an Englishman, was a unique, highly prized item, largely produced by skilled American artisans.[46]

Left: *Spotted Eagle, a Miniconjou Sioux, photographed by L. A. Huffman in the 1880s. He wears a distinctive quilled shirt and has armbands of grizzly bear claws. Of particular interest, however, is the long, slender gunstock club with three knife blades set in the upper edge. These clubs were particularly favored by the Plains Sioux from about 1860 onward.*

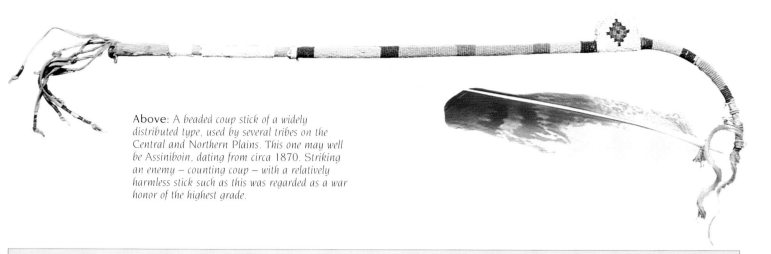

Above: *A beaded coup stick of a widely distributed type, used by several tribes on the Central and Northern Plains. This one may well be Assiniboin, dating from circa 1870. Striking an enemy – counting coup – with a relatively harmless stick such as this was regarded as a war honor of the highest grade.*

References

1 See particularly Peterson (1971: 4-6) for a detailed discussion of the terminology applied to axes, war clubs, hatchets, and the so-called 'squaw axe'.
2 Brasser, 1961: 77.
3 For illustrations of both war clubs and batons of the Northwest Coast tribes, together with detailed descriptions, see Arima and Dewhirst, 1990: 401.
4 Underhill also makes the point, however, that such paddles were mainly used to anchor the canoes to the beach (Underhill, 1945: 91).
5 Sturtevant and Taylor, 1991: 87.
6 Kroeber, 1904: 184.
7 W. C. Sturtevant (Washington, November 1999) drew my attention to the use of unusual carved wooden staves exhibiting this shape and used by the Creek as illustrated by Swanton (1922).
8 Champlain's explorations in Huron and Iroquois country in the period 1609-16, is concisely described in Goetzmann and Williams, 1992: 58-59.
9 Brunius, 1995: 158.
10 Brasser, 1978: 87.
11 At that time, Sweden then comprised not only present-day Sweden but also Denmark and Norway.
12 The hafts of both of these clubs are decorated with wampum which, on the Copenhagen club, is more intact. The use of wampum to adorn tomahawks was recorded for the Virginia tribes as early as 1700. See Brunius, 1995: 156.
13 Although Brasser has dated both these clubs as 'probably pre-1650' (Brasser, 1978: 87), Brunius' subsequent researches establish that the earliest reference to the Stockholm specimen is 1686, whilst the Copenhagen club was first documented in 1725 (Brunius, 1995: 157-58).
14 Brasser, 1961: 79.
15 One observer, Thomas Hariot, in 1585 recorded that the tribes of the North Carolina coast used 'flat-edged wooden truncheons, which are about a yard long' (Brasser, 1961: 80).
16 Less than a decade ago the author collected a sword-type club from the Florida Seminole that is clearly related to this ancient weapon.
17 Brasser (1961) documents, albeit briefly, the description left by early explorers in the Southeast, such as Thomas Hariot (1585), Captain John Smith (1607), and Du Pratz (1758), who make reference to the use of a 'sword', 'scimitar', or 'halfmoon'-shaped clubs of wood, emphasizing the early use and importance of this style of weapon in the region.
18 Several of these tribes were either forcibly or by treaty, moved west; some, such as the Delaware moved to Texas as early as 1820 (Hodge, 1907: 385). The date of appearance of the distinctive notched quirt amongst the western tribes, was probably at least well before the mid-1800s. A piece collected by Duke Friedrich Paul Wilhelm of Würtemmberg and now in the British Museum, dates from this time. Of interest is the fact that it was probably collected in Texas from the Kiowa or Comanche (Gibbs, 1982: 59).
19 Lyford, 1945: 45.
20 Phillips, 1987: 86.
21 Brasser, 1961: 82.
22 (a) Feest (1983: 110-15) describes in detail, the distribution and early styles of this club.

Amongst the earliest, are those now in the Ashmolean Museum, Oxford.
(b) For a details discussion of those in the Swedish and Danish collections, see Brunius (1995: 159-63).
(c) I am indebted to Scott Meachem for this information (Woodlands Conference, British Museum, London, February 1999).
23 See for example: Phillips, 1984; Sturtevant, 1989; Bankes, 1999; and King, 1999.
24 Peterson, 1971: 88.
25 (a) Peterson describes and illustrates a fine specimen collected from the Teton Sioux about the middle of the nineteenth century. He comments, however, 'at which time it must have been relatively new' (ibid.).
(b) Certainly by the 1830s, some Middle Missouri tribes had the gunstock type club, as attested by Karl Bodmer's paintings of the Arikara, *Pachtüwa-Chtä* at Fort Clark (Hunt, Gallagher and Orr, 1984: 283) and the Hidatsa, *Ahschüpsa Masihichsi* (ibid: 316).
26 This particular specimen is illustrated in Peterson, 1971: Plate 23. The three bowie-knife blades dating from circa 1850, are stamped on their ricassos with 'MANHATTAN/CUTLRY CCMP/SHEFFIELD'. The wide range steel knives, hatchets and tomahawks which were early manufactured in England for the Fur Trade, is discussed in Woodward (1965).
27 Lewis and Clark, Coues ed., 1893: 230.
28 ibid.
29 Peterson, 1971: 23.
(a) If the pictographic robe showing scenes of Mandan warfare (circa 1797), collected from the Mandan by Lewis and Clark is to be believed, several warriors are carrying the Missouri war axe in battle (See Ewers, 1957: Plate 1). The robe is now in the Peabody Museum at Harvard University.
(b) See also Fig. 16 of a pictograph by the Mandan chief, Four Bears, using a Missouri war axe in battle with a Cheyenne chief.
30 Excellent renderings of Missouri war axes being carried by distinguished warriors were made by Karl Bodmer at Fort Clark in 1834. See particularly Hunt, Gallagher and Orr, 1984: Plates 318 and 326.
31 This is reproduced in American Anthropologist X. No.1 (1910),11. Additionally, Kurz sketched a warrior (Hidatsa?) carrying what appears to be a Missouri war axe and decorated with a fringed handle (Kurz, Hewitt ed., 1937: Plate 31).
32 Peterson, 1971: 23.
33 ibid: 26.
34 Other terms used to describe this style, were 'dagger bladed', 'diamond bladed' (ibid: 24).
35 It was reported that the Mandans specifically requested the blacksmith of the Lewis and Clark expedition, to make them such blades. I recall, Ralph Williams of Culdesac, Idaho, showing me in 1977, two spontoon-type blades in his possession. These had been found at early Nez Perce burial sites. Mr. Williams then drew my attention to Lewis and Clark's report on reaching the Nez Perce in September 1805, where they found such tomahawks made by their own blacksmith at Fort Mandan – a few months earlier and some two thousand miles to the east! (For discussions of the complex and efficient Indian

trade, see Taylor, 1984 and Swagerty, 1988).
36 Peterson, 1971: 26.
37 Holmes in Hodge ed., 1910: 773-74.
38 Feest, Macgregor ed., 1983: 113.
39 Pohrt discusses the confusion which was arisen regarding the use of the word 'tomahawk', pointing out that the term originally described a weapon of war although, on occasions, some authors also applied the term to a variety of native stone implements, as well as wooden hand weapons. He offers a definition of the tomahawk: 'a weapon with a metal blade, usually iron or steel, hatchet-like in form, and designed or decorated in such a manner as to be distinguishable from a common hatchet. Tomahawks, whether undecorated or ornate, exhibit a refinement and finish not generally extended to the ordinary hatchet of the time' (Pohrt, 1986: 55-57).
40 Henry Timberlake In Peterson, 1971: 33. He also adds that the pipe tomahawk possessed the symbolic power of the mace for ceremonial functions.
41 Arthur Woodward's researches on the evolution and distribution of the tomahawk in North America, quotes a reference as early as the 1650s to the use of a metal tomahawk amongst the Indians in the vicinity of New York – possibly the halberd or hatchet-type. (Woodward, 1946: 4).
42 Presentation pipe tomahawks which displayed superior craftsmanship and often highly decorated with inlays of silver and occasionally gold were, of course, far more valuable. For a discussion of such styles with specific examples, (see Pohrt, 1986: 59-60).
43 (a) ibid: 57.
(b) The handle of a pipe tomahawk needs to be drilled for smoking; lacking the tools to bore a handle which could be 2ft (60cm.) or more in length, Indians generally used ash, the pith could thus be burned out with a hot wire. Alternatively, the handle could be split lengthwise, the pith removed, and the pieces glued back. Ash, as Pohrt has noted, was a favorite wood for pipe-stems where similar techniques were used.
44 I am indebted to the late Russell Robinson of the Royal Armouries, for generously giving me copies of his notes relating to trade goods. These he had researched at the Beaver House, London, prior to the records being transferred to Canada in the late 1960s.
45 Pohrt, 1986: 57.
46 (a) The late Milford G. Chandler was amongst the last of skilled tomahawk makers with an intimate knowledge of fabrication techniques learned from individuals who had directly made or had knowledge of the methods employed by agency blacksmiths (See Chandler in Peterson, 1971).
(b) The late Russell Robinson who was Senior Armourer at the Tower of London, demonstrated to me almost forty years ago, the various metal forging techniques, including the fabrication of pipe tomahawks, which would have been identical to those employed by rural blacksmiths in North America. Some of Mr. Robinson's tools are still in the collections of the Royal Armouries.

CUTTING WEAPONS

FROM TIME IMMEMORIAL, cutting weapons of various styles have been used throughout North America. Many, of course, were used as tools and utensils whilst others were specifically designed for warfare. Essential for survival was the need to scrape, saw, bore, and cut various materials and naturally, the type of tool for these processes varied considerably; not only in shape and size, but also in the choice of material for the cutting edge.

In general, scrapers – a tool of very wide distribution in North America – resembled a chisel blade, invariably with a beveled edge and made of a siliceous stone such as chert, jasper, agate, or basanite. The simplest scrapers were held in the hand, generally with some padding, whilst more elaborate versions were set into handles of wood, bone, or horn. Those used for tanning hides or shaping wood were particularly well developed in several cultural areas, such as on the Great Plains and Northwest Coast, where hide-tanning and wood-carving reached a very high degree of perfection.

The same was true of both sawing and boring tools, the former with a serrated edge, the latter a sharp pointed edge, and either held directly in the hand or provided with a haft so that the boring could be achieved generally by vibration or rotation. Relatively soft stone such as argillite or catlinite[1] could be shaped and perforated with some ease, as could various types of wood, bone, and horn. In the hands of a skilled artisan, ancient – mainly stone – tools largely satisfied the needs of the North American Indian, although even this comparatively sophisticated stone-age technology obviously had its

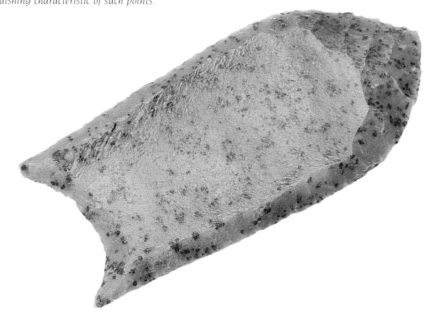

Below: *Chipped flint and chert were used for a variety of sharp-edged tools. This Folsom blade is of a style used 11,000 years ago in the region of present-day northeast Colorado. The fluting is a distinguishing characteristic of such points.*

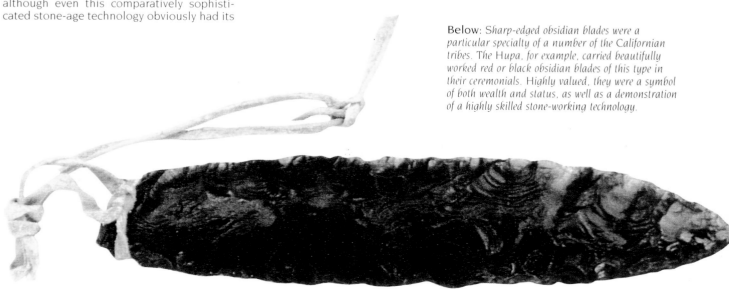

Below: *Sharp-edged obsidian blades were a particular specialty of a number of the Californian tribes. The Hupa, for example, carried beautifully worked red or black obsidian blades of this type in their ceremonials. Highly valued, they were a symbol of both wealth and status, as well as a demonstration of a highly skilled stone-working technology.*

limitations; flint tools often broke or were easily blunted and remaking or sharpening them was a lengthy process.

The production of knives particularly tested the skill of the maker, with great ingenuity being displayed in both the selection of suitable material and in the shaping of the blade. Whilst virtually every material capable of taking an edge was used – such as teeth, bone, horn, shell, wood and, on occasions, native copper and possibly meteoric iron – it was stone, as with the scraping, sawing, and boring tools described earlier, which was predominately the favored material.

The technique of flaking was an essential, skilled process to be used in the production of a sharp-edged knife or dagger. Here, the natural edges or forms of the stone[2] were modified by fracturing with a specially made flaking tool. The 'flaker', as it was commonly called, had a blade generally of antler, ivory, or hard bone, set in a wooden handle. This was applied to the stone edge and, with a quick movement (at the same time exerting a strong pressure), a flake of the stone was forced off. A skilled individual worked rapidly, moving along the outline of the blade, producing a razor-sharp, although fragile, cutting edge.

Not only were such knives of great practical value in both the hunt and war, but there was also considerable ceremony and symbolism associated with a number of them. In California, for example, ceremonial knife blades 20in (50cm.) or more in length and some 2½in (6cm.) broad at the widest part were carried in ceremonials such as the Hupa White Deerskin Dance.[3] They were generally made of chipped obsidion and commonly wrapped with a buckskin handle to prevent cutting the hands; large ones, it is said, 'can not be purchased at any price'.[4]

One recent scholar has observed that the ancient stone knives and blades – some dating back to at least 12,000 BC – were 'flint art-form masterpieces… |which| are a tribute to the skills of the earliest American |Indian| knife maker'.[5]

The use of copper

Although various types of stone were used very early on by the indigenous Americans, it is recorded that some time before the arrival of Europeans to the region of the Great Lakes and south to the Mississippi valley (circa 1600), copper was already being used. Thus, the stone age was gradually giving way to an era of metal: the processes of flaking and pecking, so characteristic of stone working, were being replaced by hammering and shaping of the copper nuggets – which had been torn from the copper-bearing rocks by glacial movement during the ice age. Whilst there is also evidence that copper was skillfully used in other regions (extending from Alaska to Florida), some of the most impressive items – celts, axes, spear-points, and knives – are predominately from the Great Lakes and Mississippi River areas.

A notable exception to this were the tribes of the Northwest Coast, who made superb copper items. Amongst the most distinctive of these were knives and daggers, many of which were highly decorated. However, the skills probably flowered with the introduction of refined copper obtained from white traders.[6]

The great value of metal over stone was clearly apparent. Blades and knives were produced which were generally long, narrow, double-edged. The knives had a convex

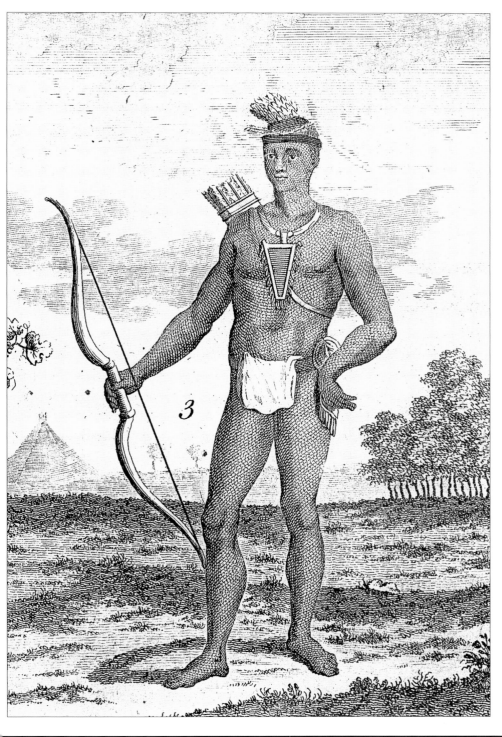

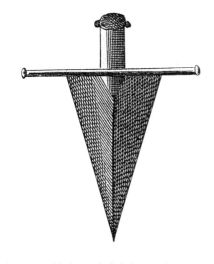

Above and left: A *chief of the Naudowessie (Santee Sioux) after descriptions by the traveler, Jonathan Carver, who traveled to the region of present-day Minnesota in 1766-67. The distinctive knife (above) worn at the neck, was described as a symbol of high rank amongst the Sioux – a concept which prevailed well into the nineteenth century.*

cross-section, often not dissimilar to those formerly of flint. The disadvantage of copper, however, was also clear to see – edges and points quickly blunted. As cutting weapons they had only limited value. It has been suggested that objects made of copper – and this included knives and daggers – were regarded as having particular and exceptional virtues, bordering on magical powers; indeed, certain early writers 'aver that some of the tribes of the great lakes held all copper as sacred, making no practical use of it whatever'.[7]

Below: A warrior of the 'Chippeways easterly of the Mississippi' after Jonathan Carver (circa 1766). More detailed than that of the Sioux on p.273 – note leggings, moccasins, gun, and tomahawk – the custom of wearing the knife in a decorated sheath at the throat, as for the Sioux, is also documented here.

Knife symbolism

The symbolic nature of the knife was referred to by the traveler, Jonathan Carver, who made his way through Chippewa and Sioux country during the 1760s. Specifically referring to the Naudowessie (Santee Sioux), Carver reported that high-ranking warriors of that tribe carried a knife in a sheath decorated with porcupine quills and hung around the neck (p.273). A point of interest is that the knife closely resembled the plug bayonet which was used by a number of [white] military forces in the seventeenth and early eighteenth centuries and, as Hanson observes, it was 'also similar in some respects to the nineteenth-century "dag", or stabber knife'[8] (see p.281). Carver reports, however, that these distinctive knives were originally made of flint or bone but, with the availability of steel from the traders, they

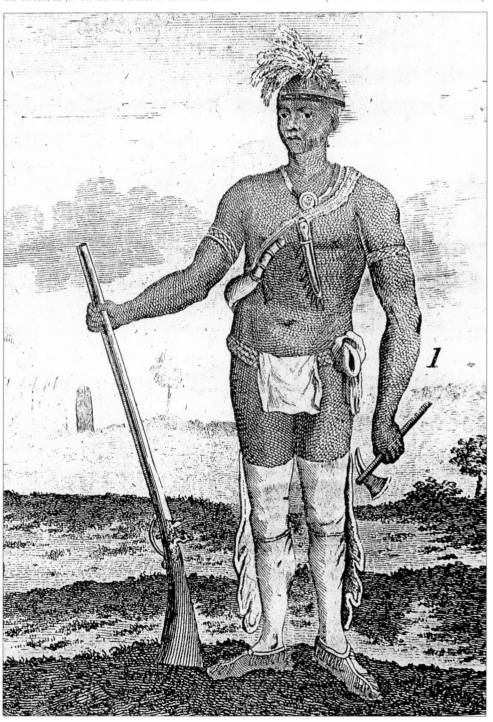

were now fabricated from metal. They were some 10in (25cm.) in length, with the blade of the knife near to the handle almost 3in (7cm.) wide; it was a double-sided keen-edge weapon which tapered to a sharp point.[9]

Although Carver refers to the custom as being a Sioux one, 'a sword worn by the Chiefs of the Naudowessie', it possibly extended to at least the Chippewa, who also carried knives in a sheath suspended around the neck.[10] The Sioux, however, later put emphasis on retaining a triangular-type neck flap on fine buckskin 'war' shirts which were worn by high-ranking individuals and such flaps resembled the original neck knife sheath.[11]

A century after Carver, the anthropologist Lewis Henry Morgan – who traveled up the Missouri in 1862 – made reference to the three oaths employed by the Plains tribes which they used to purge themselves from some charge. One of these oaths was swearing by the knife. They raised 'a knife in the right hand and point towards heaven saying "I have stated the truth." They then draw it between the lips and are required to touch the tongue to the blade. Those who swear falsely in this way attempt to avoid touching the tongue, which appears to be necessary to complete the oath'.[12]

Knife symbolism, with complex ritualistic ceremonies, is perhaps nowhere better illustrated than with the Blackfeet Bear Knife Bundle. Although the style of knife used appears not to have been exclusive to the Blackfeet – their friends the Gros Ventre also had such knives – the rituals associated with the bear knife itself and its association with warfare appear highly developed by the Blackfeet.[13]

The chief object in the Bear Bundle was a large dagger-like knife, to the handle of which was attached the jaws of a bear. Although the power of such a knife was considered to be very great – so great 'that its owner was seldom killed, for its appearance frightened everyone into submission, after the manner of bears'[14] – few individuals owned these bundles. One reason given was the brutality of the transfer ritual. Thus, the recipient was required to catch the knife thrown violently at him and also to lie naked on a thorn bed whilst being painted. At the same time, he was beaten with the flat of the knife.

In battle, the owner was not allowed to use any other weapon than the knife; he was required to walk forward toward the enemy, singing the war songs associated with the Knife Bundle and to never retreat. Little wonder that few warriors were prepared to shoulder such awesome responsibilities!

Knives of the Northwest Coast tribes

The distinctive copper knives referred to earlier as a feature of the Northwest Coast tribes were considerably elaborated upon with the introduction of iron and steel by the Russian, English, and American traders who came in pursuit of profit in the lucrative maritime fur trade, which commenced in the late eighteenth century. The major demand was for the pelts of the sea otter, an animal endowed with a lustrous coat of thick fur which 'became by far the most valuable fur on the world market'.[15]

In less than a decade, now potentially able

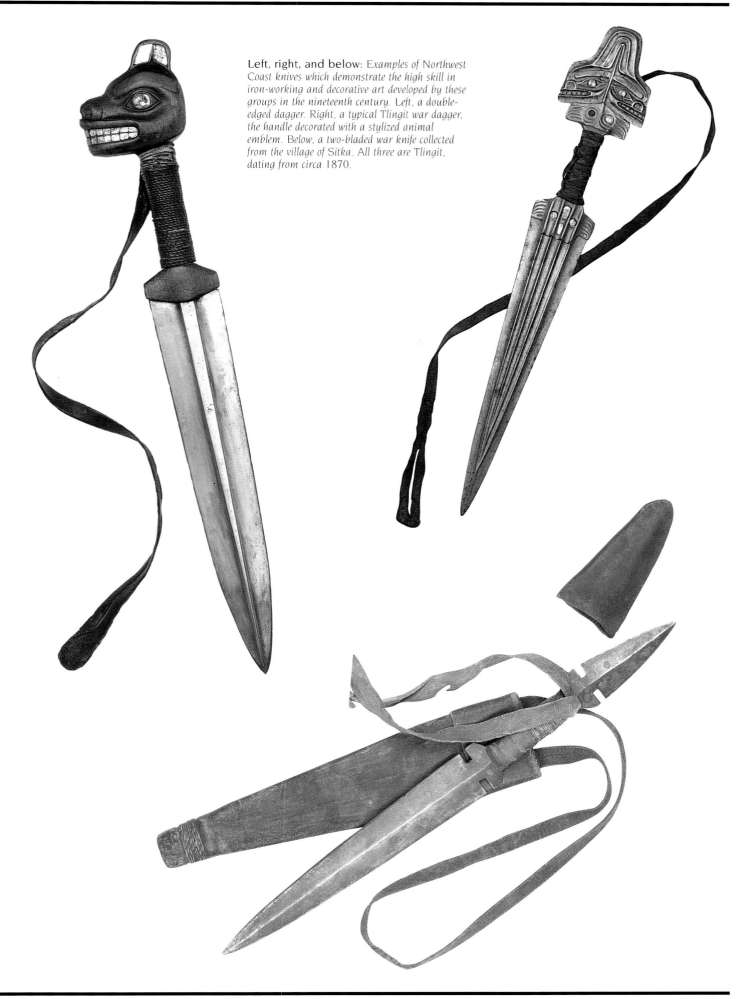

Left, right, and below: *Examples of Northwest Coast knives which demonstrate the high skill in iron-working and decorative art developed by these groups in the nineteenth century. Left, a double-edged dagger. Right, a typical Tlingit war dagger, the handle decorated with a stylized animal emblem. Below, a two-bladed war knife collected from the village of Sitka. All three are Tlingit, dating from circa 1870.*

Left: Eight styles of knives and knife sheaths from the Great Plains and Eastern Woodlands, dating from circa 1800-1900. Two of the upper sheaths are decorated with square shanked brass tacks. The blade of knife 2 is from a file, and has an elaborate horn handle. Both are identified as Blackfeet, circa 1875. The two central sheaths are beaded and the knives have wooden handles. Knife 3 is probably Cheyenne or Arapaho, circa 1870, 4 is possibly Santee Sioux, circa 1850. The superb presentation of knife 5 includes a horn handle and sheath embellished with quillwork. Probably Cree, circa 1830. Knife 6 is of Eastern Plains (Santee?) origin, circa 1840. Knife 7 could be a Menominee quilled sheath, the horn handle exhibiting a finely carved turtle emblem, circa 1780. Knife 8 is a Blackfeet DAG with distinctive beaded sheath. The knife is circa 1810, the sheath circa 1880.

Below: A fine knife and sheath, total length 14in (35cm.), probably circa 1830 and from the Chippewa. The steel-bladed wooden handled knife is in a sheath decorated with pony beads and porcupine quills. The embellishments almost certainly make reference to sky and underwater powers.

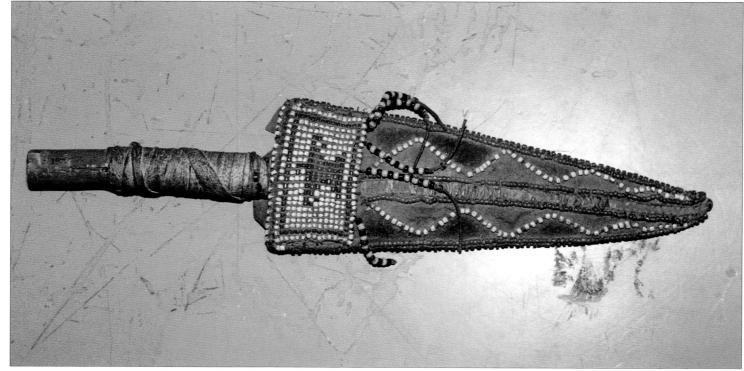

to exploit the superiority of iron[16] over copper, the demand for the former metal was high on the list of goods sought by the Northwest Coast tribes. In 1778, it is reported that the crewmen on Captain James Cook's third voyage traded 'scraps of iron' for sea-otter skins[17]. Later came various trade goods of iron, such as pots, scissors, knives, axes, and files, as well as pieces of iron and steel. This led to a new style of native industry where fish hooks, arrow and lance heads, chisel blades, and daggers, were now fabricated from iron, rapidly replacing the use of bone, shell, and stone.

The hand-fighting weapons, especially knives and daggers, were now developed to a high degree and those of the Northern tribes such as the Tlingit were particularly distinctive. A number were made from trade files, others from trade iron being hammered out on crude native forges. The blades were generally of a dagger form: some of the knives had a blade at each end, the smaller of which featured an animal head, the eyes being invariably inlaid with abalone shell. The handle was usually wrapped with heavy twine and then covered with tanned elk skin. Blades exhibited a midline ridge, concave or convex surfaces, or were fluted, and the handles were nearly always terminated by the family or clan crest, such as a bear, beaver, or Thunderbird.

These weapons were not only for show. Wearing moosehide shirts over which was an armor of rods or slats, and covering their bodies from the neck to the knees, Tlingit warriors were formidable opponent – especially with a war helmet and visor and with the fighting dagger in hand. The smaller blade was generally used to slash the face, so distracting the combatant; the larger blade was then employed to finish him off![18]

Another distinctive knife used by the Northern Northwest Coast tribes had a dagger-like blade and a spiral-hilt, sometimes described as 'volute-handled' knives (p.278). These, however, were almost certainly trade items, obtained from the Athapaskan tribes further to the north in the Yukon Valley. Tribes such as the Kutchin and Tanana made such knives either from old files or gun barrels; others were trade items from the Russians. The latter, however, were considered to have notable limitations in comparison to the native-made ones. The trader Alexander Hunter Murray observed of the Athapaskans who went to trade at Fort Yukon in 1848: 'Their knives are made of iron, but the fancy handles and fluted blades are of more value to them than the temper of the knife; they complain of ours being too hard and the difficulty of sharpening them.'[19]

Little is known about the native technology that produced these knives, which have been described as 'most expert' and 'sophisticated' – the metals in many specimens show both heat treatment and stress hardening.[20] The handles of the knives were wrapped with a split plaited cane or heavy elk skin and were carried either in the belt (p.278) or in

quilled or beaded knife sheaths, some of which might be hung around the neck, as described for the Chippewa and Sioux earlier. They were considered highly valued accoutrements in the Arctic and Subarctic regions.

Trade knives

The knives – which were traded by whites to the North American Indian in considerable numbers by the early 1600s – became both an indispensable tool and weapon.[21] The range of knives that were traded, even at this early period, was immense. The archaeological record documents both pocket and sheath knives, though the latter were generally of the type with a fixed and larger blade which was best for 'heavy-duty cutting and for fighting'.[22] Some of the best knives had fine bone handles, many inlaid with metal or horn. 'Scalping' knives are listed in trade goods accounts; these generally had narrow blades which could be worked up between the skull and scalp after the initial incision had been made. In practice, however, almost any form of knife might be used.[23]

Two styles of knife which became particularly popular, and which appear to be predominately of English make, were the single-edged butcher or carving knife and the dagger. The former came in a wide variety of styles and many early ones were made in Sheffield and London, often bearing the maker's imprint. These included 'Manson-Sheffield', 'Lowcock of Cornhill (London)', 'Wiggiams, Smithfield, London', and 'V.R. (Victoria Regina) Sheffield'.[24] One of the more distinctive of these trade knives seems to have been much coveted, probably because of its elaborately decorated handle of black horn and brass. Such a knife is shown (p.279) in the series of knives offered by the Hudson's Bay Company as well as in the portrait of the Menominee chief, also on p.279.

After about 1840, however, American knives began to displace the English variety. Many were produced by such companies as the John Russell Company at the Green River Works in Deerfield, Massachusetts, who started production as early as 1834.[26] These 'Green River' knives became widely used trade items not only for hunting and warfare, but also for everyday use. Many were recycled; the steel blades, now often thin and sharply pointed, might be given new handles of horn or bone by the owner, a common type butcher knife then taking on a distinctive, personalized form.

Additionally, knives were fabricated by local blacksmiths, using a variety of iron-based metals. Each had its definite characteristics and the quality of the finished product was well recognized. Wrought iron, which was easily forged, produced good blades, but the edge and point dulled easily; cast iron

Right: *An ornate sheath of heavy leather, decorated with blue, red, and orange beadwork in the overlaid stitch. Note the triangular-shaped slot for attachment to the belt. This piece, which dates from circa 1880, was collected from the Sarcee.*

Right: *A superb example of a volute-handled knife, dating from about 1860 and of a style used by the Subarctic Athapaskan groups such as the Kutchin and Tanaina of the Yukon-drainage region.*

held its edge and point better but was brittle; whilst steel in its various forms obviously maintained a good cutting edge – but was expensive. One old 'knife saying' apparently, was: 'You can't always trust your neighbor, but you can always trust a good piece of steel.'[27]

The 'DAG' or 'Beaver-Tail' knife

One distinctive style, initially introduced as a lance point, was the DAG. Known variously as the 'beaver-tail knife', 'Hudson's Bay DAG', or the 'stabber', they were considered a favorite weapon for hand-to-hand combat.

DAG blades were first introduced in the Great Lakes area in the mid-1700s and soon became widely used. The long, wide blade was double-edged, coming to a sharp point, and resembled ancient styles of flint spear-heads. Indeed, one student has recently observed, 'Perhaps the original designer fashioned these notched spears from the general shape of stone spear points found being used by the Indians'.[28]

The blades were generally sold without handles, being manufactured in large numbers. Many were produced in England for the Hudson's Bay Company, becoming a standard and important item in the fur trade. Later, in 1821, when the Hudson's Bay Company merged with the North West Company (of Montreal), the simpler, thin-bladed DAG was replaced by a style which was thicker and exhibited a distinctive median ridge.[29] The handles, most of wood but some of bone or horn, were generally put on by their Indian owners, the double or single notches either side of the blade and near the tang facilitating the hafting. The exceptionally wide range of blades – which vary in both length, width, tang, and notches – underlines the fact that many, as with the pipe tomahawk, were also manufactured by local blacksmiths.[30]

Very fine versions of this knife, however, were also made as presentation pieces 'much like presentation medals'.[31] Examples of such knives are shown on pp.276 and 281. Here, the handles are of black horn, with inlays of bone and brass. They were almost certainly made in Sheffield, England, and the main

Right: *A Kutchin warrior and his wife, after a sketch by Alexander Hunter Murray, who traveled to the Yukon in 1848. Note the volute-handled knife in the belt of the warrior, which is virtually identical to that shown above.*

Left: A series of trade knives which were offered by the Hudson's Bay Company during the fur trade era in Canada. Most of these knives were manufactured in Sheffield, with blades of high quality steel and handles of wood or bone. Some were elaborate and expensive, such as that on the extreme right. Here, the handle is brass, inlaid with horn.

Above: An unusual sheath and knife, possibly Chippewa and dating from circa 1860. The knife appears to be made from an early style of French plug bayonet. The snakeskin, together with the beadwork designs, suggest a highly symbolic combination.

Left: The Menominee chief, Kitchie-ogi-man, painted by Paul Kane in 1845. The use of the neck-knife is well illustrated here. Made of black-dyed buckskin and elaborately embellished with porcupine quills, it houses an English trade knife very similar to that shown above.

outlet in the early 1800s seems to have been through the Hudson's Bay Company.[32]

Peterson observed of these DAGS, that a 'modern student of knife-fighting would reject these daggers as clumsy and inefficient'.[33] Nevertheless, the Indian developed his own techniques: in combat, the knife was held with the blade below the hand and with a sidewise stroke he aimed at the ribs or stomach. Another method was a downward chopping-like stroke to stab behind the opponent's collar bone. In any event, a DAG-carrying warrior was, without doubt, a most formidable adversary!

Knife sheaths

While the blade of an Indian knife could well be of white manufacture, we have seen that the handles would often be adorned with the personal stamp of the owner – wood, bone, horn, antler, and other material was subsequently used to haft the finished product. Similarly, the sheaths used to house the knives were, with few exceptions, of indigenous manufacture – the shape, materials used, as well as the mode of decoration were distinctively American Indian. The wide range of such sheaths is shown in both the Introduction to this section and in this chapter.

The most common examples conformed to the shape of the most widely used blades – straight on one side, curved on the other. A distinctive feature of most Indian-made sheaths is a structural design which not only houses the blade but also the majority of the handle, only an inch or so being proud at the top of the sheath. This type of design obviously reduced the likelihood of losing the knife, particularly if – as in the case of many – a buckskin thong was tied around the protruding top of the handle.

Another relatively common sheath shape followed the contour of a DAG-type blade and was therefore curved on both sides. This shape is rather reminiscent of those sheaths which were hung around the neck (see Sioux knife symbolism on p.274 and also above).

Sheaths were decorated with porcupine quills and later, of course, with beads. On occasion, shells – particularly dentalium – were used in combination with blue and red trade pony beads. Whilst such sheaths have been identified from the Missouri River region, they are of a style much favored by the Northern Athapascans, such as the Kutchin and Naskapi.[34]

An interesting feature of some knife sheaths is that a pattern of the blade and the handle is sometimes worked in quills or beads on the surface of the sheath. Although this feature does occur on the Cree knife sheath shown left, it was particularly well

Above: *A Teton Sioux warrior wearing an elaborate quilled shirt from a painting by Zino Shindler, circa 1870. Knife symbolism is emphasized here; note the neck flap quillwork embellishment, which is almost certainly symbolic of knife handle and blade.*

developed by the Sioux and was commented on by the anthropologist, Frank G. Speck in papers relating to the structural basis to ornamentation amongst the Oglala.[35]

Sheaths for the early DAG were invariably ornamented with porcupine quillwork, with both floral and geometric designs used. In the case of the latter, superb examples (such as that shown above right) were embellished with bands of loom-woven quillwork, the finest of which – requiring very considerable skill – followed the pointed contour of the sheath.

Use of the sword

There are many references in literature – descriptions, drawings, photographs and pictographs – of the use of swords by North American Indians. Many of them were probably English, Model 1796, light cavalry swords which were surplussed after the Napoleonic Wars. These were sold throughout the American West, and one outlet in the 1840s was the Bordeaux Trading Post near present-day Chadron, Nebraska.[36] They became a type of status symbol, particularly amongst some of the Plains tribes, perhaps in imitation of white soldiers – the Long Knives.

The establishment of authority by the use of the sword was described in the 1890s for the Yankton Sioux chief, To-ka-cou, 'He that inflicts the first wound'. Thus, on the arrival of distinguished visitors, chiefs such as To-ka-cou would take the strangers under their protection. Outside the visitors' lodge would be placed the chief's war club, or his sword; 'the sign is well understood, and no Indian ventures to intrude'.[37]

Below: *The Kansas warrior, Meach-o-shin-gaw, "Little White Bear," after a painting by George Catlin, 1832. Note that as with the previous portrait, the knife is prominently displayed – obviously symbolic of warrior prowess. The metal blade appears to be double-edged, the handle of wood with metal inlay.*

Above: *A superb presentation type DAG. These were manufactured in Sheffield, England, for the Hudson's Bay Company in the early nineteenth century. The handle is of black horn inlaid with bone and the sheath is decorated with loom quillwork. Almost certainly Cree, circa 1840.*

Above: *Early Blackfeet pictograph, circa 1830, of a warrior on horseback. Much detail is shown here, such as the scalp-lock and horse heart line. Of particular interest is the rendering of the warrior's gun, being captured; at the same time, he is stabbed in the chest with a large-bladed knife.*

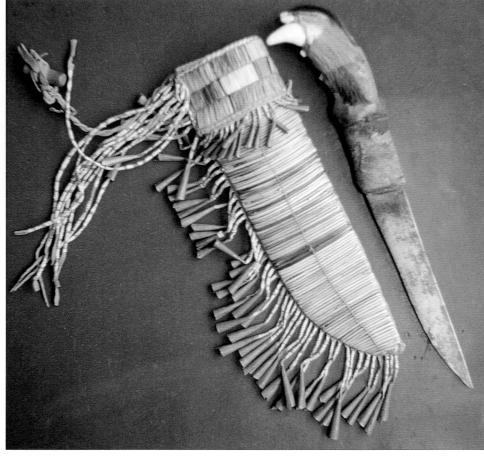

Right: *An early 'bear knife'. Although previously identified as Blackfeet, recent research (Klann, 1999:45), suggests that it is actually of Assiniboin or Eastern Sioux origin. It was collected by Duke Paul Wilhelm of Württemberg, probably at Fort Union (1829-31). The elaborate sheath is embellished with split bird-quills, an Eastern Plains rather than Northern Plains decorative art form.*

Right: *The Yankton Sioux chief, Moukauska, 'Trembling Earth', from a portrait painted in Washington in 1837 by G. Cooke. Swords were carried and prominently displayed as a sign of status and authority. Although seldom employed in actual warfare, they could be used to symbolically protect strangers. Some were housed in decorative cases.*

Above: *A fine Bowie knife, the single-edged blade having the clipped point which is one distinctive feature of such knives. Although invented in America in the 1830s, many such knives were made in Sheffield, England. This one has a horn handle and was said to have belonged to the Hunkpapa Sioux leader, Sitting Bull.*

Sword, or sabre, symbolism extended to several other Plains tribes and possibly beyond. The Crow, for example, used sabres in the ceremonial-sacred context. The Crow leader, Wraps-Up-His-Tail, was said to have cut down pine trees with a sweep of his sword, 'as he intended to do in mowing down the soldiers',[38] and the focus of his supernatural power was said to be a red painted cavalry sabre. Swords, as well as lances, were proudly carried in mounted parades by the wives of successful warriors and were generally housed in beautifully decorated rawhide cases.[39]

Cases such as these were made of rawhide and were almost certainly invented by the Crow; it seems that they were exclusive to this tribe. Several factors also suggest that they were highly sacred in nature and for this reason they were not adopted by other tribes. Few were actually produced and they may well have had their origins in 'an instructive dream or vision'.[40]

Prior to the introduction of trade swords, these cases were exclusively used to house a lance. Hence the shape, which one student of

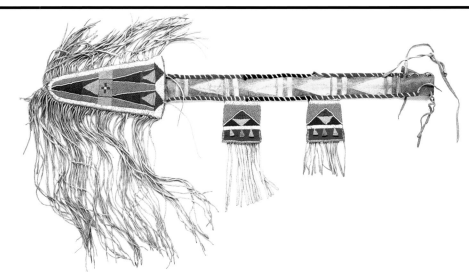

the Crow has suggested is reminiscent of ancient styles of stone-pointed spears[41]. Generally, the cases exhibit a series of arrowhead-like symbols running sequentially along the case.[42] They are magnificent examples of Crow art.

Above: *Crow sword or lance case, dating from circa 1890. Such cases – very typical of the Crow – were made of rawhide, cut into a form resembling that of a spade with a handle. The case was as shown here, decorated with incised designs, trade cloth, and beads.*

References

1 a) Argillite – generally black and much favored by the Northwest Coast tribes whose favored source was the deposits on Queen Charlotte Islands.
(b) Catlinite – named after the artist and explorer, George Catlin – is mainly found in Minnesota. It was much favored for making pipes but ceremonial-type objects, such as tomahawks and knives were also produced.
    Both argillite and catlinite were fine-grained, relatively soft when first quarried, but hardened on exposure; both materials could be highly polished.
2 int is classed as a variety of chalcedony; it originally referred to the materials found in the chalk beds of several European countries. The term has, however, now been extended to include all those stones which are principally of a silica base. Impurities, and the original manner of formation, give rise to a variety of colors and shades enhancing the beauty of the final product. An illustration of a number of chipped blades and points showing the beauty of the stone work is in Baldwin,1997:2.
3 A photograph of this dance showing one participant carrying such a knife blade, is reproduced in Taylor, ed.,1994:78.
4 Holmes in Hodge, ed., 1907-10, Part I: 718.
5 a) Baldwin, 1997: 2.
(b) A detailed discussion of flint knives and blades appears in Hothem, (1986), particularly Chapters I–VI.
6 Holmes has suggested that the manufacture of daggers of both copper and steel was modelled after both Europeans and Asiatic patterns (Holmes in Hodge, ed.,1907-10, Part I: 375. Of interest, is that the early style of *Dague a Rouelle*, carried in Nepal with the national sword (the Kora), resembles those made by the Northwest Coast tribes (See Stone,1934: 19).
7 Holmes in Hodge, ed.,1907-10, Part I:346.
8 a) Carver's encounters with both Chippewa and Sioux in the winter of 1766 were with bands in the region of Leech Lake and Belle Plaine (near the Blue Earth River in present-day Minnesota). (See Carver, Parker ed.,1976: 90-102.)
(b) Hanson, 1975: 11.
9 Hanson suggests that these knives were similar in some respects to the DAG or 'stabber knife', which was sold by the Hudson's Bay and North West Companies and supplies 'to nearly all the Canadian Indians and Eskimos' (ibid.). The DAG is discussed later in this chapter.
10 (a) Carver, Parker ed., 1976: 97.
(b) Alfred Jacob Miller saw the Teton Sioux wearing neck knife sheaths some two generations later when he traveled to the Plains with Sir Drummond Stewart in 1833-34 (Ross,1968: 79).
11 I have discussed this in some detail in Taylor, McCaskill ed., 1989: 247. The triangular neck flaps of some Sioux shirts exhibit patterns worked in quill or beadwork which resemble the knife blade, perhaps

also even the handle (see p.280 this chapter). This may be indicative of a particular status of the individual involved and relate to the early symbolism reported by Carver.
12 Morgan, White ed., 1959: 175.
13 Bear Knife power was not, however, inclusive to the Blackfeet. John C. Ewers found that it prevailed – in various degrees – amongst Siouan, Algonquian, and Athapascan linguistic groups. The Bear Knife was used by at least six tribes within these groups (See Ewers,1968. Table I: 143).
14 Wissler, 1912. Part I: 134.
15 Gibson in Washburn ed., 1988: 375.
16 The Tlingit, in particular, *did* have access to iron prior to white contact, being the closest middlemen to sources of Asiatic iron. It was, however, considered a 'precious' commodity (ibid:376).
17 Together with the skins trade for glass beads, they were subsequently 'sold in Canton for £90... [all for] an investment of one shilling'! (See Lloyd and Anderson, 1959: 21-22).
18 For a succinct description of the Tlingit-style warfare – which can be largely extended to the Northwest Coast tribes in general – see De Laguna, Suttles ed., 1990: 215-16.
19 (a) Murray, Burpee ed., 1910: 85.
(b) As the temperature of metals decreases, the Modulus of Elasticity increases. Copper would thus be inclined to hold its edge at Arctic temperatures whereas iron and steel would become both hard and brittle.
20 Witthoft and Eyman in Krech, 1989: 98.
21 An approximate 1% content of carbon in iron reduces dislocations and produces high grade steel suitable for knife blades, axes, tomahawks, and the like. The high carbon steels may be hardened by heating and quenching in water or oil – a process which could be relatively easily carried out by local blacksmiths or native artisans.
22 Peterson, 1957: 119.
23 Scalping was practised in North America prior to white contact (Owsley and Jantz, eds., 1994: 335-43). It involved the removal of the Indian's scalp-lock only or, under some circumstances, the entire scalp. It was not necessary fatal (See Taylor, 1980: 23 and 1997: 21).
24 The Bowie knife, which refers to a fairly substantial knife with a straight blade, single-edged with a clipped point and possibly a false edge, was mainly produced in England by Wolstenholm and Rodgers & Sons, both of Sheffield. The finished product was expensive and probably for this reason it found limited favor with American Indians (See Coe, Connolly et al, 1989: 108-12).
25 A trade knife of this type was collected by Sir George Simpson during his travels across Canada in the 1840s; it is now in the Ethnographical collections of the British Museum, London (King,1982: 92). See also

Baldwin (1997: 38) who illustrates a fine specimen which he dates at about 1800; it was made by Greaves and Sons of Sheffield.
26 The John Russell Company of Deerfield, Massachusetts, is still in business today.
27 Baldwin, 1997: 56.
28 (a) See ibid: 44 and 48 for observations and illustrations relating to the wide range of DAGS produced both in England and also by local American blacksmiths.
(b) DAGS hardly figured in the weaponry of the Teton Sioux (Hanson, 1975), emphasizing the Northern and Eastern distribution of the style.
30 The technique of manufacture of such blades was demonstrated to me by the late Russell Robinson, Senior Armourer at The Royal Armouries, Tower of London and an expert on metal-working, almost forty years ago. He used relatively simple tools to hand-forge the blades which seem to be mainly of mild steel (carbon content approximately 0.15% to 0.3%). He did not use case hardening.
31 Painter, 1992: 36.
32 John Painter documents the location of similar knives (ibid: 36-37). The associated Indian-made sheaths with these knives, suggest a popularity with Cree and Metis groups and dating prior to 1850.
33 Peterson, 1957: 121.
34 (a) See ibid. who illustrates such a sheath which is now in the Smithsonian Institution, Washington (specimen number 5417).
(b) See Taylor, Idiens et al., 1974: 130.
35 Wissler, 1904: 251 and Speck, 1928: 5. It is of interest to note that Speck associates such knife sheaths with Oglala *women*. He also suggests that this was somewhat distinctive in Sioux arts and is [absent] 'in the bead ornamentation of knife-scabbards among other Plains tribes...' (ibid: 6).
36 (a) Personal correspondence, Jim Hanson, Museum of the Fur Trade to C.F.T. 10 August 1999.
(b) See also Taylor, 1999 (In Press).
(c) As Hanson has observed, swords were sold to the tribes of the Eastern Woodlands as early as the seventeenth century. Although falling into disuse as weapons, they were 'symbols of rank for officers' (Hanson, 1975: 45). Sword belts, elaborately embellished with porcupine quillwork, were early produced by such tribes as the Iroquois (Brasser, 1976: 143).
37 McKenney and Hall, 1933, Vol.I: 416.
38 Lowie, 1935: 238.
39 See Galante, 1980 and Wildschut, Ewers ed., 1959 for further details on Crow sword and lance symbolism.
40 Galante, 1980: 65.
41 Wildschut in ibid:67.
42 Cowdrey, 1995:19-20

'The moon gave us the bow, the sun gave us the arrow'
(PAWNEE LEGEND).

PIERCING WEAPONS

LEAF-SHAPED CHIPPED STONE heads found in archaeological sites, as well as large points of bone and shell, give clear evidence that spears have long been used throughout North America, both as an implement of the chase or in warfare.[1] The spear appears to have developed into several varieties to match the environment, the habits of its animals, and the warfare tactics employed. In the case of the Eskimo, for example, who lived in a habitat characterized by a wide variety of animal life, a large number of spear forms were developed. In other areas, however, a simple form of spear was retained, although the point itself in historic times was made of trade metal and often of a more elaborate form.

Early descriptions of the use of spears by pedestrian tribes refer to a weapon as being some 5 or 6 feet (1.5 or 1.8m.) in length. Blackfeet informants told the ethnologist John C. Ewers that such weapons – the head of which could be up to a foot (30cm.) long – were attached to the end of a wooden shaft which was bound at intervals with otter fur to serve as grips. When used in hand-to-hand combat, the shaft was grasped with both hands, the warrior bringing it down with a quick, oblique downward stroke which combined both thrusting and swinging. As Ewers observed, 'The weapon could kill or cripple an opponent if skillfully used'.[2]

The atlatl

The need to effectively strike at a distance – to not only reduce the potential risk of personal danger but also to produce surer results – led to the development of a number of forms of propelling missile weapons by the American Indians. The sling, for example, was used extensively in Middle and South America and, to a more limited extent, by some of the Californian coastal tribes such as the Miwok and Pomo. Another weapon applied from a distance was the blow tube, which was used by the Cherokee, Choctaw, Seminole, and other tribes in the Southeast where hollow cane could be easily obtained.[3]

More effective, however, was a weapon of ancient origin and with a very wide distribution. This was a special form of throwing stick which was generally referred to as a spear-thrower or atlatl. It is almost certain that the spear-thrower was in use many thousands of years prior to the development of the bow. Indeed, it has been speculated that some of the ancestors of the American Indian brought the idea across the Bering Strait at least as early as thirteen thousand years ago. This would be some nine to ten thousand years prior to the introduction of the bow in North America.[4]

Above: *A petroglyph on rock, showing rider and horse, at Joliet, Montana. Probably produced by a Crow warrior in the early nineteenth century, it shows the rider carrying a bow-lance, combined piercing weapons of ancient origin.*

Below: *Use of the atlatl (the Aztec word for 'spear-thrower'). It is thought that Early Americans brought such devices across the Bering Strait at least 13,000 years ago. Used in both the hunt and war, they released the projectile with tremendous force to make the kill. The atlatl was one of the earliest compound weapons invented by man.*

Above: *The Crow warrior, He-who-jumps-over-everyone, painted by the artist George Catlin on the Upper Missouri in 1832. The long lance is typical for this period: the head could well be made from a cavalry sword blade, a popular item obtained from traders at an early period. Many were surplus after the Napoleonic Wars. Here, the lance was probably more for show than for practical use.*

Above: *The Assiniboin warrior, Pitätapiú, painted by the artist, Karl Bodmer, at Fort Union on the Upper Missouri in June 1833. He carries a ceremonial long bow-lance which is tipped with a metal head of a popular style and obtained from white traders. The lance is embellished with ribbons of soft, cured bear entrails which have been smeared with red sacred paint.*

The atlatl was about 18in (45cm.) in length and consisted of the main body – which was generally grooved on its upper side to take the spear shaft – the grip or handle, and a hook or socket to engage with the end of the shaft. The basic design was greatly enhanced by carving, painting, or other embellishments. Some of the most elaborate, such as those observed by Hernando Cortez amongst the Aztec, also seem to have 'served as war clubs or shields as well'.[5]

Right: *Keokuk, chief of the Sauk and Fox Indians, with his son, Musewont. The elaborately decorated lance probably commemorates the killing of a distinguished mounted Sioux warrior. This portrait was painted during their trip to Washington in 1837.*

Right: Little Smoke, a Sauk and Fox boy (?), carrying a bow and arrows. Boys were taught to use the bow at an early age, practising their skills by shooting small birds and animals. For safety, arrows were blunt-headed or had sticks bound crosswise on the lower part of the shaft.

The spear-thrower added an extra joint to the arm, thus increasing the efficiency of the hurl; additionally, the weapon's forward momentum was markedly increased by attaching a stone weight to the main body of the atlatl.[6] Even after the invention of the bow, the atlatl had its own advantages: not only could it project a missile which was several times heavier than an arrow but also, because only one hand was needed, it could be used more effectively from a canoe or kayak than the bow which, of course, demanded the use of both hands.

The atlatl was a lethal weapon in skilled hands. Thus, as one chronicler of the ill fated De Soto expedition observed of an Indian-Spanish encounter in the early 1540s: 'One soldier was wounded with... a dart |which|... is thrown with a wooden strip or a cord. Our Spaniards had never seen this weapon before that day in any part of Florida through which they had traveled... The strip |atlatl| is of wood two-thirds of a yard in length, and is capable of sending a dart with such great force that it has been seen to pass completely through a man armed with a coat of mail. In Peru, the Spaniards feared this weapon more than any others the Indian possessed for the arrows there were not so fierce as those of Florida.'[7]

The lance

Strictly speaking, this is a horseman's spear and was in general considerably longer than those used by pedestrian hunters and warriors. Although amongst some of the earliest groups to acquire the horse, the Plateau tribes appear not to have favored the use of a lance. For example, in the case of the Coeur d'Alêne – an important Salishan Plateau tribe – the spear, some 5 to 7 feet (1.5 to 2m.) long and having a flint head, 'went out of use as a weapon soon after the introduction of the horse and the beginning of buffalo hunting on the plains'.[8] Likewise on the Northern Plains. Thus, the Piegan last made use of the lance in warfare in the 1860s.[9]

By contrast, the Southern Plains tribes made very extensive use of this weapon in mounted warfare, possibly due to contacts with Spanish-Mexican soldiers, most of whom were highly skilled lancers. The Southern Plains tribes, however, as well as Southwestern tribes such as the Apaches, developed their own techniques of handling the lance in mounted combat. Of the Apache, for example, one observer commented, 'they charge with both hands over their heads, managing their horses principally with their knees. With this weapon they are considered an overmatch for the Spanish dragoons single handed...'.[10]

Comanche informants said that lance heads could be up to 'thirty inches long by one inch wide (75 by 2.5cm.) tapering to a point at the end away from the shaft'.[11] Lances, the Comanche said, were 'never hurled javelin-wise but |were| always thrust from under the arm'. Only a brave man

carried such a weapon as it 'meant hand-to-hand combat'. The brother of the Comanche informant, Breaks Something, gave up his war lance following the Battle of Adobe Walls, much to the relief of his family, as they all agreed such a weapon 'is a big responsibility'.[12]

With the passage of time the spear and lance, traditionally of important practical use, took on a religious significance – it began to be used in ceremonies and as society regalia, particularly amongst many Plains tribes. For this reason, the bow lance became the significant regalia of a number of distinguished individuals (see pp.285).

The bow

Although, as we have seen, the atlatl was the most effective weapon in skilled hands, it was gradually replaced by a more portable and, in general, more accurate, projecting device – namely, the bow. Although irrefutable data is lacking, archaeological evidence suggests that the bow was 'introduced into North America relatively recently – possibly as late as AD 1000...'.[13] Nevertheless, by the time the first white man arrived in the Americas, it was a weapon which was widely distributed 'from the far North to the tip of South America'.[14]

The most commonly used bow type was the so-called self-bow, which was made of a single piece of hard, elastic wood. The type of wood depended on the locality but it was always 'the best that could be found'.[15] The self-bow seems to have been the only type employed east of the Mississippi, it being an area of extensive forests which furnished abundant supplies of bow woods, such as ash, hickory, and black locust. There was little need for alternative bow designs.

A similar bow type was the sinew-lined or reinforced bow. As with the self-bow, this consisted of a single stave of wood but as an addition the back was covered with a thin sheet of sinew which was securely glued to the surface. Such bows, unlike the eastern self-bow which could be up to 6ft (1.8m.) in length, seldom exceeded 45in (1.2m.); they were widely used on the Great Plains as well as in California.

These styles contrast markedly in the Arctic region. Here, the Inuit people were forced to make do with what was to hand. Drift, and other wood pieces, were ingeniously joined together, the joints being reinforced with splints, bridges, and wedges. The weapon was then bound and backed with a complexity of braided and twisted sinew cords – hence the description 'sinew corded bow'. It was a style used 'almost exclusively by the Eskimo'.[16]

Similar in some respects because of the

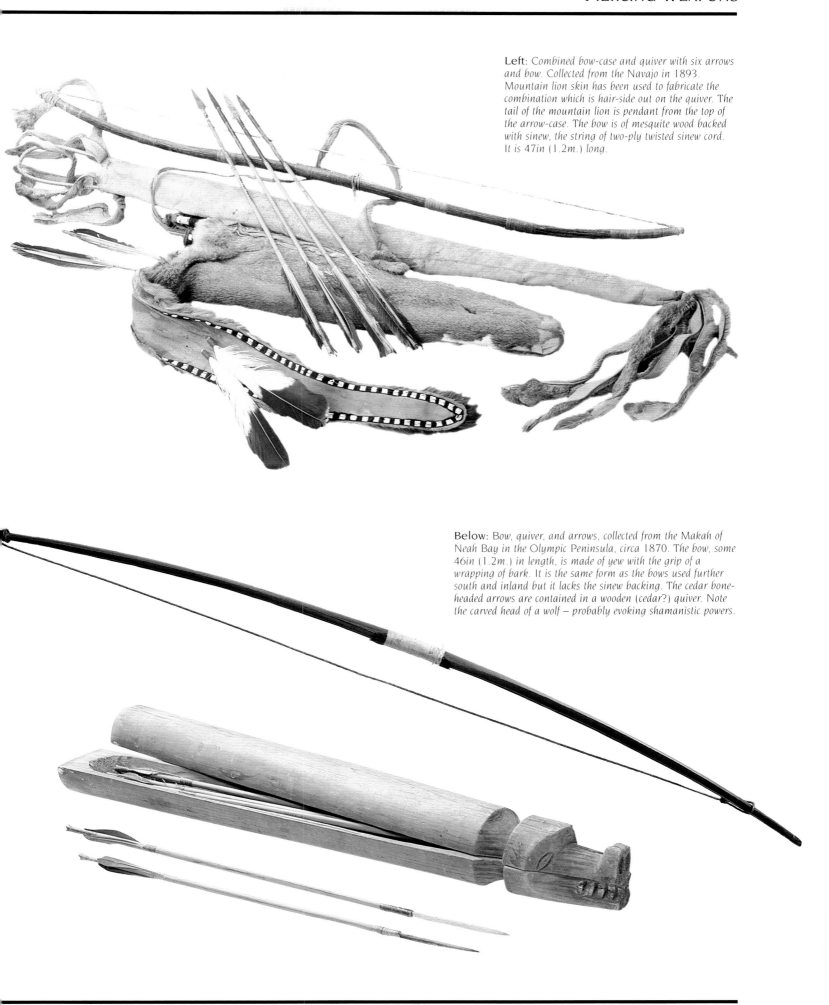

Left: *Combined bow-case and quiver with six arrows and bow. Collected from the Navajo in 1893. Mountain lion skin has been used to fabricate the combination which is hair-side out on the quiver. The tail of the mountain lion is pendant from the top of the arrow-case. The bow is of mesquite wood backed with sinew, the string of two-ply twisted sinew cord. It is 47in (1.2m.) long.*

Below: *Bow, quiver, and arrows, collected from the Makah of Neah Bay in the Olympic Peninsula, circa 1870. The bow, some 46in (1.2m.) in length, is made of yew with the grip of a wrapping of bark. It is the same form as the bows used further south and inland but it lacks the sinew backing. The cedar bone-headed arrows are contained in a wooden (cedar?) quiver. Note the carved head of a wolf – probably evoking shamanistic powers.*

MAKING AN ARROW

i) Knocking off chips from obsidian by free hand or direct percussion – the first step in shaping.

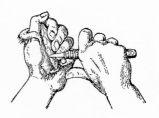

(ii) Pressing off flakes from a portion of obsidian by means of a bone flaker.

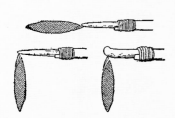

(iii) Shaping the flint arrowhead with a bone tool; on occasions, bone pincers were used.

iv) An alternative and very effective method of flaking, the operator holding the head upon a stone.

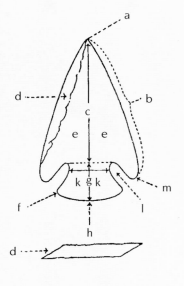

Left: Arrowhead nomenclature. (a) Point (b) Edge (c) Face (d) Bevel (e) Blade (f) Tang (g) Stem (h) Base (i) Notch (k) Neck (m) Barb or Shoulder.
The majority of arrowheads were notched; these were set in a slot at the end of the arrowshaft and tied in place with sinew or cord which was passed through the notches and around the end of the arrowshaft.

Right: A finished flint arrowhead showing the attachment cord running through the notch.

Below: (a) A high quality finished arrow, probably Mandan, a tribe who were particularly well known for their skill as arrow-makers. (b) An arrow-straightener of bone, from the Mandan village of Ruhptare on the Missouri River and dating prior to circa 1837.

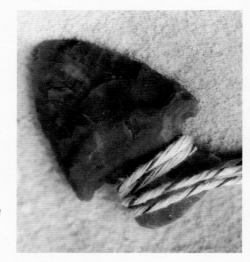

complexities of production, was the so-called 'compound bow' which was made of antler, horn, baleen, or bone, backed with a heavy lining of sinew. These bows were much favored by the Plateau tribes, although they were not entirely exclusive to that region.

The self-bow
Some of the earliest illustrations (c.1585) by John White of the Indians of present-day North Carolina and Virginia, show bows which, at a conservative estimate, were 5ft 6in to 6ft (1.7 to 1.8m.) in length. Of relatively simple construction and resembling the English longbow, they were undoubtedly of a style which extended back at least a further 500 years.

Within a century of contact with whites, however, the bow was being rapidly replaced by the gun. As one scholar has observed, 'it can safely be said that by 1700 every Indian

from the Atlantic to the Mississippi had heard of the gun and was clamoring for one, and the art of making good bows went into a rapid decline'.[17]

Astonishingly, except for one archaeological find of a badly decomposed bow, only one other bow of early and good provenance from this area is to be found in the various collections. Referred to as the 'Sudbury bow'[18] and identified as Wampanoag – a tribe who greeted the Pilgrim Fathers at Plymouth, New England, in 1620 – it is nearly 5ft 6in (1.7m.) in length, made of hickory, and finely finished. A replica of this bow, made in the 1920s, was found to have a 'weight of 46 pounds at 28 inches of draw and a cast of 173 yards.' It was described as 'soft and pleasant to shoot, and could do effective work either as a hunting or a war implement'.[19]

Clearly, many attributes were lost with the introduction of the gun, not least stealth in

hunting or approaching the enemy, but it is obvious that as far as the eastern tribes were concerned, the advantages of ball and powder outweighed those of the arrow and bow in a woodland environment – far less so in other regions.

The sinew-lined bow
Often referred to as a sinew-backed bow, this type of bow was popular on the Great Plains and, unlike in the Eastern Woodlands, it was retained when firearms were introduced to the Plains region, being particularly affective on horseback. Such bows, seldom more than 3ft 6in (1.1m.) in length, had layers of finely shredded sinew glued on the back, as Mason describes it, 'laid on so that it resembled bark'.[20] A Blackfeet bow described in the 1920s is typical of the Plains style for the mid-nineteenth century. Up to 3ft 4in (1m.) in length, it was of a flat oval cross-section. The

Right: *The techniques of arrow release, where the arrow nock is held a certain way and then let loose in the shooting. As shown here, four techniques were used by Indian tribes north of Mexico: the tertiary release was most commonly employed by the Plains tribes. The three others were used in the Northeast and Southwest.*

sinew lining tended to draw it into a reflexed position when not braced. The string was of two strands of twisted sinew, tied with half-hitches in the lower nock and a slipknot at the upper nock. Even though of considerable age, when it was braced it was found to be 'a springy, vigorous weapon' and when 'drawn 20 inches it weighs 40 pounds and shoots 153 yards'.[21]

A wide variety of woods were used on the Plains to make the sinew-lined bow; unlike the self-bow where the elasticity of the wood determined the bow's characteristics, it was the sinew which was the main contributing factor to the weight of the lined bow rather than the wood itself. As long as the wood was able to withstand the compression which occurred on drawing the arrow, requirements were largely satisfied. Suitable woods were continually sought. As Mason observed more than a century ago, 'it has been often averred that an Indian was always on the lookout for a good piece of wood… These treasures were put into careful training at once, bent, straightened, steamed, scraped, shaped, whenever a leisure moment arrived. No thrifty Indian was ever caught without a stock of artillery stores'.[22]

The Hidatsa, Wolf Chief, himself a skilled bowyer, said that chokecherry, wild plum, cedar, and iron-wood was not infrequently used; however, ash was one of the most

Below top: *A Ceremonial bow and single arrow, collected from the Haida at Skidegote, in 1883. The elaborate carvings on these unique pieces probably make reference to family history and would be carried during tribal ceremonials.*
Bottom: *A ceremonial bow from the Chippewa or Ottawa of the Michigan region and dating from the mid-nineteenth century. It is embellished with carvings of three otters, one of which is emerging from the water with a fish, symbolic of good hunters and protective spirits.*

METHODS OF ARROW RELEASE

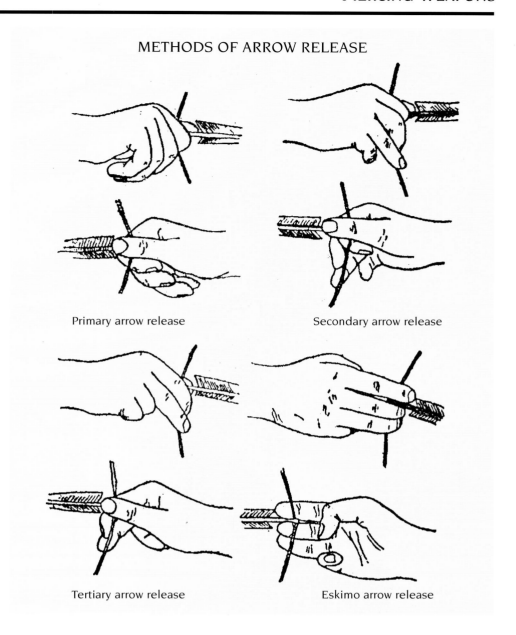

Primary arrow release

Secondary arrow release

Tertiary arrow release

Eskimo arrow release

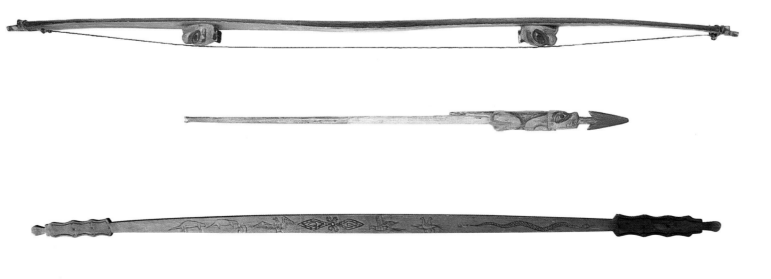

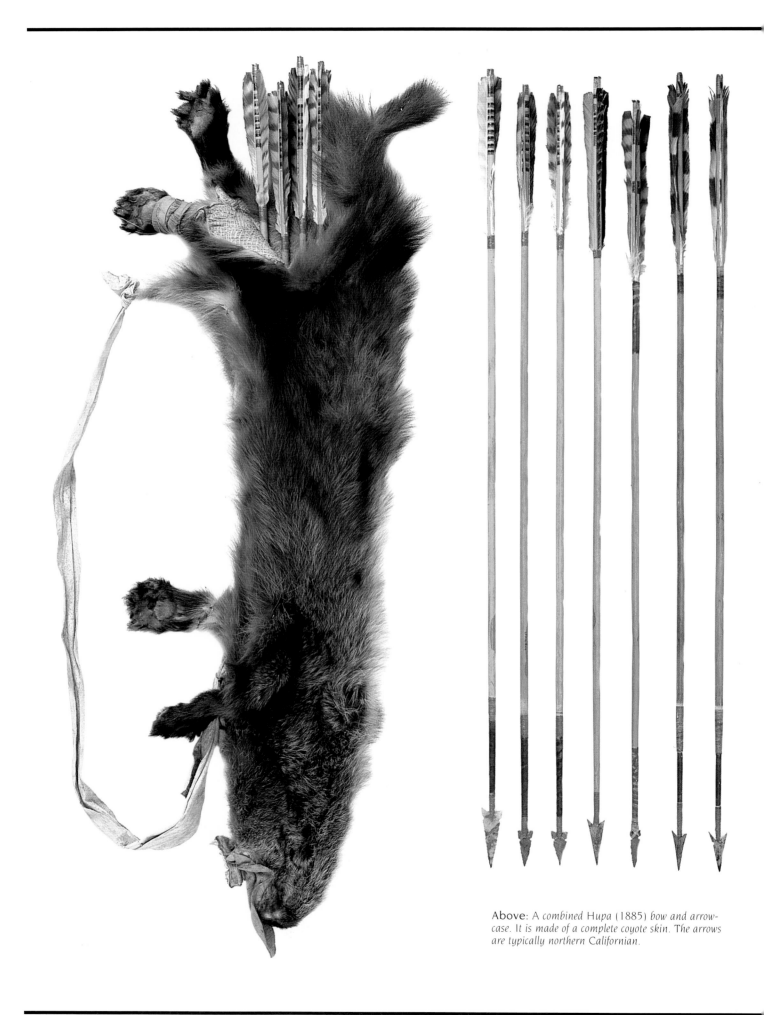

Above: *A combined Hupa (1885) bow and arrowcase. It is made of a complete coyote skin. The arrows are typically northern Californian.*

Right: *Apache warriors photographed circa 1880. All armed, the righthand warrior carries a flintlock gun, the others more traditional weapons – lance and bow. Note the long arrow, so typical of the Apache, held by the central figure. The shafts were generally of reed, the foreshaft of a harder wood.*

popular woods since it was relatively abundant on the Plains. A limb or trunk some 3in (7cm.) in diameter was generally cut in the winter, but the right raw material was not always easy to find and indeed one modern scholar of the Plains bow expressed the opinion that the 'rarity of usable wood of sufficient length and straightness might be one of the reasons for Northern Plains bows being mostly short'.[23]

The bows made by many of the tribes in California and were structurally similar to the Plains sinew-lined bow. However, at mid-limb, the width was generally greater than that of a Plains bow and yew or juniper – rather than ash – was commonly used. A distinctive feature of the coastal California bows was that many were elaborately painted with repeating geometrical designs such as diamonds, triangles, and bands, generally in blue and red. As has been observed, 'These California bows, as a class, excite the admiration of anyone who has every made a successful self-bow'.[24]

The horn bow

As discussed earlier, the power of a sinew-lined bow pivoted largely on the sinew which was attached to the back of the bow. When drawn, the sinew was stretched and the wood of the bow limbs which supported it was compressed. The thicker the sinew layer, the more powerful the bow. However, there is a limit to the amount of compression wood can withstand; beyond that, it permanently deforms and can no longer support the sinew-lining for efficient action.[25]

The problem was largely overcome by the use of horn, which can withstand far higher compression than wood. Thus, layers of the sinew lining were built up to far greater thicknesses, giving a proportional increase in bow strength. Such bows were often surprisingly short, certainly very seldom greater than 3ft 4in (1m.), with the majority in the region of 3ft (90cm.).[26] Even so, they were impressively powerful for their size. As the traveler Alfred Jacob Miller commented in 1834 when he observed Shoshone warriors using such bows, 'With an Elk-horn bow, they sometimes drive an arrow completely through a Buffalo, its propelling power being greater than that of a Yew bow'.[27]

The construction of the horn bow, one scholar has commented, is 'among the great triumphs of human ingenuity... Because of the limitations under which the Indian bowyer had to work, it is only natural to wonder how he managed to produce such a weapon'.[28] The tools available to prepare the horn were limited to say the least and, prior to the introduction of metal knives and hatchets, it is highly probable that very few, if any, horn bows were produced. A date of 1700 has been suggested for the first appearance of the horn bow and this coincides well with the arrival of trade knives and other tools in great numbers to the Plateau tribes.[29]

The horn used was from the elk or mountain sheep ram; with their complex turns and twists, neither satisfy the criteria suggested by Faris and Elmer who, in their detailed studies of horn bows, commented that 'a prime requisite of the horn for a bow should be that in its original state on

Above: *Armed Californian Indians, probably Hupa, circa 1840. In addition to the interesting rendering of hair styles, the arrow, the technique of release, and the details of the bow (with the broad middle tapering towards the ends) are accurate for the Hupa. The quiver is very similar to that shown on p.290.*

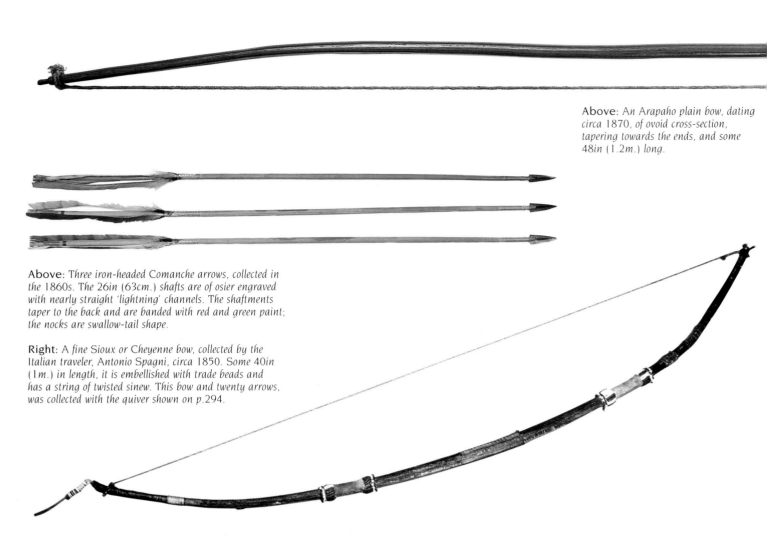

Above: *An Arapaho plain bow, dating circa 1870, of ovoid cross-section, tapering towards the ends, and some 48in (1.2m.) long.*

Above: *Three iron-headed Comanche arrows, collected in the 1860s. The 26in (63cm.) shafts are of osier engraved with nearly straight 'lightning' channels. The shaftments taper to the back and are banded with red and green paint; the nocks are swallow-tail shape.*

Right: *A fine Sioux or Cheyenne bow, collected by the Italian traveler, Antonio Spagni, circa 1850. Some 40in (1m.) in length, it is embellished with trade beads and has a string of twisted sinew. This bow and twenty arrows, was collected with the quiver shown on p.294.*

the head it should have only a simple curvature in one plane'.[30]

The techniques of construction of an elk horn bow were described by the Hidatsa, Wolf Chief, who, as a fifteen-year-old teenager, had watched his father, Small-ankles, make one over a period of some two weeks. The horns, which were picked up after being shed, first had the tines cut off; then the horn was worked down with a sharp knife to an even thickness.

It was then heated in a soil trench for some twenty-four hours, which softened the horn and allowed it to be further worked down, shaped, and then polished. Two bow limbs were so produced and these in turn were spliced together. The notches for the bow string were cut. Then, after scoring the back of the horn, layers of shredded sinew were successively built up with glue between each layer, so producing a sinew back which, on most bows, was 'approximately half the total thickness of the limb'.[31] The twisted sinew bow string was attached permanently at one end whilst a loop at the other end of the string enabled the bow to be braced for use.[32]

The procedure for making a mountain sheep horn bow was similar, the main criteria being a crush resistant platform to which the elastic sinew could be attached.[33]

As already mentioned, Alfred Jacob Miller (1834) was clearly greatly impressed with the horn bow, not only in the very efficient use of it by his Shoshone companions but also by the obvious skill which went into its making.[34] He observed: 'Now if an Elk-horn was carried to the smartest Yankee we have, with a request to make a bow of it, the probability is, that, for once, he would not find it convenient to attempt it.'[35]

The use of arrows

The structure of an arrow is made up of six parts: nock, feathering, shaftment, foreshaft, shaft, and head. Each differed in technique of assemblage, materials used, sizes, and decoration according to the region in which it was made. Arrow-making was a skilled occupation involving such activities as the selection of the wood, straightening and polishing the shaft, cutting and attaching the feathers and arrowhead, shaping the nock and notch, and channeling or painting the shaft and shaftment.[36] All required lengthy experience and practice to ensure the production of an effective missile which would have a devastating effect on animal or man.

During the period of the Plains Indian wars, considerable interest was taken by army surgeons and others regarding the power of the bow and the wounds inflicted by arrows. Many stories were related in regard to the force of arrows shot by Indian bowmen and several border on the bizarre. An example is the case of the Kiowa chief, Satamore,

who, in 1862 near Fort Larned, Kansas, was wounded after being shot in the buttocks by a Pawnee. The shaft was withdrawn but it left the arrowhead in his body. Satamore passed bloody urine but the wound healed quickly and within a few weeks he was able to go on the hunt for buffalo. For more than six years he continued at the head of his band, 'leading it in all its travels and adventures or the chase'.[37]

The presence of the arrowhead, however, troubled him somewhat and in August 1869 he conferred with a military surgeon at Fort Sill. On examination it was revealed that the arrowhead had penetrated deep into Satamore's bladder producing a large vesical calculus. Two surgeons performed a lithotomy and the calculus was removed. It was more than 2½in (6.2cm.) in length and, when cut in two, revealed the presence of the arrowhead as its nucleus. All evidence suggests that Satamore fully recovered from this somewhat unpleasant sequence of events – set in train by the Pawnee arrow some seven years before!

Others were less fortunate, such as Private Spillman of the 7th Cavalry who was wounded by a Kiowa war-party in a skirmish which took place near Fort Dodge, Kansas, in June 1867. The soldier received three arrow wounds, the worst going through the right lumbar region and penetrating some 8in (20cm.) into the abdominal cavity. With

generally being tied with sinew which passed through the notches.

Stone arrowheads were produced with great skill and patience by a process of chipping and flaking (p.288); of a naturally brittle material, they were liable to shatter on impact and for this reason those made of iron rapidly replaced the earlier, natural materials.[44]

Quivers and bow-cases

The style of quiver and bow-case varied greatly from one region to the next. Not only did it depend on the size of the bow and arrows but also on materials readily available. Sealskin was used in the Arctic by such groups as the

Above: *The effect of a steel-headed arrow on the human body. A pierced vertebra found on Little Bighorn, 1877.*

difficulty, the arrow was removed; however, the wound proved mortal.[38]

In less severe cases, Indians had their own techniques of removing arrowpoints when embedded in the body. A willow stick was split, 'the pith scraped out, and the ends rounded so that they may readily follow the arrow track. The pieces are introduced so as to reach and cover the barbs; they are then adjusted, bound to the arrowshaft, and all withdrawn together'.[39]

Tribal origin, and perhaps even a particular craftsman in some notable cases, could often be identified from the arow.[40] Thus, in 1833, when writing of Plains Indian types of weaponry, the German traveler Maximilian, observed: 'Though all their arrows appear, at first sight, to be perfectly alike, there is a great difference in the manner in which they are made. Of all the tribes of the Missouri the Mandans are said to make the neatest and most solid arrows. The iron heads are thick and solid, the feathers glued on, and the part just below the head, and the lower end, are wound round with very even, extremely thin sinews of animals... The Manitaries make the iron heads thinner, and not so well... The Assiniboins frequently have very thin and indifferent heads to their arrows, made of iron-plate'.[41]

Arrowshafts were of straight wood, stems, cane, or reeds depending on the region.[42] A notable exception was in the Arctic where the shaft might be of pieces of bone or driftwood bound together with sinew. Owing to the scarcity of materials, the shafts of arrows in this region were generally short, although the foreshaft which served the double purpose of making the front of the arrow heavier than

the rear and gave a more effective means of attaching the arrowhead, tended to extend the overall length of a typical Arctic arrow.

The shaftment of the arrow – that part of the shaft upon which the feather is fastened – varied greatly in length, form, and ornamentation. It was this part of the weapon upon which bands, and other marks, often for identification purposes, were usually placed.

As is well known, feathering is an important feature of any arrow, its main function being to retard the rear end of the missile and cause it to move straight. Thus, most North American arrows were fletched, generally with two or three split feathers.[43] An alternative, however, was to use a relatively massive head on the arrow which also served to keep the missile straight. Such was the case with some Eskimo groups who, with an elaborate foreshaft/arrowhead combination, dispensed with fletching altogether. This contrasts markedly with arrows from the Plains and Southwest region where the fletching feathers on the shaftment were often 6in (15cm.) or more in length.

Most arrowpoints were usually made of some material firmer and heavier than the shaft. Not only, of course, did this give greater penetrating power to the arrow, but it also tended to increase both the projectile's accuracy and its range. Many arrowheads were constructed of flint and other varieties of stone, as well as horn, bone, antler, wood, shell, and copper. The last was used by tribes in the region of Lake Superior and to a lesser extent by those in Alaska and British Columbia. Shapes were usually triangular and mostly notched to facilitate attachment in a slot at the end of the shaft, the head

THE POWER OF THE ARROW

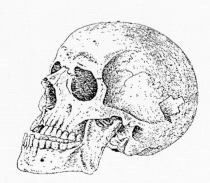

Skull of US cavalryman pierced by Comanche iron arrowhead, near Fort Concho, Texas.

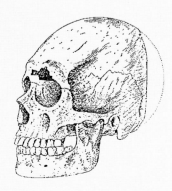

Skull of a Mexican killed in an Indian fight 75 miles northwest of Fort Concho, Texas, 1868.

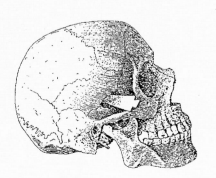

Skull of a white man pierced by arrow-point in Indian fight near Pecos River, Texas, 1870.

Above: *Cheyenne warrior, circa 1880. A combined bow-case and quiver is being carried with the strap across the left shoulder. The combination is of buffalo hide with the hair-side out. Similar examples are extant in the collections.*

Above: *A superb combined bow-case and quiver, partially made of otter hide and embellished with blue and white pony beads. This was collected by the Italian traveler, Antonio Spagni, in about 1850, who identified it as Sioux. Such arrow and bow-cases, with the long decorated triangular flap, were popular items at this time.*

Above *A bow-case and quiver with associated arrows and bow (Sioux?). Made of buffalo hide with the fur-side out, it was collected by the traveler Friedrich Köhler, about 1830. Both bow-case and quiver are bound with red trade cloth and decorated with blue pony beads.*

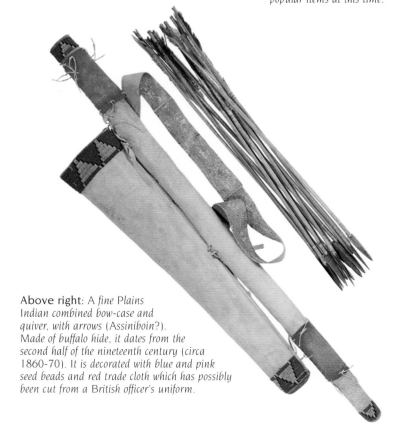

Above right: *A fine Plains Indian combined bow-case and quiver, with arrows (Assiniboin?). Made of buffalo hide, it dates from the second half of the nineteenth century (circa 1860-70). It is decorated with blue and pink seed beads and red trade cloth which has possibly been cut from a British officer's uniform.*

Above: *A fine combined bow-case and quiver made of otter skin with the fur-side out. Dating from circa 1880, it was originally identified as Nez Perce, but is probably Crow. The buckskin is embellished with red, blue, green, and white beads. Length of bow-case is 20in (50cm.).*

Central Eskimo; on the West Coast, some quivers were of cedar wood whilst various animal skins and pelts were used by the Plateau, Plains, and Woodland tribes and also to a lesser extent by those groups in the Southwest, who sometimes also used soft basketry.

Styles varied considerably, but the most common was a combined bow-case and separate arrow-case which were laced together and which generally had a strap which went over the shoulder. Some bow-case-quiver combinations were particularly elaborate, such as the elegant and richly decorated ones

made from three otterskins with two heavily beaded flaps attached – one at the mouth of the bow-case, the other on the arrow-case. Such magnificent accoutrements have been firmly associated with both the Plateau and Plains tribes, particularly the Nez Perce and Crow[45] (See bottom right, p.294).

References

1 Superbly shaped flintwork producing both spear and arrowheads is represented by such points as Clovis, Folsom and Eden – after the locations in which they were found. Some date from more than thirteen thousand years ago (see Turner, 1977: 7).

2 Ewers, 1955: 201.

3 An interesting comment by the Victorian ethnologist, Otis Mason, relating to tube projectile devices, was that the blow tube with the dart, driven to the mark by 'the elasticity of the breath, should be the antecedent and parent of the gun, pistol, and cannon'. He commented, however, that the inventors of gunpowder probably never saw an American or Malayan blow tube (Mason, 1894: 634).

4 Atlatl is an Aztec word for spear-thrower. It is a term now adopted by most American anthropologists. The Australian aborigines referred to them as *woonera*. Spear-throwers were used throughout the world and Hamilton comments that they were 'in use in Asia and Europe for tens of thousands of years' (Hamilton, 1982: 13).

5 Tate, 1986: 3.

6 These generally perforated stones are often referred to as 'banner stones' as they were formerly thought to be totems or clan emblems. Simple physics calculations relating to effects on both momentum and kinetic energy of projectile with an atlatl, suggest at least 4 to 5 fold increase in comparison without its use. A banner stone attachment would enhance this effect even more.

7 Garcilaso, 1951: 597.

8 Teit, Boas ed., 1930: 115.

9 Ewers, 1955: 201.

10 Pike, 1810: 10-11.

11 (a) A favorite point for lance heads in the historic period, was a sword blade, which according to Dodge was 'procured in great number from the Mexicans' (Dodge, 1959: 21).
(b) An examination of a series of lances in the reserve collections of the Smithsonian Institution, most of which were from the Southern Plains, revealed that more than 70% had sabre blades as points. Several were clearly of high grade steel. (Discussions with John C. Ewers, Smithsonian Institution, Washington. August 1962, and subsequent studies at the S.I., October 1999.)

12 Although the lance appears to have been used only to a limited extent in actual combat by the Central Plains tribes in the historic period, a notable exception was the Hunkpapa leader, Sitting Bull, who favored the lance above all weapons. It was described as made of ash and 7 or 8 feet in length, 'with an eight-inch notched iron blade' (Utley, 1993: 19).

13 (a) Hamilton, 1982: 26.
(b) Laubin's studies relating to the history of bow use in North America, indicate that there was no evidence of its use by the *earliest* cliff dwellers, (circa 2000 BC.), although 'it does show up in later ones'. He concludes that the North American bow seems to 'be of Asiatic origin but was brought over in later migrations, rather than in the early ones' (Laubin, 1980: 1).
(c) A recent paper by the scholar of American Indian archery, Roland Bohr, gives a somewhat more earlier date than Hamilton and states that 'The oldest undisputed archery artifacts of North America date from about AD 500' (Bohr, 1996: 2).

14 Laubin, 1980: 1.

15 Mason, 1894: 634.

16 ibid.

17 Hamilton, 1982: 29.

18 This was so named because it was taken from an Indian who was shot in Sudbury, Mass., in 1660.

19 Hamilton, 1982: 32.

20 Mason, 1894: 643.

21 Hamilton, 1982: 64.

22 (a) Mason, 1894: 638
(b) Obviously the geographical location of a tribe tended to largely dictate the type of wood used. Osage orange or *Bois d'arc* was widely recognized as amongst the hardest, finest, and most durable of

timbers. It was straight-grained and ideally suited for bow making. This tree was plentiful along the Arkansas and Canadian rivers, and near Comanche country in Texas. It was commonly used by the Comanche for their bows (Wallace and Hoebel, 1952: 100) and was sought after in trade by other tribes. The Omaha referred to *Bois d'arc*, as 'yellow wood' and the Blackfeet called the tree itself 'smooth bow' but 'bow dark' seems to have emerged as a universal terminology (Taylor, 1975: 50).

23 Bohr, 1996: 4 and personal communication, February 1999.

24 Hamilton, 1982: 69.

25 The reflexing of a sinew-lined bow refers to the bow limbs sweeping backwards from the grip when the bow is relaxed (unstrung). To some extent this is due to the sinew-lining on the back of the bow. Such bows can reverse themselves in string during the years of laying in museum storage and errors are made as to which side the sinew was originally fastened. I have seen such bows in collections, incorrectly restrung and even used the wrong way – with the sinew on the inside and hence compressed in use. (See also ibid: 9 and 59.)

26 Detailed descriptions of ten horn bows in the United States National Museum, were supplied to the scholar T. M. Hamilton, by Dr. W. R. Wedel. These had been made by George Metcalf, a careful and meticulous technician at the Museum. Mr. Metcalf made one error in thinking that some of the bows were of cow horn. Bill Holm's subsequent studies, identified the material as mountain sheep horn (Holm to Taylor, 1992). These useful and interesting statistics are reproduced in ibid: 140-43.

27 (a) Ross, ed., 1968: 60.
(b) Miller took a particular interest in the horn bows used by warriors whom he saw practising with them at the Shoshone Rendezvous in 1833. Not only did he illustrate their target practice but he also made a careful sketch of a strung and unstrung horn bow (See DeVoto, 1948: Plate XLIX and ibid: 7).

28 Hamilton, 1982: 92-93.

29 Metcalf in ibid: 92.

30 Faris and Elmer, 1945: 161.

31 Hamilton, 1982: 89.

32 The bow string was, of course, one of the most important parts of the bow itself and required considerable skill in its manufacture. Most were made from the heaviest sinews of the deer, elk, or buffalo; others, such as in the Southwest and sometimes in the Basin, were of twisted fiber. A decided disadvantage of sinew was loss of elastic properties in conditions of high humidity. For this reason, most men carried a carefully wrapped spare string and horn bows – in particular – were completely covered with a rattlesnake skin (See Taylor, 1975: 51).

33 *Mahpiya Kinyeyapi*, 'Flying Cloud', better known as Judge F. B. Zahn, of Sioux descent and who lived at Fort Yates, North Dakota – an excellent scholar who I corresponded with almost fifty years ago – reported that his old-time informants (such as Spotted Bear, aged 96 years) said that some Sioux bows were made of buffalo ribs and heavily backed with sinew. The bows were said to be 'excellent' and were protected with a canvas cover 'so that rain or moisture would not soften the sinew and thus loosen the bows' splicing' (Zahn in Hamilton, 1982: 102).

34 (a) Several students of the American horn bow have made replicas and tested their properties (See Laubin, 1980: 77-78 and Holm in Hamilton, 1982: 116-34).
(b) The performances of bows collected from widely spaced tribes in North America, such as the Navajo, Apache, Hupa, Cree, Blackfeet, Osage, Sioux, and Cheyenne (and which included a composite sinew-backed replica), were compared with those from other parts of the world – including a bow from the 'Mary Rose' which sank in Portsmouth Harbour in 1545. A replica of an English long bow of yew had a weight of 75lb (34kg.). A sinew-backed Cheyenne bow had a weight of 80lb (36kg.). The composite had a weight of 85lb (38.5kg.). Bill Holm's second sheephorn bow was

30in (1.1m.) long measured along the curve with a weight of 55lb (30kg.) at full draw of 22in (0.55m.) and maximum range 235 yards (212m.). He found it difficult to hold at full draw and concluded that such bows were 'ordinarily drawn and shot in one motion'. Over a period of some twelve years, he reported that the reflex on the unstrung bow had increased (Personal communication, 1992). (See Pope, 1923 and Hamilton, 1982: 137-39. For the Holm references, see ibid: 120-23.)

35 Ross, ed. 1968: 7.

36 (a) As is discussed in the main text and some captions, the material used for arrow shafts depended on the locality. Thus, Apache arrows were generally of easily obtainable straight marsh reeds with a heavy foreshaft of hard wood. The Apaches called the reed *klo-ka*, meaning 'arrow grass' and the hard wood, *kk-ing*. Pawnee arrows were, according to Dunbar, a reliable and early observer, of dogwood (*Cornus stolonifera*), those of the Shushwap were of service berry whilst those of the Haida and Bella-Coola have been described as of cedar (See Mason, 1894: 669, 674 and 676).

37 (a) Wilson, 1901: 527.
(b) Flint arrowheads could be more wounding than the later metal ones. Several skulls and bones exhibiting flint arrowhead wounds have been found in prehistoric sites; in some cases the arrowpoints were unusually long, having drill-like characteristics (ibid: 517-18).

38 ibid: 524-35.

39 ibid: 531.

40 For example, amongst the Mandan only a few individuals were taught by certain bundle owners, to make arrows. The teachings were, that those in need of arrows bought their supplies from them. Special rituals were observed in both the collecting of raw materials and in making the arrows (See Bowers, 1950: 283).

41 Maximilian, Thwaites ed., 1906. Vol. 23: 354.

42 Care was taken to ensure that the shaft was straight for an accurate flight path. The 'arrow straightener' was a perforated bone, ivory or wooden device, which could be used in a lever-type mode to remove localised distortions. See p.288 for an example from the Mandan which is typical of those used in several cultural regions.

43 The form of the feathers varied considerably. Sometimes they were used whole, as with many of the Eskimo groups and some of the Southwestern tribes. In other areas, the feather was split lengthwise. Feather length also varied considerably; Plains arrows have long – up to 6 or 7in (15 or 18cm.) fletching on a relatively short shaft of hard wood. In the Southwest, however, the feathering was short on the long reed shafts with heavy foreshafts. Feathers were set on the shaftment, either flat or radially, secured with sinew at the ends. Sometimes, but not always, glued down. (See Mason, 1891 and 1894 for terminology and more details; Hough (1891: 62-63) who refers to rifling techniques of the Pima; and Bourke (1891: 71-73) who not only discusses (with considerable authority) Apache arrows but fletching techniques of widely spaced tribes, such as the Pima and the Iroquois.)

44 The Hudson's Bay Company lists arrowheads under Trade Goods offered at York Factory in 1813 – for trade to Canadian Indians. According to Garretson (1938: 180), hundreds of thousands were manufactured yearly by eastern traders to be exchanged for furs. They were put in packages of one dozen each and cost the trader six cents a package. Usually one package was exchanged for a buffalo robe. Additionally, some were also made by local blacksmiths and by the Indians themselves. A Sioux informant (White Hawk), said that in his hunting days, arrowheads were frequently cut from 'thin frying pans sold by traders or used by the soldiers' (Densmore, 1918: 438).

45 Holm 1981: 60.

DEFENSIVE WEAPONS

FOLLOWING CHRISTOPHER COLUMBUS' first voyage to the 'new' American continent in 1492, the Spanish, under Juan Ponce de León, skirted the coast of a region known as *Bimini*. It was Easter Week – *Pasque Florida* – and that name became attached to an area of the Southeast which is now known as Florida (but at the time also included parts of present-day South Georgia and East Carolina). The date was May 1513. On the west coast, in the vicinity of present-day Tampa Bay, the Spanish sailed into a natural harbor. Here, they met the Calusa, a powerful tribe which dominated the region.[1]

The use of body armor

What repeatedly comes through in reports from the Spanish, and later from the French and English, is that the Calusa were fierce and

Above: *A Huron warrior from an early eighteenth century print. He wears armor made from slats of wood bound together with cords. Both chest and back are adequately covered. Effective against enemy arrows, such armor rapidly fell into disuse with the introduction of firearms.*

determined fighters, that warfare was very much a way of life, and that their offensive weapons – bows, clubs, perhaps also the spear and atlatl – and their warfare tactics, were very effective against most enemies. There is, however, little data regarding the Calusa's defensive weapons.[2]

In addition to the sword, lance, and later the gun, the Spaniards were well aware of the value of body armor, the conquistadors commonly wearing metal breast and back plates as well as a 'kettle' hat, chin plates, and sometimes leg-guards. It is probable that the use of this type of protective weaponry, as was the case later in the Spanish Southwest, on the Northwest Coast and in Alaska, was adopted and modified by the Calusa and other tribes in the region, utilizing the native materials readily available to them.

This possibility aside, however, there is also good evidence to suggest that various forms of body protection were independently developed by North American Indians. If the

Above: *Tlingit armor collected in 1880 (but probably older), combining two styles – wood slats and rods. Such armor was restrictive to body movement but the heavy slats offered considerable physical protection.*

early renderings which we have of such armor are to be believed much, and perhaps not surprisingly, it was similar in basic design – chest and back covering, helmets, leg and even chin plates (see above) – to that worn by the Europeans.[3]

An illustration attributed to F. J. Bressani, and produced prior to 1660, shows a Huron warrior wearing armor made of tightly laced osier rods or bark strips, the unit tightly laced together with sinew or buckskin thongs.[4] More than half a century later, it had not radically changed (see left).

Styles of body armor

Native American armor has been categorized into five basic types, which were largely

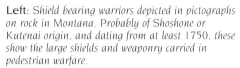

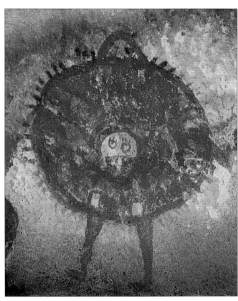

Below: *In addition to the slat armor worn by Huron warriors (left), they carried large circular shields made of cedar bark, as shown in this early engraving. Note the substantial carrying straps and that the shield covers both head and body.*

Below: *One of three large rawhide shields found in a cave near Torrey in Utah in 1925. Carbon 14 techniques date them from circa AD 1500. Almost 3ft (1m.) in diameter, these enhance details in the style shown in early pictographs (above). Note the elaborate symbolic paintings.*

Above: *A pictograph – paint on a rock surface – depicting a pedestrian shield-bearing warrior in present-day Wheatland County, Montana. Note the similarity to the Huron warrior (below, left). Many of the shields in this type of rock art display, as here, the medicine signs of the shield owner.*

determined by materials available in a particular region. For example, that of the Inuit and Eskimo groups, where wood was scarce, was generally made of overlapping plates of bone, ivory, and later – after contact with whites – of iron.[5] On the Northwest Coast, California and, as has been discussed, to the east amongst the Huron as well as the Iroquois and Indians of Virginia, body armor was either wooden slats or rods tightly bound together.

Body garments of hardened or multilayered hides were widely used, being attributed to Northwest Coast tribes such as the Haida, Chinook, and Tlingit as well as to Plateau and Plains tribes (Shoshone and Pawnee). This armor style has also been described for such widely spaced tribes as the Mohawk to the east of Lake Ontario and the Navajo more than three thousand air miles to the Southwest in present-day New Mexico.[6]

Below: *A Cheyenne warrior dressed in the regalia of the Red-Shield Society, one of the five original warrior societies of the great Prophet. He carries the distinctive shield of the Society made from a buffalo hide with the tail left on. The shirt is reminiscent of the early style, pedestrian body armor.*

The impact of the gun
The various, largely indigenous, armor styles were effective against native weaponry but far less so against gun-armed opponents and although the impacting ball would lose some of its power, native armor rapidly fell out of favor with the advent of the gun. As the Blackfeet, Weasel Tail, observed to the ethnologist John Ewers, armor was adequate protection against arrows but it was unable to ward off bullets from early firearms. Consequently, the Blackfeet 'abandoned its use after their enemies became armed with guns'.[7] This was a sentiment implied, if not stated, in other regions and, largely for this reason, such armor fell into disfavour, becoming a relic of the past. However, in the case of one dominant Plains tribe, the Sioux, it was retained as a single-layered, decorated garment and became the symbol of high-ranking office, that of 'Shirt Wearer'[8] (see 'Symbolic Weapons' chapter).

Early styles of shield – rectangular-shaped shields
Early descriptions of the shields used in North America refer to a large circular style made of heavy hide, basketry, wooden rods, or bark, or heavy multilayered elk hide. There were, however, some notable exceptions. Thus, a shield collected in the 1930s from Kagamil Island – one of the Aleutian Islands – and made sometime prior to white contact, is actually rectangular. Made of two heavy wooden boards laced together with thongs, it is embellished with geometrical designs – obviously highly symbolic to the owner – rendered in red paint.[9]

South of the Plateau region, amongst such tribes as the Coeur d'Alêne and Okanagon, several ancient styles of shields have been described, one of which was oblong and about 5ft (1.5m.) long. It was made of a single piece of heavy elk hide and was said to 'sometimes [be] moistened with water when about to be used' and that 'one side often carried painted designs'.[10] None of the oldest living Indians amongst these tribes, however, could remember the use of these ancient forms of shields, observing that they 'went out of use after horses were employed, as they were not adapted for riding.'[11]

The circular shield
In addition to the slat armor described earlier, the Huron also carried circular shields.[12] These shields we're at least 3½ft (1.2m.) in diameter with two carrying handles and, it appears, had a wooden hoop around the circumference (p.297). Some two centuries later, in the 1720s, Lafitau described the Iroquoian styles of shield: 'Their shields were of ozier or bark covered with one or many *peaux passées*; there are some made of very thick skin. They had them of all sizes and all sorts of figures.'[13]

Shields of this type were well suited to pedestrian warfare, as illustrated by the many petroglyphs and pictographs found on rock faces throughout the Plateau and Plains region. Most conspicuous are the large shields carried by the pedestrian warriors together with long bows, spears and clubs. The shields were up to 3ft (1m.) in diameter and are shown embellished with designs which probably represented the protectors and helpers of the warriors who carried them. Some of these designs are semirealistic, others more abstract, suggestive of the development of a complex system of symbolism.

These shield-bearing warrior motifs are particularly numerous at rock art sites on the Northwestern Plains and generally predate the appearance of the Blackfeet alliance.[14] These warrior figures were almost certainly of Shoshone and Kutenai – tribes who dominated the Northern Plains area prior to circa 1740.[15] Support for this suggestion comes from the finding in 1925 of three large hide-painted shields, in a dry cave near Torrey, Utah. Referred to as the 'Pectol shields' – after the finder Ephraim Pectol – mass spectrometry and radio carbon techniques date them to circa AD 1500.[16] Arm loops at the back of each shield, similar to those shown on the Huron shield (p.297), offered some support, but the greater weight, it appears, was eased with a neck strap.[17]

Such shields were certainly not exclusive to the prehistoric Northwestern Plains. Early Spanish explorers on the Southern Plains describe 'large buffalo hide shields to cover the entire body,'[18] whilst early painted hides rediscovered in Switzerland some fifty years ago, show pedestrian warriors (probably

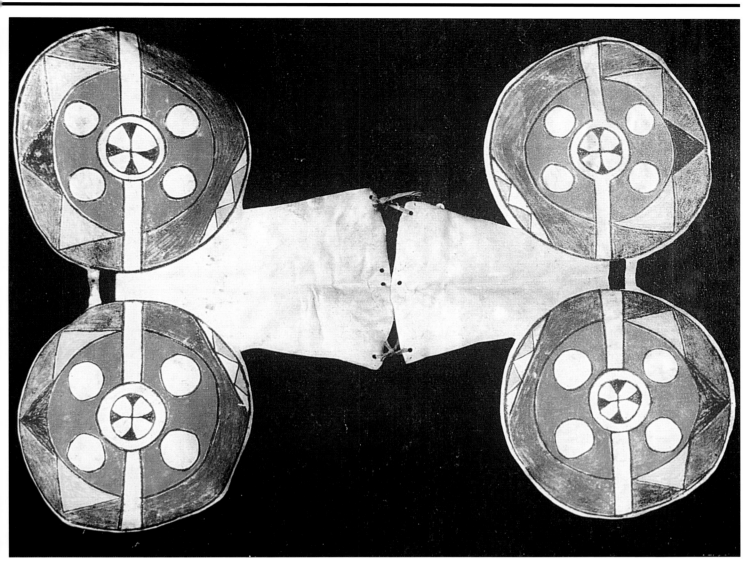

Above: *Horse armor, probably Crow, circa 1870. Such accoutrements seem to have been of indigenous origin and unrelated to Spanish-type horse armor which was used on the Southern Plains. The discs exhibit symbolic paintings suggesting the evoking of the sky's protective powers aided the actual mechanical protection of the rawhide itself.*

Plains Apache), their torsos entirely hidden behind their shields.[19]

The designs on the Pectol shields, as well as those documented in Rock Art, suggest ancient traditions of extensive religious concepts and mythology of the type identified by Clark Wissler and Robert H. Lowie for the historic Plains tribes[20]... protective and other designs associated with sky and earth powers, animal powers, metamorphosis, and even, perhaps, lunar designs.[21]

As was discussed earlier ('The use of body armor'), a form of hide body armor was worn by the pedestrian Plains tribes; this, together with the large rawhide shields, made them formidable opponents. A battle between similarly armed groups which took place about 1720, was described by the elderly Saukamappee, an adopted member of the Piegan who were moving into the Plains and progressively forcing the Shoshone to retreat to the Rocky Mountains. It refers to the method of using large shields and their effectiveness against arrows.

Warfare by pedestrian shield-bearing warriors

A combined force of some three hundred and fifty Cree and Piegan were confronted by a similar number of Shoshone in the vicinity of the Eagle Hills in present-day Southwest Saskatchewan. A few guns were owned by the Piegan but, because of the shortage of ammunition, these were reserved for hunting. Thus, both sides were armed with ancient styles of offensive and defensive weapons – lance, bows and arrows, and large shields. There was much pre-battle ceremonial feasts in a great War Tent, together with speeches and dances. A war chief was selected who then led the foot warriors towards the Shoshone. Saukamappee related: 'Both parties make a great show of their numbers, and I thought that they were more numerous than ourselves. After some singing and dancing, they sat down on the ground, and placed their large shields before them, which covered them: We did the same, but our shields were not so many, and some of our shields **had to shelter two men**' [author's stress].[22]

Saukamappee described the Shoshone bows as superior to their own; generally, they were shorter and sinew-backed. Their arrows, however, were less effective as they had flint heads which shattered on impact, whilst those of the Piegan and Cree were of iron, the arrows sticking into the rawhide shields but not penetrating them. Several were wounded on both sides. but none severely, and

nightfall put an end to the battle. Saukamappee reported that not a scalp was taken on either side and observed, somewhat wryly, 'in those days such was the result'.[23]

This was not always the case, however, for at other times, after a period of relatively ineffective archery fire, another stage might be the substitution of 'shock for fire'.[24] The war chief led the whole line in a charge; often, this was preceded by the singing of a war song, the charge itself being initiated by a war cry. Hand-to-hand fighting then took place, the main weapon being a stone-headed war club – the outcome was generally brief and bloody. Territory was thus gained, together with loot, trophies, and scalps.

An alternative strategy, and one most preferred, was for a large war-party to locate a small, isolated enemy camp, creep up on it during the night, and make a surprise attack at dawn, slaughtering the inhabitants. As Saukamappee put it: 'The great mischief of war then, was as now, by attacking and destroying small camps of ten to thirty tents, which are obliged to separate for hunting...'[25] The outcome was not much different to the ancient warfare on the Missouri River, where archaeological evidence indicates entire villages might be destroyed.[26]

Archaeological evidence and early engravings – such as that of the Delaware village in Sasquesahanok (p.304) – prove that

Above: *Keokuk or 'The Watchful Fox', chief of the Sauk and Fox. Portrait from life by George Catlin when he visited Keokuk's village in 1834. Less nomadic equestrian people than the Plains tribes further west, Catlin's portrait suggests that the Sauk and Fox retained the large, early type of rawhide shield so typical of early pedestrian warriors (p.297). Here, Keokuk carries a shield (some 3ft (1m.) in diameter) on his left arm, together with a highly decorated staff of office.*

Above: *A warrior on horseback, both horse and man covered with hide armor. Writing-On-Stone in the Milk River Valley of southern Alberta. Possibly Shoshone, sometime prior to 1800. The Shoshone are the only Northwestern Plains/Plateau tribe to have used this style of horse armor, which is probably an influence from their relatives, the Comanche in the south.*

many settled communities in the eastern part of North America commonly fortified their villages. Generally, there was a protective palisaded wall of upright wooden poles, bound together with rawhide or roping. This enclosed the bark longhouses which surrounded a central square or plaza. Outside the palisade were cleared areas for growing crops.

Such arrangements were replicated as far west as the Missouri River: thus, the early Huff site, a Mandan village which dates from circa 1500 (and is still to be seen some eighteen miles southeast of the town of Mandan in present-day North Dakota), encloses an area of about seventeen acres. The fortifications were complex, consisting

not only of a high, fort-like palisade but with bastions at the corners, a deep, wide surrounding ditch and a type of *chevaux de frise* of sharpened stakes. Defensive fortifications of this type indicate concern for protection from outside groups and it is reasonable to suppose that this show of force was matched by an increase in group solidarity.[27]

Such fortifications were obviously not used by nomadic Plains groups, as Lt. James Bradley observed of the Blackfeet (and which, he said, extended to other Plains tribes), '[they] never fortified their camps, and it was rare that they chose them with any reference to their possibilities of defense...'.[28] As Ewers observed, Plains Indians, it seems, relied very heavily upon their dogs to bark and waken them 'if enemy raiders entered the camp at night'.[29]

Horse corrals, however, were commonly used by the Plains and Plateau tribes. Lowie[30] refers to the Northern Shoshone keeping their horses inside their camp circles, which implies a form of corral being used similar to that described for the Crow who, it is reported, made corrals of brush piled between the lodges to enclose the centre of the camp.[31]

Horses corralled this way, in the centre of a Flathead tipi village, are illustrated on p.304. The episode recorded here suggests that it was not always an effective way of preventing loss of good horses to a determined horse thief!

Warfare tactics in the Northeastern Woodlands
Similar methods of pedestrian warfare to those described by Saukamappee for the Plateau and Plains, but modified by terrain

Above: *A Tonkawa Indian, circa 1830. The Tonkawa were neighbors of the powerful Comanche, and this gun-carrying warrior is dressed in an attenuated form of body armor which gave freer movement on horseback than earlier styles. These garments were described as being painted red, green, or blue; further decoration on this example seems to be porcupine quillworked discs.*

Below: *Crow shields, both dating from the early nineteenth century. Examples of spiritual and mechanical protection: the shield of Rotten Belly, a distinguished chief of the Mountain Crow (left); and the shield of Shot-in-the-Hand, made of buffalo hide and embellished with the feathers and a head of a Canada goose (right).*

Left: *Plains Indian shield, Crow (?), circa 1850. Some 19in (48cm.) in diameter, the shield has several covers, each embellished with protective paintings, perhaps to match the situation. The symbols appear to make reference to sky and bear powers – highly significant to the Crow.*

constraints, also prevailed in the Great Lakes region and beyond. There are descriptions such as the use of body armor, large shields, shock weapons, and the bow, but this ancient style of fighting rapidly went out of fashion with the introduction of the gun to the Woodlands early in the seventeenth century. As Secoy observed[32], warfare tactics were now organized not only by reference to a forest environment but markedly conditioned by the use of guns. Now it was more expedient to scatter forces, so allowing individual warriors to take best advantage of nearby cover – but still effectively support each other by fire. Thus, Woodland military tactics at this time maintained no regular formation; the warriors kept close enough together to support one another and, when hard pressed, retreated to the nearest available patch of woods where this style of warfare could be used to best advantage. Further, the shield and body armor, effective against the arrow and spear in earlier days but no longer a protection against the penetrating power of a bullet (as well as being cumbersome for rapid movement), were largely abandoned.

Although war tactics were similar throughout the Woodlands, some definite cultural separations did occur between the

Right: *Model of a Kiowa shield collected (1891-1904) by the ethnologist, James Mooney, as part of a project relating to Plains Indian heraldry. This is the shield design of Padalti, grandson of Dohasan, and head chief of the Kiowa until his death in 1866.*

Far Right: *Model shield, design of Tsonkiada, a distinguished Kiowa warrior. Mooney's studies of Kiowa heraldry established a similarity in the overall appearance of their shields which was indicative of a close camaraderie. These warriors also wore similar body paint, observed the same ceremonial taboos, and used the same war cries.*

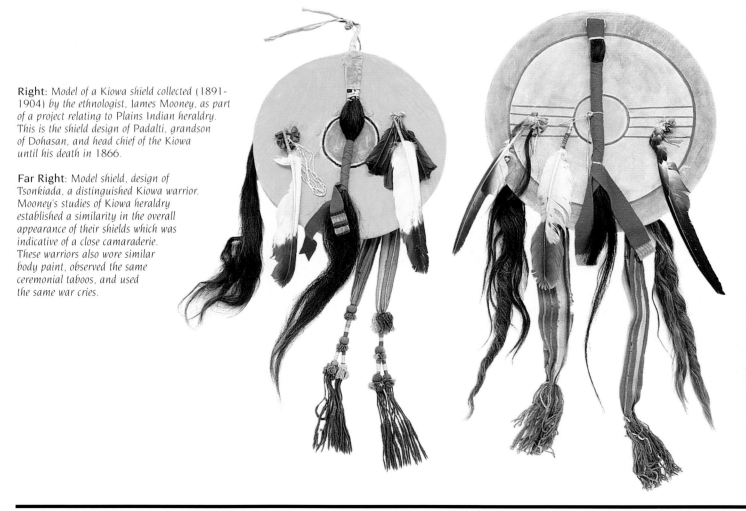

Eastern and Western groups. Specialized torture and cannibalism, which were a practice of both the Iroquois and the Huron,[33] were virtually absent amongst the more Western Woodland peoples.

Tribes such as the Santee Sioux, who in the 1600s commonly both traded and warred with such tribes as the Ottawa and Huron, had a form of institutionalized crying as an honorable manner of greeting people. To the Eastern tribes, this was regarded as a 'final loss of manhood and a weakness that they tried not to give way to, even under torture by the enemy...'.[34] The Ottawa and Huron first regarded the Sioux as weak and cowardly; it was, however, a notion which later military conflicts 'painfully contradicted'.[35]

The impact of the horse on defensive weapon styles

The ancestor of the horse probably originated in the Americas over forty million years ago. It was then a relatively small creature and there is no evidence that it was ever domesticated by the ancestors of the American Indian – rather, it was hunted and eaten. The creature, however, dispersed to the Old World via the land bridge to Siberia, eventually reaching Europe and disappearing in the Americas.[36]

Some ten thousand years or so later, after the horse had been reintroduced to North America, it was the Spanish stock-raising settlements in the Southwest which became the major source of horses for the Southern Plains tribes, notably the Comanche. By the early 1700s, a combination of trade, raids, and wild horse herds led to a gradual movement northward of a creature which radically changed the lifestyle of the indigenous population – not least, warfare tactics.

As the horse spread northwards from the Southern Plains to the Plateau, tribes such as the Shoshone, Nez Perce, Coeur d'Alêne, and Kutenai in turn traded them – by a complexity of links to the Crow, Blackfeet, and later to the Upper Missouri Village tribes.

Equestrian travel demanded freer use of arms and legs and this led to a modification of weaponry, not least that used for defence, and there were great changes. The late eighteenth century equestrian tribes, such as the Yankton Sioux, were now wearing an attenuated multilayered garment with sleeves which extended only to the elbows, and they carried smaller shields. The main reason for this was that the foes of the Sioux to the west and south 'still lacked guns, and hence used bows during this early period, so that these elements of the leather armor complex still had defensive value in battle against them'.[17] Other styles of attenuated armor which could be worn on horseback were also used by such tribes as the Shoshone, Blackfeet, and Plains Apache; these were sleeveless, some being painted red, green, or blue. The garments must have looked similar to that worn by the Tonkawa warrior sketched by Lino Tapia in Texas in 1829 (p.301).

Horse armor

Although, as discussed earlier, there is still some debate regarding the possible influence of the Spaniards on indigenous American warrior protective armor styles, there seems little doubt that the use of horse armor was an idea introduced from Europe.[18]

The use of horse armor by the Shoshone was commented on by Lewis and Clark in 1805, who observed: 'They have a kind of armor something like a coat of mail, which is formed by a great many folds of dressed antelope-skins, united by means of a mixture of glue and sand. With this they cover their own bodies **and those of their horse** [author's stress], and find it impervious to the arrow.'[19] This type of horse armor had a much more limited distribution amongst the horse-using tribes in the Southwest, Plateau and Plains. It appears not to have spread very far beyond those tribes who were in close

Left: *A Mescalero Apache chief, photographed circa 1885. As shown here, the shields of this Athapaskan-speaking Southwestern group frequently display abstract and striking paintings. Generally, the designs make reference to the mountains and the spirits which dwelt there – (Gan), lightning, wind, snakes, and the stars and planets. Shields such as these were carried by high-ranking leaders whose powers had been obtained from the supernatural world of the Apache people.*

Left: *The Delaware village of Fort Sasquesahanok, showing bark longhouses and the village fortified by use of a palisaded wall. Similar defenses were recorded for the Virginia Indians in 1585 and were also used by Missouri Indians as late as the 1880s.*

contact with the Spanish and seems seldom employed by tribes on the Central and Northern Plains – probably because of the relatively early introduction of the gun into these regions, which would render such armor virtually useless. As with the warshirt, however, the armor tradition was retained with the adoption of single-layered horse masks and caparisons – now adorning, rather than protecting, the horse.[40]

Another style of horse armor was also in vogue on the Plateau and Central and Northern Plains, and it differed considerably

Below: *A Flathead campsite in the Rocky Mountains, as depicted by Sharp, a young Piegan artist in the 1890s. It shows an outstanding exploit of White Grass who captured horses from within the tipi camp circle. Camp circles were not infrequently enclosed to corral horses at night.*

Above: *War lodge, probably Crow, circa 1880. This was photographed in the Montana wilderness by the author in 1993. These were the vital 'headquarters' of war-parties.*

Above: *Comanche warriors sketched by George Catlin, 1834. Such scenes depicted the great skills of the Comanche in handling horses. Here, in a sham battle, a horse is being used as a shield – a dangerous feat seldom used in actual warfare.*

Below: *A shield said to have belonged to the Oglala Sioux war chief, Crazy Horse. Some 22in (60cm.) in diameter, it was captured by Lieutenant Henry Lawton in 1877. The general layout of the design conforms to Wissler's informant's description of traditional Sioux shields and evokes several desired protective powers of fleetness and strength (Wissler, 1907). Some symbols, however, such as the red and black power motifs (extreme left), are decidedly Cheyenne. Crazy Horse was a close associate of the Cheyenne Dog Soldiers.*

from the Spanish type. It was made of a single layer of thin, white/yellow rawhide and exhibited four shield-like discs, often elaborately decorated (p.299). It is certain that these date from at least 1820, but were still used by the Crow in dress parades as late as 1910; the evidence suggests that such coverings put more emphasis on protection of the horse by the symbolic designs, rather than the mechanical protection of the rawhide.[41]

Shields carried by equestrian warriors
Large shields were unwieldy on horseback and not popular – although there were notable exceptions, particularly on the Southern Plains.

Large shields were still popular amongst the Southern Plains tribes as late as the 1830s, even though tribes such as the Comanche had been equestrians for more than a century. Paintings by Catlin[42] and Berlandier[43] confirm the use of shields 3ft (90cm.) or more in diameter. Possibly, as with the lance, it was the influence of the Spanish which encouraged the retention of shield styles, although the actual method of construction differed. Thus, Pfefferkorn[44] described the Spanish soldiers' shields for the mid-nineteenth century as 'egg shaped' and being made of several layers of rawhide which were riveted together. In contrast, most Plains shields were circular and generally of a single unreinforced thickness of buffalo rawhide. There were, however, exceptions to this and again the idea was possibly due to Spanish influence. It has been reported that one style of shield favored by the Comanche was the use of two discs of rawhide which were laced together around the edge of a wooden hoop. The space between the discs was then packed with hair, feathers, grass, or other material, to reduce the momentum of the impinging missile. One can only speculate as to the effectiveness of such

Left: *Pictograph by the Hunkpapa Sioux leader, Sitting Bull, circa 1880. This probably shows an episode in the killing of the mail carrier, MacDonald, near Fort Totten in 1868. The shield carried by Sitting Bull brings together a number of elements in a single circle of defensive, protective, and supernatural powers of the Sioux cosmos.*

dexterously done, the skin is kept tight whilst it contracts to one-half of its size, taking up the glue and increasing in thickness until it is rendered as thick and hard as required (and his friends have pleaded long enough to make it arrow, and almost ball proof), when the dance ceases, and the fire is put out. When it is cooled and cut into the shape that he desires, it is often painted with his *medicine* or *totem* upon it…'.[46]

Catlin, as well as others, reported on one of the important aspects of many shields which are the symbolic designs which were considered to give supernatural protection to the owners; there was also much ceremonial, in their production,[47] and often associated ritual and taboos, such as with the famous shield owned by the Crow chief, Rotten Belly (p.301). For these reasons, it is recorded, white traders were entirely unsuccessful in their

shield styles from the ball of a muzzle-loading flintlock; however, there was a demand for suitable packing material by the Comanche. Anglo-American pioneers, it has been reported, were puzzled by the Comanche's apparent sudden interest in books. The dichotomy was later explained after a Comanche shield was captured in battle – it was found that, instead of the usual packing material between the rawhide layers, there were scores of pages from a book dealing with the complete history of Rome![45]

It is obvious that early observers were impressed with techniques of shield production. Catlin, for example, described the elaborate ceremonial of 'smoking the shield', which he thought was 'very curious, as well as an important one… For this purpose a young man about to construct him a shield, digs a hole of two feet in depth, in the ground, and as large in diameter as he designs to make his shield. In this he builds a fire, and over it, a few inches higher than the ground, he stretches the rawhide horizontally over the fire, with little pegs driven through holes made near the edges of the skin. This skin is at first, twice as large as the size of the required shield; but having got his particular and best friends (who are invited on the occasion), into a ring, to dance and sing around it, and solicit the Great Spirit to instil into it the power to protect him harmless against his enemies, he spreads over it the glue, which is rubbed and dried in, as the skin is heated; and a second busily drives other and other pegs, inside of those in the ground, as they are gradually giving way and being pulled up by the contraction of the skin. By this curious process, which is most

Right: *Pictograph on a buffalo robe, probably Cheyenne, circa 1860. Recent research (Cowdrey 1995) suggests that the horn-like hair-style identifies the individual as of Suhtaio descent – a tribe that merged with the Cheyenne in the early nineteenth century. The shield conforms to known Cheyenne styles (Nagy, 1994). Note the two Thunderbird-type motifs attached to the shield.*

attempts to introduce polished metal shields to the Blackfeet,[48] and they were certainly never adopted by any other equestrian tribes. Very elaborate and highly symbolic shield designs were a characteristic of some Apache, as well as Pueblo, groups (p.303).[49] Western Apache shields are described as imbued with great protective and concealing powers and could only be made by men with knowledge of the appropriate 'power'.[50] (See the Symbolic Weapons chapter).

Such elaborate shields were matched on the Plains by the Kiowa and Kiowa Apache and so intrigued the anthropologist, James Mooney, that he attempted (but never completed) a detailed study of Plains Indian Heraldry.[51] For the two tribes, he identified some fifty (painted) shield patterns and recorded that all the warriors carrying shields constituted a close brotherhood, with similar war cries, body paint, and ceremonial taboos and regulations – sentiments which could surely be echoed for most of the warrior fraternities throughout North America from time immemorial.

Right: *White Horse, a noted Kiowa chief and war leader, photographed shortly before his death in 1892. He holds his famous cow shield which exhibits stylised renderings of the powerful and aggressive longhorn which the Kiowa viewed with awe, valuing it highly as a source of supernatural power. White Horse carried this shield in successful battles against both Navajos and Texans prior to 1875. It was one of the last available shields known to have been used by a prominent Kiowa leader.*

References

1 At first they traded with the Spanish but within a short time fighting broke out, a fleet of some eighty canoes attacking Ponce de León, compelling him to withdraw.
2 The Calusa not only practised human sacrifice of captives on a wholesale scale – both scalping and dismembering their enemies – but were also cannibals. Subsequent further contacts with the French, English, as well as other Spanish expeditions, invariably ended in bloodshed and it took more than two centuries to subdue them, most of the remnants – some three hundred and fifty souls – being removed to Havana.
3 (a) On occasions, such armor was actually adopted by the whites in their warring against hostile tribes. Thus, when fighting Indians in the vicinity of the Chesapeake, Captain John Smith and his companions, at the suggestion of friendly Indians, protected themselves with an efficient form of Massawomek armor which was made of 'small sticks woven betwixt strings of their hempe, but so firmly that no arrow can possibly pierce them' (Chamberlain In Hodge ed., 1907-10. Vol.I: 88). The idea was highly successful and the English 'securely beat back the Salvages from off the plaine without any hurt' (ibid.).
(b) As early as 1540, members of the Coronado expedition also adopted native armor. As Aiton recorded, 'The great majority wore native buckskin suits of armor, cueras de anta, which were much more comfortable on the march and quite effective against Indian weapons' (Aiton, 1939: 558-59).
4 Heidenreich, Trigger ed., 1978: 386.
5 The ivory plate armor of the Inuit and Eskimo peoples was believed by Boas to be an imitation of the iron armor of the Siberian Chukchi and he also commented that other styles of plate armour were of Japanese origin (Boas In Hodge ed., 1907-10. Vol.I: 88).
6 Leather body armor had intercontinental distribution in the Americas. A partially tailored, multilayered buckskin garment in the British Museum (specimen number 1831, 4-16, 18), which was for years labelled as 'Plains Indian' and confounded several experts, was finally identified as from Patagonia (See Taylor, 1999). In style it is very similar to Lewis and Clark's

description for the Shoshone in 1805 – as mentioned in the main text of this volume.
7 Ewers, 1955: 204.
8 Secoy, 1953: 74.
9 This particular shield from the Aleutian Islands is illustrated in Bancroft-Hunt, 1995: 195.
10 Teit, 1930: 117.
11 ibid.
12 The Huron, a very powerful tribe at the time, were first described by Jacques Cartier when he wintered at their village of Stadacona on the St. Lawrence River in 1535.
13 Hough, 1893: 631.
14 The Blackfeet alliance (which later included the Sarcee and Gros Ventre) with the Piegan at the forefront, entered the region of present-day Alberta and Montana in the mid-nineteenth century (Lewis, 1942: 13).
15 (a) Keyser, 1975: 213.
(b) The Blackfeet move to the Northern Plains was partially due to pressure from the gun-armed Cree to their east and, no doubt, to the possibility of obtaining horses from the western tribes.
16 Loendorf and Conner, 1993: 222.
17 McCoy, 1984: 5.
18 Hammond and Ray, 1953: 841.
19 Hotz, 1970: Plate 6.
20 Wissler (1910) and Lowie (1935).
21 I have considered the aspect of lunar and sky power designs on shields in an article published in *Patrick Moore's Year Book* (2001) *of Astronomy* (In Press). Additionally, the scholar Mike Cowdrey has considered some Crow shield designs and their lunar connections (Cowdrey, 1995 and personal correspondence).
22 Secoy, 1953: 35.
23 ibid.
24 ibid.
25 ibid.
26 Robarchek, Owsley and Jantz eds., 1994: 311.
27 Taylor, 1996: 17.
28 Bradley, 1923: 286.
29 Ewers, 1955: 207.
30 Lowie, 1908: 208.
31 Marquis, 1928: 149.

32 Secoy, 1953: 68.
33 Sturtevant and Taylor, 1991: 236.
34 Secoy, 1953: 65.
35 ibid: 66.
36 At the end of a complex and roundabout route, in 1493, Columbus finally brought the horse back to the Americas. It was now something of a changed animal; by good management and selective breeding, it was at least twice the size of the ancient wild horse, last seen in North America more than ten thousand years ago. It was largely the Spanish stock-raising settlements of the Southwest which became a source of horses to the Southern Plains tribes. By the early 1700s, a combination of trade, raids, and the wild horse herds became the major source of horses for the Southern Plains tribes, notably the Comanche, who traded them to their kinsmen, the Shoshone.
37 Secoy, 1953: 74.
38 (a) Thus, some types of Spanish horse armor consisted of heavy leather covers, not only for the entire body of the horse but also extending to cover the head and with apertures cut for the eyes. The overall style is reminiscent of the description by Lewis and Clark for the Shoshone (see main text).
(b) The Segesser I and Segesser II paintings, now in the Palace of the Governors in Santa Fe and which were discovered in Switzerland in 1945 and subsequently researched by the late Swiss scholar Gottfried Hotz, show depictions of this style of horse armour (Hotz, 1970: particularly Plates 5 and 6).
39 Lewis and Clark, Coues ed., 1893. Vol. 2: 561.
40 Taylor, 1944 (b): 123.
41 Taylor, 1995: 39-49.
42 See Taylor, 1994 (b): pp.17 and 219.
43 Berlandier, Ewers ed., 1969: Plate 3.
44 Pfefferkorn, 1949: 291.
45 Wallace and Hoebel, 1952: 106.
46 Catlin, 1926: 271.
47 ibid: 271-72.
48 Ewers, 1955: 203.
49 Wright, 1976 and 1992: 44-51.
50 Ferg, 1987: 140.
51 McCoy, 1995: 64-71.

'In all of these conceptions we find less appeal for the direct destruction of enemies than for a shielding protection to enable the man himself to be the destructive agent.'[1]

SYMBOLIC WEAPONS

INTERTRIBAL CONFLICT, extending over hundreds if not thousands of years, had been a way of life for the American Indian.[2] The closing of the frontier, however, in the late nineteenth century all but saw the end of both defensive and aggressive warfare.

The ordinary physical training of young men – and occasionally women – fitted them to endure the demands and hardships of the war trail and from the commencement of joining a war-party, the individual was obliged to discipline himself and to accept the various duties given by the leader. Only when the war-party was disbanded were these obligations considered fulfilled.

In most cultural areas, rank was gained by an individual's achievements and these were moderated by a complex system of ceremonials conducted by respected officials and society leaders. For example, war honors,

Right: *Choctaw ball game. Referred to as 'Ish ta boli', the game was described as 'The Little Brother of War' - many pre- and after- game ceremonials resembling those used on the warpath. George Caitlin, who painted this scene in 1834, recorded that there were 'almost superhuman struggles for the ball'.*

Left: *This pair of Magic Horns was worn by a Northern Cheyenne warrior in both the Battle of the Big Bend of the Rosebud, 17 June 1876, and in the Custer Battle on the Little Bighorn River, 25 June 1876. The horns were devised by the medicine men of the tribe and a warrior wearing a pair of these was believed to be bulletproof.*

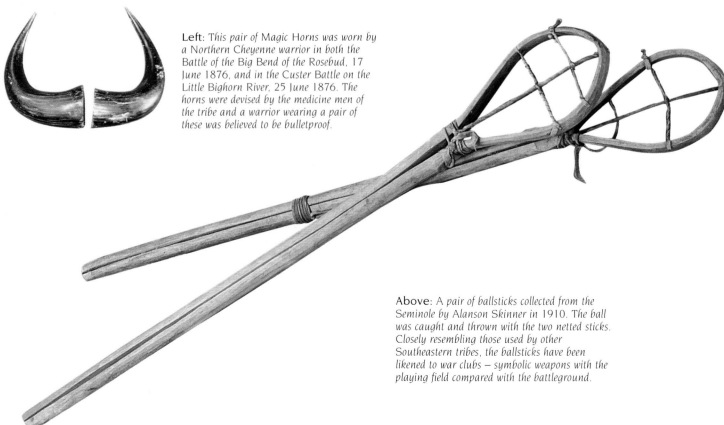

Above: *A pair of ballsticks collected from the Seminole by Alanson Skinner in 1910. The ball was caught and thrown with the two netted sticks. Closely resembling those used by other Southeastern tribes, the ballsticks have been likened to war clubs – symbolic weapons with the playing field compared with the battleground.*

Above: *Sioux protective symbols, circa 1850. The man on horseback carries a long-stemmed pipe which identifies him as the leader of the war-party depicted. The evocation of the bravery of the crane, the speed of a centipede, and the death-dealing power of lightning are illustrated by the motifs on the warriors head and shield and the tail of the horse.*

Right: *An appeal to bear-power; a Blackfeet medicine man (1832) attempting to save the life of a wounded warrior. The great strength and tenacity of the bear – desirable qualities of any warrior – were widely recognized throughout North America.*

nature of insignia, rank, and status were sanctioned by the society in which the individual lived. At that time, war honors were public tokens of an individual's courage and ability. They were regarded as important credentials when considering that person's ability to perform a particular duty or hold a position of service or responsibility.[3]

Society ethos, relative to war, extended far beyond individuals. Thus, amongst such tribes as the Osage and the Omaha, there was a special ceremonial – the Wate'gictu, 'the gathering together of facts accomplished', where war deeds were solemnized.[4] Keepers of the four Packs Sacred to War, reminded the men to state the truth, for the bird messengers contained within the packs (see p.311), would report their deeds to Thunder, the God of War. For each of the honors he was to claim, and hence don the accepted insignia, a warrior painted a small red stick which, when called upon to recite his deed before the assembled tribal members, was held above the Pack of War. At a given signal, he dropped the stick into the pack; if the deed had been disputed or the stick fell to the ground, it was believed that the man had not spoken honestly and 'the man lost the honor he had sought to gain'.[5]

The Keepers of the Sacred War Pack were themselves distinctively identified by elaborate tattooing, part of which made reference to the strength of the enemy who had been killed. Symbolically, their unexpended warrior days accrued to the War Pack Keeper (see also p.311).

Such elaborate tattooing signified rank, status, achievement, and power, and was an ancient and widespread custom used throughout North America.[6] Less permanent, often more personal, but still making powerful symbolic statements (particularly relating to warfare and often emphasizing

protective symbolism), was the use of body and face paint. The use of symbols of protection and power in the form of painting was, in the case of the Plains Indians, extended to their horses. There is some evidence to suggest that the concept was extended to the embellishment of canoes by the Woodland and Northwest Coast tribes.[7]

Societal involvement matters relating to war extended to many tribes. For example, both the Iroquois and the Pawnee – more than a thousand miles to the west of the Iroquoian territory – subjected unfortunate captives to a number of horrendous ordeals[8] and, in the Pueblos of the Southwest, extensive religious rituals relating to departure on the warpath came under a complex and authoritative priesthood which was largely tribally elected.[9] Little wonder then that without the obligations of warfare and the associated ritual, ceremonial, and society organization which went with it, most tribes found themselves in an anomic state – the old values no longer had any meaning and many of the conditions necessary for self-

Below: *A Crow war-pipe dating from the mid-nineteenth century. The pipe was smoked in ceremonial before battle as an appeal to the higher powers for success and protection.*

fulfilment and the attainment of happiness were no longer present.

The war game

The losses accrued with the elimination of warfare also extended to the tangible manifestations of symbols of power, status, protection and achievement, which were so much the fabric of American Indian society. Their original meaning and values were largely lost and adjustments were made to accommodate the imposed changes. In the case of the Crow, where symbols of war achievement were no less important than with other Plains Indians, the cessation of intertribal warfare demanded that a new way had to be found to give young men the right to display the attainment of some type of warlike success; the solution was ingenious. In pre-reservation days, a warrior who had taken a gun from the enemy, or struck an enemy first, was entitled to wear a warshirt. Striking an enemy, considered the most important of the four major coups also, according to Crow informants, entitled the shirt-wearer to attach to the shirt, four quilled or beaded bands, one each over the shoulders and down the arms of the buckskin garment. Even as late as 1927, no Crow would publicly wear such a shirt unless he was entitled to it – it was a great distinction to be so adorned.

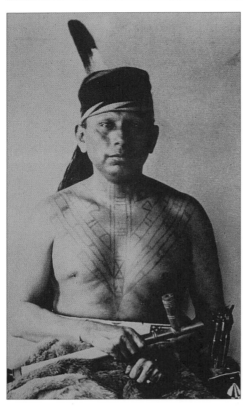

Left: *Star That Travels, Osage, 1897. He is tattooed with the 'mark of honor', designating him as the Keeper of the Pack of War. The central tattoo represents a stone knife.*

Right: *Examples of face painting, Ojibwa, circa 1880. A wide range of face and body painting was used throughout North America in both war and peace ceremonial, much being distinctive to a particular occasion. Some, however, was more personal, the use and meaning acquired in a vision or vivid dream.*

The new, largely imposed, conditions were accommodated by warrior consensus and a new way was found 'to give the ambitious youth the right to wear these shirts'.[10] Thus, a number of young Crows, led by an older experienced man, offered a visiting Indian of a different tribe valuable gifts to persuade him to act as an enemy. The enemy, riding a good horse, then rode out from camp in the evening. Before dawn of the next day the Crows started on his trail and the individual who first managed to undertake and strike the first coup was then entitled to display the honors which were formerly earned by this act in actual combat. There was, it seems, little 'watering down' of the obligations because four times, and on different occasions, it was necessary for the same young Crow to 'strike the first coup, which is usually done by hitting the "enemy" lightly with a stick or with the hand, before he is entitled to wear the decorated war shirt. This is one reason why they are valued very highly by the Crows...'.[11]

Below: *There were a number of impressive shrines in the mountain regions of Zuni territory. This one, photographed in 1893, shows the carved wooden effigies of the Elder God of War which were located in the Twin Mountains, near the Peublo of Zuni in present-day New Mexico.*

The Little Brother of War

The change in tactics, while retaining much of the earlier symbolic war concepts as described for the Crow, was far from unique and, in fact, had parallels amongst the League of the Iroquois and other tribes, centuries earlier, in the ball game lacrosse. Played with a small ball of deerskin stuffed with moss or hair, or with a wooden ball, together with one or two netted rackets somewhat resembling tennis rackets (see p.308), lacrosse was the favorite athletic game of most, if not all, the eastern tribes from the Hudson Bay to the gulf of Mexico.[12] The game could be, and often was, played on an almost tribal scale, with two settlements playing against each other and up to hundreds on each side. High stakes were wagered on the outcome.

As early as the 1630s, white missionaries such as the French Jesuit priest, Father François Joseph Le Mercier, reported on the obsession of the Huron with lacrosse – not only the game itself, but also its associated rituals and ceremonials, as well as the use of

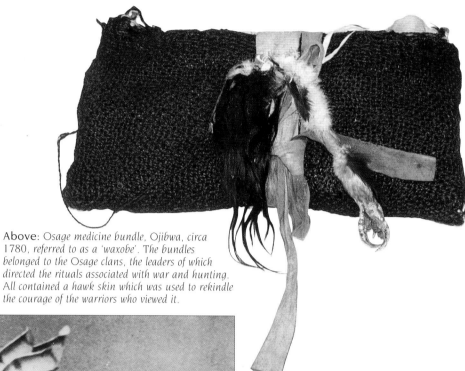

Above: *Osage medicine bundle, Ojibwa, circa 1780, referred to as a 'waxobe'. The bundles belonged to the Osage clans, the leaders of which directed the rituals associated with war and hunting. All contained a hawk skin which was used to rekindle the courage of the warriors who viewed it.*

Left and below: *Various decorated hats made of buckskin were worn by men of the Southwestern tribes; the two examples shown here were collected from the Navajo. The upper is embelished with owl feathers and abalone shells and the lower, which is of black buckskin, has two eagle feathers attached. The man is wearing a typical Western Apache hat of the type used in battle.*

charms and talismans, some in the form of miniature lacrosse sticks. Obtained in dreams or ritual, these could be used to ensure success against the opposing team. The parallels to warfare are obvious; exhausting dance and song, fasting, and finally the contest itself where the scoring posts could be miles apart, all point to the fact that many Southeastern tribes recognized that pent-up energies of virile young men needed demanding expenditure!

The ethos of the game was reinforced by the teachings of the distinguished prophet, Handsome Lake, a half brother of the Seneca, Chief Cornplanter. In the early summer of 1799, Handsome Lake experienced the first of a series of visions in which he received instructions from the Creator regarding future religious obligations of his people. He subsequently founded the Longhouse religion amongst the Iroquois. Its teachings expressly forbade violence and warfare and many former rituals connected with the warpath were forbidden.

Recent research reveals the similarities between lacrosse and warfare, almost certainly enhanced with the cessation of intertribal conflict and influence of Handsome Lake's teachings. Thus, in lacrosse, participants enter a world of 'belief and magic', where players sewed inchworms into the innards of lacrosse balls and medicine men gazed at miniature lacrosse sticks... to predict future events... bits of bat wings were twisted into a stick's netting... famous players were (and still are) buried with their sticks'.[13] Likewise, the similarities between Ojibwa and Iroquois war clubs and elaborate versions of lacrosse sticks – for example, a clasped hand and dog image carved on an ancient Cayuga lacrosse stick – all point to an underlying ethos of war. 'In the game we continue to wage war on our enemies' – a sort of secret emblem [which reinforced] the warfare/lacrosse analogy.[14]

Thus, a lacrosse stick, similar in shape to a drumstick and war club, and at times elaborately decorated to emphasize the relationship, was a symbolic weapon which signified the hidden ritual between game, music, and warfare: the playing field was analogous to the battlefield. These conclusions are reinforced by a consideration of the way the Southeastern tribes referred to lacrosse – 'brother to war' or the 'little brother of war'.[15]

War-pipes and war whistles

The earliest white travelers throughout North America repeatedly made reference to the custom of 'fumigation of a peculiar kind'; it was a practice not easily understood by Europeans. In all important undertakings – as a compliment to visitors, before or during ceremonials, in the vision quest, prior to hunting or war – the pipe was smoked by all those present. When Cortés traveled through the Southwest in 1540-42, he was received with honor and 'met' by persons carrying vessels with lighted coals to fumigate him.[16] In this region, amongst such tribes as the Hopi – but certainly not unique to them – smoke was always offered during ceremonials to the sacred powers; the pipe was handled with great reverence and care, an assistant attending the leader, ceremonial lighting of the pipe, transfer in a set manner and offerings to the world quarters. Because of the remarkable similarity in the smoking customs throughout North America, it was recognized early on that the practice was of great antiquity and important to all undertakings, not least war.[17]

Pipe styles varied considerably. Amongst the Iroquois, a number were of wood and elaborately carved,[18] whilst those of many of the Plains tribes were of catlinite or black steatite.[19] Most commonly used, particularly in the east, was soapstone, the bowls frequently elaborately carved, the long stems

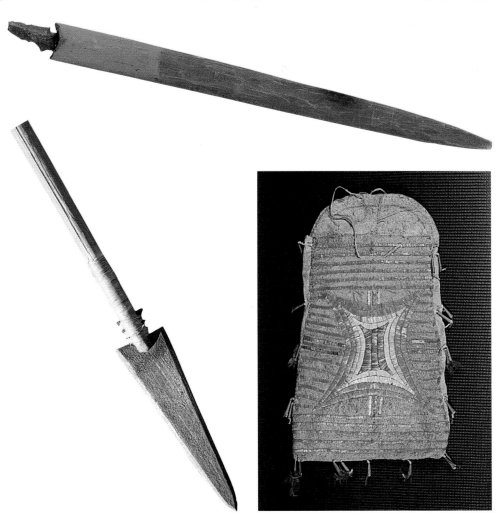

Top left: A Diegueno shaman's wand which was used to 'throw pain' into a tribal enemy. The wooden handle has a stone projectile point and is believed to date from before 1500 BC. The Diegueno were a Yuman linguistic group of Southern California.

Far left: Details of an arrow, probably Mandan, circa 1830. The iron blade is sharp-edged and bound into the shaft with sinew, producing a formidable missile. The power of lightning is evoked by a channel engraved on the shaft.

Left: The spider web symbol worked in porcupine quills on a Lakota bag dating from circa 1880. Such designs were said by the Lakota to possess great protective power, embodying the observed fact that a spider's web is not destroyed by arrows or bullets – they simply pass through it, leaving only a hole.

understood... even in the heat and noise... where all are barking and yelling... the commands of their leader |would still be heard|'.[25] Similar descriptions of the use of the war whistle in battle have been made by other observers.[26]

The war whistle, generally made from an eagle wing bone, however, had a deeper symbolic meaning on the battlefield. In 1807, whilst mapping for the North West Company and traveling to the Upper Columbia and into present-day Idaho, the distinguished explorer, David Thompson, 'the Astronomer', observed of his Indian companions: 'Before daylight I set off with five Indians... This caused a halt, as we were surrounded and began to suspect that the enemy had planned to cut us off. The Indians put on their war-caps, uttering some few words which I could

Below: (Left) Nesouaquoit or 'The Bear in the Forks of a Tree', a Fox chief, circa 1840 in a poncho of bearskin. Whole skins were used to signify the powers of the animal, in this case the prowess of a grizzly. (Right) The Seminole chief Osceola (1833). Guns were adopted early by the tribes of eastern North America, some of whom thought at first that they possessed thunder powers.

embellished with quillwork, hair, and feathers.[20] Associated pipe or tobacco bags were, particularly in early days, of complete otter or beaver pelts; later, they were of buckskin, quilled, or beaded.

Most widely distributed was the 'straight pipe', a simple tube of clay, chlorite, steatite, catlinite, or bone.[21] Of ancient origin, it was gradually replaced by the more elaborate styles but still retained in ceremonial and certainly, with a number of the Plains tribes, used on the war trail – hence the term 'war-pipe'. Of the war-pipe, the German scientist, Maximilian, commented in 1833: 'The Indians on the Upper Missouri have another kind of tobacco pipe, the bowl of which is in the same line as the tube, and which they use only on their warlike expeditions. As the aperture of the pipe is more inclined downwards than usual, the fire can never be seen, so as to betray the smoker, who lies on the ground, and holds the pipe on one side.'[22]

More specifically, Crow war leaders' medicine bundles contained tubular or straight pipes, either of catlinite or blackened stone, some accompanied with war effigies. Prior to battle, the consecrated pipe was ceremonially smoked, rituals performed, the effigies unwrapped, and prayers made to the higher powers to evoke help and ensure success of the expedition. In this context, the pipe was a symbolic weapon. Such sentiments and ceremonials were widely recognized and used throughout North America from time immemorial.[23]

Of the war whistle, George Catlin noted that this was made of bone, ornamented with porcupine quills, and carried by the leader into battle, 'suspended generally from his neck, and worn under his dress'.[24] Its practical use in battle was emphasized: when blown it was a sound that was 'distinctly heard and

Right: *A Lakota Ghost Dance shirt, circa 1890. Such garments were generally made of muslin but sinew sewn; they were elaborately painted with symbols which appealed to the higher powers for protection. The blue is symbolic of 'Taku Skan-skan', the energy or moving force of the Lakota universe. Motifs representing hail and lightning evoke the thunder powers.*

not hear distinctly, and then began to whistle with a small bone instrument which they hung around their necks for that purpose'.[27]

Years later, the anthropologist, Clark Wissler, drew attention to the fact that amongst all the Indians of the Plains, the thunder is usually associated with military exploits. Thunder was regarded as a bird – usually symbolized as an eagle. Eagle bone whistles generally had a zigzag line, usually in red, scratched down the sides (as representative of thunder power), and attached feathers of the yellow-winged woodpecker, a creature considered to be an associate of the Thunderbird.[28] The shrill tones from the whistle were considered to symbolize the cry of the eagle as representative of the Thunderbird and, as Wissler put it, 'In battle, or sometimes in stress of great trial, they are sounded to call up the power of the thunder to rescue the unfortunate one'.[29] Thus, attack or retreat in battle, the shrill of the eagle bone whistle[30] was more than a mere mechanical action – it was also a call to the higher powers for help and protection to overcome the enemy.

Thunderbird concepts and images were, as with the pipe, widely used throughout North America. For example, as well as with the Plains Indians, tribes of the Northwest Coast did magnificent renderings in wood, tattoos, and paintings of this mystical creature (see p.316) and the Eastern Woodland people from the Winnebago to the Iroquois embellished regalia – particularly bags and pouches – with motifs of the Thunderbird in quill or beadwork. Often associated with underwater mythical beings, much of the symbolic ethos was associated with warlike activities and an appeal to the supernaturals for help and protection.[31]

Below: *Pictograph of a Lakota warrior in battle drawn by Little Big Man. This possibly depicts the war leader, Crazy Horse, wearing a warshirt which is embellished with eagle feathers and lightning symbols - a sign of his rank and an appeal to the thnder for aid in overcoming the enemy.*

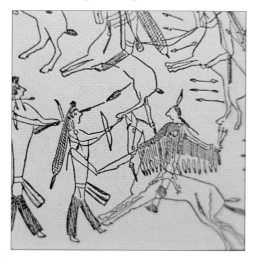

Above: *'Testing the powers of the Ghost shirt.' The use of symbols for spiritual protection is nowhere better illustrated than by the painted and embellished garments once worn tribes such as the Sioux and Arapaho when the Ghost Dance religion swept the Plains in the late nineteenth century.*

War shrines and war packs

Many indigenous settlements throughout North America had a plaza for gatherings, most of which contained a central shrine or pole, as symbolic of village unity. The concept was obviously ancient – watercolors produced in 1585 by the Englishman, John White, of the 'towns' of Secoton and Pomeiooc of the North Carolina Algonquians, show these features.[32] Westward, to tribes such as the Mandan on the Missouri River, there are very similar descriptions and illustrations, particularly in the 1830s, of a central and highly symbolic shrine.[33]

Likewise, in the Southwest – although shrines were generally in more secluded places – such as with the Zuni[34] where the War Gods are important deities and are the patrons of the Bow Priest cult whose duty it is to keep the scalps taken in war and the associated war fetishes.[35] Complex ceremonials associated with such Gods ensured protection from evil forces. A similar ethos permeated through the Pueblos and camps of the Southwest in a complexity of ritual and ceremonial and there were strong associations with Thunder and Sky powers (such as the Morning Star) – religious concepts associated with war which had many parallels in other cultural areas.[36]

Amongst one of the best descriptions of the need of a community unity by such shrines has come from the classic studies of the Omaha and Ponca tribes by Alice Fletcher and Francis La Flesche.[37] Here, both the sacred

Above: *A painted shield cover circa 1850. Although unidentified, it is probably Cheyenne. The horns appear to be giving protection from missiles in flight toward the wearer.*

Above: *Pictograph, probably Cheyenne, collected by the Englishman William Blackmore on the Platte River in 1874. The wounded warrior on the left carries a bow-spear and is wearing a buffalo horn headdress. 'Buffalo Power' was particularly important in Cheyenne religion and protective symbolism.*

Below: *A crow shield dating from about 1840. The desire to utilize the protective powers of the bear is almost certainly the inspiration for the dominant red image painted on this shield. There are no missiles below the outstretched paw, suggesting protection of the vulnerable young.*

pole and cedar pole had anciently served for aeons as a symbol of provider, protector, and source of spiritual power to the people. The warlike association was underlined by a close link with the Tent of War, War Packs and, as mentioned earlier, the tattooing of the honorary keeper.[38]

The poles were closely associated with the thunder, ancient mythology making reference to the Thunderbirds as envoys of the Thunder Gods and endowing them with supernatural powers. 'As a result', the Legend says, 'the people began to pray to the Pole for courage and for trophies in war and their prayers were answered'.[39]

Te'xi ehe gthito^{n}ba
Wagthito^{n}bi, wagthito^{n}bi, te'xi ehe gthito^{n}ba
(Their Sacred, Sacred Pole,
With reverent hands, I say, they touch the Sacred Pole before thee)
(PART RITUAL SONG. OMAHA)[40]

The gun

As discussed, the power of the thunder and lightning was viewed with awe in most cultural areas; symbols of Thunderbird, lightning, and associated spirits such as the underwater monsters were replete on much religious and military regalia and accoutrements. Little wonder that the gun had great impact on those tribes who first encountered its use. The defeat of the Mohawk in 1609 at Ticonderoga by a combined force of Huron, Montagnais, and Ottawa (with the help of arquebus-armed French under Samuel de Champlain) forcibly demonstrated the practical advantages of gunpowder over native weaponry. But it was more than this: there is good evidence which suggests that this curious hollow rod, which made such a thunderous noise when a little lever was pulled and which hurled a missile so swiftly that it was impossible to even see it fly (and caused such havoc in its wake), inspired terror and awe in the minds of most of the Indian people. As Nicholas Perrot observed in the late 1600s, the 'guns so

Left: *Peace medal with image of Andrew Jackson, President of the United States. Made of bronze and generally 4in (10cm) in diameter, the medals were given to prominent leaders, as a symbol of the peace and friendship desired by government officials in their dealings with, in the main, Woodland, Prairie, and Plains tribes. The peace medal and the American flag were coveted and adopted by a number of tribes to demonstrate peaceful intentions and symbolically protect the community. As with many 'spiritual powers', they were not always successful.*

the use of these weapons, to medicine power rather than their abilities as marksmen. Thus, when the French trader, François Larocque, met a party of well armed Crow Indians in the summer of 1805, their lack of success with their guns was attributed by the chief to the fact that 'someone had thrown bad medicine on our guns and that if he could know him he would surely die'.[44]

Some thirty years later Maximilian, on visiting the Mandan and recording their complex and rich ceremonials and culture, was told of a Mandan ceremonial for consecrating firearms. There is little doubt that gun power was viewed as strong 'medicine' and, certainly in early days, endowed with great spiritual offensive and defensive powers.

Animal protective powers

The likes of the regenerative powers of the apparently lifeless and tiny cocoon, the swift and mysterious dragonfly, the fragile spider web, the flight of the kingfisher to the swift and resilient pronghorn, the wise and powerful buffalo, and awesome bear – to name but a few – were woven into religious and military symbolism of the North American Indian. Special regalia and accoutrements such as buffalo horn and eagle

Below: *An early sketch (circa 1800) showing a returning Iroquois war-party carrying scalps and escorting a prisoner. The leader has two scalps on the staff, the one with longer hair indicating a male, the shorter hair, a female. The prisoner has a gourd rattle tied to his arm which would betray him should he try to escape. This prisoner is constrained by cords although some prisoner 'ties' merely symbolized a subservient enemy.*

Above: *Haida rendering of a double Thunderbird. Symbolism associated with this mythical creature occurred in most of the cultural areas in North America. Generally viewed as a giant bird, the flapping of its wings produced the thunder and the flashing of its eyes, the lightning; the potential destructive power was held in awe. Impressive, often abstract depictions of the Thunderbird were, as shown here, produced by the tribes of the Northwest Coast, being indicative of rapport with this sky power.*

which was out of all proportion to its effectiveness as a lethal instrument'.[43]

Of interest is that even after the tribes owned a considerable number of guns, some of them attributed their success or failure in

astonished' the Indians of the Lake Superior region that they declared 'there was a spirit within the gun, which caused the loud noise made when it was fired'.[41] Later, he reported that when the Sioux visited the Ottawa and witnessed their firing of some guns, the report of these weapons so terrified the Sioux that they said it was the thunder or the lightning of which the Ottawas had made themselves master 'in order to exterminate whomsoever they would'.[42] Other references in the literature describe the panic created when guns were used and often, it seems, it was the noise and smoke which did more harm than the bullets. As the ethnologist John C. Ewers observed, 'Indians gained a respect for the old muzzle-loading, smoothbore trade musket

PRISONERS OF THE IROQUOIS

feather headdresses (see p.312), decoration with horsehair and plumes and pelts of various creatures, as well as elaborate shirts and mantles, evoked and appealed to these powers. For example, an early nineteenth century deerskin headdress – complete with ears and antlers – was described at the time of collections in the Great Lakes region as associated with shamanistic performance relating to hunting and warfare; the iconographic features 'are the upper world motif of paired opposed double hooks and the red disk with a serrated edge... probably a representation of the sun manito'.[45] Almost a century later, similar powers were being evoked with the complex designs on the so-called Ghost Dance shirts (see p.314).

Nowhere are many of these concepts better illustrated than in the widely distributed bear symbolism. The strength, ferocity, and great bravery of the bear, particularly the grizzly, were desired qualities of a warrior. Stylized images, often the paw, appear on costume and accoutrements such as on the regalia of Nesouaquoit (see p.313), a high-ranking Fox (Prairie) chief who belonged to the Bear Society of his tribe. Bear paws, the complete hide, and often bear claws all evoke or make references to the powers of this awesome animal.[46]

Likewise, the Plains Indians evoked bear power[47] for at least two purposes, treating the incapacitated and as war medicine. The artist, George Catlin, in the summer of 1832 near Fort Union on the Upper Missouri, depicted a Blackfeet Bear Medicine man performing rites over a wounded man (see p.309).[48] Similar rituals were widely used by the Plains Indians which also extended into the Subarctic region and beyond.[49] Incised images of bear figures and bear tracks on widely scattered sites, both in the Rocky Mountains on the Great Plains and into the Woodlands region, suggest that the concepts of bear power were very widespread and ancient. One such petroglyph, it has been suggested, depicts the bestowal of supernatural power 'upon a man by a bear'.[50] In addition, necklaces of bear claws, as well as renderings of bear images in tipis, war clubs, in quillwork and beadwork, and the use of a bear jaw for the handle of a highly coveted stabber knife, all attest to the desire of Plains Indians to acquire bear powers.[51]

The supernatural protective power of the bear is nowhere more emphasized than on a shield (see p.315) collected prior to 1841, from an Upper Missouri tribe (possibly Crow). Here, a large paw, painted in red and outlined in brown, dominates the design; it appears to be warding off enemy fire and protecting smaller bears – perhaps its offspring. These were situations often faced by the Plains warrior, particularly in the period of the Indian-White confrontation where warfare and attacks against village communities were a stark reality. Warriors not only needed to simply fight the enemy, but had also to protect their wives and children; under such circumstances, as in most cultural areas for time immemorial, a man needed to evoke additional spiritual help from the higher powers!

References

1 Wissler, 1907:53.
2 See Owsley and Jantz, eds., 1994: particularly Chapter 24: 27-30.
3 Leading a war-party was a big responsibility and even some of the best warriors cracked under the strain. Thus, one Kiowa war-party leader, *Tokuléidl*, who started out with a small company of about ten men, is reported to have 'apparently lapsed into some type of schizophrenic condition, obsessed with the delusion that all of his men were horses. On one day he stopped the party, lined up the warriors and examined the teeth of each man. Another day he forced all of them to bray in chorus threatening to shoot any man who did not bray or obey him or who deserted. The upshot was that the party was ambushed and practically exterminated' (Mishkin, 1940: 33).
4 Fletcher and La Flesche, 1911: 434.
5 ibid: 437.
6 (a) This is well illustrated in the case of the tribes of the Northwest Coast. Here, tattooing was practised by the higher classes being heraldic, totemic and, on occasions, personal crests of the wearers (see Taylor, 1997: 61 for illustrations of the Haida and a further discussion).
   (b) Amongst the Omaha, a warrior who had won war honors in battles was entitled to the privilege of tattooing his body or that of his wife or daughter, as a mark of distinction. The tattooing was done by a man who was expert in the rituals connected with the ceremony and the needles used had the rattles of the rattlesnake attached (see Fletcher and La Flesche, 1911: 221).
   (c) For an excellent discussion relating to tattooing practices of the Cree and other northern tribes, see Light, 1972.
7 (a) See Sturtevant and Taylor, 1991: 112 and 170.
   (b) See also Adney and Chapelle, 1964: in particular the reference to a Passamaquoddy war canoe motif (p.82).
8 (a) Sturtevant and Taylor, 1991: 236 (Iroquois) and Taylor, 1994 (b): 67-74 (Pawnee).
   (b) See also Seaver, 1982: 103-15.
9 See, for example, Hoebel, Ortiz, ed., 1979: 414 (Zia Pueblo) and Ladd, Ortiz ed., 1979: 488 (Zuni) for reference to the place of the religious leaders in war matters.
10 Wildschut, Ewers ed., 1960: 38.
11 ibid.
12 Culin refers to Lacrosse as Racket and emphasizes that it was mainly a man's game. Shinny, he reports, was 'especially a woman's game' and it was 'frequently referred to in the myths' (Culin, 1907: 562 and 626-17).
13 Vennum, Jr., 1994: xv.
14 ibid: xiv.
15 ibid: 213.
16 McGuire in Hodge ed., Vol. 2, 1910: 603.
17 McGuire emphasizes that 'Every individual engaging in war, hunting, fishing, or husbandry... made

supplication to the gods by means of smoke, which was believed to bring good and to arrest evil [and] to give protection from enemies...' (McGuire in ibid: 604).
18 King, 1977: in particular plates 1-14.
19 For a discussion of the stone, catlinite, see Catlin, 1926, Vol.II: 233-34 and for black steatite, see Ewers, 1963: 45 who refers to the best type of 'calcareous shale'. This was located at Pipestone Cliff on the south side of the Two Medicine River, about 1½ miles (2.4km.) below its junction with Badger Creek in present-day Montana.
20 In 1540, Alarcon found the Indians on the lower Colorado River, employing 'small reeds for making perfume' and likened them to 'the Indian *tobagos* of New Spain' (McGuire in Hodge ed., Vol. 2, 1910: 603).
21 A Blackfeet drawing of a straight pipe is reproduced in Wissler, 1912: 170-71). This had been taken from a Beaver Bundle of ancient origin. Straight pipes, according to Ewers' informant, Green-Grass-Bull, were considered 'very holy object[s]' and were used in the oath of swearing 'by the pipe'. A straight pipe specifically associated with war medicine and with the Blackfeet Catcher's Society Pipe Bundle, has also been documented by Ewers (1963: 36-37).
22 Maximilian in ibid: 38.
23 The complexities of pipe rituals are well illustrated with the ceremonial manner of smoking the Sacred Pipes during council deliberations of the Omaha Seven Chiefs Society (Fletcher and La Flesche, 1911: 207-09).
24 Catlin, 1926, Vol. I: 273.
25 ibid.
26 The use of the war whistle by the Comanche and Cheyenne is discussed by Ewers (Berlandier, Ewers, ed., 1969: 176).
27 Thompson in Wissler, 1907: 47.
28 Wissler reports that his Dakota informants said that when a storm was approaching, the yellow-winged woodpecker gave 'a peculiar shrill call not unlike the sound [of the eagle bone war whistle]' (Wissler, 1907: 47).
29 (a) ibid.
   (b) Wissler said that the United States emblem of the eagle with outstretched claws, holding arrows and the lightning, was regarded by the Dakota 'as an appeal on our part to the thunder-bird' and that 'statements to the contrary are usually interpreted as white men's lies to deceive the Indians and to guard the power' (ibid: 48).
30 Berlandier, Ewers ed., 1969: 176.
31 Phillips, 1984: 42-43.
32 Hulton, 1986: Figs. 24 and 35.
33 Such shrines evoked protective symbolism with the Manda. See Taylor, 1996: 66.
34 It was, however, the Deer and Bear clans who performed the public ceremonies for the War Gods (see Ladd, Ortiz, ed., 1979: 488).
35 Acoma mythology makes reference to the weapons of war being given to young warriors by the Sun (see

Parmentier, Ortiz ed., 1979: 615).
36 (a) On a more personal level, Kachina dances were sponsored by the ill person or his family to help in curing (see Stanislawski, 1979: 598).
   (b) See Taylor, 1994(a): 44-45 (Thunder and sky powers of the Plains tribes): ibid: 91 (Sky powers of the Northwest Coast tribes): ibid: 115 (The Arctic).
37 Fletcher and La Flesche, 1911.
38 This also extended to hunting rituals. The ancient Cedar Pole, which was preserved in the Tent of War, stood adjacent to the tent which housed the White Buffalo Hide which was directly associated with buffalo hunting (ibid: 229).
39 (a) ibid.
   (b) The complexities of the ceremonials and mythology relating to the Sacred Pole are recorded in ibid: 245-51.
40 233-34.
41 Ewers, 1967: 38.
42 ibid.
43 ibid.
44 ibid:39.
45 Phillips, 1984: 51.
46 Not all cultural areas, it seems, held the gun in such awe. As Bill Holm has observed, 'Guns came into early use [on the Northwest Coast]. I don't think they were ever rated *wakan*. Most NWC tribes had traditions of a death bringer, which was easily related to the gun, and seemed almost familiar. Vancouver's men shot a seagull on the wing to impress local Puget Sound viewers, who responded with 'poo poo' as if inviting them to do it again! Vancouver found every canoe at the Nimkish village armed with a gun (the chief owned 8 muskets!) and they had never before seen a white man! There are a number of accounts of trading guns...' (BH to CFT, personal correspondence, 18 April 1999).
47 Bear power for the Northeast is nowhere better illustrated than in the photograph of Keokuk and his son, Moses Keokuk (see Sturtevant and Taylor, 1991: 245). Both wear magnificent bear claw necklaces. That of Moses, is now in the National Museum of Denmark, Copenhagen (catalogue number Hc397).
48 George Catlin described this man's costume in great detail (Catlin, 1926. Vol. 1: 46). ewers reported that the Plains Indians who acquired bear power not only used it to treat the sick and wounded, but also as war medicine (Ewers, 1982: 38).
49 Ewers, 1968:
50 Ewers, 1982: 38.
51 The artist, DeCost Smith, reports his conversation with Topompy, chief of the Lemhi Shoshone. Topompy refers to warriors being 'friends with bears' and communication with bears 'in a dream' (Smith, 1943: 120-21). A painted buffalo robe, identified as Sioux, depicts a bear 'as a source of a successful war party leader's power' (Ewers, 1982: 42).

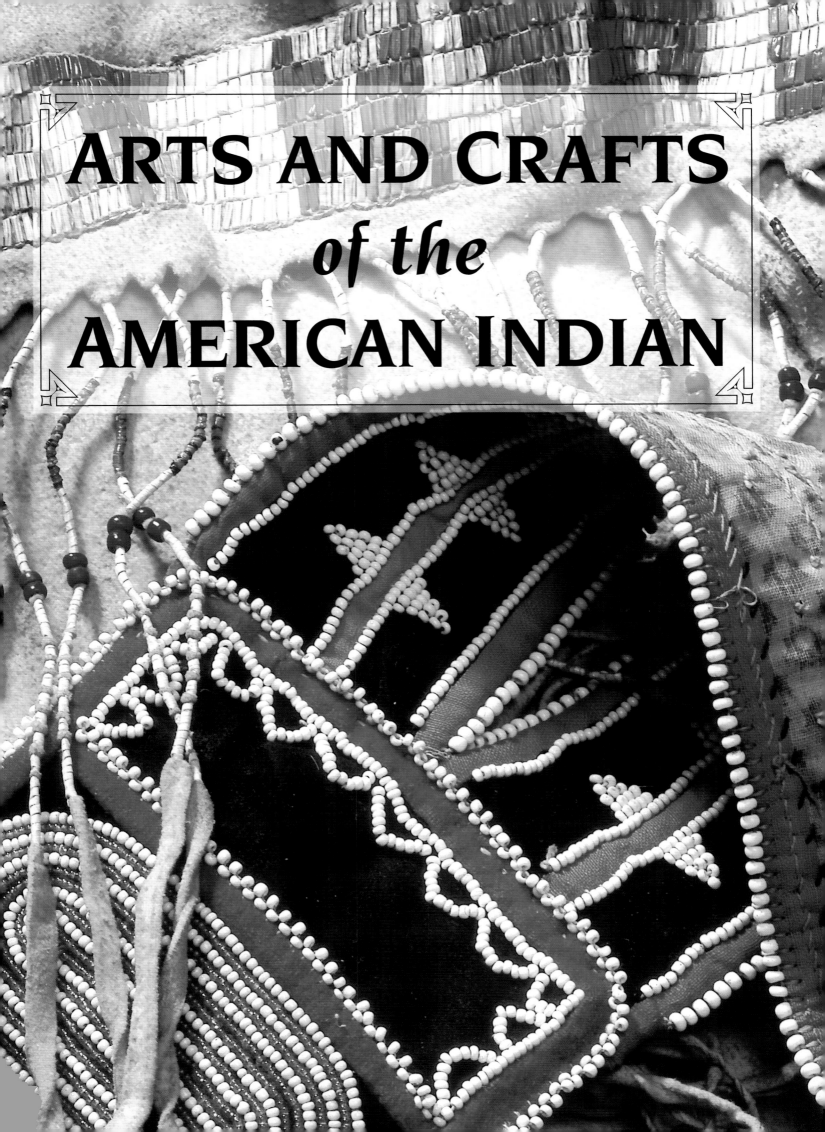

ARTS AND CRAFTS
of the
AMERICAN INDIAN

INTRODUCTION

THE DIVERSIFIED and numerous abilities of the North American Indian are reflected in the great skills in arts and crafts which are the subject of this section. Since, however, in one section it is impossible adequately to cover the wide variety of arts and craft skills practised in the nine cultural areas of North America, the approach here has been to select some of the finest of their work from the Historic Period and, in several instances, to bring it up to the present day. In all cases the attempt has been both to elucidate and illustrate the craft and artistic endeavors of the indigenous people of North America. A combination of inherited skills born of economic, social, and spiritual existence, they illustrate the innate artistry of the Indian and underline the Indian's place as the creator of North America's indigenous folk art – although, as one respected scholar has pointed out, to the individual tribesman 'art for art's sake was incomprehensible'.[1]

Nevertheless, crafts were not limited purely to the material conditions of their lives, techniques being developed so that the esthetic sense was satisfied and the art became ancillary to both ceremonial and social institutions. In all these endeavors, the North American Indian maximized the use of the mineral, animal, and vegetable wealth around him, it being developed and modified to match environmental requirements of the particular culture's area.

Thus, for example, waterproofing and extensive use of animal hides and fur for clothing and transportation were vital for survival to the Inuit, while technically fine baskets, which could be used for winnowing and even carry water, were essential to the lives of the Southwestern tribes, such as the Hopi and Navajo. All this developed over a period of many thousands of years and, in consequence, it should be recognized that the products of their labors which now repose in the museum collections of the world generally represent the best of the arts and crafts of 'The People'. They reflect the efforts of countless generations who by trial and error achieved, by inheritance, an end product which not only satisfied practical and physical needs but often esthetic and spiritual ones as well.

Unfortunately, not all is well-represented in the ethnographical collections, much being destroyed at the instigation of zealous missionaries, such as occurred among the Nez Perce[2] or by brutal army campaigns waged against the Plains tribes. Typical is

Right: *Collecting reeds for mat making was an occupation not only of the Indians of the woodlands, but also of the Plateau. In both areas the mats served various purposes, including both floor and dwelling covering.*

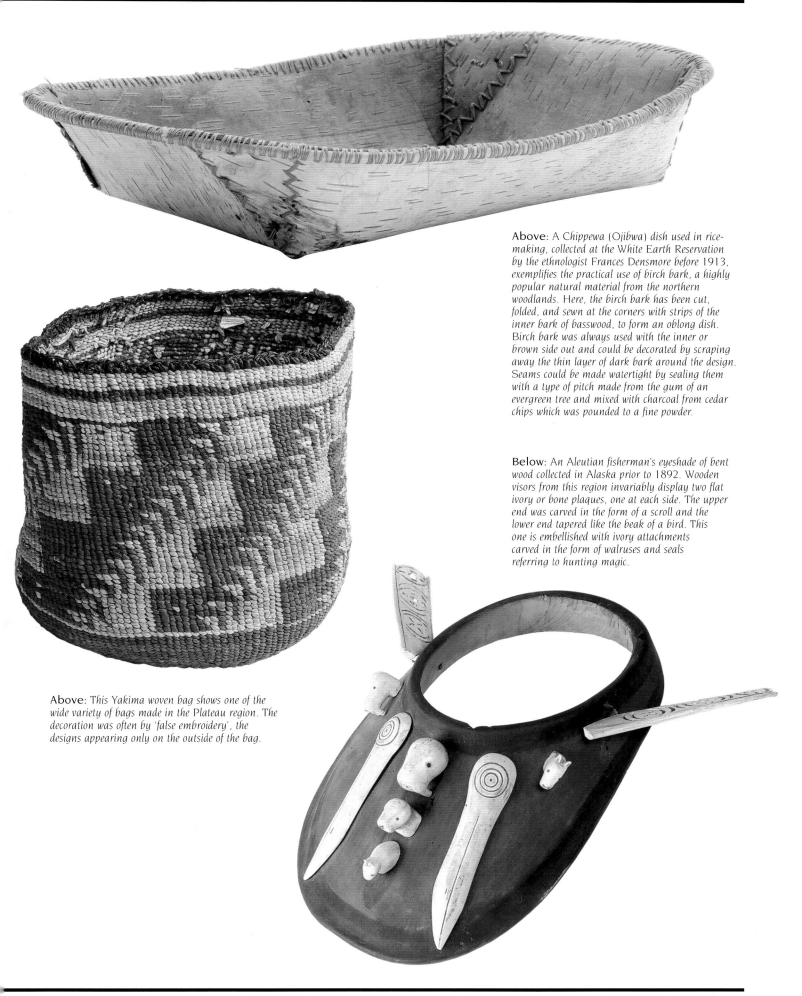

Above: A Chippewa (Ojibwa) dish used in rice-making, collected at the White Earth Reservation by the ethnologist Frances Densmore before 1913, exemplifies the practical use of birch bark, a highly popular natural material from the northern woodlands. Here, the birch bark has been cut, folded, and sewn at the corners with strips of the inner bark of basswood, to form an oblong dish. Birch bark was always used with the inner or brown side out and could be decorated by scraping away the thin layer of dark bark around the design. Seams could be made watertight by sealing them with a type of pitch made from the gum of an evergreen tree and mixed with charcoal from cedar chips which was pounded to a fine powder.

Below: An Aleutian fisherman's eyeshade of bent wood collected in Alaska prior to 1892. Wooden visors from this region invariably display two flat ivory or bone plaques, one at each side. The upper end was carved in the form of a scroll and the lower end tapered like the beak of a bird. This one is embellished with ivory attachments carved in the form of walruses and seals referring to hunting magic.

Above: This Yakima woven bag shows one of the wide variety of bags made in the Plateau region. The decoration was often by 'false embroidery', the designs appearing only on the outside of the bag.

Above: *A Yeibichai Ye'ii dancer of the Navajo, one of the impersonators of the supernatural beings, displays much of Navajo arts and crafts – hard-soled moccasins, wolf mask, featherwork, and silver conchas with turquoise, all typical of the tribe.*

Bourke's report on the aftermath of an attack on Dull Knife's village in the winter of 1876, when the troopers of the 3rd and 4th cavalry 'toiled and burned, wiping off the face of the earth many products of aboriginal taste and industry which would have been gems in the cabinets of museums'.[3]

Right: *A knife sheath collected from the Han, a tribe of the Subarctic Athapaskans. Such sheaths were worn around the neck and hung on the chest. This one is made of heavy, tanned caribou skin embellished with dentalium shells in combination with red, white, and blue trade beads. The dentaliums were very highly prized shells which were first obtained from the Northwest Coast tribes; later, white traders imported large quantities into the Subarctic region where they were used in profusion, adorning the hair, worn as earrings, and used to embellish various items of costume such as shirts, leggings, and mittens.*

Left: *A spruce-root hat made by the Haida of Queen Charlotte Islands in British Columbia, was collected by J. G. Swan at Masset in 1883. Some 2ft (60cm.) in diameter, it is painted with designs in black, red, and blue and displays the crest of the wearer. These hats were generally worn on ceremonial occasions when the family's honors were displayed, consistent with rank and the structure of Haida society. The crown itself is strengthened by an inner wooden framework and leather straps tie under the chin to hold the large hat on the head.*

Nevertheless, much has been saved and reconstructed and by good fortune, amazing 'gems' of sources have from time to time been discovered, such as in the case of Ishi, the sole noble survivor of the Yahi of California. Ishi spent the last five years of his life, from 1911 to 1917, at the Museum of Anthropology of the University of California, where he demonstrated the intricate craft skills of his tribe, all of which were systematically recorded for posterity by the anthropologists, Kroeber and Waterman.[4] It was to the credit of such scientists, who in the late nineteenth century were mindful that dynamic, enviable cultures were fast vanishing in North America, that a program of 'salvage' anthropology was instigated. Thus, august institutions such as the Smithsonian Institution in Washington,[5] the American Museum of Natural History in New York, the Field Museum in Chicago, and the Brooklyn Museum in New York, sent the young anthropologists Wissler, Lowie, Dorsey, Kroeber, Cushing, and Culin and others into the field to document and collect the remnants of the destroyed cultures.

Typical of such activities were the expeditions led by R. Stewart Culin,[6] a founder member of the American Anthropological Association. A close colleague of Culin's was George A. Dorsey, a Harvard-trained anthropologist who became curator of anthropology at the Field Museum in 1897. Between them they organized expeditions in the field to the Southwest, California, Northwest Coast, and Oklahoma. From these four cultural areas they collected a wide range of objects which illustrated the range and wide diversity of the arts and crafts of the indigenous inhabitants. Such artifacts as Kachina dolls – carved from one piece of wood – were collected from the Hopi; hand-spun garments from the Zuni; and coiled

baskets from the Western Apache[7] as well as superb examples of bowls and pitchers representing an earlier culture of the region – the Anasazi and Sikyatki – dating from the fifteenth century or earlier. From California came the superbly woven basket hats of the Hupa, carved horn spoons of the Yurok, seed flails of the Pomo, and dance capes and headbands of eagle, hawk, and red-shafted flicker feathers. From the Northwest Coast were collected impressive carvings – figures, houseposts, totem poles, kerfed chests, spoons, and rattles of cedar wood, all elaborately painted with abstract designs typical of the area.

Similar expeditions were those made by Wissler, Lowie, Dorsey, and Spinden to the Plains and Plateau regions in the period 1890-1915, when superb examples of art and craft work in feathers, beads and quills – even skin-painted tipis – were obtained.

Their legacy, however, superb anthropological studies and systematically collected objects representing the best of tribal arts and crafts, was – together with the artifacts collected in an earlier era – all but ignored for more than half a century, except by the dedicated scholar and perceptive connoisseur.[8]

The 1950s saw a resurgence of interest in the material culture and decorative craftsmanship of American Indians.[9] In the last two decades[10], scholars have become increasingly aware that many of the artifacts produced by Indians, from whatever cultural area, exhibit those attributes used to evaluate any work of craftsmanship or art – formal structure, expressiveness, virtuosity, and transcendence[11]. An ensemble of North American Indian material can, if the effort is made to interpret, give deep insights into the ethos and culture that produced it.[12]

The following pages will demonstrate that

materials found naturally and in rich supply in a particular culture area – wood, bone, ivory, furs and hides, shell, stone, and feathers – were used by the (largely) unnamed craftsmen and women[13] to produce impressive objects which were functional and essential to the life of the people. In addition, they demonstrate that the western concepts of artistic propriety were frequently crossed and recrossed without concern; little was rendered directly from life but more from memory or through mystic communication, and stunning emblems not infrequently made visible the invisible. Thus images – those of the Northwest Coast or the Plains, for example – were painted and rendered as if they floated and all animal images were flatly generalized as if caught on the move.

Sculptures too – be they from shell of the Southeast, catlinite from the Great Plains, wood or steatite from the Northwest Coast, or the clever ivory miniatures from the Arctic or Subarctic regions – made both religious and social comment. In addition, traditional beadwork, quillwork, painted pottery, and the like, not infrequently reflected abstract and subtle metonymic thought.

The legacy is a tribute to a strong and remarkable people who, despite great suppression, tenaciously maintained their values and beliefs. The wonder of it all is – given the profound anomic state of most tribes in all the cultural areas during the second half of the nineteenth century – that they retained and produced so many things of beauty. This is a theme which not infrequently continues in the creations of present-day Native Americans,[14] many of whom draw inspiration from their heritage. However, as Spinden observed: 'The ideas of beauty which arise in the red man's consciousness move with the times, and the spiritual forces behind them are not held to the trail of the vanished buffalo.'[15]

References

1 Seton, 1962:vi
2 Taylor, 1981: 42-53
3 Bourke, 1890: 29
4 Kroeber, 1987: 179-205
5 Most objects herein are from the Smithsonian.
6 Stewart Culin wrote the monumental *Games of the North American Indians.*
7 The Western Apache used twining almost exclusively when making burden baskets but all their other

baskets were made by coiling (see Whiteford, 1988: 62-92).
8 Northwest Coast carvings and paintings were early described as 'Art' by Franz Boas (see Boas, 1927: 183).
9 Feder, 1965
10 The influential *American Indian Art Magazine* was first published in November 1975.
11 Coe, 1976: 13-20

12 Taylor 1989: 237-57. Such recognition is now demanding of scholars that a revaluation be made of the large number of American Indian artifacts reposing in museum and other collections.
13 There were, however, men and women who excelled in their individual crafts and whose names are now renowned.
14 See Coe, 1986
15 Spinden, c.1930 in Farge, 1931: 74

THE SOUTHEAST

THE STORY OF Southeastern Indian arts and crafts is different from that of other Native Americans. When Europeans first penetrated the Southeast in the early sixteenth century, the Indians had reached a social, political, and religious development more akin to the grand civilization of the Mesoamerican Aztecs than to other North American Indian groups. Between about AD 1000 to AD 1540, the Mississippian Period, the Southeastern Indians' political order consisted of large and small chiefdoms presided over by a priestly elite who could command the construction of large temple mounds and other impressive earthworks. This system was supported by intensive riverine corn agriculture and maintained through warfare.

The Mississippian way of life suffered swift deterioration after European contact. European diseases, to which the Southeastern Indians had no natural immunity, were deadly foes causing a sharp population decline, the destruction of the chiefdom political order, and social dislocation as people relocated and reorganized. During this time, the better-known historic Southeastern Indian groups such as the Cherokee, Choctaw, Catawba, Creek, Chickasaw, and Seminole formed out of the wreckage of the chiefdoms. Their societies bore little resemblance to the past.

Following on the heels of the introduction of disease, an equally profound force for change occurred when the Southeastern Indians were incorporated into the European economic system through trading deerskins. Throughout the seventeenth and eighteenth centuries, the Southeastern Indians regularly encountered, lived among, were dependent upon, intermarried with, and, occasionally, fiercely resisted whites. By the nineteenth century the cotton agriculture and the plantation economy came to dominate the Old South. Unlike the deerskin trade, the plantation economy did not need the Indians; it needed their land. No longer necessary to the market system, the Indians became an obstacle, and this ultimately led to Removal, when almost all of the southern Indians were forcibly relocated to western territories.

Southeastern Indian art reflects their history. The highest artistic achievements of the Southeastern Indians undoubtedly occurred during the Mississippian Period. The people who lived during the Mississippian Period displayed a pageantry and rich ceremonial life unparalleled anywhere in Native North America. Mississippian accoutrements are lavish, eloquent, and highly crafted. Mississippian art is explicitly iconographic. Design motifs, although varying stylistically, are elements in what is termed the Southeastern Ceremonial Complex. These motifs include the bi-lobed arrow, the falcon-man, the forked-eye design, sun circles, crosses and swastikas, winged serpents, and animals with mythological or social significance such as the bear, woodpecker, raptorial bird, and rattlesnake.

This artistic expression, so closely tied to ceremony and elite authority, declined along with the chiefdoms after European contact.[2] In the Ceremonial Complex, art was inextricably associated with religious, social, or political life. During the Historic Period, Southeastern Indian ceremonial life took a

Above: *The pieces shown here illustrate the Southeastern Indian's penchant for color and rectilinear and curvilinear designs. The beaded sash, made by the Koasati of Alabama, is made from red and black stroud onto which the beadwork is embroidered. The basket was made by the Chitimacha of Louisiana, the most famous of Southeastern Indian basket makers, in the early twentieth century. The chain effect of connecting diamonds is a typical design motif for Southeastern Indian basketry. The shirt is a man's big shirt made by the Seminoles of southern Florida. The swastika design is an ancient motif found also on Mississippian Period objects.*

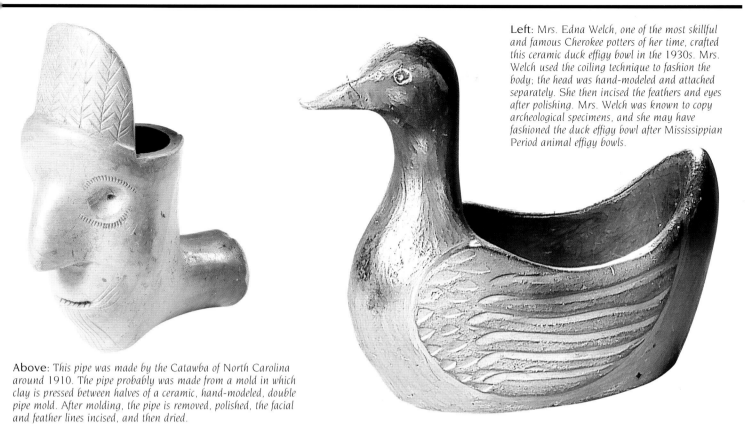

Left: Mrs. Edna Welch, one of the most skillful and famous Cherokee potters of her time, crafted this ceramic duck effigy bowl in the 1930s. Mrs. Welch used the coiling technique to fashion the body; the head was hand-modeled and attached separately. She then incised the feathers and eyes after polishing. Mrs. Welch was known to copy archeological specimens, and she may have fashioned the duck effigy bowl after Mississippian Period animal effigy bowls.

Above: This pipe was made by the Catawba of North Carolina around 1910. The pipe probably was made from a mold in which clay is pressed between halves of a ceramic, hand-modeled, double pipe mold. After molding, the pipe is removed, polished, the facial and feather lines incised, and then dried.

more egalitarian turn and did not require the trappings of a priestly elite. In the Historic Period, European trade provided most of the material items of daily life.

Ceramics

Southeastern Indian ceramic art during the Mississippian Period was unsurpassed in North America. Southeastern Indians did not possess the potter's wheel, and women, who were the masters of this medium, used coiling and hand modeling to fashion their wares. Although there are no descriptions of Mississippian potters at work, contemporary Catawba potters still practice a variant of the coiling method, and it is reasonable to suppose that Mississippian women followed similar procedures.

In the coiling technique, lumps of clay are rolled on a board until they form rounded fillets of uniform thickness and length.[3] Each piece of rolled clay is pinched together to form one long, continuous fillet which is then wound around and up to form the rough shape of the vessel.[4] The ware is then smoothed and further shaped and the walls thinned with a spoon-shaped gourd rind or mussel shell.[5] After allowing the ware to air dry, Catawba potters finish the surface by using a smooth mussel shell or kitchen knife to scrape the inside and outside of the ware and to cut and smooth the rim.[6] Handles, spouts, lugs, pedestals, legs, necks, and so on are hand-molded and attached separately. Before fire-drying, the potter polishes the surface with a worn, smooth pebble.[7] Catawba women prize their polishing stones; the more worn and smooth ones are considered irreplaceable and are often handed down from generation to generation.

Mississippian ceramics were made in an interesting array of forms. Utilitarian wares, usually undecorated, vary from small bowls to cooking and storage pots that hold up to six gallons. Ceremonial and mortuary objects have elaborate decorations and forms. Some of the most outstanding ceremonial forms are the human and animal effigy bottles and bowls, especially the noticeable 'dead-head' effigies which obviously represent a dead person.[8] The bottles were shaped into full figures of animals or into a usually kneeling human form. The bowls have miniature

Left: This picture, taken in the late nineteenth century, shows two Cherokee potters at work. The potter shapes her wares in her lap, outdoors, and in the company of others. The woman on the left is coiling a fillet of clay with one hand, and pinching the coils together and smoothing the seams with the other hand.

ceramic human or animal heads attached to the rim.[9] Other ceremonial bottles are globular bottles with relatively long necks and decorated with geometrical or curvilinear incising or polychrome painting. Many of the ceremonial containers are incised or painted with Southeastern Ceremonial Complex motifs such as the sun circle, the hand and eye motif, and the winged serpent.[10] All of the archeological and ethnohistorical evidence points to a drastic decline in ceramic art after the arrival of Europeans and, especially, after the Indians had access to metal pots, pans, bowls, cups, and dishes. The historic groups

continued to make ceramic utilitarian wares, but not in such quantities, and certainly without the mastery of their ancestors. Ceremonial ceramic wares further ceased being made. Around the turn of the twentieth century, with an increase in tourist trade and collector interest, Catawba and Cherokee women returned to ceramic manufacturing as an art form.[11]

Stonework
The stonework of the Southeastern Indians, like their ceramic art, reached its height during the Mississippian Period. Stone working was almost certainly a man's domain. Mississippian men knew the attributes and limitations of a vast variety of stone for sculpting and chipping. Men quarried local stone sources such as chert, steatite, greenstone, shale, quartz, granite, diorite, slate, hematite, limestone, and marble.[12] Especially valued high grade stone was traded throughout the Southeast.

The primary techniques in stonework were chipping and grinding. The chipping technique was used mostly in the manufacture of cutting tools. Flakes were struck from the stone being shaped with another stone or a piece of deer antler to give it the desired form and thinness. Smaller flakes were removed by applying pressure with smaller tools to refine the shape and sharpen the edges.[13] In the grinding technique, the stone to be worked was simply pecked and ground into shape and then polished with sand mixed with oil or water.[14] To fashion the more intricate stone objects such as effigy pipes, men used a soft, easily carved stone such as steatite, and then used stone chisels, drills, and scrapers to carve highly detailed forms with deeply incised lines.[15] The pipe holes were then drilled and the pipe polished.

Although many tools for daily life were made of stone, stonework became a true art form in the production of ceremonial and religious objects. Chipped stone war clubs, blades, and batons are so finely crafted, delicate, and unmarred, that they could not have been used in actual hand-to-hand combat. Grinding produced some marvelously sculpted objects, the most noteworthy being the kneeling-human mortuary figures carved out of limestone, sandstone, or marble. These figures, which may have represented mythical or real ancestors, were kept in the charnel houses which were the repositories of the elite dead; some were interred in high-status burials.[16]

The chunky game, played well into the Historic Period, required a ground-stone gaming piece or chunky stone. These pieces are discoidal stones, sometimes with concave centers on both sides; the finer ones are highly polished and perfectly round. Chunky stones, although probably used frequently, are works of art in themselves, showing a gracefulness of line and beautiful symmetry.

After European contact there was a dramatic decline in stonework.[17] Southeastern Indians readily replaced stone tools with European-made metal tools and weapons. Men continued to make stone tools, but these did not have the same attention to detail and craftsmanship as those from the

brandishing a war club. These plates appear to have been intended only as grave offerings to the elite dead.[22]

On gorgets, designs were incised on the smooth interior using sharpened stone awls and needles. Shell cups and dippers usually were engraved on their outside portions. Some shell gorgets and cups have incised designs representing human figures like those on the copper plates but most of them represent rattlesnakes, woodpeckers, spiders, or mythological beings such as the underwater panther and the winged serpent.[23] Gorgets may have been worn as political or military insignia. For instance, the Citico gorget, which depicts a coiled rattlesnake-like being, is only found in those Mississippian Period archeological sites that once comprised the chiefdom of Coosa.[24] The shell cups and dippers were probably used to serve black drink, a herbal tea drunk as a sacrament at political and religious events.[25]

With the abrupt disruption of the Mississippian ceremonial and political life, copper-

Mississippian Period. After all, the flintlock gun was now the weapon of choice.

Men, however, never completely lost the artistry of grinding and carving. Chunky stones from the Historic Period are as finely crafted and beautiful as those from the Mississippian Period. Tobacco pipes played an important role in Historic Period Southeastern Indian ceremonial life, and a great deal of care and attention went into the artistry of Historic Period steatite pipes.[18] The Cherokee were famous for their fine tobacco pipes. Historic Period pipes are usually carved with an animal effigy on the stem. Animal figures exhibited on the pipes are often bears, although panthers and frogs are also common. Pipes occasionally have a reclining human carved on the stems or, reportedly, even men and women in explicit sexual poses.[19]

Metal and Shellwork

During the Mississippian Period, shell and metal, primarily copper, were scarce in the southeast, and that which was available was traded throughout the area. Traders brought copper from the Lake Superior region and from the Tennessee Valley, and shells from the coastal areas were commonly traded to interior peoples.

The techniques used in copperwork were fairly simple. The coppersmith placed a copper nugget on a piece of buckskin laid over a hard surface, and hammered out the nugget with a hammer stone and then cut it into shape.[20] A smooth cobble or piece of stone was then used to smooth further the surface on both sides. Shellwork was usually done on large conch shell (*Busycon perversum*). The conch shells were hollowed out for use as cups or dippers, or the smooth interior portions of the shell were cut into circles for use as gorgets which were worn around the neck, over the breast or collarbone.

Shell and copper objects are almost all ornaments – beads, necklaces, hairpins, masks, gorgets, earspools, headdress emblems, and so on. Except for the jewelry, these ornaments were used as part of ceremonial or religious dress or as grave

offerings to accompany the elite dead. Sheet copper, laminated over celts, axes, earspools, or other stone and wood objects, have been discovered in elite burials. Sheet copper also was cut into silhouettes of war clubs, bi-lobed arrows, or feathers that were worn in the ceremonial headdresses of the elite.[21] Coppersmiths devoted special skill and time embossing figures of men in various poses and dances on copper sheets. The most prominent of these are the copper plates from the Etowah site in Georgia in which a falcon-man is depicted in full ceremonial regalia and

Below: *The most difficult task in basketry is form, and Southeastern Indian women are masters in achieving symmetrical and proportional forms as shown in this double-lidded Cherokee split-cane basket made around 1900. This particular basket form is a modern style.*

over and under, at right angles, until a mat base is formed. Then all the splints are turned up to form the warp of the sides.[31] Twilling is a diagonal weave in which each element of the weft is woven over two or more warp splints at an oblique angle.[32] The most difficult and skillful twilling technique is the double-weaved twill, in which the weave is doubled over at the rim and continued inside the basket. In this way so-called double weave baskets are made.

Southeastern Indian basketry is noted for its mastery of color and design. Cane splints are colored with vegetable dyes made from black walnut and butternut for a deep brown or black, puccoon root for a red or orange, bloodroot for a redbrown, broom sedge for a burnt orange, and yellowroot for a deep yellow.[33] A variety of geometrical and curvilinear designs are formed by varying the width and color of cane splints and the

and shellwork virtually ceased.[26] Historic Period Southeastern Indians appreciated fine metals and purchased trade ornaments such as crescent-shaped gorgets, hairpins, arm bands, turban bands, earrings, and rings. The Southeastern Indians continued to drink black drink throughout the Historic Period, but shell cups and dippers were replaced by European metal ones.

Basketry

Southeastern Indian basketry is perhaps the only craft that continues from the prehistoric past until the present.[27] River cane (*Arundinaria tecta* and *A. macrosperma*) is the preferred material for basketry.[28] Despite the difficulty in cutting and processing river cane splints, the women never forfeited the distinct shiny gloss of river cane for easier material. The sheer abundance of river cane also probably contributed to its popularity, since a woman would not have had to search far for her supplies.[29]

To prepare cane splints, a stalk is split lengthwise, usually into four splints. The shiny outer material is then pulled from the coarse inner fiber. The inside of the splint is then scraped of any remaining inner fiber and trimmed along the edges to a uniform width. The famous Chitimacha basketry has distinctively narrow, delicate cane splints, a technical feat in itself.

The women employ primarily two types of weaving techniques – checkerwork and twilling – both of which were used in prehistoric times.[30] In checkerwork, a number of splints are placed side by side to·make the warp; weft splints are woven in one at a time,

Right: *During the Historic Period, the Southeastern Indians decorated their military-style shirts with applique strips along the hems and necks. After removal, the Seminoles who remained in Florida elaborated on applique design by sewing applique designs over most of the shirt. After the sewing machine became available, applique gave way to the more intricate patchwork design, and Seminole women created distinctive and characteristically Seminole fabrics. The shirt style is also particular to the Seminole. This is a Seminole man's big shirt which is derived from the military-styled shirts popular among Southeastern Indian men during the Historic Period. Seminole big shirts are blousy, open, all-over garments reaching to just above the knees. Seminole men wore patchwork big shirts well into the twentieth century. Nowadays, these shirts are worn for special occasions and sold on the tourist market.*

number of over and under turns. Because of their intricate designs, the most famous basket makers in the Southeast are the Chitimacha women of southern Louisiana and the Cherokee women of North Carolina. Chitimacha women weave distinct, colorful design bands that criss-cross or curve over the whole of the basket.[34] Cherokee women prefer simple geometric lines forming squares, triangles, diamonds, and crosses over the whole basket.[35]

Women make small baskets with handles, sieves for sifting hominy, hampers, and mats for sitting, sleeping, or as wall hangings.[36] The most striking basket form of the Southeastern Indians is the burden basket. These are large, sturdy baskets with a flared opening. They were carried on the back with a leather tumpline attached to the sides and placed across the chest or forehead. Choctaw, Chitimacha, and Creek women fashion 'cow nose' or heart-shaped baskets, which are small, triangular baskets remarkably similar to the pouches of the Ceremonial Complex.[37]

Fabrics and Clothing

Daily clothing for Southeastern Indian men and women was a simple affair. Women wore knee-length skirts and men wore breechclouts, and both usually went without upper garments. They wore leggings which are long, wide pieces of single cloth wrapped around each leg and suspended by garters from a belt. In cold weather, men and women wore 'matchcoats' which were cloak-like garments worn draped over the shoulders. Europeans often compared textiles from the late-Mississippian Period through most of the Historic Period to finely-made European fabrics. These textiles were made from various types of animal fur, grasses, and bark, particularly the inner bark of the mulberry tree which produced a fine, pliable cloth similar to linen.[38] Animal skins from deer, bison, bear, and smaller animals were used to fashion moccasins and matchcoats.[39] Handmade textiles were either dyed with vegetable dyes or painted with mineral paints. Skin matchcoats were sometimes painted with geometric designs, animals, or military exploits.

As soon as European textiles became available in any appreciable quantity, men and women substituted them for handmade textiles.[40] Buckskin continued to be used through most of the eighteenth century for moccasins, but the Southeastern Indians soon preferred European woolens for their matchcoats. Men eschewed European-style pants until the nineteenth century; but they quickly adapted the knee-length, military-style European jackets and shirts and began wearing these blousy, open shirts as part of their daily and fancy wear.[41] These shirts were decorated with colorful applique strips along the bottom, and often they were covered with various ornaments of beads, silver, ribbon, and so on. Women began using European textiles for their skirts and began

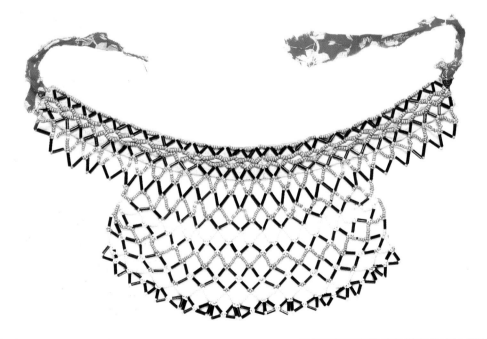

Left: *The Choctaw beaded collar as seen here is a modern innovation using pan-Indian beadworking designs. This collar, made around 1940, was worn around the neck of a dress shirt as a substitute for a man's tie.*

wearing calico bodices in the late eighteenth century. Both skirts and bodices were fully ornamented with beads, bells, rattles, and ribbons.

After Removal, most Southeastern Indians began wearing American-style dress, except for the Seminoles. Those Seminoles who escaped Removal moved into the Florida Everglades where they remained isolated for a long time. American-style clothing was not readily available to them, and Seminole women made ankle-length skirts, bodices with capes, and military-style men's shirts into the twentieth century.[42] After the manual sewing machine became available, applique gave way to the patchwork garments which have become the national dress of the Seminole.[43]

In Seminole applique, single strips of printed cloth are sewn directly onto the garment. In patchwork, patterned cloth is first torn into long strips which are then sewn together to produce a band of striped cloth. The band is then snipped into several pieces which are arranged side by side or offset and sewn together into a long band. This technique allows for an astonishing variety of designs, and a woman usually uses several bands of varying designs in making one garment.[44] The bands are then sewn together, to form a whole piece of cloth that can be cut into patterns and sewn. The final product is a very colorful patchwork garment, with a variety of intricate, detailed designs.[45]

Beadwork and Featherwork

Except for the delicate feather wands and fans, beads and feathers were used as clothing decorations or for personal adornment. Southeastern Indian women produced finger-woven, tasselled sashes, belts, and garters, and they did so in the Mississippian Period as evidenced by the engraved figures on shell gorgets and copper plates. Sashes and belts constituted part of their clothing throughout the Historic Period as well, and to the present day the Choctaw and Creek are noted for their beaded belts.[46] Sashes were worn over one or both shoulders, crossing diagonally or criss-crossing across the chest and tied at the waist with tassels and cords hanging down, often below the knees. In the late Historic Period, belts worn about the waist served to fasten the

buttonless military-style shirts. Women also made finger-woven garters with which to fasten leggings and the fancy, beaded, men's pouches (their clothing usually did not have pockets).

In finger-weaving, yarns are attached to a single bar and the threads are intertwined by the fingers alone.[47] This technique only allows for the manufacture of relatively narrow strips of cloth, hence the predominance of sashes and belts made with this technique. With beaded sashes and belts, beads are slipped onto the threads during the weaving process. Designs are constructed by varying the color of threads and weave. In examining the design motifs of belts and sashes, two style areas emerge. The Eastern style area, typified by the Seminole and Yuchi, is characterized by simple, all-over geometric designs of diamonds, Vs, Ws, and crosses. In the Western style area, comprising the Choctaw, Chickasaw, Koasati, and Alabama (the latter two were both historic Creek groups), curvilinear designs are laid out in a panel against a monochrome background.[48]

Without doubt, feather matchcoats were the finest featherwork products from the Southeast.[49] Basically, these were made of woven or mulberry cloth nets into which hundreds of feathers were twisted or tied. Turkey feathers, which have opalescent brown, red, purple, and blue hues were the preferred feathers. The feather down, of course, made these cloaks particularly good outerwear during cold weather.[50]

Finally, feather wands and fans were made from the Mississippian Period through the Historic Period. These wands were usually made of eagle feathers arranged fan-like and fastened at the quills with a leather handle or attached to a fan frame or a carved sourwood rod.[51] The eagle was a revered emblem of peace, and eagle feather fans were frequently used during ceremonial occasions and dances.[52] Fans made from other feathers such as turkey apparently were used as everyday fans.

Woodwork

Because wood preserves poorly in the acidic Southeastern soils, one can only estimate the importance of this medium to the Southeastern Indians. Although some wooden artifacts have been found elsewhere, the largest cache of Mississippian wooden artifacts are from the Key Marco site in Florida, from which many utilitarian and ceremonial wooden objects have been recovered from the saltwater marsh muck. Of these, the painted masks and tablets, animal figurines and naturalistic animal heads are the most noteworthy.

Masks and figurines were carved and chiseled from a single piece of wood using shell chisels, sawfish-tooth blades, and stone scrapers and drills. They were then smoothed with sand or sharkskin to remove all traces of tool scars.[53] Wooden animal heads sometimes were made of several pieces. For instance, a deer head has detachable ears and an alligator has a separate lower jaw that articulates with the upper jaw. These wooden pieces are painted, incised, and inlaid with shell.

How the people of Key Marco understood or used the animal figurines and heads is unknown since, for the most part, these are not representative of the Southeastern Ceremonial Complex. However, masks were worn by Southeastern Indians in various dances and ceremonial affairs from the Mississippian Period through the Historic Period. Some were used as decoy masks for hunting, in which a hunter donned an animal skin and mask and mimicked, with astonishing fidelity, the movements of his prey. Some decoy masks also were used in performing hunting dances.

Masks also were used to impersonate mythical beings, other humans, or to characterize esteemed personal traits such as bravery and fierceness in war.[54] The falcon-man motifs of the Southeastern Ceremonial Complex clearly depict masked creatures. The rattlesnake-dance masks of the Cherokee reportedly indicate the dancer's bravery since he would be obviously unconcerned about

Right: The Cherokee also make masks out of gourds, such as the child's Booger Dance mask of a 'funny' buffalo. The horns and nose are gourd necks stuck through cut-out holes. For the painted features, the mask maker uses a dye made from black walnut or charcoal (for black) and applies the paint with his fingers. Other Southeastern Indian dances require their own special paraphernalia.

the rattlesnake carved on the forehead.[55]

Historic Cherokee masks are the most well-known. Cherokee masks may seem crude in comparison to those from the northwest coast or from the northeast. Certainly the detail is missing. However, the Booger Dance masks show a finesse in caricature that is truly artistic. The Booger Dance was a burlesque dance performed by the Cherokee of North Carolina that re-enacted the arrival of white people. The Boogers wore masks representing what the dancers perceived as grotesque attributes of white men.[56] These masks were carved with grimaces and leering smiles and topped by shaggy, unkempt hair and mounds of facial hair. One mask, made in the mid-twentieth century by Will West Long, depicts in perfect caricature a quite distressed Indian.

References

1 Hudson, 1976: 376.
2 Contemporary artists and craftspeople, submitting to market demands for 'traditional' crafts, have, however, relearned old techniques.
3 Contemporary Catawba women dig clay from local clay pits noted for the purity and consistency of the clay. After the clay is prepared the potter breaks off suitable quantities and either uses them immediately or wraps them in damp cloth or leaves for storage (Fewkes, 1944: 73).
4 Fewkes, 1944: 113. Catawba women use ring coiling, rather than true coiling. They lay rings one on top of another to build a cylinder (Fewkes, 1944: 78).
5 Fewkes, 1944: 83.
6 Fewkes, 1944: 88.
7 Fewkes, 1944: 83. The Southeastern Indians did not possess the kiln. Catawba potters gradually dry their wares by placing them progressively closer to an open fire, finally placing the whole piece on the coals (Fewkes, 1944: 89).
8 Haberland, 1964: 195.
9 Animal effigies were representations of various animals common in the Southeastern Ceremonial Complex. It is unknown what or whom the human effigies represented.
10 Fundaburk and Foreman, 1957: 168-83.
11 Harrington, 1908: 401-03; Speck, 1920: 63. Contemporary Catawba trade pottery is especially noted for its fine craftsmanship.
12 Mississippian men usually extracted stone from local quarries by chiseling out large chunks. They then chipped them into suitable sizes.
13 Fundaburk and Foreman, 1957: 116. In fashioning the rough shape of a chipped stone tool the stoneworker held the stone to be worked in a piece of buckskin in his palm and struck it with a cobble or the butt end of a length of antler.
14 Fundaburk and Foreman, 1957: 116. In the grinding technique, the stone worker pecked and fractured the stone using a cobble of harder stone so that it gradually wore off the surface of the former. To refine the surface, the stoneworker used a grinding technique in which a harder stone was rubbed against the softer stone, wearing the softer stone and giving finer lines to the form and smoothing the surface. Finally, the object was polished to a high sheen using an abrader.
15 West, 1934: 387-88. Mississippian men made a variety of carved effigy pipes, some in the shapes of animals, most predominantly the owl, bear, and frog. The most distinctive and outstanding Mississippian effigy pipes, however, are the human effigy pipes.
16 Brose et al., 1985: 104.
17 Contemporary Southeastern Indians do not practise

much stonework, except in the tourist demonstration villages. But in the past few decades, the Eastern Band of Cherokee in North Carolina have revived this art form (Leftwich, 1970: 119).
18 Witthoft, 1949: 54-55.
19 Witthoft, 1949: 47.
20 Cushing, 1894: 100. Copper plates were usually cut into the outline of the figure or design intended for the finished product. Southeastern Indians, up to the present day, value bilateral symmetry in their designs.
21 Haberland, 1954: 200.
22 Hamilton et al., 1974: 5.
23 Haberland, 1964: 199-200.
24 Hally et al., 1990.
25 Hudson, 1976: 372-73.
26 The Creek people of Tuckabatchee owned a number of metal plates in the form of celts similar to those of the Southeastern Ceremonial Complex (Hudson, 1976: 400). These plates were only brought out during the Green Corn Ceremony. They were taken to Oklahoma during Removal and have been, over the years, buried in the graves of beloved men and women (Howard, 1968: 65-74).
27 Only remnants of Mississippian and early Historic Period baskets have been recovered, but these show good craftsmanship and design.
28 Choosing the right cane requires an intimate knowledge of cane and its growth patterns. Generally, basket makers choose stalks of cane about two years old, the diameter of a thumb, and with long, straight shafts between knots.
29 In recent years river cane has become scarce, forcing basket makers to use substitutes such as white oak and honeysuckle. See Leftwich, 1970.
30 Mason, 1904: 221-29. Basket making has two basic techniques – weaving and coiling. In recent years some Southeastern Indian women have begun making coiled baskets out of coiled pine needles or certain types of grasses.
31 Leftwich, 1970: 30.
32 Speck, 1920: 60.
33 Dixon and Domjanovich, 1992: 41; Leftwich, 1970: 29. Vegetable dyes are processed by first pulverizing the roots, bark, or leaves in a mortar and pestle, and then mixing the powder with water and boiling it. Cane splints are placed in the boiling water and occasionally stirred to ensure an evenness of color.
34 Turnbaugh and Turnbaugh, 1986: 102.
35 Leftwich, 1970: 51; Turnbaugh and Turnbaugh, 1986: 106.
36 Porter, 1990: 84.
37 Porter, 1990: 86. In the 1920s and 1930s Chitimacha, Choctaw, Creek, and Cherokee women, although

never having abandoned basketry altogether, began producing a variety of forms for the tourist trade.
38 Carr, 1897: 401. These materials were pounded and separated and then hand spun either with a hand spindle or by simply spinning the pieces together on the knee and pulling with the other hand. European eyewitness accounts from the eighteenth century also describe women using suspended, two-bar looms for producing broad pieces of cloth and as using finger-weaving for narrow sashes and belts (Dockstader, 1967: 54, 61).
39 Carr, 1897:401. Animal hides were soaked, scraped, and treated with pulverized animal brains to make them soft, supple, and of a uniform, desired thickness.
40 The outstanding fashion era for the Historic Southeastern Indians occurred in the late eighteenth, early nineteenth centuries, just prior to Removal. At this time, Southeastern Indian men and women reckoned fashion and clothing as a true expression of esthetics and national identity, combining colors, materials, and ornamentation in fancy wear to achieve an overall appearance of color, coordination, and elegance to their costumes.
41 Wood, 1981: 52.
42 Downs, 1979: 38-40; Sturtevant, 1967: 161.
43 Sturtevant, 1967: 171.
44 Downs, 1979: 34-35.
45 Seminole men's clothing until around 1930 consisted of knee-length big shirts, which were, in effect, knee-length dresses, and Seminole men usually went bare-legged until around 1930.
46 Medford, 1975: 46.
47 Dockstader, 1978: 57.
48 Goggins, 1967: 173. Interestingly, the Western style motifs closely resemble prehistoric pottery designs. It is uncertain whether these designs have been continual or were copied later.
49 Southeastern Ceremonial Complex falcon-men representations show men wearing feather capes in the form of falcon wings. A fragment of textile from the Spiro Mound in Oklahoma clearly has a wing design, but whether or not others were made of feathers is not known.
50 Part of the Mississippian ceremonial dress included feather headdresses with copper emblems. Feathers rarely preserve however.
51 Medford, 1975: 42; Speck, 1951: 39.
52 Speck, 1951: 39-44, 94.
53 Gilliland, 1975: 47-48.
54 Speck, 1951: 1-13.
55 Speck, 1951: 63.
56 Speck, 1951: 24.

> 'O our Mother the Earth, O our Father the Sky, Your children are we, and with tired backs we bring you the gifts that you love.
> Then weave for us a garment of brightness; May the warp be the white light of morning. May the weft be the red light of evening.
> May the fringes be the falling rain, May the border be the standing rainbow...'
>
> TEWA SONG[1]

THE SOUTHWEST

Above: *The bright colours and skilled workmanship of the Southwest are represented by the beautiful black, green, and red woven woman's manta from San Juan pueblo and green turquoise Navajo necklace. Both are items from crafts for which the region is renowned — jewelry and weaving.*

THE AMERICAN SOUTHWEST has one of the most harsh and difficult climates of any area on the North American continent, yet for thousands of years it has supported a culturally active and spiritually integrated Native American population. The arid climate has naturally produced religions which are fixed upon water, control of water, and water in its many various forms: snakes, frogs, clouds, and long cotton tassels on white dance sashes which evoke the rain falling from the high clouds.

The greater part of this area is arid or semi-arid, with extreme variations from high forested mountain ranges, from which springtime run-off of the heavy winter snows provides an important part of the waters of the Rio Grande, the Colorado, and the Pecos. A major part of the area is plateau, steep-sided sandstone mesas, deep canyons with intermittent streams, and scattered clumps of piñon and juniper trees. The southern half of the area is marked by broad areas of nearly level, hot, dry desert separated by steep, rocky mountains of limited extent which break up the flat land.

This varied Southwestern habitat offered its prehistoric occupants – the Anasazi, Hohokam and Mogollon, Basketmakers and Mimbres cultures – an enormous variety of resources, many of them to be found only in very restricted zones. This encouraged the development of greatly differing lifestyles, each adjusted to the resources available and taking advantage of several different micro-environments. To take advantage of this diversity, the peoples of the Southwest were knitted together by interlocking networks of economic and social relationships.

These ancient cultures all produced pottery, basketry, weaving, carving in wood, and some small carvings in shell and stone, some of them very beautiful and sophisticated. The study of the Southwest and its arts and crafts is influenced by the knowledge that the present Indians are the descendants of those who made the great cities in the desert such as Chaco and Mesa Verde. In the Southwest it is possible to observe in use the same loom that was used prehistorically, the same sash, the same basket... and this also gives insight into the meaning of these things within their original culture.

Crafts in the Southwest have maintained their high standards, techniques, and esthetic vision, and are still an important source of income for Native American people. Many of them sell their arts and crafts to supplement their income. There is an artisan in almost every home, and the importance of their arts and crafts is appreciated. Until the twentieth century the finest objects were made for ceremonial purposes, for the gods, and to ensure the continuation of human life. Today often the very best of their arts and crafts are most frequently destined for collectors or museums.

Although their lives often reflect the stress of living in two cultures, the Indians of the Southwest maintain their traditional way of life, and it is possible to glimpse the way these people lived 500 years ago. A quiet moment at a ceremonial dance, with the drum beat which has gone on and on all day, and the long lines of dancers stretch back to earliest days of the Anasazi, when the plaza dancers heard the same songs and drums. The past is not distant here; there is an occasional pot shard, a broken bit of flint, or the discovery of a ruin, tucked away in a cliff to remind us that there were people here long ago.

The arts are one of the strongest and most visible links to this past. The bestselling articles are made in the old traditional ways. Everything is done by hand, and with

Left: *Ceremonial aspects were never neglected either and many things were made with rituals, dances, etc, specifically in mind. The buckskin hat with beadwork decoration was bought from the Apache, among whom it belonged to a war shamen for use in the Gun Ceremony when amulets were given protective powers.*

source of continued life. The vessel holds the water; the source of life accompanies the water, hence its dwelling place is in the vessel with the water.'³

Potters have a respected place in contemporary Pueblo society, apart from the economic role. The ability to make a pot is an integral, even a sacred, part of everyday life:

'Despite the changes which have engulfed the Pueblo world, there remains the underlying world view that recognizes a spiritual dimension to every phase of life, to all common objects and everyday activities. This world view is expressed by the still vital ceremonial calendar and is embodied in items fashioned by hand from the materials provided by the earth.'⁴

To make a pot (or a figurine, spindle whorl, charm, or fetish), an Indian woman goes to her traditional clay source, which every pueblo has, and then to her own part of the source and digs out as much clay as she needs. She then dries it and puts it through a sieve or screen to get rid of the rocks and roots. After the clay is clean, she will add some sort of temper, old pot shards, volcanic earth, or ground mica, which keeps the clay from expanding too fast and cracking, and then add water so that the clay is workable. Pots are made not on a wheel but by coiling ropes of clay one on another, and then pinching them together. The clay is then smoothed, often with a piece of gourd, so that no joints are visible. The clay is then sanded and smoothed again. This may end the process or, at this point, the slip, or a paint made from clay and usually of a different color, is applied, and quickly the burnishing begins. The slip is a fine clay dissolved in water so that it is really like a paint. Slips can be of red or white clay. Production methods differ little between pueblos; the temper of the clays may differ but the main visible difference is in the decoration and thickness of the walls of the pots.

materials which are available if one knows how to pray for them, where to find them, how to process them, and to respect them.

Ceramics

Of all the arts of the Southwest, pottery may be the most definitive. It is still made using the same methods that have been used for thousands of years, and ceramics of great beauty and sophistication have been produced. The pottery of the Mimbres, Anasazi, Hohokam, and the historic and contemporary pueblos are some of the best known of the crafts of the American Indian. There is a clear stylistic link between the present and the past in Pueblo pottery, and prehistoric designs are often reused; for example, the Mimbres-influenced pottery designs of Lucy Lewis in Acoma. It has always been a central feature of the Pueblo world, serving both utilitarian and ceremonial functions and tying social life to the natural environment in a fundamental way. And Pueblo pottery accounts for probably 90 percent of all Southwestern pottery and thus typifies the region.

In centuries past, many vessels were hand-painted with elaborate designs, and simple kitchen items – storage jars, pitchers, and

ladles, canteens, seed jars, and serving bowls – were executed with the care and creative genius that characterize works of art. Like many traditional craftspeople, Pueblo potters have a remarkable ability to instill in a common household object a life and spirit of its own, and the so-called utility wares are exemplars of this quality.² Traditionally, pottery has also been viewed as possessing power and the ability to take on the attributes of the substance it holds. Thus water, a sacred element, transfers its power to the pottery vessel that holds it: 'Water contains the

Right: *Black on black burnished pottery is strongly identified with the late Maria Martinez of San Ildefonso pueblo and it was she who manufactured the classic piece seen here. Maria made the pots and her husband decorated them, achieving the delicate patterned effect clearly visible here. This piece was made in the late 1940s.*

Left: *This Laguna woman epitomizes the Pueblo relationship with clay, standing by her adobe home with a jar that will be used to carry water – the essential for life. The jar itself is adorned with geometric designs.*

Polishing pottery is a long and tiresome process. Small polishing stones, sometimes dinosaur gizzard stones frequently found in the arroyos or dry stream beds, are used to press and stroke the surface of the new pot until it begins to gleam. These small, smooth stones are treasured and passed down from generation to generation. Once the polishing is started it cannot be stopped, so the effort required to polish a large pot takes a small team of people. If the pot is to be painted, then it is not polished. Before firing it will be covered with a slip and it can then be decorated and polished.

The pot is then fired. Sheep manure provides a good fuel, burning evenly and slowly. The ashes retain their initial form and hold the heat of the fire. Some potters today in very windy locations like Acoma, high on a mesa, are using electric kilns which are easier to control. Firing is the most delicate part of the potting process, and pots are usually fired in the morning when there is little wind.

There were no glazes in the Southwest but the lack of a glaze was not considered to be very important. It was understood that the pottery would let the water evaporate slowly. The clay gives the water a sweet taste, and many Pueblo people think that the best water comes from these pots, called ollas, which keep the water cool and tasty.[5] There are, as mentioned, many decorative variations in the Pueblo pottery of the Southwest. If a black ware is desired, the fire is smothered after it has burned down, and covered with sheets of

Right: *Pots varied greatly in size, shape, and color, although combinations of these are usually enough to enable the pueblo of manufacture to be identified, both today and historically. This large black jar is from Santa Clara earlier this century, black wares being typical of the Tewan Rio Grande pueblos.*

tin or any fireproof material so that the heat and smoke are held in the fire and forced into the body of the pottery. Today this black ware is made in New Mexico by San Ildefonso and Santa Clara pueblos, but prehistorically this sort of pottery was more widespread. This black ware is burnished to a metallic sheen and had almost disappeared but was revived by Maria Martinez of San Ildefonso; today her lustrous black pottery is highly prized by

collectors. Maria and her husband Julian, who decorated her pots when she began to make pottery for sale, became the best known of many teams of potters whose production was designed for the market.

The relationship between market desires and the potter's designs is recurrent; tourist tastes have strongly influenced pottery designs. For example, the decorative use of floral motifs which have been incorporated into pueblo designs, particularly those of the Southern pueblos, Acoma, Laguna, Zuni, Zia, Santa Ana, San Felipe, and Cochiti. Many of the designs which now seem traditional may have been adapted from things which the nineteenth century potters saw on imported crockery – flowers, parrots, and bands which separated areas of the pot – in order to make the pottery more saleable to outsiders.[6] More traditionally, the decoration was distinctive if a pot was to have some role in an internal ceremony, often including water symbols, frogs, tadpoles, and clouds. Since men were in charge of religion they may have produced and painted all the pottery for *kiva* use, or, as Dillingham suggests, occasionally it was made by a woman who had been struck by lightning and lived, thus qualifying her to make *kiva* pottery.[7]

The shapes of pots have evolved gradually. The olla, or water vessel, was designed to be balanced on the head of a woman carrying water from a stream or spring to her house. It generally has a shoulder, which spreads the weight of the water, and a narrow neck, to keep the water from spilling and evaporating.

Above: *In modern-day Zuni many artistic items are produced for sale to tourists, much of it beautifully designed and crafted, drawing inspiration from traditional forms. Ceramic owls similar to this one are popular with today's buyers; this particular piece, however, was collected by the Hayden Survey in the 1870s.*

Other types of pottery produced continuously are seed jars, small globe-like pots with very narrow openings, canteens, which were introduced by the Spanish and, occasionally, effigy jars. Prehistorically the Anasazi produced mugs and pitchers, but those shapes, like the black pottery, had disappeared until these forms were revived for tourists.[8] A later, unintended effect of the popularity of the pueblo pottery was that the pottery library at the pueblos was depleted by institutions such as the Smithsonian, who purchased enormous amounts of material and shipped it into museums. In cultures where innovation is not greatly valued, this produced more changes than might have occurred otherwise, since it removed the collective memory bank of the potters of a pueblo.[9]

The Pueblos share a way of life, a world view, and a landscape, but they speak half a dozen languages and live in more than thirty villages. Although several pueblos may share a language, internally they may have different societies and clan structures, so that they are not alike in organization. There are, naturally, several distinct styles of pottery.

Down along the Rio Grande the Tewa pueblos of San Ildefonso and Santa Clara are known today for their black and red wares. San Ildefonso, the home of Maria Martinez, produces mostly black pottery, but earlier in the twentieth century when Maria was a young woman, she produced a fine black on white ceramic ware. Today no one in San Ildefonso makes the black on white pottery which was once so common. Maria's switch to

black on black (a reduction-fired clay which is burnished and then painted which leaves certain areas matte) has become the standard for San Ildefonso. Similarly, no white-slipped pottery is made at neighbouring Santa Clara.

The Tewa pueblo of San Juan produced pottery which was mostly undecorated; today's new style is really a reinterpretation of ancestral shards, combining incised lines in unslipped tan on a middle band between a polished top and bottom. In northern New Mexico the Tiwa speaking pueblos of Taos and Picuris are the home of an unslipped micaceous ware which usually comes in the form of a lidless beanpot. This is used for cooking stews and beans, and the clay is thought to impart a special, delicious flavor.

In the early part of this century potters from the Tewa pueblo of Tesuque made pottery which was black on white and looked like that being made at the same time in San Ildefonso. In the 1940s and '50s it produced a lot of low-fired work painted in unfired, bright commercial tempera paint to appeal to tourists visiting nearby Santa Fe. Paradoxically, it remains a conservative Pueblo maintaining a rich ceremonial life.

The Keresan pueblos to the south of Santa Fe make a thinner walled ceramic which is slipped white and decorated with black and red. This is called polychrome because it has several colors. The Keresan-speaking pueblos of Cochiti, Santo Domingo, Santa Ana, Zia, Laguna, and Acoma all produced large bowls and ollas. Their pots all have a red band at the base, then a design area which is white with black and red designs, often birds and flowers. The top band is either a continuation of the middle panel or geometric.

In Cochiti Helen Cordero invented, or more accurately revived, a figure called a story-teller. She remembered her grandfather singing to his children and began to produce

sitting figures with open mouths and many small children sitting and listening to the story or song. Helen Cordero, like Maria Martinez and the Hopi Nampeyo, has opened many economic doors for the pueblo potters. Story-telling figurines are changing rapidly and may be considered folk art. Very popular, they have been copied extensively.

Santo Domingo is a few miles south of Cochiti and it is a very conservative Pueblo. Even recent designs are likely to be variations of designs which were popular in the 1700s. These designs are described as simple geometric. Santo Domingo leaders forbid the representation of the human figure and other designs are not allowed on pottery for sale. Santo Domingo pots continue to be used on feast days and in the *kivas*, but today's production is limited.

To the west were, and are, more great potters, in the three Keresan-speaking pueblos of Zia, Laguna, and Acoma, and in Zuni. These have much in common; all use white slip and black and red decorations. The clay around Acoma is special, dark and dense, and it has a tendency to pit, which has made some modern Acoma potters resort to commercial clay. The pottery of Acoma has been especially enhanced by looking at the designs of their ancestors in the Mimbres valley. Prehistorically the potters of this western part of New Mexico excelled at black on white designs, and the tradition is carried

Below: *Arguably the greatest Hopi potter, and certainly one of the best known in the region, was Nampeyo from Hano. This large jar is 16.5in (41cm.) deep and shows her sense of form and great decorative skill. the designs are derived from older forms found as shards at Sikyatki ruins. It is a classic example of geometric polychrome design elements. Her descendants still make excellent pottery today.*

on today. In the past twenty-five years Acoma has developed this distinctive style, and the distinguished potter Lucy Lewis and her descendants have inspired a younger group of potters to continue their traditions and innovations.

Zuni is a separate language, although Zuni pottery appears to be closely related to the Keresean model. Historical Zuni-related pottery is called Tularosa Black on White and St. Johns Polychrome, although at other sites there are polychrome pieces which have a glaze decoration. After the Pueblo Revolt in 1680, the Zunis consolidated in one pueblo which is called Zuni. Historical Zuni ware has a white slip and three bands of design. The Zuni designs of this century have concentrated on the rosette and deer with what is called a heart line, from the mouth to the heart of the deer. Zuni ceramics were in decline in the early part of the twentieth century, but are currently being revived and young Zunis are making pottery again, although most choose to make jewelry.

Hopi pottery from about 1300 was not distinct, but there was an artistic explosion in the 1450s which produced black on white and black on orange wares. These early Hopi designs are characterized by sweeping curvilinear motifs, birds, animals, and human representations. The free designs are different from all other pottery designs in the Pueblo world, with the possible exception of the Mimbres in western New Mexico.[10] The Hopi have always used coal to fire their pottery and

are the only group to do so, although it crops up all over the Pueblo world.

The Hopi pottery renaissance is partly due to a woman named Nampeyo who lived a century ago in the Hopi village of Hano and was extremely skilled at making symmetrical vessels. In 1890 Nampeyo saw some of the pot shards from the excavation of black on yellow pots being excavated at Sikyatki and was inspired to reproduce these fragments as pots. Sikyatki Polychrome uses unbalanced design areas, dynamic color fields, stippling, engraving, and other textures. Nampeyo was a Tewa whose ancestors moved to Hopi as a result of Spanish pressure in New Mexico in the seventeenth century, so her pottery is Hopi/Tewa. Today the Hopi pottery she revived is characterized by its golden slip and polychrome decoration, elements derived from Sikyatki. Nampeyo's great fame came from her elegant design sense, which took elements of the past and reused them on contemporary pottery. Today there are many potters at Hopi who have been inventive and produced very simple variations of the traditional designs.

Other pottery in the Southwest is not as well known. The Athapaskan Navajo and Apache did make some early pottery but it is impossible to identify today.[11] Although the Pueblos continue to dominate pottery today, there is an increasing production of some unslipped, pinched rim pottery made by the Navajo. The Navajo are also making low-fired ceramic figurines of Navajo going about their

daily life. These figures are very lively and appealing and are being sought by folk art collectors. Apaches, too, have produced some ceramics, but their efforts so far have been limited to undecorated pieces, red slipped canteens, and other small pieces.

The Pima and Papago of Arizona produced a red ware pottery using the paddle and anvil and the coil technique, although they are much better known for their basketry. Their neighbors, the Maricopa, made a red and black were using coils. Maricopa ware shows some Mexican influence; they paint black designs around the necks of the pots in unbanded designs. The Maricopa and the other Rancheria tribes including the Yuma, the Cocopa, and Mojave, also make clay figurines which wear clothes and beads.

Jewelry
Among humans the urge to ornament is universal. In the Southwest, body paint was probably the most common ornament in the past, with jewelry scarce but popular. Most of this jewelry was made of stone or shell, the latter obtained by travel or trade which

Below: *The work of Navajo silversmiths was very elegant and often quite stunning in its beauty and skill; it is even better appreciated when it is considered how very basic were the tools used and the surroundings worked in. The smith pictured here in 1915 is working on a small anvil set up temporarily on a blanket in a small dwelling. His tools are clearly visible.*

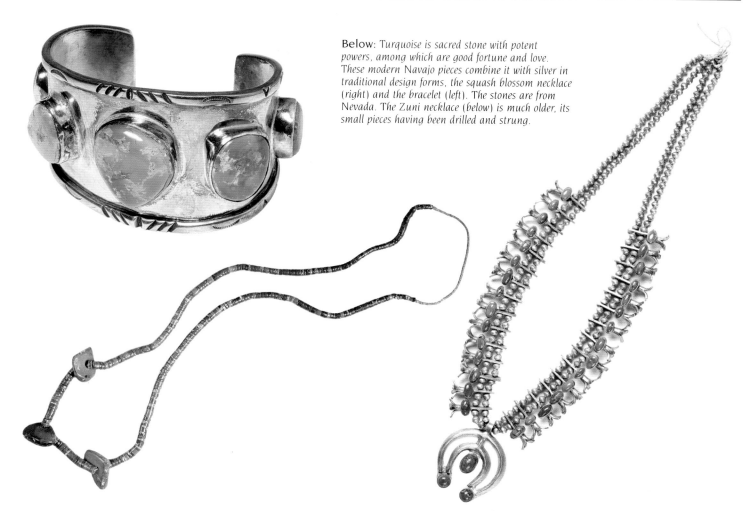

Below: *Turquoise is sacred stone with potent powers, among which are good fortune and love. These modern Navajo pieces combine it with silver in traditional design forms, the squash blossom necklace (right) and the bracelet (left). The stones are from Nevada. The Zuni necklace (below) is much older, its small pieces having been drilled and strung.*

contributed to a wide distribution of marine shell varieties. The only non-marine shell used was the terrestrial snail (gastropod). All other shells were worked to some extent; the most common use was to make beads from the small olivella shell. Shell was made into beads, rings, and bracelets by abrading it against a harder surface. Objects of ornaments are rare before AD 500 and become more popular in later periods. In the southern parts of the area there are some copper bells which were probably traded up from Mexico. By AD 900-1200 there was an increase in jewelry in the Southwest – stone and bone rings, copper bells, turquoise, jet and stone pendants, stone and shell beads and shell bracelets. In both the Hohokam and later in the Anasazi/Chaco area there was beautiful mosaic inlay. Shell was cut into the shape of birds and animals, and acid and wax etching was done on shell pendants.

Turquoise was the favorite stone of all Southwestern Indians and has many variant colors, from green to robin's egg blue, depending on the mine and the mineral composition. Because of this demand, it was traded over great distances; turquoise from the Cerrillos mines in New Mexico – controlled today by Santo Domingo Indians[12] – went into the inlaid Aztec masks from Tenochtitlan. The Santo Domingo Indians have a myth that when their people emerged from the underworld two other groups came with them, and that before they parted to go their individual ways, the Santo Domingo promised to make beads for the other

Indians. To this day, they love to trade and whole families are engaged in the production and distribution of turquoise and beads of other materials.

The manufacture of these beads, called *hishi*, is still a very important skill. The shaping of turquoise, and other materials like shell or stone, into beads is done by rolling it on tufa or sandstone to smooth all the edges. The beads are then assembled into graduated necklaces or *jaclos*, a very old and simple necklace form that has been unchanged since prehistoric times. Beads found in the Anasazi burials at Chaco Canyon are indistinguishable from beads made now. Beads and amulets were holed in the center by the use of a pump drill; the string of rough beads was then rolled on a wet slab of sandstone. This time-consuming technique is still used because it produces beads which fit together in a comfortable way.

When the Spanish first came into the Southwest looking for gold, the Indians did not have a word for metal. They were, however, quick to appreciate the bright and enduring qualities of it, and small pieces began to appear as necklaces or rings, or as additions to a shirt, although it was not worked until the middle of the nineteenth century.[13] The Native Americans had to learn to work metal in the most primitive conditions. The early techniques for silversmithing were very simple. Some coals were taken from the fire, and a torch was used to heat the silver. The coals caught the heat and acted as a small furnace, melting the

metal. As soon as the metal was hot, it was placed on an anvil and pounded into shape. As it cooled, it was reheated with bellows and reworked. The tools needed were an anvil, a hammer, several die stamps for decoration, some silver, some solder, and a fire.[14]

The original Navajo bellows were made of goat hide and served to keep the coals glowing.[15] Decoration was added after the piece was shaped. Often differently shaped dies were stamped into the silver. If the die was cut too deep, it could slice through the silver, so the artist had to be careful. Many of these dies were originally made in Spain or Mexico to stamp Mexican leather saddles, bags, and costumes. The Navajo discovered that the dies worked beautifully as silver decoration but they also learned to make their own dies using files to cut designs. The early Navajo silver work was very straightforward, and is characterized by its pure sense of design.

The influence of Mexicans who occupied New Mexico and Arizona was strong, their love of ornament being adopted by the Navajo. This is evident in several examples: the concha belt, the squash blossom necklace, the naja, and the use of ornamental buttons were all related to the Mexicans. The Navajo found that coins pounded into a domed shape and with a loop soldered to the back made both a decoration and a purchase at the trading post. The conchas, which means shells in Spanish, were originally round or oval silver plates which were larger than buttons and were attached by straps.

These were used to decorate belts, spurs, or a jacket, and the shape and design of the concha belt were fixed as early as 1880: 'The grand prize of the dandy Navajo buck is his belt... this is of leather completely covered by immense elliptical silver plaques.'[16] Navajos owned concha belts long before they learned how to make them. The Utes, Comanches, Kiowas, and other Southern Plains Indians with whom the Navajo feuded wore belts strung with plaques of copper, brass, or German silver (a non-ferrous alloy of copper, nickel, and zinc), and a Navajo might take a belt from a slain enemy or, in peacetime, obtain it in trade. Even before their capture and exile in the 1860s at the Bosque Redondo, the rich Navajos wore concha belts. White influence has reduced the size of the conchas and other forms alternate with traditional ones. Today these belts are very popular both with the Native Americans and the visitors to the area.

Another design element which the Navajo borrowed from the Mexican is the naja which is a crescent-shaped ornament used to decorate the centre of a horse bridle. It appeared on Navajo horses about the same time as concha belts became common. The naja may derive from the Moorish crescent moon, or another Moorish symbol, the hands of Fatima. Crescent-shaped figures were also popular with the Plains Indians, and the Navajo may have found it in their hunting and raiding there. The design of the naja occurs all over the world, but the most likely source for the Southwest is the Spanish/Moorish route. The naja was a popular pendant and for the Navajo was used almost exclusively, although the cross was also used, sometimes in combination with a naja, the cross symbolizing the morning star.

In addition to decorating the horse bridle, the naja is part of every squash blossom necklace. The squash blossom is a fertility symbol for the Pueblo people, and the name has become associated with this necklace although the actual flower in the necklace is a pomegranate blossom, which is also a fertility symbol. The pomegranate was a popular bead shape on Mexican trouser and jacket ornaments and has been a favorite Spanish decorative motif for centuries. The combination of pomegranate-shaped ornaments with a naja, spaced with shaped silver beads, has a hybrid beauty. This design, along with the concha belt, has come to be thought of as distinctively Navajo.

By the 1890s the Navajo had begun to add turquoise to their jewelry and were setting turquoise in simple bezels. Some of the first traders to the Navajo even imported turquoise for their silversmiths. The trader Lorenzo Hubbell at Ganado was selling fine Persian turquoise to the Navajo in 1890.[17] Hubbell also often supplied the Navajo with Mexican pesos which were pure silver and easy to work as in 1890 there was a prohibition against defacing United States coins which had previously supplied the silver necessary to make jewelry. The Navajo silversmiths were supplied partly by the traders and partly by their old trading partners in the Pueblos.[18] In addition to making and selling jewelry, the Navajo love to wear jewelry which they make. The display of wealth in the form of necklaces, belts, bracelets, rings, earrings, buttons, and silver-decorated horse bridles was, and is, important to the Navajo culture.

Among all the pueblos, the pueblo of Zuni is most noted for its jewelry. The Zuni probably learned to make jewelry from the Navajo. In 1880 they were making simple forms but by 1910 they had evolved the style which is recognizably Zuni. In contrast to the Navajo, the Zuni generally had more modern jewelry tools, which they got from their trader C. J. Wallace. Their work is more intricate and uses more and smaller stones than that of the Navajo. The tools included fine pliers which are essential to make the small bezels for the small turquoise stones which characterize Zuni jewelry in the style known as Needlepoint. The other important tools were the vise and the emery wheel, which makes polishing turquoise and silver much easier. The small rows of turquoise stones in Zuni bracelets may be inspired by rows of kernels of blue corn (a crop with sacred significance). Zuni jewelry is usually lightweight and the silver serves as a base to hold the turquoise rather than as an important design element. Commercial from an early stage, the sale of their jewelry has made a big difference to the economic well-being of Zuni.

In the late 1930s the Hopi began to make jewelry, but there were not many silversmiths until after 1946. The work done before that is not distinctive from that of the Zuni or Navajo. The best-known Hopi jeweler was Charles Loloma from Hotevilla. He used secret settings of different stones – turquoise, coral, sugulite, and obsidian – to make colorful bands inside the curves of his rings and bracelets, so that they could only be seen by the wearer. His design sense was very strong and clear. Today many of the Hopis make jewelry which is inspired by Loloma and

his teachings. Other pueblos make some jewelry, but most of the production is from Zuni, Hopi, Santo Domingo, and, of course, the Navajo Nation.

Weaving

Prehistorically textiles were made by a number of ingenious processes from whatever suitable plant or animal fibers came to hand. After cotton was introduced these processes were still retained. Non-loom techniques can be divided into two categories: finger-weaving of the single element which requires no tools or only simple devices; and finger-weaving using netting and looping, and coil without foundation, or warp-weft weaves involving two sets of elements worked at right angles to each other. It is interesting to note that knots had great ceremonial and cultural importance, and are carefully rendered in the murals of the *kivas* at Pottery Mound and Kuaua.

Surprisingly large and complex textiles can be made with these simple processes. Non-loom warp-weft weaves are made without a loom with heddles. These were favored by the basketmakers to make narrow bands, sandals, soft bags, and fur or feather robes. This process involved winding a sturdy yarn continuously around two supports. The yarn between these loops was separated and treated as warps. More complicated weaves such as tapestry weaves were employed by the Anasazi Basketmakers for apron fronts, tump-lines and other bands. The Anasazi and Mogollon sites also produce warm, weft-twined blankets of fur or feather cord. In these the warps are established by winding one continuous fur or feather cord back and forth. Pueblo weaving on looms goes back to at least AD 700 when cotton first began to appear in the Southwest. The loom was introduced from Mexico, and by AD 1100 vertical looms were found all over the Southwest. The vertical loom of the Pueblos was used exclusively with cotton yarns, a medium in which the Hopi excelled, creating a distinctive form known as Beautiful Design which consists of embroidered colors on a white cotton background.

There was a division of labor between the Pueblo men and women in weaving, the men

Below: A ceremonial sash forms part of the full dress of the Hopi flute priest. Woven by men, the sash is of the same typical embroidered design as pieces worn as girdles or breechcloths. It is thought that the patterns might represent the mask of one of the guardian kachinas, with diamonds for eyes and zig-zags for bared teeth.

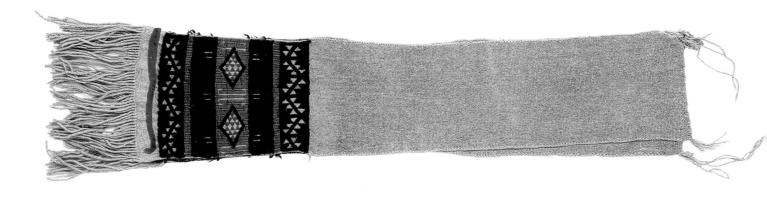

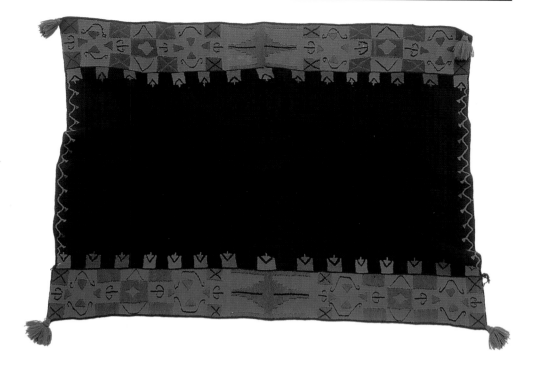

producing most of the weaving. Men wove on their looms in the *kivas* (although they also made non-loom ceremonial belts and tump-lines). A Hopi groom's male relatives were expected to weave his bride's wedding dress. Groups of women working together made fur and feather blankets, which were non-loom weaving. The use of the upright loom with heddles has now almost died out in the pueblos, but there is still non-loom weaving, now done by men.

The Navajo probably learned to weave from the Pueblo Indians no more than 300 years ago – although they weave wool rather than cotton using women rather than men – and today they are the best-known weavers. The Navajo textiles are closely related to Pueblo cultures in their use of balanced formal designs; indeed the distinctive banded design style of Pueblo blankets and shawls is an obvious influence on much Navajo work. The loom which they use, an upright loom, is related to the loom used by Pueblo men. The interchange between Pueblos and Navajo is hard to trace, but the twill and diamond designs appear in Pueblo weaving from long ago and the Navajo may have learned from the Pueblos and then later given the technique back. The woman's dress, or manta, for both Pueblo and Navajo is black wool with a red border, but blue at Zuni. It is woven in two pieces, joined at the side and fastened over one shoulder. Today the women wear a cotton calico undergarment, but on feast days the garment is worn as it was prehistorically. It may be that the diamonds in the weaving represent the different worlds in which the Indians lived and passed through to arrive in this, the world of living people.

Left: *A newly married Pueblo woman was presented with a wedding sash, along with other textile items, which had been woven by male relatives of her husband. These were treasured until death. This gray-white sash with the long tasseled fringe is from Jemez and dates from 1890. It is patterned with interlaced striped and diamond designs.*

Above: *Woven mantas, from the Spanish for blanket, were worn as both dresses and shawls by Pueblo women in the mid- to late nineteenth century. This example is from San Juan. The black background is embroidered on opposite sides in a green and red pattern, with tassels in each corner.*

The Navajo loom is made from any wood which is at hand. The main supports are two posts which are set upright in the ground. A set of beams is then lashed horizontally at the top and bottom forming a roughly rectangular frame.[19] Usually a woman weaves outside her home or *hogan*, in the shade of a tree. She weaves when there is time, when the baby is asleep, when the sheep are not demanding care, or when the meal is over. It is a stop and start process. Navajo weaving is characterized by the use of what are called lazy lines. These are breaks in the weaving which are the result of a sitting woman weaving only as far as she can reach, then scooting over and weaving another section. They are so-called because they save energy for the weaver who is sitting in the shade, and not working her entire loom.

The Navajo value weaving highly and say that they learned to weave as a gift from Spider Woman. Baby girls are prepared with a special ritual for their future as weavers. In Navajo legend it is said: 'When a baby girl is born to your tribe you shall go and find a spider web which you must take and rub on the baby's hands and arms. Thus when she grows up she will weave and her fingers and arms will not tire from the weaving.'[20] In deference to such origin stories the women used to leave a hole at the center, like a web, but traders stamped out the practice and a 'spirit outlet' replaced it; this is a thin line or flaw from the center to the edge.

Early Navajo blankets were banded and serrated with limited amounts of red used carefully as a color accent. These are the early blankets which are woven to be worn with the stripes around the body. They are woven with a very tight weave, which makes them somewhat waterproof, and warm; the colors

had a border, an element missing in traditional Navajo weaving. Finally, the Navajo began to weave some of their stories, and occasionally some of their religious ceremonial designs. Navajo sandpaintings, which were used in curing ceremonies, were woven into wall hangings. (These rugs, especially those woven in the 1930s by the great Hosteen Klah, are the core of the collection at the Wheelright Museum of the American Indian, and are quite rare – only a medicine man could weave them.)

Today many copies of old Navajo rug and blanket designs are being produced in Mexico, using cotton weft or inferior wool, but following Navajo colors and designs. These copies of Navajo rugs sell very well, since the cost of a fine Navajo rug has gone up, and fewer young weavers are entering the market. The traditional Navajo way of life, the language, tending sheep, and living in isolation, and the importance of ceremonies are all under stress as the modern world makes more inroads on the reservation. There are signs of a weaving revival, but the time and patience required to produce a rug are not easily assimilated into the life of today's teenage Navajo. For the Navajo, the two skills of making jewelry and weaving blankets and rugs have formed the basis of present day Navajo arts and crafts. These are both arts which appeal to the nomadic soul, are useful, and portable.

In the Pueblos, however, weaving has almost stopped. The pueblos of Acoma and Zuni were weaving wool mantas, which are used to make dresses and can also act as heavy shawls, until after 1900, but the availability of ready-made clothes at the trading post hurt the Pueblo weaving trade. The fine diamond weave designs on mantas with embroidered borders which were done for ceremonial use and are still used for dances are handed down as ceremonial heirlooms.

derived from various hues in the wool (white, black, gray) and vegetable dyes (yellow, red, indigo). Because the Navajo were nomadic and far-flung in their remote region, we know little about the chronology of their weaving but it appears that by 1863 the level of technical sophistication in Navajo weaving was very high.[21]

The categories of First, Second, and Third Phase Chiefs' Blankets are somewhat misleading. These handsome blankets were not worn by Chiefs, or even exclusively by men, but there is no question that these blankets were valued highly (and ownership lent a connotation of power) and that weaving such a blanket was a mark of prestige. It appears that these Chief blanket patterns were woven concurrently with more complicated design patterns and other weaving which was for internal use and was not as fine.

In 1868 many Navajo were allowed to return to their homes from their imprisonment at Bosque Redondo and a small group of merchants moved onto the reservations to trade the Navajo's manufactured goods (jewelry and blankets) for items the Indians needed in their new economy. In an attempt to help the Navajo two traders, Lorenzo Hubbell and J. B. Moore, and others began to suggest more commercial patterns which the Navajo might weave. They, and traders in other parts of the vast reservation, were responsible for the development and marketing of Navajo crafts, as well as changing the way it looked. Their trading posts were also another way of moving crafts

to market and other posts began to appear on the Navajo reservation.

The new designs came from books showing oriental rugs, probably mostly Turkish, thought to be more in keeping with the then tastes of American consumers. The Navajo women looked at the pictures of the oriental rug designs, memorized them, and wove them. These designs took the name of their regional trading posts and are called Crystal, Ganado (red, black, gray, and white geometric designs), Tuba City (storm designs with lightning), Shiprock (which produced a distinctive *Yei* design of the Navajo gods in long dancing rows), the Two Gray Hills (noted for its very fine tight weave and black, gray, and white wool), Wide Ruin (soft, natural colors), and others. There are more than a dozen different areas; the actual design, however, is always different because it is the product solely of the individual weaver. The rugs were more colorful than before and often

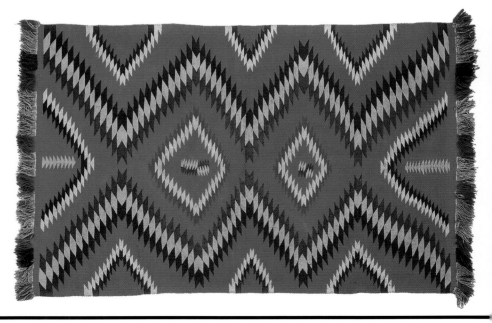

Right: *This Zuni blanket is recorded as having been made in 1879 by a boy aged twelve. The design for it was carried entirely in the boy's head. Because of its Navajo rather than Zuni influences, it is reasonable to conclude that the boy may have been a captive of the Navajo at some point. It is not, however, an authentic Navajo design for it contains an uneven number of design elements; perhaps this was done deliberately so as not to incur bad luck. Whatever the case it is a remarkable work for a supposedly first effort.*

Basketry

Baskets represent a vital aspect of American Indian life from the standpoint of survival as well as artistic expression. Along with the working of stone and bone, basket making was probably a basic technical skill of the first occupants of the North American continent. Because basketry materials are so perishable not many relics survive, but in the dry climate of the Southwest, especially in caves, many baskets and basket fragments have been preserved, with some radio-carbon dates going back more than 10,000 years.

There was a large prehistoric group in the Southwest called the Basketmakers during the period from 100 BC to AD 700. The technical level of their baskets is unsurpassed. From this period there are large storage baskets, sandals, aprons, and mats, and practically every article they used which was not stone or bone, was a type of basketry. The extensive reliance on basketry declined with the introduction of ceramics about AD 700, but baskets were still used for washing grain, winnowing and for starting pots.

The earliest basketry technique is twining, where the moving elements, or wefts, twist around the foundation elements, or warps. Several thousand years later the coiling method came into being. In coiling a hard or soft core element, which makes the coil, is wound round and round in a spiral fashion and held in place by thin wrapping elements, the stitches. A third technique is plaiting, where the warps and wefts merely go over and under each other in a particular pattern which varies from simple to complex. Within these three basic groups large regional variations occur and significant differences can be used to identify each region and tribe.

Before any basket can be made, the weaving materials have to be gathered and prepared. This takes a great deal of time and knowledge, not only in the careful selection of choice raw materials such as willow, grass, and reeds, but because the materials have to be gathered seasonally and to have reached a particular point in their growth cycle. Once the materials have been assembled, before weaving can be started there usually has to be some preparation in the form of cleaning, stripping, splitting, or treatment by applying heat or liquids. These procedures are complicated and time-consuming. In some cases the roots of plants are specially treated by heat by being buried in hot sand for a day or so in order to make them more pliable and more durable. Occasionally the fibers may be twisted into cordage for warps or wefts. Stems, shoots, and twigs are often split, necessitating great skill to produce long and even-sized elements. Colors and dyes have to be prepared, or the materials may be treated directly, for example, by being buried in mud.

When all the materials are prepared, the basket maker makes a decision about the size and decoration of the basket. Working out a design requires concentrated effort. Gathering materials may be somewhat routine, but thinking up the design takes more effort. It must be fitted to the size and shape of the basket; all the elements must work out evenly, so there has to be mathematical proportion and symmetry with accurate calculations. The weaver has to keep in mind all the details of the various elements of the pattern: where they are design elements, how they are placed, and their relationship to each other as the weaving progresses. The variations in length, size, and shape of the design and the spaces between require many permutations and intense concentration. In many cases the weaver cannot keep track visually because she (both historically and at the present, most basket weavers are women) cannot see the opposite part of the basket. For true quality work, the weaver cannot begrudge either time or patience. The finished basket is usually a marvel in geometric and mathematical perfection.

Baskets are versatile and are woven in many shapes. Woven water bottles were common all over the Southwest, many of them made by the Paiute and traded to the Hopi, Zuni, and Navajo. These woven water bottles are covered with pinion pitch so that they do not leak. It is also possible to cook in a basket, by filling the basket with hot water and food, and dropping hot rocks into the basket. This method of cooking was still used by the Paiutes as late as 1900. The unbreakable and lightweight nature of baskets made them the best choice for portable cookware. Basketry may be the mother of pottery. Today a shallow basket is sometimes used to hold the clay as a pot is first begun. It is possible that the use of coils to make ceramic vessels came from the experience of using coils to make baskets.

The Hopi of Second and Third Mesa are probably the best known contemporary basket makers in the Southwest. (The other Hopi Mesas do not make baskets.) The Hopis weave by coiling or plaiting, using yucca over grass or shredded yucca bundles; they plait baskets either with yucca strips or with rabbit brush wefts and wild currant warps. The flat baskets best serve as trays or sifters – or as well plaques. Deep baskets with flared sides of rabbit brush and Native or aniline-dyed designs are also decorative and useful items for sale to tourists. The Hopi use coiling to make circular trays or plaques and

Below: *Hopi basketry trays or coiled plaques using traditional designs are still produced today by the women of Second Mesa. Made of galleta grass and yucca leaves, the green ones come from the outside of the plant, the other colors come from natural dyes – such as black from sunflower seeds. This plaque was made in about 1895, and its pattern may represent the four corners of the world or may be a whirlwind design.*

Above: *Of all the Southwestern basketmakers the Pima and Papago number among the very best. Their designs and patterns are similar. This Papago woman is weaving objects almost certainly destined for the tourist trade, but the Papago also maintain many of their traditional ways and continue to make and use baskets for their own domestic functions such as gathering fruit from the giant cactus.*

storage baskets in various sizes. Hopi flat trays of wicker are used for carrying the sacred corn meal, and serving the flat piki bread. Some of the best of these come from the village of Old Oraibi.

When a Hopi girl is about to be married, she asks her female relatives to help weave all the baskets which will be required for her dowry. It may take several years to weave all the baskets. The requirement for this skill in a wife shows both the economic and ceremonial importance of basket making to the Hopi. Wedding baskets are important for the Navajo too, but they require only one basket for the wedding and it is an important part of the ceremony, not the dowry. This basket is a shallow bowl which is coiled with the basic colors of red, black, and natural vegetation color.[22] The material is of sumac stitched over a three-rod willow foundation. This design band is said to illustrate the hills and valleys of this world and the underworld. There is a break in the design which is the path that spirits take between the two worlds. According to tradition the end of the coil must line up with this break: this provides an easy method of locating the opening which must face east during the ceremony.

Many other fine basket-making groups live in the Southwest. The Havasupai are Hokan-speaking Yumans who live in a secluded branch of the Grand Canyon which has beautiful waterfalls. They are known for their weaving, which has continued to the present day. The Walapai are close relatives who live in northwestern Arizona, making baskets by coiling and twining. They frequently use sumac twigs since sumac grows all around their reservation. The Hualapais and Yavapais are similarly active.

A much larger group, the Apaches, are close Athabaskan relations to the Navajo and probably came into the Southwest with them. They are well known for their excellent baskets. These were nomadic peoples who did not want to settle down on reservations; baskets were easy to move and did not break. Today they live on reservations, but their main craft remains basket making, although that skill is not being passed on to the next generation. Apache basketry has been commercial since the 1880s, traditionally crafted from yucca, sumac, and mulberry, made to simple and utilitarian designs, and colored with reds, yellows, and blues. The three traditional types are round, shallow trays; tall burden baskets; and vessels made watertight with pitch.

There are two principal divisions in the Apache, a result of their nomadic past, each with several main bands: the Western Apache comprises the San Carlos, White Mountain, Cibecue, and Northern and Southern Tonto; to the east are the Mescalero, Jicarilla, and Chiricahua groups. The Western Apache traditionally practised more farming and were culturally closer to the Navajo, the San Carlos Apache in particular having produced many examples of beautiful basketry.

The Jicarilla still weave some baskets, partly thanks to Lydia Pena, a remarkable weaver who has done a good job in restoring interest in basket making among the tribes. She teaches classes and sells most of her produce, but it is hard work and it is difficult to price the baskets high enough to cover the time involved.

The work of the Western Apache is mostly coiled trays, large burden baskets, and storage baskets. The designs are mostly geometric, but the use of human and animal forms is common. It is interesting to note that these most nomadic of the Southwestern Indians continued making baskets like burden baskets for practical use in moving materials around, rather than using baskets for ceremonies or specific processing of food as was the case in the pueblos. This survival of baskets in such ceremonial use makes anthropologists think that basketry is very old in the Southwest, since the ceremonial use of objects is usually very conservative.

There are two groups of Indians in southern Arizona who are specially noted for their baskets: the Pima and the Papago. These people live in the very hot and arid desert and their basket work is closely related. Pima baskets are made from willow and devil's claw over a foundation of tule. Since the 1890s the Papago have changed material, and now yucca has replaced willow in Papago work, which makes it easier to distinguish between them. The start of the baskets is also different, with the Papago basket starting at a cross, and the Pima a plaited knot. Probably the most recognizable Papago basket is the burden basket.

Today's Papago probably make more baskets than any other tribe with animal and plant forms as their favorite decorative elements. Since the Papago basket is pounded as it is woven, their baskets tend to be flatter and wider than a Pima basket. Pima baskets are close to Apache baskets in the excellence of their weave. Their designs are usually geometric patterns in swirls or a quadrant layout. Most designs are based on squash blossoms, whirlwinds, or a maze. These are frequently shallow baskets which were used for winnowing seeds or ground wheat.

Sculpture and Leatherwork

There has been sculpture in the Southwest since prehistoric times. Soft stones have been carved, and figurines in stone, wood, clay, and shell were common throughout the Anasazi times: there is a carved stone Hohokam ram which may have been a palette, or designed for some ceremonial use. One form of carving still much in evidence is the Zuni art of fetish making from minerals and semi-precious stone. The animal figures are very important in regional culture, being used in the hunt societies and as part of medicine bundles. Carved from turquoise or soft stone, the fetishes are usually small for portability and concealment. They often have bundles of sage or feathers tied around them. Today, fetishes have become popular charms for tourists.

One of the most notable losses during the early Spanish period was that the kachinas, the masked gods, disappeared from the Rio Grande pueblos, although they still appear in Zuni or Hopi. Many small carvings of the sacred kachinas have been made from dried cottonwood by the Zuni and the Hopi for the past few centuries.[23]

In the nineteenth century Zuni kachinas were often dressed in real cloth and leather, while Hopi kachinas had their clothing carved out of the wood. Zuni kachinas also usually have taller bodies, and their limbs are articulated. Today, the lines between Zuni and Hopi kachinas are somewhat blurred, and the situation is further confused because the Navajo have been making kachinas since 1985 for sale to tourists.

The kachinas embody the spirit of many different ideas and things. For the Zuni and the Hopi the kachinas come to bless and to chastise people. It is important to know what kachina you are seeing, and so the dolls are made to teach the children to recognize and to invoke these special beings. This is especially true for girls, since boys will learn to recognize the kachinas in the *kivas*.

Kachina dolls today can be elaborately

Above: *The rawhide saddlebag of the Apache was leatherwork par excellence. Its patterned cut-work decoration reveals the red strouding underneath; and conical metal tinklers and long fringes add further to its distinctive appearance.*

carved, but a century ago they tended to be simple. They have always been sought by collectors since they portray the rich religious life of the Pueblos in a tangible way. Simple, wooden kachina dolls were traditionally given to Hopi children as their first toys, the mother kachina, or *Hahay'iwuuti*, being hung over the cradle to bring good health. Today, the technical excellence of all the carvers has increased and most of the production of kachinas is for the market. There are many kachinas, and different ones appear seasonally. Spending half a year with the Hopi, the kachinas bring them rain and prosperity. Each kachina has different attributes and subtle changes in costume. It is important to all the Pueblos that the kachinas do not disappear, and the depiction of the kachinas is one way of reminding people of who the kachinas are, their special functions, and, as important, who the Pueblo people themselves are.

As well as kachinas, gambling and gaming objectives were carved, ceremonial sticks prepared and painted, and figures created to form part of the altar screen in the *kiva*. Tablitas or flat headdresses were also made and painted for women's dances; the Butterfly Dance or the Corn Dance, for instance, may use different tablitas.

Another craft associated with the Apache in the last century was the manufacture of

Right: *Carved fetishes and kachinas were, and are still, among the most typical of Southwestern items. The bear (left) and mole (right) are two very popular choices. The attachment of an arrow to the back is traditional.*

handsome, cut leather shirts and dresses. Whole skins of deer or antelope were tanned, then fringed and pierced with circles or square holes in order to create designs made by the cutaway portions of the skin. The leather might be dyed and ornamented with shells or feathers to add beauty and/or protective medicine. Many fine examples of dresses and saddle bags are held in various museum collections.

References

1 Reichard, 1968: 167.
2 Dillingham, 1992: 5.
3 Cushing, 1886: 511.
4 Dillingham, 1992: 8.
5 Before the Spanish arrived in 1598, some pueblos had developed a low melting point lead glaze which was used as decoration, not as a seal. When the Spanish returned after the 1680 Revolt, the use of lead glaze disappeared and the pottery of the southern pueblos and Hopi was slipped with a clay that fired to a matte finish, and decorated with red and black which is still in use today.
6 The American entrepreneur, Fred Harvey, brought good food and quick service to the travelers on the railroads which were pushing west. He also saw that he could make money selling Indian arts and crafts. His agent, Herman Schweizer, went around the reservation buying and sometimes commissioning things which could be sold. The railroad of the late 1880s also led to a reduction in the size of many of the large vessels. Tourists wanted things of a size that they could pack to take home.
7 Dillingham, 1992: 10. This is interesting because it indicates the strong sex-linked roles in these traditional cultures, that being struck by lightning is a clear transformational experience, and that only then could one cross a sex line to perform tasks which were culturally assigned. That division, however, has broken down.
8 We believe there was a change in the shape of vessels when the Spanish introduced wheat. Bread dough needs a big open bowl to rise, and although the market for big dough bowls may have been steady under the Spanish, the American troops who arrived in 1848 were all bread, not corn tortilla, eaters, and the best known of the bread bowls, the

Santo Domingo dough bowl, was probably produced to make wheat and yeast bread for the tastes of the American Army. Information from David Snow in an unpublished manuscript.
9 Margaret Harding, an anthropologist at the Lowie Museum, University of California, brought back photographs of the insides of pots to Zuni in the mid-1980s. These were pots which had disappeared from Zuni when Frank Hamilton Cushing in mid-1880 had collected almost every pot in Zuni and taken them to the Smithsonian in Washington. Verbal communication with Margaret Harding in 1985.
10 Sturtevant, 1979: 517.
11 Personal communication with David Snow, Southwest ceramic specialist.
12 They got control of the great turquoise mines from the pueblo of San Marcos, which emigrated to Santo Domingo when San Marcos was abandoned.
13 During the Bosque Redondo in 1864-68, one man, *Atsidi Sani*, or Old Smith, first began to work iron and fix the bridles for the soldiers and cowboys.
14 'All the smithing was done outside beside a campfire. Sometimes an apprentice would watch and help. If a young man has a father who is a silversmith, he will begin to help him with the work when he is about fourteen years old... As he grows older and becomes more experienced in working metal, his father gives him more to do, and within a period of a year or two he is able to make silver by himself and sell it at the trading post.' Adair, 1962: 76
15 It is thought the masterful Navajo learned the craft from the Pueblos who gained it from the Spanish; there was, however, metalworking among the Athapaskan kin of the Navajo in the north, so their knowledge may predate their migration.
16 Bloom 1936: 226.

17 Adair, 1962: 15.
18 Herman Schweizer had pre-cut turquoise given to Navajo smiths who were working for traders. The Harvey company sent the material to trading posts to be made into bracelets, beads, and other jewelry.
19 A second pair of horizontal beams holds the weaving. These are laid on the ground and the warp, the vertical threads, is strung continuously in a figure-eight conformation between the beams. This is then raised and fastened inside the rectangular frame. It is not attached at the top beam, but is lashed to an intermediate pole, the tension beam. This intermediate beam creates a more even tension for the warp. The lower warp is then tied directly to the bottom of the frame. Then the heddles, which are used to raise and lower the weaving, are made. They open a temporary space, or shed, between the two planes of the warp threads through which the yarn passes. After the yarn has passed, the batten – a wide flat stick – is removed, and the yarn is beaten into place with a weaving comb or a firm stroke of the batten. Berlant and Kahlenberg, 1991: 41-42
20 O'Bryon, 1956: 56.
21 Personal communication with Mary Hunt Kahlenberg, 1994.
22 The Apache say that they use the Navajo basket because once when an Apache chief was sick, a great Navajo medicine man helped his Apache brother with the curing ceremony. The patient recovered, and when the Apache thanked his helper and asked the secret of his power, the Navajo said the basket was important.
23 The kachina is made from the dried cottonwood root, the center of which must also be the center of the kachina.

THE PLAINS

PERHAPS MORE than any other peoples, the Indians of the Great Plains of North America – the Blackfeet, Sioux, Crow, Kiowa, and Comanche to name a few – have captured the imagination of the world. Resplendent in costume, picturesque in appearance, and romantic in their customs, these equestrian nomads roamed the prairies and plains living in tipis and hunting the buffalo. The fundamentals of the culture, however, were due largely to two momentous imports of the white man – the horse, which came from the Spanish settlements in the southwest, and the gun from the French in the northeast.

The Plains stretch some 2,000 miles (3,386km) from present-day Texas to Alberta and from the Mississippi/Missouri to the base of the Rocky Mountains. The tribes who dwelt there shared enough traits to be classed together as representing a distinct way of life although some, such as the Mandan and Pawnee, lived in more permanent earth-lodge dwellings. Dominant however, was the dependence on the buffalo which not only provided food but hides for clothing, receptacles, and dwellings; during at least part of the year, Plains Indians lived in tipis with a seasonal grouping in a large circle when the scattered groups united for the great ceremonials.

A characteristic of Plains culture was to put great emphasis on the interrelationship between ceremonial, costume, adornment, and song – a holistic world view where everything was linked in a complex pattern of mythology and ritual: as one Blackfeet ceremonialist put it, 'My clothes are my medicine'.[2] Throughout the region, women displayed a high degree of skill in the preparation of animal hides for use in the fabrication of many household objects, clothing, and dwellings. This craft gave a decided common thread to the culture: the emphasis in artwork, however, differed considerably among the areas. Thus, northern and central Plains tribes did some exquisite porcupine quillwork, while on the southern Plains such work was almost entirely absent. Later, with the introduction of beads in the early nineteenth century, definite identifiable area – even tribal – styles were developed. Likewise, skill and emphasis in such fields as carving, pipe-making, featherwork, and pictographs varied from one part of the Plains to the next. Nevertheless, in all cases the end product reflected the concern and skill and dedication of the craftsman or woman to produce an object which was a thing of beauty and in harmony with its environment even though, as the opening quote suggests, the work might be carried out under the most adverse conditions.

Porcupine Quillwork

Although sometimes considered a gastronomic delicacy, the most important use of the porcupine in North America was as a source of material for quillwork. The North American porcupine, *Erethizon dorsatum*, was commonly found on the northern and western Great Plains and the quills were a significant trade item to those tribes who did not have direct access to the animal.[3] The pelage of the porcupine is a dense, woolly undercoat and white-tipped guard hairs and quills on the heads, back, and tail. The quills are white stiff hollow tubes with brown to black barbed tips and those used for quillwork range in size from about 2-5in (30-140mm.) in length and 1-2mm in diameter. In addition to porcupine quills, bird quills were also occasionally used, particularly by those tribes on the Missouri River, such as the Hidatsa, Mandan, and Arikara and, perhaps to a lesser extent, by the Santee and Yankton Sioux and Ojibwa along the upper Mississippi River.[4]

Archeological evidence suggests that

Above: *Colorful beadwork and skilled leatherwork of an Arapaho craftswoman, embellish a mirror bag from circa 1890. Attached to the bag is a heavily beaded band for passing over the arm, whilst small brass bells, acquired by trade, garnish the lower edge of the bag above the fringe. Pendents at the top are looped buckskin thongs tightly bound with red porcupine quills. Plains Indian skill in carving is displayed by the wooden spoon with a turtle effigy as a crest on the handle.*

porcupine quillwork has long been practised in North America, the main evidence for this coming from the region of Utah and Nevada where artifacts preserved in caves show the use of quills as a bonding element; such items date to c.500 BC, while moccasins decorated with quillwork and dating from the thirteenth and fourteenth centuries have been reported from various archeological sites.[5] It has been suggested that quillwork possibly had its origins in Asia, with examples of woven mats and baskets found in Asia exhibiting the same basic weaving and sewing techniques as used in quillwork in North America.[6]

Highly formalized quillworkers' guilds have been identified among such tribes as the Cheyenne and Arapaho,[7] and these guilds used certain designs which were considered sacred and could only be produced by the initiated women. Similar customs appear to have prevailed among the Blackfeet,[8] whom it has been reported, traditionally at least, put considerable emphasis on the religious significance of quillwork.[9] Guilds appear to have been less formalized among the Siouan tribes such as the Lakota, Mandan, Hidatsa, and Crow but several of these tribes – in common with the Plains Algonquian – explain the origin of quillwork in mythological terms.[10]

In preparing the quills for use, they were first softened by the application of moisture, generally by being placed in the mouth, and they were then flattened by being drawn between the teeth or finger nails; while some elaborately carved bone or antler quill flatteners are to be found in the collections, it is probable that they were actually ceremonial in function. In early days, the sources of dye were various roots, berries, and mosses, but later, colored trade cloth was used – when cloth and quills were boiled together, the color from the cloth penetrated the quills. Commercial dyes obtained from white traders were increasingly used after 1870.

Some sixteen porcupine quill techniques

Below: *A superb shirt fringed with buckskin dating from circa 1860. It is identified as 'Sioux' in the museum records but the plaited quillwork technique, displaying the typical line of demarcation running lengthwise through the center of the strip and the complex patterns worked with the technique, suggests that it is of Hidatsa or Crow make, possibly a trade item. The triangular flap at the neck is of red and black cloth and parallel lines in blue paint embellish the body and arms of the shirt, features which are not uncommonly found on Lakota regalia.*

were used by the Plains tribes, of which eight were very common and in combination they can frequently be utilized to determine both the tribal origin and age of a particular specimen. The tools used were relatively simple and in addition to the possible use of a quill flattener, a woman quillworker used a bone marker, awl, knife, and sinew threads. The marker either simply impressed the surface or was dipped into a colored fluid and then used as a pen. The sinew thread was used to secure the quills to the hide. Wrapping techniques on rawhide strips were common and widely used in the decoration of hair ornaments and pipe-bags, both being particularly favored by the Sioux. Woven quillwork was used by the Cree and possibly in early days by the Blackfeet and it also occurs on at least one shirt from the Santee Sioux now in the Nathan Jarvis collection in the Brooklyn Museum. The technique is of particular interest since it utilized a small loom, the exquisitely finished work having the appearance of being made from fine cylindrical beads. More specialized methods such as the plaited technique and quill-wrapped horsehair were particularly well-developed by the Crow and appear on shirts, leggings, and moccasins. Although such work was also found on similar items collected from the Hidatsa, Mandan, Arikara, and Nez Perce, in most cases this was probably due to trade with the Crow.[11]

With the wholesale introduction of beads to the Plains tribes in the mid-nineteenth century, quillwork was progressively displaced as a decorative medium. However, fine traditional costumes decorated with quillwork were still being produced in limited quantities as late as the turn of the century on both the central and northern Plains, the Hidatsa in particular excelling in this skill. An exhibition of contemporary Sioux quillwork was assembled in 1974 at the Sioux Museum in Rapid City, South Dakota, and since that

Above: *A magnificent doll 31in (78cm.) high completes the selection of craft items. She wears a dress of blue strouding with rows of elk teeth. On the belt is a knife sheath and a beaded cradle.*

time, a number of Sioux quillworkers have found a 'ready market for their wares'.[12]

Beadwork
Until approximately 1830, porcupine quillwork predominated over beadwork even though beads were introduced to the Plains tribes in the early 1800s. Thus, when the trader François Larocque traveled to the Crow in the vicinity of the Yellowstone River in 1805, he reported that they already possessed small blue glass beads which had come from the Spaniards in the southwest and probably via Shoshoni intermediaries. The Crow were so fond of these beads that they were willing to give a horse for one hundred of them; in consequence their high value at this time limited their use to the edges of porcupine quillwork strips. This, however, was the beginning of the so-called 'Pony Beadwork' phase on the Great Plains.

Pony beads – so called because they were transported on pony pack trains – were large, somewhat irregular china and glass beads which were made in Venice and were about one-eighth of an inch (3mm.) in diameter. The colors were limited, blue being the most popular but white, black, and red were also used. By 1840 these beads were being used in great profusion – often in combination with a colored cloth – and they were applied to pipe-bags, moccasins, leggings, shirts, and buffalo robes. On clothing, the beadwork was generally carried out on a separate band, perhaps 3-4in (7.6-10cm.) wide and then sewn to the shirt or leggings, although on buffalo robes, the bands could be up to 8in (20cm.) wide. Patterns consisted of tall triangles, bars, squares, and diamonds and often reflected the designs used in earlier quillwork. The pony beadwork period lasted until about 1855 when a smaller type of bead became popular; referred to as 'seed' beads they varied in size from one to three-sixteenths of an inch in diameter and gradually displaced the pony beads as a working medium.[13]

Two main methods of sewing beads to a surface were employed by the Plains tribes:

the overlaid or spot stitch which was popular on the northern Plains, and the lazy stitch which was much favored by the central Plains tribes. In the overlaid or spot stitch, the technique was similar to that used in quillwork: here, a thread of sinew was strung with a few beads which was then attached to the surface by another thread sewn across it at intervals of every two or three beads. If a broad surface was to be covered, line after line was attached with the lines laid close together. In the lazy stitch, a number of beads were strung on a thread of sinew which had been fastened to the skin, and then a perforation was made to attach the sinew at the end of the row of beads. As in the overlaid stitch, the perforation did not completely pass through the skin but ran just below the surface so that no stitches appeared on the back of the work. The same number of beads were again strung on the sinew which was carried back to the starting point and passed through another perforation adjacent to the first one. Varying colors could be introduced and so arranged as to produce a design.

The tribal differences both in technique and style may be illustrated by reference to the beadwork of the Blackfeet on the northern Plains and that of the Sioux on the central Plains.[14] Almost without exception, the

Blackfeet employed the overlaid stitch, patterns being built up of scores of small squares or oblongs which were united to form larger patterns with the borders which were invariably an arrangement of different colored squares or oblongs. The large figures were generally squares, diamonds, triangles, or slanted bands with long, stepped sides. The inspiration for this style of beadwork seems, at least in part, to have derived from earlier quillwork designs, particularly in woven quillwork.[15] Floral designs were also used by the Blackfeet, possibly influenced by the Cree and Ojibwa and, with the increased use of seed beads in the late nineteenth century, floral designs on moccasins became common. As J. C. Ewers has observed, 'Photographs of Piegan Indians in the 1880s indicate that moccasins beaded in flowered patterns were then about as common as ones decorated with geometric designs'.[16] Additionally, floral designs were commonly used on saddles, saddle bags, and martingales: less commonly they appear on men's shirts and leggings. In contrast, the Sioux seldom used floral designs – the lazy stitch which they almost exclusively employed in their beadwork tending to restrict the patterns to blocks, crosses, tall triangles and particularly after c.1880, figures consisting of thin lines, terraced and forked, which were spread out on a white or, less commonly, blue background. The inspiration for this type of work, it has been suggested, came from the patterns which appeared on Caucasian rugs brought in by white settlers.[17] About 1890, some craftswomen began embroidering live figures such as men, horses, and elk – markedly different to the earlier traditional geometrical designs – and these figures were commonly worked on men's waistcoats and pipe-bags.[18] Crow

beadwork is particularly distinctive, the style appearing more massive than that of other tribes with large triangles, hourglasses, and lozenges in various combinations. A definite characteristic of Crow beadwork was the outlining of many of the patterns with white beads so setting them off from the background. A similar type of beadwork also prevailed among the Nez Perce and Shoshoni, the inspiration coming, at least in part, from those designs which commonly appeared on painted parfleches.[19] Men's and women's dress clothing, containers, robes and blankets, moccasins, as well as riding gear, were commonly decorated with this distinctive style of beadwork.[20]

In marked contrast to those tribes on the central and northern Plains, the beadwork of such tribes as the Kiowa, Comanche, and Southern Cheyenne on the southern Plains, was generally restricted to single lanes – perhaps seven or eight beads wide – along the edges of leggings, shirts, and women's dresses. The work was always of a high quality, the beads being both small and carefully selected, presenting a neat and expertly finished artifact. Some exceptions were the exquisite fully beaded bags and awl cases which, particularly among the Kiowa, invariably exhibited a distinctive glassy red bead background.

Carving and Engraving

The large carved house posts, totem poles, and the like so common and well-developed by the Indians of the northwest coast of America, found virtually no place in Plains Indian carving, the majority of which was rendered in the miniature. An exception to this was the use of human effigy spirit posts carved by Plains Cree and Ojibwa. These were observed as early as 1799 by the fur trader, Peter Fidler, in the vicinity of the Beaver River in what is now eastern Alberta. The posts were generally life-size and had crudely carved heads being referred to as *Mantokans* which derives from the Algonquian *maniot*, a term used for the mysterious life powers of the universe. Peter Fidler said that they were erected by Indians in the hope that 'the great *Menneto* will grant them and their families health while they remain in these parts'.[21] While the nomadism of most typical Plains tribes does go a long way to explaining the desire for small three-dimensional artwork, even among the semi-sedentary Plains tribes such as the Mandan, Hidatsa, and Omaha of the Missouri River, no large carved sculpture was found.[22]

Prior to the arrival of the Europeans, the production of carved artifacts was carried out by the use of stone implements although bone and pieces of copper obtained in trade might have been used. While appearing primitive, they were clearly more efficient in the hands of a skilled craftsman than might be imagined; thus the shaping of lance and flint arrowheads – the so-called Folsom and Clovis points – by early Plains inhabitants, demonstrates that great skill and workmanship was possible without the use of iron tools.

It can only be speculated as to how much wooden carving the early Plains tribes produced since wood rapidly deteriorates in the ground and no archeological sites on the

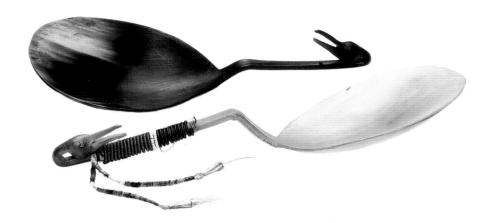

Plains have yielded wooden effigies; however, stone carvings of catlinite (a soft red stone) produced prior to the fifteenth century have been found and some of the finest Plains Indian carvings were of catlinite.[23] Additionally, shell and bone effigies which may date as early as AD 1000 have been found in sites associated with the ancestral Mandan.[24]

By the middle of the nineteenth century, and probably earlier, wooden carved animal effigies were associated with medicine hunts, tree-dweller ceremonials, and war medicines. War clubs, courting flutes, pipe-stems, Sun Dance dolls, children's toys, and effigy horse figures were also carved and widely distributed across the Plains.[25]

Horse effigies were often depicted on mirror-boards and pipes, but the most elaborate carvings of horses were used in victory dances and were highly symbolic. Thus, when Walter McClintock visited the Blackfeet in 1898, he observed 'One of these dancers named Rides to the Door carried the carved wooden figure of a horse to remind people of his bravery and skill in raiding enemy horses'.[26] Such effigies had wide distribution being used by the Sioux, Crow, Hidatsa, Ute, Blackfeet, Gros Ventre, Blood, Assiniboin, and Cheyenne.[27] A famous carver of horse effigy dance sticks was the Hunkpapa Sioux, No-Two-Horns, and a particularly fine carving (one of several extant) by this man is now in the Medora Museum, North Dakota. It seems to have been made to commemorate an event in the Custer Battle when No-Two-Horns' horse was wounded seven times and died in action. The wounds are indicated on the carved horse by triangular areas of red flowing from a wound at the apex of the triangle. No-Two-Horns was also known to be adept at other types of carving, producing dolls and miniature weapons for his grandchildren.[28]

In addition to carving, several items used by the Plains tribes were engraved such as the riding quirts or roach spreaders of elk antler. This was a material which was relatively easy to work and could be shaped and finished with simple tools. When used for quirts, there seems to have been some preference for the prongs which protruded forward on each side of the main rack just above the skull.[29] Such prongs could be made into handles with the minimum of effort; in turn these handles were not infrequently engraved with war exploits, life figures, and geometric and curvilinear patterns, the process being carried out by use of an awl or knife point. Deeper lines were made with the cutting edge of a knife blade or a file;[30] roach spreaders were engraved in a similar way. Before about 1870, they were usually made of a flat plaque of antler, often displayed military exploits, and were carefully shaped, matching the contours of the roach base. Later, they were made of wood, metal, or rawhide. Roach spreaders had a multifold purpose – to spread the roach farther apart, support the plume holder such that the eagle feathers stood out from the back of the roach, and to beautify the roach further with the engravings which were on it.

Horn spoons with elaborately carved handles displaying effigies of snakes, beaver, bighorn, birds, and elk were much favored by the Western Sioux, particularly during the second half of the nineteenth century and, after the buffalo were virtually exterminated in the 1880s, the effigy spoons were made of cowhorn from those animals slaughtered as rations for Indians on the reservation. Typical is an elk-head spoon of cowhorn on which the handle is bent at the end, the elk head facing the same direction as the bowl of the spoon; the carver has taken pains 'to show the animal's open mouth and lightly incised nostrils and eyes, as well as its spreading horns'.[31] Elk power was associated with sexual prowess by many Plains tribes. As the English sportsman, John Palliser, observed in 1847, 'In the breeding season the wapiti chants the most beautiful musical sound in all the animal creation; it is like the sound of an enormous soft flute, uttered in a most coaxing tone'.[32] Thus, in seeking elk power, the Sioux fabricated elaborately carved flutes of cedar wood, which not infrequently displayed a carved elk head at one end in the act of calling his mates.

Pipes

The ceremonial use of tobacco was widespread in North America and had supernatural associations; the ritual of smoking was said to lift one's thoughts to the spirits above, linking earthbound man with the sky above. Pipes used by the Plains Indians were made of various workable stones – limestone, steatite, and chlorite – but the most favored was a red stone quarried in the area of present-day Minnesota and referred to as catlinite after George Catlin who first visited the quarry in 1835 and who brought a sample of the stone back for scientific analysis. This pipestone was known to the Indians of the region from prehistoric times and prior to c.1700 was in the territory of the Oto and Iowa. After this time, the Sioux took over the quarry and by the mid-nineteenth century they were its sole owners, the stone rough blanks or finished pipes then being traded to other tribes.[33]

North American Indian pipes have been divided into two major categories depending upon their form: one style is tubular in which the smoke travels in one plane, the other is elbow in which it travels in two planes.[34] Both types were found on the Plains in the Historic Period. More recently this classification has been extended to the five most common forms – the tubular or straight pipe, the modified Micmac pipe, elbow pipe, prowed pipe with flaring-bowl, and the calumet or inverted T-shape.[35] A number of these pipes were particularly elaborate exhibiting effigies of animals and humans; some of the finest in the category were made by the Sioux and Pawnee. George Catlin expressed the opinion that the Pawnee were probably the 'most ingenious' of all the Plains tribes in the production of such articles. Effigy bowls were of high artistic quality with imaginative designs, the likenesses of humans and animals usually being carved so that they faced the smoker; some made social comments such as the effects of liquor on Indians.

The carving of a pipe from catlinite or other stone was a formidable task and, before the introduction of steel tools by Europeans, the stone was fashioned using flint or other hard materials, the bowl being drawn on the stone and the excess cut away. The holes for tobacco and stem were a particular problem as Catlin observed: 'The Indian makes the hole in the bowl of the pipe, by drilling into it a hard stick, shaped to the desired size, with a quantity of sharp sand and water kept constantly in the hole.'[36] The bowls were then finally shaped and polished with flint, quartzite and fine sand. Buffalo tallow and other animal fats gave the finished piece its polish.

The modified Micmac style of bowl was so named because it was the Micmac of Nova Scotia who were first observed by Europeans using this type of pipe. The style traveled west in trade and was a distinctive shape having a bowl not unlike an inverted acorn upon a keel-like base. The Plains Cree, Crow, Assiniboin, and, in particular, the Blackfeet, utilized pipes of this type, although there were many variations on the basic style.

Ewers found this modified form of Micmac pipe still being made as late as 1947 and he obtained an example of such a pipe from his Piegan informant and interpreter, Reuben Black Boy, who had fabricated it a short time previously. It resembled a pipe first illustrated by Carl Bodmer more than a century earlier

Above: *Mountain Chief a Blackfeet warrior photographed in 1913, wears a fine straight-up headdress typical of the featherwork of his tribe. Here, the traditional feathers from the immature golden eagle – white with brown or black tips – are set upright in a folded rawhide headband. Each feather is embellished with ermine and hair-locks at the tips and the band profusely decorated with brass studs and ermine fringe. Note also the 'hackle plume' at the center of the headdress; this red-colored plume may indicate membership of the Blackfeet military Horns Society. Mountain Chief also carries a carved wooden horse effigy, probably to commemorate his bravery and skill in raiding enemy horses: this is a good example of Blackfeet wood carving. Note the miniature figure of a warrior astride the horse.*

(1833) and was referred to by the Blackfeet as a 'real pipe'. The technique of manufacture had, however, changed markedly – Reuben was now using a pencil to outline the shape of the bowl, a wooden vise to clamp the slab, a hacksaw to rough out the bowl, a carpenter's brace to drill the holes, a wood rasp to get the final shape, and the exterior was smoothed with commercial sandpaper. The final blackening of the bowl, however, followed more traditional lines. Reuben built a fire of green buckbrush and, placing a stick in the pipe-stem hole, he held the bowl over the fire for about fifteen minutes. After the stone had cooled, he rubbed the surface with his hand, giving it an even, shiny surface.[37]

Most of the pipes so far described had stems which, for ceremonial purposes, could be up to 3-4ft (1-1.3m.) in length. The stems were made of ash, oak, or hickory, the pith in their center being burned out with a hot wire. An alternative was to split the stem lengthwise, scrape out the pith, and then glue the pieces together. Flat pipe-stems were most popular on the central Plains while round ones were used on the northern Plains. Some had open work 'puzzle stems' where only the carver knew the true pathway of the smoke as it zig-zagged from bowl to mouthpiece, by-passing the decorative and symbolic designs which were carved on the stem. Other stems were of the spiralling variety where rounds stems were carved with a knife and file, sometimes a double spiral being produced. The stems were not infrequently decorated with porcupine quillwork, generally in the so-called braided technique with additional decoration in the form of horsehair, feathers, beaks, and paint. Although both bowl and stem were considered to be endowed with sacred power, the pipe itself was not considered activated until the two parts were brought together and, when not in use, stem and bowl were taken apart and stored in a bag, beautifully embellished with beads and porcupine quills.

Featherwork

As early as the mid-sixteenth century, a crown of feathers came to indicate Indian identity in most of the Americas.[38] Such headdresses generally consisted of a simple band with the feathers of the wild turkey, hawk, heron, or eagle attached so that they stood upright around the head. Similar to this early style was the headdress of the Blackfeet of the northern Plains which, by the profuse combination of eagle feathers and ermine skins, turned the ancient and simple headband style into an imposing form of warrior and society regalia. This style, referred to as a 'straight-up bonnet', was said to have originated with the ancient Bulls Society of the Blackfeet.

Headdresses of this type were made from a piece of thin rawhide or heavy tanned skin 6in (15cm.) or so in width and of sufficient length to fit the wearer's head. It was then folded along its long dimension and holes were cut in the edge of the fold through which the eagle feathers were passed.[39] Some twenty to thirty feathers were attached to the band either by cutting the feather quill and tucking it back into itself so as to form a loop or, alternatively, a small wooden pin was pushed into the hollow quill of the feather. The feathers were then fixed in place by the use of a lacing thong which went through the quill loop or over a groove in the wooden pin. A second thong usually passed through the quill about halfway up the feather which held it in place and gave shape to the bonnet. The headdress was then covered with red cloth which was decorated with brass studs or, occasionally, beadwork. Long ermine fringes were hung from the sides and back and additional decoration in the form of narrow strips of rawhide wrapped around with porcupine quills were sometimes attached to the quills of the eagle feathers with small fluffy plumes at the base of each. Finally, the ends of the band were joined by tying them together at the back and carefully adjusting so that it fitted snugly on the head. Such headdresses were worn on ceremonial occasions, in dances, and parades. They were also worn in battle but this was considered a particularly brave act since it made the wearer exceptionally conspicuous and a more than likely target for enemy fire.

The use of the straight-up headdress progressively decreased after c.1895 and by the 1940s very few such bonnets were then worn, having been replaced by the Sioux style of flaring bonnet.[40] Elderly Blackfeet explained this by saying that the straight-up bonnet was considered very sacred regalia and that few people had the right to wear it.[41]

The Sioux-style warbonnet contrasted with the Blackfeet style, having a cap of soft buckskin which fitted loosely to the head. To it were attached feathers to form a circle, but unlike the Blackfeet style where the feathers were fixed rigid and upright, the feathers were at an angle, flaring both upward and backward from the wearer's head and having freedom of movement.

The development of the Sioux style flaring bonnet can be traced through early travelers' accounts to the Plains tribes beginning with the French explorer, La Verendrye, to the Mandan in 1738 who referred to feather headbands; while later, in 1811, the English explorer, Brackenridge, refers to Arikara headdresses with the feathers arranged as a kind of crown.[42] It seems that by 1820 the flaring style of warbonnet was well-developed, clustering among tribes who put emphasis on coup designation by the use of eagle feathers, such as the Dakota, Arikara, Pawnee, Hidatsa, Mandan, Crow, and Omaha. There were slight variations within the style, but of them all, the Sioux version – where the feathers swept back from the brow and the middle side feathers were approximately 45 degrees to the vertical – typifies the style. Some thirty or more feathers were used, the foundation being a buckskin cap. The feathers were first carefully prepared and most important was the formation of a loop at the bottom of the feather. This was either made by cutting the quill as one would for a pen and tucking the quill back into itself, or alternatively leather or rawhide strips were bound to the quill leaving a loop at the bottom. The feathers were further embellished with buckskin or colored cloth at their base together with several fluffy plumes while the tips were decorated with horsehair.

The feathers were then laid out in the order that they would appear on the bonnet, the two longest and straightest being at the center. Then they were laced to the cap by running a buckskin thong through the loop and pairs of slits cut in the cap. Another thong was run through the feathers part way up the quill, holding the feathers in place and enabling the bonnet to be set so as to become a balanced and uniform spread. A 'major plume' was then attached to the center of the cap, originally in the form of a power amulet such as the skin of an animal or bird. In later years – 1870 onward – it was replaced with a long stripped quill cut and embellished in a certain way to distinguish the owner. The headdress was completed by the addition of a quilled or beaded brow band with rosettes on each side from which were hung ermine and colored ribbons.

Traditionally, the flaring style of bonnet could only be possessed and worn by the consent of a man's fellow warriors – by an individual who had gained both war honors and the respect of the leading men in the community. Among the Omaha each feather stood for a man, the tip of hair fastened to the feather and dyed red, representing the man's scalp-lock. Before a feather could be fastened on the bonnet, a man had to count the war honor which actually entitled him to wear the feather and so enabled him to prepare it for use in decorating the bonnet. When the warrior counted his honors he held up the feathers which were to represent them, saying 'In such a battle I did thus'.[43] Thus, the wearing of a warbonnet by a privileged individual did not refer exclusively to that individual's feats of arms, rather it signified the best warrior and underlined the interdependence of men.

Buckskin Garments

While the most typical garment for Plains Indian women in the mid-nineteenth century was a one-piece sleeveless dress, a closer study of women's costumes indicates that despite this general pattern there were considerable variations in tribal styles. Thus, on the northeastern Plains an early style was the 'strap dress' which consisted of two long pieces of buckskin sewn at the sides and held up by straps over the shoulders with the addition of separate cape-like sleeves which were connected by thongs across the front and back. Another early style on both the northern and central Plains was the 'side-fold dress' which consisted of a wide rectangular piece of hide folded on one side, the other being sewn with the top turned down to form a type of cape. A hole was made for the arm on the folded side and the dress was sewn or laced at the shoulders.

By 1830, however, both these styles of dress were beginning to go out of fashion, being replaced by the 'two-skin dress' probably due to influences from the Plateau tribes farther west. This was made by sewing two deerskins together with the hind legs at the shoulders, a few inches – which included the tail – being folded down.[44] Thus, the natural shape of the tanned hide was retained – a good example of how the form of a costume is determined by the material used. Piercing, trimming, additional inserts, and mode of decoration on this basic garment were often indicative of tribal origin. On the southern Plains, however, among such tribes as the Southern Cheyenne and Arapaho, Kiowa, and Comanche, three skins were used in the construction of a woman's dress. Here, two deerskins were cut straight a few inches below the forelegs; these skins became the skirt of the dress, a third skin being folded lengthwise and sewn to the other two skins at the waist. A hole was cut into the top of the fold to allow the head through. The Southern Cheyenne and Arapaho tended to decorate such dresses with bands of beadwork about 3-4in (7-10cm.) wide on both the shoulders and across the chest, while the Kiowa and Comanche often painted their dresses and used only a limited amount of beadwork at the edges.

In the fabrication of clothing, a common practice among Plains Indians was maximum use of material at hand with minimum wastage. In this respect, the style of leggings used by men was no exception. Hides from the white- or black-tailed deer or prong-horned antelope were commonly used in the

manufacture of leggings. An excellent contemporary account of Plains-style leggings was given in 1805 by the explorers, Lewis and Clark:

'The leggings are generally made of antelope skins, dressed without the hair and with the legs, tail, and neck hanging to them. Each legging is formed of the skin entire and reaches from the ankle to the upper part of the thigh and the legs of the skin are tucked before and behind under a girdle around the waist. It fits closely to the leg the tail being worn upwards, and the neck highly ornamented with fringe and porcupine quills, drags on the ground behind the heels. As the legs of the animal are tied round the girdle the wide part of the skin is drawn so high as to conceal the parts usually kept from view, in which respect their dress is much more decent than that of any nation of Indians.'[45]

Such styles of leggings were widely used on the central and northern Plains, but farther south tribes such as the Kiowa and Comanche began to make leggings which were more tailored than those used farther north. The most popular form of skin legging in the second half of the nineteenth century, was the so-called 'tab and fringe' style. Here, the legging was made from a single hide folded lengthwise to form a double flap, after a tailored leg seam had been sewn. The flap was then cut into a fringe leaving a whole portion near the top; referred to as the 'tab', this was generally tastefully decorated with paint and beads.[46]

Embellished buffalo robes, certain styles of headgear, special forms of leggings, and, in particular on the central and northern Plains, the ceremonial shirt, were all important ways of communicating an individual's position within the social and political strata. Thus, among the Pawnee, the wearing of the skin shirt was 'one of the outstanding symbols of high status... very few men were privileged to wear them' and even able chiefs might be excluded.[47] The sacred character of a special style of hair-fringed shirt among the Sioux was emphasized by the elaborate rituals developed relating to its conferment and, as late as the reservation period when such shirts were being made for collectors, special rituals were still performed during both its fabrication and transferral.[48]

Traditionally, the Sioux ceremonial shirt was made of two deer, bighorn, or antelope skins; about one-third of the top was cut off each skin which was then folded to make the sleeves, the lower two-thirds becoming the front and back of the shirt. The head portion from each skin was then used as a decorative flap on the front and back. The sides of the shirt were generally left open and the sleeves sewn from the wrist to the elbow only. Most of these shirts have quilled or beaded bands over the shoulders and often two – generally narrower – bands down the arms. These were invariably, although not exclusively, worked separately on a leather base and then sewn to the shirt. Human hair fringes were attached to the edges of these shoulder and arm bands which represented the war deeds – or perhaps a mark of allegiance – of

Right: *A three-skin dress from the Southern Cheyenne and dating from about 1890 is embellished with elk teeth on the heavily fringed and yellow painted cape. The skirt is decorated with two single lanes of seed beadwork and an additional scalloped effect pattern at the bottom, below which the buckskin is painted red. Note the cone jingles.*

Left: *A painted buffalo robe, probably Lakota and dating from before 1840. This is a superb example of early Plains Indian pictography which in dramatic graphic form documents the war exploits of the owner and his followers. Details of costume and accoutrements, such as pipes, headgear, weapons, hair styles, quirts, shield,s and horse equipment are accurately rendered by the imaginative artist. This is both a cultural and historical 'document' par excellence, giving important insights into the complex culture that produced it.*

the members of the Chiefs' Society or individuals who sanctioned the wearing of such garments by outstanding leaders.[49] A typical garment in this class was worn by the Oglala leader, Red Cloud, and others when they visited Washington in the 1870s.[50]

Petroglyphs and Pictographs

The communication of ideas by means of petroglyphs and pictographs is of ancient origin in North America. Petroglyphs have been defined as pictures 'upon a rock either in situ or sufficiently large for inference that the picture was imposed upon it where it was found'.[51] Pictographs, on the other hand, were pictures upon skins, bark, pottery, and later on woven fabrics such as linen cloth and muslin as well as paper, the latter producing, in the late nineteenth century, a proliferation of so-called ledger book art.[52]

Recent studies of Plains petroglyphs – now popularly referred to as Rock Art – have identified two major styles, Ceremonial and Biographic, the first being of considerably greater antiquity than the second.[53] A variety of techniques were employed in producing the petroglyphs but most commonly the rock surface was scratched. Alternatively, the surface was pecked with a small sharp-edged stone, but both methods removed the darker weathered surface.[54]

Pictographic work on hides was generally carried out using 'brushes' made of the spongy, porous part of the buffalo's leg bone, one edge of which was sharpened to make narrow lines while the flat side was used to spread color over larger surfaces.[55] Colored earth and clay and some vegetable materials were used for paints, these being ground into a powder and mixed with a gluey substance which was obtained from boiling hide scrapings or the tail of a beaver. As with petroglyphs, painted art work on skins was both geometric and representational;

generally, the former was done by women and the latter by men.

One of the most popular geometric designs used by women was the so-called 'box and border' and much favored by the Sioux and Arapaho. This exhibited two distinctive features – a continuous border which surrounded all four sides of the hide together with an enclosed rectangular, decorated field, usually located just above the center of the hide and always elongated horizontally. An associated style was the 'border and hourglass' pattern; here, the central pattern tended to be variable in detail but its essential form was always broad at the ends and constricted in the middle – a form suggestive of an hourglass.[56] It is suggested that such designs were stylized representations of the buffalo showing its internal structure. As Hail has observed, 'It was easy for the people of hunting cultures to visualize internal organs, as they were accustomed to butchering their kills and distributing the parts. This is true especially of women, since they were responsible for cutting up the meat that the hunters brought in. The joys of a full stomach and relief from the fear of starvation for her children would be part of her pleasure in drawing these designs'.[57]

The earliest documented painted robe showing extensive detail of inter-tribal warfare among the Plains tribes and obviously in the category of an autobiographical treatise, was collected by Lewis and Clark from the Mandan in 1805. It was reported that the pictographs depicted a battle fought about 1797 between the Mandan and Minnetaree against the Sioux and Arikara.

Analysis of robes of this type leads to the conclusion that the subject matter of early Plains Indian representative painting was overwhelmingly that of humans and horses, while the episodes recorded put emphasis on the stealing of horses or the counting

of coup on the enemy.

Horses were represented in a variety of ways, a stick-like leg with a hooked hoof – actually representing a hoof print – being typical of hide painting done prior to 1850. Later, horses are shown in a more realistic way, the eyes, phallus, tail, and sometimes the mane being depicted, while the running horse was conventionalized to forelegs extending forward and hind legs backward.[58] Early depictions of human figures were knob-like heads which were generally devoid of features although hair-styles were not infrequently shown. Arms and legs were stick-like with simple triangular and rectangular bodies.

There were several notable exceptions to this early style – in particular the work of the Mandan chief, *Mato-tope* (c.1833) whose pictograph technique was possibly influenced by white artists.[59] In the second half of the nineteenth century, there was considerable refinement of human proportions, an abundance of detail, increase in richness of colors, some experimentation with spatiality, and the appearance of new themes and subject matter.[60]

Rawhide

Rawhide has great strength and versatility and because of these qualities it was highly prized by Plains Indians and used in a variety of ways.

The preferred hide for making rawhide was that of the buffalo and although elk, moose, and domestic cattle hides were used – particularly during the reservation period – buffalo was considered to be more elastic and fibrous and 'long use of a piece of buffalo rawhide made it somewhat like heavy, firm cloth'.[61] There were considerable variations in the production of rawhide but the end product was always the same – a clean hide devoid of fleshy material and hair which, on drying, was white and opaque. A widespread technique was to stake the hide out by putting pegs through slits cut around its edge and to use a chisel-like bone (later metal) tool called the 'deflesher' to remove fat and tissue from the inner part of the hide.[62] The hide was then turned over and with an adze-shaped tool, the hair was carefully scraped away. Finally, it was thoroughly washed and left in the sun to dry and bleach.

While rawhide was used in the fabrication of such items as shields, drums, knife sheaths, saddles, cruppers, horseshoes, burden straps, hats, doors of tipis, mortars, decorative and symbolic cut-outs, and even cradles, its commonest use was in the production of the parfleche[63] which was a flat, rectangular and expandable case in which clothing, food, and other materials were placed for storage and transportation.[64]

Parfleches were generally made in pairs from a buffalo hide which had already been cleared of fat and tissue during the rawhide production process. The flesh side of the staked out hide was marked out using peeled willow sticks of different lengths defining the parfleche shape and the geometrical patterns which were to be painted on it. A bone 'brush' was used to draw the outlines of the patterns which were generally in a single color; the larger areas were then filled in with the desired colors.

The surface was then covered with a thin coat of glue or size which gave a gloss to the paint and protected it from wear and tear when in use.[65] After the paint and glue had dried, the hide was turned over and the hair removed in the usual way: finally, the parfleche was cut out from the rawhide to the desired shape.

Regardless of tribal origin, most of the patterns on parfleches consisted of geometrical designs made up of rather massive rectangles, squares, triangles, and hourglass-type figures. There were, however, some definite tribal variations; thus the Blackfeet frequently used curved lines, the Crow put emphasis on using straight lines, and the Sioux used a mixture of both. Some of the finest parfleches were made by the Cheyenne, whose designs were unusually delicate and the combination of colors particularly distinctive.[66]

Moccasins

With the exception of the sandal-wearing tribes of the Southwest and Mexico, moccasins were universally worn throughout most of North America. The true moccasin – the term originating from eastern Algonquian dialects – was a type of footwear in which the 'soft sole and the upper, or part of the upper, are continuous, passing upwards from under the foot, forming a well-constructed foot covering which always has a back seam'.[67] There were considerable variations within this basic style but typical for the Plains Indians in the early nineteenth century is Larocque's (1805) description of Crow moccasins, which he said were 'made in the manner of mittens having a seam round the outside of the foot only without |a| pleat'.[68] The Blackfeet referred to this earlier one-piece soft-soled moccasin style as the 'real moccasin'.

Since soft-sole moccasins wear out quickly in the harsh Plains environment, a modification in the form of an additional piece of leather was sometimes added to the sole but the basic pattern survived to at least the beginning of the reservation period (c.1870), being preferred for winter wear when buffalo hide with hair inside was used.

Around the middle of the nineteeth century, another style progressively came into use. This was the two-piece moccasin which had a rawhide sole with a soft buckskin upper. Although this style came to have wide distribution on the Plains, even toward the end of the nineteenth century, some tribes – notably the Crow – were still using both types. As the army officer, Captain W. P. Clark observed in the 1880s, 'the Crows make their moccasins of one piece sewed at the heel, though some have separate soles'.[69]

On the southern Plains from around 1860 onward, a high-topped style, particularly popular with the Kiowa and Comanche, was in use; a tube legging was attached to the moccasin, the seam being covered by a single lane of beadwork. The moccasins were always of the hard-sole variety and these, together with the attached legging, were painted yellow or green. Heavy German silver discs were usually attached to the leggings and the edging beadwork exhibited intricate patterns worked in small seed beads.

A floral design was invariably worked on the instep of Kiowa high-topped moccasins, a feature seldom used by their close allies, the Comanche.[70]

References

1 Pond, 1986: 42.
2 Waugh, 1990: 70.
3 Best and McClelland, 1977: 4.
4 Feder, 1987.
5 Loud and Harrington, 1929: 24. Libby, 1951: 276. Martin, Quimby and Collier, 1947.
6 Some of the earliest extant examples of quillwork are to be found in the European museum collections, such as the elaborately quill-embellished shirt now in the Ashmolean Museum, Oxford (Turner in MacGregor ed., 1983: 123-30) and the collection of early moccasins and headdresses in the Musée de l'Homme, Paris (Fardoulis, 1979).
7 Grinnell, 1923, Vol.I: 163. Kroeber, 1902-07.
8 Ewers, 1945: 29.
9 Dempsey, 1963: 52.
10 Possibly the earliest account of porcupine quillwork from the Plains region was by Dr. Samuel Lathan Mitchell, who has described in great detail an Assiniboin quilled *wapiti* skin collected before 1817. (Fenenga, 1959: 19-22. Orchard, 1926: 64).
11 Taylor, 1962, 1981. Quillwork on bark, very common among the Micmac and Ojibwa, was not found on the Plains; however, the use of moosehair while firmly associated with Woodland tribes was, on occasions, also utilized by the Plains Cree.
12 Bebbington, 1982: 30.
13 The pony bead still continued to be used in Idaho, northwest Montana, and eastern Washington even as late as 1900.
14 Lanford (1990) has recently put forward ideas relating to the origins and precursors of symbolic and decorative beadwork motifs among the central Plains groups.
15 Pohrt (1989) has further references relating to North Plains beadwork.
16 Ewers, 1945: 38.
17 Lyford, 1940: 71.
18 Lessard (1991) has a detailed discussion of pictographic Sioux beadwork which includes identification of the producers.
19 Lowie, 1954: 143.
20 A discussion of the origins of Crow Indian beadwork designs appears in Wildschut, 1959 and more recently in Feder, 1980.
21 MacGregor, 1966: 116.
22 Robert Ritzenthaler's survey (1976) of Woodland sculpture demonstrates that carved objects were rarely more than a foot in length and that woodworking was carried out by men. Several parallels have been found between Woodland carving

and that from the Plains (Ewers, 1986: 11).
23 Ewers, 1986: 12 and 15.
24 Ewers, 1986: 41.
25 Ewers, 1986: 18 pictures a human effigy Tree-Dweller Medicine, said to have been for some 200 years in the Wabasha (Santee Sioux) family. It is 6in (15cm.) high and of painted wood.
26 McClintock, 1937: 13.
27 West, 1978: 64.
28 West, 1979: 295 and 299.
29 Pohrt, 1978: 63.
30 Pohrt, 1978: 63.
31 Ewers, 1986: 177.
32 Palliser, 1969: 146-47.
33 From time immemorial, the area was considered to be neutral ground and anyone could visit the quarry in peace and mine the stone (Catlin, 1841, Vol.II: 169). The pipestone and finished product was widely traded, pipe bowls of catlinite having been found in seventeenth century Iroquoian sites. The Pipestone National Monument was established in 1937 and the exclusive right to the use of the quarry by Native Americans only was established.
34 Douglas, 1931.
35 Ewers, 1986: 50.
36 Catlin, 1841, Vol.I: 334. Experiments show that such work was very time-consuming. To drill a cone-shaped hole some 1in (25mm.) deep into catlinite employing the method described by Catlin took one hour (West, 1934, Vol.I: 341-42).
37 Ewers, 1963: 42 and 50.
38 Sturtevant, 1992: 28.
39 Golden or 'calumet' eagle feathers were the most prized for headdresses. These came from the immature bird and were white with dark brown or black tips. Such feathers were considered exceedingly valuable. (See Denig, 1930: 589.)
40 Ewers reported that when the Sioux-style bonnet was introduced among the Blackfeet in about 1895, it became so popular as to replace the traditional Blackfeet style almost entirely (Ewers, 1945: 61).
41 Ewers, 1945: 61.
42 Taylor, 1994: 23.
43 Fletcher and La Flesche, 1911: 447. (See Taylor, 1994: 91-99 for a more detailed discussion relating to the symbolism.)
44 The cutting, lacing, and beadwork embellishment associated with the Blackfeet woman's dress has been considered by Conn (1961: 114-17). See also Ewers (1945:42).
45 Lewis and Clark, 1904, Vol.II: 129. Further

descriptions and a discussion of the various styles of leggings used on the northern and central Plains are in Taylor (1961).
46 Cooley, 1983.
47 Weltfish, 1977: 375.
48 Wissler, 1912(b): 40.
49 Taylor, 1989: 247.
50 238 human hair and 68 horsehair locks embellish this shirt which is now in the collections of the Buffalo Bill Historical Center, Cody, Wyoming.
51 Mallery, 1893: 31.
52 Petersen, 1971 and 1988.
53 Conner, 1971 and Keyser, 1987. In pre-reservation times, petroglyph sites were regarded as special places and imbued with spiritual power.
54 Some petroglyphs were colored with earth paints enhancing the image but unless the petroglyph was protected this coloring faded.
55 A number of bone 'paint brushes' have been found in early Pawnee and Mandan sites (Ewers, 1939: 36).
56 Ewers, 1939: 9-10.
57 Hail, 1983: 40.
58 Ewers, 1939: 19-21.
59 Taylor, 1973.
60 Arni Brownstone has recently compared traditional Blackfeet pictography and nineteenth century European painting, identifying two distinct pictorial systems. See Brownstone, 1993: 29.
62 A favored source for making metal defleshers was the sawn-off end of the old northwest gun.
63 The term 'parfleche' is of doubtful origin but it appears in French narratives as early as 1700 and is probably from some old French root, possibly from *parer* 'to parry', *fleche* 'arrow' in reference to the shield, or body armor of rawhide.
64 See Spier, 1931: 82 for a definition of the parfleche.
65 A beaver tail was often boiled to make a sticky glue (See Ewers, 1945:17).
66 Morrow, 1975: 78. Torrence, 1994.
67 Webber, 1989: 4 considers the theories of the development of the moccasin.
68 Larocque, 1910: 27.
69 Clark, 1885: 259. For a detailed analysis of Crow, Sioux and Arapaho moccasins, see Wildschut 1959 and Kroeber 1902.
70 Wissler's (1927) studies of moccasin decorations covers the 25-year period 1890-1915 and considers both partially and fully quilled and beaded moccasins and their distribution.

PLATEAU AND BASIN

THE PLATEAU AND GREAT BASIN culture areas cover a vast and diverse area of the interior of western North America. The traditional Native cultures of the Plateau evolved in the upper Columbia River Basin in the present states of Washington, Oregon, Idaho, Montana ,and adjacent sections of the province of British Columbia between the Rocky Mountains on the east and the Cascade Mountains on the west. Numerous tribes, including the Wasco/ Wishram, Cayuse, Umatilla, Yakima, Palouse, Spokane, Nez Perce, Coeur D'Alene, Kutenai, Kalispel, and Flathead all lived in the Plateau area. This location enabled them to draw artistic inspirations and materials from the Native people of the buffalo plains east of the Rockies as well as from the maritime cultures west of the Cascades. They did this both through extensive trade networks with other Native people and with Euro-Americans, as well as by extensive travel themselves. Central and eastern Plateau people, particularly the Nez Perce and Flathead, regularly made the difficult and dangerous journey east across the Rockies to the buffalo plains of Montana to hunt and trade. The people practised a lifestyle that revolved around hunting, fishing, and gathering wild foodstuffs on a seasonal cycle, and they were consummate horse people after the mid-eighteenth century. Trading and direct inter-tribal contacts with other culture areas resulted in Plateau arts and crafts that are a unique synthesis of equestrian and maritime cultures. Native Plateau artisans worked with a wide range of materials and media to produce objects of utility and beauty.

The Great Basin is an even larger area between the Sierra Nevada Mountains on the west, and the Rocky Mountains on the east. It is centered geographically in the present states of Nevada, Utah, Oregon, and Idaho. The traditional cultures of the Great Basin are diverse, varying from the desert-dwelling hunter-gatherers in the south and west to the big-game hunting, horse-mounted nomads in the north and east. Great Basin ethnography is sometimes confusing because groups of people with the same tribal name developed widely varying cultures. The Northern Shoshonis, Northern Paiutes (Bannocks), and the Utes of the semi-arid and mountainous areas of eastern Idaho, western Wyoming, eastern Utah, and eastern Colorado developed a nomadic horse culture that was very similar to those of the Great Plains. They lived principally by big-game hunting and often ventured on to the plains after buffalo. By contrast, the Washoe, Paiute, Western Shoshoni, Goshute, Southern (Utah) Ute, and other desert dwellers of southern Oregon, western Idaho, Nevada, and western Utah

never became horse nomads. Theirs was a naturally harsh and difficult arid environment which was one of the last areas of North America to be dominated by the Euro-Americans. The desert dwellers had the ingenuity to live and prosper there for generations, and through most of the nineteenth century continued to practise their ancient pattern of seasonal hunting and gathering, relying upon a wide variety of

Above: *The Plateau and Basin regions, bordered as they were by five other cultural areas, tended to reflect their influences in their own tribal cultures to a greater degree than was the case in other regions where fewer interactions existed. Beadwork and quillwork were both predominant on the neighboring Great Plains but gained their own distinctive expression in the Plateau and Basin, as shown in the Umatilla floral design moccasins and Ute beaded and quilled hide robe.*

Above and right: *Plateau people in the 19th century made and used a variety of highly decorated horse equipment for festive occasions. This double beaded bag (right) — actually two complete bags joined at the top — could have been placed over the saddle horn so that one side hung on each side of the horse, similar to the rectangular bags in the photograph (above). It was collected from the Yakima and dates from about 1870. The beadwork is in the classic Plateau contour beaded style in which the background was beaded in rows that follow the outlines of the curvilinear designs.*

animal and plant foods. Their possessions tended to be few and light and this in turn had a significant impact upon their arts and crafts.

In both the Plateau and the Basin traditional arts and crafts were produced primarily by women. Basketry, porcupine quillwork, parfleche decoration, hide-tanning, and clothing were all produced almost exclusively by women. Objects of stone, wood, and horn, realistic hide painting, and weapons were produced primarily by men.

Beadwork

The Plateau people already valued and used glass beads acquired in trade even before the time of their first recorded contacts with Euro-Americans in the early nineteenth century. The earliest surviving pieces of Plateau beadwork date from the 1830s and are heavily embroidered with predominantly black and white beads 3-4mm in diameter.

These beads, now called 'pony' beads, were manufactured largely in Venice and were acquired in trade from other tribes or from Euro-Americans.[2]

Plateau pony beadwork produced before 1850 was usually executed in only a few primary bead colors, including translucent sky blue, white, black, and rose (a translucent red with an opaque white center), although a variety of other colors such as shades of green, shades of blue, pink, translucent

cranberry, and yellow were occasionally used. The beads were usually sewn onto a hide backing with animal sinew thread or sometimes with native fiber cordage. The geometric designs were simple and bold with strong color contrast. Womens' dress yokes, moccasins, shoulder and sleeve strips on men's shirts, men's legging strips, blanket or robe strips, cradle boards, and a variety of horse gear were among the items commonly decorated with early pony beadwork. The

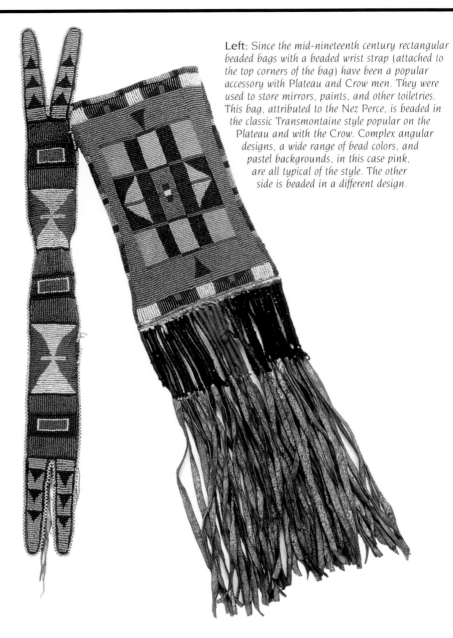

By about 1860 curvilinear beadwork was very popular on the Plateau. Bold, colorful, symmetrical, abstract floral designs were set against a light color background that was beaded in the same contours as the adjacent curved motifs. The texture of the background bead rows produced a subtle radiating or halo effect around the primary beaded designs. By the end of the century very realistic floral designs predominated, with outlined, filled-in designs set against a fully beaded background in horizontal, not contour, rows. On many late nineteenth and early twentieth century beaded pieces, particularly women's flat hand bags and men's vests, realistic, often asymmetrical, bead designs included not only floral but also animal figures.[6]

At the same time that Plateau women were perfecting the use of curvilinear, floral, and animal designs, they were also perfecting what has come to be known as the Transmontaine style of beadwork. This term reflects the fact that this distinctive beadwork style was produced by women on both sides of the Rocky Mountains: principally by the Crow along the Yellowstone River, and by many of the Plateau tribes in the upper Columbia River, the foremost probably being the Nez Perce.[7]

One of the hallmarks of this style in its fullest development is the optical ambiguity created between what is a design element and what is 'background'. This is much like the line drawing which may first appear to be a vase and may then appear as the profiles of two faces. Transmontaine beadwork designs are closely related to painted parfleche designs, discussed below. The same design elements, design layout, and to a certain extent the same colors were used in both painting and beading, at least in the 1860-1900 period. A wide variety of objects were beaded in the Transmontaine style, including large bandoleer bags, otter bowcase and quiver sets, men's shirt and legging strips, cradle boards, horse equipment, gun cases, moccasins, and men's flat mirror bags.[8]

The beadwork traditions of most Great Basin people have never been thoroughly studied and are poorly understood. The available evidence indicates that little or no porcupine quillwork was produced in the area and that beadwork was not a major art form among the western, desert-dwelling tribes. The women of the eastern Great Basin tribes – the Shoshoni, Bannock, and Ute – were active beadworkers, although only among the Ute was beadwork as prominent as it was in the Plains and Plateau. There are some surviving pieces of Ute pony beadwork which probably date from before 1850, and it is probable that the Great Basin beadworkers went through the same transition from pony to seed beadwork, as did the women of the Plains and Plateau.

Late-nineteenth century photographs of Shoshoni and Bannock people often show little or no beadwork, even though the people are wearing a variety of other types of ornamentation. The beadwork that appears is often executed in simple, blocky designs on light backgrounds. Historic photographs also show Shoshoni and Bannock people using curvilinear beadwork (usually on an open hide or cloth background), and occasionally with beadwork in the classic Transmontaine

visual impact of pony beadwork with its simple designs and strong color contrasts could be dramatic. About 1840 an observer noted that a 'young lady... in one of these dresses, upon a fiery horse well equipped with saddle & crouper, makes a fine appearance'.[3]

By the middle of the nineteenth century Plateau women began to use fewer of the larger pony beads and incorporated smaller (1-2mm diameter) glass 'seed' beads. Seed beads were also manufactured primarily in Venice, and were used in a much wider range of colors than pony beads.[4] The small size and color variety of seed beads, used alone or in conjunction with the larger beads, allowed Plateau women to create more delicate and complex designs than was possible with pony beads alone. By at least the mid-1840s they were creating beadwork employing curvilinear designs, first in pony beads and later in seed beads. The earliest Plateau curvilinear beadwork in the 1840-60 period usually employed outlined, symmetrical designs based upon a double-curve motif on a hide or dark fabric background.[5]

There were several bead sewing techniques

most commonly used. The lane stitch or 'lazy' stitch was used, for example, on the broad bands on women's dress yokes and on narrow bands outlining beaded panels. A stitch was taken in the foundation material, a sufficient number of beads were strung to cover the desired width, and a second stitch was taken to secure the row. These stitches were continued side by side to complete the band of beadwork. Curvilinear beadwork was done in a two-thread applique or spot stitch. Beads were strung on one thread, and a second thread was stitched between every second or third bead to secure the beadwork to the foundation. A third major technique was the 'Crow' stitch in which bands of lane stitch were completed and then secured to the foundation by a second thread that looped around the lane stitch at right angles between every four to six beads.

Lane stitch produces slightly humped or ridged rows of beadwork, while the spot stitch and Crow stitch both produce smooth, flat beadwork. Lane stitch and Crow stitch were both used to produce geometric designs, while the spot stitch could be used for either geometric or curvilinear designs.

style common to Crow and Plateau beadworkers. It may be that Shoshoni and Bannock women produced beadwork in all three of these styles in the last half of the nineteenth century.

Ute women were prolific beaders who had regular contact with people from the Great Basin, the Plains, and the northern Rio Grande Pueblo areas. The best known Ute style was characterized by bold, simple, geometric designs in only a few colors on a light, usually white background. This style, which lasted from about the 1820s until the 1890s, is very reminiscent of early geometric design pony

beadwork of the Plains and Plateau. Ute women worked first in pony beads and then in seed beads by the 1860s, and used both lane stitch and flat stitch techniques. Shoulder and arm strips on men's shirts, men's legging strips, women's dress yokes, women's leggings, and men's tobacco bags were all commonly decorated in this style.[9]

Ute women were also fond of the Transmontaine style of beadwork, and Ute people sometimes used pieces 'imported' from the Crow or Plateau. However, Ute women also practised this style of beading in small but significant numbers of pieces. Ute beadwork

in this style usually incorporates a Transmontaine-style panel bordered by distinctly Ute panels in multi-row geometric lane stitch. Men's tobacco bags were often decorated in this fashion. Ute women also produced curvilinear beadwork, usually in symmetrical abstract floral motifs with cloth or hide for the background. This technique is most often seen on distinctive Ute cradles with wicker hoods, but also on other items such as horse gear and moccasins.

Porcupine Quillwork

Decoration with porcupine quill embroidery was a uniquely Native American art form. While early descriptions of Plateau decorative arts mention the use of quillwork, it is clear that Plateau women largely, but not completely, abandoned quillwork by the mid-nineteenth century. Therefore, little is known about early Plateau quillwork that would distinguish it from early quillwork from other areas.

One rare quillwork technique that persisted late into the nineteenth century in the Transmontaine (Plateau and Crow) art area was quill-wrapped horsehair. Quills were wrapped around parallel bundles of horsehair about one-eighth of an inch in diameter, and were sewn between the hair bundles as they were attached to the hide backing. These quill-wrapped bundles were sewn side by side to form decorative strips. Simple blocky designs were produced by altering the colors of the quills, or by wrapping with colored yarn instead. These strips, always edged with a single lane of beadwork, were used for the decorative strips on men's shirts and leggings, for blanket or robe strips and occasionally for moccasins.[10]

Plateau women may also have used other techniques of porcupine quill decoration, particularly multiple-quill plaiting. This technique involved weaving multiple flattened quills together to form decorative bands an inch or more wide. Usually two such bands of plaiting were worked parallel to each other and were bordered with a single lane of beadwork on each edge, just like quill-wrapped horsehair. Some extant pieces of early quillwork, primarily blanket or robe strips and mens' legging strips, consist of quill-wrapped horsehair rosettes separated by rectangles of multiple-quill plaiting.

Hide Painting

The women from most Plateau tribes produced quantities of storage containers made from parfleche, which was cleaned, dehaired, but untanned hide, usually buffalo or elk.[11] The most common parfleche containers were envelopes folded from large rectangles of hide, but smaller flat envelopes and tubes with closed ends were also produced.[12] The outer surfaces of parfleche containers provided a smooth, hard surface which was decorated in two different ways. In

Left: *This woman's hide dress (top) was collected from the Utes by the explorer Powell in the 1870s. The cape is beaded in typical Ute fashion in few colors and simple geometric designs. Ute cradles (left) had a board foundation covered with hide (yellow buckskin in this instance), and a twined wicker hood shielded the infant's head. The decorative beadwork is most attractive to look at.*

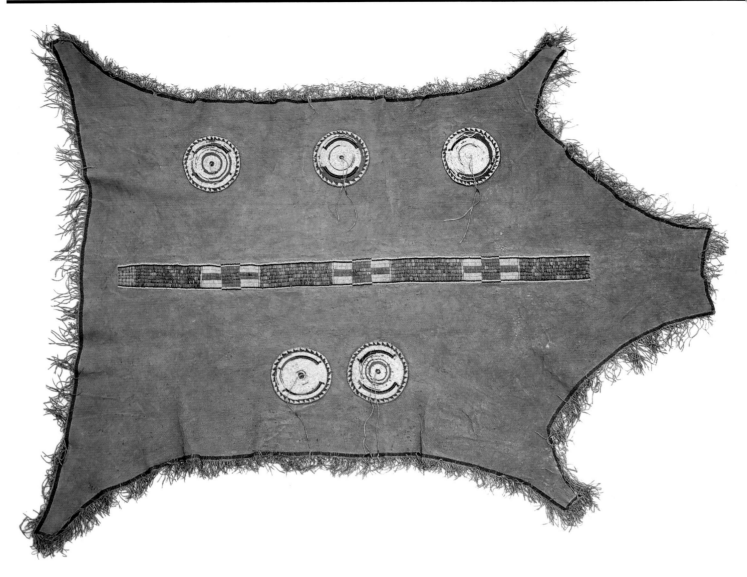

Above: *Powell collected this hide from the Utes as a horse cover, but it was more likely worn as a robe. The 'pony' beaded rosettes wre probably recycled from a Plains or Plateau blanket strip. The presence of the central panel of porcupine quillwork is very unusual for a Ute piece. While Ute women produced quantities of beadwork in the late nineteenth century, they seem to have seldom done quillwork.*

the first, designs were painted onto the wet, skin-side surface of the hide while it was stretched flat.[13]

A second, possibly older technique of parfleche decoration on the Plateau employed the dark brown epidermis on the hair side of buffalo hides. Designs were cut or scraped just through the surface of the wet hide, and when the hide dried the cut lines opened to show the lighter layer of the hide underneath. The design consisted entirely of light and dark areas of hide, and usually no paint was used. When buffalo hides were not available, the women used elk or other hides and darkened the epidermis with animal blood before incising the design. Traditionally the incised parfleche was used for food storage, while the painted parfleche was used for storing clothing and food supplies. Surviving incised parfleches are now extremely rare.[14]

The horse-mounted nomads of the Great Basin – the Shoshoni, Bannock, and Ute – shared the painted parfleche container tradition with the people of the Plains and Plateau.[15] The Northern Shoshoni parfleches were made of buffalo, elk, and later, of cattle hides, and were very similar to those of the Crow and Nez Perce. Shoshoni women usually painted a three-panel or nine-block design layout using straight lines, blue outlining of the design elements, and a major central geometric design element. Ute parfleches were made of the same materials but the painting was different: thin brown or black lines outlined the design elements; designs composed of blocks within blocks; rectangles filled with squares; and overall designs not enclosed by a border.[16]

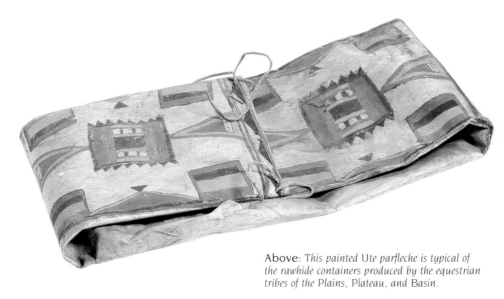

Above: *This painted Ute parfleche is typical of the rawhide containers produced by the equestrian tribes of the Plains, Plateau, and Basin.*

Fiber Arts and Basketry

A variety of baskets and other fiber objects played an important part in the lives of the Plateau people.[17] The two Plateau basketry types most well known today are the 'cornhusk' bag and the 'Klickitat' basket, both of which were produced by the women of several tribes in the area. The cornhusk bag was a flat basket originally woven from native hemp cordage by a simple twining technique. Decoration was applied by false embroidery using dyed grass as well as cornhusks and later, wool yarn. The earliest bags were large rectangles (up to 2 by 3ft (0.6 by 1m.)) with an opening at the top that closed with a drawstring, and were used primarily for food storage. Designs on these early bags were repeated simple geometric forms in soft natural browns and tans, typically arranged in horizontal bands across the bag. Decoration was almost always different on each side of the bag.

In the latter part of the nineteenth century, as traditional food gathering and storage became less important, cornhusk bags were produced in smaller sizes that were more square than rectangular and which were used primarily for women's decorative hand bags. Brighter dyed natural materials and wool yarn were used for the false embroidery, and

commercial twine began to replace native hemp cordage. By the end of the nineteenth century, designs became more complicated, employing symmetrical geometric forms and realistic figures such as humans, animals, and plants. The earlier practice of asymmetrical designs on the two sides was retained, as was the uniqueness of virtually every bag design.[18]

Women from many Plateau tribes wove tall, round baskets using the wrapped twining technique. The designs were usually rather simple colored bands, although more

Right: *Wasco/Wishram women on the Columbia River were producing finely twined round containers like this at the time of earliest contact with Euro-Americans. Similar distinctive human and animal designs are found on prehistoric bone and stone sculptures from the same area.*

elaborate designs in false embroidery were used. The Wasco/Wishram round baskets were often decorated with distinctive stylized human and animal figures very similar to those used in woven beadwork. Plateau women also produced coiled spruce root basketry, usually decorated by imbrication. While these are usually referred to as 'Klickitat' baskets, they were produced by several other Plateau tribes including the Yakima and Nez Perce. The designs were usually executed in simple, natural colors,

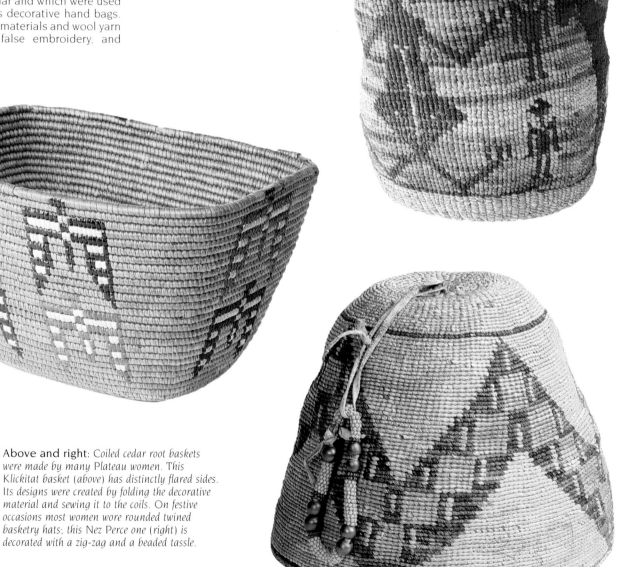

Above and right: *Coiled cedar root baskets were made by many Plateau women. This Klickitat basket (above) has distinctly flared sides. Its designs were created by folding the decorative material and sewing it to the coils. On festive occasions most women wore rounded twined basketry hats; this Nez Perce one (right) is decorated with a zig-zag and a beaded tassle.*

but in elaborate geometric as well as stylized realistic designs. In the southern Plateau coiled baskets tended to be rounded oblongs with two small 'ears' or lifting loops on the top rim. In the northern Plateau the coiled baskets were similar, but tended to be more globular and rectangular in shape, sometimes with lids.

Basketry has been called one of the technological hallmarks of the Great Basin,[19] and the extremely arid conditions in much of the area have preserved samples of highly developed basketry from prehistoric periods. This aboriginal skill in basketry continued throughout the Basin in the Historic Period, although production and use tended to decline among the northern and eastern tribes that adopted the horse.[20]

Traditional Great Basin basketry was produced in several well-defined forms that

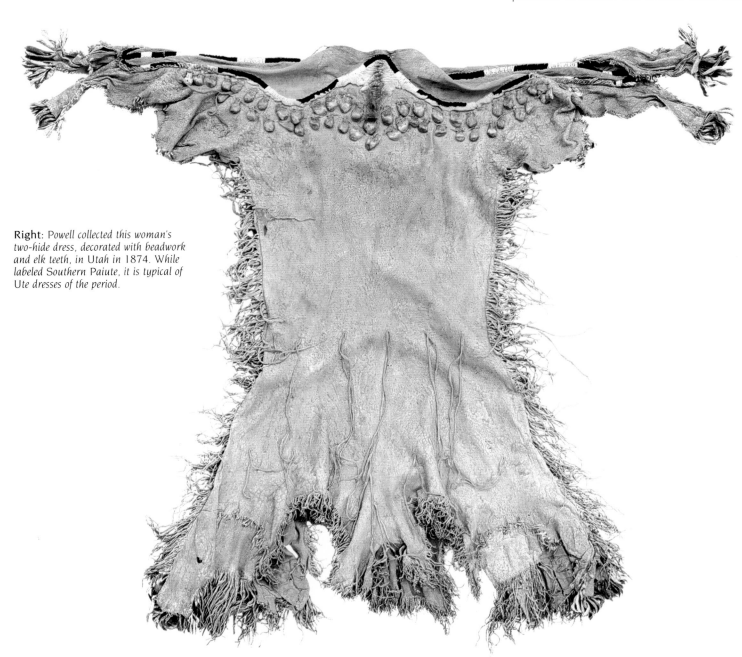

Right: *Powell collected this woman's two-hide dress, decorated with beadwork and elk teeth, in Utah in 1874. While labeled Southern Paiute, it is typical of Ute dresses of the period.*

reflected their utilitarian role in a hunter-gatherer society. Wild plant foods – especially seeds, berries, and pinenuts – were important parts of the diet of the Great Basin people, and specialized basketry forms were developed to gather, process, store, and consume them. The largest baskets were conical burden baskets, usually twined, which women carried on their backs using an attached tump-line or carrying strap across the shoulders or forehead. While gathering wild plant foods, women used a smaller conical or rounded gathering basket to do initial collecting, dumping it into the burden basket as it filled. Elongated, fan-shaped seed beaters were used to dislodge seeds and berries for gathering, while flattened trays were used for nut and seed gathering, sorting, winnowing, parching, cleaning, and serving. Basket bowls were used for mush cooking (using hot rocks) and eating.

Tightly-woven water bottles waterproofed with evergreen pitch were widely used throughout the area. Great Basin women also wove and wore basketry hats much like those worn on the Plateau, but usually covering more of the head. Finally, most Great Basin cradles were made of twined willow rods, usually with a curved rod sunscreen and were often covered with buckskin.

Other Arts and Crafts

The Native people of the Plateau and Great Basin traditionally produced for themselves everything needed to sustain their life and economy. They continued to do so on a significant scale even after widespread trade allowed the substitution of Euro-American materials for many native materials. Tanning large animal hides for clothing and other uses, for example, was a constant chore at which most Plateau and Basin women were experts even after the general availability of cloth in the mid- to late-nineteenth century. Even where cloth replaced hides for clothing, the garments were still largely handmade by the women.

Left: A Wasco/Wishram carver made this bowl from the horn of a bighorn sheep. The zig-zag border and concentric square designs are typical. These durable vessels, as well as horn ladles, were treasured heirlooms and were widely traded throughout the Plateau.

The Plateau and horse-mounted Great Basin people produced a wide variety of horse equipment such as saddles, stirrups, ropes, halters, and cruppers. Canoes built on a bark-covered wooden frame were extensively used on the Plateau. These canoes were covered with cedar, birch, white pine, and other barks, and had a unique long, pointed 'sturgeon nose' shape. Plateau people commonly made containers for temporary and more permanent use out of folded bark sewn with cedar root.

Plateau people also made extensive use of the horn of the bighorn sheep, carving and shaping it into bowls, ladles, and hunting bows. Several varieties of local stone were carved into cooking vessels and pipe bowls used with wooden stems. The earliest pipe bowls were straight tubes, while the later ones were a curved elbow shape, sometimes embellished with lead inlay.

Most Great Basin people wove light, warm, twined rabbitskin blankets out of thin strips of hide with the hair left on, and also made robes of multiple small animal skins sewn together. Mountain sheep horns were used to make short, strong, sinew-backed bows. Ladles and bowls were made from sheep and buffalo horns. Large vegetable fiber hunting nets and rush, feather-covered duck decoys have been found preserved in several caves, and were still in use into the twentieth century. Small stone, wood and clay figurines have also been found.

The Great Basin is also an area rich in representational and geometric rock art, produced since prehistoric times by painting and by inscribing into the rock surface.

References

1 Devoto, 1953: 246.
2 In 1805 Lewis and Clark recorded that the people along the Columbia River were very eager to trade for blue and white beads. However, surviving pieces of beadwork reliably dated to before 1850 are very rare today.
3 Rev. Spalding, quoted in Wright, 1991: 36.
4 While the popularity of seed beads increased as the nineteenth century progressed, they never completely replaced the earlier pony beads. In the 1840-70 period Plateau women often incorporated both in the same piece of beadwork.
5 The development of curvilinear beadwork on the Plateau may have been influenced by the beadwork worn by eastern Indians who participated in the fur trade in the west as early as the 1820s.
6 Elk, deer, horses, and even fish were most common in the earlier part of the period.
7 The Transmontaine style is characterized by the use of a wide range of bead colors to produce large diamond, hourglass, and triangular design motifs in a flat stitch. Major design elements were often outlined in a single line of white beads or by a lane of dark blue beads or both, set against a light field. The Transmontaine style also makes extensive use of red wool cloth as a background.
8 Another distinctive beadwork style was produced by a small group of Wasco/Wishram women on the western edge of the Plateau. Usually found on small

flat bags, this work appears to be 'loomed' but was woven with a loose warp technique. Bead colors were usually very simple, with designs in one color of dark beads on a white background. Distinctive animal, human, and skeletonal human 'X-ray' designs were popular.
9 Classic Ute blocky-design seed beadwork after about 1870 is virtually indistinguishable from Jicarilla beadwork of the same period.
10 Experts disagree whether quill-wrapped horsehair was produced exclusively by Plateau women, by Crow women, or both.
11 The natural range of the buffalo extended into the southern Plateau and northern Great Basin areas. Buffalo were found there in small herds until they were killed off in the 1830s.
12 One of the earliest surviving pieces of Plateau art is a painted, flat, fringed parfleche envelope collected in 1841 and now in the Smithsonian.
13 Liquid paint was made from powdered natural or trade pigments mixed with a medium such as glue. It was usually applied to the hide with a porous bone 'brush' or stylus. Alternatively, powdered pigments were mixed with a glue medium and allowed to dry into small cakes, which were used to draw directly on to the damp hide.
14 Parfleches filled with food, clothing, and other articles were commonly given away in large numbers during inter-tribal events on the Plateau, such as

marriages. This factor, plus the fact that many Plateau tribes have shared reservations for over a hundred years sometimes make distinct tribal styles of parfleche design hard to differentiate.
15 Shoshoni men also practised the Plains tradition of realistic paintings on soft hides, depicting their war exploits.
16 The Southern Paiutes may have made some parfleches, but parfleche use was not prevalent among non-horse people.
17 Mats were made from tule stems twined and sewn together side by side with hemp cordage. These mats were used primarily for longhouse coverings, as well as for a variety of other household purposes.
18 Cornhusk bags filled with roots were common gifts at both inter- and intra-tribal occasions on the Plateau so it is difficult to identify a particular cornhusk bag design with any particular tribe. The same materials and weaving techniques were used to produce a wide variety of other objects such as horse gear (saddle drapes and martingales), belt pouches, and occasionally clothing.
19 Fowler and Dawson, 1986: 705.
20 Those people, principally the northern and eastern Shoshoni, Bannock, and Ute, adopted Plains-style parfleche and tanned hide containers for transport and storage.

CALIFORNIA

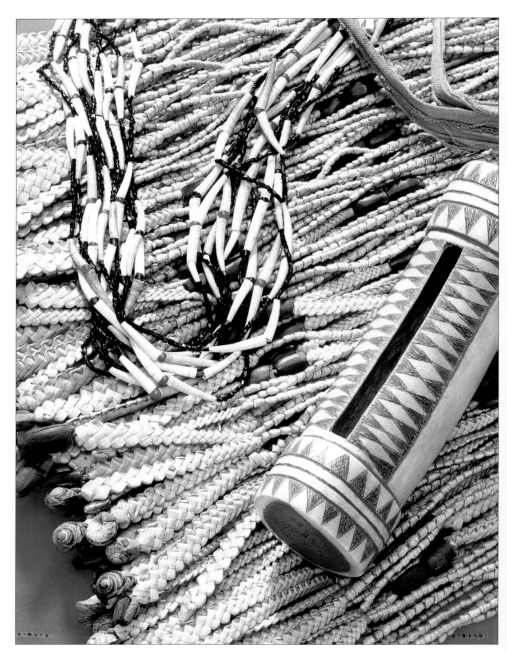

THE AREA NOW KNOWN as California was one of the most linguistically and culturally diverse areas in the world prior to 1800; more than sixty 'tribes', all with their own languages and material culture, made their homes in the California region. For the sake of this discussion of arts and crafts, the California culture area can be divided into several major regions which share similarities in their arts and crafts: northwest (including Yurok, Karok, Hupa, Tolowa, Wiyot, and neighboring tribes); northeast (including Achomawi, Atsugewi, and Shasta); central (including Pomo, Maidu, Yuki, Miwok, Yokuts, Patwin, Wappo, and others); and southern (including Chumash, Cahuilla, Tipai-Ipai, Gabrielino, ·Juaneño, Luiseño, Cupeño, Serrano, and Tataviam).

In northwestern California, people shared a rich culture which relied on salmon, animals (such as deer), and a great variety of plants. Women made fine twined baskets of hazel or willow shoots and conifer root, overlaid with patterns in black maidenhair fern stem and shiny yellow bear grass. The men were skilled craftsmen, producing dugout canoes, split-plank houses, finely incised antler purses, and exquisite dance regalia.

In the northeastern part of the state, people had varied material cultures influenced by extreme variations in elevation, climate, and vegetation in the region. From deserts, coniferous forests, swamps, and meadows, the Achomawi, Atsugewi, and their neighbors obtained a vast array of plant and animal resources to provide for their subsistance. They also produced a distinctive style of fine twined basketry, using some of the same, and some different, materials as people in northwest California. Their baskets were similar in appearance to those of the Klamath River, except that overlaid patterns were evident on both the inside and outside of the baskets. Men in this region made fine sinew-backed bows, which were an important trade item, and dance regalia, though it was not as highly developed an art as it was in the northwest. After the arrival of non-Indians, woven glass beadwork became firmly established in this area, and thousands of woven strips were made utilizing a limited repertory of patterns executed in hundreds of different interpretations.

People in the central portion of California relied on acorns as an important food source along with hundreds of other plant foods. Animals, including deer, elk, squirrels, and various birds, were also important in their diets. The Pomo peoples made and used a great variety of twined basketry, primarily reserving coiled basketry for fancy baskets, often made as special gifts. Some of these baskets, fully covered with small, brilliantly

colored feathers, have become the best known of Pomo arts. Coiled basketry for everyday use assumed more prominence among peoples to the east and south of the Pomo, including the Maidu, Patwin, Miwok, and Yokuts. Men among the Maidu, Patwin and Pomo produced exquisite dance regalia, including flicker-quill headbands, belts woven of native hemp and ornamented with green and red feathers and white shell beads, and a myriad of feathered headpieces and cloaks.

Above: *The skill of native Californian artists is evident in this display of Hupa wealth. An 1870s' woman's apron of woven bear grass, snail shells, and pine nut beads, an incised elk antler purse used to store tusk-shaped dentalium shell money, and a dentalium and glass bead necklace owned by the Hupa Shoemaker Robinson during the early twentieth century show the array of materials used to create objects of lasting beauty. Glass beads were used by many other peoples in California and woven glass beadwork reached its greatest development in the north.*

In southern California, the Chumash on the coast utilized the wealth of the sea, while tribes living inland adapted to their more arid environments. Inland tribes used the various resources offered by the desert, including clay, which was formed into elegant and useful pottery vessels. In basketry, coiled baskets were made and used almost exclusively. Women from the Chumash, Cahuilla, Tipai-Ipai, Gabrielino, Juaneño, Luiseño, Cupeño, Serrano, and Tataviam made elaborately coiled baskets which sometimes incorporated three colors. Men, apparently, executed the polychrome rock art characteristic of the Chumash region. A tradition of beautifully carved, steatite utilitarian ware and sculptures was centered in the Chumash-Gabrielino region.

Basketry

Basketry is perhaps the best-known art of California, and Native women have become well-known for it the world over. It is an ancient skill in California, and there are marked differences in baskets from different regions. Basket-making was primarily a woman's art; generally men made only a few coarse-twined baskets, like fish traps. Women took great pains to produce their baskets according to traditionally dictated methods and ideals, although each basket was unique and identifiable as the product of a specific individual.[2] Weaving skills took many years to develop, and young girls were encouraged and expected to participate in gathering and preparing basket materials as well as weaving. By the age of ten or twelve, most girls were capable of good basketry.

Baskets were indispensable in the lives of California Indian people and they were woven in a multitude of shapes, each designed to function in a special niche of the Native lifestyle. Specific baskets were made for cooking and food preparation, storage, carrying loads, and cradling children.[3] Prized baskets, often made especially for the occasion, were given as gifts or burned or buried with the dead, and baskets were frequently burned during mourning ceremonies to honor the dead.

The study of basket form, manufacture, and change over time does not extend far into the past, as baskets do not usually survive in archeological sites.[4] Different styles of

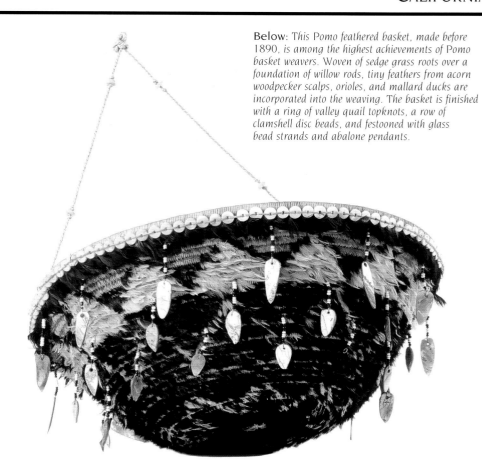

Below: This Pomo feathered basket, made before 1890, is among the highest achievements of Pomo basket weavers. Woven of sedge grass roots over a foundation of willow rods, tiny feathers from acorn woodpecker scalps, orioles, and mallard ducks are incorporated into the weaving. The basket is finished with a ring of valley quail topknots, a row of clamshell disc beads, and festooned with glass bead strands and abalone pendants.

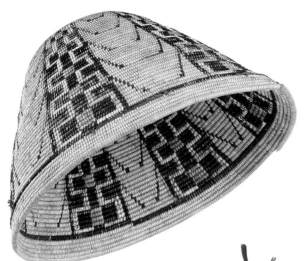

Left and below: A few coiled baskets use animal materials as part of their decoration. The Tubatulabal woman's cap (left), with patterns outlined in white porcupine quills, is a rare example of this type of basketry. The Chukchansi Yokuts basket (below left) by Mrs. Graham uses split orange quills of the flicker, while the Pomo coiled basket from the late nineteenth century (below), is ornamented with the red scalp feathers of the acorn woodpecker, quail topknots, and shell beads.

Right: *This late-eighteenth or early-nineteenth century Chumash basket, tightly woven of split juncus, was used to stone-boil acorn mush.*

basketry developed in distinct areas, and people often regarded their own style as the 'correct' one. The words of the Karok woman, 'Imakyanvan (Mrs. Phoebe Maddux), in about 1930 embody this principle:

'Each new year ceremony my deceased mother would go to Clear Creek to attend the new year ceremony. She would pack upriver two pack basket loads of bowl baskets and openwork plates, and dipper baskets; she would trade them for blankets, Indian blankets, and upriver hats, and juniper seeds, for all kinds of things, upriver things. They used to give us those upriver hats sometimes, but we did not wear them, it does not look right on us.'[5]

Mrs. Maddux's comments describe not only how desirable her mother's baskets were as trade items, but also how these Karok women viewed the women's basketry hats from upriver tribes such as the Achomawi as not quite 'right'.

Weavers of northwestern California produced baskets in plain twining with decoration overlaid on the baskets' exterior. Mush bowls, twined with conifer roots on a foundation of hazel sticks, were embellished with a horizontal band of design in shiny yellow bear grass. More elaborate baskets, such as the dress caps worn by women, were further ornamented with shiny black maidenhair fern stem and woodwardia fern stem dyed to a rust color with alder bark. Only the most highly prized women's caps were further ornamented with additional overlay in yellow-dyed porcupine quills. The quills surrounded by the shiny black of the maidenhair fern stem made a striking contrast to the lighter yellow bear grass background.[6]

A handful of Yurok baskets collected by members of the Vancouver voyage in 1793 are preserved in British museums, but otherwise few baskets exist from this region from before 1890. After that date, the tradition of destroying an individual's possessions (and, therefore, baskets) upon their death fell increasingly into disuse, so more baskets survived. Additionally, women started to make baskets specifically for sale to non-Indians. Many of the baskets produced after

1890 for non-Indians were made with patterns and shapes specifically designed to make the baskets more saleable, including motifs of realistic arrows and swastikas, and innovations such as pedestal bases and knobbed lids. In baskets made for their own use, as well as in most made for sale, women of this region still adhered to time-honored ideas of 'correct' patterns and basket forms. Some innovative weavers, such as Elizabeth Hickox (born in 1873), achieved a previously unrealized fineness and beauty by applying Karok patterns to a unique, lidded basket form. Her yellow-on-black baskets are among the finest from northwestern California.[7]

Baskets of northeastern California were produced in plain twining with a decorative overlay that shows on both the basket's interior and exterior. Like the Karok and Hupa to the west, women among the Wintu and Atsugewi wove their baskets on stiff warps of willow or other sticks. Some Achomawi women used twisted cordage (made from the sheath of the tule) for their warps, as did Klamath and Modoc people to the north, resulting in flexible baskets. By the early-1900s, some weavers were making changes in their baskets to make them more saleable to non-Indians. Many women wove large baskets with patterns that had previously only been evident in smaller baskets. Others experimented with new forms (such as oval baskets) and/or patterns (such as eight-pointed stars and serrated diamonds, patterns that reached the area with the arrival of woven beadwork). Some weavers covered their completed baskets with loose-warp-woven beadwork, producing striking objects that were a blending of ancient basketry with more recently learned glass beadwork technique and patterns.

Women in central California wove both twined and coiled baskets. Colored patterns were produced by substituting colored weaving strands for the background color strands. Pomo women excelled in both twined and coiled basketry, and they also produced feathered baskets. In these baskets, small feathers – such as scarlet woodpecker-scalp feathers, bright-blue bluebird feathers, brilliant-yellow oriole or meadowlark feathers, and iridescent-green mallard duck

scalp feathers – were incorporated into the basket, held in with the basket's stitching. Thus, a completed basket's exterior was covered with a velvet-like coating of fine feathers. Such baskets were further embellished with abalone shell pendants and clamshell disc beads.

Many supreme Pomo artists created exquisite works of basketry art. While it was unusual for men to weave, both William Benson (1862-1937) and his wife Mary (c.1878-1930) wove baskets of a quality rivaling the best produced anywhere; some of the coiled baskets had a stitch count of over thity-two stitches per inch.

The Bensons, weaving for the non-Indian market, pushed basketry beyond the traditionally-accepted Pomoan style and made it into textile sculpture.[8] Similarly, others weavers such as Joseppa Dick (c.1860-1905) produced exquisitely designed basketry with fine stitching (sometimes as many as forty-one stitches per inch).[9] Cache Creek Pomo-Patwin weaver Mabel McKay (1907-93) was renowned for her feathered and beaded baskets, and she taught the art of basketry to both Indian and non-Indian weavers, helping to ensure the art's survival.

Other central California peoples also produced excellent baskets; the Patwin and Maidu were renowned for their fine coiled baskets. The Patwin made baskets in both single-rod and three-rod coiling (like their Pomo neighbors to the east), but the Maidu produced only three-rod baskets. Farther south, the Yokuts and Western Mono made coiled baskets using a foundation of bunch grass stalks, and the Miwok made baskets using all of the above-mentioned coiling techniques.

Just after the turn of the century, Yosemite Valley, in Southern Miwok territory, became an important locale for the development of basketry into an art form produced solely for sale to non-Indians. Around 1910 weavers of mixed Southern Miwok and Mono Lake Paiute ancestry (Mono Lake Paiute people had come across the Sierra Nevada into Yosemite Valley) began to create a fancy style of three-rod coiled basketry with black and red patterns. The design style was encouraged by the Yosemite Indian Field Days, a rodeo-fair event held in Yosemite during summers of the 1920s; basketry contests at the Field Days spurred weavers to produce baskets with extremely fine stitching (sometimes exceeding thirty stitches per inch) and complex patterning. Individual women such as Lucy Telles, Carrie Bethel, Nellie and Tina Charlie, and Leanna Tom were recognized as artists, and collectors eagerly sought to acquire their baskets.[10]

Women in southern California wove both coiled and twined baskets, though fewer twined baskets were made (they included winnowers, sieves, seed beaters, and asphaltum-coated water bottles |made by the Chumash|). A wide variety of baskets, many very finely woven, were made with coiling. A highly developed design style evolved in certain Chumash groups; specific patterns and design placement were rigidly followed (for example, alternating colors of stitching on a basket's rim and the principal design band's placement on the upper part of the basket).

As early as the late eighteenth century, southern California Indian women began to make baskets for foreigners. Spanish officials stationed there often obtained Chumash baskets as gifts for visiting European dignitaries, thus excellent examples of Chumash basketry are contained in museum collections in Germany, Spain, and England. By the end of the nineteenth century, when basket collecting became a fashionable hobby in the United States, southern California weavers again filled the demand by weaving thousands of baskets for non-Indian patrons.[11]

Right: *The Pomo artist William Benson (1862-1936) created this elegant man's hairpin of incised deer bone and tiny woodpecker, bluebird, meadowlark, and quail feathers bound with deer sinew.*

Ceremonial Regalia

Ceremonial dances were an important part of Native people's existence throughout California. Dances often manifested supernatural power; they were extremely complex performances and were usually considered prayers in visible form. A great array of carefully crafted ceremonial regalia was indispensable to these dances.[12]

In central California, dance regalia differed among dances. Flicker-quill headbands were used in most of them, however. These bands were made with salmon-pink scraped-feather quills of the common flicker (a woodpecker-like bird) and each band required the feathers from twenty to sixty birds. Many of the dances also required dancers to wear feather capes (most often men wore them on their backs). The capes were made from large feathers obtained from hawks, eagles, vultures, condors, or various waterfowl.

In addition to flicker-quill headbands, a wide variety of headgear was worn in different ceremonial dances, with many styles reserved for specific spirit impersonators. Pomo women sometimes wore fur-covered forehead bands decorated with short, projecting quills. Each quill was ornamented with a small mat made of sewn flicker quills and beads. Both men and women wore feather bunches on their heads. These were made of feathers tied and coiled into a bristling tuft.

The Patwin, Valley Maidu, and Pomo made a headpiece known as the 'bighead' which was worn by spirit impersonators in the Hesi ceremony. The headpiece was over 4ft (1.2m.) in diameter and made up of about a hundred stripped willow shoots. The shoots were usually painted red and tipped with white waterfowl feathers, then thrust into a bundle of tule tied on to the dancer's head. The headpiece looked like an immense pincushion.

Elaborately decorated, woven feather belts were perhaps the most remarkable achievement in ceremonial regalia of central California. The belts, produced primarily by the Valley Maidu (Konkow) and Patwin, averaged 6ft (2m.) in length and about 5in (12cm.) in width. They were woven of native milkweed or hemp fiber in a weft-face weave; included in the weaving were small, scarlet scalp feathers of about five-hundred acorn woodpeckers, and iridescent-green scalp feathers of some hundred male mallard ducks. These feathers were arranged in alternating panels, and the red panels were further ornamented with small olivella-shell disc beads which had been baked in ashes of a fire to turn them white. Such a belt was the most expensive item in the trade economy of central California, worth three large feathered baskets, several bearskins, or over a thousand clamshell disc beads.[13] The belts, which were worn by men in ceremonial dances such as the Hesi, testified to the group's wealth and dedication to using their best when dancing to ask for the spirits' protection.

In northwestern California, featherwork was also an important part of dance regalia. Woodpecker scalps (from pileated, or less commonly, acorn woodpeckers) were considered a visible manifestation of an individual's wealth and they were used in a myriad of ways: headbands worn by men in the Jump Dance required more than thirty pileated

Left: *Dance regalia differs greatly among California Indian groups. This trident-like hairpin was popular with a variety of groups in central California. This example is most like those used by Pomo dancers.*

or two-hundred acorn woodpecker scalps; albino deerskins carried in the White Deerskin Dance and otter-fur quivers carried in the Brush Dance were trimmed with them; most hairpins worn by male dancers, and some women's basketry caps and braid ornaments were also ornamented with either entire scalps or individual tufts of scarlet feathers.

Women's dance regalia in northwestern California was elaborate, and produced its own music from the hundreds of shells and shell beads used in necklaces and as decoration on dance aprons. Women wore a front apron, which was often made of bear grass woven over buckskin cords and pine nuts or glass beads. This was worn with a back apron ornamented with beargrass and maidenhair fern stem with an upper fringe of beads and abalone shell pendants, and a lower fringe of fine buckskin thongs. The

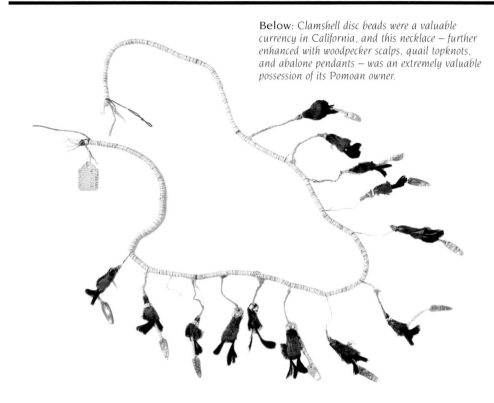

Below: *Clamshell disc beads were a valuable currency in California, and this necklace – further enhanced with woodpecker scalps, quail topknots, and abalone pendants – was an extremely valuable possession of its Pomoan owner.*

rustling of the shells against one another produced a pleasing sound that is inseparable from the music of the dances on the lower Klamath River region.

Dance regalia in southern California was more limited than that to the north. Perhaps the most elaborate regalia in the region was produced among the Chumash and their neighbors. Skirts were made of strings twisted from native fiber incorporating eagle down, so that each string became a white, fluffy streamer; these were often tipped with sections of jet-black crow feathers or cinnamon-colored mature red-tailed hawk tail feathers. Men sometimes wore a high feather crown of magpie or roadrunner tail feathers surrounded with black crow feathers, and then with a band of white eagle-down tied across the brow. The headpieces also bore testimony to the owner's wealth and to the abundant bird life of the region, as only the center feathers from magpie tails were used in the headpieces, and more than fifty birds were needed to manufacture a single headpiece.[14]

Quill bands, similar to those of central California, were made by the Chumash and their southern neighbors. These bands differed, however, from the flicker headbands made farther north, as they were usually used as streamers and attached to poles at ceremonial sites, or worn as bandoleers. They also differed in that the section of stripped quills was narrow (averaging about 2in/5cm.) and were solidly bordered by the unstripped feather. The bands were made of feathers not only from flickers, but also from crows and jays, as well as small feathers of pelicans and condors.

Also worn by Chumash men, and by the Cahuilla, Tipai-Ipai, and neighboring groups, was a net skirt which had a lower edge fringed with eagle or condor feathers. The skirt, worn with a headband of owl fluffs and head plumes of stripped great horned owl feathers, comprised the costume for the Whirling Dance.

Beadwork

Beads were an important part of the economy of Native California long before the arrival of Europeans. Among the Yurok, Karok, Hupa, and their neighbors, tusk-shaped dentalium shells (obtained in trade from the north) were a standard currency. Beads of bull pine nuts and juniper seeds were used by women to decorate ceremonial regalia.[15] The Pomo and Coast Miwok just north of San Francisco Bay were the primary suppliers of clamshell disc beads to northern and central California.[16] The Pomo also produced highly valued, pink stone beads made from magnesite. On the southern coast near Santa Barbara, the Chumash produced olivella-shell disc beads as well as soapstone beads.

Glass beads were brought to California as early as 1542 with the explorer Juan Rodriguez Cabrillo, but they did not become common until they were distributed as a result of missionary activities between 1769 and 1800. By the first half of the nineteenth century, opaque, white glass beads and translucent green glass or white glass beads coated with a red exterior, along with less common green, blue, and black beads were widely used in central California.

It was not until sometime in the later half of the nineteenth century, however, that woven beadwork bands were first produced in California. Woven beadwork technique, and many patterns, reached California from the Wasco and their neighbors in the Columbia River region through interior groups in Oregon. The method of making woven beadwork bands using a 'loose-warp' technique was quickly assimilated by the Klamath, Modoc, Achomawi, Wintu, and their neighbors, probably sometime around or just before 1870.[17]

Along with the technique of making woven beadwork strips, certain patterns and forms came to California from the Columbia River Region. Eight-pointed stars, serrated diamonds and pairs of triangles linked together along a central dividing line were among the most enduring of motifs to be used in California. One form which was used in California with little change was the multi-tab, octopus bag of the Wasco. Produced entirely in woven beadwork, the Wasco bag was usually multicolored with a variety of designs. The Wintu version of the bag was somewhat changed, incorporating a closing flap at the top (usually produced with red, black, or blue designs on a white ground), and making use of only a few simple, but striking, geometric patterns.[18]

By the 1890s, Paiute people along the eastern flank of California were also producing woven beadwork bands, although they often made them using a bow loom. Their use of this style of beadwork facilitated the introduction of beadwork to groups such as the Southern Miwok and Maidu across the Sierra, although beadwork never gained a strong foothold with either.

Beadwork is still produced today by members of many groups in California; some of it still relating to the earliest techniques, but much more of it is wholly new.

Sculpture

The archeological record in California provides ample proof of the antiquity of stone sculpture. While various types of plummet-shaped charms are known to have been produced since perhaps 2000 BC in central California, the most elaborate stone carvings were produced in the Chumash and Gabrielino areas.

A wide variety of effigies were produced by the Chumash, primarily from steatite (soapstone). Some were small models of

Below: *Woven glass beadwork, such as this Wintu shot bag collected in 1872, was popular in northern California. Bold designs and use of only a few colors characterize beadwork among the Wintu and their neighbors in the 1870s.*

plank boats. The little boats were highly prized charms for boat builders, ensuring good luck in fishing. The charms' owners sometimes kept several to be assured of fishing success. When the owner died, the small charms were buried with him.

Other sculptured effigies are representations of specific animals, but there is great variation in the degrees of realism with which they were made. Many of the charms represent whales: some clearly and accurately detail the mammal's anatomy, while others are more abstract representations, lacking fins, eyes, and other details. Other effigies are phallic in nature, or represent fish, seals, and birds.

In the northwest corner of California, the Yurok, Karok, Hupa, and their neighbors produced a limited amount of utilitarian sculpture. Men carved sleek redwood canoes with elegant prows and sterns, each made from a single tree; the boats were the primary mode of conveyance on the Klamath River. Wooden trunks, carved from a solid block of redwood, were used to store ceremonial regalia and other valuables. Tubular pipes were made from dense yew wood, usually fitted with soapstone bowls. So exquisite was the workmanship on these pipes that early explorers marveled at their symmetry and thought they must have been turned on a lathe.

Antler provided another medium for sculpture among the peoples of the lower Klamath River. Sections of elk antler were scraped, carved, polished, and incised to produce what the Native people called purses: small boxes with fitted lids used to store dentalium shell money. The section of the antler that attaches to the elk's skull was used to carve elaborate spoons that had intricately carved handles decorated with delicate cut-out patterns. These spoons were used by men to eat acorn mush and served as an elegant symbol of the people's wealth and prestige.[19]

Rock Art

Although rock art is found throughout California, it appears to be concentrated in specific areas. Both petroglyphs (patterns pecked, abraded, or ground into stone) and pictographs (patterns applied to the stone with paint or pigment in one or more colors) are found, although there seems to be little overlap in the two techniques.

Rock art seems to be an ancient style of art in California, so old that in most areas Indian

Below: *The Hupa and their neighbors, perhaps more than any other Californian group, made beautiful and functional objects from antler. These spoons, carved from the base of an elk's antler, were used by men for eating acorn soup. Highly valued, only one pair could be made from an adult bull-elk's antlers, since the bone at the top of the skull was needed to make the bowl of the spoon.*

people ascribed the rock art to people who lived in the area before them, or to legendary beings. One of the few areas for which information exists about the ethnographic use and production of rock art is among the Chumash.[20] Chumash rock-paintings were probably produced by elite shaman-priests. They seem to incorporate astronomical data as it was associated with Chumash cosmology and mythology. The production of such paintings, at least among some of the Chumash, was tied to the time of the winter solstice.

One Chumash story tells of a neighboring Gabrielino sorcerer who caused a famine and many deaths by producing a painting on rocks of many falling men and women who were bleeding from their mouths.

Indeed, some of the finest rock art in North America is found in the Chumash area. In the mountains north of Mount Piños, in the territory of the Emigdiano Chumash, is the most elaborate extant Chumash rock art site: it comprises four shallow caves, each of which has walls covered with finely executed paintings of large circular motifs with concentric rings, anthropomorphic and zoomorphic figures, dots, bifurcated and zig-zag patterns in black, white, yellow, cream, green, blue-green, red, and orange. The green and orange are unique, among the Chumash, to this single site. It has been speculated that the colors were obtained from Mexican sources during the revolt of 1824, and that the use of these 'foreign' colors may have been an attempt to gain supernatural power over the Mexicans during the revolt.[21]

Today

Many of the arts discussed are no longer produced in California, while some skills, such as basketry, survive among some groups. On the lower Klamath River, weavers such as Susan Burdick preserve and continue the fine weaving that characterizes the area, just as Konkow Maidu weaver Rella Allen and Maidu weaver Lily Baker make the traditional coiled basketry of their region.

Some skills, such as the manufacture of steatite carvings in southern California, had not been practised for many years until they were revived in the past decade by William Pink (Cupeño) and L. Frank Manriquez (Tongva-Ajachme[22]); they produced pieces of high quality that rival the best of prehistoric examples. Similarly, Hupa-Yurok artist George Blake's fine sinew-backed bows, elk-horn spoons and purses, redwood trunks and canoes are among the finest extant examples of these objects.

Traditional artists demonstrate their skills to the public at special events and at recreated Native villages in many locations throughout California. Perhaps the best-known demonstrator today is Julia Parker, a Pomo woman who has demonstrated the traditional skills and basketry of her husband's Miwok-Paiute family to visitors to Yosemite National Park since 1960. An accomplished basket weaver, Mrs. Parker says:

'I always say I wouldn't be what I am and couldn't weave like I do without the women who came before me. I feel like a little bit of them comes out in me whenever I weave.'[23]

References

1 Kroeber, 1925: 194.
2 For perhaps the most complete discussion of ethno-esthetics among Yurok and Karok basket weavers, see O'Neale, 1932.
3 For a discussion on the use of a variety of baskets in processing acorns for food, see Ortiz, 1991.
4 Bates, 1982: 33-34 and Bates and Lee, 1990: 39-40.
5 Harrington, 1932: 128.
6 O'Neale, 1932.
7 Mrs. Hickox was actually the daughter of a Wiyot woman and a non-Indian man, although she identified as Karok. See Fields, 1985.
8 Their lives are detailed in McLendon, 1990.
9 For more on Joseppa Dick see Smith-Ferri, 1993.
10 Bates and Lee, 1990.
11 Dawson and Deetz, 1965.

12 Bates and Bibby, 1985.
13 These belts continued to be produced into the first quarter of the twentieth century. Belts made in the late nineteenth century often used commercial cordage for the weft and glass beads for decoration. For additional information on the belts, see Bates, 1981a, Bates and Bibby, 1983, and McKern, 1922.
14 This style of headpiece was commonly used by Yokuts people, by people as far north as the Coast Miwok of the Bodega Bay region, and by people as far east as the Paiute of western Nevada. The use of these magpie headpieces does not seem to have spread farther south than the Chumash.
15 A discussion of the manufacture and use of pine nut beads is in Ferris, 1992.
16 For clamshell disc and magnesite bead manufacture

among the Pomo, see Hudson, 1897.
17 There is very little published on the spread of glass beadwork to California. Most of the known primary sources are cited in Bates, 1981b.
18 These octopus bags among the Wasco were probably produced in imitation of Cree-Meti bags, brought west during the fur trade in the 1830s and 1840s. See Schlick and Duncan, 1991.
19 For a lengthy discussion see Kelly, 1930.
20 Grant, 1966; Hudson and Underhay, 1978.
21 Lee, 1979.
22 L. Frank Manriquez uses these village names to identify herself, rather than the Spanish names of Gabrielino and Juaneño.
23 Bates and Lee, 1990: 171.

'It is easy to become entranced by the soft curtain of age, seeing this instead of what it obscures...
This is not what their creators intended. These were objects of bright pride, to be admired in the newness of their crisply carved lines,
the powerful flow of sure elegant curves and recesses — yes, and in the brightness of fresh paint.'

BILL REID (HAIDA)[1]

THE NORTHWEST COAST

SOPHISTICATED, vital, and brilliant, the Northwest Coast visual arts have captivated the imagination and appreciation of foreign visitors for over two-hundred years. It is this time period Euro-Americans have designated as 'traditional' but which represents merely an epoch in an art tradition that has spanned hundreds, if not thousands of years. Contact with Euro-Americans resulted in a florescence in the art, and it is from about 1749 until the present that our most impressive museum collections of Northwest Coast art derive. As with most non-western cultures, the Northwest Coast languages did not have a word for 'art', though by no means did their culture lack esthetic values, principles, or appreciation of the practice of the visual arts. Indeed, their culture had specialists in art production – both men and women – who enjoyed long careers and held inter-tribal reputations for excellence. Almost every aspect of their extensive material culture inventory was or could have been embellished by any number of the decorative arts. Art on the Northwest Coast was a fact of everyday life rather than simply reserved for the elite or in special locations.

The people and cultures of the Northwest Coast occupied the narrow strip of island-dotted land from Yukatat Bay in Alaska to the Columbia River in what is now the state of Washington. Facing the Pacific Ocean to the west and confined to the coastal waters by the towering and most impenetrable coastal range of mountains on the east, the people evolved a distinctive cultural response to their largely maritime environment. The northern groups were the Tlingit of the Alaskan coast, the Tsimshian of the inland coastal waterways of the Nass and Skeena Rivers, the Haida of the Queen Charlotte Islands, and their relatives, the Kaigani Haida of the Prince of Wales Archipelago. The Wakashan or central groups of the coast between the Tsimshian in the North and the Kwakiutl in the south were the Bella Bella (or Northern Wakashan), and the Salishan-speaking Bella Coola. On the north and eastern shores of Vancouver Island and adjoining mainland were the group of tribes known as the Kwakiutl. The west coast of Vancouver Island and the tip of the Olympic Peninsula were occupied by the Nuu-chah-nulth (formerly the Nootka or Westcoast) and their relatives the Makah. The southernmost tribe was the Coast Salish of the Puget Sound and lower mainland.

The Practice of Art
If we could take a journey back in time, travel by an elegant wooden canoe to our hosts' home, we would pull up on the pebble beach of the village's protected cove. The dense cedar forest rises dark, huge, and formidable behind the row of houses glowing in the silver patina of their weathered cedar facades. Massive gabled houses lining the beaches and monumental crest poles creating a veritable curtain of images in front of the houses further diminish our human dimensions. Experience of the monumental is precisely the theme underlying the production of the material culture of these

Above: *The Tsimshian ceremonial T'Kul rattle, carved in fine grained wood, depicts supernatural frogs springing from the eyes of the Wind Spirit. Robes or tunics were often worn for ceremonies. Here we have a woven Chilkat tunic upon which the rattle rests. Using a painted 'pattern board' as the guide, formline designs, as seen on the tunic, were meticulously copied with all their intricate and subtle curves. The weavers were able to combine various sophisticated techniques with different weights of weft threads to render a technically exceptional tapestry.*

366

Left: This beautiful crest hat was worn by a high-ranking member of the Chilkat tribe. A collaboration between a weaver and a carver, this hat is painted with a killer whale on its brim. The Raven's cry is almost audible from the animated carving on the crown. A tribute to the weaver's skill, some Tlingit carvers of solid wooden clan helmets (right) imitated the skip-stitched twined patterning of woven hat brims.

Left: This scowling face was made more fearsome by a bristling facial hair of inlaid bear fur; locks of human hair were pegged into place above the forehead.

coastal cultures.[2] Harnessing the invisible forces of society, nature, and the supernatural by making them visible was a task particularly relished by Northwest Coast artists. Challenged by the task, these artists translated the idea of monumental not only in the size of their artistic productions, but by the degree of spiritual and material complexity in their arts. The same theme of monumentality may be found in a giant crest pole or in a tiny ivory charm; the conception guiding the artist's eye and hand is larger than a single human life and the art makes visible the contemplation of the invisible.

Who were the artists? As a general observation, women were the weavers of the Coast while men were the carvers and painters. There were exceptions, but generally women wove the garments, baskets, and mats to furnish the comfort of daily life and enrich the spectacle of ceremonial life.[3] Men carved primarily in wood, though also in stone, bone, and ivory, often combining their three-dimensional art with two-dimensional painted designs. Their arts formed the massive structures found in the material culture as well as the smaller embellished instruments of the hunt, food preparation, and ceremony. Not infrequently, the arts involved varying degrees of collaboration as the weaver's talents were combined with those of the carver.

There were distinct though shared artistic conventions on the Coast, each with their own principles of composition and esthetic rules. Northwest Coast artists' adherence to these rules over large geographic areas through the centuries is impressive – and forms a stunning chapter in world art history. Forging metals and making and firing pottery were virtually unknown in traditional times. Yet, with few and relatively simple tools, Northwest Coast artists employed a myriad of techniques to manipulate mostly wood and wood fibers into an astonishingly large inventory of cultural objects that served all the purposes of life.

Throughout the region, the visual images were almost entirely representations of animals or humans.[4] Though the exact

meaning of an image might be restricted to those who know the artist's intent, learning the basic vocabulary of forms gives the viewer access to a visual syntax of tremendous depth. Conventionalized identifying features distinguish one animal from another: the long, slender, straight beak of Raven differs from the heavy, sharply down-curved beak of Eagle; Killer-Whale's long, upright dorsal fin marked with a circle contrasts with the smaller, blunt dorsal of Gray Whale; Beaver's image is characterized by long incisor teeth and a cross-hatched tail (for the scales), whereas Grizzly Bear is known by a square snout and large-toothed mouth with prominent canines and a protruding tongue. The system of identification is relatively simple when the artist chooses a simple, naturalistic representation, but becomes more complex when these conventionalized features become hidden in the design or when the design itself is of a lesser known natural or supernatural creature. A sea-monster, for example, may have a wolf or bear head, but dorsal fins on its back, and flippers or fins on the joints of limbs that end in claws. Subtle variations in the depiction of an

anatomical part such as a beak may identify the specific species of bird.[5]

Esthetic considerations governed the arrangement of these conventional features of the subjects. Artists distorted, exaggerated, and rearranged the anatomy of whatever was being portrayed to fit the design field. Artists composed designs through such conventions as: x-ray imaging where ribs, backbones, organs, and joints are made visible; split-representation where the body image is split to show the frontal and back views or both sides of a figure simultaneously; and visual punning where one ambiguous feature may result in an image being read as two different subjects. Complexity of form was matched by complexity of iconography. Recorded information about what the art meant to owner and carver is surprisingly meager.[6] We cannot always know the full constellation of meanings surrounding a given object; some levels of meaning were personal and specific to a particular time and place. Yet understanding only some of the fundamental forms, techniques, and principles of design opens lenses to a richness and complexity in

Left: Elaborate serving spoons and ladles were made from mountain goat and mountain sheep horn. The most ornate and most complex of these were the two-piece horn spoons. The handle was made of intricately carved mountain goat horn that preserved the natural shape of the arched tapered horn. Brass or copper rivets attached the dark, luminous handle with its three-dimensional carvings of the family's crests to a delicate amber bowl of mountain sheep horn that had been steamed to a simple, yet elegant bowl. These horn spoons were made by master artists and reserved for formal feasts.

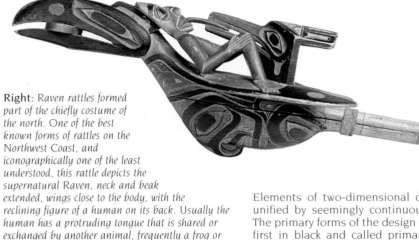

the practice of Northwest art that allows stirring insight into some of those meanings and into the potential for innovation, invention, and excellence.

One of the most distinctive and sophisticated design elements known by northern artists was first academically analyzed by the art historian, Bill Holm, in his definitive work on northern two-dimensional design. Holm described the calligraphic-like line found in northern design as the 'formline', a broad line with a single pulse that started and finished with a tapered point.

Elements of two-dimensional designs were unified by seemingly continuous formlines. The primary forms of the design were defined first in black and called primary formlines. Secondary formlines, in red, further elaborated the form. The remaining spaces were either unpainted background spaces, or tertiary forms that were outlines with thin black or red lines, or were sometimes painted blue. Formline design included distinctive elements given visually descriptive names by Holm: ovoids (and their elaboration, salmon-trout heads), to depict eyes and the joints of the body; U-forms (and the variation Split U-forms), to depict ears, flukes, and fin shapes; and S-forms (and the variation Split S-forms), to depict ribs and feathers.[7]

Remarkably, this design system, given its economy of elements and conventions, permitted a limitless range of images and interpretive innovations. Though genres of

objects – for example, spoons, boxes, dancing robes, frontlet headdresses – evolved specific design codes, and individual artists varied their interpretation of the codes. Personal interpretation of the tradition resulted in the stylistic signatures of individual artists that can be identified from preliterate times.[8]

Less well-defined, but no less significant or impressive, are the Nuu-chah-nulth and Makah two-dimensional design systems. Though clearly related to the northern design conventions, there are other design elements unique to the area: curlicues, thin crosses, and rows of dots, and discontinuous, though sensuous, thin lines of solid color. Figures tended to be less abstract, more representational, and portrayed in dramatic profile with asymmetrical eyelid forms. Coast Salish design was primarily expressed in three dimensions. Arguably, the Coast Salish were influenced by the pervasive northern design, for ovoids and U-forms with conventionalized cuneiform-like gouges in their centers were sometimes employed in low relief carvings, though their geometric compositions were freer in spatial organization than in the north. Usually, Salish three-dimensional design is characterized by bold geometric elements, broad flat planes intersecting one another, and generalized, though fluid, limbs, and torsos.

Unfortunately we know much of this art from the objects that rest silently in museum and gallery collections; they serve as dramatic memories of voices, times, and places in the not-too-distant past. We connect and reconnect the objects with the artists, the artists with the cultures, mindful that our attempts to contextualize and reconstruct usually fall short of a complete appreciation of that time of monumental achievements in making the social and the supernatural worlds visible. It will be useful to scan some of these high achievements, these 'objects of bright pride', to glimpse not only the tremendous power and elegance of their expression, but to gather perspective on an art that was a way of life.

Houses – Containers of the Cosmos

Virtually all of the early Euro-American explorers on the northern Pacific Coast were astonished and impressed by the huge dwellings of the Northwest Coast peoples. The massive structures towered against the forested stands, occupying the thin strips of beach on protected coves and bays. Planked and gabled, the houses were made of cedar and were large enough to hold several families. Usually arranged in a single row along the beach, or two rows if the frontage property was restricted, the rectangular structures imposed a built reality to the misty coast. Northwest Coast people lived in these permanent villages almost year-round, sometimes having a summer village location as well as a winter one.

Red cedar (*Thuja plicata*) was the material favored by Northwest Coast builders. The huge trees were selected, harvested, prepared, and assembled by skilled craftsmen working under the directions of one or more

specialists. In traditional Northwest Coast society, the building of these massive structures was a complicated and expensive undertaking requiring the commissioning of a coordinating architect who supervised the selection, felling, and transportation of large cedar logs to the building site, the splitting of planks, and forming of posts and beams. The owner of the house fed, sheltered, and compensated the workers at every stage of construction, from the assembling of materials to the raising of the posts and beams. Frequently artists were employed to embellish posts and beams with adzed flutes or carved crest images of animal spirits. Wealthier house owners commissioned massive paintings representing clan figures that covered entire house fronts. In postcontact times almost every northern-style house had a huge carved 'totem' pole gracing its facade.

The final expense was the ceremonial occasion or potlatch that marked the completion of the structure with feasting and the naming of the house.[9] Some families took years to build a house, and only the wealthy could begin such a commission after assembling and committing the resources of all the members of their extended family. The labor was intensive, traditionally undertaken with simple tools and without the benefit of tack or pulleys. Using levers, fulcrums, ropes, and raw human strength, posts were set into the ground, beams hoisted to their lofty summits, and massive planks then attached to the structures. If the labor to build a house was based on brute strength, the resulting architecture was simple yet elegant in thought and form. Northwest Coast houses were not only functionally durable, but they were also ingeniously suited to the environmental, spiritual, and social needs of the occupants.

Fundamentally there were two kinds of architectural constructions for the post and beam framed houses of the coast: the northern type with house planking that was integral to the structure, and the southern type with planked walls structurally separate from the main framework.[10] The southern type had two variations: the shed-roofed house, with rectangular posts, and the Wakashan house style with posts supporting two eave beams and one or two larger central ridge beams. Typically found in southern areas including the Coast Salish, Southern Kwakiutl, Nuu-chah-nulth, and Bella Coola, both the shed-roofed house and the Wakashan house had walls of wide horizontal planks hung and lashed between pairs of vertical poles placed along the outside of the house's frame posts.

The northern post and beam house built by the Tlingit, Haida, Tsimshian, and Northern Wakashan people had gabled roofs formed by massive roof beams. In contrast to the southern type houses, northern houses for the most part had thick vertical planks up to 2ft (60cm.) wide whose tapered ends slotted into grooves in the roof beams and ground level sills.[11] The interior of the house was similar in concept to southern houses, with raised platforms for seating and sleeping. At least one house in every village, usually that of the village chief and therefore the largest house, had an excavated interior. Entry into

these houses was at ground level with one or two levels of concentric platforms surrounding the subterranean central fire. The chief's family occupied the rear of the house, their quarters often separated from the rest of the house by a large screen of painted planks. Families of lesser rank were to the left and right of the screen, with those of the least rank next to the front door. The roof planks of these houses were often secured with rock-weighted boards and there was a movable opening in the roof to provide optimum ventilation for the central fire. Doors were traditionally at the front of the house, often through a central or portal house post. Other doors at the rear of the house were provided for emergency exits, and a special door was made in the rear of a house to remove the body of a deceased family member after the period of lying in state.

The house remains one of the most impressive of Northwest Coast artifacts, splendid in design and execution of its form, and astonishingly monumental in its concept and function. The wonder of the early travelers to the coast is mirrored by all those who encounter Northwest Coast houses for the first time. The structures were massive, made from massive materials. Strangers, after suffusing their wonderment, ask why? Surely a people with such impressive technology for splitting and building shelters could have built smaller, single family dwellings.

The answer is cultural rather than technological. From a sociological viewpoint, a Northwest Coast individual was part of an extended family, a lineage. As such, the house sheltered more than one's parents and children; it sheltered the lineage. In contemporary terms, the Northwest Coast house was more of a small apartment building than a nuclear family home. The house was for part of the year a profane place, site of the mundane stuff of everyday life: fish and game hung drying in its smoky rafters; people slept, ate, and worked in its roomy shelter; and interior platforms provided

Above: *This view of the eastern end of the Haida village of Cumshewa illustrates some of the variety in forms of 'totem' or crest poles. Here house frontal poles were interspersed with single mortuary and memorial poles. The house on the right, named 'House That Makes a Great Noise', has a frontal pole with three Skils or watchmen at the top. House names, crest images, and the songs, stories, and dances associated with them were the exclusive property of the owners and demonstrated the history and hereditary prerogatives of the lineage.*

hidden storage space for clothing, foodstuffs, tools, hunting, and ceremonial paraphernalia. Attached porches and semi-attached decks provided warm-weather spaces for gambling, gossiping, and otherwise enjoying the company of others.

From a ritual and ceremonial viewpoint, the house was transformed in the dark months of winter into a site of sacred events. Figuratively and literally the house became the center of the universe as the people gathered to witness the speeches, songs, dances, masked performances, and rituals that enacted and validated their ancestral claims to the lineage's supernatural origins, property rights, wealth, and traditions. Painted screens and interior houseposts carved with clan images heightened the sense of bringing together and making visible the social and the supernatural. New members of the lineage were thus socialized into the interrelationships of family and the supernatural; strangers and newcomers were educated to the valid claims of the lineage to supernatural ancestry and inherited social prerogatives that formed the exclusive property of the lineage. In this way lineages confirmed their relationship to every other lineage, to the larger clan units, and ultimately to the cosmos. The names of some of the larger houses frequently referred to the vaunted position of the lineage's claims: The Monster House, House Split-in-Two-by-the-Sun, Thunder-Rolls-Upon-It, House-Chiefs-Peep-at-from-a-Distance, and Mountain

Above: *Originally this Kwakiutl house pole was the only entrance to a magnificent painted house front. The opened long bill of Raven served as a door to the communal house; outspread wings of the Raven were painted on the house front. Above the Raven are Bear, the Cannibal-bird Hokhokw, Wise One, Wolf, Killerwhale, and Thunderbird. The pole, erected in about 1899, belonged to Chief Wawkius of Alert Bay and was carved for the princely sum of 350 white blankets with black borders. In later years the pole was moved to Stanley Park in Vancouver, a reminder of its past glory.*

House. The names are fitting to the sizes of the houses, but also to the monumentality of their social and symbolic function in Northwest Coast cultural life.

As quickly as Northwest Coast technology and culture changed with exposure to Euro-American culture, innovations to housing also appeared. Grander houses featured European-style doors and windows, gingerbread gables, and even picket fences. With missionization and the dramatic decimation of the population through disease in the late-nineteenth and early-twentieth century, the building of large communal houses eventually gave way to

smaller, though often no less grand, two-story frame houses. Some of the villages, such as those of the Haida at Ninstints, Tanu, and Skedans, suffered such extreme losses that the villages were abandoned before the houses could ever be built. Posts, beams, and planks have decayed – melted back into the forest that gave them life. In one site, fluted house beams that once supported the roof of the cosmos lie shrouded in the moss of the forest floor, giving new life to spruce. Skeletal is the wrong word to describe these fallen giants. For the Haida, they are fulfilling their destiny to complete the cycle of being first part of the natural world, then the cultural world, before returning – transformed and part of our memory – to nature.

Crest Poles – Heraldic Monuments in Cedar

The monumentality of the great planked houses of the Northwest Coast was complemented by the massive carved sculptures commonly but improperly called 'totem poles'.[12] The term 'crest poles' reflects what even the earliest Euro-American seamen knew: the images on the poles were never worshiped or part of religious ceremonies, but were a visual record of the

owner's hereditary ancestors, a heraldic device that proclaimed for all to see the social positioning and antiquity of the family lineage.[13] Crest poles came in many forms and had various functions; generically, however, a pole was made from a large vertical cedar shaft and covered with interlocking images of supernatural clan ancestors.

There are various types of crest poles. The most frequently depicted is the free-standing singular crest pole. Depending on its function, the pole depicted the crests of a living family or commemorated the memory of a recently deceased person of high rank. Other memorial poles among the northern groups were sometimes simply tall cedar shafts, topped by a single massive crest animal such as Thunder-bird, Raven, Bear, or Eagle. Crest poles were also features of house architecture. Some were attached directly to the front of a house. When these house frontal poles had an entrance carved in the lower portion of the pole – usually through the belly or mouth of the lowest creature – the pole was a house portal or entrance pole. Usually these kinds of entrances were considered highly symbolic as orifices of the house and were thus used only on ceremonial occasions. Separate doors were placed beside the pole for every day use. Corner posts and interior house posts were also appropriate spaces to place crest carvings.

Welcoming figures, such as those found among the Kwakiutl, were placed on the beach to welcome guests. These large human or animal forms were carved from a single log and had attached extended arms. Similar monumental sculptures have been recorded among the Haida as ridicule or shaming poles, where the purpose was not to welcome guests, but to humiliate them. Mortuary poles were most common among the Haida. The single mortuary pole had a cavity carved in the large end of the pole to receive a box containing the remains of the deceased. The tapered end of the pole was placed in the ground and a plank placed across the top of the pole to cover the opening. Double mortuary poles consisted of two poles with a platform between them to hold several burial boxes. As with the single pole, the covering plank was often carved in high relief and painted with the owner's crests.

Wealth was the key to demonstrating great social and supernatural power on the coast, and it was only the wealthy person who could afford the monumental sculptures adorning and surrounding the great houses. Crest poles were commissioned from recognized artists. Their reputations were well-known on the coast, and some traveled not only to other villages to fulfill commissions, but inter-tribally as well. As with house building, every aspect of making a crest pole, from selection, felling, and transportation of the log to the carving and raising of the pole, was paid for by the owner.[14] Compensation for this portion of the task was considerable.

Carving a crest pole was a lengthy process.[15] The prone log was stripped of bark and flattened on its back.[16] Large elbow adzes and chisels roughed out the preliminary shapes, and successively finer adzes and knives were used to refine the images. The artist used chisels to fashion mortise and tenon joints to attach appendages to the cylinder of

emerging figures. Straight and curved knives completed the detail work: incised lines around the eyebrows and lids, cross-hatching on beaver tails, and undercuts for claws and wings. Small adzes gave some texture to large expanses; carvers preferred the precise, rhythmic, parallel adzing marks over smooth 'unfinished' wood.[17] From early accounts, paint was used sparingly, if at all. Natural black, red, white, and blue-green pigments were used to accent eyes, eye sockets, eyebrows, lips, tongues, and nostrils. After glossy commercial marine paints became available, southern artists added other colors to their palettes – greens, blues, yellows, and whites – and painted most of the surfaces of their poles with gusto.[18]

When the pole was finished, the owner hosted a substantial potlatch. Invited guests assembled to admire the pole, to witness and validate the owner's claims to the crests depicted in the carvings, and the pole was carried to the site where it was to be erected by scores of men.[19] Drumbeats matched heartbeats as the pole inched up, dancing in the tension of ropes being pulled over the scaffolding and holding the unwieldly and precious column in balance. From a distance, the artist and his apprentices watched, their necks and waists circled with twisted cedar bark rings to which their carving tools have been attached. When the pole was up, the carvers danced at its base while those who hoisted on the ropes rested and celebrated the satisfaction of raising the pole and the triumph of its new owners.[20]

The florescence of crest pole carving probably lasted less than a century, for eventually the wealth diminished and the death rate increased. By 1920 the art had all but vanished, though almost every major museum in the Western world boasted a huge 'totem pole' in their grand entry halls. Crest poles are again being made, some for important art commissions, others to serve the age-old practices of commemorating one's claims to ancient heraldic crests and prerogatives. From lofty heights, Eagles and Ravens, Killer-Whales and Wolves, Thunderbirds and Grizzly Bears claim their places against the open skies and are cherished in the hearts of the people as emblems of a living culture.

Canoes – Monuments of the Seas

More than the principal means of transportation, the canoe was yet another feature of monumentality on the coast. Embellished with carving of prows and painted bows and sterns the canoe was more than a functional object. A floating artistic statement of rare grace and brilliant design, it is little wonder that the canoe was one of the principal measurements, along with the house and the crest pole, of a family's material wealth. The finished canoes ranged in size from large ocean-going vessels 50 to 70ft (up to 21m.) in length with beams of 6 to 10ft (up to 3m.). Family canoes were smaller, in the 18 to 35ft (up to 10m.) range and holding fifteen to twenty people, while smaller canoes were constructed to be handled easily by as few as two people. From the Kwakiutl north, canoes were broad in the beam with both bow and stern ends swept upward; a vertical fin under the bow cut the waves. Nuu-chah-nulth, Makah, and Quilleute hunting and fishing canoes were generally flatter on the bottom, with low rising vertical sterns and their concave prows rose dramatically into a distinctive 'snout' that abstractly resembled the head of a wolf.[21] Both of these styles of canoes had a groove in the prow to hold masts or harpoons.[22]

Carved from single massive cedar trees, the canoe required much the same expertise and expense of houses and crest poles.[23] Deep in the forest, master carvers would select sound trees with few knots, and then rough out the top and narrow the ends of the canoe. With hull, bow, and stern adzed into perfect symmetry, the unfinished canoe was left over the winter to season. The following spring the canoe was righted, the interior hollowed with chisels and adzes, or on some parts of the

Below: *The Haida village of Tanu was still a thriving populated village at the time of this 1878 photograph. It helps to show the relative scale of monumental houses to enormous but graceful seagoing canoes. The small fishing canoe on the left is protected by a mat.*

Above: *Before undertaking the monumental task of carving a giant cedar into the intricate and complex crest figures found on 'totem' or crest poles, the carver would make a smaller version of the sculpture for the approval of the person commissioning the pole. Such maquettes also served in measuring and placing the figures on the larger pole. In later years, when pole carving was in decline, this functional item was converted to an art form – destined for the art market. Without knowing the specific family that owned these crests, it is impossible to render an exact interpretation of these images because they represented an individual's specific hereditary crests. However, this Bella Coola pole may be generically read, from top to bottom, as Raven, a Woman with labret, a Transforming Bear, and Eagle. Intriguingly, the lower figure is a supernatural being grasping an extended nose that enters the mouth of the upturned human face on the base. The ambiguity of the figures speaks to Northwest Coast artists' ability to convey the power of the supernatural made visible. Typical of Bella Coola art, the pole is painted brilliant ultramarine blue.*

coast, the interior was excavated using controlled burning with rocks heated red-hot in a fire.

Precision was the hallmark of the master canoe-builder. Symmetry of the exterior was matched by the even thickness of the hull.[24] The final step in making large vessels was to fill the canoe with water, drop red-hot stones into it to boil the water, and gently spread the softened wood at the gunwales. On larger canoes, prow and stern extensions were carved then pegged or sewn into place. The final embellishment of a canoe was done by a master artist who painted crest designs on the vessel. Some canoes were painted red or white in the interior; some had exteriors painted black. Others were fitted with elaborately carved crested figures that were lashed to both sides of the bow and/or stern.

Canoes were highly valued possessions, carefully protected from the elements so they would not split, lovingly and effectively patched when damaged, and handled cautiously so that they would last a decade or more. As with houses, canoes were often given hereditary names. At a potlatch, a canoe was an extravagant gift and similarly the destruction of a canoe during a potlatch was an ostentatious display of conspicuous consumption that enhanced the owner's status. Their value and grace inspired songs and their elegance inspired myth images for the mind's eye of great wealth and power.

Bowls, Boxes, and Baskets

Bowls of cedar, yew, alder, maple, and other woods were sculpted into various geometric and anthropomorphic shapes using many of the same carving tools that were used to make canoes and crest poles. Wooden bowls could range in size from small personal feast dishes to enormous bowls used for potlatches that required several people to carry into the feast house. Animal-shaped bowls, bowls that imitated birch bark containers, bowls with supernatural human and monster figures, as well as bowls with geometric contours reminiscent of canoe shapes were all part of the repertoire of Northwest Coast artists. Sometimes the rims

of bowls were inlaid with opercula[25], sea otter teeth, or small pieces of abalone shell. Some wooden bowls were painted with crest designs, but most were not. Given the propensity of the wood to soak up the fish and sea mammal oils of foods served in the bowls, little more embellishment of the carved surfaces was needed. The glossy patina of well-used, oft-handled vessels was rich and mellow; the sensitive fit of the bowls' surfaces to the embrace of human palms was timeless.[26]

So different from the bowls that were carved from single pieces of wood, the bent box or bowl with its kerfed corners and inlaid base was perhaps one of the most distinctive aspects of the Northwest Coast people's culture and technology. Using bent-wood construction, men created containers from cedar planks for everything a person would use from cradle to coffin. The cedar bent box technology was used for obvious constructions such as storage and furniture and less obvious functions such as drumming and cooking. Bent bowls were made in the same manner as boxes, but begun with a plank that was pre-shaped with elegantly undulating rims and bulging contours with hollowed interiors. Boxes and chests were sometimes fitted with lids inlaid with opercula, while bowls often had complex overhanging rims. Finishing touches to kerfed containers could include painted formline designs (flat or deeply incised), nearly three-dimensional carving in high relief, and/or abalone shell inlay.

Sometimes the weight and rigidity of a box was more than necessary for containing the stuff of life. Baskets were woven by women to function in almost all the same ways a box was used.[27] Lighter than wooden boxes, baskets were no less durable. Some baskets were designed to be flexible and even collapsible when not in use. Some baskets were of a generalized form, others were created for specific tasks; elegance of form frequently matched the ingenuity of function. There were baskets for holding babies, for collecting shellfish, for cooking, storing, and serving food stuffs,[28] for carrying the tools and

implements of the hunt or the harvest, for holding treasures, or for simply displaying the weaver's virtuosity. After contact with Euro-Americans and responding to a new market for their woven arts, women created basketry items that mimicked objects from the foreign culture: suitcases, dollies, lamp shades, bottles and lidded jars, plates and platters, and even tea cups and saucers.[29] Interestingly, though, they were never intended for the indigenous use, these 'tourist' baskets nonetheless demonstrated some of the finest examples of the basket makers' art. Within Northwest Coast culture, well-made basketry items were valued trade items and prestigious potlatch gifts; many baskets on the coast were found far from their places of origin.

Besides the ubiquitous cedar bark, withe, and root, the Northwest Coast women harvested and used many natural materials for making their fine baskets. While no one fiber was specific to a given area of the coast, some groups had preferences. Spruce root was a favorite of northern weavers, especially the Tlingit and Haida. Nuu-chah-nulth women produced a very different kind of basketry from the many species of sedge grasses.[30] Cedar bark was an abundant and favorite construction material of the Coast Salish. Various grasses and reeds were employed by the weavers as foundation materials and for making the woven surface decoration on the baskets known as imbricating, where tucks of light grasses and shiny bark strips were caught under the stitches on the basket's outer surface. Another decorative technique was known as false embroidery where bleached or dyed fibers were wrapped around the wefts at every stitch to form bands of geometric designs.[31]

The weavers used many techniques for basket making: coiling, plaiting, two- and three-strand twining, skip-stitch twining, twilled two-strand twining, warp twining, diagonal warp twining, wrapped crossed warp, and flat weaving. While talented fingers did most of the work in creating the fine, regular surfaces of the baskets, the weaver's tool kit might also include a sharpened bone awl for piercing coiling strips, hard wood

Right: *This beautiful Haida lidded container is a product of superb joinery. A cedar plank was cut with three deep, grooved undercuts or kerfs that traversed its width in three precisely measured places, dividing it into four sections. The plank was then steamed and the softened wood bent 90 degrees at each kerf (see detail, above) to fold the groove into itself, resulting in four sides. The open corner was then pegged.*

Above: *Bowls of animal horn were made by cutting away the hollowed base of the horn and using moist heat to spread the sides of the bowl.*

Left: *Worn only by the high-ranking people of the Tlingit, Haida, Tsimshian, and Kwakiutl these dancing robes represented the hereditary crests of their owners. All Chilkat blankets have a border of black and yellow wool, a deep white fringe, and a large design field filled with the crest of the owner. Chilkat weaving probably originated with the Tsimshian, as did the entire chiefly costume with the raven rattle and frontlet headdress.*

consummate master carvers. Appropriate to the ritual at hand, masks were accompanied by intricately carved rattles, puppets, speakers staffs, headdresses, drums, whistles, and other ceremonial paraphernalia to complete their presentation. Consummate in the art of suspending disbelief, the artists restored and reinforced belief in the social, natural, and supernatural.

The panoply of mask types was massive for each group along the Northwest Coast, except for the Nuu-chah-nulth and the Coast Salish. Cataloging that impressive array would be a monumental task. For every crest, for every lineage, for every ancestor, for every personal hereditary property or heraldic event, for each member of the culture there could be, and probably was, at least one if not several artistic interpretations commissioned by that lineage. The inventory was staggering if not infinite, bound only by our imagination – and that much can be concluded from museum collections alone. Museum collections, made mostly from the decades surrounding the turn of the century, contain mere samplings of what must have existed.[43]

From the Tlingit, powerful shaman's masks seem to freeze the human face in a moment of the healing trance.[44] The Haida were renowned for a kind of mask Euro-Americans have called the 'portrait' mask that depicted in wood with sensuous accuracy the skin stretched or

Below: *This early Tlingit frontlet was collected in about 1870 and depicts Bear and Frog, important crests of the Wolf and Raven clans. Frogs were associated with shamanism and witchcraft, while bears figure in many mythical events.*

implements to press against smooth stones for flattening and smoothing the surface of twined strands, and bark splitting tools.[32]

Basketry designs were achieved with tremendous skill and dexterity. The catalogue of named designs seemed endless. Some representational designs included recognizable animal and human forms: 'wolf', 'merganser', 'man', 'dragonfly', and 'butterfly'. The Nuu-chah-nulth weavers frequently depicted whaling scenes showing a harpooner standing in a canoe, his line firmly attached to a gray whale. Other design terms are more enigmatic, and seem to have a closer connection with the meanings given by the individual weaver rather than springing from a large, universal iconographic system. The names of the designs give some insight into the complex, precise woven arts that came from these consummate artists. The elegance of their artworks is matched by the poetry of the word images describing the design elements: Crow's shells, leaves of the fireweed, blanket border fancy picture, fern, porpoise, between-the-dice, double war club, mouth-rack of the woodworm, half the head of a salmonberry, and fish flesh.[33]

Woven Clothing

If boxes and baskets were containers of life, then blankets were the containers of people. Northwest Coast women wove botanical and animal fibers on upright looms to create blankets, tunics, and robes that graced the human form. Labor intensive from the gathering and processing of raw materials to the manufacturing process, weaving was a specialist art that took years to master and perfect.

Everyday clothing appropriate to the raincoast had to be water-repellent, comfortable to work in, and warm. The ingenious response of all the Northwest Coast people was to turn again to the cedar tree.[34] Shredded bundles of yellow cedar were hung on an upright loom and the weaver twined them at intervals with wefts of cedar bark, nettle, or wool string. Soft yet durable clothing was produced; its multi-layers were

worked with oil to shed the water easily, and wet surfaces could be dried quickly.[35] A versatile garment, the cedar bark robe could be fastened as a cape or skirt. Often adorned with fur or feathers, some had designs worked in dyed fibers and a few had edgings worked in mountain goat wool. Some robes were painted with elaborate crest images and were probably for ceremonial use by high-ranking individuals.[36]

On the northern Coast, Tlingit, Tsimshian, and Haida women created ceremonial robes known as Chilkat blankets for high-ranking people.[37] Myth records the Chilkat blanket as originating with the Tsimshian,[38] though it was developed by the Chilkat tribe of the Tlingit.[39] It took a master weaver a full year to complete the robe. Woven on an upright loom, on a warp of spun cedar bark and mountain goat wool with a weft of pure white, black, yellow, and blue-green dyed mountain goat wool, the five-sided blankets resembled the shape of an upside down house front.[40] Part of the sumptuous chiefly costume of frontlet headdress with its 6ft (3m.) train of ermine, raven rattle, and dance apron, the Chilkat blanket had a deep double fringe that flared around the dancer's body.[41] As Bill Holm said of the blankets: 'No more royal robe ever draped a king…'.[42]

Masks and Ceremonial Paraphernalia

Without a doubt masks, headdresses, and their associated ceremonial paraphernalia were and are one of the most distinctive cultural features of the Northwest Coast. The earliest explorers were struck by the elaboration and variety of the masking complex found all along the coast from the Salish in the south to the Tlingit in the north. Cognizant with every aspect of the art of mask making and masked performance, the artists of the Northwest Coast explored the concept of making transformation visible and credible through the construction of elaborate hinged, movable, and mutable masks. Masks that metamorphosed, grew, shrank, spoke, danced in thin air, and were even destroyed and resurrected were due to the skills of

wrinkled over the bones of the skull.[45] The *naxno'x* ceremony required masks of the Tsimshian carvers known as the *Git'sontk* or 'the People secluded' who created all the paraphernalia for the most sacred part of their potlatches.[46] From their hands, humanoid masks with movable eyes and mouths were exceptional and in the dim light of the fire, terrifyingly realistic. The Northern Wakashan and Bella Coola artists championed in the creation of bold bird masks with sloped foreheads, large overhanging brows, and piercing eyes: a stunning blend of stylized abstraction and naturalism.

The Kwakiutl's propensity for the theatrical and for flamboyance has been characterized by Holm as fundamental to their 'distinct and aggressive' culture.[47] The masks created for the *Hamatsa* or Cannibal Society dances fit the drama and prestige of portraying human encounters with the monumental supernatural birds at the edge of the universe.[48] The narrow elongated beaks of the *Hokhokw* were said to crush men's skulls; the beaks of some of these masks ranged in length from a modest 2 or 3ft (up to 1m.) to up to 10ft (3m.). These masks required the aid of a body harness and rigging, concealed by heavy fringes of shredded cedar bark, for the skillful dancer to carry the weight of the mask while snapping the movable mandibles of the supernatural birds. The neighboring Nuu-chah-nulth used a unique blend of smooth, spare sculptural form and decisive, abstract, painted forms to create the subtle images of wolves with large nostrils, raptor-beaked thunderbirds, and slender-nosed lightning snakes for the *Klookwana* ceremony.[49] The Coast Salish had but one mask, the *Sxwayxwey*, that appeared always with three others of its kind. Huge and spectacular, the *Sxwayxwey* had large peg eyes that projected from the facial plane, with no lower mandible and a vertical flange below the nose.[50]

Frontlets were not masks. They were the individualized, exquisitely carved wooden portion attached to the front of headdress worn by high-ranking Tlingit, Tsimshian, and Haida chiefs.[51] The headdress was almost always worn with the other prestigious items fitting the owner's high rank: a Chilkat blanket, dancing aprons, and leggings, and the enigmatic, complex Raven rattle. This impressive raiment, reportedly used in 'welcoming dances', represented the synthesis of the supernatural and social power of the chief. It was, in effect, the crown jewels and a bishop's miter all in one. In the ritual occasion for displaying the headdress, the chief acted as head of state and like a shaman; the roles were merging into a spectacular display of social and spiritual power.[52]

Increasingly, non-Native and Native people have discovered and rediscovered a fascination for these traditional arts and it is a fascination built not only on an appreciation of form. The images are timeless. They speak through the culture and across cultures, and hold our imagination. As anthropologist Wilson Duff observed, Northwest Coast art has this power because '[These] images seem to speak to the eye, but they are really addressed to the mind. They are ways of thinking, in the guise of ways of seeing. The eye can sometimes be satisfied with form alone, but the mind can only be satisfied with meaning, which can be contemplated, more consciously or less, after the eye is closed... The meaning is in the relationships being expressed... Images hold ideas apart so that they can be seen together'.[53]

The Tradition Continues

Living traditions change and develop and the visual art tradition of the Northwest Coast is no exception. The Euro-American trade brought new materials, new technologies, and new wealth. The result was nothing short of a cultural revolution as social, economic, linguistic, religious, material, and artistic ideas felt the impact of the foreigners. There were subtle changes in the art resulting in the decline of some forms and the rise of others.

The Northwest Coast people had skilfully hammered copper nuggets into items of personal adornment in precontact times, and after contact with Euro-Americans, they purchased commercial copper wire to make some of the same items: bracelets, anklets, earrings, nose-ornaments, and beads. Engraving techniques were well-known to the early Haida and Tlingit artists, and when gold and silver coin was introduced to the Northwest Coast, these techniques were used on the new materials to create expertly crafted silver bracelets and other jewelry.[54] With a revival in the 1950s, the tradition continues to the present, with bold, finely carved formline designs sweeping across mirror-bright surfaces.

Unique to the Haida, a new art form emerged in the early nineteenth century: the carving of a slate-like, soft stone known as argillite. In the early years of contact, argillite was much sought after by Euro-American seamen and commanded high prices, only to be scorned in later years as an art of acculturation. As Holm noted, 'In fact, some of the great masterpieces of Haida art as well as some of the most trite souvenirs' were produced by canny Haida artists who created and developed an exclusive market for this rare stone.[55] Carved with woodworking tools, argillite takes on a high luster.

The earliest carvings were 'pipes' (though most could not be smoked) with clusters of Haida images and/or Euro-American ship motifs. Later new forms emerged as images of the people and materials from foreign visitors were faithfully, if not mockingly, carved in free-standing sculpture. A third period in the art, which occurred after 1865 when the Haida population was decimated by disease in less than a generation, marked a dramatic return to bold sculptural images of Haida life and mythology. The art failed to develop for a while, then was revived in the 1960s by Haida artists reestablishing connections to the past. Today, argillite sculpture is a flourishing art form, still created primarily for sale to non-Natives and still making dynamic artistic statements about all that it means to be Haida.

After contact, commercial blankets replaced cedar bark clothing and the art all but disappeared. While plain commercial blankets were worn over Euro-American clothing, a new style of ceremonial blanket was developed with goods introduced shortly after the time of contact.[56] The spectacular robe was known as a 'button blanket' and it took the place of painted cedar bark, hide, or sail canvas robes, replacing their use all over the coast by the turn of the century. Adapted to an older concept of a dancing robe with elaborate borders and a central crest figure rendered with an outline of abalone shell, the button blanket was constructed of dark blue or black Hudson's Bay Company blankets and a broad border of red melton cloth. Red cloth was used to create an appliqued crest image in the center of the blanket. Mother-of-pearl buttons were sewn along the edge of the red border and along the outlines of the appliqued formline design; sometimes buttons alone were used to render the crest figure. Great care was given to selecting buttons of regular size, color, and shape. These elegant ceremonial robes, worn with the design at the back, flashed with the brilliance of a matador's 'coat of lights' in the fire light of the winter house.[57]

The renaissance of Northwest Coast art is wonderfully exemplified in the thriving serigraph studios in the Pacific Northwest.[58] This is an example of a new art form – the silk screen print – being adapted to the tradition of two-dimensional formline design. Begun in the latter half of the twentieth century, this new tradition draws directly on earlier forms. With a vast visual library of published images, Northwest Coast serigraph artists have been able to draw inspiration from their prolific ancestors to create a body of work that reflects a continuity between past motifs and styles, and exciting innovations of contemporary minds.[59]

Of course all the other traditions of carving and now even weaving are alive and well – thanks to their resurrection by dedicated and innovative Northwest Coast artists and art schools such as the school of art at 'Ksan, Hazelton. In the dedication to their first art catalogue, the artists have written:

'Walk on, walk on, walk on, on the breath of our grandfathers. These words follow the *wsinaax*, the songs we sing beside our dead. The words proclaim our strong sense of continuity, our belief in the constant reincarnation of thought, deed, and man; our knowledge of the presence of yesterday in today, of today in tomorrow.'[60]

References

1 Duff, 1975.
2 Ryan and Sheehan, 1988.
3 Blackman (1982) records that Florence Davidson painted canoes carved by her husband Robert.
4 Sometimes plant, insect, celestial phenomena, tides, and even the wind were represented; frequently they were given personified forms, though pure formline design elements could be used to portray their natural forms.
5 Frank Boas was one of the first ethnographers to publish the vocabulary of visual forms enabling Euro-Americans to 'read', at a pre-iconographic level, the fundamental images in Northwest Coast art, 1951:183-298. For a contemporary version of his interpretations see Stewart, 1979.
6 Fortunately, there were a few such as Marius Barbeau who made a special effort to identify artists not only by name, but by their works. Barbeau, 1929 and 1957.
7 Three-dimensional design of the north is strongly two-dimensional in concept: in some works, essentially flat design was wrapped around a form, and carved in high relief. Some objects were more sculptural in concept, though still decorated with formline designs. Southern Kwakiutl and Bella Coola artists used a somewhat more flamboyant version of the northern formline design system. Holm, 1965, has the most in-depth analysis.
8 Again, Holm and his students have been at the forefront in the identification of individual Northwest artists through their stylistic signatures. Holm, 1983.
9 Some Haida named the individual beams and posts as well; in some instances a house could have more than one name.
10 For house types see Stewart, 1984: 60-75.
11 Sometimes the Tsimshian houses used the slotted plank technology to create horizontal house planking between vertical squared timber posts.
12 The antiquity of crest poles has long been debated. Scholars do know that the early European visitors to the coast recorded the presence of large house frontal poles and massive free-standing carved poles, though their mention is sporadic. It is likely that with increased contact, and access to technology and wealth, there was a flourishing of crest pole carving. Barbeau, 1929 and 1990; Inverarity, 1950; Keithahn, 1963; Halpin, 1981; Macdonald, 1983.
13 The concept of *totemism* acknowledges a special relationship between humans and animals marked by an avoidance of the animal for food, or even for interactions. *Totemism* implies animal worship by humans. This cultural practice was not found on the Northwest Coast.
14 Physically the undertaking was complex and required the services of many experienced men to harvest a 60-80ft (18-24m.) red cedar. The trees most suitable for poles (as well as houses and canoes) were deep in the forest, straight and free from knots. Stewart, 1990.
15 Selection of the artist alone was a complicated matter. Initially a family member (usually from another lineage) might be given the hereditary honor of carving the pole though his involvement was nominal and in fact the actual carving was carried out by a professional artist. Maquettes or miniatures of the pole were sometimes carved and submitted to the patron for approval. Given artistic license in interpreting the crests, the artist nonetheless followed the conventions of three-dimensional representation and formline design.
16 Particularly if the sculpture was to be a house frontal or portal pole, the log's heartwood was excavated from the back of the pole, leaving it 'C'-shaped in the cross-section. This made it possible to use very large logs for poles, as they were considerably lighter without the heartwood and, moreover, were less likely to rot, split, or check.
17 House planks were adzed in a similar manner, the builders claiming that the long parallel rows of adze marks gave a 'finished' appearance.
18 The northern artists, maintaining a traditional restraint, were far less flamboyant than their southern colleagues who sometimes painted rather than carved some of the crest details.
19 The method of raising a pole has not changed over the centuries – even contemporary poles are raised in the age-old manner. The heel of the pole was placed into the hole and ropes tied to the upper portion were strung over a crossbar supported by sturdy scaffolding. Under the direction of an experienced person counting time with a drum, the pole was slowly raised by dozens of people hauling and pulling.
20 Few poles ever fell, but if they did, they were left where they lay, for to raise the pole again would require the same level of potlatching it would take to raise a new pole. Economics and practical wisdom opted for the new pole.
21 Smaller canoes were constructed using the same methods as the larger ones, but were not steamed and usually lacked prow and stern additions.
22 Holm notes that there is considerable debate on whether or not Northwest Coast mariners 'sailed' before Euro-American contact. He believes the debate is a matter of semantics. Holm, 1987: 98.
23 Stewart, 1984: 52-60. Duff, 1976; Arima, 1975.
24 Small holes were drilled in the roughed out hull and filled with measured pegs of darkened wood or lighter yellow cedar. The carver then removed wood from the inside of the hull to the uniform depth of the pegs, creating an even thickness.
25 An operculum is the small white shell 'trap door' on the opening of the red turban snail.
26 Sturtevant, 1974.
27 Gender bias in traditional ethnographies has perhaps robbed women of full credit for this ingenious and elegant art which was as prevalent as men's woodworking arts and just as highly prized by their society.
28 Cooking baskets were woven with such tight construction methods that they could be used for stewing and steaming in much the same way as bent wood boxes.
29 Holm, 1987: 222.
30 Stewart, 1984: 128.
31 Cherry bark, horsetail fern roots, cattail leaves, leaves of beargrass, reed canary grass, and swamp grass, to name a few, were employed in the construction and embellishment of baskets.
32 All of these techniques and materials are discussed with photographs in Lobb, 1978.
33 Emmons, 1903; Kaplan, 1986; Holm, 1987.
34 In the spring, after the offering of appropriate prayers, long strips of bark were taken from tall, living trees. (Taking the strips did not kill the tree.) The inner bark was separated from the outer, and beaten to soften and separate layers.
35 Early mariners reported that the people wore two pieces of bark clothing, loose blankets, or capes about the shoulders covering a blanket or skirt belted on the lower body.
36 A splendid painted cedar bark robe is in the British Museum. Likely Nuu-chah-nulth, it was collected by Capt. Cook in 1780. See King (1979).
37 Chilkat weaving was also used to produce tailored sleeved or sleeveless tunics, dance aprons, leggings, and shamans' headgear.
38 See Dawson, 1880: 120; 127-28. Samuel's monumental work *The Chilkat Dancing Blanket* remains the authority on the history and construction techniques. Samuel, 1982.
39 Holm notes that 'Classic Chilkat blankets date only to the beginning of the nineteenth century. Their predecessors were geometrically patterned tined robes of which only a handful have survived'. Holm, 1987: 182; Samuel, 1987.
40 'The blanket is shaped like a house worn upside down. Metaphorically, the house-shaped blanket which engulfs the dancer is *GonaquAde'ts* under-world house.' Sheehan, 1977: 226-27.
41 In Tsimshian, all the words connected with this dancer have the same root word, *halait*, which roughly translates as 'dancer', 'shaman' 'power', and 'sacred'; the dancer is *Wihalait*; the blanket, *Gweshalait*; the frontlet headdress, *amhalait*; and the Raven rattle as *Hasem semhalait*. All are stored in a Chief's box or '*anda amhalait*. Halpin, 1973: 213.
42 Holm, 1984: 182.
43 Fane, et al, 1991; Holm, 1987; Gunther, 1966; Kaplan, 1986; Dempsey, 1991; Jonaitas, 1988.
44 Jonaitas, 1986.
45 Emmons, 1914, was one of the first to discuss 'portraiture' on the coast, though the Euro-American concept of portraiture may not have the same connotation. See also the discussion of portrait 'masks' by Haida artist Charles Gwaytihl in Macnair, et al. 1984: 70-71; and King, 1979.
46 Halpin, 1973: 75.
47 Holm, 1984: 89.
48 A photographed account of a twentieth century *Hamatsa* ceremony may be seen in Macnair, 1984.
49 For descriptions of the Kwakiutl masks see Hawthorn, 1967 and 1979; and Holm 1972.
50 The nose of the *Sxwayxwey* was either a head of a bird or it merely had skeletal nasal passages; two birds with elongated necks rose over the forehead of the *Sxwayxwey*. A wide ruff circled the mask and long reeds with tips of downy feathers bobbed from the perimeter. The four dancers, on a healing mission, carried hooped rattles hung with huge Pacific sea scallop shells. Salish art is described in Kew, 1980, and Suttles, 1982, describes the masks of the Halkomelem (Coast Salish) *Sxwayxwey*.
51 In the early nineteenth century, the hereditary right to this headdress was passed by marriage to a Kwakiutl family, the Hunts, where it is worn to this day. Later, it was also obtained by some Northern Wakashan and Bella Coola tribes.
52 Sheehan, 1977.
53 Duff, 1975: 12.
54 Euro-American motifs such as floral patterns and the American eagle were used along with traditional formline designs prior to 1900. Harris, 1983: 132-36.
55 Holm, 1983: 106.
56 Holm, 1984: 186.
57 Jensen, 1986. Innovating on appliqued blankets, Haida artist Dorothy Grant has created contemporary fashions. Blackman, 1992.
58 Hall, et al 1981.
59 Blackman & Hall, 1982: 30-39.
60 Guédon and MacDonald, 1972.

'The leather is neatly painted and fancifully worked in most parts with porcupine quills, and moose-deer hair:
the shirts and leggings are also adorned with fringes and tassels; nor are the shoes and mittens without somewhat
of appropriate decoration, and worked with a considerable degree of skill and taste.'

SIR ALEXANDER MACKENZIE, 1801[1]

THE SUBARCTIC

THE SUBARCTIC REGION of North America, as the name implies, lies directly south of the Arctic. A vast area of approximately 2,000,000 sq miles (3,219,000 sq km.), it includes interior Alaska and most of interior Canada. The predominant features of the landscape are barren tundra to the north and dense forest to the south, but there are also areas of open woodland and swamps, mountains, river valleys, and lakes. The winters are long and bitterly cold, with limited daylight, heavy snowfalls, and piercing winds. The short summer is warm and humid, but plagued by swarms of biting insects. A harsh and inhospitable land, it has, nevertheless, supported small bands of nomadic hunters and fishermen for thousands of years.

These bands were composed of two linguistic groups: the Athapaskans or Dene in the basins of the Yukon and Mackenzie Rivers, and the Algonquians in the regions south of Hudson Bay and the highlands of Labrador. Their lives were regulated by the abundance and seasonal migration patterns of the animals they hunted. Caribou, for example, were hunted in summer on open ground and in winter in the forests where both humans and animals could find shelter. Yet food resources were unpredictable and starvation and death were not uncommon, particularly in the winter months. Mobility was essential to survival. In providing mobility, even in deep snow, snowshoes were perhaps the most important Subarctic invention. Indeed, it might be claimed that it was only the use of snowshoes which enabled people to survive the bleak, often bitter, Subarctic winters.[2]

Besides food, animals also supplied raw materials in the form of hides for tents and clothing, bone and horn for tools, sinew for thread and bowstrings. Nearly all remaining materials – wood, bark, and plant fibers – came from the forests. It was a lifestyle which encouraged self-reliance and children were instructed at an early age in the skills required for later life. Boys, for example, were taught to hunt and fish, to build houses and canoes, and to make tools and weapons. Girls learned to tan hides and make sinew thread, to sew and decorate clothing, and to make baskets and bark containers. Naturally, some became more proficient than others and were recognized as being so. However, such a meager subsistence economy did not permit the luxury of full-time specialists in particular arts and crafts.

Women were the main craftworkers and were thus best able to demonstrate artistic skills. Such skills, however, were expected to operate within established traditions. Esthetic values were based on respect for

technical competence and good craftsmanship and there was little room for imagination or innovation for its own sake. It is this basic conservatism which helps to make regional preferences identifiable. Nevertheless, within these traditional confines artistic expression flourished, and the decorative art of the Subarctic is at its richest and most sophisticated in the painted designs, quillwork, and embroidery in moosehair, beads, and silks created on clothing and other utilitarian objects.

Above: *The skill and ingenuity with which Indian women utilized both traditional materials and those introduced by traders is illustrated by this Kutchin shirt and Tahltan knife sheath. The shirt, of caribou skin stitched with sinew, is decorated with a band of dyed porcupine quills, red ochre, and quill-wrapped fringes. The knife sheath is also of caribou skin, but covered with blue and red trade cloth and embroidered with glass beads. The geometric design imposed by the quills contrasts with the more fluid effect of the beadwork. Other materials came from the forests.*

The Prehistoric Period

Although documentary sources for precontact life are meager – limited to the relatively few accounts by early travelers, fur traders, and missionaries – there can be little doubt that the artistic traditions which, in many cases, only began to be recorded in the eighteenth century, had been an integral part of Subarctic life for centuries.

Unfortunately, at many sites, any organic matter has been destroyed by the acidity of the soil so that, while stone tools for working skin, bone, antler, and wood have survived, the materials for which they were intended have not. There are a few exceptions where unusual conditions have led to a greater degree of preservation. For example, bone tools engraved with plain or ticked parallel lines have been excavated from prehistoric sites in northern Yukon. One of the most attractive objects recovered is a carved fish effigy – probably a fishing lure. Whether the engraved lines were intended simply as ownership marks or whether they should be regarded as symbolic – perhaps as stylized representations of animals or natural phenomena – remains a matter for conjecture.[3]

Sites around copper deposits such as those on Lake Superior and in the Copper River area have produced a range of objects hammered from copper nuggets in the form of arrowheads, knives, fishhooks, awls, chisels, beads, and other ornaments. Evidence from sites elsewhere shows that such items were widely traded throughout the Subarctic.[4]

The shards of decorated pottery which also appear in prehistoric sites point to the development of a distinctive pottery-making tradition in Manitoba and Ontario.[5] In western Alaska the pottery made around the time of historic contact by the ancestors of the Ingalik and Koyukon reflects the influence of their Eskimo neighbors.[6]

Changes to traditional Algonquian culture began early in the sixteenth century when British, French, and Portuguese fishermen came ashore to process the fish they had caught on the Newfoundland Banks. Trading metal knives, hatchets, and kettles for meat and furs, they soon attracted hundreds of Indians to the north shore of the Gulf of the St. Lawrence every summer. As a result, tools and utensils of iron and brass came to replace stone and bone over much of northeastern America during the sixteenth and seventeenth centuries.

European contact began for the Athapaskans in the late seventeenth century with the establishment of trading forts on the southwestern shores of Hudson Bay. During the eighteenth century trapping and trading activities extended westwards, with the Cree, Chipewyan, Yellowknife, and Dogrib acting as intermediaries between the traders and the northwestern groups. By the early nineteenth century the fur trade had reached the Tanaina, Tanana, and western and northern Kutchin, although some Alaskan Dene on the uppermost reaches of the major rivers did not actually set eyes on a white man until about 1900.[7]

While the disruption caused to traditional society by imported diseases and missionary activity contributed to the discarding of old ideas and activities, practical considerations

Below: *Regular trading links existed between the Ingalik and their Eskimo neighbors, with the Ingalik exchanging their wooden dishes and ladles for seal skins and oil. The Ingalik food tray (below), painted with the face of a stylized animal, was collected from an Eskimo village in the 1870s. The painting was done with red ochre and charcoal mixed with seal blood, which helped to fix the colors. Birch bark containers do not appear to have been items of trade, although, intriguingly, an Ingalik bone knife (left) used for stripping birch bark from the tree, is etched with typical Eskimo designs, including the raven's footprint motif.*

should not be underestimated. There can be little doubt that the advent of European technology greatly eased the workload of Indian women. The merchandise offered by traders – metal tools and cooking pots, woven textiles and ready-made clothing, decorative materials like beads, silk thread, and ribbons – was both attractive and labor-saving. Moreover, the possession of trade goods and the wearing of fur-trade fashions conferred considerable social status and prestige. It is hardly surprising that by the end of the eighteenth century Sir Alexander Mackenzie was able to report of the Cree: 'They are fond of European articles and prefer them to their own native commodities.'[8]

Wood and Bark

It was from the forests that people, quite literally, built their lives. The forests supplied the materials for building shelters, whether substantial log houses or simple pole frameworks covered with skin or bark. They supplied materials for transport – for sleds, toboggans, and snowshoe frames, and for canoes made of sheets of bark fitted over a wooden frame, the seams stitched with spruce root and caulked with spruce gum.

Bark and roots, as well as wood, were used for hunting and fishing equipment. Fishing lines and nets, for example, were made from willow bast, cut while green and torn into strips, then rolled on the naked thigh to

produce a strong and durable twine. A fishing net made from willow twine could last a year or more.

Dishes, ladles, and cups were carved from solid pieces of wood and decorated with notching or with incised or painted designs. In some areas, water buckets or cups were made from thin wooden slats (usually of spruce or larch) steamed and bent into circular or oval shapes. The overlapping edges were stitched with split spruce root and pieces of wood were cut and fitted in order to form the bases.

Not all woodwork was so utilitarian. For their winter ceremonials, the Ingalik of Alaska carved elaborate wooden masks, often painted and decorated with feathers and beads. Some had moveable appendages with which the wearer could imitate the movements of the being represented. Both the style of the masks and the ceremonies in which they were worn were greatly influenced by those of the neighboring Eskimo.

Baskets, both for cooking and storage, were made from sheets of birch bark and from twined spruce root (watape). Sir Alexander Mackenzie spoke approvingly of the spruce root baskets made by the Sekani in the late eighteenth century: 'Their kettles are also made of watape, which is so closely woven that they never leak, and they heat water in them by putting red hot coals into it.'[9]

Bark was cut from the tree in spring, while it

Above: *Carved and painted wooden masks were worn during the Ingalik Mask Dance, held to honor the game animals and to ensure their continued availability.*

was still flexible enough to be folded into the desired shape. The sides of the basket were stitched with strips of spruce root, which was also used to bind the rim. Baskets for cooking or for storing liquids were made watertight by applying spruce gum to the seams. Those intended to hold trinkets and other small objects sometimes had a buckskin top, closed with a drawstring.

Regional differences are apparent in both the shape and the decoration of bark containers. Those made in the Yukon and interior Alaska took the form of a bucket with a curved rim. Decoration consisted of horizontal or diagonal bands of lines and triangles, formed by scraping away the dark outer layer of bark to expose the paler bark underneath.[10]

Elsewhere in the Subarctic, bark baskets (referred to as 'mococks') had rectangular bases, sloping sides, and oval rims. The sides (and lid, if one was attached) were often decorated with stylized plant or naturalistic animal motifs. In this case, decoration was achieved by scraping away the background, leaving the design in dark relief.[11]

According to the eighteenth century explorer Samuel Hearne, the making of a complete set of Chipewyan winter clothing could take as many as eleven caribou hides.[12] A hunter required a new set of clothing at least once a year and a new pair of moccasins every two to three weeks. It is small wonder then that for Indian women dressing skins was a constant occupation.

It was also a laborious occupation, involving de-hairing (if the skin was to be used for summer clothing), along with repeated scraping, soaking, stretching, and rubbing with animal fat and brains. Finally, the skin was often smoked over a smoldering fire to give it a golden brown color. This last process also helped to make the skin waterproof and items like tent covers and moccasins were always produced out of smoke-tanned skin.

A whole range of items, including gun cases, quivers, tump-lines, baby carriers, dog packs, and bags of various forms, were made from skins. Babiche, thin-cut lines of rawhide, was (and still is) one of the most versatile of traditional resources. It was used for snares, for snowshoe lacings and for infilling ice-scoops, for making strong, yet light, netted bags, and for fastenings and lashings of all kinds. When modern technology fails, it has been used to make running repairs to chainsaws and outboard motors.[13]

The most important use of skins, however, was in the manufacture of clothing. Everyday clothing was similar for both sexes – a shirt or parka (generally longer for women), leggings or trousers, and moccasins. Some western groups like the Kutchin wore trousers with footwear attached. A cap or hood, mittens, and a fur-lined robe or coat were added in cold weather.

The skins were cut up with a sharp flint or obsidian (later metal) knife and the pieces

Left and below: *Baskets took various forms, ranging from the open-twined storage bag to the closely-woven and watertight Chilcotin cooking vessel (below), to this Cree birch bark container with its tightly-fitting lid (left).*

Right: *The French term 'babiche' refers both to finely cut strips of rawhide and to the webbing made from it. Throughout the Subarctic area, babiche was used in the making of snowshoes. Netted babiche bags were made in different sizes for a variety of purposes. This Tahltan example has loops for attaching a carrying strap. Even such a utilitarian object is decorated with horizontal stripes of red pigment.*

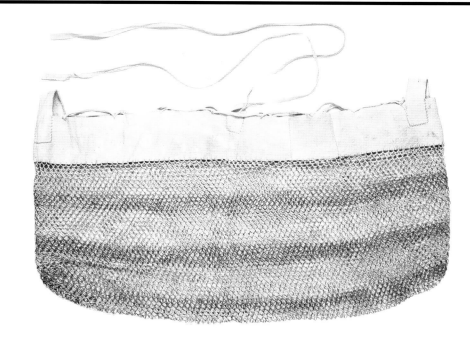

stitched together with sinew threaded through small holes punched along the seam lines with an awl.[14] Different types or parts of skin were preferred for different items of clothing – leg skins for mittens and moccasin uppers, for example, and calfskin for undergarments. When large game was scarce, shirts and robes might be made from rabbit skins, cut into strips and woven to make a warm fur fabric.[15] Fish skin was used in some parts of Alaska, where the Kolchan, for example, wore rain capes made of salmon skin.

With the establishment of trading posts, people increasingly came into contact with European manufactures, including ready-made clothing of wool and cotton. As early as 1809, David Harmon, a trader among the Beaver, noted that 'the greater part of them are now clothed with European goods'.[16] By the beginning of the twentieth century, traditional everyday skin clothing – apart from a few items like mittens and moccasins – had more or less disappeared, replaced by garments of European style and fabric.[17]

Painting

Paint, most commonly red and black, was used to decorate a variety of objects, including snowshoes, sleds, canoe gunwales, drums, dishes, and garments, particularly along the seams. Red, the most popular color, was originally obtained from local earth pigments, but vermilion – brighter and clearer – was supplied by traders from the earliest period of contact. Black was probably derived from burnt bones or charcoal.

Designs tended to be highly symbolic. In the early 1770s Samuel Hearne watched Chipewyan warriors painting their shields with red and black designs in preparation for battle:

'...some with the figure of the sun, others with that of the moon, several with different kinds of birds and beasts of prey and many with the images of imaginary beings... I learned that each man painted his shield with the image of that being on which he relied most for success in the intended engagement.'[18]

Perhaps the best-known examples of Subarctic painted decoration are to be found on the caribou-skin coats which were worn by Montagnais-Naskapi hunters at least from the eighteenth century until the 1930s.[19] Part of their interest lies in the way in which they reflect the changing styles of European fashion during this period. In fact they illustrate a trend found all over the Subarctic (although generally not until the nineteenth century) whereby garments, while continuing to be made from traditional materials, began to borrow European stylistic features such as centre front openings, collars, and cuffs.

The main significance of the Montagnais-Naskapi coats, however, lies with the designs, for these coats were made and worn in order to enlist supernatural aid in hunting the

Right: *The supreme importance of the caribou hunt to the Naskapi, Montagnais and Cree of the Quebec-Labrador Peninsula is reflected in their painted caribou-skin coats. By wearing such coats, decorated with powerful symbols, hunters hoped to enlist supernatural aid to bring them success in the hunt. Caribou-bone tools were used to apply the red, blue, and brown painted designs on this Naskapi hunter's summer coat.*

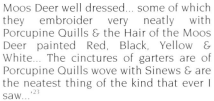

Above: *Porcupine quill weaving was highly developed in central Canada and Alaska. Designs created by the Athapaskans of the Yukon and North West Territories were of particular fineness and complexity, in contrast to the bolder patterns produced by Algonquian groups such as the Cree. Besides woven quillwork, various forms of braided and sewn work were also done, producing strong geometric bands of color. Quilled panels like those decorating these Cree leggings were often so highly valued by their owners that they were transferred to new garments when the old ones wore out.*

Below: *As the nineteenth century progressed, European designs, as well as materials, became increasingly incorporated into Indian art. At the same time, traditional materials were adapted for the souvenir market. The unusual form of this Montagnais birch bark box, together with its floral quillwork decoration, reflects European influence and it may in fact have been made for sale rather than for use. The quills were applied to the bark by being pushed through tiny holes in the surface and then covered with an inner lining to keep them from working loose.*

all-important caribou. A hunter received instructions in dreams concerning the symbols which would give him the special power he needed. He passed the dream instructions to his wife, who translated them into visual form by painting the skin.[20]

The designs themselves – intricate combinations of double curves, crosses, dots, lozenges, triangles, leaf- and heart-shaped motifs, among others – were applied to the coats with tools made of caribou antler or bone. The pigments used were yellow (derived from sucker fish roe), red (locally obtained hematite or vermilion), black (possibly burnt bone), and blue (indigo supplied by traders and, from the mid-nineteenth century, laundry blue).[21]

The layout of the painted designs is remarkably standard and clearly subscribes to established tradition, the main pattern areas being the hem, the center back and fronts, and the collar. The most important constant feature of the coats is the back gusset, a narrow triangle of skin inserted where another triangle of skin has been cut out. As Dorothy Burnham has suggested, this painted area is almost certainly the symbolic centre of the coat's power, representing 'the Magical Mountain where the Lord of The Caribou lived and from the fastness of which the caribou were released to give themselves to the hunter'.[22]

Quill and Hair Embroidery
Although very few precontact examples survive, quillwork was among the very earliest artifacts collected by European explorers, and from their comments it is evident that quill weaving and embroidery were already well-developed and sophisticated crafts by the time of contact.

Mackenzie, at the end of the eighteenth century, expressed admiration for the work done by Slavey and Dogrib women:

'They make their Clothing of the Rein or

Right: *At the onset of puberty girls underwent a period of ritual seclusion, during which they were subject to a number of rules governing their food, clothing, and general behavior. When they emerged from seclusion, they were regarded as ready for marriage. This skin-covered collar was worn by a Tahltan girl during the period between puberty seclusion and marriage. The collar is decorated with dentalium shells, red and blue glass beads, and tassels of colored wool or worsted.*

Moos Deer well dressed... some of which they embroider very neatly with Porcupine Quills & the Hair of the Moos Deer painted Red, Black, Yellow & White... The cinctures of garters are of Porcupine Quills wove with Sinews & are the neatest thing of the kind that ever I saw...'[23]

Quills included both porcupine and split bird quills, usually goose, and hair included moose and caribou, although where both were available the former was preferred. All these materials could be colored with dyes derived from plant or mineral sources, but the natural colors were used as required. Quills were sometimes dyed black or dark brown by being tied up and boiled with lichen. A later variant of this technique was to boil quills with blue or red trade cloth so that they absorbed the color. In modern times crepe paper has been used in the same way to produce red, green, and yellow quills.

There were various ways of using quills, the most straightforward being to lay them in parallel rows, each being held by a stitch in the middle and at either end. This was the method applied to the stiffer, less malleable bird quills, and was used for items like belts and tump-lines.

The simplest method of decorating clothing was by wrapping flattened porcupine quills around thong fringes. More complex techniques involved folding the quills over and under one or two sinew threads to produce lines or bands of color which could be combined to make patterns of rectangular blocks, stepped triangles, and crosses. However, undoubtedly the finest porcupine quillwork was that which was woven either on a bow loom or directly on to the skin ground on a sinew cross-weft. Almost certainly, it was woven quillwork which so impressed Mackenzie.

Traditional woven and applied quillwork produced intricate geometric patterns, but during the nineteenth century curvilinear and floral patterns, first produced in eastern Canada via the European embroidery tradition, moved rapidly westwards.[24] By1850 Dr. John Rae had acquired, probably from the Cree, a guncase decorated with double-curve moosehair scrolls.[25] Ten years later, Andrew Flett of the Hudson's Bay Company collected

for the Industrial Museum of Scotland a pair of Kutchin mooseskin moccasins embroidered with a floral motif in red and blue porcupine quills edged with moosehair.[26]

By that time, too, Indian women had acquired steel needles and silk thread and, influenced by fort life and mission schools, were producing skin moccasins, mittens, gloves, bags, and other items decorated with silk floral embroidery entirely in the European tradition.[27] When both silks and quills are used to decorate the same object, the stiffness and formality of the quillwork is in striking contrast to the exuberance of the embroidery. Although quillwork continued to be used to decorate clothing, it is clear that Indian craftswomen had come to recognize its limitations and that, as European materials became more freely available, it would increasingly be relegated to a secondary position.

Beadwork

Beads made of bone, shell, copper, seeds, and dried berries were used as jewelry and to decorate clothing in precontact times and into the historic period. After European contact, imported glass beads and metal ornaments began to be found alongside native materials.

'All the natives of the interior,' wrote Lieutenant Zagoskin, visiting the mouth of the Yukon River in the 1840s, 'are passionately fond of finery and bright colors. They have contrived to adorn their simple clothing by sewing on porcupine quills, deer hair, borders of threaded beads, shells, pendants cut out of copper, little bells, and so on...'[28]

Glass beads came in a range of colors and sizes. The large beads, supplied by Russian traders on the North Pacific coast from the end of the eighteenth century, varied from 'necklace' beads (7mm. or more in diameter), to 'pony' beads (3-4mm). Further east 'seed' beads (2mm or less) were in use by the mid-eighteenth century, becoming widespread by the second half of the nineteenth century.[29] Faceted metal beads became popular towards the end of the nineteenth century, the 'silver' beads being polished iron and the 'gold' ones brass or copper.

As beads became more readily available in the nineteenth century, they were incorporated into the established geometric design tradition and it is possible to trace the continuity from quilled designs to very similar ones produced with beads or by combinations of beads and dentalia shells.[30] Kutchin garments and accessories collected in the 1860s show dentalia and glass beads being used in equal proportion to produce chequered bands of color on the yoke seams and cuffs of dresses and shirts and down the seams of leggings.

Beads were attached to skin and cloth using a two-thread couching technique, whereby the beads, strung on one thread, are stitched to the surface at intervals by a second thread passing between every two or three beads. This technique allowed the beadworker greater flexibility of design since the strung beads could be turned in any direction desired and this, together with the introduction of steel needles and cotton thread, led to the great development of floral beadwork throughout most of the Subarctic region in the latter half of the nineteenth century.

Some of the far western groups like the Tahltan did retain more geometric patterns adapted from quillwork and basketry and their bold, rectilinear beadwork designs are in strong contrast to the conventionalized floral and curvilinear designs being produced elsewhere. The woven beadwork in some areas also retained the rectilinear designs necessitated by the weaving technique.

Present-day beadworkers continue to practice and develop floral beadwork, although always within the established design tradition, because 'that is how it is done'. The respect for technical quality remains, with emphasis on matching beads for size and color, even stitching and symmetry of design. It is these qualities which Indian craftswomen find esthetically pleasing; in the words of a modern beadworker, Minnie Peter of Fort Yukon, 'I like to make something bright. If I want to sew, I like to make something pretty'.[31]

References

1 Mackenzie, 1970:133.
2 Many explorers and traders found, often after initial scepticism, that native technology had much to commend it. Dr. John Rae, who explored the western shores of Hudson Bay in the 1840s, wrote: 'At first I could not be persuaded that a person could walk better with such great clumsy looking things as snowshoes on his feet crunching knee deep in snow, but it did not require very long practice to decide this question in favour of the snowshoes.' Quoted in Idiens & Wilson, 1993: 80.
3 It has been suggested that the decoration of ritual equipment with incised lines (for example, items used during periods of puberty seclusion or mourning) may imply that at least some of this was more than merely decorative. (Thompson, 1987: 146.)
4 None of the native peoples lived in isolation prior to European contact. All were part of an elaborate and long-established inter-tribal trading network.
5 According to the archeologist J. V. Wright, 'It has been somewhat of a problem to determine from where this pottery came. It is not part of any of the ceramic complexes to the south, and there exists a broad zone to the northwest completely lacking in and thereby precluding a possible Asiatic origin. The only reasonable alternative is that the idea of pottery was adopted from the south via stimulus diffusion and that the Archaic populations of the Shield evolved a distinctive ceramic complex after they had acquired the essential techniques of manufacture'. (Helm, 1981: 89.)
6 Koyukon and Ingalik continued to make clay lamps and cooking pots into the Historic Period and into the twentieth century.
7 The effect of Europeans was felt long before they actually appeared and western manufactured goods were traded through the existing aboriginal networks to become part of the cultural inventory of groups far from the point of source.
8 Mackenzie, 1970: 133.
9 Mackenzie, 1970: 291. A traditional method of cooking was to fill a container with food and water and drop in heated stones until the water boiled.
10 It has been suggested that this style of decoration may in fact pre-date European contact because of its similarity to the earliest known woven quillwork, although the few bark trays so far recovered are undecorated. (Duncan, 1989: 26.)
11 Perhaps the most unusual method of decorating bark is that still practised today by Cree women in Manitoba and Saskatchewan. By folding a piece of bark and biting it, a skilled worker can create a range of intricate patterns which is revealed when the bark is unfolded.
12 Quoted in McMillan, 1988: 219-20.
13 Savishinsky, 1974: 21.
14 Eyed needles for sewing appear to have been unknown in the Subarctic until introduced by traders, although eyed needles for lacing snowshoes have been recovered from prehistoric sites.
15 Whole rabbit skins were too flimsy for clothing.
16 Quoted in Duncan, 1989: 38. It was, of course, in the trader's interest that people should bring him their furs and dressed skins rather than turn them into clothing for themselves. When Alexander Murray established Fort Yukon in 1847, he reported: 'Blankets, axes, knives, powder horns, and files went off rapidly enough, but it was hard to dispose of the clothing as they consider their own dresses much superior to ours both in beauty and durability, and they are partly right, although I endeavoured to persuade them to the contrary.' Quoted in Nelson, 1973: 205.
17 There are still certain areas where traditional materials triumph. The anthropologist Joel Savishinsky records a Hare hunter comparing the skin slippers made by his wife with a pair of store-bought woolen socks: 'Two weeks ago all I had were those lousy woolen ones from the store, but they weren't worth a damn. It was forty or fifty below and my feet were freezing. Then I had Lena make me these. That's some difference I'll tell you. I put these on and I don't care if it's sixty below – it's like I don't feel anything and my feet never hurt.' Quoted in Savishinsky, 1974: 21.
18 Quoted in Thompson, 1987: 147.
19 Because the style and decoration of these painted coats proved attractive to travelers and collectors, a number have survived from quite an early date. Several of those now in European museums have been dated as early as 1700 – largely on stylistic grounds, since documentation is often lacking.
20 While the designs clearly had very powerful symbolic meaning for the hunter who dreamed them and had them painted on his coat, it is impossible at this remove even to guess what that meaning might have been. (Burnham, 1992: 59.)
21 It has been noted that, in general, the earlier coats display finer, more detailed painting. Dorothy Burnham has suggested that, before the arrival of Christian missionaries, when hunters were able to have several wives, one might have been released from her other duties to concentrate on painting her husband's coat. (Burnham, 1992: 3.)
22 While in coats of similar European cut, gussets are introduced to give added fullness to the skirts, this is not necessarily the case with these painted skin coats. On some of the later coats, the insert is actually narrower than the piece it replaced. Thus, the influence of contemporary European fashion, although strong, is more visual than structural. (Burnham, 1992: 11-12.)
23 Mackenzie, 1970: 184.
24 The floral designs which have dominated Subarctic art since the mid-nineteenth century are entirely European in origin.
25 National Museums of Scotland L.304.127.
26 National Museums of Scotland 563.1.
27 White women who exerted influence on native communities – nuns, schoolteachers, the wives of clergymen, and traders – actively encouraged Indian women to learn European domestic crafts such as embroidery and lace-making, which they regarded as having a civilizing effect.
28 Quoted in Duncan, 1989: 38. Zagoskin is of course describing ceremonial or 'dress' clothing. Everyday wear in this area, as elsewhere, was not decorated apart from a few fringes and perhaps a patterned belt. Because such costume was everyday, it was rarely commented on or collected.
29 Venice had the monopoly of glass bead production until the 1880s, when Bohemian (Czech) beads became available and were imported.
30 The shells mentioned by Zagoskin were almost certainly dentalia or 'tooth shells', which were widely traded from the Pacific coast all over the interior. They were highly prized as decoration and as a form of currency and conspicuous wealth.
31 Quoted in Duncan & Carney, 1988: 34.

THE ARCTIC

THE NORTH AMERICAN Arctic features a surprisingly varied land mass with distinct ecological and cultural zones. The extensive coastline and tundra interior encourages mixed maritime and inland hunting economies. Major river systems penetrate the interior; their fertile deltas provide rich feeding grounds for fish, seals, and small mammals. In Alaska and on Baffin Island, ranges of snow-capped mountains rise majestically from low-lying coastal plains. The treeline marks a meandering route staying within 250 miles (402km.) of coastal Alaska but sloping sharply south beyond the Mackenzie Delta. Marked with patches of dwarf willow, the central Canadian Arctic features a seemingly boundless expanse of tundra. Rich in vegetation, the tundra provides summer grazing land for herds of caribou and musk oxen, as well as migratory wildfowl.

For over 2,000 years, Aleutian, Yup'ik, and Inupiat-Inuit peoples, descendants of the Eskimo-Aleut linguistic family, have skillfully exploited local resources, sustaining a remarkably productive life in a wide range of environmental conditions.[2] At the time of contact with Russian explorers in 1741, the Unangan (Aleuts) occupied the Aleutian archipelago, clusters of islands which extend from the Alaskan peninsula 1,300 miles (2,092km.) towards Asia. With scarce land resources, Aleutian hunters pursued whales, sea lions, fur seals, and sea otters by baidarka (kayak) in coastal waters. Fish, nesting birds, and marine life collected on beaches provided additional food and raw material.

The Yup'ik-speaking cultures of southwestern Alaska constructed villages of semi-subterranean houses on the Bering Sea coast and off-shore islands, and along the Yukon and Kuskokwim Rivers. The Yukon-Kuskokwim Delta, a crescent-shaped area extending from Norton Sound to Kuskokwim Bay (and 200 miles (322km.) inland), is the heartland of Central Yup'ik country.[3] The river deltas provide rich sealing areas, while the rivers and their tributaries offer access to fish and wildlife resources in the interior.

The Inupiat-Inuit peoples of northern Alaska, Arctic Canada, and Greenland share a common language with a continuum of regional dialects. Scattered in camps and villages across an extensive territorial range, they too developed distinctly regional hunting economies. During the spring migration of bowhead whales, Inupiat in northwestern Alaska, for example, conducted a highly ceremonialized form of whalehunting under the direction of *umialit*, whaling captains.[4] Across the Canadian Arctic, Inuit families lived in camps of extended kin, shifting location in response to the seasonal

movement of game. From coastal communities on Baffin Island and along the west coast of Hudson Bay, kayak hunters pursued whales, walrus, and narwhal. They seal-hunted at breathing holes in winter and hunted caribou inland in spring and fall. Fish (fresh, frozen, or dried) provided an important food source throughout the year.

In tandem with extreme winter temperatures, the Arctic experiences a dramatic seasonal change in light and animal resources. As the sun disappears in early fall, caribou, whales, geese, and ducks abandon the north. They return each spring to give

Above: *Both skilled and decorative craftwork of the Arctic region are represented by the Aleutian and Inupiat parkas, together with the Greenland Eskimo boot of sealskin embellished with thin stips of red, yellow, and black painted skin applique. The magico-religious art so characteristic of the culture is illustrated by the pierced hand from a wooden tunghak mask. Of extreme importance for survival in a hostile environment was the production of the waterproof outer parka, which vividly underlines the remarkable employment of natural materials to best effect. Made of strips of walrus or seal intestine, they were joined by an ingenious waterproof sinew-sewn seam.*

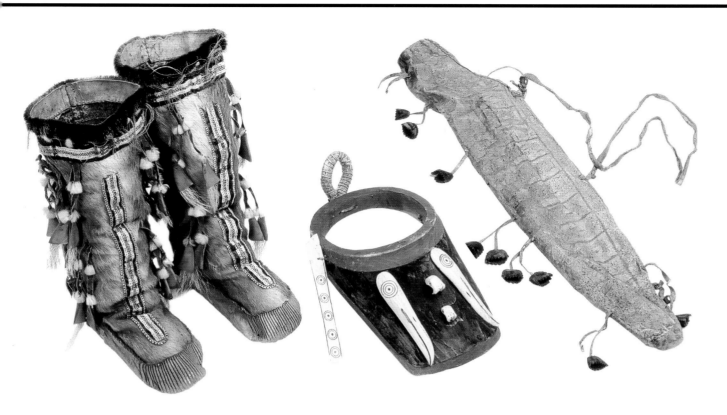

Above: *Great effort went into producing children's clothing, especially for ritual and social occasions. This pair of child's boots (above left) was collected from the Yup'ik prior to 1866. They exhibit the highly technical and decorative craftwork in leather and fur so characteristic of the region. The Aleutian child's shade (left center) has a talisman of diving waterbirds of carved ivory. The combined bow-case and quiver (right) contains a bow and eight arrows for hunting small game. The symbolic decoration alluded to the child's role as a prospective hunter.*

birth and nurture their young. This annual cycle of light and dark, scarcity and abundance, makes the Arctic a land of sharp contrasts. In winter, families relied on available game and reserves of stored food. Through social gatherings and ritual ceremonies, they appeased spirit forces which controlled the supply of animals. The sun's reappearance in spring, accompanied by the return of the whales, migratory birds, and thundering herds of caribou, heralded a period of regeneration and renewal.

Historical Art Forms
Flawlessly designed implements, produced from wood, bone, antler, ivory, and stone, comprised the remarkably efficient toolkit that enabled hunters to procure game on land or sea. With ingenuity and technical

Right: *A Bering Strait Eskimo carver uses a traditional style of bow and drill on a walrus tusk, the end product almost certainly being to satisfy the demand of early white traders. Such work was produced by the Nome Eskimo where this man was photographed in 1912 (though the mouthpiece technique demonstrated here goes back centuries). Large objects are not representative of early Eskimo sculpture, much of which was done in the miniature with a fine eye for detail. The parka has the sinew-sewn seam attractively decorated with small feathers and tassels.*

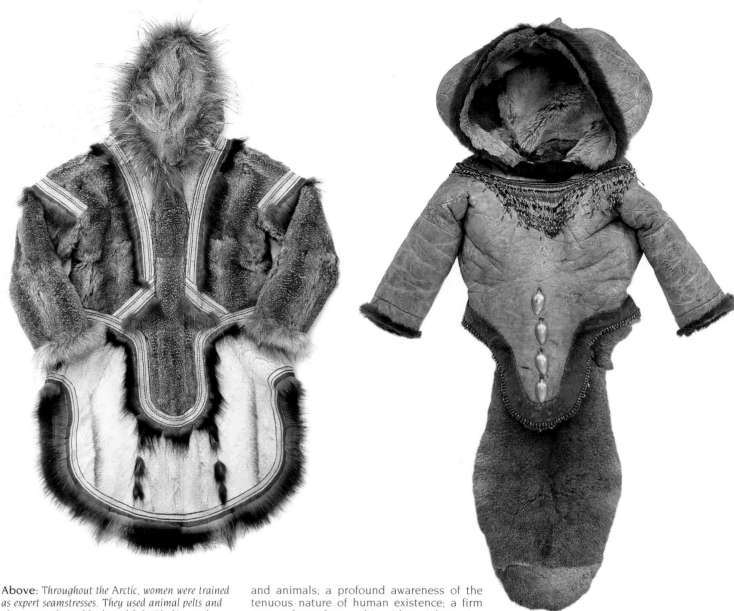

Above: *Throughout the Arctic, women were trained as expert seamstresses. They used animal pelts and skins, even those of birds and fish. Clothing styles identified gender and region. Men's parkas had references to the role of hunter, women's that of the procreative, maternal role. These parkas are both women's. The Inupiat one (left) is made of squirrel and sealskin and was collected by E. W. Nelson prior to 1897. In contrast is the Inuit one (right) of caribou skin collected by Lucien Turner in the early 1880s and heavily embellished with trade goods including pewter spoons, lead drops, and seed beads. Both garments, however, underline the importance of efficient clothing to cope with the harsh Arctic environment.*

expertise, women used sewing skills to fashion objects necessary for everyday use. Animal hides and furs furnished women with raw material for clothing, tents, umiak and kayak covers, quivers, storage bags, and various hunting and domestic equipment.

Despite clear regional differences in language, dialect, hunting pursuits, and social practices, Arctic cultures shared broadly similar ideological concerns which imbued the production of traditional art forms. These are an intimate physical and metaphysical relationship between humans and animals; a profound awareness of the tenuous nature of human existence; a firm respect for craftsmanship with social prestige vested in skill and productivity; and a deep love of children and desire to impart the knowledge and skills necessary for them to achieve a productive life in an exacting, and often unforgiving, environment.

Arctic peoples believed that well-crafted objects pleased spirit forces and secured good will toward the maker and his/her family.[5] Impeccably tailored clothing, and finely carved hunting tools, provide evidence of the value placed on the artistic combination of form and function. Today, well-made, skillfully decorated clothing remains a treasured gift from a seamstress to her husband, daughter-in-law, or grandchild.

Clothing as Art
'A parka is a beautiful art form. It is our cultural heirloom, which we call *paitaq*. The parka is pieced together from the animals of our area... It's all the life forms coming together through the hands and skills of a seamstress.'
MARIE MEADE (YUP'IK) 1990[6]
Throughout the Arctic, extraordinary time, skill, and talent were invested in clothing production. Women possessed expert knowledge in treating animal skins to maximize warmth or waterproof garments. Rendered from animal products, clothing underscored human dependence on the animal. Clothing design was functional as well as symbolic. Since clothing styles were regional, they served as an important sign of social identity and collective cohesion.[7]

Waterproof garments made from sea mammal intestine were used for maritime hunting throughout the Aleutians, coastal Alaska, St. Lawrence Island, and the eastern Canadian Arctic.[8] Yards of tubular intestines were scraped, inflated, and dried. Treated as such, the gutskin appears as translucent parchment, seemingly fragile but surprisingly resilient when oiled. On St. Lawrence Island gutskins were bleached in freezing temperatures to achieve their creamy color and soft texture. To fashion the parka, bands of gutskin were laid in horizontal tiers or vertical columns. The seams were folded over and stitched without fully penetrating the skin. Whale or walrus sinew was often used for thread; it swelled when wet, helping to seal the hole.

Gutskin garments were frequently decorated with alder-dyed hair of unborn seals, cormorant feather tufts, or tiny auklet crowns, inserted at regular intervals in the seams. Such decoration was both visually pleasing and profoundly symbolic. Cormorant feathers alluded to the bird's diving and fishing ability; the hair of unborn seals symbolized the propagation of the species. Women, as well as men, wore exquisitely decorated gutskin parkas. These served a utilitarian function as rain cover, but were also featured in ceremonial contexts.[9] In the wake of European contact and trade, bits of red, blue, and green yarn replaced traditional forms of decoration.

Although apparently regarded as a poor man's clothing choice, bird skins provided an important source of parka material, particularly in areas of limited resources. Eider duck, emperor goose, murre, puffin, squaw duck, loon, and cormorant skins made lightweight and water-repellent parkas. Certainly, the doll of a Yup'ik hunter, dressed in a cormorant parka with elaborate personal adornment, presents an image of affluence and prestige.

In general, Yup'ik seamstresses preferred ground squirrel (marmot), mink, otter, and muskrat furs for parka material. Flensed, dried, and scraped to soften, the small pelts were laid in horizontal rows, sometimes with tails intact. Traditionally, Yup'ik parks were long, dress-like garments, often hoodless with a high standing collar. Today, women's parkas (atkupiaq) are hooded with a 'sunburst' trim of wolverine and wolf similar to hood styles in northern Alaska.[10] Plates of white calfskin (formerly pukiq, white caribou fur) are fixed with wolverine, otter, or mink tassles and attached in horizontal tiers across the parka front and back. They are highlighted with decorative stitching (kelurqut) on thin strips of black or red painted skin. 'The red earth paint is called uiteraq or kavirun. It is the representation of the blood of our ancestral mother An'gaqtar. An'gaqtar, who some people say is the daughter of Raven, the Creator, left pockets of her menstrual blood in various [sacred] places in southwest Alaska.'[11]

Caribou fur and ground squirrel were preferred by the Inupiat of northern Alaska. Men's parkas were thigh-length with slightly rounded hems in front and back. Trousers and boots completed the outfit. The creamy white mottled fur of domesticated Siberian reindeer, obtained from itinerant Chuckchi traders or St. Lawrence Island middlemen, was considered extremely valuable.[12] Wolverine or wolf tails, an eagle feather or loon's head were often attached to the parka back, evoking respect for the subject's predatory skill and serving as a talisman for the wearer.[13]

Caribou fur provides exceptional hypothermal protection and was favored by Inuit throughout Arctic Canada.[14] While traveling or hunting in winter, the parka was worn in two layers. The uniform design of the outer parka signified one's regional and gender identity, while the inner parka was decorated with amulets which alluded to the wearer's personal relationship with spirit forces.[15]

Sealskin parkas were prevalent in Greenland, Baffin Island, and Labrador. Lightweight and water-repellent, they were worn especially during the wet spring and warm summer months. The sealskin was scraped on the inside, then stretched and laced to a drying rack to air dry. For parkas and trousers, the hair was left intact. Women took great pride in contrasting the skin's silver tone with dark decorative inserts. As Lucien Turner notes, 'The woman may be several years in getting the right kind [of sealskin] and may have effected many exchanges before being suited with the quality and color'.[16]

Clothing styles contained specific design elements which identified the wearer as male or female. Inuit women's parkas, for example, were identified by a back pouch (amaut) used to carry a baby. The amaut emphasized the woman's maternal role on both a functional and symbolic level.[17]

Trade played a prominent role in the design of clothing and personal adornment. Blue trade beads from China, purchased from itinerant Siberian traders, decorated labrets, clothing, needlecases, and hunting implements.[18] Russian and European explorers, whalers, and traders, introduced manufactured cloth and beads. Tartan shawls, wool berets, and calico covers became the height of fashion in different areas. In Greenland, women devised an elaborately netted collar of colored beads in bold geometric patterns. Strands of beads formed variegated color bands that were draped from shoulder to shoulder on women's parkas on Baffin Island and in northern Quebec. In the central Arctic, seamstresses created narrative and abstract designs by sewing seed beads to a stroud backing attached over the chest, shoulders, wrists, and hood. The woman adhered to regional design norms, but the pictorial images were the creation of each seamstress.[19]

Carving and Graphic Arts

While women's art was primarily demonstrated through sewing,[20] men were proficient in producing hunting equipment and household implements. As noted earlier, superior craftsmanship was believed to please the souls of prey and enhance the efficacy of an object. Moreover, Arctic cultures believed that animals possessed a soul (Yup'ik: yua; Inupiat: inua). In response to the respect paid to the animal and its spirit, animals allowed themselves to be captured. A hunter demonstrated his respect for the animal by virtue of his moral character, personal appearance, and the care taken in producing and maintaining hunting equipment.

Hunting equipment was often designed to attract prey. Ivory fishinghooks were carved as

Right: In western Alaska women carried sewing implements in decorated bags known as 'housewives'. This bag (far right) exhibits beadwork in large blue beads. The needle-case (center) consists of an ivory tube through which runs a thong of rawhide in the folds of which the needles were kept. The comb (left) is of bone. All carry symbolic references to animals, signifying the seamstresses' dependence on animal resources.

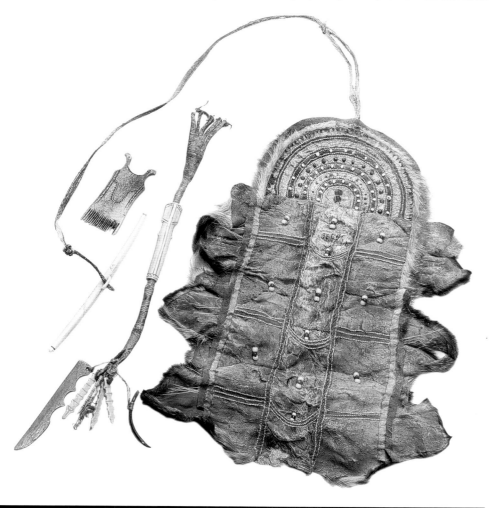

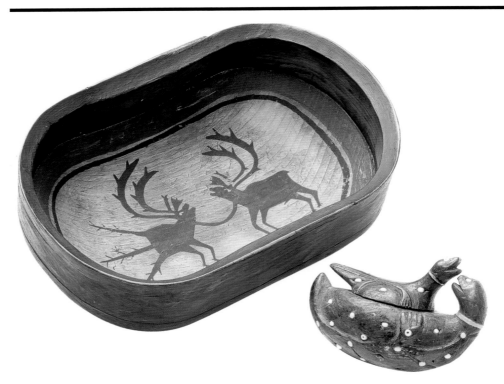

The pair are incised with skeletal markings studded with white trade beads, a design recalling the practice of marking joints, the site of souls, with nucleated circles.[24] Its function as a snuff box also demonstrates the hunter's generosity in sharing his valuables, and serves as a form of spirit propitiation.

In the central Arctic, Inuit were reluctant to accumulate unnecessary personal possessions. Moving seasonally from camp to camp, families used caches, marked by stone formations known as *inukshuit*, to store food and unneeded seasonal goods. Wood, a scarce commodity, was reserved for kayak and umiak frames, sleds, tent poles, and essential hunting equipment. In its place, Inuit relied heavily on stone, bone, antler, ivory, and animal skins. Among the Copper Inuit, musk ox horn was boiled, carved, and shaped into ladles; bone marrow picks were handsomely rendered with decorative finials; and seal hide, bird skins, and ducks' feet were sewn into exquisitely designed containers. Families traveled widely to trade and to obtain raw materials. Indigenous names for places and social groups often derived from the most prominent resource available in a region.

Dolls and Models

Throughout the Arctic, parents fashioned ivory, wood, and skin figures, as well as model umiaks, kayaks, hunting, and domestic equipment for the entertainment and instruction of children. Ivory storyknives, carved by male relatives in the *qasgi* (men's house), were used by Yup'ik girls to depict mythological and historical epics, and to relate personal narratives.[25] More than an entertaining pastime, these stories served a key educational function. Similarly, girls learned the pattern designs (and decorative codes) of adult clothing by sewing miniature replicas for their dolls. Model-building allowed an older generation to convey details of large-scale construction to children and grandchildren.[26]

Thus, child-scale equipment was produced with exceptional care. The future hunter's quiver and visor replicated their full-scale counterpart, even in details of magico-religious decoration.[27] Also, time was reserved in social gatherings for children to

Above: *Wood could be worked as skillfully as ivory. This oval dish (above left) from the region of Nulok Tokok, Alaska, is made of a bottom piece and separate wooden rim, the outer and inner sides of the rim being painted red. Mythical reindeers, linked by a symbolic power line and painted in black, embellish the slightly concave bottom. The superbly carved and inlaid snuff box (above right), is a sea otter at play with her cub.*

fish with precious blue trade beads for eyes. Arrow straighteners took the form of complacent caribou. Passing repeatedly through the device, the arrow became used to the caribou's body while the animal learned to accept the hunter's weapon.[21]

In Alaska, hunting gear was stored in covered wooden boxes. The interior was often painted with hunting trophies, mythological beings, and explicit sexual images. The sexual energy conveyed in these pictographs also empowered the hunter. In fact, the hunt itself was frequently perceived in sexual terms.

Sexual abstinence was encouraged, for a woman's smell was believed to be abhorrent to the animal. Young men were discouraged from looking at women in order to preserve and intensify their hunting vision.[22]

Meat trays with painted pictographs also combined pragmatic and spiritual functions. The wood was carved, steamed, bent, and fitted. Seams were stitched with spruce root. Trays and ladles were painted with mythological images in the early fall and accompanied men in the ritual sweatbath in order to fix the pigment.[23] Food contained in these trays fed spirits, deceased ancestors, and other guests. The painted images alluded to spirit forces and animal procreation. For example, a bentwood tray shows two figures, a male caribou and its *inua*, energized by a mystical power line. The exposed penis sexually charges the image, emphasizing the fecundity of the species. A delicately carved snuff box takes the form of a mother sea otter, playfully carrying her offspring on her belly.

Right: *A unique style of kayak was developed by the Aleutian Eskimo to transport non-Native travelers. This ivory model of a three-hole baidarka shows the split prow kayak with three figures; the man in the middle is lighting his pipe whilst the two Aleuts prepare to throw harpoons.*

Right: *This pair of Alaskan Eskimo dolls show elaborate Arctic costume in the miniature. Such dolls were not mere playthings but were used to instruct girls in the techniques of patterning and sewing to enable them to produce practical and esthetically pleasing costume demanded by the Arctic environment and culture. The male doll (left) is from Tuniakput and the female doll (right) from Bristol Bay.*

Right: *This pair of Alaskan Eskimo dolls show elaborate Arctic costume in the miniature. Such dolls were not mere playthings but were used to instruct girls in the techniques of patterning and sewing to enable them to produce practical and esthetically pleasing costume demanded by the Arctic environment and culture. The male doll (left) is from Tuniakput and the female doll (right) from Bristol Bay.*

demonstrate their novice skills. This practice continues today and serves as an important occasion of social pride in the physical and cultural development of a new generation.

Magico-Religious Art

Arctic cultures acknowledged their dependence on spirit forces through an annual cycle of ritual ceremonies. Their complex cosmology demanded that respect be paid to celestial beings, the spirit of animals, and deceased ancestors. Festival gatherings, ritual or secular in nature, consisted of appropriate combinations of songs, dance, social play, comic scenes, and dramatically staged masked performances.

The extensive resources and large settled populations in the Yup'ik area supported an impressive ceremonial cycle. Ceremonies included food offerings made to children (Qaariitaaq), gift exchanges between men and women (Petugtaq), formal thanks for the annual harvest of seals (Nakaciuq), memorial celebrations dedicated to the spirits of the deceased (Elriq), elaborate gift distributions in honor of a child's first catch (Kevgiq), and ritual feasts (Keleq) directed by shamans for ensuring a 'time of plenty'.[28] The qasgi (men's house) served as the ritual center in which ancestor and animal spirits were hosted by those present. New clothing, bentwood trays, and ladles were made in early fall at the start of the ceremonial calendar.[29]

Nakaciuq, the Bladder Festival, took place over a five-day period in December, known as cauyarvik: 'time for drumming.'[30] Hunters reserved the bladders of seals they had caught throughout the year. Bladders lost or destroyed by dogs were replaced by the stomach or other organ. Participants washed in urine, rinsing their bodies in the snow. During Nakaciuq the inflated bladders were displayed in the men's house; their souls (yua) were feted with food, song, oratory, and dance. At dawn following the full moon, the hunters returned the bladders to the sea through a hole chipped in the ice. Confident of being well-treated, the seal's spirit – contained in the bladder – returned to the hunter the following season.

During Elriq namesakes received gifts of food and clothing presented to honor the deceased. Bits of food were dropped through the floorboards to ancestor spirits gathered beneath. For Keleq, the Inviting-In Feast, one village hosted another with several days of masked performances staged to please animal spirits and thus ensure a plentiful hunt. Masks, commissioned from carvers, were often made under the direction of shamans. The masks illustrated supernatural visions, personal narratives, or symbolized the relationship between a participant and an animal yua.[31] Bird feathers often surrounded the mask. In ritual contexts birds served as messengers between the natural and supernatural worlds. Large-scale tunghak masks were grotesque impersonations of the spirit force which controlled the supply of animals. Frequently depicted with a leering grin, the tunghak's hands were characteristically pierced with an unopposable thumb, signaling its benign authority in releasing animals to the hunter.[32] Wooden carvings of select species were placed tauntingly about the tunghak's face.

An assembly of seated male drummers accompanied the dancers. The drum covering was struck with a long narrow baton. When women danced, they performed with downcast eyes, holding a pair of finger masks

Above: *Finger masks were small wooden masks carved with human, bird, or tunghat features. Danced as pairs by women, the images were either identical or complementary. These are from the region of the mouth of the Togiak River, Alaska. The embellishment of fur, feathers, or caribou hair accentuated the movements of the hands.*

which served as their surrogate eyes.[33]

Dance styles between the south and north differed radically. In the early twentieth century, Hawkes contrasted the 'raw vigor' of northern dance with the graceful, fluid motions used in the south.[34] Moreover, the material richness of festivals in the western

Arctic contrasted sharply with the more austere gatherings of Inuit in Arctic Canada.

In the eastern Canadian Arctic, early ethnographic accounts provide some evidence of communal ceremonies with skin masks, transsexual costuming, and the formal propitiation of animal spirits.[35] However, few references fully describe annual ritual cycles. Social gatherings provided a context for shamanistic performances in which the shaman (*angakuq*) was called upon to heal the sick, locate game, predict or change the weather, and ascertain metaphysical causes for any disaster confronting the community. Dances were held to greet visitors and to establish relationships between hosts and guests. Accompanied by the resounding pulse of the large skin-covered drum (almost a meter in diameter), a male or female dancer performed stylized movements of birds and animals, sang songs of hunting exploits and personal experiences, or lampooned themselves or a joking-partner.

Transformations in Artistic Expression

From the early twentieth century, and particularly following the Second World War, Arctic peoples have faced an increasingly cash-dependent economy with few employment opportunities for unilingual individuals. In this context, one cannot underestimate the economic importance of independent artmaking or community-based, often government-supported, art and craft programs. Yet it is only now that we are beginning to appreciate their cultural and historical importance. For example, small ivory carvings once produced for whalers, missionaries, and traders are often dismissed as 'souvenir art'. The ivory model of a bidarka (p.386), however, embodies significant historical and cultural information. The center hole carries a European-dressed figure

Above: *This Eskimo mask was probably carved at the request of a shaman who, during a trance or journey into the unknown, encountered supernatural beings and spirits. This particular mask, a tunghak, was believed to impersonate the spirit forces which had control over the supply of animals (note the carvings of species above his face).*

Below: *A carved model depicting an episode in the ancient Bladder Festival. The model was collected from the Eskimo of Nushagak and is made of walrus ivory, wood, sinew, gut, nails, and trade cloth. The winter festival lasted several days and was held to propitiate seals whose skin, meat, blubber, and other parts were essential to survival.*

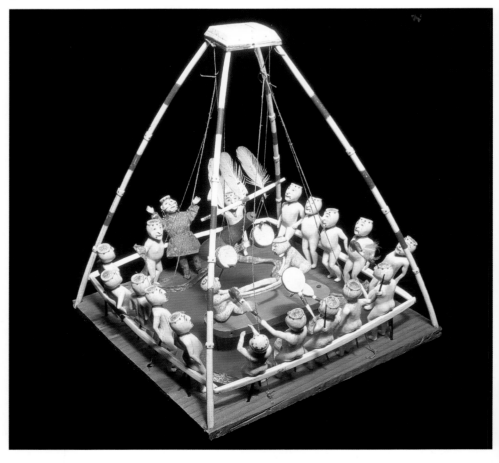

lighting his pipe while two Aleuts paddle. There is humor and irony in this depiction, particularly in a cultural setting that places a high value on self-sufficiency and deplores indolence and pretentious authority.

The work of contemporary sculptors, print-makers, and textile and graphic artists throughout Alaska, Arctic Canada, and Greenland comprises a valuable source of personal and collective history. Stone and wood carvings, works on paper, and textile art offer perceptive, first-hand insights into the social, spiritual, economic, and intellectual life of northern peoples.[36] Research among elders by native and non-native ethnographers affirms that the rich

mythological and cosmological traditions of Arctic societies remain a vital cultural force.[37] Furthermore, scholars point out that despite centuries of trade and culture contact, imported materials were often syncretically adopted, bringing about superficial rather than substantive changes in material culture.[38] Thus, as Aleutian, Yup'ik, and Inupiat-Inuit peoples seek to rediscover and reclaim cultural traditions as a vital source of knowledge, the testimony of elders, the witness of museum artifacts, and the creative work of contemporary artists all serve as essential resources in ensuring the continuing strength of indigenous Arctic cultures.

Above: *This modern fabric art from the Baker Lake region in the Canadian Arctic is called One Man's Dream and was made by Inuit Marion Tuu'Luuq. Made of felt, stroud, and cotton thread, the image illustrates a myth widely known in the Arctic region. It refers to a girl who takes a lover in a darkened igloo. To find out who he is, she marks his face with soot, only to discover it is her brother. In shame, she takes up a blazing torch and is carried up to the sky where she becomes the sun. Her brother pursues her but his torch grows faint and he becomes the moon. In myth and art, the Inuit associate the female with procreative power. Here, from the tattooed face of a woman, emanate ever-expanding circles of land and sea animals, birds, transformed beings, plant forms, and human life.*

References

1 Kay Hendrickson, Nunivak Island, as quoted in Morrow, 1984: 124.
2 For a full discussion of the prehistoric and historical development of Arctic cultures, see Damas (ed.), 1984.
3 Burch, 1984: 5.
4 Lantis, 1947; Lowenstein, 1993; Spencer, 1959: 332-53; Fitzhugh and Crowell, 1988.
5 Rasmussen, 1929; Fitzhugh and Kaplan, 1982; Fienup-Riordan, 1990: 167.
6 Meade, 1990: 230.
7 Driscoll, 1987: 176-87.
8 For a description of gutskin parkas and treatment, as well as examples of extant garments, see: Nelson (1983); Turner, 1976 (1894): 56-58; Moore, 1923; Jochelsòn, 1933; Collins, et al., 1973; Fitzhugh and Kaplan, 1982; Hickman, 1987; Bockstoce, 1977; Black and Liapunova in Fitzhugh and Crowell, 1988; Chaussonnet in Fitzhugh and Crowell, 1988.
9 Morrow, 1984: 125, 137.
10 Meade, 1990: 231.

11 Meade, 1990: 231-34.
12 Fitzhugh and Kaplan, 1982: 220; Nelson, 1899: 228-32.
13 Driscoll, 1987: 176-82.
14 See Stenton, 1991, for an excellent description of the hypothermal qualities of caribou clothing.
15 Driscoll, 1987.
16 Turner, 1976 (1884): 49.
17 Driscoll, 1980, 1987.
18 For artifact examples, see: Ray, 1977, 1981; Fitzhugh and Kaplan, 1982; Driscoll, 1987 (Vol. 2).
19 Driscoll, 1987: 193-99.
20 Aleutian women were especially known for their production of finely woven grass baskets, an area outside the scope of this chapter. See, for example, Ray, 1981; Black, 1982.
21 Fitzhugh and Kaplan, 1982: 56, 107.
22 Fienup-Riordan, 1994: 168.
23 Morrow, 1984: 124.
24 See Morrow quoted in Fienup-Riordan, 1990: 53; see also Fitzhugh and Kaplan, 1982: 166.

25 Ager, 1974; Fitzhugh and Kaplan, 1982:156-159
26 See also Laughlin, 1980; Fienup-Riordan, 1994.
27 See, especially, Black, 1991 for analysis of the symbolic implications of hunting hat decoration
28 Morrow, 1984 offers an excellent summary of Yup'ik ceremonialism based on research among elders collected by Elsie Mather, a native Yup'ik speaker.
29 Morrow, 1984:124
30 Morrow, 1984:123-127
31 Hawkes, 1914
32 Fitzhugh and Kaplan, 1982:202-205
33 Fienup-Riordan, 1990:49-67
34 Hawkes, 1914
35 Boas 1964:197
36 For a comprehensive discussion of the development of Inuit art in the Canadian Arctic, see Swinton, 1992; for an exceptional analysis of a specific theme in contemporary Canadian Inuit art, see Blodgett, 1979.
37 Morrow, 1984; Fienup-Riordan, 1990, 1994
38 Black, 1981

THE NORTHEAST

WITH THESE WORDS, this Mesquakie (Fox) artist establishes the essential significance that the arts and crafts of the Northeast Woodlands and Great Lakes region hold for these people. Not only do the words exemplify the Native understanding of the complementary halves of reality and spirituality, of the visible and the invisible, of the past and the present, but they also reflect the reality of two separate, yet strongly interactive worlds of Indians and Europeans. While we, as non-Natives, may see the visible part presented in the tangible forms of Native arts and crafts, much still remains hidden from view, evoking a desire to learn more. Wanatee's final words also attest to the role that tribal women held, and continue to hold, in the transference of cultural knowledge through material expression. These words also imply women's adaptability and innovative skills which incorporated trade goods and non-Native features into these works of art endowing them – whether for tribal use or as trade items – with a distinctively Native voice.

The Northeast Woodlands and Great Lakes area, extending from the shores of the Atlantic Ocean in the east to the western shores of the Great Lakes, was the first region to be exposed to continuous European contact. Beginning in the early 1500s, Basque fishermen were soon followed by traders, missionaries, French and British officials, and adventure-seekers. With them came trade goods to be exchanged; first for furs and then for exotic items. An historical overview of indigenous arts and crafts reflects the impact of this early interaction. The ability of the various groups to adapt Native materials and techniques to provide satisfactorily the exotic and the practical to fulfill European perceptions of esthetics and requirements, attests to the flexibility and fluidity of native culture and establishes an innate entrepreneurial spirit. At the same time, Native Americans continued to create material objects to fulfill their own needs, esthetic values, and religious expression. It was through this transformation of intangibles into dynamic and symbolic aspects of material culture that both individual tribes and broader culture areas established and maintained their identity.

Despite overlaps of art forms, techniques, and materials, there is often a distinctive art tradition that has become associated with a specific group and/or area. Differences can be attributed to divergent subsistence economies, access to materials restricted by environmental features, encroachment of Europeans onto Indian lands, and any number of social, economic, and political circumstances. Examples presented here

underscore several of these elements. Certainly economic necessity and a local non-Native market stimulated the expansion of the traditional woodsplint basketry craft among the Algonquian-speaking New England tribes on the southeastern Atlantic Coast. Farther up the Atlantic Coast, the Micmac (also Algonquian) shifted their porcupine quillwork techniques from decorating native birch bark objects to decorating forms more acceptable to European tastes. In the St. Lawrence Lowlands, Iroquois, Huron, and Abenaki,

Above: *Combining indigenous materials with those acquired through trade to create items for their own use and for the tourist market, echoes Native responses and interactions with the non-Native newcomers to the Northeast. The heavily beaded Chippewa (Ojibwa in Canada) bandoleer bag (background) colorfully illustrates the incorporation of European trade beads into a traditional Native art. The late nineteenth century Micmac moccasins (top), made expressly for the tourist trade, demonstrate the skilful amalgamation of local deerskin and porcupine quill decoration on a cloth-covered birch bark vamp with imported beads, silk ribbon, and silk lining.*

having been taught the fundamentals of true embroidery using indigenous materials by the French Ursuline nuns, refined this skill into the production of a made-for-trade commodity. To the south of the Great Lakes, the horticultural Iroquois carved wooden masks for performance in public and private tribal rituals. As the Chippewa moved westward into the northern Great Lakes area, they adapted quillwork techniques to create elaborate beadwork items. The tribes of the Great Lakes region, comprising both Algonquian and Siouan speakers, continued to twine fiber bags according to prehistoric traditions. Concurrently, these same groups adeptly transformed European trade textiles into a distinctly Native art form.

Thus each and every art and craft form voiced the Native esthetics, innovations, creativity, and complementary roles of men and women that constitute the essence of dynamic artistic expression.

Birch Bark Biting

Creating pictures on folded sheets of very thin layers of birch bark with the teeth was a ubiquitous art form throughout the entire region wherever the white birch tree (*Betula papyrifera*) grew. Historical accounts from the seventeenth, eighteenth, and nineteenth centuries establish the antiquity of this unusual craft and ethnographic accounts of the early twentieth century continue to record the practice.[2] More recently, recognition of birch bark dental pictographs as both an entirely Native and an endangered art form has prompted collectors and museum curators to acquire the work of the very few contemporary artists who possess the ability to create these bitten bark transparencies.

According to current knowledge, bark is collected in the spring when the sap first starts to run. Criteria for the selection of the perfect tree entail the color (which should be pure white), the correct age and size, freedom from imperfections and knots. From this

Below: *Using readily available products of their forest environment, Algonquians such as the Chippewa bit thin sheets of folded birch bark to create symmetrical designs. It became a magical moment bringing awe and delight to young and old as the bark was unfolded and held up so that the light would suffuse it with a golden glow and shine through the tiny perforations.*

living source the bark (the best is ten layers thick) is removed and is then painstakingly peeled into fine paper-like pieces, of which only half may be suitable. The sharpest pictures result by biting the prepared bark while it is still fresh. However, written accounts of frozen birch logs releasing tissue-thin layers of bark as they thawed by the fire and of warming pieces of bark from dried logs would have ensured a winter supply as well.[3]

Various folding procedures determine the configuration of the designs. Most of the bark is folded in half to make an oblong and in half again to form a square, and finally folded from corner to corner to form a triangle. Holding the folded bark with the fingers, the point is inserted into the mouth. Using the incisor and canine teeth to make impressions in the folded bark, the piece is moved about in the mouth with the help of fingers and tongue. After the biting is completed, the bark is unfolded to reveal an intricate symmetrical design formed in the translucent medium. A second method of folding begins with a rectangular piece folded in half lengthwise, the upper third folded down and then diagonally to form a triangle. Teeth impressions are made along the hypotenuse thus formed. The bottom third of the oblong is folded only once on an oblique angle. The result resembles similar patterns of flowers with leaves and stems worked on moccasin vamps. By leaving the bark unfolded and biting it according to the position of the artist's fingers, single realistic and/or asymmetrical figures can be produced. Those with expertize can, by regulating the force of the bite, produce a shaded effect. In a matter of minutes a pattern emerges that may be geometric, abstract, or representative of particular life forms, handsomely revealed when the pieces of bark are held up to sunlight or campfire light.

Several recorded accounts suggest that dental pictographs were made purely for pleasure.[4] Certainly as a diversion around the camp fire or stove, women and children (and occasionally men) derived great pleasure from this creative activity. By imitating their mothers, aunts, and grandmothers, children learned new skills and absorbed new ideas and cultural values. Although results varied in artistic quality depending on expertize, most if not all efforts were consumed by the fire. If, as some researchers have suggested, these bitten patterns were used as guides for making beadwork designs and scraped patterns on birch bark, a few would have been kept.[5]

Bitten bark designs constitute a truly ephemeral art, providing pleasure only for the moment. However, the implications that arise are significant. It has been considered by some to be the only example of 'art for art's sake' among Native North Americans.[6] As an art form, it demonstrates the multiplicity of designs possible, and lends itself to design experimentation. More importantly, it affords insights into the cognitive skills that utilize mental templates in the designing of an artifact. 'A woman never copied one pattern from another – it was original work, and a peculiarity was that **the pattern was clear in the mind of the worker before she made her first fold**. She said that she knew how the finished work would look before she began to

Above: *Some objects were unaffected by trade with non-Natives. This carved miniature Delaware mask, for example, was inspired by a dream.*

Below: *Carefully fashioned from birch bark with seams stitched together and covered with spruce gum, this small, watertight mokuk was commonly used by the Chippewa for collecting and storing maple syrup, wild rice, or berries. Only the bark stripped from the tree in the spring has the soft cambium inner layer which can be scraped away to reveal the whiter bark. Containers intended to be decorated have this brown layer on the outside. Although a bark template is often used to trace a pattern onto this soft surface, the geometric design seen here was created freehand. Once the design has been traced, either the background area or the design itself is scraped away to create a negative or positive design. As the cambium darkens over time the contrast increases.*

work...'[7] The 'portability' of such a capacity was of supreme value to earlier hunting and foraging groups who, out of necessity, carried their worldly goods with them. The capability to recreate objects using 'the mind's eye' diminished the burden of excess material culture.

In its own small way, this art form establishes Native creativity and innovation to set the stage for other forms of arts and crafts utilizing either indigenous or foreign materials for personal use or for exchange purposes.

Woodsplint Basketry

Prevalent throughout the Northeast Woodlands, it was among the New England tribes of the eastern Maritime regions that woodsplint basketry attained its greatest expression. First developed through an intimate knowledge of the woodland environment, basketry became an integral aspect of maize horticulture and the related preparation of maize foods. Baskets also served traditional needs as eel and fish traps, containers for berry picking, and for a multitude of uses as storage containers. Later, basketry skills provided necessary products for early European settlers and as such, continued as a source of subsistence income for the Indians. Within the Native community, basketry, as a means of communication, became a source for regional, ethnic, family, and individual identity.

The processes involved in creating a basket begin with the initial steps of preparing the flat sturdy strips of wood splints, usually undertaken by a man. Selection of the preferred black ash (*Fraximus nigra* Marsh.), or 'basket' tree growing in bogs and along streams is done in the spring when the sap is running. Tobacco offerings propitiate the spirit of this slow-growing hardwood as it stands straight, its trunk marred by few knots, before it is cut down. Once felled and the bark removed, the entire circumference of the log is pounded with overlapping strokes using a wooden maul. This releases anywhere from one to six annual growth layers, called grains, 6 to 10in (15 to25cm.) in width at one time.[8]

Below: *Pictured in 1900, Abenaki basket maker Caroline Masta is shown weaving fancy baskets with splints and sweetgrass sent to her by relatives in the Canadian province of Quebec. The products of her efforts were sold to tourists.*

This process is continued until the heartwood is reached. As black ash is a ring-porous hardwood, the cells laid down during the rapid growth period in the spring are coarser and less dense than those laid down during the summer. When the log is pounded, these coarser cells collapse, allowing the grains to separate easily.[9] The rough, grainy remains of the soft cellular tissue between each ring are scraped off to reveal smooth, light wood. These splints can be separated further into finer splints, and then divided into widths appropriate for the type and size of basket desired. Specialty but non-essential tools in the form of splitters, scrapers, basket gauges and forms introduced during the mid-nineteenth century, continued to ease the preparation process and establish uniformity in materials.

Prepared splints are then transformed into baskets of innumerable shapes, sizes, and purposes, decorated and plain. Primarily three weaving techniques were used: 'checker', in which the warp and weft have the same thickness and pliability and are woven one over, one under; 'twill', in which the warp and weft alternate at a ratio other than one to one, creating a diagonal pattern; and 'wicker', in which flexible, narrow splints are woven onto a wide and inflexible warp in a basic one over, one under pattern. Occasionally 'twining' is used in which two or more flexible wefts are twisted around individual warps.

The addition of color in various ways comprised early decorative applications. Splints could be completely permeated by dyes, swabbed on one side with color before weaving, block stamped with designs cut from potatoes, turnips, or wood, and dipped into pigment, or hand-painted with a brush or chewed twig on the finished basket. Textural patterns, generated by alternating scraped and unscraped splints – or those created by using narrow and wide wefts – were also intentional decorative devices. Greater texture and shadow were added when basket weavers began to incorporate secondary twisted or 'curlicue' wefts into their baskets. In this latter technique the outermost of a pair of wefts is twisted to form patterns of

loops or curls, commonly referred to as 'porcupine', 'shell', and 'diamond'.

Regional, cultural, individual, and blended styles can be distinguished through materials, techniques, form, decoration, and function during specific time periods. Regional styles are composites of ideas and techniques used by two or more contiguous groups living in an area. Cultural styles reveal the ethnic identity of specific groups. Imbedded within these styles are individual or family expressions recognized through certain features or innovations. An overlapping or combining of traits from two styles is called blended.

By way of illustration, baskets made by the Schaghticoke, Mahican, and Paugusett peoples of the southwestern New England region during the eighteenth and nineteenth centuries were woven with both wide and narrow wefts of black ash and decorated by swabbing and/or stamping. In contrast, during the same period, the baskets of the southeastern New England Mohegan, Pequot, Niantic, Nipmuck, and Wampanoag were constructed with wide wefts of white oak enhanced with elaborate painted designs. From the late nineteenth century onward, both regions began to produce virtually identical undecorated narrow-weft splint baskets.

Cultural styles such as those evident in the painted designs of the Mohegan also reveal temporal changes reflecting native reactions to changing political and social environments. During the period of forced removal from their lands, basket decoration acknowledged their resistance by enclosing a traditional four-domed medallion or rosette symbolizing the Mohegan people inside a boundary or enclosure. Outside the ancestral lands, Mohegans were often represented as a strawberry or a flower. Thus, through continued use of symbols on their basketry, Mohegans maintained their sense of ethnic identity and documented their grief.

Individuals and families of basket makers gained recognition with the intensification of their skills in response to an increasing tourist market. As specialty tools (gauges, splitters, and blocks) became commonplace, weavers transformed the exceedingly fine narrow splints into elaborate, Victorian-inspired styles, eagerly purchased as souvenirs. With the development of summer tourist resorts certain individuals or families retained rights to these areas to sell their winter's production.[10] Elaboration was expressed in both the form of the baskets, encompassing everything from novelty items to fancy household items to serviceable shopping bags, and in the decorative elements of ingeniously twisted and curled splint. Children learned the craft through observation, producing small rimless baskets and they developed their marketing skills by selling these for five cents during the early twentieth century.

Micmac Quillwork

Unique to the Micmac of the Atlantic Provinces is the decorative insertion of dyed porcupine quills into birch bark found primarily on covered boxes. The fairly complete chronological sequence for this quillwork affords insights into the development of forms, styles, decorative

Above: *Fanciful shapes and new decorative techniques illustrated by this Central Algonquian splint basket (top right) were developed to meet the increasing Victorian tourist market. By way of contrast, the tiny covered trinket basket (above), with its narrow weft and simple decorative elements, remained a favorite tourist item long after the more elaborate styles lost favor. This piece is probably Abenaki made.*

Right: *The oversized ring handles on this undecorated Penobscot basket woven with narrow splints suggest that its intended purpose was more ornamental than practical.*

techniques, motifs, and functions. While early historic documentation establishes that the Micmac used five different techniques of quillwork, by the beginning of the seventeenth century all but insertion appears to have fallen from use.[11] It was this fast and easy technique that became the basis for the Native entrepreneurial spirit. The Micmac response to the eighteenth-century European desire for souvenirs and curiosities was to continue to use Native materials in the production and decoration of European forms. By 1750 a distinctive Micmac style was already evident in the round and rectangular lidded containers completely covered with dyed quills. As the Victorian mania for tourist items took hold over the following century, the repertoire of forms expanded to include such novelty items as tea cosies, lamp shades, fire screens, fans, cigar cases, purses, and chair seats.

Materials were birch bark, porcupine quills, spruce roots, and the occasional use of thin wooden box liners. The bark of *B. papyrifera* or white birch was harvested by the men from the living tree during the latter days of July when the bark is pliable.[12] Porcupine quills, actually modified hairs with tiny barbs on the points, are plucked from the dead animal's back by the women, separated from the other hair, and sorted according to size.[13] Coarser tail quills were also used for specific finishing details. Prior to the 1860s, quills were dyed predominantly red, yellow, black, or white (the natural quill color) from vegetal sources. Additional sources provided blue and violet. After that time, inorganic aniline dyes from trade sources expanded the color palette but increased the susceptibility to color fading. From the black spruce (*Picea mariana*) came long, slender roots split lengthwise into fibers for sewing birch bark and for decorative applications. The colors of dyed spruce roots faded rapidly, producing a more or less uniform soft brown tone. In the production of quilled boxes and purses, the softwood of pine, spruce, or cedar was used for bases, pegs, linings, handles, and hoops. The addition of sweetgrass (*Hierochloe odorata*) as a finishing edging imparted a sweet, long-lasting fragrance.

Round and oval-lidded boxes, the most frequently encountered forms, are also the simplest to construct. A piece of birch bark cut to shape is rolled into a cylinder, the ends held together with quills. Once quilled, this cylinder is stitched with spruce root to a bark base or pegged to a wooden base. Into this is inserted a bark liner (or for rectangular boxes, a thin wooden liner) extending above the box height equal to the depth of the box lid. The sides of the lid were then flush with those of the box. The lid itself was composed of a top of quilled bark sewn to a root-wrapped or quillworked bark ring side. For some boxes the bark liner served as the foundation over which root-wrapped rings were built up to form the exterior.

The insertion of the dyed quills into the birch bark to produce the typically vibrant mosaic patterns entailed a number of steps. Both bark and quills were worked while slightly damp, the bark being dipped into warm water before beginning and the quills moistened as needed. A tiny insertion hole was made from the outer side of the bark with a beaver incisor or bone awl (and more recently with a darning needle). Once the quill was inserted into the hole, the bark contracted as it dried, holding the quill tightly in place. The process was repeated for either end of each quill until the desired area was covered with closely inserted parallel rows. On the underside the barbed ends of the quills were burnt and all remaining ends were cut flush with the surface.[14]

Further steps in the design process built upon the basic principles of running quills all one way within a single color area and by contrasting colors or design areas by placing quills at angles to other sections. The break created by these placements was filled in first with a single quill-width, then two, and eventually this 'fill' developed into a complete design element such as that used to divide a pattern into four quarters. Also possibly introduced during the nineteenth century are designs of flattened quills overlaid on solidly quilled areas. Readily recognizable is the lattice-like design first used as an overlay, but which evolved into being used alone on bare bark. Checkered patterns on root-wrapped rings were obtained by weaving natural

Below: *Superbly crafted, this cylindrical birch bark-lidded container is decorated with undyed porcupine quills. A bundle of sweetgrass stitched to the bottom rim adds a pleasant fragrance. The form and quillwork suggest that it is a Chippewa item made for sale at Niagara Falls or some other tourist attraction.*

Above: *The form and application of dyed porcupine quill on this rectangular birch bark box have been borrowed from the Micmac. A turn of the century tourist piece, the use of indigenous materials enhanced with brightly colored quillwork in a 'portable' size made this an appealing souvenir from the Northeast Woodlands.*

colored quills into the vertical warp of the roots. Border edges were often finished with lengths of flattened tail quills or bundles of sweetgrass with fine spruce root.

Similar to other groups, early Micmac dream-inspired designs rendered tangibly on material items provided protection, healing, and power. The symbolic meaning of these designs has become lost over the years and all of the traditional names forgotten, except for an eight-pointed star called *gogwit* or *kagwet* (Eight-Legged Starfish) and a fan-shaped motif called *waegardisk* (Northern Lights). The earliest dated design of 1760 has a double two-dimensional arch or rainbow which by the twentieth century had degenerated into a token arched line incorporated into a central design element. Often found in combination with this double rainbow is a stepped design. The most common motif is the chevron (and the variant, half chevron) traditionally found on the sides of lids and boxes.[15] Over time the visual dominance of the chevron pattern gave way to zig-zag lines created visually through the use of color. The chevron also occurs in a half form as well as integrated with diamonds and triangles. Circles, crosses, stars, double curves, squares, 'fylfot', and several realistic forms comprise the majority of the design elements.[16] With the introduction of aniline dyes, the intricacy of earlier designs was replaced with stronger ones placed on a white background to accentuate the brilliant colors.

Although virtually all the quillwork produced over the centuries was for trade, this art form is so strongly identified with the Micmac nation that they themselves have come to regard it as a traditional form.[17]

Moosehair Embroidery

The use of animal hair – moose, caribou, and reindeer – as a widespread medium of artistic expression among northern aboriginal groups became the medium of instruction used by the Ursuline nuns to demonstrate French embroidery techniques to young Native girls. By the early 1700s in the St. Lawrence River Lowlands, Iroquoian (most notably the Huron) and Algonquian artists had become adept at creating exquisite floral designs and pictorial depictions of Native life. These moosehair masterpieces, embroidered on to black tanned hide,[18] trade cloth, and birch bark, formed the basis of a strong commercial venture.[19]

Moosehair, the primary decorative material, was procured from the winter pelage of the moose (*Alces alces*). Fine white hairs, 4 to 5in (10 to 13cm.) in length, with long tapering black tips, removed from the dead animal's cheeks, mane, rump, and 'bell' were washed and then dyed. Initially, the dyeing process involved steeping the hair in hot vegetal infusions to acquire various shades of red, blue, and yellow to be used in combination with the natural white ones. These indigenous organic ones were quickly replaced when the introduction of aniline dyes offered an easier process and a wider selection of colors. Tied into bundles for storing, dyed hairs merely required moistening in the mouth to be ready for use.

Three precontact techniques of line-work (spot stitching or appliqueing bundles of the moosehair into straight, curved, or zig-zag lines on to a background), loom weaving, and false embroidery were supplemented by the European introduction of true embroidery which relied upon steel needles threaded with a filament (in this case, moosehair). The continued use of line-work can be recognized by the distinctive bead-like effect created by the slight twisting of the hair bundle just before the couching thread is pulled tight. However, with the new technique of needle

embroidery, depth, shading, and further three-dimensional texture were achieved through color variation and various embroidery stitches. Simple patterns soon became elaborated into complex designs and earlier non-representational motifs became dominated by floral ones.

By the beginning of the nineteenth century, Huron floral-decorated items epitomized the height of this expression. Rich colors and intricate designs, accentuated by their background of black tanned hide, were rendered on mittens, moccasins, pouches, and leggings. Cloth panels enhanced with floral designs were sewn to collars, cuffs, epaulettes, lapels, and borders of hide and cloth coats. Similar decorations appeared on 'pockets' formed from the lower legs of moose and caribou, knife sheaths, belts, garters, and bandoleers. Although long considered as items made solely for the tourist market, their native forms suggest probable indigenous functions as well.

A second genre, well-developed by the first half of the nineteenth century, was moosehair embroidery on birch bark items. This souvenir work was either entirely floral in design or depicted narrative vignettes of native life enhanced with flowers and trees. Traditionally-garbed Indians were embroidered in romanticized settings in canoes, in front of wigwams, smoking peace pipes, hunting in the forest, juxtaposed with larger-than-life flowers and berries – all designed to appeal to the then current European notion of the Noble Savage. Imbedded within these images, however, are invaluable iconographic details of Native ideals concerning the environment, establishing individual and group identity through clothing, and such symbolic referents as strawberries with their association of an idyllic afterworld. Decorated with either flowers or pictorials, the forms of this second genre are non-traditional containers, boxes, whimsies, cigar cases, bases for women's reticules, and so on, designed specifically for trade and as gifts for foreign dignitaries.

Iroquoian Masks

Two types of Iroquoian masks – classified according to materials used – are carved wooden ones associated with the False Face Society, and those woven of cornhusks for the Husk Face or Bushy-heads' Society. Individually each form reflects one half of the complementary features that comprise the synergistic whole of Iroquoian culture. False Faces are carved by men from the material of the forest domain, while Husk Faces are woven by women from products of their horticultural endeavors. Together, the False Face and Husk Face Societies, men and women, hunting and horticultural, function to ensure the health and well-being of the society.

Origins of the False Face masks arose as a result of a mythic contest between the Great Creator and the First Hodo'win, the most powerful of the forest faces.[20] To test the strength of their powers they each attempted to summon a mountain to them; success would acknowledge supremacy. The first to try, Hodo'win achieved only partial success. So anxious was he to see what the Creator was achieving, Hodo'win turned sharply, striking his face on the mountain which had appeared directly behind him. The impact broke his nose; his mouth twisted from the pain. The successful Creator, recognizing the strength of the loser, entrusted him to assist humans to combat illness and other evil influences. Henceforth, as the Great Doctor, it became Hodo'win's responsibility to instruct men in the art of carving masks and in the ceremonies in which they were to be used.

As a mask was carved from a living tree to acquire the earth power and sky power imbued within this cosmic axis, this necessitated ritual preparation of both carver and tree. In order to retain the potency and spirit of the basswood or other softwood tree, three days were spent ceremonially feeding tobacco (Nicotiana rustica) and tobacco smoke to the Tree Spirit and entreating forgiveness for the impending injury. Appeased, the Tree Spirit requested that its life spirit be continued in the mask to be carved and hewn from its trunk.

Before the introduction of steel tools, woodworking was accomplished by burning the area and scraping away the charred wood. With steel tools, carving was performed directly on the wood. Once the bark was removed, the face was roughed out, and only when the carving was nearly completed was the mask released from the tree. The finished mask was smoothed inside and out, metal eye rings were attached, the face was painted, and long hair inserted into holes. If the carving of the mask was begun in the morning, it was painted red; black was indicative of an afternoon start. These colors represented the belief that the daily journey of the first False Face followed the sun; therefore his face appeared red in the morning as he came from the east, and black in the evening as he looked back from the west. A mask painted half-red and half-black represented a divided being – half-human, half-supernatural – whose body was split in two and who stood facing south, his red cheek to the east, black one to the west.

The features of masks vary according to their intended function, dream visions experienced by the carvers, and local styles. Generally, the masks possess deep-set eyes accentuated with metal 'whites', large noses bent in imitation of the Great Doctor's, and often a deeply creased forehead. The mouth is the most variable feature, leading to contemporary classifications based solely on this feature.[21] The twisted mouth of the Great Doctor is replaced alternatively with a smile, a grimace with teeth showing, a pucker as if whistling, a pucker with spoon-like lips, or with lips distended to blow ashes. A number display protruding tongues.[22]

Sanctification of completed masks consisted of a number of steps. A tiny bag filled with tobacco was attached to the forehead of the mask; its face rubbed with sunflower oil to feed it; and then it was placed near the fire and tobacco was thrown into the fire. As the mask became suffused by wood and tobacco smoke, the carver told the mask what it was supposed to do.[23] The mask was then ready to perform in curing rituals. Periodic feeding of sunflower oil and tobacco continued to maintain the strength of the mask as long as it was used. Boys learned to carve by first making small masks.

Visually and tactilely pleasing, the significance of the masks rests, however, in their power, which is especially efficacious in healing rites. The best-known, although not the most important, curing rituals were performed by the False Face Society. When a person fell ill, the members of the Society would don their masks and creep toward the sick person's home. There they scraped their snapping turtle rattles against the wooden door frame before entering the house, shaking the rattles all the while.[24] Using sacred ashes and tobacco in specific rites, the masked healers effected a cure. Once cured, the patient became a member of the Society along with anyone who had an appropriate visionary dream. Although most curing sessions were held privately, the False Faces also performed curing rituals during the public Midwinter Festival.

Below: Collected during the 1830s by artist-traveler George Catlin, this marvelous hide garment exhibits period Indian iconography and decorative techniques. In addition to the painted border motifs and the woven quillwork on the top of the sleeve, a band of pony beads on front and back utilizes trade goods.

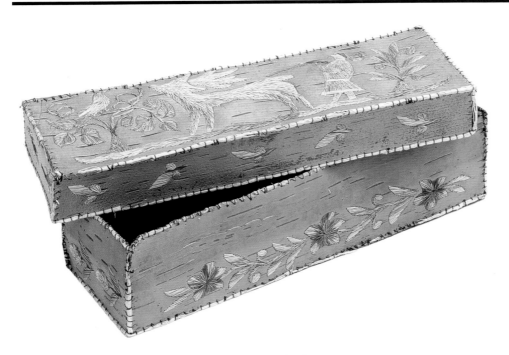

Above: *During the nineteenth century, Micmac and Huron Indians produced quantities of moosehair embroidered birch bark objects such as this rectangular box. The iconography of these items addressed two audiences simultaneously. For the European collectors, the depictions of natives in traditional clothing performing stereotypical ways in an Eden-like setting was romantic and exotic. To the Native viewers the use of a conceptual scale reducing the size of humans and enlarging the flora and fauna signified the importance of the spiritual powers inherent in the natural world.*

The Society of Husk Faces or Bushy-heads are earthbound spirits, who in their capacity as messengers of the Three Sisters – corn, beans, and squash – taught agricultural practices to humans. Although not as integrated or prominent as their counterparts, the False Faces, they shared certain functions. Under a condition of remaining mute, members of this group, nevertheless, possessed their own tobacco invocation, a medicine song, and the power to cure by blowing ashes. Wearing cornhusk masks, they appeared at the Midwinter Festival to dance with the people and beg for food.

The fabrication of these masks by the women is based on an ancient craft technique wherein cornhusks are shredded and braided. Two different methods are used to give them the desired shape: sewing of coiled husk braids, and twining. In the first, long strips of cornhusk braid are sewn into three coils to form the eyes and mouth, and the nose, which is often a sheathed corncob, is attached; after this the the fringe is then added.

Twined masks were begun at the nose with eight warps which were later extended by twisting on new elements. A pair of wefts was twisted around each warp until the rim was reached.

At first sight there appears to be little variety in these faces, which are always surrounded by husk streamers, but closer inspection reveals a high level of individuality. Paint was only occasionally applied to these masks.[25]

Beadwork

A kaleidoscope of colors and patterns dominates Chippewa (Ojibwa) beadwork. With the introduction of glass trade beads early in the seventeenth century, techniques already in use for porcupine quillwork were easily adapted to accommodate this exciting new medium of artistic expression. First 'pony' beads and later tiny 'seed' beads, pinpoints of light and color, readily lent themselves to the complex forms of woven and appliqued beadwork. Through the subtle blending of vividly-colored transparent, translucent and opaque, round or faceted seed beads, artistic masterpieces emerged. For more than two centuries beadwork was a major artistic focus for the Chippewa, and continues to gain them as much recognition from within their own culture area as it does from non-Native audiences.

Loom-weaving produced beadwork in which the fibers carrying the beads are also the sole foundation of the finished item. The earliest loom was the bow loom, a flexible stick with birch bark or hide heddles to hold and separate the sinew warps fastened at each end. Exchanging beads for porcupine quill, women wove beaded bands suitable for garters, belts, headbands, and decorative strips to be sewn on to articles of clothing. Limitations in length and width of finished pieces led to the development of the simple rectangular box loom, devised of four pieces of wood fastened together at the corners. On this loom one continuous warp thread is strung evenly-spaced around the frame, including one warp row more than the number of beads required for the width of the pattern. To weave the beads on either loom requires a long, fine beading needle, threaded and with one end tied to an outside warp. The appropriate number of beads for one width are strung onto this weft thread.

First the threaded and bead-strung needle is passed under the warp to the opposite side. Holding the thread tight, each of the beads is pushed up between a pair of the warp threads all the way across so that the holes in them are above the level of the warp threads. The threaded needle is then passed back through all the beads while they are in this position, thus weaving the first row. All subsequent rows follow this procedure. Loose ends are woven back into the beadwork to produce a stronger foundation. Sometimes the warp threads are braided or woven into fringes. The introduction of the box loom expanded the earlier repertoire of beadwork with longer and wider forms. Wider pieces were sewn whole on to bandoleer bags and smaller pouches. Understandably, this technique of square weaving dominates design, creating motifs and patterns which are basically geometric. Even floral motifs are reduced to the artificial 'curves' of tiny square steps.[26]

Appliqued beadwork involves the stitching of beads to another material such as hide or cloth which serves as the foundation. Basically, a line of sinew-threaded beads is sewn to the foundation by means of a second thread tacking (spot stitching or couching) the first one after every two or three beads. In contrast to woven beadwork, this beadwork application permits the design to dominate the technique. As a result, a wide range of decorative possibilities abound: curves pose no problem; both outline patterns and solid areas are beaded with equal ease; and colors can be changed at will. Great examples appear on clothing, ceremonial items, cradle boards, and bags.

Below: *This Upper Cayuga version of Hadu'i was carved in 1943. Worn by shamans and dancers in ways that were revealed to them in dreams, it personified the essence of the spiritual being.*

Both types of beadwork appear together on bandoleer bags, 'the apex of the beadworker's art'.[27] A shoulder strap or 'baldric' of woven or appliqued beadwork was attached to a rectangular pouch of heavy floral applique work and to the bottom of this was stitched either a fringe or a wide loom-woven panel. Asymmetrical patterns on the strap with motifs and configurations changing at mid-point in the length, serve as an identifying feature. These ornate bags, worn cross-wise over each shoulder in ceremonies and dances, once served as fire bags carrying smoking pipes and tobacco. As their significance and popularity increased, esthetic properties supplanted practical ones and the bags were made without true pouches. Ultimately they became a symbol of wealth with an individual wearing anywhere from the usual one or two to as many as twelve or more. Sometimes referred to as 'Friendship Bags', bandoleer bags were presentation gifts at tribal and inter-tribal gatherings, enhancing the prestige of artist, donor, and recipient alike.

Twined Fiber Bags

All the Great Lakes and Northeast Woodlands tribes were proficient at twining fiber bags for their own use. Regional evidence dating from at least AD 300 establishes this craft's relationship to widespread ancient finger-weaving techniques which no machine can duplicate.[28] It is the people of the Great Lakes area – Fox, Sauk, Menominee, Winnebago, Potawatomi, Ottawa – whose inventory of materials and finger-weaving techniques showed the greatest variety. Decoration, somewhat limited by the twining technique, was restricted to patterns formed through the use of contrasting color fibers and complex methods of twining. Stripes, geometric shapes, and stylized birds, felines, deers, and humans constituted the basis of the imagery. While coarser utilitarian bags that functioned as harvesting and storage containers were sometimes decorated with colored patterns, it is the smaller, softer bags that have received greater attention.[29]

These softer bags were made of fine *Apocynum* fibers.[30] The stalks of this plant were first soaked in stagnant water until the fleshy parts could be beaten off, leaving fibers 3 to 4ft (1 to 1.3m.) in length. Rolling these fibers into an S twist on the knee yielded strands that were then twisted together to produce the two-ply cords preferred for weaving. Dark brown buffalo wool was sometimes used for natural color contrast. As trade with the Europeans increased, these native fibers were replaced with colored yarns.

To twine the bags, prepared warp elements are hung over a stick suspended horizontally. Beginning closest to the stick, two weft cords are passed one in front of a warp element and one behind it and then twined (twisted) at each crossing. This procedure is continued from left to right in a continuous spiral around the loose-hanging warps. Weaving is discontinued 4 or 5in (10 or 13cm.) from the ends of the warp elements. These ends are braided horizontally to form the opening of the bag. By removing the stick from between the warps, a seamless bag results.

Decorative elements are created by setting up double warps of light and dark contrasting colors. Whichever of these two warp colors is pulled forward during the weaving process is the one that appears at that point on the

Above: *A Chippewa version of a colorful, loom-woven beaded bag. Of particular interest are the two distinct patterns used for each half of the strap.*

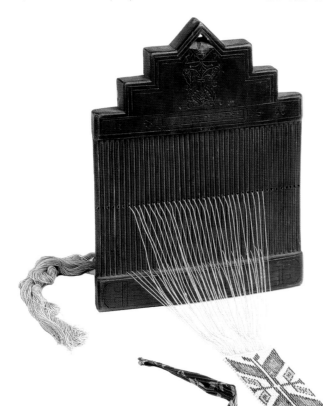

Left: *The Fox (Mesquakie) bead loom illustrated here is an artwork in itself. Carved in the late-1800s from hardwood and incised with designs on both faces, its technology is more sophisticated than the smaller looms normally used for beading straps. In this example, half the warp threads passing through perforations in the middle of the heddle are held firm while the other half passing between the heddles are free to move up and down. The sheds thus created allow the warp to be interwoven so that the pattern appears the same on both sides.*

Above: *Floral beaded moccasins with silk ribbon appliqued ankle flaps are most often associated with the tribes of the Great Lakes region. This pair was collected at Niagara Falls in the mid-nineteenth century. Note the different colored pattern of silk on either flap.*

surface of the bag. Due to the limitations of the twining technique, motifs tend to be angular, with representational figures rendered in a stylized manner.

The imagery on a number of bags reflects the cosmology of the Great Lakes area. Birds and felines appearing on opposite sides of these bags are interpreted, respectively, as depictions of the mythical Thunderbird and the Underwater Panther. The Thunderbird is most often depicted as two triangles joined to form a stylized hourglass shape to which down-thrust wings are attached. In some

Below: *This flat bag is an early example of a twined bag utilizing fine strips of lindenwood (basswood) bast and was acquired from the Fox (Mesquakie) Indians in Iowa. The body of the bag, decorated with simple stripes of natural and black, is finished with false braid on the margin of the opening. The attached strap and tassel are also made from bast.*

versions the hourglass is filled with concentric triangles, chevrons, or diamonds. A central diamond on the torso indicates the heart. Often associated with a large central Thunderbird figure are smaller thunderbirds and recurrent geometric patterns in the form of parallel zig-zag lines representing lightning or thunderbolts. On the other side of the bag the Underwater Panther (or group of Panthers), as the key figure, is depicted with horns, ribs, dorsal scales, and an exceedingly long tail coiled around the cat-like body. Associated with this figure are elongated hexagonal forms identified as representing sacrifices of food in bark dishes as well as zig-zag, wavy, or castellated lines interpreted as wavy or roiled water.[31] These associated geometric designs become significant in the absence of life figures on some bags; for wherever these non-representational geometric designs are present, they can be construed as symbolic of manitous.

Both the Thunderbird and the Underwater Panther were extremely powerful manitous who, respectively, controlled the Sky World and the Under World. The power of each was manifested in both beneficent and malevolent aspects with the Thunderbird

responsible for rain and victory in war but who also caused devastating storms. Balancing the Underwater Panther's malevolent forces that roiled the waters and drowned the unwary were its curative powers that could heal and prolong life. Mythic accounts place them as opponents in a continuing battle. Conflicts of power and strength between these two opposing manitous are mediated by elements of the Earth zone represented by the vegetal and animal fibers of the bag. By this means a balanced tri-partite cosmos is rendered tangible in these fiber bags.

Twined bags functioned within the societies as containers for individual personal medicines or as components of larger medicine bundles. Intriguing are those bags that were 'rigged with internal mechanical devices and used by medicine men to perform spectacular tricks in public performances, such as the appearance or disappearance of seemingly live but actually wooden snakes or puppets'.[32] Only after their power was no longer efficacious were these personally significant Native-made bags of indigenous materials acquired by non-Natives.

Ribbonwork

Ribbonwork is the art of cutting and sewing brightly colored silk ribbon to trade cloth for decorative purposes on clothing and other paraphernalia. The technique, first developed in the early eighteenth century, initially had a wide distribution throughout the entire cultural region. However, it is among the Great Lakes tribes that it reached its apogee and continues there today as an important art form. While the development of this art form was entirely dependent upon the introduction of trade goods – cloth, ribbon,

Below: *Collected from the Menominee of Wisconsin in 1908, this small bag is twined from yarns dyed with bloodroot and other plants. Once used by a medicine woman to hold herbs gathered for healing, the alternating colored stripes and the herringbone pattern of the bag itself create a dynamic sense of an inherent energy that complements the potential medicinal power of its herbal contents.*

thread, scissors or knives, and needles – the origins, forms, motifs, color selection, and intended use, are totally Indian.

Silk ribbons, first presented as gifts to the Indians, continued to be available through trade. Early ribbons were narrow, often only one-half to one-and one-half inches in width. Later ones reached widths of 3 and 4in (up to 10cm.). Woolen trade cloth, providing backgrounds of black, dark blue, or red, was fashioned into women's blankets (shawls) and skirts, men's shirts, leggings, moccasins, and other miscellaneous items.

In its simplest form, the ribbonwork technique consists of cutting a design into a silk ribbon of one color, hand sewing it on to a background panel of another color, and then stitching the panel to the fabric of the garment. Mirror images, repetition, and asymmetrical designs are typical. Positive and negative styles are identified by pairs of ribbons sewn to produce a bilaterally symmetrical four-ribbon strip. The distinguishing feature is determined by the layer in which the figure is created. Positive style is identified by the cut and sewn top layer which is perceived to be the design. Negative style is created when the top parts of the ribbon are cut away to reveal the bilaterally symmetrical figure on the bottom layer of ribbons.[33] Around 1850 these basic styles became elaborated with design units larger, more varied, and more complicated in shape and incorporating several layers of various colored ribbons. Simple geometric designs in earlier work were later augmented with intricate curvilinear ones. Patterns to create these designs were cut from birch bark or paper, and a collection of these became a woman's most treasured personal possession.[34]

Preference in ribbon colors was given to those with symbolic meaning in addition to their esthetic value. For the Menominee, colors from the realm of Sky Woman were associated with the cardinal points: red for east; white and yellow for south; blue for west; and black for north.[35] For Mesquakie Ada Old Bear, red signified the Fox clan and black was associated with spiritual enlightenment and prayer.[36] Color selection performs as an integral aspect of the interplay between foreground and background, between dark and light, and between pattern form and color. This interplay and the tensions of mirror images and pattern reversals creates a dynamic vitality, the carefully balanced designs changing as the perspectives of the viewer shift. Creativity, innovation, and a common regional esthetic of these Native artists is superbly demonstrated through this manipulation of non-Native textiles.

It is fitting that many contemporary examples of ribbonwork shirts and skirts are made especially to accompany the dead,[17] for in this way the metaphor of duality, of a whole being split – half in this world, half in the spirit world – is brought to life as the corporeal body transforms into the spiritual one, as the past world becomes the new world.

Below: *The richness of color captured in silk became the artistic palette of the Great Lakes Indians. Cutting and stitching this trade material into geometric and curvilinear designs to create vibrant mirror image or appliqued work is illustrated here by the woman's shawl from Minnesota. This combination of Native artistry and European materials reflects reconciliation of the Native's split social world.*

References

1 Torrence and Hobbs, 1989: 19.
2 In the fall of 1687, Jesuit Father Beschefer sent 'Pieces of bark, on which figures have been marked by the teeth' to France (Thwaites 1959: 287).
3 For example, Friedl, 1944: 150.
4 See Speck 1937: 74-80. He also suggests that these dental pictographs might have been a source for what he calls 'phytomorphic' (literally, plant forms) art decorations (Speck, 1937: 77-78).
5 Davidson, 1928, Moody, 1957, Speck, 1937, and innumerable others have suggested this and yet there is no concrete evidence.
6 For instance, William H. Holmes as cited by Densmore 1941: 679.
7 Densmore, 1941: 679 (emphasis added). A number of other sources reinforce this ability.
8 Bardwell, 1986: 54.
9 Wetherbee, 1980: 197.
10 Speck (1947: 22) lists several individuals and their rights to specific resorts in New England. Mason (1904: Plate 120) provides a photograph of Caroline Masta, an Abenaki who made baskets at Belmar, New Jersey from splints and sweet grass supplied by her family in Quebec (Canada). These she sold at Asbury Park and Boardwalk in New Jersey (Pelletier, 1982: 6).
11 R. H. Whitehead (1982) provides the definitive study and analysis of Micmac quillwork from the historical evidence to the current situation.
12 If the bark is removed properly at the correct time, the tree is not killed.
13 When possible, the quills were taken during the

spring before they became filled with an oily fluid as the summer progressed.
14 The burning of the barbed end turns the quill into ash, effectively removing it from being caught on the hands or bare feet (Whitehead, 1982: 100n3).
15 Whitehead suggests that this might have been considered a conventionalized representation of a fir tree (1982: 146n304).
16 Whitehead (1982: 193) uses this term to distinguish the motif from the right-angled swastika. However, linguist Peter Bakker (1991: 21), recognizing the motif as identical to the Basque national symbol, calls it by the Basque term *lauburu*.
17 It is important to note here that Ursuline nuns located in Quebec convents are known to have produced similar quillwork from circa 1773 until the 1830s. Poor quality and differences in motifs serve to differentiate these from the work of the Micmac.
18 Once a hide had been scraped, it was soaked overnight in a solution of butternut shells or alder bark before tanning. Although there are some indications that this was done for 'special' garments, it was most assuredly an esthetic intent.
19 Native people first taught the nuns how to work in birch bark and moosehair. However, not only did the nuns utilize these materials to provide instruction in European methods of embroidery, they also commercially exploited this bark and moosehair art form by producing and selling similar wares themselves for a brief period of time (Phillips, 1991: 22).

20 Forest Faces were mythological semi-human beings appearing as disembodied heads with long, snapping hair who darted from tree to tree in the forest. They are constantly hungry for tobacco.
21 Fenton (1987) has suggested a classification scheme which not all Iroquoianists accept.
22 Another set of wooden masks represents a variety of forms from pigs to clowns and for specialized societies.
23 Fenton, 1987: 177-78.
24 This replicates the action of the Great Doctor who scraped his rattle on the cosmic (World) tree to absorb its strength.
25 Fenton, 1987: 54-59.
26 Bowdoin Gil, 1977: 50.
27 Pohrt, 1990: 25.
28 Whiteford, 1977: 52.
29 See for example, Feest 1984; Phillips 1989; Whiteford 1977; Wilson 1982.
30 One species used is the Spreading Dogbane (A. *androsaemi folium*) and the other, Indian Hemp (A. *cannibinum*).
31 Skinner, 1921: 260n3.
32 Feest, 1984: 15.
33 Abbass, 1986
34 Hartman, 1988: 41; Torrence and Hobbs, 1989: 18.
35 Skinner, 1921.
36 Torrence and Hobbs, 1989: 19.
37 Torrence and Hobbs, 1989: 49.

BIBLIOGRAPHY

THE AMERICAN INDIAN PEOPLE

Introduction

Fagan, B. M. 1987. *The Great Journey: The Peopling of Ancient America*. London: Thames and Hudson.

MacNeish, R. F. 1986. The Preceramic of Middle America. *Advances in World Archaeology*, vol.5, 93-130.

Martin, P. S. 1973. The Discovery of America. *Science*, vol.179, 969-74.

Martin, P. S. and R. Klein 1974. *A Pleistocene Revolution*. Tucson: University of Arizona Press.

Turner, C. 1984. Advances in the Dental Search for Native American Origins. *Acta Anthropogenetica*, vol.8 (1&2), 23-78.

Williams, R. C. et al 1985. Gm allotypes in Native Americans: Evidence for Three Distinct Migrations Across the Bering Land Bridge. *American Journal of Physical Anthropology*, vol.66, 1-19.

The Southeast

Note: This short list is intended to guide the reader to four invaluable sources of information on southeastern Indians.

Fagan, Brian M. 1991. *Ancient North America: The Archeology of a Continent*. New York: Thames and Hudson.

Hudson, Charles 1976. *The Southeastern Indians*. Knoxville: University of Tennessee Press.

Smith, Marvin T. 1987. *Archeology of Aboriginal Culture Change in the Interior Southeast: Depopulation during the Early Historic Period*. (Ripley P. Bullen Monographs in Anthropology and History Number 6.) Gainesville: University Presses of Florida.

Swanton, John R. 1946. *The Indians of the Southeastern United States*. *Bureau of American Ethnology Bulletin 137*, Smithsonian Institution. Washington, D.C.: U.S. Government Printing Office. [Reprinted 1979 by Smithsonian Institution Press.]

The Southwest

Bahti, Tom 1968. *Southwestern Indian Tribes*. Flagstaff: KC Publication.

Baldwin, Gordon 1965. *The Warrior Apaches*. Globe: Dale Stewart King.

Ball, Eve 1970. *In the Days of Victorio*. Tucson: University of Arizona Press.

Bunzel, Ruth 1932. Introduction to Zuni Ceremonialism, Zuni Kachinas, Zuni Ritual Poetry, Zuni Prayers. *47th Annual Report of the Bureau of American Ethnology*. Washington D.C.: Government Printing Office.

Collier, John 1947. *Indians of the Americas*. New York: W.W. Norton and Company.

Dobyns, Henry F. and Robert C. Euler 1971. *The Havasupai People*. Phoenix: Indian Tribal Series.

Dutton, Bertha 1975. *Indians of the American Southwest*. Englewood Cliffs, New Jersey: Prentice-Hall.

Eggan, Fred 1950. *Social Organization of the Western Pueblos*. Chicago: University of Chicago Press.

Euler, Robert C. 1972. *The Paiute People*. Phoenix: Indian Tribal Series.

Goodwin, Grenville 1942. *The Social Organization of the Western Apache*. Chicago: University of Chicago Press.

Hewett, Edgar Lee and Bertha P. Dutton 1945. *The Pueblo Indian World*. Albuquerque: University of New Mexico Press.

Hoijer, Harry 1938. *Chiricahua and Mescalero Apache Texts*. Chicago: University of Chicago Press.

James, Harry C. 1956. *The Hopi Indians*. Caldwell, Idaho: The Caxton Press.

Johnston, Bernice 1970. *Speaking of Indians*. Tucson: University of Arizona Press.

Kluckhohn, Clyde and Dorothea Leighton 1962. *The Navajo*. Garden City, New York: Doubleday and Co.

Lumholtz, Carl 1902. *Unknown Mexico*. New York: Charles Scribner's Sons.

Lurie, Nancy O. and Stuart Levine eds. 1968. *The American Indian Today*. Deland, Florida: Everett/Edwards.

Matthews, Washington 1897. *Navaho Legends*. New York: American Folklore Society.

Opler, Morris E. 1938. *Mescalero and Apache Texts*. New York: Memoirs of the American Folklore Society, vol.31.

Opler, Morris E. 1941. *An Apache Way of Life*. Chicago: University of Chicago Press.

Ortiz, Alfonso 1969. *The Tewa World*. Chicago: University of Chicago Press.

Ortiz, Alfonso ed. 1979. *Handbook of North American Indians*. vols 9 and 10. *Southwest*. Smithsonian Institution, Washington, D.C.

Parsons, Elsie Clews 1925. *The Pueblo of Jemez*. Andover, Mass: Phillips Academy.

Reichard, Gladys A. 1963. *Navajo Religion*. New York: Pantheon Books.

Smith, Anne 1965. *New Mexico Indians Today*. Santa Fe: Museum of New Mexico.

Sonnichsen, C. L. 1958. *The Mescalero Apaches*. Norman, Oklahoma: University of Oklahoma Press.

Spicer, Edward 1962. *Cycles of Conquest: The Impact of Spain, Mexico, and the United States on the Indians of the Southwest. 1533-1960*. Tucson: University of Arizona Press.

Spier, Leslie 1928. *Havasupai Ethnography*. New York: American Museum of Natural History.

Underhill, Ruth M. 1938. *Singing for Power*. Berkeley: University of California Press.

Weaver, Thomas ed. 1974. *Indians of Arizona. A Contemporary Perspective*. Tucson: University of Arizona Press.

White, Leslie A. 1935. *The Pueblo of Santo Domingo, New Mexico*. Memoirs of the American Anthropological Association, no.43.

The Plains

Bell, W. 1869. *New Tracks in North America*. London.

Bourke, Capt. John G. 1890. *Mackenzie's Last Fight With The Cheyennes*. Governor's Island, N.Y.H. (Reprint The Old Army Press, Bellevue, Nebraska. 1970).

Brasser, Ted J. 1982. The Tipi as an Element in the Emergence of Historic Plains Indian Nomadism. *Plain's Anthropologist*, vol.27, no.98. Lincoln, Nebraska.

Brasser, Ted J. 1987. By The Power of their Dreams, in *The Spirit Sings*. Toronto: McClelland and Stewart.

Butler, Colonel W.F. 1891. *The Great Lone Land*. London: Sampson Low, Marston & Company.

Carver, Jonathan 1976. *The Journals of Jonathan Carver: and Related Documents 1766-1770*. Edited by John Parker. St. Paul, Minnesota: Minnesota Historical Society Press.

Catlin, George 1926. *The North American Indians*. 2 vols. Edinburgh: John Grant.

Dempsey, Hugh A. 1972. *Crowfoot, Chief of the Blackfeet*. Norman, Oklahoma: University of Oklahoma Press.

Dodge, R.I. 1876. *Hunting Grounds of the Great West*. London: Chatto and Windus (reprinted 1976).

Hassrick, Royal B. 1964. *The Sioux, Life and Customs of a Warrior Society*. Norman, Oklahoma: University of Oklahoma Press.

Hughes, Thomas 1909. History of Blue Earth County, in *Minnesota Historical Society Collections*, vol.XII.

Johnson, Barry C. 1989. 'A Captain of Chivalric Courage': Thomas H. French, 7th Cavalry. The Brand Book, vol.25 nos 1 & 2. 1987/88. London: The English Westerners' Society.

Kroeber, Alfred L. 1939. Cultural and Natural Areas of Native North America. *Publ. Amer. Archaeol. and Ethnol.* vol.38. University of California.

Laubin, Reginald and Gladys 1957. *The Indian Tipi*. Norman, Oklahoma: University of Oklahoma Press.

Lavender, David 1965. *The American West*. Harmondsworth, Middlesex: Penguin Books.

Lewis, Oscar 1942. The Effects of White Contact Upon Blackfoot Culture. Centennial Anniversary Publication, American Ethnological Society 1842-1942. University of Washington Press, Seattle.

Mackenzie, Charles 1889. *The Mississouri Indians. A Narrative of Four Trading Expeditions to the Missouri 1804-1805-1806*. in Masson, 1889. vol.I.

Masson, L. R. ed. 1889. *Les Bourgeois de la Compagnie du Nord-Ouest*, vol.I.

McCann, Lloyd E. 1956. The Grattan Massacre. Reprint from *Nebraska History*, vol.XXXVII, no.1, March 1956.

McDonald, J. Douglas, A. L. McDonald, Bill Tallbull and Ted Risingsun 1989. The Cheyenne Outbreak Revisited: The Employment of Archaeological Methodology in the Substantiation of Oral History. *Plains Anthropologist*, vol.34, no.125:265-9. Lincoln, Nebraska.

Miles, N. A. 1896. *Personal Recollections and Observations of General Nelso A. Miles*. Chicago and New York.

Neihardt, John G. 1932. *Black Elk Speaks*. New York: William Morrow.

Nye, Wilbur Sturtevant 1968. *Plains Indian Raiders*. Norman, Oklahoma: University of Oklahoma Press.

Pakes, Fraser J. 1989. *Making War Attractive*. The Brand Book, The English Westerners' Society, vol.26, no.2, London.

Smith, DeCost 1943. *Indian Experiences*. Caldwell, Idaho: The Caxton Printers.

Smith, Rex Alan 1975. *Moon of Popping Trees: The Tragedy at Wounded Knee and the End of the Indian Wars*. Lincoln: University of Nebraska Press.

Swanton, John R. 1952. *The Indian Tribes of North America*. Bulletin 45. *Bureau of American Ethnology*. Smithsonian Institution, Washington, D.C.

Taunton, Francis B. 1977. *Sufficient Reason?* Special Publication No.5, The English Westerners' Society, London.

Taunton, Francis B. 1986. *Custer's Field: 'A Scene of Sickening Ghastly Horror'*. In collaboration with Brian C. Pohanka. The Johnson-Taunton Military Press, London.

Taylor, Colin 1975. *The Warriors of the Plains*. London: Hamlyn.

Taylor, Colin 1980. Ho, For The Great West! Title Essay in The Silver Jubilee Publication of the English Westerners' Society, London. Edited by Barry C. Johnson.

Taylor, Colin 1981. *Crow Rendezvous: The Place of the River & Mountain Crow in the Material Culture Patterns of the Plateau & Central Plains circa 1800-1807*. American Indian Studies Series No.1, English Westerners' Society, London.

Taylor, Colin 1984. Crow Rendezvous, in *Crow Indian Art*. Edited by D. and R. Lessard. Mission, S. Dakota: Chandler Institute.

Thompson, David 1916. *David Thompson's Narrative of His Explorations in Western America, 1784-1812*. Edited by Joseph Burr Tyrell. The Champlain Society Publications, vol.12, Toronto.

Utley, Robert M. 1963. *The Last Days of the Sioux Nation*. New Haven: Yale University Press.

Utley, Robert M. 1967. *Frontiersmen in Blue: The United States Army and the Indian, 1848-1865*. New York: Macmillan.

Utley, Robert M. 1973. *Bluecoats and Redskins: The United States Army and the Indian, 1866-1891*. London: Cassell.

Vestal, Stanley 1948. *Warpath and Council Fire*. Norman, Oklahoma: University of Oklahoma Press.

Vestal, Stanley 1957. *Sitting Bull: Champion of the Sioux*. Norman, Oklahoma: University of Oklahoma Press.

Wallace, Ernest and E. Adamson, Hoebel 1952. *The Comanches: Lords of the South Plains*. Norman, Oklahoma: University of Oklahoma Press.

Wissler, Clark 1904. Decorative Art of the Sioux Indians. *American Museum of Natural History*, vol.XVIII, New York.

Wissler, Clark and D. C. Duvall 1908. Mythology of the Blackfoot Indians. *Anthropological Papers of the American Museum of Natural History*, vol.II, New York.

Plateau and Basin

Brady, Cyrus Townsend 1916. *Northwestern Fights and Fighters*. New York: Doubleday, Page.

Brown, Mark H. 1967. *The Flight of the Nez Perce: A History of the Nez Perce War*. New York: Putnam's Sons.

D'Azevedo, Warren L. ed. 1986. *Great Basin*. Vol.II of *Handbook of North American Indians*. Smithsonian Institution, Washington, D.C.

De Smet, Pierre Jean 1905. *Life, Letters, and Travels of Father Pierre-Jean De Smet*. Edited by Hiram M. Chittenden and Alfred T. Richardson. 4 vols. New York: F. P. Harper.

Ewers, John C. 1955. The Horse in Blackfoot Indian Culture. *Bureau of American Ethnology Bulletin 159*. Smithsonian Institution, Washington, D.C.

Fletcher, Robert S. 1930. The Spalding-Allen Indian Collection. Reprint from *The Oberlin Alumni Magazine*, Oberlin, Ohio.

Fowler, Catherine S. 1986. Subsistence, in *Handbook of North American Indians*, vol.II, *Great Basin*: 64-97. Edited by Warren L. Azevedo. Smithsonian Institution, Washington, D.C.

Garcia, Andrew 1977. *Tough Trip Through Paradise*. Edited by Bennett H. Stein. London: Abacus, Sphere Books.

Harper, Kimball T. 1986. Historical Environments, in *Handbook of North American Indians*, vol.II, *Great Basin*: 51-63. Edited by Warren L. Azevedo. Smithsonian Institution, Washington, D.C.

Henry, Alexander and David Thompson 1897. *New Light on the Early History of the Greater Northwest. The Manuscript Journals of Alexander Henry and David Thompson 1799-1814*. Edited by Elliott Coues. 3 vols. New York.

Hultkrantz, Åke 1968. *Shoshoni Indians on the Plains: An*

Appraisal of the Documentary Evidence. Sonderdruck: Zeitschrift für Ethnologie, Band 93, Heft 1 u.2, Braunschweig.
Hultkrantz, Åke 1986. The Peril of Visions: Changes of Vision Patterns Among the Wind River Shoshoni, in *History of Religions*, vol.26, no.1. Chicago: University of Chicago Press.
Lewis, Meriwether and William Clark. 1893. *The History of the Lewis and Clark Expedition*. Edited by Elliott Coues. 3 vols. New York: Dover (reprint).
Lowie, Robert H. 1909. The Northern Shoshoni. *Anthropological Papers*, vol.II, part 2. American Museum of Natural History, New York.
McWhorter, L. V. 1940. *Yellow Wolf: His Own Story*. Caldwell, Idaho: The Caxton Printers Ltd.
Mooney, James 1896. The Ghost-Dance Religion and the Sioux Outbreak of 1890. *14th Annual Report of the Bureau of American Ethnology to the Smithsonian Institution 1892-3*. Washington D.C. New York: Dover (reprint 1973).
Ross, Alexander 1855. *The Fur Hunters of the Far West: A Narrative of Adventure in the Oregon and Rocky Mountains*. 2 vols. London: Smith, Elder.
Shawley, Stephen Douglas 1974. *Nez Perce Dress: A Study in Culture Change*. University of Idaho.
Spinden, Herbert Joseph 1908. The Nez Percé Indians. *Memoirs of the American Anthropological Associations*, vol.II, part 3. Millwood, New York: Kraus Reprint Co. (1974).
Teit, James A. 1930. The Salishan Tribes of the Western Plateaus. Edited by Franz Boas. *Extract from 45th Annual Report of the Bureau of American Ethnology to the Smithsonian Institution*, Washington, D.C.
Trenholm, Virginia Cole and Maurine Carley 1964. *The Shoshonis: Sentinels of the Rockies*. Norman, Oklahoma: Univesrity of Oklahoma Press.
Wildschut, William 1959. *Crow Indian Beadwork*. Edited by J. C. Ewers. Museum of the American Indian, Heye Foundation, New York.
Wissler, Clark 1910. Material Culture of the Blackfoot Indians. *Anthropological Papers of the American Museum of Natural History*, vol.V, part 1, New York.
Wissler, Clark 1915. Costumes of the Plains Indians. *American Museum of Natural History*, vol.XVII, New York.
Wood, C. E. S. 1884. Chief Joseph, The Nez-Percé. *The Century Magazine*, VI. New York.

California

Bannon, Francis ed. 1974. *Bolton and the Spanish Borderlands*. Norman University of Oklahoma Press.
Bolton, Herbert E. ed. 1976. *Historical Memoirs of New California by Fray Francisco Palou*, O.F.M. 4 vols. Berkeley: University of California Press.
Burnett, E.K. 1944. *Inlaid Stone and Bone Artifacts from Southern California*. New York: Museum of the American Indian, Heye Foundation.
Casebier, Dennis G. 1972a. *The Battle at Camp Cady*. Norco, CA: Dennis G. Casebier.
Casebier, Dennis G. 1972b. *Carleton's Pah-Ute Campaign*. Norco, CA: Dennis G. Casebier.
Chartkoff, Joseph L. and Kerry Kona Chartkoff 1984. *The Archeology of California*. Stanford: Stanford University Press.
Clark, Cora and Texa Bowen Williams 1954. *Pomo Indian Myths*. New York: Vantage Press.
Cook, Sherburn F. 1976a. *The Conflict Between the California Indians and White Civilization*. Berkeley: University of California Press.
Cook, Sherburn F. 1976. *The Population of California Indians, 1769-1870*. Berkeley: University of California Press.
Crampton, C. Gregory ed. 1975. *The Mariposa Indian War 1850-1851 Diaries of Robert Eccleston: The California Gold Rush, Yosemite, High Sierra*. Salt Lake City: University of Utah Press.
Cullin, Stewart 1975. *Games of the North American Indians*. New York: Dover Publications, Inc.
Davis, James T. 1974. *Trade Routes and Economic Exchange Among the Indians of California*. Ramona, CA: Ballena Press.
Edwards, Malcolm ed. 1970. *The California Diary of E. D. Townsend*. N.P.: The Ward Ritchie Press.
Federal Writers' Project 1943. *California: A Guide to the Golden State*. New York: Mabel R. Gillis.
Geiger, Maynard and Clement W. Meighan 1976. *As the Padres Saw Them: California Indian Life and Customs as Reported by the Franciscan Missionaries 1813-1815*. Santa Barbara: Santa Barbara Missions Archives.
Heizer, Robert F. and M. A. Whipple comp. and ed. 1971. *The California Indians: A Source book*. Berkeley: University of California.
Heizer, Robert F. ed. 1974. *The Destruction of the California Indians*. Santa Barbara and Salt Lake City: Peregrine Smith, Inc.
Heizer, Robert F. ed. 1978. *Handbook of North American Indians*. Vol.VIII *California*. Washington, D.C.: Smithsonian Institution.
Heizer, R. F. and Adan E. Treganza 1972. *Mines and Quarries of the Indians of California*. Ramona, CA: Ballena Press.
Kroeber, A.L. 1970. *Handbook of the Indians of California*. Berkeley: California Book Company Ltd.
Kroeber, Theodora 1976. *Ishi in Two Worlds*. Berkeley: University of California Press.
Lang, Kathryn M. 1979. Golden Gate National Recreation Area: The Indian and Hispanic Heritage of a Modern Urban Park. San Francisco: Golden Gate National Recreation Area, National Park Service.
Mason, Tufton 1976. *Aboriginal American Indian Basketry*. Santa Barbara: Peregrine Smith, Inc.
Members of the Potomac Corral of the Westerners 1966. *Great Western Indian Fights*. Lincoln: University of Nebraska Press.
Merrill, Ruth E. 1980. *Plants Used in Basketry by the California Indians*. Ramona, CA: Acoma Books.
Reid, Hugo 1926. *The Indians of Los Angeles County*. Los Angeles: privately printed.
Rolle, Andrew F. and John S. Gaines 1979. *The Golden State: A History of California*. Arlington Heights, IL: AHM Publishing Corporation.
Thompson, Erwin N. 1971. *Modoc War: Its Military History & Topography*. Sacramento: Argus Books.
Tuska, Jon and Vicki Pierkaski 1983. *Encyclopedia of Frontier and Western Fiction*. New York: McGraw-Hill.
Utley, Robert M. 1984. *The Indian Frontier of the American West 1846-1890*. Albuquerque: University of New Mexico Press.
Wax, Murray L. 1971. *Indian Americans Unity and Diversity*. Englewood Cliffs, NJ: Prentice-Hall.
Webb, Edith Buckland 1952. *Indian Life at the Old Missions*. Los Angeles: Warren F. Lewis.
Wissler, Clark 1966. *Indians of the United States*. Garden City, NY: Anchor Books.

The Northwest Coast

Bancroft-Hunt, Norman and Werner Forman 1979. *People of the Totem*: The Indians of the Pacific Northwest. New York: Putnam's Sons.
Brown, Steve. From Taquan to Klukwan: Tracing the Work of an Early Tlingit Master Artist, p.173, in Peter L. Corey, ed., *Faces, Voices and Dreams: A Celebration of the Centennial of the Sheldon Jackson Museum*. Seattle: Division of Alaska State Museums and Friends of the Alaska State Museum, 1987.
Carlson, Roy L. ed. 1976. *Indian Art Traditions of the Northwest Coast*. Burnaby: Simon Fraser University Archeology Press.
Cole, Douglas 1985. *Captured Heritage: The Scramble for Northwest Coast Artifacts*. Vancouver: Douglas & McIntyre.
Cole, Douglas and Ira Chaikin 1990. *An Iron Hand upon the People: The Law against the Potlatch on the Northwest Coast*. Vancouver: Douglas & McIntyre.
Cook, Warren L. 1973. *Flood Tide of Empire: Spain and the Pacific Northwest*, 1543-1819. New Haven: Yale University Press.
Duff, Wilson 1964. *The Indian History of British Columbia, Volume 1: The Impact of the White Man*. Anthropology in British Columbia, Memoir No.5. Victoria: Provincial Museum of British Columbia.
Duff, Wilson 1975. *Images: Stone: B.C.: Thirty Centuries of Northwest Coast Indian Sculpture*. Seattle: University of Washington Press.
Fisher, Robin 1977. *Contact and Conflict: Indian-European Relations in British Columbia, 1774-1890*. Vancouver: University of British Columbia Press.
Fisher, Robin 1977. Missions to the Indians of British Columbia, in John Veillette and Gary White, *Early Indian Village Churches: Wooden Frontier Architecture in British Columbia*. Vancouver: University of British Columbia Press, pp1-11.
Fladmark, Knut 1986. *British Columbia Prehistory*. Ottowa: National Museum of Man.
Gunther, Erna 1972. *Indian Life on the Northwest Coast of North America as seen by the Early Explorers and Fur Traders during the Last Decades of the Eighteenth Century*. Chicago: University of Chicago Press.
Gustafson, Paula 1980. *Salish Weaving*. Vancouver: Douglas & McIntyre.
Halliday, W. M. 1935. *Potlatch and Totem and the Recollections of an Indian Agent*. Toronto; J. M. Dent.
Hinckley, Ted C. 1982. *Alaskan John G. Brady: Missionary, Businessman, Judge, and Governor, 1878-1918*. Ohio State University Press.
Holm, Bill 1965. *Northwest Coast Indian Art: An Analysis of Form*. Seattle: University of Washington Press.
Holm, Bill 1983. *Smoky-Top: The Art and Times of Willie Seaweed*. Seattle: University of Washington Press.
Holm, Bill 1987. *Spirit and Ancestor: A Century of Northwest Coast Indian Art at the Burke Museum*. Thomas Burke Memorial Washington State Museum Monograph 4. Seattle: Burke Museum and University of Washington Press.
Holmberg, Heinrich Johan 1985. *Holberg's Ethnographic Sketches*, edited by Marwin W. Falk and translated by Fritz Jaensch. Fairbanks, Alaska: University of Alaska Press.
Hou, Charles undated. *To Potlatch or Not to Potlatch: An In-Depth Study of Culture-Conflict Between the B.C. Coastal Indian and the White Man*. Vancouver: British Columbia Teachers' Federation.
Jackson, Sheldon. *Alaska, and Missions on the North Pacific Coast*, New York: Dodd, Mead.
Jonaitis, Aldona 1986. *Art of the Northern Tlingit*. Seattle: University of Washington Press.
Knight, Rolf 1978. *Indians At Work: An Informal History of Native Indian Labour in British Columbia*, 1858-1930. Vancouver: New Star Books.
Laguna, Frederica de 1972. *Under Mt. Saint Alias*. Washington, D.C.: U.S. Government Printing Office.
LaViolette, Forrest E. 1973. *The Struggle for Survival: Indian Cultures and the Protestant Ethic in British Columbia*. Toronto: University of Toronto Press.
Lobb, Allan 1990. *Indian Baskets of The Pacific Northwest and Alaska*. Portland: Graphic Arts Center Publishing Company.
MacDonald, George F. and Richard I. Inglis 1976. *The Dig: An Archeological Reconstruction of a West Coast Village*. Ottawa: National Museum of Man.
Macnair, Peter L. et al 1984. *The Legacy: Tradition and Innovation in Northwest Coast Indian Art*. Vancouver: Douglas & McIntyre.
Pethick, *First Approaches to the Northwest Coast*.
Samuel, Cheryl 1982. *The Chilkat Dancing Blanket*. Seattle: Pacific Search Press.
Sewid-Smith, Daisy 1979. *Prosecution or Persecution*. Nu-Yum-Baleess Society.
Stewart, Hilary 1973. *Artifacts of the Northwest Coast*. Vancouver: Hancock House Publishers.
Stewart, Hilary 1977. *Indian Fishing: Early Methods on the Northwest Coast*. Vancouver: Douglas & McIntyre.
Stewart, Hilary 1979. *Looking at Indian Art of the Northwest Coast*. Seattle: University of Washington Press.
Stewart, Hilary 1984. *Cedar: Tree of Life to the Northwest Coast Indians*. Vancouver: Douglas & McIntyre.
Tennant, Paul 1990. *Aboriginal Peoples and Politics: The Indian Land Question in British Columbia, 1849-1989*. Vancouver: University of British Columbia Press.
Vaughan, Thomas and Bill Holm 1982. *Soft Gold: The Fur Trade and Cultural Exchange on the Northwest Coast*. Portland: Oregon Historical Society.
Wyatt, Victoria 1984. *Shapes of Their Thoughts: Reflections of Culture Contact on the Northwest Coast*. New Haven: Yale Peabody Museum of Natural History and University of Oklahoma Press.
Wyatt, Victoria Alaskan Indian Wage Earners in the 19th Century: Economic Choices and Ethnic Identity of Southeast Alaska's Frontier, *Pacific Northwest Quarterly* 78(1-2):43-9.

The Subarctic

Boudreau, Norman J. ed. 1974. *The Athapaskans: Strangers of the North*. National Museum of Man, Ottawa.
Bourque, Jim 1986. *This Land Is Our Life*. Government of the Northwest Territories, Yellowknife, NWT.
Brasser, Ted J. 1976. *Bo'jou, Neejee!*. National Museum of Man, Ottawa.
Brody, Hugh 1990. Hunters and Bombers, in *The Independent*, 30 June 1990.
Cameron, Agnes D. 1912. *The New North*. New York: Appleton and Company.
Cory, Harper 1935. *Grey Owl and the Beaver*. London: Thomas Nelson.
Dickason, Olive Patricia 1972. *Indian Arts in Canada*. Department of Indian Affairs and Northern Development, Ottawa.
Dickson, Lovat 1973. *Wilderness Man: The Strange Story of Grey Owl*. Toronto: Macmillan.
Duncan, Kate C. 1989. *Northern Athapaskan Art: A Beadwork Tradition*. Seattle: University of Washington Press.
Duncan, Kate C. and Eunice Carney 1988. *A Special Gift: The Kutchin Beadwork Tradition*. Seattle: University of Washington Press.
Godsell, Philip H. 1935. *Arctic Trader*. London: Putman.
Godsell, Philip H. 1938. *Red Hunters of the Snows*. London: Robert Hale.
Grey Owl (Wa-Sha-Quon-Asin) 1935. *Pilgrims of the Wild*. London: Lovat Dickson.
Hail, Barbara A. and Kate C. Duncan 1989. *Out of the North: The Subarctic Collection of the Haffenreffer Museum of Anthropology*. Brown University, Bristol, Rhode Island.
Hatt, Gudmund 1969. Arctic Skin Clothing in Eurasia and America: An Ethnographic Study. *Arctic*

Anthropology, vol.V, no.2. University of Wisconsin Press.
Hearne, Samuel 1958. *A Journey from Prince of Wales's Fort in Hudson's Bay to the Northern Ocean in the Years 1769, 1770, 1771, and 1772*. Edited by R. Glover. Toronto: Macmillan.
Helm, June ed. 1981. *Subarctic*. Vol.6 of *Handbook of North American Indians*. Smithsonian Institution, Washington, D.C.
Honigmann, John J. 1981. Expressive Aspects of Subarctic Indian Culture, in *Handbook of North American Indians*, vol.6. *Subarctic*: 718-38. Edited by June Helm. Smithsonian Institution, Washington, D.C.
Hosley, Edward H. 1981. Intercultural Relations and Cultural Change in the Alaska Plateau, in *Handbook of North American Indians*, vol.6. *Subarctic*: 546-55. Edited by June Helm. Smithsonian Institution, Washington, D.C.
Hubbard, Mrs Leonidas, Junior 1908. *A Woman's Way Through Unknown Labrador*. London: John Murray.
Irving, Susan et al 1985. *Trapline Lifeline/Sur La Piste Des Trappeurs*. Prince of Wales Northern Heritage Centre. Northwest Territories Culture and Communications.
Kerr, Robert 1953. For the Royal Scottish Museum, in *The Beaver: A Magazine of the North*, Outfit 284. June 1953. Hudson's Bay Company, Winnipeg.
Murray, Alexander Hunter 1910. *Journal of the Yukon 1847-48*. Edited and annotated by L. J. Burpee. *Publications of Canadian Archives*, no.4. Government Printing Bureau, Ottawa.
Orchard, William C. 1916. The Technique of Porcupine Quill Decoration Among the Indians of North America. *Museum of the American Indian, Heye Foundation*. New York (reprint 1971).
Rogers, Edward S. and Eleanor Leacock 1981. Montagnais-Naskapi, in *Handbook of North American Indians*, vol.6. *Subarctic*: 169-89. Edited by June Helm. Smithsonian Institution, Washington, D.C.
Rogers, Edward S. and James G. E. Smith 1981. Environment and Culture in the Shield and Mackenzie Borderlands, in *Handbook of North American Indians*, vol.6. *Subarctic*: 130-45 Edited by June Helm. Smithsonian Institution, Washington, D.C.
Skinner, Alanson 1911. Notes on the Eastern Cree and Northern Saulteaux. Edited by Clark Wissler. *Anthropological Papers of the American Museum of Natural History*, vol.IX (1912) New York.
Smith, Donald B. 1990. *From the Land of Shadows: The Making of Grey Owl*. Western Producer Prairie Books, Saskatoon, Saskatchewan.
Smith, James G. E. 1978. Economic Uncertainty in an 'Original Affluent Society': Caribou and Caribou Eater Chipewyan Adaptive Strategies. *Arctic Anthropology*, vol.XV, no.1., University of Wisconsin Press.
Smith, James G. E. 1981. Chipewyan, in *Handbook of North American Indians*, vol.6. *Subarctic*: 271-84. Edited by June Helm. Smithsonian Institution, Washington, D.C.
Speck, Frank G. 1925. Central Eskimo and Indian Dot Ornamentation. *Indian Notes*, vol.2, no.3. Museum of the American Indian, Heye Foundation, New York.
Speck, Frank G. 1930. Mistassini Notes. *Indian Notes*, vol.7, no.4. Museum of the American Indian, Heye Foundation, New York.
Speyer, Arthur 1968. *Indianer Nordamerikas 1760-1860*. Deutschen Ledermuseum-Deutsches Schuhmuseum, Offenbach.
Thompson, Judy 1983. Turn-of-the-Century Métis Decorative Art from the Frederick Bell Collection, in *American Indian Art*, Autumn 1983, Scottsdale, Arizona.
Thompson, Judy 1987. No Little Variety of Ornament: Northern Athapaskan Artistic Traditions, in *The Spirit Sings*. Toronto: McClelland and Stewart.
Turner, Geoffrey 1955. *Hair Embroidery in Siberia and North America*. Pitt Rivers Museum, University of Oxford, Oxford.
VanStone, James W. 1981. Athapaskan Clothing and Related Objects in the Collections of the Field Museum of Natural History. *Fieldiana Anthropology*. New Series no.4, Field Museum, Chicago.
Webber, Alika Podolinsky 1983. Ceremonial Robes of the Montagnais-Naskapi, in *American Indian Art*. Winter 1983. Scottsdale, Arizona.
Webber, Alika Podolinsky 1989. *North American Indian and Eskimo Footwear: A Typology and Glossary*. The Bata Shoe Museum Foundation, Toronto.

The Arctic

Bergsland, Knut and Moses L. Dirks, eds. 1990. *Aleut Tales and Narratives collected by W. Jochelson*. Fairbanks, Alaska: Alaska Native Language Center.
Black, Lydia T. 1980. Early History, in Morgan, Lael ed. *Alaska Geographic – The Aleutians*, vol.7(3): 82-105.
Black, Lydia T. 1983. Some Problems in the Interpretation of Aleut Prehistory. *Arctic Anthropology*, vol.20(1): 49-78.
Black, Lydia T. 1984. *Atka: An Ethnohistory of the Western Aleutians*. Kingston, Ontario: The Limestone Press.
Black, Lydia T. 1988. The Story of Russian America, in Fitzhugh, William W. and Aron Crowell. *Crossroads of Continents: Cultures of Siberia and Alaska*. Washington, D.C.: Smithsonian Institution Press, 70-82.
Black, Lydia T. and R. G. Liapunova 1988. Aleut: Islanders of the North Pacific, in Fitzhugh, William W. and Aron Crowell. *Crossroads of Continents: Cultures of Siberia and Alaska*. Washington, D.C.: Smithsonian Institution Press, 52-7.
Brody, Hugh 1987. *Living Arctic: Hunters of the Canadian North*. Vancouver: Douglas & McIntyre.
Chaussonnet, Valerie 1988. Needles and Animals: Women's Magic, in Fitzhugh, William W. and Aron Crowell. *Crossroads of Continents: Cultures of Siberia and Alaska*. Washington, D.C.: Smithsonian Institution Press, 209-26.
Collins, Henry B. Jr. 1945. The Islands and their People, in Collins, Henry B. Jr., Austin B. Clark and Egbert H. Walker. *The Aleutian Islands: Their People and Natural History*. Washington, D.C.: Smithsonian Institution Press.
Colombo, John Robert ed. 1981. *Poems of the Inuit*. Ottawa: Oberon.
Comer, George 1906. Whaling in Hudson Bay, with notes on Southampton Island. *Boas Anniversary Volume: Anthropological Papers Written in Honor of Franz Boas*. New York: G. E. Stewart, 475-84.
Damas, David 1963. Igluligmiut Kinship and Local Groupings: A Structural Approach. *Anthropological Series 64, National Museum of Canada Bulletin*, 196.
Dumond, Don E. 1984. Prehistory: Summary, *Handbook of North American Indians*, vol.5, *Arctic*: 72-9. Edited by David Damas. Smithsonian Institution, Washington, D.C.
Dyson, George 1986. *Baidarka*. Edmonds, Washington: Alaska Northwest Publishing Company.
Eber, Dorothy, H. 1989. *When Whalers were up North: Inuit Memories from the Eastern Arctic*. Kingston, Ontario: McGill-Queen's University Press.
Fienup-Riordan, Ann 1988. Eye of the Dance: Spiritual Life of the Bering Sea Eskimo, in Fitzhugh, William W. and Aron Crowell. *Crossroads of Continents: Cultures of Siberia and Alaska*. Washington, D.C.: Smithsonian Institution Press, 256-70.
Fitzhugh, William W. and Susan A. Kaplan 1982. *Inua: Spirit World of the Bering Sea Eskimo*. Washington, D.C.: Smithsonian Institution Press.
Freuchen, Peter 1961. *Peter Freuchen's Book of the Eskimos*. Cleveland, Ohio: The World Publishing Company.
Guemple, D. Lee 1961. *Inuit Spouse Exchange*. Chicago: Department of Anthropology, University of Chicago.
Hansen, Craig A. 1982. Exploration and Development, in Henning, Robert A. ed. *Alaska Geographic – Islands of the Seals: The Pribilofs*, vol.9(3): 75-85.
Heath, John D. 1987. Baidarka Bow Variations, in Corey, Peter L. *Faces, Voices and Dreams: A Celebration of the Centennial of the Sheldon Jackson Museum*. Juneau, Alaska: Division of Alaska State Museums, 93-6.
Houston, James 1972. *Songs of the Dream People: Chants and Images from the Indians and Eskimos of North America*. Toronto: Longman Canada Ltd.
Hudson, Raymond L. 1987. Designs in Aleut Basketry, in Corey, Peter L. *Faces, Voices and Dreams: A Celebration of the Centennial of the Sheldon Jackson Museum*. Juneau, Alaska: Division of Alaska State Museums, 63-92.
Hughes, Charles C. 1984. Siberian Eskimo, in *Handbook of North American Indians*, vol.5, *Arctic*: 247-61. Edited by David Damas. Smithsonian Institution, Washington, D.C.
Jochelson, Waldemar 1968. *History, Ethnology and Anthropology of the Aleut*. Oosterhout, The Netherlands: Anthropological Publications.
Kan, Sergei 1988. The Russian Orthodox Church in Alaska, in *Handbook of North American Indians*, vol.4. *History of Indian-White Relations*: 506-21. Edited by Wilcomb E. Washburn. Smithsonian Institution, Washington, D.C.
Krauss, Michael E. 1988. Many Tongues – Ancient Tales, in Fitzhugh, William W. and Aron Crowell. *Crossroads of Continents: Cultures of Siberia and Alaska*. Washington, D.C.: Smithsonian Institution Press, 145-50.
Lantis, Margaret 1970. The Aleut Social System, 1750-1810, from Early Historical Sources, in Lantis, Margaret ed. *Ethnohistory in Southwestern Alaska and the Southern Yukon: Method and Content*. Lexington, Kentucky: University Press of Kentucky.
Lantis, Margaret 1984. Aleut, in *Handbook of North American Indians*, vol.5, *Arctic*: 161-84. Edited by David Damas. Smithsonian Institution, Washington, D.C.
Laughlin, William S. 1980. *Aleuts: Survivors of the Bering Land Bridge*. New York: Holt, Rinehart and Winston.
Lyon, George F. 1824. *The Private Journal of Captain G. F. Lyon, of H.M.S. Hecla, during the recent voyage of discovery under Captain Parry*. London: John Murray.
Mary-Rousselière, Guy 1954. Issingut. The starvation camp. *Eskimo*, vol.33(December): 9-13.
Mary-Rousselière, Guy 1984. Iglulik, in *Handbook of North American Indians*, vol.5, *Arctic*: 431-46. Edited by David Damas. Smithsonian Institution, Washington, D.C.
Mather, Elsie 1985. *Cauyarnariuq*. Bethel, Alaska: Lower Kuskokwim School District Bilingual-Bicultural Department.
Mathiassen, Therkel 1928. Material Culture of the Iglulik Eskimos. *Report of the Fifth Thule Expedition 1921-24*, vol.6(1). Copenhagen: Gyldendalske Boghandel.
McCartney, Allen P. 1984. Prehistory of the Aleutian Region, in *Handbook of North American Indians*, vol.5, *Arctic* 119-35. Edited by David Damas, Smithsonian Institution, Washington, D.C.
Merck, Carl Heinrich 1980. *Siberia and Northwestern America 1788-1792: The Journal of Carl Heinrich Merck, Naturalist with the Russian Scientific Expedition led by Captains Joseph Billings and Gavrill Sarychev*. Kingston, Ontario: The Limestone Press.
Michael, Henry N. ed. 1967. Lieutenant Zagoskin's Travel in Russian America, 1842-44: The First Ethnographic and Geographic Investigations on the Yukon and Kuskokwim Valleys of Alaska. *Anthropology of the North: Translations from Russian Sources 7*. Toronto: Published for the Arctic Institute of North America by the University of Toronto Press.
Morgan, Lael ed. 1980. *Alaska Geographic – The Aleutians*, vol.7(3).
Morrow, Phyllis 1984. It is Time for Drumming: A Study of Recent Research on Yup'ik Ceremonialism. *Etudes/Inuit/Studies*, vol.8:113-40.
Nelson, Edward W. 1899. *The Eskimo about Bering Strait*. Washington, D.C.: Smithsonia Institution Press.
Netsvetov, Iakov 1980. *The Journals of Iakov Netsvetov: The Atkha Years, 1828-44*, Kingston, Ontario: The Limestone Press.
Parry, William E. 1824. *Journal of a second voyage for the discovery of a Northwest Passage from the Atlantic to the Pacific: Performed in the years 1921-22-23, in his Majesty's Ships Fury and Hecla, under the orders of Captain William Edward Parry, R.N., F.R.S., and Commander of the Expedition*. London: John Murray.
Pierce, Richard A. 1988. Russian and Soviet Eskimo Indian Policies, in *Handbook of North American Indians*, vol.4, *History of Indian-White Relations*: 119-27. Edited by Wilcomb E. Washburn. Smithsonian Institution, Washington, D.C.
Rasmussen 1929. Intellectual Culture of the Iglulik Eskimos. *Report of the Fifth Thule Expedition, 1921-24*, vol.7(1). Copenhagen: Gyldendalske Boghandel.
Robert-Lamblin, Joelle 1982. Women's Role and Power within Traditional Aleut Society. *Folk*, vol.24: 197-202.
Ross, W. Gillies 1975. *Whaling and Eskimos: Hudson Bay 1860-1915*. Publications in Ethnology no.10. Ottawa: National Museums of Canada.
Shalkop, Antoinette 1987. The Russian Orthodox Church in Alaska, in Starr, S. Frederick ed. *Russia's American Colony*. Durham, North Carolina: Duke University Press, 196-217.
Stager, John K. and Robert J. McSkimming 1984. Physical Environment, in *Handbook of North American Indians*, vol.5, *Arctic*: 27-35. Edited by David Damas. Smithsonian Institution, Washington, D.C.
Stefansson, Viljhalmur 1946. *Not by Bread Alone*. New York: MacMillan.
Steller, Georg Wilhelm 1988. *Journal of a Voyage with Bering, 1741-1742*. Stanford, California: Stanford University Press.
Tennant, Edward A. and Joseph N. Bitar, eds. *Yupik Lore: Oral Traditions of an Eskimo People*. Bethel, Alaska: Lower Kuskokwim School District.
Turner, Christy, G. II 1988. Ancient People of the North Pacific Rim, in Fitzhugh, William W. and Aron Crowell. *Crossroads of Continents: Cultures of Siberia and Alaska*. Washington, D.C.: Smithsonian Institution Press. 111-16.
VanStone, James W. 1967. *Eskimos of the Nushagak River: An Ethnographic History*. Seattle, Washington: University of Washington Press.
VanStone, James W. 1984. Mainland Southwest Alaska Eskimo, in *Handbook of North American Indians*, vol.5, *Arctic*: 224-42. Edited by David Damas. Smithsonian Institution, Washington, D.C.
Veniaminov, Ivan 1984. *Notes on the Islands of the Unalshka District*. Kingston, Ontario: The Limestone Press.
Woodbury, Anthony C. ed. 1984. *Cev'armiut Qanemciit Qulirait-llu: Eskimo Narratives and Tales from Chevak, Alaska*. Fairbanks, Alaska: Alaska Native Language Center.

Woodbury, Anthony C. 1984. Eskimo and Aleut Languages, in *Handbook of North American Indians*, vol.5, Arctic:49-65. Edited by David Damas. Smithsonian Institution, Washington, D.C.

Yesner, David R. 1988. Effects of Prehistoric Human Exploitation on Aleutian Sea Mammal Populations. *Arctic Anthropology*, vol.25(1): 28-43.

Zimmerly, David W. 1986. *Qajaq: Kayaks of Siberia and Alaska*. Juneau, Alaska: Division of State Museums.

The Northeast

Adney, Edwin Tappan and Howard I. Chapelle 1964. *The Bark Canoes and Skin Boats of North America*. Museum of History and Technology, Smithsonian Institution, Washington, D.C.

Bedford, June et al 1985. *Mohawk Micmac Maliseet... and other Indian Souvenir Art from Victorian Canada*. Canada House Cultural Centre Gallery, London.

Biard, Pierre. See J.R.

Bishop, Morris 1949. *Champlain: The Life of Fortitude*. London: MacDonald.

Bock, Philip K. 1978. Micmac, in *Handbook of North American Indians*, vol.15, Northeast: 109-122. Edited by Bruce G. Trigger. Smithsonian Institution, Washington, D.C.

Brotherston, Gordon 1979. *Image of the New World: The American Continent Portrayed in Native Texts*. London: Thames and Hudson.

Butler, Eva L. and Wendell S. Hadlock 1957. *Uses of Birch-Bark in the Northeast*. The Robert Abbe Museum, Bar Harbor, Maine.

Catlin, Geo 1841. *Letters and Notes on the Manners, Customs, and Condition of the North American Indians*. 2 vols. Egyptian Hall, Piccadilly, London.

Cleland, Charles E. 1973. *Art of the Great Lakes Indians*. Flint Institute of Arts, Flint, Michigan.

Densmore, Frances 1910 & 1913. *Chippewa Music. Parts I and II*. Bureau of American Ethnology Bulletins 45 and 53. Smithsonian Institution, Washington, D.C.

Densmore, Frances 1929. *Chippewa Customs*. Bureau of American Ethnology Bulletin 86. Smithsonian Institution, Washington, D.C.

Fenton, William N. 1978. Northern Iroquoian Culture Patterns, in *Handbook of North American Indians*, vol.15, Northeast: 296-321. Edited by Bruce G. Trigger. Smithsonian Institution, Washington, D.C.

Hilger, Sister M. Inez 1951. *Chippewa Child Life and its Cultural Background*. Bureau of American Ethnology Bulletin 146. Smithsonian Institution, Washington, D.C.

Hodge, Frederick Webb ed. 1907-10. *Handbook of American Indians North of Mexico*. 2 vols. Bureau of American Ethnology Bulletin 30. Smithsonian Institution, Washington, D.C.

Hodge, G. Stuart 1973. *Art of the Great Lakes Indians* (Foreword). Flint Institute of Arts, Flint, Michigan.

Hoffman, Walter J. 1891. *The Midewiwin or 'Grand Medicine Society' of the Ojibwa*. 7th Annual Report of the Bureau of American Ethnology for the Years 1885-6. Washington, D.C.

J.R. = Thwaites, Reuben G. ed. 1896-1901. *The Jesuit Relations and Allied Documents: Travel and Explorations of the Jesuit Missionaries in New France, 1610-1791*. 73 vols. Burrows Brothers, Cleveland. (Reprint: Pageant, New York, 1959.)

Kenton, Edna ed. 1954. *Black Gown and Redskins: The adventures and explorations of the first missionaries among the North American Indians*. London, New York & Toronto: Longmans, Green.

King, J. C. H. 1982. *Thunderbird and Lightning*. London: British Museum Publications Ltd.

Lyford, Carrie A. 1945. *Iroquois Crafts*. United States Indian Service, Haskwell Institute, Lawrence, Kansas.

Lyford, Carrie A. 1953. *Ojibwa Crafts*. Bureau of Indian Affairs, Haskwell Institute, Lawrence, Kansas.

Mallery, Garrick 1893. *Picture Writing of the American Indians*. 2 vols. 10th Annual Report of the Bureau of American Ethnology. Government Printing Office, Washington, D.C.

Palmer, Rose A. 1949. *The North American Indians: An Account of the American Indians North of Mexico, Compiled from the Original Sources*, vol.4 of The Smithsonian Series. Edited by Charles Greeley Abbot. New York: The Series Publishers.

Parkman, Francis 1883. *La Salle and the Discovery of the Great West*. Boston: Little, Brown.

Pelletier, Gaby (ed.) 1977. *Micmac & Maliseet Decorative Traditions*. The New Brunswick Museum, Saint John, NB.

Phillips, Ruth B. 1989. Souvenirs from North America: The Miniature as Image of Woodlands Indian Life, in *American Indian Art*, vol.14, no.2, Scottsdale, Arizona.

Pohrt, Richard A. 1986. Pipe Tomahawks from Michigan and the Great Lakes Area, in *Bulletin of the Detroit Institute of Arts*, vol.62, no.1, Detroit, Michigan.

Quimby, George Irving 1960. *Indian Life in the Upper Great Lakes, 11,000 B.C. to A.D. 1800*. Chicago: University of Chicago Press.

Ritzenthaler, Robert E. 1953. *The Potawatomi Indians of Wisconsin*. Milwaukee Public Museum Bulletin, vol.19, no.3, Milwaukee, Wisconsin.

Ritzenthaler, Robert E. 1978. Southwestern Chippewa, in *Handbook of North American Indians*, vol.15, Northeast: 743-59. Edited by Bruce G. Trigger. Smithsonian Institution, Washington, D.C.

Ritzenthaler, Robert E. and Frederick A. Peterson 1956. *The Mexican Kickapoo Indians*. Milwaukee Public Museum Publications in Anthropology, no.2, Milwaukee, Wisconsin.

Rydén, Stig 1963. A 17-Century Indian Head Dress from Delaware. Ethnos 2-4. The Ethnographical Museum of Sweden, Stockholm.

Speck, Frank Gouldsmith 1945. *The Iroquois: A Study in Cultural Evolution*. Cranbrook Institute of Science. Bull.23, Bloomfield Hills, Michigan.

Strong, William Duncan 1938. *The Indian Tribes of the Chicago Region*. Field Museum of Natural History, Anthropology Leaflet 24, Chicago.

Tooker, Elisabeth 1978. The League of the Iroquois: Its History, Politics, and Ritual, in *Handbook of North American Indians*, vol.15, Northeast: 418-41. Edited by Bruce G. Trigger. Smithsonian Institution, Washington, D.C.

Trigger, Bruce G. 1969. *The Huron: Farmers of the North*. New York: Holt, Rinehart and Winston.

Trigger, Bruce G. (ed) 1978. *Northeast*. Vol.15 of *Handbook of North American Indians*. Smithsonian Institution, Washington, D.C.

Turner, Geoffrey 1955. *Hair Embroidery in Siberia and North America*. Pitt Rivers Museum, University Press, Oxford.

Webber, Alika 1978. *Wigwamatew*: Old Birch Bark Containers, in *American Indian Art*, vol.4, no.1, Scottsdale, Arizona.

Whitehead, Ruth Holmes 1982. *Micmac Quillwork*. The Nova Scotia Museum, Halifax.

WEAPONS OF THE AMERICAN INDIAN

Adney, Edwin Tappan and Howard I. Chapelle *The Bark Canoes & Skin Boats of North America*. Washington: Museum of History & Technology, Smithsonian Institution. 1964.

Aiton, Arthur S. Coronado's muster roll. *Amer.Hist.Rev*, Vol. 44, No.3: 556-570. 1939.

Arima, Eugene and John Dewhirst. Nootkans of Vancouver Island in *Handbook of North American Indians*, Vol.7 Northwest Coast: 391-411. Ed. Wayne Suttles. Washington: Smithsonian Institution. 1990.

Baldwin, John *Early Knives and Beaded Sheaths of the American Frontier*. West Olive, Michigan: Early American Artistry-Trading Company. 1997.

Bancroft-Hunt, Norman *Warriors: Warfare and the Native American Indian*. London: Salamander Books Ltd. 1995.

Bankes, George *North American Woodlands Art in the Manchester Museum Collections*. Paper given at Museum of Mankind, London – Native Art of the North American Woodlands Conference. 26 Feb. Unpublished. 1999.

Berlandier, J. Louis *The Indians of Texas in 1830*. Edited by John C. Ewers. Washington: Smithsonian Institution. 1969.

Birket-Smith, Kaj. Some Ancient Artifacts from the Eastern United States. *Journal de la Société des Americanistes de Paris*. 12–13. 1920.

Bohr, Roland *Plains Indian Archery Gear of the Historic Period*. Seminar Paper. Bismarck: University of North Dakota. 1996.

Bourke, Captain John G. *Remarks. Arrows and Arrow-Makers*. Vol. IV: 71–74. The American Anthropologist. 1891.

Bowers, Alfred W. *Mandan Social and Ceremonial Organization*. Chicago, Illinois: University of Chicago Press. 1950.

Bradley, James H. *Characteristics, habits and customs of the Blackfeet Indians*. Vol. 9. Montana Hist. Soc. Contrib. 1923.

Brasser, Theodore War Clubs. *American Indian Tradition*. Vol. 7. no. 3: 77–83. Alton, Illinois. 1961
Bo'jou, Neejee! Ottawa, Ontario: National Museum of Man. 1976.
Early Indian-European Contacts in *Handbook of North American Indians*, Vol. 15 Northeast: 78–88. Washington: Smithsonian Institution. 1978

Brunius, Staffan. Some Comments on Early Swedish Collections from the Northeast in *New Sweden in America*: 150–168. Ed. Hoffecker, Waldron, Williams & Benson. Newark: University of Delaware Press. 1995.

Carver, Jonathan *The Journals of Jonathan Carver: and Related Documents 1766-1770*. Ed. John Parker. St. Paul: Minnesota Historical Society Press. 1976.

Catlin, George *North American Indians*. 2 Vols. Edinburgh: John Grant. 1926

Chandler, Milford G. *The Blacksmith's Shop*: 55–77 in Peterson. 1971.

Coe, Connolly et al *Swords and Hilt Weapons*. London: Weidenfeld and Nicolson. 1989.

Cowdrey, Mike *Spring Boy Rides the Moon: Celestial Patterns in Crow Shield Designs*. Privately published by author. 1995

Culin, Stewart *Games of the North American Indians*. 24th Annual Report of the Bureau of American Ethnology, 1902-03. Washington: Smithsonian Institution. 1907. (Reprint. 1975: New York: Dover Publications).

De Laguna, Frederica. Tlingit in *Handbook of North American Indians*, Vol.7 Northwest Coast:203-228. Ed. Wayne Suttles, Washington: Smithsonian Institution. 1990.

De La Vega, Garcilaso *Florida of the Inca*. Translated by John and Jeannette Varner, Houston: University of Texas Press. 1951

Densmore, Frances *Teton Sioux Music*. Bull.61, Bureau of American Ethnology. Washington: Smithsonian Institution. 1918.

DeVoto, Bernard *Across the Wide Missouri*. London: Eyre and Spottiswoode. 1948.

Dodge, Col. Richard Irving *33 years among our Wild Indians*. New York: Archer House, Inc. 1959.

Ewers, John C. *The Horse in Blackfoot Indian Culture*. Bull.159, Bureau of American Ethnology. Washington: Smithsonian Institution. 1955.
Early White Influence Upon Plains Indian Painting: George Catlin and Carl Bodmer among the Mandan, 1832–34. Vol. 134, No. 7. Misc. Colls. Washington: Smithsonian Institution. 1957.
Blackfoot Indian Pipes and Pipemaking. Anthro. Papers, no. 64. Bureau of American Ethnology. Washington: Smithsonian Institution. 1963.
The White Man's Strongest Medicine. Reprint. St. Louis(?): Bulletin of the Missouri Historical Society. 1967.
Indian Life on the Upper Missouri. Norman: University of Oklahoma Press. 1968.
The Awesome Bear in Plains Indian Art. *American Indian Art*. Vol. 7, No. 3: 36–45. Scottsdale, Arizona. 1982.

Faris and Elmer *Arab Archery*. Princeton: University Press. 1945.

Feest, Christian Essay in *Tradescant Rarities*: 110–115. Ed. Arthur Macgregor. Oxford: Clarendon Press. 1983.
Jacques Le Moyne Minus Four. *European Review of Native American Studies*, 2: 1: 33–38. Vienna. 1988.

Ferg, Alan (ed.) *Western Apache Material Culture: The Goodwin and Guenther Collections*. Tucson: The University of Arizona Press. 1987.

Fletcher, Alice C. and Francis La Flesche *The Omaha Tribe*. 27th Annual Report of the Bureau of American Ethnology. Washington: Smithsonian Institution. 1911.

Galante, Gary. Crow Lance Cases or Sword Scabbards. *American Indian Art*. Vol. 6, No.1.: 64–73. Scottsdale, Arizona. 1980

Garretson, Martin, S. *The American Bison*. New York. 1938.

Gibbs, Peter. The Duke Paul Wilhelm Collection in the British Museum. *American Indian Art*. Vol. 7, no. 3: 52–61. Scottsdale, Arizona. 1982.

Gibson, James R. The Maritime Trade of the North Pacific Coast in *Handbook of North American Indians*, Vol. 4 History of Indian-White Relations: 375–390. Ed. Wilcomb E. Washburn. Washington: Smithsonian Institution 1988.

Goetzmann, William H. and Glyndwr Williams *The Atlas of North American Exploration*. New York: Prentice Hall General Reference. 1992.

Hamilton, T. M. *Native American Bows*. Special publications No. 5. Columbia: Missouri Archaeological Society. 1982.

Hanson, James Austin *Metal Weapons, Tools, and Ornaments of the Teton Dakota Indians*. Lincoln: University of Nebraska Press. 1975.

Heidenreich, Conrad E. Huron in *Handbook of North American Indians*, Vol. 15 Northeast: 368-388. Ed. Bruce G. Trigger. Washington: Smithsonian Institution. 1978.

Hodge, Frederick Webb (ed.) *Handbook of Americans Indians North of Mexico*. 2 Vols. Bull. 30, Bureau of American Ethnology. Washington: Smithsonian Institution 1907–1910. (Reprint. 1965: New York: Rowman and Littlefield Inc.).

Hoebel, E. Adamson Zia Pueblo in *Handbook of North American Indians*, Vol. 9 Southwest: 407–417. Ed. Alfonso Ortiz. Washington: Smithsonian Institution. 1979

Holm, Bill. The Crow-Nez Perce Otterskin Bowcase-Quiver. *American Indian Art*. Vol. 6, No. 4: 60–70. Scottsdale, Arizona. 1981.

Hothem, Lar *Collecting Indian Knives. Identification and Values*. Alabama: Books Americana. 1986.

Hotz, Gottfried *Indian Skin Paintings from the American Southwest*. Norman: University of Oklahoma

Press. 1970.
Hough, Walter *Arrow Feathering and Pointing in Arrows and Arrow-Makers*. Vol. IV: 60–63. The American Anthropologist. 1891.
Primitive American Armor. Washington: Smithsonian Institution. 1893.
Hulton, Paul *America* 1585. *The Complete Drawings of John White*. University of North Carolina Press & British Museum Publications. 1984.
Hunt, David C. and Marsha V. Gallagher and William Orr *Karl Bodmer's America*. Joslyn Art Museum & University of Nebraska Press. 1984.
Keyser, James D. A *Shoshonean Origin for the Plains Shield Bearing Warrior Motif*. Vol. 20, No. 69. 1975. Plains Anthropologist.
King, J. C. H. *Smoking Pipes of the North American Indian*. London: British Museum Publications, Limited. 1977.
Thunderbird and Lightning. London: British Museum Publications, Limited. 1982.
Clubs and Tomahawks: the Inversion of Function and Meaning in the 19th Century. Paper given at Museum of Mankind, London – Native Art of the North American Woodlands Conference. 26 Feb. Unpublished. 1999
Klann, Kilian. Die Sammlung indianischer Ethnographica aus Nordamerika des Herzog Friedrich Paul Wilhelm von Württemberg. Wyk auf Foehr:Verlag für Amerikanistik. 1999.
Krech, Shepard III A *Victorian Earl in the Arctic: The Travels and Collections of the Fifth Earl of Lonsdale* 1888-89. Seattle: University of Washington Press. 1989.
Kroeber, Alfred L. *The Arapaho*. New York: Bulletin of the American Museum of Natural History. 1902–1907.
Kurz, Rudolph *Journal of Rudolph Friedrich Kurz*. Bull. 115, Bureau of American Ethnology. Ed. J. N. B. Hewitt. Translated by Myrtis Jarrell. Washington: Smithsonian Institution. 1937.
Ladd, Edmund J. Zuni Social and Political Organization in *Handbook of North American Indians*. Vol. 9 Southwest: 482–491. Ed. Alfonso Ortiz. Washington: Smithsonian Institution. 1979.
Laubin, Reginald and Gladys *American Indian Archery*. Norman: University of Oklahoma Press. 1980.
Lewis. Meriwether and William Clark *The History of the Lewis and Clark Expedition*. 3 Vols. Ed. Elliott Coues. New York: Francis P. Harper. 1893. (Reprint. Dover Publications Inc., New York).
Lewis, Oscar *The Effects of White Contact upon Blackfoot Culture*. Centennial Anniversary Publication. The American Ethnological Society 1842–1942. Seattle: University of Washington Press. 1942.
Light, D. W. *Tattooing Practices of the Cree Indians*. Occasional Paper No. 6. Calgary: Glenbow-Alberta Institute. 1972.
Lloyd, Christopher and R. C. Anderson (eds.) A *Memoir of James Trevenen*. London: Navy Records Society. 1959.
Loendorf, Lawrence L. and Stuart W. Conner The Pectol Shields and the Shield-Bearing Warrior Rock Art Motif. *Journal of California and Great Basin Anthropology*. Vol. 15, No. 2.: 216–224. 1993.
Lowie, Robert H. *The northern Shoshone*. Anthrop. Paper, Vol. 2. Pt. 2. New York: American Museum of Natural History. 1908.
The Crow Indians. New York: Farrar & Rinehart, Incorporated, on Murray Hill. 1935
Lyford, Carrie A. *Iroquois Crafts*. Lawrence, Kansas: United States Indian Service, Haskell Institute. 1945.
Marquis, TB 1957. *"Wooden Leg; a warrior who fought Custer"*. University of Nebraska Press. Lincoln.
McCoy, Ronald *Circles of Power*. Vol. 55, No. 4., in 'Plateau' series. Flagstaff: Museum of Northern Arizona. 1984.
Miniature Shields: James Mooney's Fieldwork among the Kiowa and Kiowa-Apache. *American Indian Art*. Vol. 20, No. 3: 64–71. Scottsdale, Arizona. 1995.
McKenney, Thomas L. and James Hall *The Indian Tribes of North America*. 3 Vols. Edinburgh: John Grant. 1933.
Marquis, Thomas H. *Memoirs of a White Crow Indian*. New York: The Century Company. 1928.
Mason, Otis T. *Arrows and Arrow-Makers*. Vol. IV. The American Anthropologist. 1891.
North American Bows, Arrows, and Quivers. Smithsonian Report (1893): 631–679. Washington: Government Printing Office. 1894.
Maximilian, Prince of Wied *Early Western Travels* 1748-1846. Vol. XXIII. Part II of *Maximilian, Prince of Wied's Travels in the Interior of North America*, 1832–1834. Ed. Reuben Gold Thwaites. Cleveland, Ohio: The Arthur H. Clark Company. 1906.
Mishkin, Bernard. *Rank and Warfare Among the Plains Indians*. Seattle and London: University of Washington Press. 1940.
Morgan, Lewis Henry *The Indian Journals* 1859-62. Ed. Leslie A. White. Ann Arbor: The University of Michigan Press. 1959.
Murray, Alexander Hunter *Journal of the Yukon* 1847-48. Publications of the Canadian Archives No. 4. Ed. L. J. Burpee. Ottawa: Government Printing Bureau. 1910.
Nagy, Imre A *Typology of Cheyenne Shield Designs*. Plains Anthropologist: 39–47.
Owsley, Douglas W. and Richard L. Jantz (eds.) *Skeletal Biology in the Great Plains*. Washington and London: Smithsonian Institution. 1994.
Painter, John W. *American Indian Artifacts: the John Painter Collection*. Cincinnati, Ohio: George Tassian Organization, Inc. 1992.
Parmentier, Richard, J. The Mythological Triangle: Poseyemu, Montezuma, and Jesus in the Pueblos in *Handbook of North American Indians*, Vol. 9 Southwest: 609–622. Ed. Alfonso Ortiz. Washington: Smithsonian Institution. 1979.
Peterson, Harold L. *American Knives*. New York: Charles Scribner's Sons. 1957.
American Indian Tomahawks. New York: Museum of the American Indian, Heye Foundation. 1971.
Pfefferkorn, Ignaz. *Pfefferkorn's description of the Province of Sonora*. Ed. Theodore E. Trentlein. Albuquerque: Coronado Cuarto Centennial Publ. Vol. 12. 1949.
Phillips, Ruth B. *Patterns of Power*. Kleinburg, Ontario: The McMichael Canadian Collection. 1984.
Like a Star I Shine in The Spirit Sings. Toronto: McClelland and Stewart. 1987.
Pike, Zebulon M. *An account of expeditions to the sources of the Mississippi, and through the western parts of Louisiana*. Philadelphia. 1810.
Pohrt, Richard A. *Pipe Tomahawks from Michigan and the Great Lakes Area*. Bulletin of the Detroit Institute of Arts. Vol. 62, No. 1: 54–60. Detroit, Michigan. 1986.
Pope, Saxton A *study in Bows and Arrows*. Publications in American Archaeology and Ethnology. University of California. 1923.
Robarchek, Clayton A. Plains Warfare and the Anthropology of War in Owsley and Jantz: 307-316. 1994.
Ross, Marvin C. (Ed.) *The West of Alfred Jacob Miller*. Norman: University of Oklahoma Press. 1968.
Seaver, James E. *The Life of Mary Jemison*. New York: The American Scenic and Historic Preservation Society (Reprint). 1982.
Secoy, Frank Raymond *Changing Military Patterns on the Great Plains*. Seattle: University of Washington Press. 1953.
Smith, DeCost *Indian Experiences*. Caldwell, Idaho: The Caxton Printers Ltd. 1943.
Speck, Frank, G. Notes on the Functional Basis of Decoration and the Feather Technique of the Oglala Sioux. *Indian Notes*, Vol. V, No. 1. New York: Museum of the American Indian. 1928.
Stanislawski, Michael B. Hopi-Tewa in *Handbook of North American Indians*, Vol. 9 Southwest: 587–602. Ed. Alfonso Ortiz. Washington: Smithsonian Institution. 1979.
Stone, G. Cameron A *Glossary of the Construction, Decoration and Use of Arms and Armor*. New York: Jack Brussel. 1934.
Sturtevant, William C. *Iroquois Hieroglyphics*. Paper given at 10th American Indian Workshop. Vienna. 1989.
Sturtevant, William C. And Colin Taylor *The Native Americans*. London: Salamander Books, Ltd. 1991.
Swagerty, William R. Indian Trade in the Trans-Mississippi West to 1870 in *Handbook of North American Indians*, Vol. 4 History of Indian-White Relations: 351–374. Ed. Wilcomb E. Washburn. Washington: Smithsonian Institution. 1988.
Swanton, John R. *Early History of the Creek Indians and Their Neighbours*. Bull 73, Bureau of American Ethnology. Washington: Smithsonian Institution. 1922.
Tate, Marcia *The Atlatl Story*. Tate Enterprises Unlimited, Inc. 1986.
Taylor, Colin *The Warriors of the Plains*. London: The Hamlyn Publishing Group. 1975.
Title essay in Ho, *For the Great West!* The Silver Jubilee Publication. Ed. Barry C. Johnson. London: The English Westerners Society. 1980.
Crow Rendezvous in *Crow Indian Art*: 33–48. Eds. D. & R. Lessard. Mission, South Dakota: Chandler Institute. 1984.
Wakanyan: Symbols of Power and Ritual of the Teton Sioux in *Amerindian Cosmology*. Cosmos 4, Yearbook of the Traditional Cosmology Society. Ed. Don McCaskill. Brandon, Manitoba: The Canadian Journal of Native Studies. 1989.
Native American Myths and Legends. London: Salamander Books Limited. 1994a.
The Plains Indians. London: Salamander Books Limited. 1994b.
Sun'ka Wakan. Sacred Horses of the Plains Indians: Ethos and Regalia. (Bilingual English/German). Wyk auf Foehr: Verlag für Amerikanistik. 1995a.
Myths of the North American Indians. London: Calmann and King Ltd. 1995b.
Catlin's O-kee-pa: Mandan Culture and Ceremonialism. The George Catlin O-keep-pa Manuscript in the British Museum. (Bilingual English/German). Foreword by W. Raymond Wood. Wyk auf Foehr: Verlag für Amerikanistik. 1996.
North American Indians. Avonmouth, Bristol: Parragon. 1997.
Hoka hey! Scalps to coups: the impact of the horse on Plains Indian warfare. Lecture given at the Buffalo Bill Historical Center, Cody, Wyoming. September. 1999. IN PRESS.
Taylor, William E., Jr. And Dale Idiens et al *The Athapaskans: Strangers of the North*. Foreword by Norman Tebble. Ottawa: National Museum of Man and Edinburgh: Royal Scottish Museum. 1974.
Teit, James A.*The Salishan Tribes of the Western Plateaus*. 45th Annual Report of the Bureau of American Ethnology. Ed. Franz Boas. Washington: Government Printing Office. 1930.
Turner, Geoffrey *Indians of North America*. Poole, Dorset: Blandford Press. 1979.
Underhill, Ruth *Indians of the Pacific Northwest*. Washington: Bureau of Indian Affairs, Branch of Education. 1945.
Utley, Robert M. *The Lance and The Shield: The Life and Times of Sitting Bull*. New York: Ballantine Books. 1993.
Vennum, Thomas Jr. *American Indian Lacrosse: Little Brother of War*. Washington and London: Smithsonian Institution Press. 1994.
Wallace, Ernest and E. Adamson Hoebel *The Comanches: Lords of the South Plains*. Norman: University of Oklahoma Press. 1952.
Wildschut, William and John C. Ewers *Crow Indian Beadwork*. New York: Museum of the American Indian. 1959.
Wildschut, William *Crow Indian Medicine Bundles*. Ed. John C. Ewers. New York: Museum of the American Indian. 1960.
Wilson, Thomas *Arrow Wounds*. N.S.3., American Anthropologist. 1901.
Wissler, Clark. *Decorative Art of the Sioux Indians*. Vol. XVIII. New York: American Museum of Natural History. 1904.
Some Protective Designs of the Dakota. Vol. I, Part II. New York: American Museum of Natural History. 1907.
Material Culture of the Blackfoot Indians. Vol. V. New York: American Museum of Natural History. 1910.
Social Organization and Ritualistic Ceremonies of the Blackfoot Indians. Vol. VII, Part I. New York: American Museum of Natural History. 1912.
Woodward, Arthur The Metal Tomahawk: Its Evolution and Distribution in North America in *The Bulletin of the Fort Ticonderoga Museum*. 3,3. 1946.
Indian Trade Goods. Portland: Oregon Archaeological Society. 1965.
Wright, Barton *Pueblo Shields*. Flagstaff, Arizona: Northland Press. 1976.
Pueblo Shields. *American Indian Art*. Vol. 17, No. 2: 44-51. Scottsdale, Arizona. 1992.

ARTS AND CRAFTS OF THE AMERICAN INDIAN

Introduction
Books
Boas, F. *Primitive Art*, 1927.
Bourke, Capt. J. G. *Mackenzie's Last Fight With The Cheyenne*, reprinted Bellevue, Nebraska, 1890.
Coe, R. T. *Sacred Circles*, London 1976.
Coe, R. T. *Lost and Found Traditions*, New York, 1986.
Culin, S. *Games of the North American Indians*, 24th Annual Report of the Bureau of American Ethnology 1902-03, Smithsonian Institution Washington D. C., 1907.
Farge, O., et al, *Introduction to American Indian Art*, Glorieta, New Mexico, 1931.
Feder, N. *American Indian Art*, New York, 1965.
Kroeber, T. *Ishi In Two Worlds*, London 1987.
Seton, J. M. *American Indian Arts: A Way of Life*, New York, 1962.
Other
Taylor, C. F. 'Costume with Quill-wrapped Hair: Nez Perce or Crow?' in *American Indian Art Magazine*, Vol. 6, No. 3, Scottsdale, Arizona, 1981.
Taylor, C. F. '*Wakanyan*: Symbols of Power and Ritual of the Teton Sioux'. Edited by D. McCaskill in *Amerindian Cosmology, Cosmos* 4, Brandon, Manitoba, 1989.
Whiteford, A. H. 'Southwestern Indian Baskets', Santa Fe, New Mexico, 1988.

The Southeast
Books
Brose, D. S. and Brown, J. A. *Ancient Art of the American Woodland Indians*, New York, 1985.
Dockstader, F. J. *Weaving Arts of the North American Indians*, New York, 1978.

Fundaburk, E. L. and Foreman, M. D. F. *Sun Circles and Human Hands: The Southeastern Indians Art and Industries*, Luverne, Alabama, 1957.

Gilliland, M. S. *The Material Culture of Key Marco Florida*, Gainesville, Florida, 1975.

Haberland, W. *The Art of North America*, 1964.

Hudson, C. *The Southeastern Indians*, Knoxville, Tennessee, 1976.

Leftwich, R. L. *Arts and Crafts of the Cherokee*, Cullowee, North Carolina, 1970.

Speck, F. G. and Bloom, L. *Cherokee Dance and Drama*, Berkeley, California, 1951.

Turnbaugh, S. P. and Turnbaugh W. A. *Indian Baskets*, Westchester, Pennsylvania, 1986.

Wood, M. *Native American Fashion*, New York, 1981.

Other

Carr, L. 'Dress and Ornamentation of Certain American Indians', in *Proceedings of the American Antiquarian Society*, Vol. 11, Worcester, Massachusetts, 1897.

Cushing, F. H. 'Primitive Copper Working: An Experimental Study' in *American Anthropologist*, Vol. 7, Arlington, Virginia, 1894.

Dixon, D. and Domjanovich, S. 'Native American Cane Basketry', in *Shuttle, Spindle, and Dye*, Vol. 13, No. 4, West Hartford, Connecticut, 1992.

Downs, D. 'Patchwork Clothing of the Florida Indians', *American Indian Art Magazine*, Vol. 4, No. 3, Scottsdale, Arizona, 1979.

Fewkes, V. J. 'Catawba Pottery Making, With Notes of Pamunkey Pottery Making, Cherokee Pottery Making, and Coiling' in *Proceedings of the American Philosophical Society*, Vol. 88, No. 2, Philadelphia, Pennsylvania, 1944.

Goggin, J. M. 'Style Areas in Historic Southeastern Art', in *Indian Tribes of Aboriginal America: Selected Papers of the XXIX International Congress of Americanists*, New York, 1967.

Hally, D. J., Smith, M. T., Langford, J. B. 'The Archaeological Reality of de Soto's Coosa', in *Columbian Consequences*, Vol. II, *Archaeological and Historical Perspectives of the Spanish Borderlands East*, Washington D. C., 1990.

Hamilton, H. W., Hamilton, J. T., Chapman, E. F. 'Spiro Mound Copper' in *Memoir of the Missouri Archaeological Society*, No. 11, Stillwater, Oklahoma, 1974.

Harrington, M. R. 'Catawba Potters and Their Work' in *American Anthropologist*, Vol. 10, No. 3, Fairfax, Virginia, 1908.

Howard, J. H. 'The Southeastern Ceremonial Complex and Its Interpretations', in *Memoir of the Missouri Archaeological Society*, No. 6, Stillwater, Oklahoma, 1968.

Larson, L. 'A Mississippian Headdress from Etowah, Georgia', in *American Antiquity*, Vol. 25, No. 1, Menasha, Wisconsin, 1959.

Mason, O. T. 'Aboriginal American Basketry: Studies in a Textile Art Without Machinery', in *Annual Report of the Board of Regents of the Smithsonian Institution*, Washington D. C., 1904.

Medford, C. 'Native Clothing of the Southeastern Indian People', in *Indian America*, Vol. 9, No. 1, Tulsa, Oklahoma, 1975.

Porter, F. W. 'Basketry of the Middle Atlantic and Southeast', in *The Art of Native American Basketry: A Living Legacy*, New York, 1990.

Speck, F. G. 'Decorative Art and Basketry of the Cherokee', in *Bulletin of the Public Museum of the City of Milwaukee*, Vol. 2, No. 2, Milwaukee, Wisconsin, 1920.

Sturtevant, W. C. 'Seminole Men's Clothing', in *Essays on the Verbal and Visual Arts, Proceedings of the 1966 Annual Spring Meeting of the American Ethnological Society*, Seattle, Washington, 1967.

West, G. A. 'Tobacco, Pipes, and Smoking Customs of the American Indians' in *Bulletin of the Public Museum of the City of Milwaukee*, Vol. XVII, Milwaukee, Wisconsin, 1934.

Witthoft, J. 'Stone Pipes of the Historic Cherokee', in *Southern Indian Studies*, Vol. 1, No. 2, Chapel Hill, North Carolina, 1949.

The Southwest

Books

Adair, J. *The Navajo and Pueblo Silversmiths*, Norman, Oklahoma, 1962.

Bedinger, M. *Indian Silver, Navajo and Pueblo Jewelers*, Albuquerque, 1974.

Berlant, A. and Kahlenberg, M. H. *Walk in Beauty*, Salt Lake City, 1991.

Brody, J. J. *Beauty From the Earth, Pueblo Indian Pottery from the University Museum of Archeology and Anthropology*, Philadelphia, 1990.

Bunzel, R. *The Pueblo Potter, A Study of Creative Imagination in Primitive Art*, New York, 1972.

Coe, R. T. *Lost and Found Traditions*, 1986.

Dillingham, R. *Seven Families in Pueblo Pottery*, Albuquerque, 1974.

Dillingham, R. *Acoma and Laguna Pottery*, Santa Fe, New Mexico, 1992.

Fox, N. *Pueblo Weaving and Textile Arts*, Santa Fe, New Mexico, 1978.

Frank, L. and Harlow, F. *Historic Pottery of the Pueblo Indians 1600-1880*, Boston, 1974.

Harlow, F. *Historic Pueblo Indian Pottery*, Santa Fe, New Mexico, 1970.

James, G. W. *Indian Basketry*, New York, 1972.

Kent, K. P. *Prehistoric Textiles of the Southwest*, Santa Fe, New Mexico, 1983.

LeFree, B. *Santa Clara Pottery Today*, Albuquerque, 1975.

Marriott, A. *Maria: The Potter of San Ildefonso*, Norman, Oklahoma, 1986.

O'Bryon. *The Dine Myths of the Navajo Indians*, Washington D.C., 1956.

Reichard, G. A. *Spider Woman: A Story of Navajo Weavers and Chanters*, reprinted Glorieta, New Mexico, 1968.

Rozaire, C. *Indian Basketry of Western North America*, Santa Ana, California, 1977.

Schaafsma, P. *Kachinas*, Albuquerque, 1994.

Sturtevant, W. and Ortiz, A. *Handbook of North American Indians*, Vol. 9, *Southwest*, Washington D. C., 1979.

Trimble, S. *Talking With the Clay: The Art of Pueblo Pottery*, Santa Fe, New Mexico, 1987.

Other

Bloom. 'Bourke on the Southwest', in *New Mexico Historical Review*, XI, 1936.

Cushing, F. 'Zuni Breadstuff' in *Indian Notes and Monographs: 8*, Museum of the American Indian, New York, 1886.

The Plains

Books

Bebbington, J. M. *Quillwork of the Plains*, Calgary, Alberta, 1982

Best, A. and McClelland, A. *Quillwork by Native Peoples in Canada*, Toronto, Ontario, 1977.

Brownstone, A. *War Paint: Blackfoot and Sarcee Painted Buffalo Robes in the Royal Ontario Museum*, Toronto, Ontario, 1993.

Catlin, G. *Letters and Notes on the Manners, Customs, and Condition of the North American Indians*: Vols I-II, London, 1841.

Catlin, G. *Indian Art in Pipestone: George Catlin's Portfolio in the British Museum*, Edited by John C. Ewers, Washington D. C., 1979.

Clark, W. P. *The Indian Sign Language*, Philadelphia, 1885.

Denig, E. T. *Indian Tribes of the Upper Missouri* Edited by J. N. B. Hewitt, Washington D. C., 1930.

Ewers, J. C. *Plains Indian Painting*, Stanford, California, 1939.

Ewers J. C. *Blackfeet Crafts*, Lawrence, Kansas, 1945.

Ewers J. C. *Blackfoot Indian Pipes and Pipemaking*, Bureau of American Ethnology Bulletin 186 (64), Washington D. C., 1963.

Ewers J. C. *Plains Indian Sculpture*, Washington D. C., 1986.

Fardoulis, A. *Le cabinet du Roi, et les anciens Cabinets de Curiosités dans les collections du Musee de l'Homme*, Paris, 1979.

Fletcher, A. and La Flesche, F. *The Omaha Tribe, 27th Annual Report of the Bureau of American Ethnology, 1905-06*, Washington D. C., 1911.

Grinnell, G. B. *The Cheyenne Indians: Their History and Ways of Life*: Vols. I-II, New Haven, 1923.

Hail, B. A. *Hau kola!* Bristol, Rhode Island, 1983.

King, J. C. H. *Thunderbird and Lightning*, London, 1982.

Kroeber, A. L. *The Arapaho*, Bulletin of the American Museum of Natural History, New York, 1902.

Larocque, F. *Journal of Larocque from the Assiniboine to the Yellowstone, 1805*. Edited by Lawrence J. Burpee, Ottawa, 1910.

Lewis, M. *History of the Expedition under the command of Capts. Lewis & Clark*: Vols. I-II, 1904.

Lewis, M. and Clark, W. *The Original Journals of Lewis and Clark, 1804-1806*: Vols. I-VIII. Edited by Reuben Gold Thwaites, reprinted New York, 1959.

Lowie, R. H. *Indians of the Plains*, New York, 1954.

Lyford, C. A. *Quill and Beadwork of the Western Sioux*, Lawrence, Kansas, 1940.

MacGregor, A. (ed.) *Tradescant Rarities: Essays on the Foundation of the Ashmolean Museum in 1863*, Oxford, 1983.

MacGregor, J. G. *Peter Fidler: Canada's Forgotten Surveyor, 1769-1822*, Toronto, 1966.

Mallery, G. *Picture Writing of the American Indians*, 10th Annual Report of the Bureau of American Ethnology, Washington D. C., 1893.

Martin, P. S., Quimby, G. I., and Collier, D. *Indians before Columbus*, Chicago, 1947.

Morrow, M. *Indian Rawhide: An American Folk Art*, Norman, Oklahoma, 1975.

Orchard, W. C. *The Technique of Porcupine Quill Decoration Among the Indians of North America*, reprinted New York, 1971.

Palliser, J. *Solitary Rambles*, Vermont, 1969.

Petersen, K. D. *Plains Indian Art from Fort Marion*, Norman, Oklahoma, 1971.

Petersen, K. D. *American Pictographic Images*, New York, 1988.

Pond, S. *The Dakota or Sioux in Minnesota As They Were in 1834*, reprinted St. Paul 1986.

Spier, L. *Plains Indian Parfleche Designs*, Publications in Anthropology, Vol. IV, No. 3. Washington D.C., 1931.

Sturtevant, W. C. and Taylor, C. F. *The Native Americans*. London, 1991.

Taylor, C. F. *Wapa'ha: The Plains Feathered Head-dress*, Germany, 1994.

Torrence, G. *The American Indian Parfleche: A Tradition of Abstract Painting*, Des Moines, 1994.

Waugh, E. H. *Blackfoot Religion: My Clothes Are Medicine*. Edited by P. H. R. Stepney and D. J. Goa, Edmonton, 1990.

Webber, A. P. *North American Indian and Eskimo Footwear*, Toronto, 1989.

Weltfish, G. *The Lost Universe: Pawnee Life and Culture*, Lincoln, Nebraska, 1977.

West, G. A. *Tobacco Pipes and Smoking Customs of the American Indians*. Milwaukee Public Museum, Bulletin 17, Milwaukee, 1934.

Wildschut, W. *Crow Indian Beadwork*, New York, 1959.

Wissler, C. *Social Organization and Ritualistic Ceremonies of the Blackfoot Indians*. Part II. 'Ceremonial Bundles of the Blackfoot Indians', Anthropology Papers of the American Museum of Natural History Vol. VII, New York. 1912 (b).

Wissler, C. *Costumes of the Plains Indians*, together with *Structural Basis to the Decoration of Costumes Among the Plains Indians*, reprinted New York, 1975.

Wissler, C. *Distribution of Moccasin Decorations Among the Plains Tribes*, Anthropology papers of the American Museum of Natural History, Vol. XXIX, Part I, New York, 1927.

Other

Conn, R. 'Blackfeet Women's Clothing' in *American Indian Tradition*, Vol. 7, No. 4, 1961.

Conner, S. and B. L. 'Rock Art of the Montana High Plains' in *The Art Galleries*, Santa Barbara, 1971.

Cooley, J. 'Kiowa Tab Leggings' in *Moccasin Tracks*, June, Vol. 8, No. 10, La Patnia, California, 1983.

Dempsey, H. 'Religious Significance of Blackfoot Quillwork' in *Plains Anthropologist*, Vol. 8, Lincoln, Nebraska, 1963.

Douglas, F. H. 'American Indian Tobacco'. *Indian Leaflet Series*, No. 22, Denver, 1931.

Feder, N. 'Introduction: Crow Indian Art – The Problem' in *American Indian Art Magazine*, Vol. 6, No. 1, Scottsdale, Arizona, 1980.

Feder, N. 'Bird Quillwork' in *American Indian Art Magazine*, Vol. 12, No. 3, Scottsdale, Arizona, 1987.

Fenenga, F. 'An Early Nineteenth Century Account of Assiniboine Quillwork' in *Plains Anthropologist*, Lincoln, Nebraska, 1959.

Keyser, J. D. 'A Lexicon for Historic Plains Indian Rock Art' in *Plains Anthropologist*, Vol. 32, No. 115, Lincoln, Nebraska, 1987.

Lanford, B. 'Origins of Central Plains Beadwork' in *American Indian Art Magazine*, Vol. 16, No. 1, Scottsdale, Arizona, 1990.

Lessard, F. 'Pictographic Sioux Beadwork, A Re-Examination' in *American Indian Art Magazine*, Vol. 16, No. 4, Scottsdale, Arizona, 1991.

Libby, W. F. 'Radiocarbon Dates, II', *Science*, 114, Washington D. C., 1951.

Loud, L. L. and Harrington, M. R. 'Lovelock Cave'. *University of California Publications in American Archeology and Ethnology*, 25.1, Berkeley, California, 1929.

McClintock, W. 'Dances of the Blackfoot Indians', *Southwest Museum Leaflet*, 7, Los Angeles, 1937.

Pohrt, R. A. 'Plains Indian Riding Quirts with Elk Antler Handles' in *American Indian Art Magazine*, Vol. 3, No. 4, Scottsdale, Arizona, 1978.

Pohrt, R. A. 'Tribal Identification of Northern Plains Beadwork' in *American Indian Art Magazine*, Vol. 15, No. 1, Scottsdale, Arizona, 1989.

Ritzenthaler, R. E. 'Woodland Sculpture' in *American Indian Art Magazine*, Vol. 4, Scottsdale, 1976.

Sturtevant, W. C. 'The Sources for European Imagery of Native Americans'. Edited by R. Doggett, M. Hulvey and J. Ainsworth in *New World of Wonder, European Images of the Americas 1492-1700*, Washington D. C., 1992.

Taylor, C. F. 'The Plains Indians' Leggings' in *The English Westerners' Brand Book*, Vol. 3, No. 2, London, 1961.

Taylor, C. F. 'Early Plains Indian Quill Techniques in European Museum Collections' in *Plains Anthropologist*,

Vol. 7, Lincoln, Nebraska, 1962.

Taylor, C. F. 'The *O-kee-pa* and Four Bears: An insight into Mandan ethnology', in *The English Westerners' Society Brand Book*, Vol. 15, No. 3, London, 1973.

Taylor, C. F. 'Costume with Quill-wrapped Hair: Nez Perce or Crow?' in *American Indian Art Magazine*, Vol. 6, No. 3, Scottsdale, Arizona, 1981.

Taylor, C. F. '*Wakanyan*: Symbols of Power and Ritual of the Teton Sioux', 1989 (See Introduction).

Turner. 'The Tradescant Shirt' in MacGregor. A. (ed.), 1983: 123-130.

West, I. M. 'Plains Indian Horse Sticks' in *American Indian Art Magazine*, Vol. 3, No. 2, Scottsdale, Arizona, 1978.

West , I. M. 'Tributes to a Horse Nation: Plains Indian Horse Effigies', in *South Dakota History*, Vol. 9, No. 4., South Dakota Historical Society, 1979.

Plateau and Basin
Books
Adney, E. T. and Chapelle, H. I. *The Bark Canoes and Skin Boats of North America*, Washington D. C., 1964.

D'Azevedo, W. L. (ed.) *Handbook of North American Indians*, Vol. 11, *Great Basin*, Washington D. C., 1986.

Devoto, B. (ed.) *The Journals of Lewis and Clark*, Boston, 1953.

Feder, N. *American Indian Art*, New York, 1973.

Gidley, M. *With One Sky Above Us*, New York, 1979.

Janetski, J. C. *The Ute of Utah Lake*, Salt Lake, 1991.

Kapoun, R. W. *Language of the Robe, American Indian Trade Blankets*, Salt Lake City, 1992.

Lomahaftewa, G. A. *Glass Tapestry*, Phoenix, 1993.

Madsen, B. D. *The Northern Shoshoni*, Idaho, 1980.

Madsen, B. D. *The Lemhi: Sacajawea's People*, Caldwell, Idaho, 1990.

Marsh, C. S. *The Utes of Colorado, People of the Shining Mountains*, Boulder, Colorado, 1982.

Morrow, M. *Indian Rawhide*, Norman, 1975.

Peterson, J. *Sacred Encounters*, Norman, 1993.

Pettit, J. *Utes, the Mountain People*, Boulder, Colorado, 1990.

Ruly, R. H. and Brown, J. A. *The Cayuse Indians*, Norman, 1972.

Schlick, M. D. *Columbia River Basketry*, Seattle, 1994.

Schuster, H. H. *The Yakima*, New York, 1990.

Smith, A. M. *Ethnography of the Northern Utes*, Albuquerque, New Mexico, 1974.

Teit, J. A. and Boas, F. *The Salishan Tribes of the Western Plateaus*, Washington D. C., 1928.

Trenholm, V. C. *The Shoshonis*, Norman, 1964.

Wheat, M. M. *Survival Arts of the Primitive Paiutes*, Reno, Nevada, 1967.

Wright, R. K. (ed.) *A Time of Gathering. Native Heritage in Washington State*, Seattle, 1991.

Other
Bernstein, B. 'Panamint Shoshoni Basketry' in *American Indian Art Magazine*, Scottsdale, Arizona, Autumn, 1979.

Chronister, A. B. 'Characteristics of Ute Beadwork 1860-1885' in *Whispering Wind*, Summer, 1992; Part 2, *Whispering Wind*, Fall-Winter, New Orleans, Louisiana, 1992.

Cohodas, M. 'Lena Frank Dick, Washoe Basket Maker' in *American Indian Art Magazine*, Scottsdale, Arizona, Autumn 1979.

Cohodas, M. 'The Breitholle Collection of Washoe Basketry' in *American Indian Art Magazine*, Scottsdale, Arizona, Autumn, 1984.

Fowler, C. and Dawson, L. 'Ethnographic Basketry' in *Handbook of North American Indians*, Vol. II, *Great Basin*, Washington D. C., 1986.

Gogl, J. M. 'Columbia River/Plateau Indian Beadwork' in *American Indian Basketry*, Vol. V, No. 2 (1985).

Gogl, J. M. 'The Archetypal Columbia River Plateau Contour Beaded Bag' in *Eye of the Angel*, Northampton, Massachusetts, 1990.

Lanford, B. 'Beadwork and Parfleche Designs' in *Crow Indian Art*, Mission, South Dakota, 1984.

Marr, C. J. 'Salish Baskets from the Wilkes Expedition' in *American Indian Art Magazine*, Scottsdale, Arizona, Summer, 1984.

Marr, C. J. 'Basketry Regions of Washington State' in *American Indian Art Magazine*, Scottsdale, Arizona, Spring, 1991.

Schlick, M. D. and Duncan, K. C. 'Wasco-Style Woven Beadwork, Merging Artistic Traditions' in *American Indian Art Magazine*, Scottsdale, Arizona, Summer, 1991.

Shawley, S. D. 'Hemp & Cornhusk Bags of the Plateau Indians' in *Indian America*, Tulsa, Oklahoma, Spring, 1975.

Shawley, S. D. 'Hide Tanning of the Plateau Indians' in *Indian America*, Tulsa, Oklahoma, Spring, 1976.

Slater, E. 'Panamit Shoshoni Basketry 1920-1940' in *American Indian Art Magazine*, Scottsdale, Arizona, Winter, 1985.

Whiteford, A. H. and McGreevy, S. D. 'Basketry Arts of the

San Juan Paiutes' in *American Indian Art Magazine*, Scottsdale, Arizona, Winter, 1985.

California
Books
Bates, C. D. and Lee, M. J. *Tradition and Innovation; A Basket History of the Indians of the Yosemite-Mono Lake Area*, Yosemite National Park, California, 1990.

Fields, V. M. *The Hoover Collection of Karuk Baskets*, Eureka, California, 1985.

Grant, C. *The Rock Paintings of the Chumash: A Study of a California Indian Culture*, Berkeley and Los Angeles, California, 1966.

Hudson, T. and Underhay, E. *Crystals in the Sky: An Intellectual Odyssey Involving Chumash Astronomy, Cosmology and Rock Art*, Santa Barbara, California, 1978.

Kroeber, A. L. *Handbook of the Indians of California*, Bureau of American Ethnology Bulletin 78, Washington D.C., 1925.

Ortiz, B. *It Will Live Forever; Traditional Yosemite Indian Acorn Preparation*, California, 1991.

Other
Bates, C. D. 'Coiled Basketry of the Sierra Miwok' in *San Diego Museum Papers*, No. 15, San Diego, California, 1982.

Bates, C. D. 'Feather Belts of Central California' in *American Indian Art Magazine*, Scottsdale, Arizonia, 1981(a).

Bates, C. D. 'Beadwork in the Far West: The Continuation of an Eastern Tradition' in *Moccasin Tracks*, La Palma, California, 1981(b).

Bates, C. D. 'Feathered Regalia of Central California: Wealth and Power' in *Occasional Papers of the Redding Museum 2*, Redding, California, 1982.

Bates, C. D. and Bibby, B. 'Collecting Among the Chico Maidu: The Stewart Culin Collection at the Brooklyn Museum' in *American Indian Art Magazine*, Scottsdale, Arizona, 1983.

Bates, C. D. and Bibby, B. 'Beauty and Omnipotence: Traditional Dance Regalia of Northern California' in *The Extension of Tradition*, Crocker Art Museum, Sacramento, California, 1985.

Dawson, L. and Deetz, J. 'A Corpus of Chumash Basketry' in *Annual Reports of the University of California Archaeological Survey 7*, Los Angeles, California 1965.

Ferris, G. J. '"Women's Money": Types and Distributions of Pine Nut Beads in Northern California, Southern Oregon and Northwestern Nevada' in *Journal of California and Great Basin Anthropology 14(1)*, Banning, California, 1992.

Harrington, J. P. 'Tobacco Among the Karuk Indians of California' in *Smithsonian Institution Bureau of American Ethnology Bulletin 91*, Washington D.C., 1932.

Hudson, J. W. 'Pomo Wampum Makers' in *Overland Monthly*, August, 1897.

Kelly, I. T. 'The Carver's Art of the Indians of Northwestern California' in *University of California Publications in American Archaeology and Ethnology 24(7)*, Berkeley, California, 1930.

Lee, G. 'The San Emigdio Rock Art Site' in *Journal of California and Great Basin Anthropology 1(2)*, Banning, California, 1979.

McKern, W. C. 'Functional Families of the Patwin' in *University of California Publications in American Archaeology and Ethnology 13(7)*, Berkeley, California, 1922.

McLendon, S. 'Pomo Baskets: The Legacy of William and Mary Benson' in *Native Peoples 4(1)*, Phoenix, Arizona, 1990.

O'Neale, L. M. 'Yurok-Karok Basket Weavers' in *University of California Publications in American Archaeology and Ethnology 32(1)*, Berkeley, California, 1932.

Schlick, M. D. and Duncan K. C., 'Wasco-Style Woven Beadwork: Merging Artistic Traditions' in *American Indian Art Magazine 16 (3)*, Scottsdale, Arizona, 1991.

Smith-Ferri, S. 'Basket Weavers, Basket Collectors, and the Market: A Case Study of Joseppa Dick' in *Museum Anthropology 17(2)* Arlington, 1993.

The Northwest Coast
Books
Barbeau, M. *Totem Poles of the Gitksan Upper Skeena River, British Columbia*, British Columbia Bulletin No. 61, Ser. No. 12, Ottawa, 1929.

Barbeau, M. *Haida Carvers in Argillite*, National Musuems of Canada Bulletin, No. 139, 1957.

Barbeau, M. *Totem Poles*, Vols 1 & 2, Canadian Museum of Civilization: Hull, Quebec, 1990.

Barbeau, M., Garfield, V. E. and Wingert P. S., *The Tsimshian: Their Arts and Music*, New York, 1951.

Blackman, M. *During My Time: Florence Edenshaw Davidson, A. Haida Woman*, Seattle, 1982.

Boas, F. *Primitive Art*, New York, 1951.

Curtis, E. S. *The North American Indian* Vol. 10 (Kwakiutl)

and Vol. 11 (Nootka), New York, 1916.

Dempsey, H. A. *Treasures of the Glenbow Museum*, Calgary, Alberta, 1991.

Duff, W. *Images Stone, B.C.: Thirty Centuries of Northwest Coast Indian Sculpture*, Saanichton, British Columbia, 1975.

Fane, D., Jacknis, I., and Breen, L. M. *Objects of Myth and Memory*, Seattle and London, 1991.

Guedon, M. F. and MacDonald, G. '*Ksan: Breath of our Grandfathers*, Ottawa, 1972.

Gunther, E. *Art in the Life of Northwest Coast Indians*, Seattle, 1966.

Hall, E. S. Jr., Blackman, M. B., and Rickard, V. *Northwest Coast Indian Graphics: An Introduction to Silk Screen Prints*, Vancouver, 1981.

Halpin, M. M. *Totem Poles: An Illustrated Guide*, Museum Note No. 3, Vancouver and London, 1981.

Hawthorn, A. *Art of the Kwakuitl Indians and Other Northwest Coast Tribes*, Seattle, 1967.

Hawthorn, A. *Kwakuitl Art*, Seattle, 1979.

Holm, B. *Northwest Coast Indian Art*, Seattle, 1965.

Holm, B. *Crooked Beak of Heaven*, Seattle, 1972.

Holm, B. *Smokey Top. The Life and Times of Willie Seaweed*, Seattle and London, 1983.

Holm, B. *Spirit and Ancestor*, Burke Museum Monograph 4, Seattle, 1987.

Holm, B., et al. *The Box of Daylight*, Seattle, 1983.

Inverarity, R. B. *Art of the Northwest Coast Indians*, Berkeley, 1950.

Jensen, D. and Sargent, P. *Robes of Power: Totem Poles on Cloth*, Vancouver, 1986.

Jonaitas, A. *Art of the Northern Tlingit*, Seattle, 1986.

Jonaitas, A. *From the Land of the Totem Poles*, Vancouver, 1988.

Jonaitas, A. *Chiefly Feasts*, Vancouver, 1991.

Kaplan, S. A. and Barsness, K. J. *Raven's Journey*, Philadelphia, 1986.

Keithahn, E. L. *Monuments in Cedar*, Seattle, 1963.

Kew, J. E. M. *Sculpture and Engraving of the Central Coast Salish Indians* Vol. 9, Vancouver, 1980.

King, J. C. H. *Portrait Masks of the Northwest Coast of America*, London, 1979.

Lobb, A. *Indian Baskets of the Northwest Coast*, Portland, 1978.

MacDonald, G. F. *Haida Monumental Art – Villages of the Queen Charlotte Islands*, Vancouver, 1983.

Macnair, P.L., Hoover, A. L., and Neary K. *The Legacy: Tradition and Innovation in Northwest Coast Indian Art*, Vancouver, 1984.

Samuel; C. *The Chilkat Dancing Blanket*, Seattle, 1982.

Samuel; C. *The Raven's Tail*, Vancouver, 1987.

Sheehan, C. *Pipes That Won't Smoke: Coal That Won't Burn*, Calgary, 1981.

Stewart, H. *Looking At Indian Art of the Northwest Coast*, Vancouver, 1979.

Stewart, H. *Cedar: The Tree of Life to the Northwest Coast Indians*, Vancouver, 1984.

Stewart, H. *Totem Poles*, Vancouver, 1990.

Sturtevant, W. C., et al. *Boxes and Bowls*, Washington D. C., 1974.

Suttles, W. *Coast Salish Essays*, Seattle, 1987.

Other
Arima, E. Y. 'A Report on a West Coast Whaling Canoe Reconstructed at Port Renfrew' in *History and Archaeology* Vol. 5, Ottawa, 1975.

Blackman, M. B., and Hall, E. S. Jr. 'The Afterimage & Image After: Visual Documents and the Renaissance in Northwest Coast Art' in *American Indian Art Magazine*, Vol. 7:2 Spring, 1982.

Dawson, G. M. 'Report on the Queen Charlotte Islands' in *Geological Survey of Canada. Report of Progress for 1878-79*, 1880.

Duff, W. 'Thoughts on the Nootka Canoe' in *The World is as Sharp as a Knife: An Anthology in Honor of Wilson Duff*. Donald N. Abbot (ed.), 1976.

Emmons, G. T. 'The Basketry of the Tlingit' in *Memoirs: American Museum of American History*, 111:3 1903.

Emmons, G. T. 'The Chilkat Blanket – With Notes on the Blanket Design by Franz Boas' in *Memoirs: American Museum of American History*, III:4, 1907.

Emmons, G. T. 'Portraiture among the North Pacific Coast Tribes', in *American Anthropologist*, n.s. 16, 1914.

Halpin, M. M. *The Tsimshian Crest System: A Study based on Museum Specimens and the Marius Barbeau and William Beynon Field Notes*, Ph.D thesis, University of British Columbia, Vancouver, 1973.

Harris, N. 'Reflections on Northwest Coast Silver' in *The Box of Daylight*, Seattle and London, 1983.

Ryan, J. and Sheehan, C. 'Monumentality and the Peoples of the Northwest Coast' in *Canada's Native Peoples*, Canada Heirloom Series, 11: 8. Charles J. Humber (ed.), Mississauga, 1988.

Sheehan (McLaren), C. *Unmasking Frontlet Headresses*, Masters thesis, University of British Columbia,

Vancouver, 1977.

Sheehan (McLaren), C. 'Moments of Death: Gift of Life. A Reinterpretation of the Northwest Coast Image Hawk' in *Anthropologica*, n.s. XX, 1978.

Sheehan (McLaren), C. 'Masks of Light: Iconographic Interpretation of the Northwest Coast Raven Rattle,' unpublished paper presented to Canadian Ethnology Society, Montreal, 1980.

Suttles, W. 'The Halkomelem Sxwayxwey' in *American Indian Art Magazine*, Vol. 8:1, 1982.

The Subarctic
Books
Burnham, D. K. *To Please the Caribou: Painted Caribou-skin Coats*, Seattle, 1992.

Boudreau, N. J. (ed.) *The Athapaskans*, Ottawa, 1974.

Duncan, K. C. *Northern Athapaskan Art: A Beadwork Tradition*, Seattle, 1989.

Duncan, K. C. & Carney, E. *A Special Gift: The Kutchin Beadwork Tradition*, Seattle, 1988.

Helm, J. (ed.) *Handbook of North American Indians: Vol. 6*, Washington D. C., 1981.

Idiens, D. & Wilson, B. *No Ordinary Journey: John Rae – Arctic Explorer 1813-1893*, Edinburgh, 1993.

Jenness, D. *The Sekani Indians of British Columbia*, (National Museums of Canada Bulletin 84), Ottawa, 1937.

Leechman, D. *The Vanta Kutchin*, (National Museums of Canada Bulletin 130), Ottawa, 1954.

Mackenzie, Sir A., *The Journals and Letters of Sir Alexander Mackenzie* (W. Kaye Lamb ed.), Cambridge, 1970.

McMillan, A. D. *The Native Peoples and Cultures of Canada*, Vancouver, 1988.

Nelson, R. K. *Hunters of the Northern Forest*, 1973.

Nelson, R. K. *Make Prayers to the Raven*, Chicago, 1983.

Orchard, W. C. *The Technique of Porcupine Quill Decoration Among the Indians of North America*, New York, 1971.

Savishinsky, J. S. *The Trail of the Hare: Life and Stress in an Arctic Community*, New York, 1974.

Turner, G. *Hair Embroidery in Siberia and North America*, Oxford, 1976.

Other
De Laguna, F. 'Indian Masks from the Lower Yukon', in *American Anthropologist*, No. 38 (4), New York, 1936.

Gibbs, G. 'Notes on the Tinneh or Chipewyan Indians of British and Russian America', in *Annual Report of the Smithsonian Institution for 1866*, Washington D. C., 1872.

Osgood, C. 'The Ethnography of the Great Bear Lake Indians', in *National Museums of Canada Annual Report for 1931*, Ottawa, 1932.

Thompson, J. 'No Little Variety of Ornament: Northern Athapaskan Artistic Traditions' in *The Spirit Sings: Artistic Traditions of Canada's First Peoples*, Toronto, 1987.

The Arctic
Books
Black, L. T. *Aleut Art*, Anchorage, Alaska, 1982.

Black, L. T. *Glory Remembered: Wooden Headgear of Alaskan Sea Hunters*, Juneau, Alaska, 1991.

Blodgett, J. *The Coming and Going of the Shaman*, The Winnipeg Art Gallery, Manitoba, 1979.

Boas, F. *The Central Eskimo* (1888), Lincoln, Nebraska, 1964.

Bockstoce, J. *Eskimos of Northwest Alaska in the Early Nineteenth Century: Based on the Beechey and Belcher Collections and Records Compiled During the Voyage of H.M.S. Blossom to Northwest Alaska in 1826 and 1827*, University of Oxford, Pitt Rivers Museum Monograph Series 1, 1977.

Collins, H. B., de Laguna, F., Carpenter, E., and Stone, P. *The Far North: 2,000 Years of American Eskimo and Indian Art*, National Gallery of Art, Washington D.C., 1973.

Damas, D., (ed.) *Handbook of North American Indians: Arctic Vol. 5*, Washington D.C., 1984.

Driscoll, B. *The Inuit Amautik: I Like My Hood to be Full*, The Winnipeg Art Gallery, Manitoba, 1980.

Fitzhugh, W. and Crowell, A. *Crossroads of Continents: Cultures of Siberia and Alaska*, Washington D.C., 1988.

Fitzhugh, W. and Kaplan, S. *Inua: Spirit World of the Bering Sea Eskimo*, Washington D.C., 1982.

Fienup-Riordan, A. *Eskimo Essays: Yup'ik Lives and How We See Them*, New Brunswick, 1990.

Fienup-Riordan, A. *Boundaries and Passages: Rule and Ritual in Yup'ik Eskimo Oral Tradition*, Norman, Oklahoma, 1994.

Hickman, P. *Innerskins/Outerskins: Gut and Fishskin*, San Francisco, 1987.

Jenness, D. *Material Culture of the Copper Eskimos*. Report of the Canadian Arctic Expedition, 1913-18, Vol. 16, Ottawa, 1946.

Jochelson, W. *History, Ethnology and Anthropology of the Aleut*, Washington D.C., 1933.

Jones, S., ed. *Eskimo Dolls*, Anchorage, Alaska, 1982.

Kaalund, B. *The Art of Greenland: Sculpture, Crafts, Painting*,

Berkeley, California, 1983 (originally published in Danish, 1979).

Kaplan, S. and Barsness, K. *Raven's Journey*, Philadelphia, 1986.

Lantis, M. *Alaskan Eskimo Ceremonialism*. Monographs of the American Ethnological Society, New York, 1947.

Laughlin, W. S. *Aleuts: Survivors of the Bering Land Bridge*, New York, 1980.

Lowenstein, T. *Ancient Land: Sacred Whale. The Inuit Hunt and Its Rituals*, New York, 1993.

Nelson, E. W. *The Eskimo about Bering Strait*. Bureau of American Ethnology Annual Report for 1896-1897, vol. 18, no. 1, Washington D.C. 1899 (reprinted 1984).

Oakes, J. E. *Copper and Caribou Inuit Skin Clothing Production*. Canadian Ethnology Service Mercury Series Paper no. 118, Ottawa, 1991.

Rasmussen, K. *Intellectual Culture of the Iglulik Eskimos*, Report of the Fifth Thule Expedition 1921-24, vol. 7(1), Copenhagen, 1929.

Rasmussen, K. *The Netsilik Eskimos: Social Life and Spiritual Culture*, Report of the Fifth Thule Expedition 1921-24, vol. 8 (1-2), Copenhagen, 1931.

Ray, D. J. *Eskimo Masks: Art and Ceremony*, Seattle, Washington, 1967.

Ray, D. J. *Eskimo Art: Tradition and Innovation in North Alaska*, Seattle, Washington, 1977.

Ray, D. J. *Aleut and Eskimo Art: Tradition and Innovation in South Alaska*, Seattle, Washington, 1981.

Smith, J. G. E. *Arctic Art: Eskimo Ivory*, New York, 1980.

Spencer, R. F. *The North Alaskan Eskimo: A Study in Ecology and Society*, Bureau of American Ethnology, Smithsonian Institution, Washington D. C., 1959 (reprinted 1976).

Swinton, G. *Sculpture of the Inuit*, Toronto, 1992.

Turner, L. M. *Indians and Eskimos in the Quebec-Labrador Peninsula: Ethnology of the Ungava District*, Quebec, 1979 (originally published, Washington D.C., 1894).

Other
Ager, L. P. 'Storyknifing: An Alaskan Eskimo Girls' Game' in *Journal of the Folklore Institute* 11(3), Bloomington, Indiana, 1974.

Black, L. T. 'The Nature of Evil: Of Whales and Sea Otters' in *Indians, Animals, and the Fur Trade: A Critique of the Keepers of the Game*, Athens, Georgia, 1981.

Burch, E. S., Jr. 'The Central Yupik Eskimos: An Introduction', in *Etudes/Inuit/Studies 8* (supplementary issue), Laval, Quebec, 1984.

Chaussonnet, V. and Driscoll, B. 'The Bleeding Coat: The Art of North Pacific Ritual Clothing' in *Anthropology of the North Pacific Rim*, Washington D.C., 1994.

Collins, H. B., Jr.; Clark, A. H.; Walker, E. H. 'The Aleutian Islands: Their People and Natural History' in *Smithsonian Institution War Background Studies*, no. 21, Washington D.C., 1945.

Driscoll, B. 'Arctic' in *The Spirit Sings*, Calgary and Toronto, 1987.

Driscoll, B. 'Pretending to be Caribou: The Inuit Parka as an Artistic Tradition' in *The Spirit Sings*.

Fienup-Riordan, A. 'The Bird and the Bladder: The Cosmology of Central Yup'ik Seal Hunting', in *Etudes/Inuit/Studies* 14(1-2), Quebec, 1990.

Hatt, G. 'Arctic Skin Clothing in Eurasia and America: An Ethnographic Study' in *Arctic Anthropology* 5(2), 1969.

Hawkes, E. W. *The Dance Festivals of the Alaskan Eskimo*. University of Pennsylvania, Museum Anthropological Publications 6(2), Philadelphia, 1914.

Hoffman, W. J. 'The Graphic Art of the Eskimos: Based Upon the Collections in the National Museum', in *Annual Report of the United States National Museum for 1895*, Washington D.C., 1897.

Holtved, E. 'Contributions to Polar Eskimo Ethnography' in *Meddelelser om Gronland* 182(2), Copenhagen, 1967.

Kroeber, A. L. 'The Eskimo of Smith Sound'. *Bulletin of the American Museum of Natural History* 12(21), New York, 1900.

Lantis, M. 'The Alaskan Whale Cult and its Affinities', *American Anthropologist* 40, Washington D.C., 1938.

Meade, M. 'Sewing to Maintain the Past, Present and Future' in *Etudes/Inuit/Studies* 14(1-2), Laval, Quebec, 1990.

Moore, R. D. 'Social Life of the Eskimo of St. Lawrence Island', *American Anthropologist*, No. 25(3), Washington D.C., 1923.

Morrow, P. 'It is Time for Drumming: A Summary of Recent Research on Yup'ik Ceremonialism' in *Etudes/Inuit/Studies 8* (supplementary issue), Laval, Quebec, 1984.

Oakes, J. E. 'Environmental factors influencing bird-skin clothing production', *Arctic and Alpine Research* 23(1), 1991.

Stenton, D. R. 'The adaptive significance of caribou winter clothing for arctic hunter-gatherers' in *Etudes/Inuit/Studies* 15(1), Laval, Quebec, 1991.

VanStone, J. W. 'The Bruce Collection of Eskimo Material Culture from Port Clarence, Alaska' in *Fieldiana Anthropology*, vol,. 67, Chicago, 1976.

VanStone, J. W. 'The Bruce Collection of Eskimo Material Culture from Kotzebue Sound, Alaska' in *Fieldiana Anthropology*, N.S., no. 1, Chicago, 1980.

The Northeast
Books
Brasser, T. J. *A Basketful of Indian Culture Change*, Ottawa, 1975.

Coleman, B. *Decorative Designs of the Ojibwa of Northern Minnesota*, Washington D. C., 1947.

Davidson, D. S. *Decorative Arts of the Tetes de Boule of Quebec*, New York, 1928.

Feest, C. F. *Beadwork and Textiles of the Ottawa*, Harbor Springs, Michigan, 1984.

Fenton, W. N. *The False Faces of the Iroquois*, Norman, Oklahoma, 1987.

Hartman, S. *Indian Clothing of the Great Lakes: 1740-1840*, Ogden, Utah, 1988.

Lyford, C. *Iroquois: Their Art and Craft*, Surrey, British Columbia, 1989.

Mason, O. T. *Aboriginal American Basketry*, Washington D. C., 1904.

McMullen, A. and Handsman, R. G. (eds) *A Key into the Language of Woodsplint Baskets*, Washington, Connecticut, 1987.

Pelletier, G. *Abenaki Basketry*, Ottawa, 1982.

Ritzenthaler, R. E. and Ritzenthaler, P. *The Woodland Indians of the Western Great Lakes*, Milwaukee, 1983.

Skinner, A. *Material Culture of the Menominee*, New York, 1921.

Speck, F. G. *Montagnais Art in Birch-Bark, A Circumpolar Trait*, New York, 1937.

Speck, F. G. *Eastern Algonkian Block-Stamp Decoration*, Trenton, New Jersey, 1947.

Speck, F. G. *Midwinter Rites of the Cayuga Long House*, Philadelphia, 1949.

Thwaites, R. G. *The Jesuit Relations and Allied Documents: Travels and Explorations of the Jesuit Missionaries in New France 1610-1791*, New York, 1959.

Torrence, G. and Hobbs R. *Art of the Red Earth People: The Mesquakie of Iowa*, Seattle, 1989.

Turner, G. *Hair Embroidery in Siberia and North America*, Oxford, 1955.

Whitehead, R. H. *Elitekey: MicMac Material Culture from 1600 AD to the Present*, Halifax, Nova Scotia, 1982.

Other
Abbass, D. K. 'American Indian Ribbonwork' in *LORE*, No. 36 (2), Milwaukee, 1986.

Bakker, P. 'The Mysterious Link Between Basque and Micmac Art' in *European Review of Native American Studies*, No. 5 (1), Vienna, 1991.

Bardwell, K. 'The Case for an Aboriginal Origin of Northeast Indian Woodsplint Basketry' in *Man in the Northeast*, No. 31, Arlington, Virginia, 1986.

Bowdoin Gil, C. A. 'Native North American Seed Beading Techniques: Part I: Woven Items' in *Bead Journal* No. 3 (2), 1977.

Densmore, F. 'The Native Art of the Chippewa' in *American Anthropologist*, No.43, New York, 1941.

Fenton, W. N. 'Masked Medicine Societies of the Iroquois' in *Native North American Art History*. Edited by Z. P. Mathews and A. Jonaitis. Palo Alto, California, 1982.

Friedl, E. 'A Note on Birchbark Transparencies' in *American Anthropologist*, No.46, New York, 1944.

Garte, E. 'Living Tradition in Ojibwa Beadwork and Quillwork' in *Papers of the Sixteenth Algonquian Conference*. Edited by W. A. Cowan, Ottawa, 1985.

Moody, H. 'Birch Bark Biting' in *The Beaver* Outfit 287, Winnipeg, 1957.

Phillips, R. B. 'Dreams and Designs: Iconographic Problems in Great Lakes Twined Bags' in *Great Lakes Indian Art*, Edited by D. W. Penney, Detroit, 1989.

Phillips, R. B. 'Glimpses of Eden: Iconographic Themes in Huron Pictorial Tourist Art' in *European Review of Native American Studies* No.5 (2), Vienna, 1991.

Pohrt, R., Jr. 'Great Lakes Bandolier Bags in the Derby Collection' in *Eye of the Angel*. Edited by D. Wooley, Northampton, Massachusetts, 1990.

Wetherbee, M. 'Making a Basket from a Tree: Splints from black ash in the Shaker tradition' in *Fine Woodworking Techniques*, Newtown, Connecticut, 1980.

Whiteford, A. H. 'Fiber Bags of the Great Lakes Indians' in *American Indian Art Magazine* No.2 (3), Scottsdale, Arizona, 1977.

Wilson, L. A. 'Bird and Feline Motifs on Great Lakes Pouches' in *Native North American Art History*, Edited by Z. P. Mathews and A. Jonaitis, Palo Alto, California, 1982.

INDEX

PICTURE CREDITS

The publishers wish to thank the following individuals and institutions who have supplied pictures for this book. Figure artworks are by Lois Sloan with additional artworks by Jeffrey Burn and maps by Janos Marffy. All black and white photographs, with the exception of those mentioned below, are courtesy of the NAA, Smithsonian Institution.

American Museum of Natural History: 189(b), 190, 194, 197, 206, 221(t), 222(b)

Anchorage Museum of History and Art: 207, 208(t), 211(tl, tr)Bancroft Library, University of California: 131(t)

Chrysalis Images: 258(bl, br), 259 (tl, b), 260(bl, bc), 261-262(all), 264(t), 268(tl), 269(l), 272(both), 275(all), 278(t), 282(bl), 283, 287(all), 290, 292(t, c), 296(r), 302(b), 304(both), 305(b), 308(c, b), 311(cr, br), 315(b), 321-399(all artefact photographs)

Joslyn Art Museum: 16, 34(l), 67(l,r), 77, 95(t), 238(t), 250(t)

Mendocino City Historical Society, Robert J. Lee Collection: 131(b)

Peter Palmquist: 137

Pitt Rivers Museum: 64, 226, 232

Royal Ontario Museum: 103(b), 104, 241(b), 279(bl)

Stark Museum of Art: 103(t), 177(t), 181, 193, 237

Colin Taylor: 254-256(all), 257(b), 258(t), 259(tr), 260(t, br), 263(b), 264(b), 265, 267(all), 268(bl, tr, cr), 269(r), 270-271(all), 273(both), 274, 276-277(all), 278(b), 279(tl, tc, tr, br), 280(b), 281(all), 282(tl, tr), 282(br), 284-285(all), 288-289(all), 291(both), 292(b), 293-294(all), 296(l), 297-301(all), 302(t), 303, 305(tl, tr), 306-307(all), 308(t), 309-310(all), 311(bl, tr), 312-314(all), 315(tl, tr), 316(all)

ACKNOWLEDGEMENTS

The Project Manager and Publishers wish to thank Ashley Brent, Paul Brewer, Stella Caldwell, Marie Clayton, Charlotte Davies, Katherine Edelston, Terry Forshaw, Colin Gower, and Stephen Mitchell for their contributions to the production of this book.